MW01201161

LAW AND ETHICS OF THE VETERINARY PROFESSION

James F. Wilson, DVM, JD

Bernard E. Rollin, PhD and Jo Anne L. Garbe, DVM, JD
Contributing Authors

Priority
Press
Ltd.

Managing Editor: Elise P. Wilson
Editor-in-Chief: Suzanne Neilson
Production: Publishers Network, Morrisville, PA

James F. Wilson, DVM, JD
   Adjunct Lecturer, University of California, Davis
   Veterinary Hospital, University of Pennsylvania

Bernard E. Rollin, PhD
   Professor of Philosophy,
   Professor of Physiology and Biophysics
   Director of Planning
   Colorado State University

Jo Anne L. Garbe, DVM, JD
   CITIES Policy Regulations Specialist
   The Office of Management Authority
   United States Fish and Wildlife Service
   Department of the Interior

Library of Congress Cataloging in Publication Data:

Wilson, James, 1943 -
   Law and ethics of the veterinary profession/James F. Wilson.

ISBN: 0-9621007-0-6

Printed in the United States of America

4 3 2 1

To my dear wife Elise,
and my children Amy and Mike

Acknowledgments

Although the conception of this book started out as a painless midlife change of career from veterinarian to author, its gestation became more and more difficult. Just because one has a law degree and a veterinary diploma does not mean that he can write. This is especially true when the task at hand consists of learning and relearning difficult legal principles and then putting them into a language and format that veterinary students and fellow veterinarians can readily comprehend.

Fortunately, I had the good sense to surround myself with caring, competent, and often compassionate assistants or this text never would have seen the light of day. By far the most important person in the evolution of this book was my wonderful sounding board, word processor, conscience, director of marketing, assistant editor, and wife, Elise. Without her unending encouragement, personal sacrifice, patience, and assistance, this book would still be a pipe dream.

The next most irreplaceable and important person was our superb editor, Suzanne Neilson. Suzanne does with a pencil what most veterinarians hope to achieve with a scalpel and sutures; i.e., carve out the unhealthy, undesirable, or useless material, reconstruct the remaining tissues so they function perfectly, and suture the area so that the end result is smooth and free of flaws. If this text is readable and understandable, it is because of Suzanne's abilities as an articulate editor.

A third key person to have a major impact on the production of this text was Connie Kellner of The Publisher's Network. Instead of telling us that novices like us never would be able to publish a book of this magnitude, Connie taught us how to do it. The cover design, internal layout and design, production, and marketing of this text were accomplished under her enthusiastic guidance.

Another important person is my father-in-law Thomas J. Prior. His endless hours of initial editing, proofreading, summarizing material, and teaching me how to write succinctly are most appreciated. His enthusiastic encouragement and occasional cocktail hour "conference on the mound" kept my spirits up and provided the humor needed to tolerate what seemed like an unending gestation for the birth of this book.

Many other people played key roles, too: Roger Cossack, JD and Jerilou Cossack Twohey, who talked me into applying to UCLA's School of Law instead of pursuing an MBA to supplement my veterinary school education; Rob Amonic, MD, who introduced us to Roger, Jerilou, and life in Los Angeles; Bernie Rollin, PhD, Colorado State University, who made the chapter on ethics come to life; Jo Anne Garbe, DVM, JD, who brought order to an unbelievable array of federal and state laws governing the care and custody of wild animals; and Michael Philbrick, DVM, whose interest in and research regarding computer-generated medical records adds special substance to the medical records chapter. Also, Lynne Kesel, DVM, Colorado State University, who put legal principles into humorous graphic illustrations, in the hope that the heaviness of the subject matter could somehow be lightened; and Bob Stover and Jim Greenhough of Quality Press who met impossible printing schedules without complaint.

Other key people included Max Crandall, DVM, and Edward Ballitch of the Food and Drug Administration's Center for Veterinary Medicine and Jerry Appelgate, DVM, of Solvay Veterinary, Inc, who carefully reviewed and rewrote parts of Chapter 9; Larry Snyder of the Drug

Enforcement Agency, who reviewed and assisted with Chapter 11; and Dave Espeseth, DVM, of the United States Department of Agriculture Animal and Plant Health Inspection Service, Veterinary Service, who reviewed Chapter 10.

All veterinarians, and especially I, owe unending thanks to the AVMA and Harold Hannah. Without Mr. Hannah's Legal Briefs published in JAVMA TX, the entire profession would still be in the dark ages regarding the impact of the law on the practice of veterinary medicine.

Thanks are also in order for Joan and Bill Schaeffler, DVMs; Jan Bellows, DVM; John Madigan, DVM; Jack Dinsmore, DVM; Lou Gatto, CPA; Alan Beck, ScD; and Gary Hill, Executive Officer of the California Board of Examiners in Veterinary Medicine, who reviewed chapters and provided food for thought. Not to be forgotten are Laura Becker, DVM, my partner at Four Corners Veterinary Hospital, who has continued to manage our veterinary practice in Concord, California while I set off on a new career as an author on the East Coast; William Pritchard, DVM, of UC Davis, whose desires to retire from teaching jurisprudence to the students there enabled me to develop a career as his replacement; Lorna McAdam, also of UC Davis, who could always get last-minute word processing done after time had seemed to run out; and Darryl Bierry, DVM, Director of Clinical Studies at the University of Pennsylvania, who found a way to get me on staff at Penn part time while I was pursuing this endeavor nearly full time.

A tribute also must go out to the wonderful clients and staff at Four Corners Veterinary Hospital in Concord, California, who taught me so much about being a happy and successful veterinarian. Much of the philosophy and material included in this text came into being through experiences gained by working on and appreciating the love they had for their animals, dealing with their complaints, and receiving their praises.

My love and thanks to our children Amy and Mike, who endured two years of life with their parents during which time they were frequently ignored while their parents were immersed in this project.

Last but not least, unending thanks are in order for my parents, Jim and Helen Wilson, who taught me that with enough perseverance and effort, I could accomplish anything I set out to do.

Preface

After graduating from Iowa State University's veterinary school and subsequently earning a law degree from UCLA, I decided not to pursue a career as an attorney but to continue practicing veterinary medicine. A career as a medical diagnostician and surgeon helping animals held a bigger challenge and joy for me than resolving legal battles between people. However, because of my law school education I found that I had developed a strong interest in and recognition of the legal pitfalls associated with the practice of veterinary medicine. When the opportunity to teach veterinary jurisprudence arose at the University of California, Davis, I took it with enthusiasm. This part-time position allowed me to own my own veterinary practice and bring everyday examples of legal obstacles to Davis's veterinary students.

The decision to teach veterinary law and ethics has provided me with an annual dose of stimulation. The support I have received from the administration and faculty at UC Davis and its students has been extraordinary, and this school continues to be one of the leading veterinary schools advocating and implementing the teaching of these materials.

The interest and concern about legal issues within veterinary associations and state boards of examiners have been a positive influence favoring the inclusion of this course of study in veterinary school curricula. I have served on many state board and veterinary association committees and have found that hardly a meeting goes by without discussion of some serious legal concern. The emphasis and volume of information on legal topics in veterinary journals also have strengthened my belief that information about the law is vital to today's practicing veterinarians.

Perhaps the strongest interest, though, is coming from veterinary students themselves. I find that students at other schools are struggling to find information and answers to their legal questions. I also find that Davis graduates serving internships and residencies at other hospitals and colleges are spreading the word to local students about the legal awareness they developed while they were students at Davis. As a result, I have received requests repeatedly for information and copies of the course syllabus we use to teach this material. Many of my former students have told me that they have used their jurisprudence syllabus more than any of their other college notes. This is one of the greatest incentives I have had for writing this book. It brought home the need to assemble this body of scattered and diverse information into an organized reference to enable veterinary students to learn about this complex topic.

It also seemed a reasonable assumption that the legal awareness of busy practicing veterinarians could be heightened if they had such a book to which they could refer. It is difficult for most practitioners to keep current with the rapid changes in veterinary medicine. It is even more difficult for them to keep abreast with the changing consumer laws, the liability of professionals under antitrust laws, the growing governmental control of activities regarding the practice of veterinary medicine or the administration and dispensing of veterinary drugs, the sober area of controlled substances, the menagerie of laws relating to animals, the changing philosophies regarding animal rights and veterinary ethics, the growth of malpractice actions and potential professional liability, the increasing liability associated with prepurchase examinations, the problems surrounding care and custody of wild animals, or even the issues relating to the maintenance of medical records or serving as an effective expert witness.

A text on this subject is long overdue. This volume is at least a modest start toward advancing the mass of material available on this subject. Meanwhile, I hope that it will prove to be helpful for veterinary practitioners and students as they gain a better perspective of the wide range of jurisprudence relevant to their profession.

In the interest of bettering our veterinary students' and colleagues' education, I will appreciate receiving your criticisms and suggestions for any improvements that can be made.

Table of Contents

CHAPTER 1
The Basics of American Law

Origins of Law	1
Laws, Ethics, and Morals	2
Enforceability	2
The Code of Ethics	3
Some Examples	3
Classification of Laws	5
Criminal Law versus Civil Law	5
Contract Law versus Tort Law	5
Substantive versus Procedural Law	6
Written versus Unwritten Laws	7
Law versus Equity	7
The Judicial System	7
Classification of Courts	8
The Legal Codification, Citation, and Library Systems	9
Legal Case Headings	9
The Adversary System of Justice	11
An Unresolvable Issue	11
An Impartial Tribunal	11
Equality in Competence	12
Equality in Adversariness	12
Attorneys	12
Selection of Legal Counsel	12
The Issue of Fees	14
The Course of Events in a Legal Action	15
The Initiation of a Civil Case	15
Service of Process	16
Pleadings	16
The Initial Stages of a Criminal Case	17
The Mid Stages of Legal Action	18
The Trial	19
The End Stage of a Legal Action	20
Enforcement	21
Alternative Methods for Solving Disputes	21
Negotiation	21
Mediation	22
Arbitration	23
Conclusion	23

CHAPTER 2
Veterinary and Animal Ethics

Bernard E. Rollin, PhD

Veterinary Medicine and Philosophy	24
Valuational Assumptions	25
Moral Value Judgments	25
The Neglect of Ethical Inquiry	26
Ethical Inquiry and Veterinary Medicine	27
Can Ethics Be Dealt with Rationally?	28
A Rational Approach to Ethical Decision Making	29
Morally Relevant Differences and Ethical Decision Making	29
Inconsistencies and Ambiguities	30
Helping People Set Ethical Goals	30
Types of Ethical Questions in Veterinary Medicine	31
Recognizing Ethical Questions	31
Sorting out Ethical Issues	32
The Four Types of Moral Problems in Veterinary Medicine	33
Analyzing Ethical Issues	36
Creating a Forum for Dialogue	37
Moral Principles	38
Justifying Moral Principles	40
Ethical Theory	41
Adjudicating Moral Issues	42
An Ethic for Animals	45
Conclusion	48

CHAPTER 3
Laws Establishing the Practice of Veterinary Medicine

The State Board	50
Mission and Jurisdiction	50
Appointments to the Board	51
Practice Acts	51
Purpose	51
Definitions	52
Additional Board Duties, Rights, Privileges, and Powers	56
Veterinary Premise Inspections	57
The Adoption of Minimum Standards	57
Record Keeping Requirements	58

The Administration of Anesthetics   58
Issuance of Licenses   58
Various Examinations   60
Reciprocity of Licensing   61
The Future of Reciprocity   62
Special Features of Practice Acts   62
Good Samaritan Acts   62
Reporting Animal Cruelty Cases   63
Duties to Report Dogs Injured in Staged Animal Fights   64
Licensing of Veterinary Premises   64
Ownership of Veterinary Hospitals   64
Dealing with Abuse of Alcohol and Other Drugs   65
Penalties for Practice Act Violations   66
Penalties for Licensed Veterinarians   67
Grounds for Disciplinary Action   67
Unprofessional Conduct   68
A New Method of Discipline   68

CHAPTER 4
Animals and the Law

Terms and Categories   72
Defining Animals   72
The Classification of Animals as Domestic or Wild   73
The New Category Called Pets   74
The Unique Position of Animals as a Form of Property   75
Limitations on Ownership   76
Animal Confinement Laws and Liability   76
Licensing Requirements   79
Rabies Vaccination Requirements   79
Liability for Animal Bites   80
Reporting Bite Incidents   81
Dangerous Dogs   82
Animal Noise as a Nuisance   83
Animal Waste Laws   84
Limitations on Numbers of Animals Owned,
    Kept, or Harbored   85
Abandoned Animal Laws   86
Liens for Veterinary Services   89
Animal Cruelty Laws   91
Rights of Animal Owners   94
Rights Embodied in Wills and Trusts   95
The Right of Stray Animals to Receive Emergency Care   96
The Requirement to Stop at the Scene of an Accident   97
Property Rights Pertaining to Animal Cadavers   98
Owners' Rights to Destroy Their Animals   102
Rights of Livestock Owners   102

Bailments   105
    Duties of Bailors and Bailees   106
Emergency Care and Euthanasia   107

CHAPTER 5
Minimizing Complaints and Settling Disputes

Causes for Complaints   111
    Breakdowns in Communications About Medical Care 111
    The Failure to Provide Satisfactory Quantity
        and Quality of Veterinary Care   117
    The Failure to Offer Referrals   118
    The Failure to Show Adequate Compassion   119
Aggravating the Potential for Complaints   120
    Emergency Clinic Personnel   120
    Specialists   121
    Veterinary School Personnel   121
    Egotistical Veterinarians   122
    When Criticism Is Appropriate   123
Avenues for Addressing Grievances   123
    Personal Contact   123
    Traditional Ethics Committees   124
    Peer Review Committees   125
    State Boards of Examiners Review   127
    Courts of Law   129

CHAPTER 6
Professional Liability

The Magnitude of the Professional Liability Problem   131
The Law of Negligence and Malpractice   132
    Negligence Defined   132
    Relating the Law of Contracts,
        Negligence, and Malpractice   133
The Elements of a Cause of Action for Negligence   133
    Duty   134
    The Standard of Care   135
    Proximate Causation   145
    Damages   145
The Duty to Refer   154
Res Ipsa Loquitur   156
Legal Defenses to Negligence Actions   157
Essential Types of Liability Insurance   160
    Professional Liability Insurance   160
    Directors' and Officers' Liability Insurance   161

Comprehensive General Liability Policies 161
Bailment Coverage 161
Veterinarian Countersuits 162
Malicious Prosecution 162
Abuse of Process 163
Negligence 163
Barratry, Defamation, Emotional
Distress, Invasion of Privacy, and
Prima Facie Tort 164
Assault and Battery 164
Defining Assault and Battery 164
Defenses 165
False Imprisonment 166
Libel and Slander 166
The Elements 167
Defenses 169
Wrongful Discharge 170
Avoiding Liability 171

CHAPTER 7
Antitrust and Advertising

Antitrust Among the Professions Prior to 1975 175
The *Goldfarb* v. *Virginia Bar* Case 176
The Sherman Antitrust Act 176
The Objective 176
Delegation of Administration 177
Language of the Sherman Antitrust Act 179
Sherman Act Exemptions 183
The Statutory Basis for Penalties 183
Professional Liability Insurance and Antitrust Suits 184
The FTC Act 184
Unfair Methods of Competition 184
Investigations by the FTC 185
Changes in the Law Regarding Advertising 185
The Beginning of Change 185
Major Changes Occur 185
The Veterinary Profession Has Its Day in Court 187
The Final Outcome 187

CHAPTER 8
Contract Law

Formation of the Contract 190
The Contract 190
Offer Under Common Law 191

The Common Law Acceptance   193
The Acceptance in Implied versus Express Contracts   193
Offer and Acceptance Under the UCC   194
Meeting of the Minds   194
Intent   194
Standard Form Contracts, or Contracts of Adhesion   195
Consideration   195
Capacity to Contract   197
Minority   197
Mental Disability   198
Intoxication   199
Statute of Frauds   199
Types of Contracts Covered   199
Remedies for a Failure to Comply   200
Parol Evidence   200
Remedies for Breaches of Contract   200
Damages   200
Specific Performance   201
Restitution   202
The Duty to Mitigate Damages   202
The Law of Quasi Contract, or Unjust Enrichment   203
Personal Service Contracts   204
Reasons Why Practitioners Avoid
    Employment Contracts   204
Problems with Recollection   204
Contract Terms   205
Sample Contracts   205
Covenants Not to Compete   205
Legal Precedents   206
The Sherman Antitrust Act   207
State Laws   212
Summary   213

CHAPTER 9
The Legal Use of Veterinary Drugs

The Regulatory System   215
Federal Regulatory Agencies and Legislation   215
State Government Regulations   216
The FD&C Act   216
Drugs in Interstate Commerce   217
Obtaining FDA Approval:
    New Animal Drug Applications   217
Drug Categories   218
Products Not Subject to Federal Regulation   218
Adulterated Drugs   218
Misbranded Drugs   218

Over-the-Counter Drugs   219
Prescription, or Legend Drugs   219
Extra-Label Drug Use   220
Drugs Prohibited for Use in Food-Producing Animals   221
Unapproved Drugs   223
Generic versus Brand Name Drugs   225
Drugs for Minor Use   225
FDA Regulatory Efforts—A Changing Scene   225
Antibiotics in the Food Chain   226
Changes in the Political Climate   226
The Veterinarian-Client-Patient Relationship
  and the FDA   227
The AVMA's Definition of the
  Veterinarian-Client-Patient Relationship   227
California's Definition of the
  Veterinarian-Client-Patient Relationship   228
Priorities for FDA Regulatory Attention   229
The FDA's Investigations and Penalties   229
FDA Inspections   229
Controversial Issues   230
Penalties for Illegally Selling or Dispensing Drugs   231
Managing Veterinary Drugs   231
Distributor Assurances Regarding Product Liability   231
Veterinary Liability for Drug Residues in Food   232
Separating Prescription Drugs from OTC Drugs   232
Hospital Policies Regarding Prescription Drug Sales   232
Keeping Abreast of the Changing Times   233
Labeling and Packaging   233
Label Requirements   233
Poison Prevention Packaging Act   234
Adverse Drug Reactions   235
Documenting Drug Reactions   235
Reporting Adverse Drug Reactions to the FDA   236
Product Liability and the Veterinarian   236
Implied Warranties   236
The Restatement of Torts View of Strict Liability   238
Foreseeability as a Part of Product Liability   239
Product Recalls   239
Avoiding Liability Problems   240
Defenses to Product Liability Actions   241
Veterinarians' Rights to Render Nonstandard Treatment   242
FDA Policies   242
Extra-Label or Unapproved Drug Use   242
Client Consent Considerations for Drug Use   243
Side Effects: The Owner's Right to Know   243
Drugs of Special Concern   243
Medical Factors Influencing the Need for Consent   245
Various Types of Client Consent   246
Administering Drugs to Show and Racehorses   248
American Horse Show Association Rules   248

State Laws on Drugs Used for Horses   250
National Association of State
    Racing Commission Rules   250
Summary   251

CHAPTER 10
The Law on Veterinary Biologicals and Pesticides

Regulation of Veterinary Biologicals   254
    The Virus-Serum-Toxin Act of 1913   254
    Interstate Commerce, Intrastate
        Shipments, and Exports   255
    Testing Procedures   255
    Testing the Products   255
    Packaging and Labeling Requirements   256
    Questions About Product Efficacy   256
    Extra-Label Use of Biologicals   257
    The Veterinarian-Client-Patient Relationship   257
    Administration of Rabies Vaccines   258
    Some Concluding Thoughts   258
The EPA and Veterinary Responsibilities
        for the Use of Pesticides   258
    The Federal Insecticide, Fungicide,
        and Rodenticide Act   258
    Basic Concerns About Veterinarians' Use of Pesticides   258
    Active versus Inert Ingredients   259
    Labels and Labeling   259
    Misbranding   259
    Risks of Liability and Uses
        Inconsistent with the Labeling   260
    State Law Application to Pesticide Uses   260
    Minimizing and Avoiding Problems   260

CHAPTER 11
Controlled Substances

The Importance of Laws Governing Controlled Substances   262
Federal Regulation of Controlled Substances   262
State Drug Control   263
Classification of Controlled Substances   263
    Schedule I   263
    Schedule II   263
    Schedule III   264

Schedule IV   264
Schedule V   264
Rescheduling of Controlled Substances   264
Registration   264
Who Must Register   265
Defining Practitioners   265
Veterinarians Working at Multiple Locations   265
Administration of Controlled Drugs
    by Nonveterinary Staff Members   266
Independent Contractors   267
Applications, Renewals, and Address Changes   267
Registration of Animal Shelters   267
Termination of Registration   268
Ordering Controlled Substances   269
Obtaining Order Forms   269
Completing Order Forms   269
Powers of Attorney to Order Controlled Drugs   272
Record Keeping   273
The Rationale for Records   273
Record Keeping Rules   273
Lending Controlled Drugs to Other Practitioners   276
Other Systems for Record Retrieval   277
Inventory of Controlled Substances   277
New Businesses or Change of Registrant   277
Biennial Inventories   277
Security of Stored Controlled Drugs   278
The Securely Locked, Substantially
    Constructed Cabinet Rule   278
Security for Potent Drugs Used on
    Exotic and Wild Animals   278
Thefts or Losses of Controlled Drugs   279
Prescriptions   279
Schemes and Shams   279
Chemically Impaired Veterinarian Programs   282
Summary   283

CHAPTER 12
The Veterinarian as an Expert Witness

Defining an Expert   284
The Duty   284
Type of Expert   285
The Constitution of Evidence   285
Types of Evidence   285
Preparation   287
Important Papers   288
The Overly Modest Expert   288

Taking Sides   288
Payment for Testimony   289
Qualifying as an Expert   289
The Questioning Process   290
Appearance in Court   291
Opinion Evidence and Hypothetical Questions   291
Attributes of Good Expert Witnesses   292

CHAPTER 13
Credit Management and Debt Collection

Debt Avoidance Techniques   294
 Contracts   295
        Implied Contracts   295
        Oral Contracts   295
        Written Contracts and Estimates   296
Credit Management   296
        Managing Client Debt   296
        The Billing System   299
        Aging Accounts   302
        In-House Collection Techniques   303
Fair Debt Collection Statutes   304
        Transactions Not Covered by the California Act 304
        Personnel Who Are Covered by the Act   304
        Communications Regarding the Debt   304
        Prohibitions Against Notations on
             Written Correspondence   305
        Other Prohibited Practices   306
        Prohibitions Against Deadbeat Lists   306
        Debtors' Responsibilities   306
Collection Agencies   307
        Pros and Cons of Collection Agency Use   307
        Types of Collection Services   307
Small Claims Court   308
        Types of Complaints   308
        Drawbacks to Small Claims Courts   308
        Factors to Consider Before Filing   309
        Filing the Claim   310
        Service of Process   310
        Answers to Small Claims Court Actions   311
        Counterclaims   311
        Venue   311
        Preparation for Trial   311
        Testimony at the Trial   312
        The Decision and Appeals   313
        Judicial Collection Devices   313
Summary   315

CHAPTER 14
Medical Records: Content, Requirements, and Legal Implications

Types of Records   316
    Medical and Business Documents   316
    Source versus Problem-Oriented Records   317
Recording Information in the Record   318
    The History   319
    The Examination   319
    The Diagnosis   319
    Treatment   320
    Other Important Entries   320
    Omissions from the Medical Record   321
    Alterations in the Record   321
Medical Record Requirements   321
    Statutory Requirements   322
    Medical Records in a Legal Defense   323
    Computer-Generated Medical and Business Records   324
    Insurance Requirements   327
    Professional Association Requirements   328
    Contractual Requirements   329
    Tax and Documentary Purposes   338
    Informed Consent Requirements   338
    Ownership, Possession, and Access
        to the Medical Record   344
    Confidentiality of Medical Records   345
    Retention of Medical Records   346
    Ownership of Radiographs,
        Electrocardiograms, and Laboratory Reports 347
    Theft of Mailing Lists and
        Computer-Generated Records   349
    Lost Medical Records   349
Improving the Routine Medical Record   350
    Timeliness   350
    Dealing with Incomplete Records   350
    Differentiating Staff Entries on the Record   350
    Flow Sheet Laboratory Forms   351
    Hospital Census List   351
    The Use of Photographs   351
    Incidental Notations   354
    Arm Twisters and Bail Outs   354

CHAPTER 15
Legal Principles Associated with Prepurchase Examinations

Terminology	359
Liability Concerns	360
Increasing Liability Risks	360
The Issue of Confidentiality	360
Conflicts of Interest	361
Areas of Legal Concern	361
The Buyer's Involvement in the Prepurchase Exam	362
Attendees at the Examination	362
The Horse's Intended Use	362
Identifying the Horse	362
Disclosing the Value of the Horse	363
Evaluating Behavior and/or Reproductive Capabilities	363
The Buyer's Consent	363
Reviewing the Components of the Exam	368
The Examination	368
The Veterinarian's Findings	368
Laws Regarding Medical Records	369
The Physical Examination	369
The Seller's Involvement	369
Disclosures by Sellers	372
Drug-Use Disclosure	372
Previous Medical Records	373
The Prepurchase Examination Record	376
Summary	377

CHAPTER 16
Wildlife Law
Jo Anne L. Garbe, DVM, JD

The Laws, Treaties, and Authorities Governing Wildlife	378
International Law	379
International Agreements	379
International Regulation of Trade	381
Federal Legislation and Regulation	383
The Permit Process Pertaining to Wildlife	388
Permit Procedures Under the Department of Interior Authority	388
Permit Procedures Under the Department of Commerce Authority	399

Procedures Under the Department of
    Agriculture Authority That Affect Wildlife   400
Permit Procedures Under the Department
    of Health and Human Services Authority   405
Federal Regulation of Other Wildlife Activities   406
    Wildlife Rehabilitation Facilities   406
    Pet Stores   406
    Wildlife Auctions   406
State Regulation of Wildlife   407
    New York Regulation of Wild Bird Importation   407
Other Areas of Concern to Wildlife Veterinarians   408
    Extra-Label Use of Pharmaceutical
        Products with Wildlife   408
    Liability of Wildlife Veterinarians   408

APPENDICES

Appendix A, Compilation of Laws Relating to
    the Practice of Veterinary Medicine   414
Appendix B, Model Veterinary Practice Act   438
Appendix C, Proposed Minimum Standards of Practice   447
Appendix D, Principles of Veterinary Medical Ethics   456
Appendix E, National Drug Withdrawal Guide   467
Appendix F, The Commonwealth of Massachusetts
    Code of Professional Conduct   469
Appendix G, Revised Contra Costa County, CA,
    Animal Control Ordinance   472
Appendix H, International Treaties   487
Appendix I, Federal Legislation   488
Appendix J, Addresses of Federal Agencies or
    Offices Issuing Wildlife Permits   489
Appendix K, Offices Involved with State Regulation
    of Wildlife   491
Appendix L, DEA Divisional Domestic Field Offices   495
Appendix M, Medical Abbreviations   499
Appendix N, AVMA Guidelines for Supervising Use and
    Distribution of Veterinary Prescription Drugs   507

INDEX   513

Trademark List

Actifed-C is a trademark of Burroughs Wellcome Company.
Cytoxan is a trademark of Bristol-Myers Oncology Division.
Darvon is a trademark of Eli Lilly and Company.
Demerol is a trademark of Winthrop-Breon Laboratories.
Desoxyn is a trademark of Abbott Laboratories.
Dexedrine is a trademark of Smith Kline & French Laboratories.
Dilaudid is a trademark of Knoll Pharmaceuticals.
Empirin is a trademark of Burroughs Wellcome Company.
Equanil is a trademark of Wyeth Laboratories.
Hycodan is a trademark of Du Pont Pharmaceuticals.
Librium is a trademark of Roche Laboratories.
Lomotil is a trademark of Searle Pharmaceuticals.
Miltown is a trademark of Wallace Laboratories.
Nembutal is a trademark of Abbott Laboratories.
Numorphan is a trademark of Du Pont Pharmaceuticals.
Ovaban is a trademark of Schering Corporation.
Percodan is a trademark of Du Pont Pharmaceuticals.
Phenaphen is a trademark of A. H. Robins Company.
Phenergan is a trademark of Wyeth Laboratories.
Ritalin is a trademark of CIBA Pharmaceutical Company.
Robitussin A-C is a trademark of A. H. Robins Company.
Sansalid is a trademark of Shell Chemical.
Seconal is a trademark of Eli Lilly and Company.
Talwin is a trademark of Winthrop-Breon Laboratories.
Tranxene is a trademark of Abbott Laboratories.
Tylenol is a trademark of McNeil Consumer Products Company.
Valium is a trademark of Roche Laboratories.

LAW AND ETHICS OF THE VETERINARY PROFESSION

CHAPTER 1

The Basics of American Law

A vast number of legal concepts and precedents are encompassed within the framework of veterinary medical practice. Although most veterinarians rarely stop to consider what these are, business relations exist and function in an orderly manner because of this network of laws.

Some laws define the rights and duties of employers. Others establish the basis for contractual relationships. Each chapter in this book focuses on one area of law that has an impact on the daily provision of veterinary services.

The laws and regulations affecting veterinary medicine are innumerable. Nevertheless, every veterinary student and practitioner should acquire a general knowledge of law and rely on both written and personal sources when specific questions related to the practice of veterinary medicine arise.

Origins of Law

The law regulating business relations is a part of a comprehensive legal system that has evolved over centuries. Various cultures have had an effect on our current law, the first being those civilizations associated with the creation of the Bible. The Greek and Roman cultures also contributed to present-day legal concepts. Trials by judges, the assistance of lawyers for those involved in the trial process, and the creation of written laws for all people to inspect comprise some of the contributions these earlier societies made to today's legal system.

The English Common Law System has had the biggest impact on American law. Unlike some other legal systems, the English common law does not rely solely on statutory law (laws created by legislatures or dictatorships). Instead, under the common law system, judges have the discretion to establish binding legal precedents by interpreting the customs and beliefs of the people as they pertain to a set of facts presented. As in all systems, the court is also charged with interpreting the language and intent of legislatively enacted laws.

Judicially created law, or *case law*, as it is called, is law derived from judicial decisions and

1

interpretations. The customs and beliefs of the times gradually become law as judges rely upon the doctrine of *stare decisis* ("the decision stands"). This legal principle means that decisions made in prior cases are to be followed in current cases and will be followed in future cases when the same set of facts exists. Because of this rule, lawyers can anticipate how courts will decide cases, and they can advise people regarding ways to avoid future legal conflicts. Nevertheless, variations in the facts associated with similar cases make predicting the outcome of these cases somewhat tenuous. Depending on these variations, courts will always have some leeway to alter their decisions. The result is that since very few sets of facts are identical, the law is frequently gray rather than black or white.

It must also be kept in mind that prior decisions are binding only in courts of the same *jurisdiction*. There are various legal jurisdictions including the federal, state, municipal, and several other court systems. Because of jurisdictional variations, what is law in Florida may not be the same as the law on a given issue in Pennsylvania. For example, money damages for the emotional distress associated with the loss of a pet are judicially allowed in Florida,[1] Hawaii,[2] Louisiana,[3] and Texas[4] but have either not been considered or have not been allowed by appellate courts in the remaining 46 states.

Laws, Ethics, and Morals

Numerous definitions of "the law" exist, but one that says it best is the following:

> *The law* is that body of principles that govern conduct and the observance of which can be enforced by courts, or that which must be obeyed and followed by citizens subject to legal sanctions or consequences.[5]

The key ingredients in this definition are "a body of principles," which govern personal "conduct," and the right to have these principles "enforced in courts" via legal "sanctions."

Moral and ethical constraints are as important as the legal constraints imposed upon the veterinary profession. In fact, the basis of all constraints in the practice of veterinary medicine is the underlying morality of each person. An individual's moral conception of right and wrong will consistently affect how that person responds to or obeys the ethical and legal constraints of the profession.

A person's moral standards are determined largely by family influences and to some degree by religious or philosophical principles. One wonders how much influence the veterinary educational process has on the professional person's morality. Traditionally, there has been little mention of this subject during the educational process. The international animal rights movement of the 1980s has changed this, though, in that the veterinarian is more than ever before in the mainstream of the issues concerning people's interactions with and responsibilities for the treatment of animals.

In the past few years many veterinary schools have added courses on law and ethics in veterinary medicine to their curricula. Thus, it appears that what Watergate did to upgrade ethics curricula in the nation's law schools, the animal rights movement is doing for veterinary schools.

Enforceability

The key element differentiating a law from a moral precept or from a component in a code of ethics is that of enforceability. The only thing that has any clout when it comes to the enforcement of a moral precept is personal guilt. The efficacy of that deterrent depends entirely on the character of the individual.

This differs somewhat from the enforcement of a principle in a veterinary code of ethics. Whereas courts have the jurisdiction and power to enforce laws, they have no such authority with regard to enforcing ethical behavior. Ethics are rules established by professional organizations or other groups intended to influence the actions of the group. Although ethical guidelines are extremely important in encouraging cooperation and respect within a profession, these codes cannot be enforced within a court of law. Courts and governments can and do, nevertheless, look to the ethical principles established by the various professional associations for guidance when legal precedents need to be updated to fit today's professional expectations.

A professional association may reprimand, suspend, or expel a member for failure to adhere to its ethical code, but it must rely on its own organizational rules, not those of the court system, to effect the expulsion. The benefit to society or the association from such action is questionable because members can continue to behave unethically even after they have been expelled. It is because of this fact that action taken against an unethical veterinarian by an association does not usually have as much impact as a court or state board of examiners decision.

The Code of Ethics

The basic code of ethics for veterinarians in the United States is the American Veterinary Medical Association (AVMA) *Principles of Veterinary Medical Ethics*.[6] Individual state veterinary associations usually adopt the AVMA code to fulfill their own needs for a script on the topic of ethics.

One writer has criticized this code as nothing more than a code of etiquette, not ethics.[7] He says that the code emphasizes relatively simple issues like what constitutes ethical advertising but does not provide guidance for the difficult ethical situations. On the other hand, another author maintains that the code is a strong, simple statement on the subject of professional behavior by veterinarians.[8] In recent years the AVMA's judicial counsel has made major changes and additions to the code in order to expand and contemporize its position on new ethical issues.

Whatever the case, issues of morality and ethics must be considered in conjunction with the law. The process of professional orientation for a veterinarian involves the voluntary conversion of an individual's attitudes and perceptions from those of an ordinary citizen to those of a medical professional. How this is accomplished and whether the attempt is successful will greatly affect the professional behavior patterns and standards by which veterinarians conduct their practices in the years to come.

Some Examples

Some commonplace examples comparing ethics, morality, and the law can help explain the overlap among these constraints on practice and the dilemmas faced by practitioners.

1. Legally, veterinarians have no duty to render emergency care to any animal examined by them unless the patient has been under their care and the current emergency is related to that care.

   Morally, it seems fairly certain that since veterinarians have been educated to help, treat, and care for animals, they should provide emergency care to any animal in need of it. Because of the financial impact associated with such an ideal, however, adhering to this moral precept is not always practicable.

   From an ethical viewpoint in this situation, one can look to Parts 1 and 2 of Section 1 of the *Principles of Veterinary Medical Ethics* for guidance. Part 1 says that one of the principles of the veterinary profession is to prevent and relieve suffering of animals. Part 2 states, "Veterinarians may choose whom they will serve. Once they have undertaken care of a patient, they must render service to the best of their ability." Although this is helpful, it does not resolve the difficult issue of what a veterinarian is to do if the owner cannot pay for emergency treatment. Since veterinarians legally are not required to provide veterinary care and, ethically, they can choose whom they will serve, there is still no requirement to provide emergency service to anyone. The encouragement to go ahead and do so certainly appears to be embodied, though, within the ethical code.

When this issue of a legal duty to provide emergency veterinary care was raised in New Jersey in 1977, the Appellate Division of the Superior Court sidestepped it.[9] They did say that a veterinarian's failure to "exhibit professional interest, compassion and empathy, and render not only skilled care, but humane concern and compassionate care as well" was not in and of itself grounds for a finding of gross malpractice or gross neglect. In this case, a veterinarian's employee (spouse) had refused to extend credit to the owners of a sick kitten in need of some emergency treatment. They went on to say, though, that although the employer veterinarian could be liable in a tort action (under the negligence theory) for the conduct of an employee, that same veterinarian, "absent proof of some participation personally in the objectionable conduct, could not be subject to censure, fines, suspension or revocation of his license for the act of his employee."

2. Morally, an employed veterinarian should report to some authority the fact that a given veterinary employer is, for example, charging clients for lab work not actually performed, knowingly administering outdated vaccines, or experiencing anesthetic deaths in patients because of outdated anesthetic protocols. Legally, however, nothing in the Veterinary Practice Acts or regulations instructs veterinary employees to do anything about such activity.

One of the recent additions to the *Principles of Veterinary Medical Ethics* specifically addresses the problem of dissatisfied animal owners who "take the initiative of going from one veterinarian to another without referral."[6] However, there are no ethical guidelines regarding problems between employed veterinarians and their employers. Only Part 5, Section 1, of the AVMA *Principles* directly addresses this issue. It says, "The veterinary profession should safeguard the public and itself against veterinarians deficient in moral character or professional competence." Perhaps future modifications of the AVMA *Principles* will assist employed veterinarians whose fears of being fired prevent them from seeking some professional assistance with moral dilemmas like the above.

3. Clients will sometimes ask veterinarians to euthanatize a perfectly healthy animal. This may be morally repulsive to many veterinarians, but animals are legally classified as property. Therefore, the owner, under current law, still has the right to humanely bring about the death of that property. When one seeks some ethical guidance in a case like this, the AVMA *Principles of Ethics* offers minimal assistance. Part 2 of the *Principles* does say, "Veterinarians may choose whom they will serve" and, therefore, they can simply refuse to serve a client with this type of request on ethical grounds. Would it be any better if the *Principles of Ethics* placed some level of stewardship on veterinarians to protect animal life, as suggested by at least one author?[10] Could any differentiation be made between animals used for economic gain and animals owned as pets?

4. Consider a case in which the veterinarian makes a mistake in the choice or dosage of a drug administered to a hospital patient and that mistake kills the patient.[11] It is quite possible that the owner will not find out what transpired and absent any

such knowledge, there will be no legal action. Legal liability for such a mistake, however, is still a distinct possibility.

The ethical requirement is to be honest with the client, although honesty could provoke a lawsuit. Morally, there is undoubtedly a heavy burden of guilt as well as a duty to tell the owner what really happened. That brings three tough questions to the fore. First, do veterinarians have a legal duty to inform the client of what actually transpired? Second, can veterinarians morally charge for all the services rendered to a patient that dies due to an error or negligence on their part? Third, will a failure to charge a fee cause the owner to suspect that something wrong happened and thus provoke a legal action? In other words, will the truth make things better or worse and for whom?

There are no easy answers to any of these interlinked moral, legal, and ethical situations. As the value of animal life continues to increase in the eyes of concerned citizens and the law, these issues will repeatedly arise within the veterinary profession. The AVMA *Principles* speak well when they recommend, "It is suggested that the teaching of ethics and professional morals be intensified in the schools."[6]

Classification of Laws

Many different types of laws exist in this country, with most having specific procedures for enforcement and an established set of remedies. Figure 1.1 charts the general types of American law.

Criminal Law versus Civil Law

One of the traditional methods for classifying law has been on the basis of what type of activity is being regulated.

Criminal law defines the boundaries of the relationship between the individual and society. Acts that are harmful to people and to the fabric of an orderly society are crimes. In conjunction with the creation of criminal laws, society has developed a set of procedures and laws allowing for the investigation of a crime, the arrest of a suspected criminal, the prosecution of such an individual, and the determination of punishment. Most criminal laws focus on acts that can injure people, go against the public interest, or offend public morality. When legal action is initiated, it is brought by society acting through a district attorney at the local level or the United States Attorney General on a national level.

Civil law pertains to the relationships among individuals within a society. A contract dispute between a veterinarian and an employee is an example of a civil law action. In some cases both civil and criminal suits occur. A horse thief, for example, could be charged in a criminal action for committing a wrong against society. In addition, the horse owner could file a civil lawsuit against the thief in an attempt to attain compensation for damages that occurred to the animal at the time of the theft.

Contract Law versus Tort Law

Civil law has two major subdivisions—contract law and tort law. Contract law deals with duties established by individuals as a result of a contractual agreement. This area of law developed because merchants needed a means to assure that promises between persons would be fulfilled. A failure to respect or fulfill the duties set forth in the contract creates the potential of a lawsuit for breaching that duty. Within contract law are laws regulating specific types of business contracts, negotiable instruments (like checks), insurance (including worker's compensation), bankruptcy proceedings, securities (stocks and bonds), etc.

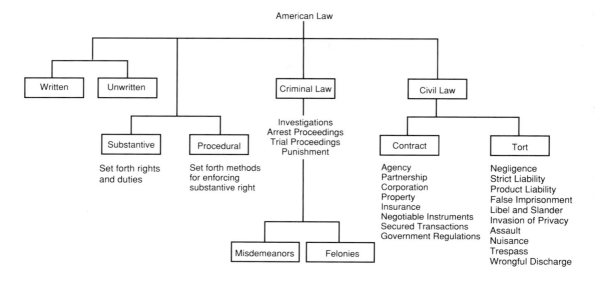

Figure 1.1   General types of American law.

Conversely, tort law deals not with duties created by the parties through a contract, but with duties toward other people that are established by law. For example, the law of negligence, a subdivision of tort law, imposes a duty upon business people to maintain the premises in a manner that will prevent injuries to any people invited to enter those premises.

Courts and legislatures have expanded tort law, creating standards to which every person in our society must adhere. Under tort law, standards of care exist for the protection of one's body, business interests, personal property, and reputation. Tort law permits people to sue for relief of an injury that occurred as a result of damages inflicted on their bodies, family, or property due to a wrongful act. In general, a legal action of this type seeks not to punish the wrongdoer, but only to obtain monetary compensation for the injury that occurred. If the action was intentional, occurred with malice, or involved gross negligence, however, large monetary awards may be allowed by the court in order to punish the individual financially.

Substantive versus Procedural Law

References to "substantive law" or "procedural law" are frequent. Each has its own function. Substantive law comprises a set of rights and duties to which a person must adhere in today's society. Tort law, encompassing personal injuries and a concurrent set of remedies, is an example of substantive law.

Procedural law comprises the rules and procedures for conducting a lawsuit. The court in which an action must be filed, the types of evidence that are admissible, and the procedure for appealing a verdict are all components of procedural law. Errors in following the proper procedures can allow a valid substantive lawsuit to be dismissed from court without being heard by a judge or jury.

The procedural laws that most commonly pose problems for attorneys are the statutes of limitations. Such laws provide that unless people commence lawsuits within a specified period of time, they lose the right to proceed with or maintain the legal action. An example is the California Statute of Limitations on Malpractice Actions,[12] which requires that legal actions for professional negligence be filed within three years after the date of the injury or within one year after the plaintiff discovers or should have discovered the injury, whichever occurs first.

Most procedural laws have a good rationale behind their existence. In the case of statutes of limitations, the theory is that evidence and witnesses tend to disappear and lose recollection as time passes. Thus, a suit must be filed within a reasonably short time after the injury occurred or was discovered. In addition, speedy resolution is important because it is not fair for defendants to be subjected to the threat of a lawsuit indefinitely.

Written versus Unwritten Laws

Written laws are rules and regulations that have been enacted by a legislative arm of government and codified (placed in a code of laws). This body of law is comprised of federal and state statutes as well as county and city ordinances.

Unwritten law, or *common law*, refers to the interpretation by our court system of written laws as well as the interpretation of previous court decisions. Therefore, even though it may appear that a particular action is not covered by a given statute, legal counsel must research the unwritten law (legal interpretations) of all pertinent cases before providing a client with a legal opinion.

Law versus Equity

As the legal system evolved, a rigid set of *remedies at law* was created for various crimes or breaches of conduct. These often involved the payment of monetary damages for an injury caused by such conduct. It soon became apparent, however, that the court needed more flexibility than this provided. In some situations a remedy at law that only allowed

a plaintiff to collect damages would be totally inadequate. Instead, a judicial remedy that, for example, prohibited repetition of the crime or the undesired action was the only way to prevent future damages. Furthermore, since very few sets of facts were ever the same, judges needed the opportunity to customize a punishment or a remedy. As a result, a second legal system evolved under English law allowing courts to develop *remedies in equity*. In today's court system, a judge can dispense either a legal or an equitable remedy.

In a case of breach of contract, instead of merely determining a dollar value for the damages, the court can order one of the parties to perform the contract in certain limited situations. This is titled *specific performance* and is an equitable remedy rather than a rigid legal remedy. For example, the court could specifically require a defendant to transfer title of a unique piece of property to the plaintiff if simply requiring the defendant to pay damages would result in an unequitable and unjust remedy.

Another example of a remedy in equity is the issuance of an *injunction*, prohibiting specific conduct or activity. If any action is taken in violation of the injunction, the defendant can be found to be in contempt of court and sent to jail.

The Judicial System

The court system plays a major role in the administration of justice in the United States. It is through the orderly, although sometimes painstakingly slow, judicial branch of government that individuals have a means to settle personal conflicts peacefully. These same courts also function to preserve the fabric of society by trying and punishing disruptive people who commit crimes against other people or society itself. Lastly, the courts seek to maintain the public's social values and traditions by interpreting the Constitution, laws, and interpersonal relations in a manner that improves society while still respecting the ever-changing customs and mores of its people.

Classification of Courts

Courts of Original Jurisdiction

There are basically two types of courts within the judicial branch of government. The first is the *court of original jurisdiction*, which has the authority to hear a case when it is first brought before the court system. One of the key elements in determining which court can hear a case involves the extent of that court's jurisdiction. Each court has a designated area of authority, granted by the Constitution or the legislature, to hear and decide cases.

The court's jurisdiction is sometimes determined by the type of legal activity involved in the suit. For example, traffic courts decide only traffic cases, while tax courts deal only with interpretations of the tax codes. The court's jurisdiction also can be governed by the dollar value of the suit. Small claims courts, for example, only deal with suits in which the damages sought are less than a certain amount, depending upon the state, and in which legal counsel is not permitted in the courtroom, also depending upon the state. The next higher court system (sometimes called the *court of common pleas*, *municipal court*, or *superior court*) may encourage or require the parties to retain legal counsel. Courts in this group have the authority to hear civil cases when the dispute does not exceed $15,000 or, in criminal cases, when the fine does not exceed $5,000 and the prison term is less than five years. In addition, there are territorial boundaries within which one or both parties to the lawsuit must reside which establish the jurisdiction of a court to hear and decide the case.

These courts of original jurisdiction are where the trials are held and where evidence and testimony are considered. They have a wide variety of designated titles from state to state, as indicated in Figure 1.2. The federal courts of original jurisdiction are entirely separate from the state courts and have their own titles. The jurisdiction in the federal ladder of courts is limited to such areas as disputes between states, conflicts between residents of various states, matters governed by federal law, patent law, and other areas as shown in Figure 1.3.

Courts of Appellate Jurisdiction

The second type of court is called a *court of appellate jurisdiction*. Appeals from courts of original jurisdiction go first to an intermediate court of appeal. Some of the various titles for these state courts are the *court of appeals*, *appellate session of superior court*, and *supreme court, appellate division*. These appellate courts have the power to review cases for errors in the admission of evidence, errors in legal interpretations by the trial court judge, and errors in instructions to juries. Appellate courts only consider transcripts of evidence presented at the trial and arguments presented by legal counsel about the law applied to the case. They do not rehear any of the evidence presented by witnesses at the trial. They can, however, *remand* the case (send it back) to the trial court for it to hear additional evidence if their review shows that legal procedures were improperly followed and some evidence was therefore incorrectly admitted or omitted.

The rights of appeal do not end at this appellate system. There are still the state supreme courts, also called *supreme judicial courts* or *supreme courts of errors* and, ultimately, there is the *United States Supreme Court*. In general, because of the significant costs incurred in the appeals process, only cases involving a considerable amount of money or critical legal principles are appealed all the way to the state or United States Supreme Court level. Fortunately, most cases against veterinarians do not contain either of these ingredients. As a result, excessive trial and appellate legal expenditures are uncommon in veterinary medicine.

For most general business law disputes involving veterinarians, ample precedents

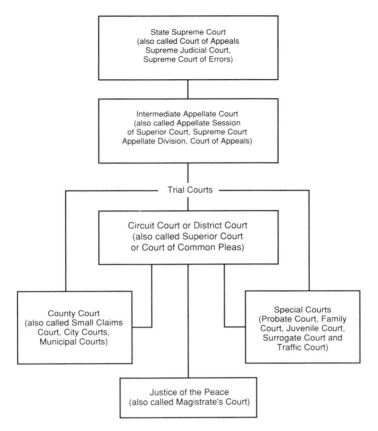

Figure 1.2 State courts of original jurisdiction.

are available so that counsel can offer sound advice. When it comes to veterinary negligence and malpractice disputes, however, relatively few cases have been tried and appealed. Since case law and precedents are only created by the writing of legal opinions at one of the appellate levels, this paucity of case law makes it difficult for attorneys to predict outcomes of veterinary malpractice cases.

follow up on these, people with even the most basic legal knowledge can use a law library. Most law libraries have a reference librarian available to assist the novice. County and city courthouses, law schools, large- and medium-sized law firms, and many public libraries all have an array of legal references for anyone who wishes to use them.

The Legal Codification, Citation, and Library Systems

Legal references and citations are scattered profusely throughout most legal writings. To

Legal Case Headings

Case titles are generally defined by the names of the parties to the lawsuit. A small "v." separates the names and stands for versus, e.g., *Brown* v. *The Board of Education*. At the trial court level, the plaintiff's name, the person bringing the lawsuit, appears first. The defendant's name, the person defending the legal actions, appears last.

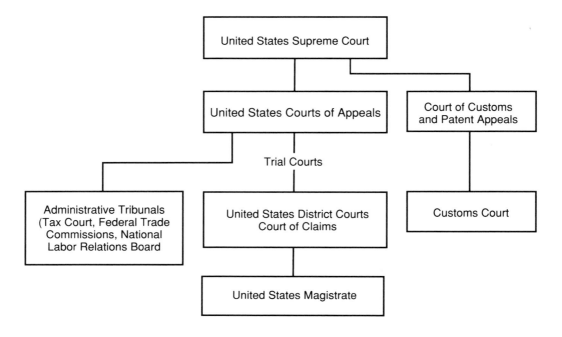

Figure 1.3   Federal courts of original jurisdiction.

If a suit is appealed after a verdict at the trial court level, the name of the party who is appealing the case appears first. If a case appears as *People* v. *Atchison*, it is most likely a criminal case brought by the local district attorney or state attorney general on behalf of "the people" in that jurisdiction.

Whenever a case is cited, the place where it can be found follows the name of the case. For example, 250 U.S. 620 (1916) means that the written report of this case can be found in volume 250 of the *United States Reports* (reporting cases decided by the United States Supreme Court) on page 620. The (1916) means that the case was decided in 1916. The year that the case was decided is virtually always a part of the citation.

Citation of a case heard by a state supreme court is slightly different. An example is *Burke* v. *Fine*, 51 NW 2d 818 (Sup Ct Minn. 1952). Although this case would most likely be reported in a book of cases solely pertaining to Minnesota, the United States has also been sectioned into groups of states. This is done for ease, so that all the cases decided by the supreme courts in each group of states

can be placed in one volume to save law libraries and law offices the need for stocking books from all 50 states.

In the example, the case cited could be found in Volume 51 of the second series of the *North Western Reporter* on page 818. Table 1 lists the courts included in each of the most commonly abbreviated citations. A citation like 287 F Supp. 840 (W.D. Va. 1968), for instance, means that the decision came from the United States district court in the western district of Virginia.

Statutes are also found frequently as components of legal citations. They follow a similar basic style. These too are easy to locate in a law library by looking at the title and the section (§) citations. An example appearing as Calif. Evidence Code §1230 would be found by locating the books of state statutory codes within a library. These are often stacked alphabetically around the perimeter of the library, while the books reporting appellate court decisions are alphabetical by state or region within the central part of the library.

The Adversary System of Justice

Several components are necessary in order for the American legal system, also called the *adversary system of justice*, to function effectively. These are an unresolvable issue, an impartial tribunal, equality in competence, and equality in adversariness.

An Unresolvable Issue

The first item is that of identifying an unresolvable issue. Almost any situation can become controversial, so finding enough substance for a lawsuit is not difficult. Examples of issues which may be unresolvable without court intervention can include whether or not the facts of a case support a plaintiff's contention that the medical care provided for their animal was below the standard for their community, their state, or for the country as a whole. In another case, the primary issue may involve a determination of the magnitude of the damages in-curred. In still others, the major unresolvable issue could be one of determining which states' laws apply to the case.

An Impartial Tribunal

The second key element needed to allow for the American legal system to function is that of an impartial tribunal. Our forefathers chose the judge and jury system to fulfill this need. Although some judgeships are elective positions, the majority of judges are appointed. Some, as in the United States Supreme Court, are appointed for life. They are therefore unlikely to be beholden to any person or business interest. Historically, the judicial system seems to have met the test of impartiality well.

To assure the maximum potential for impartiality, however, the Constitution also established trial by a jury of one's peers. Not all legal actions are open to this option, but most serious offenses for large-dollar suits may have a jury trial. Courts such as traffic court and small-claims court do not have the full protection of a jury trial.

Table 1.1   Common Abbreviations for Case Reports

Abbreviation	Title	Courts Included
U.S.	*United States Reports*	United States Supreme Court
F.	*Federal Reporter*	Federal circuit courts of appeals
F.		
F.Supp.	*Federal Supplement*	United States district court decisions
A.	*Atlantic Reporter**	Pa., Md., Del., N.J., Conn., Vt., N.H., Maine, R.I.
A.2d†		
N.E.	*North Eastern Reporter**	Mass., N.Y., Ohio, Ind., Ill.
N.E. 2d		
N.W.	*North Western Reporter**	Mich., Wis., Minn., Iowa, N.Dak., S. Dak., Neb.
N.W. 2d		
P.	*Pacific Reporter**	Kans., Okla., N.Mex., Colo., Wyo., Mont., Idaho, Utah, Nev., Ariz., Calif., Oreg., Wash., Alaska, Hawaii
So.	*Southern Reporter**	La., Miss., Ala., Fla.
So. 2d		
S.E.	*South Eastern Reporter**	W.Va., Va., N.C., S.C., Ga.
S.E. 2d		
S.W.	*South Western Reporter**	Tex., Ark., Mo., Tenn., Ky.

*These regional reporters include decisions of all appellate courts in these states.
†The abbreviation 2d means the second series of volumes collecting specific reports (e.g., F2d means *Federal Reporter*, second series).

Equality in Competence

The third component for a fair and effective legal system is reasonable equality in the competence of legal counsel on each side of the case. It is in this area that the system is most likely to break down. Overburdened counsel working for the public defender's office of a county or city court system may not have resources sufficient to defend individuals against well-directed police evidence or aggressive district attorneys. On the other hand, the district attorney's office may be underbudgeted and undermanned to compete with wealthy defendants who can hire top attorneys and private investigators.

The old adage "you get what you pay for" is as apropos in the legal world as in any other area of the free-enterprise marketplace. Veterinarians in need of legal counsel should anticipate spending $50 to $300 per hour for an attorney's services depending upon the complexity of the legal problem, the need for experienced senior counsel versus less-seasoned junior counsel, and whether they live in a metropolitan or rural area. It should be kept in mind that good legal care is as important as good medical care, depending on the seriousness of the legal issue.

Equality in Adversariness

The fourth essential ingredient for the effective application of justice is equality in adversariness. The English system of justice is based on what is termed *the adversary system of justice*. The continental system, used generally throughout Europe, is not an adversary system.

The English and American systems allow the attorneys for each side of the case to ask nearly all the questions of the witnesses and to select expert witnesses. In the continental system, the judge is the primary interrogator, with attorneys presenting written questions and arguments on behalf of their clients to the judges. As the action proceeds in the continental system, the judge may interject new theories and new legal and factual issues,

thus reducing the disadvantage of the party with the less competent lawyer.[13] In addition, the court may obtain evidence from expert witnesses on its own initiative. Neither of these is likely to occur in the American system.

It is because of the adversary element in our system that law students are taught to represent their sides of cases to the maximum of their abilities. They are instructed not to determine or assume anything regarding the guilt or liability of their clients; that job is up to the tribunal, i.e., the judge or jury. The attorney's duty is to present the facts and arguments in the case as effectively as possible regardless of what the clients said or did.

One cannot help but wonder what effect some of the procedures inherent in the continental system might have on the issues of adversariness. In that system costs of litigation are taxed in such a way as to discourage hopeless or frivolous cases and, as a rule, the defeated party bears the cost of litigation including attorney's fees.[13]

Although the adversary system has worked satisfactorily for years, it is because of the adversary element that many legal controversies which start out as small matters ultimately become huge lawsuits. The parties to the lawsuit often become enemies engaging in war instead of individuals seeking to negotiate amicable solutions that are satisfactory to each. Too often both parties end up losing and, because of the legal fees incurred, the attorneys are the biggest winners.

Attorneys

Selection of Legal Counsel

Selecting an attorney is as difficult a task as choosing an auto mechanic, physician or, for the animal owner, a veterinarian. Because many veterinarians think that they cannot afford attorneys, they are often undercounseled regarding the law. Practitioners who seek legal counsel should consider the following in making their choice:

1. The candidate's reputation in the community. Due to the huge number of attorneys in practice, this may be difficult to ascertain. If questioning a few other attorneys familiar with the lawyer being considered is not feasible, it may help to ask the candidate for a reference of someone with a legal problem similar to the one at hand.

2. Find out what the candidate's record for punctuality has been. Time is very important in certain veterinary activities such as a proposed partnership or corporate buy in or buy out, and an inordinate delay can kill a deal.

3. Determine the candidate's reputation for returning phone calls. The frustration of being unable to contact one's legal counsel within a reasonable time after the need arises can also create ill will. It may be best to casually ask a secretary in the attorney's office this question as well as question the attorneys themselves.

4. Establish, as well as possible, how adversary minded the attorney is. Questions that focus on the attorney's flexibility regarding solutions to a given legal problem can help one estimate this characteristic. Sometimes practitioners need a very adversary-minded attorney who will dogmatically look after their best interests. Other times they will merely want counsel to assemble the papers for a business deal as expeditiously as possible. It helps to find out if candidates are willing to meet with both of the parties to a proposed business deal or if they wish only to work with the opposing counsel. If the case is, for example, a contract negotiation that definitely requires independent legal representation for each side, a call to the opposing attorney to see how well the two attorneys can work together may also be worthwhile.

5. Assay competence by posing questions to references provided by the attorney. When very little background information about an attorney exists, it might be worthwhile to ask for the names of some clients with similar legal problems who could provide some references. In addition, asking question that determine how much experience the candidate has with legal issues like the ones under consideration allows at least some measure of competence to be determined.

6. Do not pick candidates randomly. Most veterinarians would be as leery about choosing an attorney by perusing the yellow pages as they would be about picking a physician that way. Assemble a list of potential candidates from references and then narrow the list to one or two choices.

Word of mouth is probably the best approach in this type of search. Asking friends who manage small businesses, local dentists and physicians, or accountants or bankers can produce a list of names for review. Often legal counsel employed by a local corporation, a government agency or a local law school can provide good, unbiased referrals. Sometimes these references may be able to advise which attorneys not to hire as well as which to consider. If no other sources are available, veterinarians can contact the local bar association. Most associations provide a referral service to members who will offer an initial fifteen-minute consultation free of charge.

Since there are as many specialties in the law as there are in veterinary medicine, finding attorneys who specialize in the type of legal counsel that is needed is worth some extra effort. The usual areas of expertise of attorneys are bankruptcy, probate and estate planning, criminal, patent, corporate, and commercial law, worker's compensation, property, litigation, and trade. Attorneys who specialize in commercial or trade law are generally best suited for business-related advice.

The Issue of Fees

As discussed earlier, the adversarial training that lawyers undergo during their legal education encourages them to "dot every i and cross every t without regard for economic realities."[14] In addition, attorneys are traditionally accustomed to taking on legal assignments without explaining to their clients what each, or for that matter, any component of the legal representation is likely to cost. Part of this habit stems from the state bar association minimum fee schedules which were common prior to the mid 1970s and covered nearly every legal procedure.

Another part of the rationale for vague fees evolves from the difficulty in ascertaining how much time it might take to research all the current legal precedents, tax ramifications, or witness testimony pertaining to the case in question. Determining the best course of action can require considerable homework, depending on the complexity of the facts. Of course, the same can be said for difficult veterinary cases, but most veterinarians were not taught to charge for medical research in the manner that attorneys and accountants have been taught to charge for legal and tax research.

Negotiations about fees are as important when choosing an attorney as many of the previous items are. The following are some points to consider in this area.

1. Discuss and negotiate fees well before deciding to hire legal counsel. Request an itemized estimate which includes, for example, the lawyer's hourly fee, charges for photocopying documents, costs for filing legal documents, and fees for secretarial services. Flat fees for some particular services can be negotiated, but occasionally this reduces the attorney's incentive to do a thorough job on more difficult cases.

   Determine whether the attorney has a minimum billing time for work performed. If the minimum billing time is 15 minutes, plan phone calls to take full advantage of the 15-minute time span that will be charged, using a clock or stopwatch to stay within the minimum billing time increments. Have a note pad readily available to write down information gathered during the conversation. Since much of the discussion will be about unfamiliar concepts, written notes are essential if one expects to be able to remember and explain what has been learned during the conversation.

   Fees may be lower in smaller firms where fewer people are involved in the case and there often is more contact between the lawyer assigned to the case and the client. Find out whether junior associates are able to resolve the case or whether more expensive senior partners will be needed.

2. Determine the type of billing. An itemized monthly bill is essential. A breakdown of the components of the legal services rendered and the time each took can help define what progress is being made in resolving the case.

3. Insist on monthly status reports in order to ascertain what type of progress is being made. If costs are escalating or progress seems too slow, remember that the person who hired the attorney is the one who should retain control of the case.

4. Do not become excessively concerned with economics. Veterinarians should always remember that the main objective in seeking legal counsel is the creation of an ideal document or providing the best possible representation for their particular interest. Penny pinching on legal fees can sometimes save money in the short run but cost dearly in terms of emotional aggravation and monetary losses in the long run.

5. Do some homework. Perhaps the best way for practitioners to control expenditures on legal fees is for them to prepare as many of their own materials as

they possibly can and then pay counsel to put it in legal terms. Providing attorneys with some sample language for a partnership agreement, for an employment contract, or for a buy-sell agreement that has been hashed over by the involved parties can greatly reduce essential legal time. Although attorneys should be able to create an agreement that establishes what the parties have agreed to, it is often helpful for those parties to thoroughly discuss and write down what they have in mind before their attorneys draft the document. If they do not do this, they may discover that what they have just paid well for does not reflect what they wanted at all. This book will provide formats for items like these so that veterinarians can discuss and attempt to resolve many of the issues embodied in them before they seek legal counsel. Those people willing to devote personal time to home preparation before seeking competent legal counsel will reap dramatic reductions in legal costs.

Opportunities for complaints lie behind every door.

The Course of Events in a Legal Action

The course of events in civil cases is different from the course in criminal cases, so each is covered separately.

The Initiation of a Civil Case

A Complaining Party

The first notice that a veterinarian usually has of a potential legal problem is in the form of a complaining or angry client, staff member, or supplier. Although this may seem to be nothing more than an irritant, be thankful

for the notice. It is much more difficult if the first notice arrives in the form of a summons rather than in the form of an upset individual. A summons is a legal document that states that the plaintiff (complaining party) has been injured because of certain acts or omissions for which the defendant is liable.

The reason that it is preferable to face a complaining person rather than a summons is because it is possible to reason and negotiate with an individual on a personal basis outside of the confines of the legal system. Once a legal summons appears, this usually is no longer an option. Instead, the reality of attorneys' fees and the judicial system are part of the future.

If the complaining parties are clients with injuries to themselves personally or to their animals, the appropriate first response for a veterinarian before doing anything besides listening quietly to the complaint is to call one's insurance agent. Only veterinarians who have good professional liability insurance will have this option, though.

Do not admit any liability or offer any type of settlement options without first notifying and consulting with a spokesperson from the insurance company. It is at this stage that good insurance representatives have the best opportunity to resolve grievances. Any comments made by the insured party that might compromise the insurer's ability to defend or settle the case must be avoided or the insurer may have the option of refusing to defend the insured party.

When the complaint is in the form of a civil lawsuit, legal counsel is generally required. Where insurance is involved, the insurance carrier will choose and pay for such counsel. If no insurance coverage is in force, e.g., a criminal action for violating the Food Drug and Cosmetic Act or an action by the State Board of Examiners for a violation of the state Practice Act, practitioners must supply their own legal representation and answer the allegations contained in the summons within 30 days.

Options for Early Settlement

Experienced insurance company personnel can often settle a grievance relatively easily because they are reasonably unemotional bystanders. In addition, it is normally in their own economic best interests to settle cases instead of sustaining major legal fees. Insurance companies have been known to procrastinate in paying claims, though, in order to forego paying for as long a period of time as possible.

Practitioners should ensure that their professional liability insurance company does not have the option of settling a claim without their approval. Any veterinarian who thinks a lawsuit or grievance is merely a nuisance action rather than a legitimate case should reserve the right to have the insurance company defend the case and not settle it.

When settlements are impossible, legal counsel should be selected as soon as possible after a suit is filed, well before what is called the *discovery phase* of the legal action begins.

Service of Process

The procedure for delivering a summons, a complaint, or a subpoena to the defendant is called *service of process*. This may be performed by the plaintiff, by a court marshall, or by someone from the office of the plaintiff's attorney. It may be delivered in person, by leaving it with someone at the defendant's residence or business or, sometimes, by publishing it in a newspaper. Each court has procedural rules specifying who may deliver the service of process and how it must be done. Improper service of process, sometimes referred to as *sewer service*, can result in a case being dismissed.

Pleadings

Once a plaintiff has decided to file a lawsuit, the defendant and the court need to know what alleged wrong needs to be righted. The *complaint* filed by the plaintiff, which sets forth the alleged facts along with a request for a remedy, is the first component of the *pleadings*. The defendant is required to answer all allegations in that document, which is why any *summons* ordering the veterinarian to appear before the court is a serious matter. In the answer to a civil suit, the defendant may admit or deny the allegations made in the complaint or claim any defenses to the charges. In addition, the defendant may file a *counterclaim*, which is a request for action to remedy a wrong caused by the plaintiff arising out of the same set of facts contained in the complaint.

The complaint, any counterclaim, the answer, any answer to the counterclaim, and any preliminary motions made by the attorneys comprise the pleadings of the case.

Preliminary Motions

To test the strength of a complaint or an answer, either party may file a *preliminary motion* requesting that the judge make a ruling or take some specific action before the case proceeds. Some motions are procedural. For example, they may attack an improper method in notification of the defendant about the legal action or allege that the suit has been filed against the wrong person.

Other motions attack the substance or the

legal theory of the case. An example is a defendant who wishes to admit the facts alleged in the complaint but deny that any injury occurred as a result. In such a situation, a motion called a *demurrer* is filed with the court. After allowing reasonable time for either side to respond to a preliminary motion and reviewing the arguments presented by the parties, the judge either overrules the motion and orders the case to proceed, upholds the motion filed and orders corrections in the documents filed with the court, or dismisses the case.

Subpoenas and Summons

A subpoena is a court-ordered command to provide testimony or to turn over particular items of evidence for examination by the opposing party.

The Initial Stages of a Criminal Case

The types of criminal activities that veterinarians would most commonly become involved in are the abuse of controlled substances or driving under the influence of alcohol or a drug. Although these abuses could involve a state law enforcement agency, procedures vary from state to state, so only federal procedures will be discussed here.

Crimes are generally classified as misdemeanors and felonies. Misdemeanors are offenses lesser than felonies, usually punishable by fines or imprisonment for less than one year. Felonies are offenses punishable by death or imprisonment for terms exceeding one year.

Complaints to the United States Attorney

The procedures in the federal court system for misdemeanor crimes can unfold in one of two ways. Most cases begin with a law enforcement agent complaint to the office of the United States attorney. That office then has a choice of proceeding either by issuing a complaint based on testimony under oath before a United States magistrate or by requesting or requiring that the evidence be submitted to a grand jury.

Grand Jury Indictments

If the grand jury decides that there is enough evidence to support a finding of *probable cause*, it will return an indictment. Probable cause exists when facts and circumstances would warrant a person of reasonable caution to believe that an unlawful offense was or is being committed. An *indictment* is a formal written accusation originating with a prosecutor and issued by a grand jury charging that the person named has done some act or been guilty of some omission that by law is classified as a crime.

In some cases the complaint or the indictment leads to a summons commanding the appearance of the accused person in court. In other cases an arrest warrant is issued.

If the offense constitutes a felony and the crime was committed in the presence of a government agent or the agent had probable cause to believe that a felony was committed, an arrest can be made immediately without a summons or arrest warrant. More commonly, though, in felony cases the United States attorney's office convenes a federal grand jury, presents the evidence, and requests that the grand jury return an indictment.

If the crime is a simple misdemeanor, the initial appearance of the defendant is made before the magistrate. For the more serious misdemeanors, the magistrate informs the defendants of their rights and adjourns the case until legal counsel can be appointed or retained.

Preliminary Hearings

If the misdemeanor or felony was initiated through the complaint process rather than by the indictment of a grand jury, a preliminary hearing will take place. This is a test of the prosecutor's evidence to determine whether there is probable cause that a crime was committed and that the defendant committed it. If a defendant is being prosecuted under a grand jury indictment, there is usually no preliminary hearing. In *United States* v. *Mase*, 556 F2d 671 (1977), the court ruled that a grand jury indictment constitutes a finding of probable cause and eliminates the need for a preliminary hearing.

Pretrial Motions

Just as in civil cases, pretrial motions are important. These raise issues that can be either procedural or substantive in nature. Some of the most common ones involve whether or not the evidence was acquired during an illegal arrest or illegal search which violated the defendant's constitutional rights. Other pretrial motions concern discovery, e.g., providing defense counsel with copies of any statements made by the defendant to government agents, results of chemical or physical tests performed on the defendant, and any information that might aid in the defense effort.

The Mid Stages of Legal Action

Discovery

The discovery phase of a case is that portion of time after a suit has been filed and after any preliminary motions have been decided. During this stage, attorneys for both sides assemble all materials that are relevant to the case. Subpoenas are used to obtain otherwise inaccessible evidence. The first items to be subpoenaed in cases involving the practice of veterinary medicine are generally the medical records related to the case; any pathology reports, radiographs, or photographs; the appointment book; and any relevant portions of the laboratory, surgery, anesthesia, or radiology log books. In an effort to expedite a dispute when veterinarians are certain they have a strong defense to any action, it may be beneficial to provide these items to the plaintiff or plaintiff's counsel before the issuance of a subpoena. This should never be done without authorization from an agent for the insurance company or from legal counsel assigned to the case. Such a demonstration of cooperation and openness is sometimes quite valuable.

After the provision of this type of information, the next step is to subpoena witnesses who have information about the incident that provoked the suit. *Interrogatories* (formal written questions) are prepared by opposing counsel for questioning during a deposition. The *deposition* stage of the case involves an informal hearing with counsel for the plaintiff, counsel for the defendant, the witness who will be questioned, and a court reporter. Questions about the witness's educational background, how the case was handled, and anything else that seems relevant are posed. Carefully thought out answers to these interrogations are essential, because when the deposition ends, the witnesses are required to sign a statement that all testimony is true. If the case goes to trial, testimony at the trial is compared with that from the deposition. Discrepancies will be clearly pointed out to the judge or jury in an attempt to impugn the credibility of the witness.

Settlement Conferences

Settlement conferences are part of civil actions and can occur at any time. If the case has not been settled within two weeks prior to the trial date, however, a mandatory settlement conference generally takes place. This includes the attorney for the plaintiff, the attorney employed by the insurance company or the defendant, and the judge.

Plea Bargaining

While the mid stages of civil actions are marked by settlement conferences, the mid stages of criminal cases involve attempts to settle using the plea bargaining process. To understand plea bargaining, one must first know the various pleas. A guilty plea means just what it says, i.e., the defendant admits that a violation of the law has transpired. The only thing left to determine, then, is the sentence. Most defendants are advised by counsel to plead not guilty because it gives counsel time to evaluate the evidence and pursue the best course of action.

Another plea that can be used is that of *nolo contendere*, or *no contest*. Such a plea may be made only with the consent of the court. It is different from a guilty plea in that a plea of no contest may not be used against the defendant in a civil action based upon the same facts, whereas a guilty plea can. No contest pleas might be used, for example, in antitrust cases in which there is a likelihood of a civil action for damages following a criminal charge of an antitrust conviction.

The only other pleas allowed are not guilty or not guilty by reason of insanity. A not guilty plea in a criminal case means that the prosecution must proceed to trial and attempt to prove *beyond a reasonable doubt* that the defendant committed a criminal act. Fulfilling this burden of proof is considerably more difficult than the burden applied to civil cases in which the requirement is to show that a *preponderance of the evidence*, i.e., more than half, supports one side of the case or the other.

In many states, a conviction of a crime pertaining to the abuse or dispensing of a controlled drug is sufficient grounds for the state board to seek a license revocation or suspension. Since a no contest plea is the equivalent of a conviction of the controlled drug violation, and that conviction is sufficient for the state board to initiate action,[15] a no contest plea provides no value to veterinarians who find themselves in this situation.

Plea bargaining is an integral component of the criminal justice system. Counsel for the defendant negotiates with the prosecutor to reduce the magnitude of the offense or the sentence depending upon the strengths and weaknesses of each side's case. Unlike civil cases, in which judges are involved in settlements, judges are forbidden from participating in these negotiations. The bargain can involve the defendant pleading guilty in exchange for either dropping some charges in a multiple-charge prosecution, or allowing the defendant to plead guilty to a lesser crime instead of going to trial for the more serious crime. It also can involve recommendations satisfactory to both sides regarding the length of the sentence for the guilty plea.

The Trial

If no settlement occurs and the case goes to trial, the first item to be determined is the choice of a jury.

Jury Selection

Potential jurors are drawn by chance from a drum containing names of people called for jury duty. From this group, a jury is selected consisting of twelve people in criminal cases and six or twelve people in civil cases plus one or two alternates. The size of the jury varies, depending upon the court and jurisdiction from which the case originates. The selection process is called *voir dire*.

In federal courts, the judge asks questions of prospective jurors. These questions generally are meant to reveal any prejudices relevant to the type of case or the defendant personally. In state courts, the judge and the attorneys for each side may ask questions. Prospective jurors are then either selected or eliminated based upon their answers to these questions.

The judge or either attorney may have grounds to remove a prospective juror because of a prejudice, in which case the request to remove a juror is called *removal for cause*. Each side also has the right to reject three potential jurors for no apparent reason at all, in which case it is called a *preemptory strike*.

Opening Statements

Once the jury has been chosen, opening statements are usually presented by both sides to describe the facts of the case to the jury. In addition, the attorneys for each side have the opportunity to summarize the evidence in the case. The plaintiff always starts out with an opening statement, but differences can occur as to when in the trial the opening statement is made on behalf of the defendant. The delivery of the defendant's opening statement depends upon the wisdom of counsel and the type of case involved, i.e., criminal or civil.

Evidence

After opening statements are completed, the actual trial with the presentation of evidence commences. The plaintiff must present evidence first. (Chapter 7 on expert witnesses gives an overview of what materials are considered evidence.) When counsel for the plaintiff has completed questioning a witness, counsel for the defense has the right to cross-examine the witness. If some issues need additional review, the plaintiff's counsel may engage in re-direct examination of the witness. Counsel for the defendant then has another opportunity to cross-examine the witness concerning the specific questions raised during the re-direct exam. At this point, witnesses may be dismissed or, with sufficient justification, requested to remain available in case they need to be recalled for further testimony.

Closing Statements and Directed Verdicts

When the attorneys for both sides have presented all the evidence and finished the cross-examination of witnesses, each one makes a closing statement. These closing remarks summarize the facts of the case for the jury and restate whatever remedy was requested by the plaintiff. If the evidence presented substantially proves one side of the case or the other, either party may request a directed verdict. If the judge agrees, the jury is directed by the judge to decide in favor of one of the parties without deliberation.

Jury Instructions

If the case does not merit a directed verdict for either party, the judge instructs the jury on how it should reach a decision about the case. This is called the judge's *charge* to the jury and includes the judge's interpretation of the relevant points of law. After the charge, the jury retires to another room to conduct its deliberations in secret. When a decision has been reached, the jury returns to the courtroom and announces its verdict.

At this time, the judge has the option of accepting the verdict and ordering appropriate remedies or rejecting the verdict. This latter decision is made only when the jury's verdict does not appear reasonable. In such a case, the judge has the option of issuing a judgment notwithstanding the verdict. Such a decision can reject all or part of the verdict or modify it. Either party to the case may request such a decision; however, the likelihood of a judge granting such a verdict is not very great.

The End Stage of a Legal Action

Appeals

Once a case has been decided and a verdict entered by the court, the losing parties must elect either to accept or reject the verdict. Losing parties that reject the verdict request a *stay of execution*, which is then applied to the case while an appeal to a higher court is in progress. Higher courts either accept cases for appeal, i.e., *grant certiorari* or refuse to consider them, *deny certiorari*. To succeed in an appeal on a case, losing parties must show that a material error was committed during the trial that might have altered the outcome of the case.

A few of the more common examples of material errors include incorrect instructions to the jury (an incorrect charge), allegations that the court failed to follow proper court procedures, incorrect omissions of or admittance of specific items of evidence, or the discovery of new evidence that might affect the outcome of the case. In some criminal cases, e.g., murder cases with death sentences, the defendant is automatically entitled to an appeal.

Appellate Procedures

The court procedures for an appeal are quite different from the course of events at a trial. Appellate courts only hear or examine points of law, not questions of fact. It is assumed that only the trial judges or the juries can decide questions of fact, since they heard and saw all the factual evidence in the case. If an appellate court finds that no substantial evidence exists to support a finding of fact by the jury, however, they may overrule the jury's finding.

Another major difference at the appellate court level is that only the attorneys for each side are allowed to present any arguments or material during the hearing. In addition, instead of only one judge being present for the hearing, there are often three judges or, in the case of supreme courts, nine judges.

The appellate court decision may affirm that of the trial court, in which case the verdict remains the same. It also may reverse the decision, or *remand* the case to the trial court for additional evidence or work. As mentioned earlier, it is the opinions written by these appellate court judges analyzing the law and other precedents that become the guidelines for judges' decisions in future cases.

Enforcement

After a case is decided and the verdict accepted, or after all appellate remedies are completed, a verdict becomes final and it is time for enforcement. It is at this point that veterinarians who have brought a legal action in small claims court for fees not paid are most likely to meet the reality of defeat. Just because parties win lawsuits does not mean they will be able to collect the monies due them.

Some remedies for a failure to pay court-ordered damages, though, do exist. First of all, upon the prevailing party's request, the court can issue *an order of execution* directing the seizure of some or all of the defendant's property to pay the judgment. If the value of that property is insufficient, the prevailing party may try a second tact, i.e., requesting that the court order a *garnishment*. If this request is granted, the court will order someone who owes the defendant money, like an employer, to pay some or all of that money to the plaintiff instead of to the defendant as a means of paying off part or all of the judgment. Keep in mind that if a counterclaim has been filed, in which case the plaintiff in the primary action becomes a defendant in the countersuit, the original plaintiff can end up owing the defendant a sum of money instead of vice versa.

Yet another option is available to people who attempt to collect a judgment. This involves placing a lien on the defendant's property. If the defendant owns property, especially a house or business, this can be an effective method for collecting a debt. *Attaching a lien* to the defendant's property means that, in the event that the defendant ever sells that property, the proceeds must go to pay off the judgment before any money can be kept by or returned to the defendant.

Alternative Methods for Solving Disputes

Very often the complexity of the legal system, the sluggish progression of cases, and the high costs of attorneys' fees for both parties in a dispute discourage people from using the judicial arm of government. Consequently, a brief review of some alternatives is in order.

Negotiation

It is not uncommon for business people to elect to resolve business disputes in a practical manner by themselves instead of through the legal system. The method for resolving disputes may be written into the business's contract, or it may be agreed upon after a dispute occurs.

An example involves a method for arriving at the value of a veterinary practice. It is very difficult to establish a monetary value for the goodwill, equipment, inventory, medical records, and other components of a veterinary practice. Although no one person has any magic formula, there are experienced professionals in the veterinary business services arena who can help in valuing practices.

One way to resolve disputes involving the valuation of veterinary practice partnerships, corporations, or sole proprietorships (in the event of a death, disability, expulsion, retirement, loss of license, bankruptcy, etc.) is to allow a court to determine value. The costs and difficulties of deciding an issue like this via a jury trial can be overwhelming, though.

An alternative to a judicial resolution to this problem is to develop a negotiated method for resolving disputes about value and make it a part of the partnership agreement or corporation bylaws when these documents are created. The following example has been a part of the author's partnership agreement for the past nine years. Its workability has been tested three times, each time resulting in the sale of or purchase of an interest in the business at the agreed-upon value:

> Annually, at a time not later than four months subsequent to the end of the partnership's (or corporation's) fiscal year, the assets of the partnership shall be valued and an interest rate to be used in a buy out determined.
>
> If the partners (or shareholders) fail to agree on such valuation and/or interest rate, the assets and liabilities of the business shall be appraised by a disinterested third party with expertise in the appraisal of veterinary medical practices, who shall be selected by agreement of the partners (shareholders).
>
> All costs of such appraisal shall be borne by the partnership (or corporation).
>
> If the parties to this agreement fail to agree on an appraiser, then each partner may select one appraiser. If an even number of owners exists, then the appraisers chosen by the owners can select one more person to reestablish an odd number of people. These appraisers shall

then decide upon a valuation and an interest rate based upon a majority vote. All costs of such appraisal shall be borne proportionately by the partnership (or corporation).

Although in this case the negotiated settlement to a dispute of this type is binding on the parties because the partnership agreement says it is, such negotiation need not be binding. It could be nothing more than a voluntary settlement conference between the parties with or without their legal counsel.

Mediation

Sometimes, because of personal animosities or a stalemate based upon "principles," negotiations between individuals are impossible. To overcome such a situation, the parties may elect to use an intermediary. This person must be a neutral party in whom both sides have confidence. The parties will not be required to accept the mediator's findings or decision, but involving such a person may well be worth the effort. The economic savings in legal fees and court costs plus the potential for an expeditious resolution may mean that a less-than-perfect solution is much better than the alternative of a lawsuit.

The following example is taken from T. J. Herron's excellent book on business law:

> A recent landlord-tenant dispute illustrates the use of mediation to solve a legal problem. A group of tenants refused to pay their rents because their landlord had failed to make repairs he had agreed to make. When the landlord threatened to evict them, the tenants threatened to file complaints with the city housing authority. Neither side wanted a prolonged struggle. The tenants only wanted the repairs made and the landlord only wanted the rents paid. Instead of pursuing the dispute through legal channels, the parties agreed to turn it over to a local minister for mediation. The parties followed the recommendation of the minister and reached an agreement about the types of repairs that were to be done and the amount of rent that was to be paid.[16]

The potential benefits of time saved and aggravation avoided alone are worth considering mediation of disputes as a viable alternative to a legal action.

Arbitration

Arbitration is similar to mediation except that the findings of the neutral arbitrator are generally binding on the parties. Under this system, for example, each party could choose one arbitrator and those arbitrators could select a third. Another method often used is to have disputes concerning contracts decided by a member of the American Arbitration Association. Still another way of gathering an unbiased group to arbitrate a contract dispute is as follows:

> Should any dispute arise concerning the scope, validity, effect, or construction of this agreement, then each party shall submit to a presiding judge in and for the county (where the business resides) a list of three attorneys, three business people, and three veterinarians. The presiding judge shall select one person from each party's list of nine proposed arbitrators, and those people selected shall comprise a panel of arbitrators to resolve such dispute. The arbitration shall be conducted pursuant to the rules of the Illinois (or whatever state in which parties reside) Code of Civil Procedure.

Although settling a dispute in this fashion may not be ideal, it is certainly faster and, in all likelihood, less costly than the legal option.

These alternative methods for resolving disputes may look attractive, but before any of them are used, the experience and advice of local counsel should be considered. After all, the legal system has evolved in a fashion intended to protect the rights of all the parties. Its function should not be bypassed without good reason.

Conclusion

This chapter provides basic background information about the law. Some of this information will be expanded upon in later chapters as one topic at a time is discussed in depth. Because laws and precedents vary so much from state to state and year to year, the necessity for the counsel of local attorneys cannot be overemphasized as readers attempt to implement ideas and suggestions that are found throughout this book.

References

1. *Knowles Animal Hospital, Inc* v Wills, 360 So2d 37 (Fla 1978).
2. *Campbell* v *Animal Quarantine Station*, 632 P2d 1066 (Hawaii 1981).
3. *Peloquin* v *Calasieu Parish Police Jury*, 367 So2d 1246 (LA 1979).
4. *City of Farland* v *White*, 368 SW2d 12 (Texas 1963).
5. Fink JL: *Pharmacy Law Digest*. Media, PA, Harwal Publishing Co, 1983.
6. *Principles of Veterinary Medical Ethics*. Schaumburg, IL, American Veterinary Medical Association, 1986, pp 3,5.
7. Rollin B: Updating veterinary medical ethics. *JAVMA* 173:1015-1018, 1978.
8. Miller EB: History and evolution of the AVMA code of ethics 1867-1940. *Calif Vet* Nov-Dec:17-20, 1985.
9. *In re Kerlin*, 376 A2d 939 (NJ 1977).
10. Tischler J: Rights for non-human animals: A guardianship model for dogs and cats. *San Diego Law Rev* 14: 484,1979.
11. *Kerbow* v *Bell*, 259 P2d 317 (Okla. 1953).
12. California Code of Civil Procedures § 340.5.
13. Glendon MA: *Comparative Legal Traditions*. St. Paul, West Publishing Co, 1985, pp 167-168.
14. How to keep a lawyer from running up your bill. *Vet Econ* (Nov): 1985.
15. California Business and Professions Code § 4883(1).
16. Harron TJ: *Business Law*. Boston, Allyn & Bacon, Inc, 1981.

CHAPTER 2

Veterinary and Animal Ethics

Bernard E. Rollin, PhD
Colorado State University

Veterinary Medicine and Philosophy

Most veterinarians, like most physicians, lawyers, artists, scientists, and other people immersed in a field of study or practice, do not spend a great deal of time pondering the philosophical assumptions upon which their chosen field is founded. Indeed, the majority of professionals do not even realize that they have made philosophical assumptions, that such assumptions are inevitable and fundamental, and that they periodically require examination, justification, and modification. Yet veterinarians and practitioners in all fields are working from a philosophical base, however little they may be aware of it.

A moment's reflection will reveal that any area of human activity, from medicine to art, from education to politics, from literature to science, rests upon certain assumptions. A clear example can be seen in high school geometry. The object of geometry is to prove certain theorems. This is done by combining and manipulating assumptions or postulates, such as "two points determine a line." Yet such assumptions are not and never can themselves be proved, since a proof is, by definition, some combination of assumptions. They are simply taken for granted.

This is the situation in all fields. Certain assumptions must be made and certain things taken for granted. Artists take for granted some notion of what constitutes a work of art; scientists take for granted the notions of fact or cause and effect; medical practitioners take for granted the concepts of health and disease; most people take for granted that what they do is worth doing, or valuable. Few such people could define or justify these concepts—they are too busy using them in order to get the job done. As Aristotle put it, if one did attempt to prove one's assumptions, it would have to be on the basis of other assumptions, which assumptions would either need to be taken for granted or else be proved on the basis of other assumptions, etc., to infinity.

The key point, then, is that people must make assumptions and take certain concepts for granted in order to operate in a given field. It does not mean, however, that the assumptions of a given field cannot and should not be probed, examined, studied, and justified. What it does mean is that when one examines one's assumptions in a given field, one is functioning not so much as a practitioner in the field, but rather as a philosopher of the field. If one engages in veterinary practice, one is functioning as a veterinarian. But in probing the assumptions made by veterinary medicine, one functions as a philosopher of veterinary medicine.

Valuational Assumptions

Among the most important assumptions one makes in life are valuational assumptions. Scientists, for example, contrary to widespread belief that science has nothing to do with values, make value judgments all the time. When physicists assume that one ought to study the quantifiable aspects of things and ignore qualitative differences, that represents a value judgment. When biologists or doctors assume that it is justifiable to cause harm to an animal in order to advance knowledge, that is a value judgment. When scientists say it is wrong to falsify data, that is a value judgment. And when veterinarians assume that their primary obligation is to the client or to the animal, that too is a value judgment.

There are many sorts of value judgments. Sometimes they are quite specialized. For example, assumptions concerning how one should proceed in a given field of inquiry, what types of explanation one seeks, or what counts as an adequate theory represent commitments to what philosophers call *epistemic values*—values shaping what we will count as knowledge. Other values are aes-

thetic, such as when we judge a surgery beautiful or evaluate a work of art. There is a wide array of value judgments in all fields, as when we talk about a worthwhile expenditure, a good colleague, a trivial diversion, a successful trip, a good advertisement, and so on. These values form the basis for making judgments in all aspects of one's ordinary and professional life, as when a government agency funds one research proposal and rejects another; a veterinarian decides on which therapeutic modality to employ; and a person chooses a charity to which to donate, a neighborhood to live in, and a profession to pursue.

Our choices often reflect our subconscious values. On one occasion, when addressing a group of Colorado ranchers, I asked them why they were in the ranching business. "Money!" they shouted, "Why else does one do anything?" "Really," I replied, "Suppose you could make three times as much money being a dress manufacturer in New York City—then I presume you would change jobs?" "No way," they responded, "not for 10 times the money." "Well then," I replied, "you can't say you are ranchers just for the money. There must be other values involved that are weighed more heavily in your mind than strictly economic ones."

Moral Value Judgments

Perhaps the most profound valuational judgments made by human beings in their personal and professional lives are those called *ethical* or *moral judgments*. These concern moral rightness and wrongness, moral good and bad, justice and injustice, and fairness and unfairness.

People are faced with ethical decisions that require that they appeal to moral notions every day. Should I tell a lie to make a profit? How should I respond to an unwarranted insult? Ought I charge a poor client less than an affluent one? Whatever decision people make in these cases, they will have implicitly (or explicitly) taken a stand on what is right and what is wrong, on how humans ought to behave, and on what sort of world we should be trying to achieve.

Veterinarians, in their professional activities, face these sorts of questions in a variety of areas. Should a veterinarian euthanatize a healthy animal for owner convenience? Should the veterinarian present all options to a client or only the best ones? Should the veterinarian do what is commonly done by other veterinarians, even if it is of little medical value, or risk a suit for malpractice by doing something innovative? Should a veterinarian devocalize or declaw an animal? Should a veterinarian "blow the whistle" on a colleague?

Indeed, although all fields are fraught with moral questions, veterinary medicine is even more problematic than most other professions. Not only must veterinarians deal with a full range of ethical questions pertaining to how one should treat human beings, they have an added burden not shared by physicians or attorneys. This is an issue long ignored by society in general yet forced on veterinarians by virtue of the very nature of their profession—the issue of the moral obligations that humans have toward animals, and how these obligations weigh against obligations toward humans when they inevitably come into conflict.

The Neglect of Ethical Inquiry

Despite the plethora of moral issues in veterinary medicine, the profession, like most others, has not devoted much attention to analysis and discussion of ethical questions and moral problems. Basically, most people are too busy to probe the assumptions upon which their field of interest rests. Instead, they use and apply traditional assumptions, including ethical ones, without question.

Veterinarians learn standard moral assumptions and practices in the field from their professors and peers in school and during their internship. As their medical educa-

tion unfolds, they do not usually question either the factual or moral elements of what they are taught. The students do not recognize their own ethical assumptions because those assumptions are shared by their peer group and are rarely discussed. It is only when these assumptions are challenged that they are noticed and made a focus of attention.

An example of the invisibility of moral assumptions is evident in that, until recently, women were almost totally excluded from the field of veterinary medicine. Many older veterinarians never saw the exclusion of women from veterinary medicine as a moral issue, but merely as a rational and inevitable practice flowing naturally from biological differences and from the "natural" role and place of women in society.

A second reason why veterinarians and other scientists have avoided exploring ethical issues in their field of practice is that science in the 20th century has been assumed to be purely objective and thus value free. Consequently, scientists and veterinarians have been taught that science has nothing to do with ethics. It is alleged that since science depends on experimentation, data gathering, and facts, ethics is irrelevant to science.

Ethics, it is further alleged, is a matter of opinion, not fact; emotion, not reason. Scientists tend to assume that value judgments in general, and moral judgments in particular cannot be dealt with objectively and empirically. Ethics is viewed as subjective, not objective, and ethical questions and positions cannot be rationally adjudicated or decided. Science textbooks and courses have ignored ethical issues and, insofar as human and veterinary medicine schematized themselves as sciences, they too have shunned dealing with ethical questions.

The cleavage between science and morality was revealed dramatically in a recent Public Broadcasting System documentary dealing with the development of the atomic bomb. When scientists who worked on the bomb were asked to comment on their ethical thoughts at the time, they replied that science had nothing to do with ethics, and that they saw their role as solving a scientific puzzle—ethics was for the politicians!

Only when society absolutely forces its concerns on the scientific community, as in the cases of research on humans and animals, or in dramatic areas like medical ethics, such as the cases of euthanasia, abortion, and transplants, does science tend to engage ethical issues. Veterinary medicine has been no exception. Indeed, so powerful is the hold that scientific ideology has over people that many people who are morally reflective in their nonprofessional lives nonetheless divorce their scientific activities from such reflection.

This untenable notion that science is value free has been buttressed by a generalized tendency in our society to equate democracy and freedom with the lack of a universal ethic. In a democracy, it is often said, everybody's ethical opinion is as good as everyone else's; ethics is a matter of individual choice and preference—of tastes—and one cannot rationally argue about taste. It has been said that one cannot study ethics rationally or objectively or criticize ethical positions.

Ethical Inquiry and Veterinary Medicine

For all of these reasons, there is a dearth of material examining ethical questions in veterinary medicine. Until very recently, veterinary medicine, like human medicine and other professions, tended to see ethics either as dealing only with blatant deviations from acceptable behavior or as a set of rules governing intraprofessional conduct.[1]

Because of this professional attitude regarding ethics as a matter of control of deviance, veterinary medicine and other professions have maintained local, state, and national ethics committees that examine charges of alleged misconduct. The most common complaints for review in veterinary medicine have included using quack remedies, doing various types of unnecessary pro-

cedures, and overcharging. In this sense of ethics, it is assumed that what is right and wrong is clear and unproblematic, and that ethics means dealing with the "bad apples." Given this view of ethics, it is no surprise that professions like veterinary medicine have traditionally ignored major ethical questions such as whether animals should be hurt for human benefit in sport and research, preferring to concentrate on ferreting out universally acknowledged "wrongs."

Alternatively, veterinary and other professional ethics have also come to mean the set of rules governing intraprofessional interactions—the etiquette of veterinary medicine, as it were. Thus the traditional code of ethics issued by the AVMA focused almost exclusively on issues like advertising (until the Supreme Court declared that restraint of advertising was illegal); how large one's sign could be to be "professional"; and whether fees could be split. The 1973 edition of the *Principles of Veterinary Medical Ethics* contained 30 entries discussing advertising and not a single one regarding the ethics of euthanasia.

Clearly, while regulation of intraprofessional conduct may be part of ethics, it is not the only or even the major part. If an adequate study of veterinary ethics is to develop, veterinarians must deviate extensively from these traditional concerns.[1] At the same time, there must be a response to the skepticism about ethics as a legitimate object of study. Common questions that must be answered include: (1) How can one study ethics objectively? (2) Isn't ethics just a matter of opinion, and are all opinions equally correct? (3) How does one decide on answers to moral questions? (4) Aren't ethical questions really economic ones?

Ethicists talking to veterinary audiences about some of the ethical questions pervading veterinary medicine, such as euthanasia of healthy animals or ear cropping, are consistently told that these are not ethical decisions, but simply matters of economics. The answers to these questions are dictated by the fact that veterinarians need to make a living.

Aside from the fact that this would absolve child pornographers, hit men, and drug dealers from any responsibility for considering the morality of what they do, since they too must make a living, a deeper point arises. The appeal to an economic basis for a decision does not enable one to avoid making an ethical decision, but is itself a debatable moral decision. In the issues of euthanasia or ear cropping mentioned above, for example, those veterinarians who say that these are solely economic decisions have made the moral decision that financial benefit is more important than the life or suffering of the animal! And if veterinarians are so desperate financially that they must do anything and everything for money, surely this is an argument for allowing only rich people into veterinary medicine, or for government subsidies for veterinarians.

Thus, before one can proceed to examine veterinary ethics in detail, the skepticism about the impossibility of the rational objective approach to ethics must be laid to rest. It is to this difficult task that we now turn.

Are you trying to tell me that animals have no rights?

Can Ethics Be Dealt with Rationally?

Is it true that one cannot deal rationally with ethics, that all ethical judgments and positions are equally correct, and that ethics (and other value judgments) are simply a matter of opinion? In veterinary education, this sort of view has been reinforced by the idea that the schools can teach only facts and techniques, i.e., "objective data," and thus must eschew the teaching of ethics.

This thesis rests upon a number of confusions, which are best illustrated with particular examples. Consider the claim that, as a science, veterinary medicine has nothing to do with values of any sort and thus surely not with moral values. We have already seen that science is indeed impregnated with values of all kinds. The absurdity of denying values to science is well illustrated by the biologist who says that science has nothing

to do with values, but that it cares only about knowledge, totally unaware that caring about knowledge is itself a value!

Even if science and veterinary medicine contain values, do they necessarily contain moral values? Everyone who believes, as most people surely would, that there should be constraints on what one can do as a scientist has made a commitment to some moral values. If it is morally wrong to falsify data, experiment on people without informing them, or steal another person's results, or if it is morally permissible to hurt animals in order to gain knowledge, one has made a moral choice, whose opposite could be asserted by someone else. The fact that such moral choices are widely shared does not mean that they are not moral choices. And to seriously entertain the idea that such choices are merely arbitrary opinions is to implicitly license others who do not share the same opinions to steal and falsify data, or to experiment on humans as they see fit.

Most people who advance the claim that all ethics is a matter of opinion and that all opinion is equally correct have not thought through the implications of that assertion. Most importantly, they have not realized that they are forced to conclude that others who say that ethics is not a matter of opinion and does contain objective validity are just as correct as those who assert that it is a matter of opinion and does not contain any objective truth—certainly an incoherent, self-defeating position. Surely no one wants to take a position which entails the equal validity of its opposite!

People who say that ethics is just subjective opinion usually are focusing on the fact that in a free society, people may say or assert whatever they choose. It does not, however, follow from this that all assertions are equally correct! In a free society, one certainly may say "you ain't going nowhere too quick." It is not true, however, that such a statement is correct, for there are rules of English grammar that preclude such a locution. By the same token, one may add 4 + 4 and get 7. If someone else argues the point and says, "No, the total is 8," it is a non sequitur to say, "It's a free country, I can say what I wish." Again, there are rules of mathematics that preclude the incorrect addition, whatever the political situation. And by the same token, there are rules of moral reasoning that are inviolable, however free-spirited one may be.

A Rational Approach to Ethical Decision Making

There is a rational approach to ethical decision making. Let us look at some specific examples where people's moral reasoning can be rationally criticized. Finding inconsistencies and ambiguities in people's ideas is one way of looking at ethics rationally and objectively.

Whenever I lecture before audiences about ethics, I try to make the point that there are rules governing moral reasoning. To convince skeptics, I ask the audience how many of them are Christians, and if those people will please hold up their right hands. After explaining that a moral relativist is someone who believes that there is no true right and wrong or good and bad, I then ask those who consider themselves to be moral relativists to hold up their left hands. Invariably there are a number of people holding up both hands, which is of course a logical absurdity, since being a Christian commits one to believing in the existence of certain moral truths, while being a relativist commits one to the position of denying their existence! One cannot be a Christian and relativist any more than one can be married and a bachelor.

On one occasion, I was arguing with a scientist about the need for legislation covering laboratory animals. "Nonsense," he said, "you are bringing ethics in where it doesn't belong. Ethics is just opinion. And you are imposing your opinion on me. Scientists have been doing as they please with animals for 300 years." "Well then," I replied, "if ethics is just opinion, and you've had your way morally for 300 years, then it's our turn for the next 300." Obviously, he held a number of inconsistent positions on the morality relevant to animal research. He failed to realize that his position was a moral position, and by his own view it could not be said to be any more true than mine.

Morally Relevant Differences and Ethical Decision Making

Morally relevant differences are another component to watch for in moral decision making. Morally relevant differences are differences that bear moral weight. Thus, suppose I owe both Dr. Smith and Dr. Jones $500 for treating my dog. I pay Smith but not Jones. "Why not?" asks Jones. "Because you are a redhead," I reply. Clearly, hair color is not relevant to my obligation to pay. Recent social history in the United States and elsewhere has been characterized by court decisions requiring society to give up its morally irrelevant differences as justifications for differential treatment. The courts and legislatures have taken the view that discrimination based upon race, color, national origin, religion, and sex is constitutionally prohibited. While teaching this to students, I have attempted to make it relevant by pointing out that in the 1970s, particular groups of students at our University had sought out hippies and stomped and beaten them, shearing their long hair and beards. "Surely," I pointed out, "having long hair and a beard does not make someone worthy of being stomped and beaten." I felt the students had been presented with a definitive example of a morally irrelevant difference and moved on.

Suddenly a hand shot up. The student said, "Oh Dr. Rollin, it is not the hair and beard, it is what it represents." "What does it represent," I queried, "that makes someone worthy of being stomped and beaten?" "Being un-American," she replied. "What does that mean?" I asked. "Being different, disagreeing with the majority," she responded, and blushed as laughter spread among the students. Obviously, her unwillingness to tolerate any deviation from the mainstream was more "un-American" than the opinions and appearance of the hippies, since protection of the unpopular minority is a key feature of our democratic system of government.

Inconsistencies and Ambiguities

Finding inconsistencies and ambiguities in people's ideas is only one way of looking at ethics rationally and objectively. More often people do not even know what they believe morally, and helping them to discover what they do believe is again a rational process. An example of this occurred during a lecture I gave to a group of ranchers about animal rights. They were quite hostile, and even booed when I was introduced. It was clear that we could not have a good discussion in such an environment, so I decided to ask them to please answer two questions in

order to clear the air. They grudgingly agreed. "Okay," I said. "First of all, do you people believe in right and wrong?" "Of course," they said. "Second question: Would you do anything at all to an animal to increase profit? For example, suppose it was discovered that you could increase weight gain by torturing a cow's eye with hot needles, would you do it?" "Of course not," they said. "Good," I replied, "then we are only haggling about price." In other words, they accepted the major assumptions that it is coherent to talk about right and wrong and coherent to apply it to animals.

It is perhaps important here to distinguish between inconsistency in moral beliefs and hypocrisy. If people believe that they ought to be Christians and relativists, they are logically incoherent. If they believe that they are Christian and yet act as if they are relativists while still believing that they ought to act like Christians, then they are weak-willed hypocrites—blameworthy perhaps, but not irrational. Philosophers are not as interested in weakness of will as in irrationality, since they are trained to deal with ideas, not character traits. For example, the ranchers had certain beliefs that they did not know they had, and the philosopher's job was to help them realize that. If, once they were aware of their beliefs, they chose to violate them, that was their choice and not the concern of the philosopher.

Helping People Set Ethical Goals

Helping people to clarify their ideas, especially moral ideas, is as old as philosophy, and that is precisely what Socrates did. That this job was both necessary and dangerous is attested to by the fact that the Athenians killed Socrates. If anything, society is more in need of help in the clarification of moral ideas today than during the era of ancient Athens. Evidence of this problem is embodied in the present-day belief that science has nothing to do with ethics, and that ethics is neither rational nor objectively studiable. The results of such a belief, coupled with the fact that virtually everything we do involves some presuppositions about good and bad, right and wrong, are inevitable. Professionals make ethical assumptions without recognizing them as such, college professors teach ethics without knowing it, and scientists take ethical positions without examining their coherence.

In previous years, when American veterinary schools taught surgery by doing multiple survival procedures on dogs, they were taking an ethical position and sending a moral message to their students without realizing it or endorsing it. When the AVMA code of ethics failed to address euthanasia of healthy animals, that lack of a statement was an ethical position. And when the veterinarian's oath commits one to the fundamentally incompatible goals of advancing medical knowledge and relieving animal suffering without prioritizing those goals, veterinarians are being asked to commit to the impossible.

Because so many ethical positions are adopted unknowingly, a number of prestigious groups studying United States higher education have concluded that a major lack therein is in the failure to teach analysis, recognition, and adjudication of value questions, especially moral ones. It is also for this reason that it behooves veterinarians to view the examination of ethical notions not as frivolous addenda to their professional lives but as a foundation to it. Once sensitive to this issue, veterinarians will realize the great extent to which their time and effort are devoted to dealing with ethical issues. According to one estimate, fully one-third of a veterinarian's time is spent on adjudicating and dealing with ethical questions.[2]

Most veterinary schools now include some element of ethics teaching in their curricula, though almost certainly not enough. What many veterinary educators are beginning to realize is that, like it or not, they are always teaching ethics, although usually without knowing it and often without endorsing the principles that are conveyed. For example, as just mentioned, during the 1970s many veterinary schools were teaching surgery by multiple successive use of animals in recovery procedures, often with limited provision for aftercare. When this was discussed with administrators and faculty, almost no one wanted to say that they endorsed the notion that unowned animals were cheap and expendable tools, and that their pain didn't matter a great deal. This, however, was precisely the message conveyed to the students.

Types of Ethical Questions in Veterinary Medicine

Recognizing Ethical Questions

One of the most important steps toward dealing rationally with ethical questions that arise in veterinary medicine is learning to recognize them. Veterinarians, like most other professionals, especially in the sciences, are not trained to recognize ethical questions. In ethics, as in any other area, people's perceptions to a great extent reflect their training.

When this point is made to veterinarians, it often elicits the response that anyone can recognize ethical questions. While it is certainly true that virtually anyone can recognize some ethical questions when they encounter them, the less obvious ethical questions are often missed because the person's attention has never been directed toward them. The case of multiple surgery previously discussed exemplifies this phenomenon. By the same token, the failure of many veterinarians to concern themselves with the pain suffered by animals from certain procedures (as reflected in the paucity of analgesic drugs and regimens for animals), is a direct consequence of an educational system that has not emphasized the importance of alleviating pain in animals.

Many veterinarians trained in the 1960s who were taught to use succinylcholine as a method of restraint for horse castrations say that the issue of animal pain or suffering never arose, and thus they never thought about it, though this drug was known to be a paralytic drug and not an anesthetic.

Many medical researchers have acknowledged that they never thought of the use of human subjects in moral terms—this despite the fact that moral concern for humans is preached to people from the time they are children, while moral concern for animals is immeasurably rarer. A striking example of this point is found in a recent article by Dr. Jay Katz, a major figure in developing federal protection for human subjects in the United States during the 1960s:

> During 1954 to 1958, two colleagues and I conducted experiments on hypnotic dreams, supported by grants from the National Institutes of Health. After we had worked out our research methodology, we became concerned that some of our volunteer-subjects, as a consequence of their participation, might experience emotional stress sufficient to necessitate a brief period of hospitalization. While we believed this to be unlikely, we were sufficiently worried to ask the chairman of our department whether, if our fears materialized, he would make hospital beds available to our subjects free of charge. He readily agreed. We were relieved, feeling that we had satisfactorily fulfilled our professional responsibility to our research subjects. It did not even occur to us that we might be obligated to disclose to our subjects our concerns about the investigation's possible detrimental impact.[3]

Detecting ethical questions is, in some ways, like detecting lameness. Prima facie, ordinary people not particularly knowledgeable about veterinary medicine would think that anyone can tell when a horse is lame and which leg is affected. In fact, when actually confronted with a lame horse, inexperienced lay people (and even veterinary students)

can at best detect that something is wrong (and sometimes not even that), but can rarely pinpoint it. This is exactly analogous to the problem of identifying ethical problems: People (sometimes) know something is problematic, but they have trouble saying exactly what it is.

Sorting out Ethical Issues

A true case embracing a multitude of ethical issues illustrates the difficulty of recognizing, sorting out, and dealing with ethical questions.

A man brought a small comatose dog with a head injury into a veterinary school clinic. He freely admitted, and even boasted, that he had struck the dog in the head with a frying pan because it barked too much. When the dog did not regain consciousness, and the man's wife became upset, he took the dog to his regular practitioner. The veterinarian advised him to take the dog to the veterinary school hospital. The dog died there, and the animal's body was brought to necropsy and presented as a case to a group of students by a pathology instructor.

Coincidentally, one of the veterinary students in that class was an animal control officer, among whose duties was investigating cruelty complaints. With the instructor's permission, the student took the client's name from the file and began to investigate the case, phoning the client's home and speaking with his wife. The client became irate and complained to both the referring veterinarian and veterinary school clinician who had taken his case that his right to privacy had been violated. The private practitioner and the veterinary school referral clinician in turn were furious with the student. The student was frightened, worried about the effect of the incident on his academic and subsequent career, and sought help.

What moral conflicts and problems does this case raise? Initially, the referring practitioner, the veterinary school clinician, and some administrators saw only one issue—the betrayal of client confidentiality by the student. As the case evolved, administrators were also troubled by the involvement of the pathologist who had "betrayed" the identity of the client. Only after much dialogue with an ethicist, the pathologist, and the student did the parties begin to realize that there were many other concurrent issues.

First, there was an animal welfare issue: The client should not be allowed to fatally beat an animal with impunity. In addition, there was a social or moral obligation to report the occurrence of a crime and, particularly, the same sort of moral obligation (now also a legal one in human medicine) as exists for health care professionals to report suspected child abuse. The pathologist argued that veterinarians ought to treat cases of suspected animal abuse the same as other health care professionals do cases of suspected child abuse. Furthermore, there was the moral (and legal) question of whether one could invoke confidentiality in a public teaching hospital, where it is implicit that cases will be discussed with students as part of their learning process. Lastly, the pathologist argued that, as a veterinary teaching institution, the school had a high moral obligation not to condone that which society as a whole has recognized as immoral and illegal.

Some veterinarians argued that the pathologist was within his rights to reveal the name, but that the student ought not to have acted upon the information. To this point, the student replied that, as a law officer, he had a sworn duty (moral obligation) to enforce the law. Some veterinarians hypothesized that if confidentiality weren't strictly observed, abusers of animals would not bring animals in for treatment. A controversy also arose over the fact that the school clinician had at least obliquely threatened the student with recriminations when he came to the clinic. Others worried that the information about the case and these issues had not been sent back to the referring veterinarian for that party to handle. The issue of a conflict of interest between being a veterinary student and serving with animal control was also raised.

Ultimately, the situation was resolved, at least for the future, by the university's drafting a formal policy that suspected abuse cases of this sort would automatically be reported to the school and government authorities. One of the valuable features of the case was its dramatic teaching value in demonstrating just how complex a single ethical problem or case can be.

The Four Types of Moral Problems in Veterinary Medicine

This case contains ethical dimensions representing every possible category of moral problems a veterinarian can confront: the veterinarian in relation to peers, clients, animals, and society in general. In the first category, veterinarians' relations to their peers, the following questions arose: Ought the school veterinarian have simply sent the case back to the original clinician? Should the pathologist have conferred with either the college's attending veterinarian or the referring veterinarian before releasing the name of the client? Should students (potential veterinarians) act on their own conscience or initiative or refer questions like this to their teachers? Should the initial veterinarian have referred the case without reporting the presence of cruelty as the cause of the injury?

The second set of questions concerning a veterinarian's relationship to a client also comprised many issues. Does or should confidentiality weigh more heavily than a crime or than animal cruelty? Should veterinarians favor their consciences over the client's interests? Are veterinarians obliged to protect their clients even when what the client has done is wrong or illegal?

The third set of questions concerns moral problems that arise regarding the veterinarian's obligations to animals. Should the client's veterinarian or the college veterinarian have reported the abuse? If the animal had lived, would it have been morally right for the veterinarians to have returned it to the owner? (Legally, of course, there is no choice. But, as will become clear, what is moral and what is legal are not always the same.) Most basic in this category, of course, is what has elsewhere been called "the fundamental problem of veterinary medicine," namely, Does the veterinarian have primary obligation to the animal or to the owner?[1]

The fourth and final sort of problem concerns the veterinarian in relation to society. Do veterinarians have special obligations to society in virtue of their profession? In this case, the pathologist claimed that a veterinary teaching institution needs to be more scrupulous about reporting cruelty than anyone else. Interestingly, a California statute requires that all medical professionals, including veterinarians, report cases of suspected child abuse, thereby acknowledging a special social obligation of veterinarians in virtue, presumably, of their medical knowledge.[4]

Every veterinarian, whether in pet practice, large animal practice, laboratory animal practice, zoo practice, or research, encounters many of these types of ethical issues daily. A problem often encountered is the failure to recognize problems as ethical questions, because veterinarians have never really been trained to think about them in these terms. Very often it is only when one encounters a new and very dramatic dilemma, pulling in two directions, that a person really becomes aware of an issue as an ethical one.

For example, a veterinary school surgeon recently had a call from a woman asking if he would declaw her dog, as the dog was tearing up the furniture and carpet. Although he had declawed many cats and thought nothing of it, declawing a dog struck him as a mutilation. On the other hand, the woman said that she would kill the dog if it weren't declawed. The surgeon felt a moral aversion to declawing, but also a desire to save the animal's life. Discussing the case with his peers, he got the idea of suggesting a behavior specialist to the woman—a suggestion she heartily embraced. Because of this unusual and nontraditional request, the surgeon is now rethinking a variety of surgeries previously taken for granted, such as cat declaws, dog devocalizations, and tail dockings.

Some Examples

There are a number of typical examples of moral problems from the above categories which are encountered fairly commonly.

Most veterinarians are familiar with problems that arise in relation to other practitioners. What should practitioners do when they have a peer who is incompetent in a given area? What should be done when a client transferring from another veterinarian comes in with a problem that is clearly the result of the previous veterinarian's error or mistreatment? What should veterinarians do when they are asked to testify in a malpractice suit? What does a beginning veterinarian do when he/she is working for an established, respected practitioner, and it becomes clear that the owner practitioner is regularly cheating or overcharging the clients?

Equally familiar, and probably most numerous, are problems that veterinarians encounter in relation to clients. Does one lie to clients? If so, when? Some veterinarians have said that they regularly lie to clients who are financially secure when it is in the best interest of the animal. These veterinarians present clients only with the best therapeutic modality if they fear that the clients may opt for the cheapest option despite the consequences for the animal. Other veterinarians report cases in which elderly people bring in animals suffering from diseases resulting from something the client has done, such as feeding an improper diet. Some veterinarians will spare the person guilt and anguish by not presenting the true etiology of the disease even if asked to do so.

Another ethical issue regarding veracity with clients would be a situation wherein one is dealing with highly emotional owners whose animal has unexpectedly died. Some veterinarians in such a case will first tell the owner that the animal has taken a turn for the worse and will shortly thereafter let them know that the animal has died. The point of this, they say, is to prepare the owners emotionally and soften the blow.

Even more difficult morally and psychologically for the veterinarian are cases wherein an animal has died and some medical mistake has been made, or a possible option was not pursued which may have more successfully dealt with the problem. The client asks what happened. How much information is the clinician morally obliged to divulge? Is it necessary to indicate that if an alternative approach had been chosen the animal might not have died? Or does it suffice to explain what did in fact happen? (Such cases frequently occur with alternative anesthetic regimens.) On the one hand, giving the client the (unrequested) information that an alternative approach might have forestalled the death can invite a lawsuit. But failure to provide that information can be seen as self-serving dissembling by omission.

Still other veterinarians will lie and break contracts with clients in instances where they are asked to euthanatize healthy animals without medical justification, such as when people wish to replace an older dog with a new puppy. If clients do not respond favorably to the suggestion that they leave the animal in the care of the veterinary hospital so that staff people can try to find a home, these practitioners will agree to euthanatize the animal and accept a fee, thereby establishing a contract, but then adopt the animal out anyway.

This latter situation raises a number of points critical to a discussion of veterinary ethics. First, it illustrates that what is legal and illegal is not necessarily what is moral or immoral. The legal system may put a contract above an animal's life, but certain moral principles would dispute that. For example, there are many things that are legal that many of us would consider to be immoral such as giving up one's children, divorcing frequently on a whim, or multiple bankruptcies that make creditors suffer. On the other hand, there are many things that are illegal which many would consider morally necessary to do, for example, breaking the old segregation laws in the South or the apartheid laws in South Africa, trespassing to picket a biological weaponry plant being put into a neighborhood, or beating up a child molester. The relationship between law and morality is very complex, and appealing to the law does not always resolve an ethical question.

The second question raised in the case of the contract-breaking veterinarian is what has been called the fundamental question of veterinary medicine.[1] To whom does the veterinarian owe primary moral allegiance—owner or animal? Does the veterinarian schematize him- or herself on the model of a garage mechanic, where if a car owner says "$1500 is too much to spend to fix it—junk it," one does so; or on the model of a pediatrician, where the focus of one's moral concern is not the person paying the bill? (We do not allow a parent to say "$1500 to fix him? Junk him, I can make a new one.") Those veterinarians who do schematize themselves as owing primary moral allegiance to the animal are in constant tension with the law, since in the eyes of the law, animals are property. Nor is this sort of dilemma restricted to the companion animal veterinarian. Food animal and laboratory animal practitioners are also troubled by the difficulty of caring for the animal itself, and not merely treating it as personal property.

This leads to the third category of ethical questions—the veterinarian in relation to the animal. What is the veterinarian's obligation if an owner wishes a healthy animal euthanatized, devocalized, declawed, or ear cropped? What does the veterinarian do when the owner refuses to pay for treatment that will maximize the health and welfare of the animal? Many such questions are the flip side of questions arising in the second category, the veterinarian in relation to client, since very often the client's interests and the animal's interests are in conflict. But there are questions that arise between veterinarian and animal alone. For example, should veterinarians deviate from standard veterinary practice, thereby running the risk of malpractice litigation, for the benefit of the animal? When it was standard practice to do equine castrations with paralytics like succinylcholine, veterinarians who did worry about pain had to do a full anesthetic procedure under less-than-ideal conditions, incurring a significant risk of malpractice litigation should the procedure fail.

Further questions are, Should a morally concerned veterinarian use analgesia postoperatively when it is commonly asserted that such analgesia makes the animal more prone to injury, because its movements are not restricted by pain? What should veterinarians who feel a direct moral obligation to animals do when animals are brought in for convenience euthanasia? If they refuse the owner's request for euthanasia, the animal may well suffer a worse fate. On the other hand, willingness to perform euthanasia may lead to perpetuation of the idea in the client's mind that animals are disposable according to convenience.

Veterinary medicine has, in euthanasia, a powerful tool for alleviating suffering and misery which human medicine lacks. But when does one employ that tool? Every veterinarian knows of cases in which clients are too quick on the trigger, or conversely, too slow to elect euthanasia. A classic case of clients wrongly wanting their animals medically euthanatized arises when a dog or cat needs a limb amputated. Some people are convinced that the animal cannot possibly function well. More perniciously, others are distressed by the idea of a crippled animal, or by their own guilt at having to look at a mutilated pet. For this reason, some veterinarians have a list of owners of amputee pets who are willing to provide positive counsel to animal owners whose pets are in need of an amputation. On the other end of the spectrum are those clients who nurture false hopes, who refuse to acknowledge the animal's misery, and who insist on keeping the animal alive for their own selfish reasons rather than considering the animal's benefit and needs.

Finally, there are moral questions that arise in virtue of the special function accorded to veterinarians by society. The public sees veterinarians as exemplary leaders of animal welfare in society. Yet those who make a living in ways that harm or exploit animals—be it scientific research or intensive agriculture—are the people who pay the bills for a substantial amount of veterinary care and employ veterinarians as a major component of their activities. How do veterinarians function in this dual, conflicting social role? This tension in veterinary medicine is reflected in the veterinarian's oath, which commits the veterinarian to incompatible goals, saying nothing about weighing them or resolving basic conflicts that grow out of this conflict. Thus, for example, the oath commits the veterinarian both to advancing scientific knowledge and animal health and to alleviating animal pain, yet sometimes scientific knowledge is gained at the expense of inflicting pain on animals or by making them sick.

This problem is exacerbated by traditional hostility, or at least mutual distrust, between veterinarians and animal welfare advocates, ranging from moderate humane societies to radical animal rights activists. It is further aggravated by tension in society itself, which demands both the benefits of animal exploitation and its diminution or elimination. The basic problem, of course, is that we have no moral tradition delineating our obligations to animals, in contrast to our long tradition of moral concern for people. Thus, neither society as a whole nor veterinary medicine in particular has yet articulated a rational ethic regarding animals, and both are buffeted by winds of emotion which blow when animal welfare issues are highlighted and assume sudden urgency in society.

Analyzing Ethical Issues

How does a morally conscientious veterinarian resolve ethical questions? One cannot respond merely according to gut feelings, for one's gut feelings may conflict from case to case or even within a given case. If practitioners relied on gut reactions alone, they might well refuse to euthanatize healthy animals if they liked a particular animal but agree to do it if they did not. Whether one likes or dislikes the animal is the only difference between the two cases, and surely that is irrelevant. That would be analogous to physicians making medical decisions on the basis of whether or not they find the patient attractive!

Each case must be rationally analyzed into its morally relevant components, as with the cruelty case presented earlier. Such an analysis is objective. The failure to accomplish such an analysis results in a very limited view of the issues involved in a given case, as exemplified by the faculty members who saw the cruelty case as raising only questions of confidentiality.

In other words, before veterinarians can decide a case involving moral issues, they must determine all of the relevant moral issues, not just the most obvious or striking ones. The situation is analogous to medical diagnosis: Just because a patient presents with obvious and dramatic symptoms does not mean that there are not other, less dramatic symptoms which need to be considered before a diagnosis can be made and treatment begun. Identifying the morally relevant components of a situation is no simpler than identifying the medically relevant ones.

Creating a Forum for Dialogue

People's vision of the world tends to be narrow, and they see things only in certain ways. They become blind to alternative solutions to problems. This tendency, in conjunction with the lack of ethical training in veterinary education, are a large part of the reason that people are unsuccessful at recognizing and rationally dealing with ethical/moral issues.

A striking example of this habituated blindness was related by a dean at a large veterinary college. A number of students had complained that a professor was requiring students to do a painful procedure in a lab using 40 rats, when the same objective could have been accomplished with eight. "So what," said the professor, "I'm funded for 40! I must have killed 10,000 rats in my time." It was only when the dean took him out to lunch and explained the situation in great detail that the faculty member even began to understand the students' concern. "Oh, I get it, they're worried about hurting more rats than I absolutely need. I never thought of that," he declared.

The best way to avoid habitual blindness is dialogue, especially dialogue with those who do not share one's perspective. Dialogue forces people to consider alternative perspectives which would never arise if each person was looking at a case individually.

As knowledge has become more technical and specialization has become common, people increasingly tend to talk to people in their own area, who more or less share their perceptions. This phenomenon extends into social realms also. Breaking provincialism is one of the major benefits of the local project review committees mandated by federal law and policy for institutions doing research on human and animal subjects. Because these committees convoke specialists from diverse areas as well as lay people from the community at large, dialogue is virtually certain, and a variety of ethical perspectives inevitably emerge. But such mandated dialogue is the exception.

A recent attempt at creating dialogue in more than one veterinary school is a phenomenon called *ethics rounds*. These are forums designed to air ethical issues and determine the significant dimensions of problematic cases. Such a model might be appropriate in a variety of contexts. Certainly laboratory animal and research veterinarians will get this input in animal care committees. Academic veterinarians can easily set up some dialectical forum for ethical analysis. For private practitioners, though, the institutionalization of dialogue is significantly more difficult.

For practitioners, local veterinary associations could provide regular meetings where practitioners present interesting cases and freewheeling dialogue is pursued, perhaps moderated by someone whose specialty is ethics. The *Journal of the AVMA* could have a regular ethics column wherein interesting issues are presented and discussed on the model of the veterinary law column.

Sensitivity to ethical issues could help reduce the likelihood of malpractice litigation and contribute to better public relations for the veterinary profession. Practitioners of veterinary medicine should be leaders in the field of animal ethics; this is particularly important in terms of the public's view of the profession. Furthermore, it is clear from what has happened in human medicine that the medical community can be forced to address medical ethics questions when mass media becomes involved and creates a public with a significant degree of sophistication on medical ethical issues.

Failing a forum for dialogue, practitioners in all areas of practice should ask themselves what assumptions they are making about right and wrong. Does the situation confronted require that judgments be made regarding good and bad or right and wrong? Does it raise options that seem to be problematic, such as lying or concealing facts? Does it pit the welfare of humans against that of animals? Do any of the choices involve the inflicting or minimizing of pain or harm? Does a conflict exist between obligations to oneself and other obligations in this case? Are practitioners being asked to violate any principles that they hold? Does something not feel right about a choice being contemplated?

Above all, if something feels wrong, even if no one else seems to recognize it, practitioners should not be afraid to heed and pursue their intuition until it is clearly articulated, since therein lies progress and creativity. How often have we all felt that something was wrong but did not articulate it for fear of looking foolish or because we felt that if there was a problem, someone else surely would have recognized it? That is not necessarily the case. The push toward conformity is strong, and concern with what everyone says is great, but it must be resisted when the situation warrants.

Moral Principles

At the most primitive level, our responses to ethical issues are quick and intuitive. An American child who sees the incredible poverty in Mexico for the first time says, "We ought to give them all the money they need." And many of us who read of particularly brutal crimes respond with a heartfelt wish that criminals could be boiled in oil. Such intuitions form the raw material out of which moral life is constructed. As has been argued elsewhere, intuitions are to ethics as perception is to science.[5]

However, just as simple perceptions cannot exclusively form our picture of the world, so simple intuitions cannot be all of ethics. One simple perception tells us that the sun is a little body not too far away in the sky; but other, more sophisticated perceptions tell us that this is not so. So to understand the world, we use reason to structure the perceptions and reconcile conflicting ones.

Exactly the same thing happens in ethics. A common instinct is to boil the child molester in oil; another instinct is to abhor torture. One intuition is to help the needy, another tells us to hold on to what is ours. We rise beyond perception by reason, to grasp regularities in perception which we call natural laws. In the same way, we rise beyond intuitions to grasp rational regularities underlying our intuitions, these being general moral principles.

Moral principles are learned from a young age from a wide variety of sources—parents, schools, friends, peers, books, television, and movies. Many of these have been incorporated into our thinking, for example, "It is wrong to steal," "Don't pick on people weaker than you," "It is wrong to lie," "All people should be given an equal chance or treated equally," "It is wrong to hurt people's feelings," "Turn the other cheek," "Don't take guff from other people," "Stand up for yourself." Interestingly, many of these principles contradict each other. There is clear tension between not taking guff and turning the other cheek, between never lying and never hurting people's feelings, between injunctions to women to be chaste and injunctions not to make men who are making advances feel badly, and between injunctions not to kill and glorification of patriotic wars. In fact, for most people, contradictions in their moral positions of the sort exemplified earlier arise at the level of principles.

And this is not surprising. Given the diverse sources of our principles, it is inevitable that they will conflict. Moral principles gleaned from watching John Wayne will not cohere with those formed from the reading of Gandhi, yet most of us do both and file the resulting principles. Since we are rarely asked or forced to make our principles consistent with one another, we rarely feel the tension between them.

So we have a multiplicity of moral principles from diverse sources, which may be in conflict, but the conflict is rarely noticed. On the other hand, there is a significant core of principles we hold in common in our society. Most people do not disagree on ethical matters most of the time. The disagreements get greater attention, but for every instance of disagreement in principles, there are hundreds of cases of consensus. Furthermore, many apparent disagreements over moral principles, for example, whether abortion is wrong or acceptable, are disagreements over nonethical, sometimes metaphysical matters. Both parties to the abortion debate would agree to the principle that it is wrong to kill humans for convenience; the disagreement arises over the obscure metaphysical question of whether fetuses are or are not human beings.

The extent to which we share rather than disagree over moral principles is evident in law, for law is often a codification of shared ethical principles or deductions from those principles. In general, if a law does not reflect shared moral consensus, it probably will not work. Thus the civil rights laws of the 1960s worked because society had been sensitized to the notion that equality of treatment and opportunity were principles that Americans endorsed deeply, though they may have

been violating them in practice. Once civil rights were stressed, as it were, in the highly visible new laws, people grudgingly acquiesced. Thus the traditional grumble often heard, that morality cannot be legislated, is wrong: Morality is legislated all the time, whether it be in zoning pornographic bookstores or in banning psychoactive drugs. What cannot be done is to legislate morality that has no basis in shared moral principles, the prohibition being the obvious case in point.

Thus we all have many shared moral principles, which may well conflict in ways exemplified above. Furthermore, these conflicts are often undetected. People inevitably apply and use these principles when occasions demand. But to decide whether one is coherent and consistent in their application requires a level of reflective analysis or philosophical examination in which many of us do not engage. Consequently, contradictions or inconsistencies in our ethical positions continually arise.

Many philosophical questions arise around the subject of moral principles. One that emerges clearly from the preceding discussion is this: Some people entertain contradictory moral principles at the same time, and such people are inconsistent and must revise their positions. But, as cited above, the principles themselves seem to be in conflict. How is this possible? How can we have some principles that tell us to protect ourselves and others that tell us to shun violence? This is an extremely difficult question. It appears that occasionally we do learn moral principles that are fundamentally inconsistent, such as *turn the other cheek* and *protect yourself and your own*, but such cases are rare, for obvious reasons. This case is explained by the fact that the principle of *turn the other cheek* is not often seriously entertained or taught; it is most often a pious, empty, ritualistic statement which grows out of religious doctrine—something people say without thinking about it.

More common are some of the other cases of conflict cited above, such as the one involving the principle against hurting other people's feelings and the one forbidding lying. These are dealt with by refining the principles or giving them different weights. Thus, the principle against taking life is usually refined to exclude cases of self-defense or protection of the innocent against the vicious. And the conflict between the principle forbidding lying and that of not hurting people's feelings is resolved by the little white lie, or by appealing to the notion of doing more harm by not telling the lie.

Another problem related to the one just discussed concerns knowing which principles apply in a given case. It is helpful to think of moral principles as analogous to a box full of socket wrenches used to fix a car. Which sockets are used, metric or SAE, depends on the nuts one is presented with, and it is difficult to know which tools to take out until one has seen the car and perhaps even tried some wrenches. By the same token, which moral principles to utilize depends on the nature of the case one is confronting.

For example, it cannot be said in advance that a given surgical procedure on an animal is always wrong. It is not that the principles change from case to case, but rather that one has to know which principles are applicable, and how much to weigh them, and these decisions depend on the details of the case. To say, for example, "devocalization is wrong" would fail to accommodate the (admittedly rare) case in which the only alternative to devocalization is death. If such a situation arises, some such principle as "life as a whole is of higher value than any given nonessential body part" would need to be invoked to do justice to the case. Thus each case must be examined in as much detail as possible to assure that all relevant principles are invoked and balanced.

Justifying Moral Principles

The most difficult question concerning moral principles is, Why should we accept their truth? What are the grounds for believing in them? Even if we share a consensus in our society, couldn't there be other societies with totally different principles, and would not those principles be just as true as ours?

These difficult questions have occupied philosophers for as long as people have thought about morality. The answers can take many different forms. Firstly, it can be argued that at least some moral principles are necessary as ground rules if people are to live together, which of course they must. Rational self-interest dictates that if I do not respect your property, you will not feel any need to respect mine. Since I value my property and you value yours, and we cannot stand watch over it all the time, we "agree" not to steal and adopt it as a moral principle. A similar argument could be mounted for prohibitions against killing, assault, etc. By the same token, the prohibition against lying could be based naturally in the fact that communication is essential to human life, and that a presupposition of communication is that in general the people with whom one is conversing are telling the truth.

Some philosophers have mounted a more ambitious case for deriving ethical principles from logic. We would all agree that the strongest way in which someone can err is to be self-contradictory. To be sensible, or rational, we must be consistent. According to some thinkers, something very like the golden rule is a natural consequence of a consistency requirement. In other words, I can be harmed in certain ways, helped in others, and wish to avoid harm and fulfill needs and goals. I see precisely the same features in you and the same concerns. Thus if I feel something should not be done to me, I am led by the similarities between us to conclude that it should not be done to you either, either by me or by another. In fact, it is precisely to circumvent this plausible sort of reasoning that we focus on differences between ourselves and others; color, place of origin, social station, heritage, genealogy, anything which might serve to differentiate you from me, us from them, so I don't have to apply the same concerns to others as to me and mine. The history of civilization, in a way, is a history of discarding differences which are not relevant to how one should be treated, like sex or skin color. In sum, some notion of justice—treat equals equally—has been said to be a simple deduction from logic.

A third attempt to ground moral principles takes the following tack: We share certain moral principles in virtue of living in the same society. One cannot doubt that these are real—they control our actions and are built into law. If one tries to imagine life without these principles, it becomes clear that chaos would ensue—we simply could not live together. In short, our moral principles work to create the possibility of smooth social intercourse. Furthermore, most of us would not wish to see society restructured without these moral principles. Thus, these principles enjoy foundational validity; however we may speculate about alternatives to them, they run our everyday lives.

Furthermore, despite the fact that skeptics do appeal to other societies as examples of cases with very different moral principles, at least a core of common principles survives even cross-cultural comparison. For example, some version of the golden rule can be found in Judaism, Christianity, Islam, Brahmanism, Hinduism, Jainism, Sikhism, Buddhism, Confucianism, Taoism, Shintoism, and Zoroastrianism. And it stands to reason that certain moral principles would evolve in all societies as a minimal requirement for living together. Any society with property would need prohibitions against stealing; communication necessitates prohibitions against lying; murder could certainly not be freely condoned, and so on.

Ethical Theory

The difficulty of explaining the basis for ethical principles and the constant need for weighing and choosing among principles have led many philosophers to try to con-

struct ethical theories. To continue the earlier analogy: It was suggested that one can compare ethics and science. Just as laws in science systematize and describe regularities in perception, principles in ethics do the same thing with moral intuitions. But in science we do not stop with laws, we try to systematize, explain, and consolidate a group of laws under a more general system called a *theory*. Thus the kinetic theory of gases explains and derives the various gas laws, Newton's theory of motion and gravitation explains Kepler's laws, and so on.

By the same token, ethical theories attempt to explain and derive moral principles. For example, utilitarianism attempts to explain and justify moral principles on the grounds that they produce the greatest happiness or pleasure (or absence of pain) for the greatest number of people. Thus utilitarianism explains moral principles in terms of their likely results.

Another theory, that of Immanuel Kant, says that results are irrelevant to what makes something moral or immoral. What is relevant is the reason that the agent performs the action. According to Kant, moral laws or principles follow from the rational nature of the human mind. Being rational means trying to grasp universal truths; that is, what science and mathematics do. Being rational in the area of conduct means measuring one's action by what it would be like if everyone did it, i.e., if it were universalized. If lying were universalized, for example, then no one would trust anyone else, and no one would believe anyone, so no one could lie. Thus universalizing lying leads to an absurdity, and hence lying is immoral. Alternatively, Kant develops his ethic in terms of respect for the dignity and freedom of individuals, and thus what is moral is what involves treating other persons "not merely as means, but as ends in themselves."

In addition to such philosophical theories of morality, social practice in our society has also attempted to organize and explain our moral principles by a theory built into our religious traditions, our common sense, and our legal and political system. The theory is expressed in our Constitution. It contains elements both of utilitarianism and Kantianism, explaining morality both in terms of general welfare and respect for the individual. In effect, it balances these major concerns. Thus, the key object of moral concern and attention in our society is the individual human being, not the church, the state, the *Volk*, the government, the aristocracy, or any other abstract notion. Not every society puts such primacy upon the individual—in many societies, the state is all important, and the individual is nothing. In our theory, a society is effectively a group or collection of autonomous, free, equal individuals each worthy of respect, not a separate or higher entity. Thus moral principles first and foremost exist out of respect for individual freedom and dignity.

When social decisions are made in our society, they respect the individual in two ways. First, such decisions are made in theory by summing the interests of all individuals (voting presumes that each individual votes his or her own interest), so that one achieves the greatest good for the greatest number. But even though such a procedure gives each individual a chance in each decision, it raises the danger of the majority riding roughshod over the minority. If the majority is conservative, it might silence liberals; if the majority is harmed by a thief who has stolen a large sum of money, it might decide to torture him to get him to reveal its hiding place.

In order to maximize moral concern for individual dignity, our system builds fences around individuals to protect them from coercion by the majority. These protective fences are called *rights*, and they protect all aspects of an individual deemed to be essential to being human—the need to speak freely, to believe as one chooses, to preserve property and privacy, to associate with whomever one chooses, and so forth. This moral theory is given the full power of law and is mobilized, often at great expense, to protect the dignity and nature of each individual.

Adjudicating Moral Issues

It remains to apply this discussion to some concrete cases, to give content to the discussion and also to point out its limitations. Let us consider first a fairly straightforward case heard from a veterinarian serving on a state ethics committee.

A companion animal practitioner had built an intensive care and convalescent unit as an annex to his hospital. Gradually, complaints from clients began to surface, because people were paying high intensive care bills, yet their animals would always die eventually. An investigation revealed that the veterinarian was taking animals that died and putting them in intensive care. When clients came to visit, he did not allow them to go into the unit, claiming that the excitement was detrimental to recovery. Instead he let them view the animal through smoked glass and talk to it through a microphone. He had attached a fishing line to the animal's tail. He pulled on this while the client talked to the animal so that the animal appeared to be wagging its tail.

What are the moral issues raised by this case? What moral principles apply? The answers to these questions are straightforward. The practitioner was lying to clients, defrauding them of money, raising their hopes falsely, utilizing his privileged position for personal gain without benefit to client or animal, and breaking trust. He was, furthermore, damaging the veterinary profession's standing with the public. Principles exist forbidding all of the above actions. Further, there were no counter principles in this case weighing on behalf of what he was doing. He was, it seems, being immoral in relation to client, peers, and society. His actions did not benefit but harmed society in general, the client, and his peers. Nor was he treating other people as ends in themselves, but simply as a means to line his pocket.

Let us modify the case a bit, hypothetically. The veterinarian is caught, but it is determined that he is not doing it on a regular basis or for profit. In self-defense, the veterinarian explains that the dog belongs to a terminally ill child who will certainly die in a few days and whose dog was suddenly taken ill and died at the clinic. The child's peace of mind is significantly tied to the dog's survival, and so the veterinarian is trying to do what he can to assure it. He has told no one for fear of a leak.

Here the assessment is very different. The veterinarian is indeed lying and defrauding people, but not for his own benefit. In addition, he is risking a great deal. So the principle against lying seems to be outweighed by a principle of compassion for the child or one of diminishing the child's suffering. One could argue that the child's autonomy and dignity are being paternalistically eroded—she deserves to know the truth, however much it hurts—but few would defend such a case.

Having examined a clear case falling into three of the categories of moral problems a veterinarian might confront, let us examine another. Two veterinarians, Dr. X and Dr. Y, were in fierce competition in the same big-city affluent neighborhood, and they hated each other. Mrs. Z had a small dog usually treated by Dr. X which became ill while X was on vacation. She took the animal to Y and it died, and he put the body in the freezer until he could do a necropsy. When X returned, she told him what had happened. X was sure that Y had fouled up and killed the dog and would fake the necropsy to cover himself. X proceeded to bribe Y's receptionist to steal the dog's body and bring it to him so that he himself could do the necropsy and prove X's negligence and incompetence. When caught, he said he was under a professional obligation as a veterinarian to expose incompetence and protect the public, which superseded ordinary moral principles.

What are the morally salient features of the case? Y bribed and corrupted someone, and in effect stole something, all actions of which are prohibited by moral principles. In his defense, he claims that he was upholding his high moral duty in virtue of being a veterinarian and wanting to expose corruption. In an ethicist's view, his position was very weak. While veterinarians or other professionals can be held to higher and more stringent principles than ordinary people in virtue of the professional role conferred by society, they surely cannot claim to be less accountable. If it is wrong for anyone to bribe and steal, it is equally wrong for a veterinarian. And can ordinary people steal if they suspect a wrongdoing? Surely not; even police, that is, those charged by society with investigating wrongdoing, cannot do so. It violates the rights (or fundamental concerns) of an individual))the right to property, privacy, a presumption of innocence until proven guilty—which are cornerstones of our social ethic.

A more complex case is the cruelty incident at the institution discussed earlier. After three days of dialogue between the student, an ethicist, a number of college administrators, the pathologist, the clinician who had received the animal, and the referring clinician, the following weighing of principles emerged: Although there is a principle of confidentiality in medicine, it is often outweighed, such as in California by the law requiring that medical personnel report suspected child abuse. Suspicion of violation of law outweighs confidentiality. In the case at hand, the violation of law was not just suspected, it was certain. In addition, the veterinary school by virtue of its social position as educator and leader, has a duty to be more scrupulous than ordinary practitioners in taking seriously virtually the only sort of action that society has forbidden in regard to animals, intentional cruelty. A number of parties to the debate argued that the veterinarian has a duty to animals that supersedes the duty to the client, exactly analogous to the pediatrician in relation to the child, but this part of the discussion was not decided.

The institution reached sufficient consensus to pursue the adoption of a policy unequivocally stating that a suspected cruelty incident will always be reported to school and humane association authorities. It is true that such a policy may deter an animal abuser from bringing in an injured or sick animal, but it was held that the risks associated with this were more acceptable than the implicit acceptance of cruelty. In addition, the institution felt that it had a duty to notify the referring clinician before any action was taken.

This case involves elements of all of the types of moral problems, for it raises questions of the veterinarian in relation to clients, society, peer groups and, to some extent, animals. Interestingly, even if practitioners do not think that they have direct duties to animals, they still can reach the conclusion that the institution did by arguing that veterinarians, like all citizens, have a moral duty to uphold the law and an obligation to respect society's view of animal cruelty.

The most difficult moral cases that arise in veterinary medicine are those that involve a clear-cut decision regarding the extent to which humans in general and veterinarians in particular are obligated to treat animals as direct objects of moral concern. The reason that such cases are so difficult is that society has not achieved a consensus of moral principles regarding animals nor a consensus moral theory regarding our obligations to animals. For a long time, it was not even a question. And although we are all brought up in much the same ethic concerning the value of human life, or our obligations to human beings, there is no agreement on the question of the value of animal life or our obligations to animals. It is for this reason that veterinary medical ethics is conceptually more interesting than human medical ethics. Human medical ethics is, after all, basically the application of well-established, widely shared, time-honored moral principles and theory to a particular area of concern. In veterinary medical ethics, on the other hand, there is no consensus ethic regarding our obligations to animals. Yet veterinarians must make decisions every day that implicitly presuppose answers to the questions of whether one is primarily obligated to animal or owner, whether animals have value themselves or merely have value as property, and whether animals enjoy any moral status, and what it is.

Veterinarians stand in the midst of a social maelstrom on this issue. Around them swirl myriad opinions with no coherent consensus, ranging from the view that animals are and ought to be tools for human use to the idea that animals are morally no different from humans. Each veterinarian must implicitly take positions on those issues every day—when asked to do cosmetic surgery which does not benefit the animal or to euthanatize a healthy animal, or to castrate or dehorn without anesthesia, or not to use postoperative analgesia on a research animal, or in a thousand other cases. Consider the case of the veterinarian mentioned previously who agrees to euthanatize a healthy pet and then fails to do so but instead adopts out the animal. He is violating some obvious moral principles since he is breaking a promise, lying, and breaking a contract by not performing a service for which he was paid. He in turn responds that if he were a Nazi doctor asked to do the same thing to unwanted human babies, he would be praised for treating the saving of a life as a higher concern than abiding by a promise, a contract, or honesty. In his view, the obligation to save the animal's life far outweighs the other obligations relevant to the case.

The fact that there is no consensus ethic in society about animals does not mean that there should not be. In fact, it grows increasingly clear that as social concern about animals grows, we need one desperately, if only to help assure that our moral and social decisions are not irrational. Without an ethic, we emerge with absurdities like that of the Animal Welfare Act wherein, for purposes of the law, rats, mice, and farm animals are not animals, but dead dogs are. Without a rational ethic, we rely on sentiment and emotion, and thus society stops the army from doing wound labs on dogs but does not blink when they are done on goats, pigs, and sheep, even though no morally relevant difference between these species can be cited. No one needs such an ethic more than the veterinarian, whose professional life consists in large part of making moral decisions relevant to animals.

An Ethic for Animals

For now, veterinarians must generate a viable ethic for the treatment of animals without a social consensus. Certainly each practitioner can generate his or her own ethic, checking it for consistency, coherence, and so on, and trying to live by it. But for a veterinarian, such a decision has daily impact on interactions with others—pet owners, researchers, farmers, etc. How can a purely personal ethic bridge the gap that separates his or her ethic from theirs? And how can busy individuals find the time to formulate their own cohesive ethic?

The task seems insurmountable, yet it is perhaps not as difficult as it appears. First of all, any ethic is an ideal, or something to aim at. We do not always achieve the ideal for humans that we share for lack of resources, weakness of will, selfishness, etc. We do not really treat people equally; all sorts of prejudices color that ideal. But we try, and judge ourselves remiss when we fail. An ethic is a yardstick, a measure of where we are deficient, or a target to aim at which sharpens our skill, as Aristotle said. Without an ideal, we confuse the way things are with the way they ought to be and are smug and complacent. Only by having an ideal to move toward can we progress beyond the status quo. It is by referring to the ideal of equality that we were able to achieve progress for blacks, women and other minorities in the past few decades. It is by appeal to the ideal of fairness that we redistribute income, or share our wealth.

The best animal ethic that our society has generated is a lowest common denominator, or something like "Don't be cruel if you don't have to be," which is hardly of much value in problematic cases. In the absence of an ethic based in reason, a vacuum is created which is filled by emotion and sentiment.

Until very recently, those who cared about animals did so largely for emotional and sentimental reasons. Hence cute, familiar animals were the focus of attention, while others were ignored. Concern for animals was seen as pity, compassion and humaneness rather than duty or obligation, an overflow of goodness coming from us rather than something owed to animals in virtue of traits they had. Abuse of animals was equated with cruelty, sadism, and perversion.

Such an approach, predictably, engenders little progress. No coherent policy emerges. Most animal abuse is not sadistic cruelty, but rather a function of habit, pursuit of profit, insensitivity, training, and lack of thought. Researchers, for example, are rarely sadistic. Mostly they just do not think about animals in moral terms, a situation that is compounded by the large numbers they work with.

So the need for an ideal for animals is manifest. Its lack is becoming painfully apparent as we try to write laws governing the treatment of animals in research, teaching, and agriculture. Even more dramatically, as laws have been passed in the United States and elsewhere requiring enforced self-regulation of animal research, monitored by local animal care committees which review projects, the absence of an ideal becomes painfully evident. When committees review research projects that use human subjects, they can appeal to a detailed social ethical ideal for the treatment of humans. Animal review committees find themselves in the position of jurors told to adjudicate cases without being given the law.

It would seem that constructing an ideal that would command widespread acquiescence would be difficult given the myriad moral views on animals. Most of the accepted views of animal ethics are not reasoned positions, however. They are prejudices, expressions of self-interest, or habit. As such, they rarely can be defended rationally. So if a rational, logically developed ethic for animals based on premises or assumptions shared by society were constructed, it would surely have to command universal attention, at least as an ideal.

Since society shares a great number of moral assumptions in virtue of living under the same moral consensus about humans, the problem becomes, then, one of extending the logic of those assumptions to animals. To effect such an extension, a technique is employed that has become very familiar over the last few decades in the course of changes in social attitudes on disenfranchised humans. During that period people asked, "What is the difference between whites and blacks, or men and women, or young and old, that justifies treating the latter groups in these dichotomies differently and worse than the former?" Certainly there are differences between black and white, such as skin color and hair type. But are these differences morally relevant? Do they justify a difference in moral status, an exclusion of these people from full moral concern, or equality, or justice, or application of our moral principles?

The same question must be asked in relation to animals: What is the morally relevant difference which, ideally and theoretically, barring pressures of convenience and practicality, excludes animals from the full scope of moral concern and rationally justifies us in failing to apply our morals to the treatment of animals? Many such differences have been suggested in the history of human thought, but in fact none stands up to rational scrutiny. If, for example, humans have immortal souls and animals do not, as is often said, one is faced with showing what this has to do with moral status, even if this could be proved, which of course it cannot.

Furthermore, this view is open to a much more striking response, first enunciated by Cardinal Bellarmine 300 years ago. True, said Bellarmine, as a Catholic I must accept Church doctrine that animals have no souls, but this has nothing to do with their being excluded from moral concern. In fact, he argued, they ought to be treated better than humans, since this is their only chance at existence, whereas wrongs to humans will be redressed in the afterlife! So the interesting point in this example is not theological, but rather the dramatic way it enjoins us to be clear about the moral relevance of the differences we point to.

Other alleged differences between humans and animals fare no better. It has been argued that we may do as we wish to animals because we are superior, but what does "superior" mean? Some have said that it means that we are at the top of the evolutionary ladder, but there is no evolutionary ladder, only a branching tree. And if it does make sense to talk about species superiority, it is only in terms of differential reproduction, species longevity, and adaptability, in which case we share top billing with many other species, like the rat, and we lose to the cockroach. If "superior" means that we are more powerful than other creatures and can in fact do as we wish with them, this is surely true, but it has no moral relevance. To say that it does is to affirm that might makes right and to destroy morality altogether, to confuse de facto authority with de jure authority. If one accepts this position, one is forced to say that the government has the right to kill people as it sees fit, since it is after all more powerful than any of us, or that the mugger or rapist is perfectly morally justified in exploiting his victim.

Other alleged differences are equally irrelevant from a moral point of view. "Man is rational, animals are not," is a favorite justification for the exclusion of animals from moral concern. But what is the moral relevance of rationality? Doubtless one needs to be a rational being to be a moral agent or actor, to be held morally responsible for what one does. But one surely does not need to be rational to be an object of moral attention and concern—consider children, the insane, the senile, the comatose, and the retarded. Furthermore, if rationality is the key feature of what makes something worthy of moral attention, why is so much of our moral concern devoted to aspects of human life that have nothing to do with rationality?

Suppose it was discovered that college professors could make their students more rational by wiring their seats and shocking them when their attention wandered. If rationality were the key feature relevant to moral concern, such behavior would not only be permissible but obligatory. Yet we would rightly condemn such behavior as monstrous, showing that rationality is not the only thing involved in being an object of moral concern. There are many other features involved, as this hypothetical case shows. It is wrong to shock the students because it causes pain and infringes on their freedom.

The key point is that while we do worry about the effect of our actions on rationality in our moral concern for humans, we also worry about many other things, namely the other needs or interests of human beings, the thwarting of or infringement upon which matters to them. The whole package of interests involved in being a human being makes up human nature, which is the object of our moral concern. Humans, by nature (at least according to the theories of human nature that serve as the basis for our ethical-legal system), are thinking beings, social beings, beings who feel pleasure and pain, who value freedom, and so forth. And from our view of human nature and our recognition that each individual human being is an object of moral concern, possessing intrinsic value, comes the set of legal and moral protections of the human individual which we call rights: freedom of speech, freedom of religion, freedom of social interaction, protection from cruel and unusual punishment, and so on. Rights, as seen earlier, protect the individual human being as an object of moral concern even when this may result in great cost to society as a whole and to the general welfare.

Clearly there are no differences between people and animals that can conceivably bear the weight of excluding animals from the scope of moral concern and from the full application to them of our moral notions. Not only are there no morally relevant differences, there are clearcut morally relevant similarities. Most important, what we do to animals matters to them: Fulfillment of their needs is attended by joy and comfort, and thwarting of their needs induces pain, fear, and anxiety, though the scientific and veterinary communities have sometimes insisted that animals do not experience such feelings.[6-9]

Animals have natures, what I have called an animal's *telos*—the "pigness" of a pig, the "dogness" of a dog. They have certain basic needs and interests which are genetically encoded, environmentally modified, and expressed and which are essential to their type of animal. These interests are as essential to the animal as ours are to us. If there is no morally relevant difference justifying us in withholding our moral machinery from animals, and we protect the essential nature of individual humans from undue encroachment, we are logically obliged to do the same for animal nature. And if this is done in our moral code by acknowledging rights, then it must be said that animals too must have rights that are legally guaranteed. They are not, of course, the same rights as people's, but are appropriate to the animal in question based on its nature.

In view of this ideal, much of our animal use is frank exploitation of the powerless, and the protection enjoyed by animals is woefully inadequate. This ideal both follows from our ethic for humans and rationally captures the ferment in society to better the lot of animals. The ideal is not a blueprint for instant social change, but a rational mandate for change, or an ideal to aim at, in research, agriculture, pets, zoos, and elsewhere. Society simply must become more sensitive to its effects on and uses of animals. At the very least, this ideal tells us that the interests of animals consonant with people's use of them must be maximized—something we are shamefully far from accomplishing. All pain killers, for example, are tested on laboratory animals but, until quite recently, no one even thought of using pain killers on laboratory animals.[8]

The bulk of laboratory animals are still not animals, according to the definitions of the Animal Welfare Act. White veal is raised in a manner that violates every principle of decency and rational medicine. Millions of healthy pet animals are killed each year.

Many zoos are grotesquely inadequate for the animals they keep, resulting in physical and psychological misery. In fact, in no area of animal use is society even close to maximizing the interests of the animals consonant with that use.

Veterinarians are pivotal people in this new social concern to elevate the moral status of animals. They are in the middle, between researcher and animal, farmer and animal, pet owner and animal. It is veterinarians who must make the daily moral decisions about animals that the rest of society, including animal advocates of the most radical sort, only think about. It is veterinarians who have chosen to devote their lives to animals. And it is they who must maximize this dim, inchoate feeling emerging in society about bettering the lot of animals. It certainly behooves veterinarians to have a rational, articulated ethic consonant with our other moral beliefs.

Conclusion

The ethic outlined in this chapter follows from humanity's most widely held principles, though many people do not like to draw those conclusions or reject them as impossible to live up to. If one accepts certain premises and commits no errors in reasoning, the resultant conclusion must be accepted, however upsetting it is. And the ethic described herein is not repulsive to most veterinarians. After all, most veterinarians entered veterinary medicine because they believe that animals are worth caring about in their own right, not just as someone's property. That is the intuition articulated by the ethical deduction above, which in essence shows that animals are worth caring about in their own right if people are.

This ethic has generated astounding changes in a brief time in veterinary schools and forums all over the world. In recent time we have seen the voluntary abolition of multiple survival surgery by many veterinary schools in the United States, the elimination of invasive laboratory exercises, the pursuit of alternatives to killing and hurting animals in teaching, and a great reduction in the numbers of animals being used unnecessarily.

Laws have been drafted for the protection of laboratory animals, providing meaningful beginnings in controlling pain and suffering. Tremendous authority and responsibility have been granted to laboratory animal veterinarians all over the world to assure the welfare of laboratory animals. And countless veterinarians are moving toward articulating and embracing the rational expression of the feeling and intuitions that drew them to care for animals.

This is not to say that all or even most veterinarians have heartily embraced raising the moral status of animals. Many fear that an ethic such as this will raise malpractice insurance in its elevation of animals above property status, destroying veterinary medicine and their livelihoods in the process. Such fears have been fueled by those who stand to lose financially if animal exploitation is constrained by rising moral concern for animals. Yet in the final analysis, these fears are groundless. As is seen in laboratory animal medicine, quite the opposite occurs. Rising social concern for animals has helped laboratory animal veterinarians: It has given them the authority of law to do their jobs, forced their hiring in all facilities using animals for research, raised their salaries appreciably, and created a context in which their knowledge and skills are esteemed, not ignored.

And the same thing will occur throughout the field of veterinary medicine. Veterinary medicine has gone from an adjunct of agriculture to a highly sophisticated science. As concern for animals in society heightens, the chances to deploy first-rate medicine will increase. As the lives, health, comfort, and happiness of all animals become of greater concern to society, so too must the work of veterinarians. And as the status of animals rises in society, so inevitably must the status of veterinarians.[10]

Veterinarians have not yet come close to

doing their utmost to better the lot of animals. To take one simple example, the major cause of death for pet animals is euthanasia for behavioral problems. Yet few veterinary schools have required courses in behavior. Most veterinarians could do a great deal of good, morally and financially, knowing how to change and understand dog behavior. Yet veterinary schools are too busy teaching monoclonal antibodies or fiberoptics, or whatever the research interests of the faculty. By the same token, veterinarians must take more time educating their clients about animals—and they should charge for it. Society is asking for education regarding their animals—who is more admirably suited to supply it? (Some veterinarians establish doctor-client relationships with clients before they choose a pet so that they can help clients choose the species, breed, size, nutrition, and temperament before a pet is acquired. Very often these people remain clients for life.)

In short, veterinarians should see the ethic articulated herein and the social ferment about animals it mirrors not as a threat to be feared, but as an opportunity. Veterinarians today have a rare opportunity to help shape a major social revolution and to eliminate practices and situations which, most veterinarians say, have bothered them since they entered the field. Rising social concern with animals is a gift to veterinary medicine, which should be embraced, yet used wisely and thoughtfully under the control of reasoned ethical thinking.

References

1. Rollin BE: Updating veterinary ethics. *JAVMA* 173:1015-1018, 1978.
2. Samuelson M: Personal communication, Small Animal Teaching Hospital, Kansas State University, Manhattan, Kansas, 1985.
3. Katz J: The regulation of human experimentation in the United States—A personal odyssey. *IRB* 9(1):1ff, 1987.
4. California Child Abuse Reporting Law § 8572.
5. Rollin BE: *Animal Rights and Human Morality*. Buffalo, NY, Prometheus Books, 1981.
6. Rollin BE: Animal pain, in Fox MW, Mickley L (eds): *Advances in Animal Welfare Science*. The Hague, Martinus Nijhoff, 1985.
7. Rollin BE: Animal consciousness and scientific change. *New Ideas Psychol* 4(2):141-152, 1986.
8. Rollin BE: Animal pain, scientific ideology, and the reappropriation of common sense. *JAVMA* 191(10):1222-1226, 1987.
9. Rollin BE: *Animal Consciousness, Animal Pain, and Scientific Change*. Oxford, Oxford University Press, 1988.
10. Rollin BE: The concept of illness in veterinary medicine. *JAVMA* 182:122-125, 1983.

Laws Establishing the Practice of Veterinary Medicine

The process of licensing veterinarians appears to have begun in California in 1893. Since then, the growing influence and prestige of the learned professions have led to increased governmental regulation of professional activities. Today all states employ statutory veterinary licensing procedures under the direction of administrative agencies called *state boards of examiners*.

The State Board

Mission and Jurisdiction

A major state licensing responsibility is to assure the public that the quality of care received from all veterinary licensees will meet an accepted minimum standard. Through their licensing authority, states have granted a legalized monopoly to that segment of the state's economy encompassing the practice of an entire profession. Therefore, most practice acts are written in a manner that allows boards to exercise much more power over the actions of licensed veterinarians than they can ever exert over unlicensed activity.

A major omission in most state board examinations, however, is the lack of testing on laws governing the practice of veterinary medicine. National board exams, clinical competency tests, and oral or practical state examinations are given to evaluate medical knowledge, but most state boards usually fail to test applicants' knowledge of the laws and codes of professional conduct governing the practice of veterinary medicine in their state. Thus, veterinarians frequently understand little about the legalities of their profession, and the legal problems they encounter often stem from their ignorance of laws regulating the practice of veterinary medicine.

Although most practice acts contain similar language and principles, details are often different. In covering veterinary practice acts in this chapter, the California Act is used as the principal example. It has been updated routinely over the past 10 years, is reasonably representative of the law in other states, and contains some innovative and progressive ways to assure that consumers are adequately protected. The California Act in its entirety can be found in Appendix A.

Most veterinarians perceive that a state board's primary mission is to prevent unqualified people from practicing veterinary medicine. Practitioners also believe that one of the board's duties is to initiate legal recourse against the unlicensed practice of veterinary medicine. Action of this type, however, is beyond the jurisdiction of all state boards except California's, where recent legislation has provided an avenue to initiate legal action.[1]

Appointments to the Board

The number of people appointed to a state board varies from three to nine.[2] Some boards are made up entirely of licensed veterinarians, others include an animal health technician (AHT), and most include both veterinarians and members of the public. In general, veterinarians must have been practicing within the state for a minimum of two to five years and be in good professional standing to be eligible to serve on the board.

Most appointments to the board are made by the governor of the state, sometimes with confirmation by one of the houses of state government. Terms generally run from 3 to 5 years. Legal counsel for the board is usually provided by the state's attorney general's office. Compensation for serving on the board is usually nominal ($50 to $60 per day plus travel) in relation to the amount of time

required and responsibilities associated with such an appointment.

Practice Acts

Veterinary practice acts establish the basic law that governs the practice of veterinary medicine. The acts can be found in a variety of state statutory codes. These include the Business and Professions Code (California), the Education Code (New York), the Public Health Code (Michigan), the Professions and Occupations Code (New Jersey), the Agriculture Code (Maryland), and the general statutes of many states. Under the authority of their practice acts, states also adopt regulations interpreting and implementing those laws. Copies of a state's most current practice act and regulations are generally available only from the licensing boards. Addresses and telephone numbers for nearly all boards can be found in the *AVMA Directory*.

Purpose

Federal, state, and local governments are all empowered to pass and enforce laws that affect the practice of veterinary medicine. The federal government has regulatory powers over practitioners' use of veterinary drugs and has established procedures that accredited veterinarians must follow when providing health certificates for interstate transportation of animals. State licensing agencies establish criteria that must be met before a person is eligible to be licensed as a veterinarian. These agencies examine the educational and technical qualifications of applicants by reviewing the applicants' education and by testing their abilities via state board examinations. Municipalities exert control over veterinarians by regulating the zoning of lands on which they might wish to practice.

The purpose of state government regulation of professionals is clearly stated in the legislative intent found in one state's practice act:

It is hereby declared that the practice of veterinary medicine is a privilege which is granted by legislative authority in the interest of the public health, safety and welfare and to protect the public from being misled by incompetent, unscrupulous and unauthorized persons and from unprofessional or illegal practices by persons licensed to practice veterinary medicine. This act is enacted in the interest of society, health, safety, and welfare of Pennsylvanians.[3]

There certainly are positive effects to veterinary licensing procedures in that they provide public assurance that people entering the profession have an acceptable level of knowledge. Some critics contend, though, that licensing acts grew haphazardly and that their emphasis today is too strongly on restricting entry into professions than on protecting the public.[4] In 1978 the chairman of the Federal Trade Commission said, "It is not unusual for boards to reject higher percentages of applicants during economic downturns when their services are in less demand."[5]

The perception that licensing was overly protectionist became most evident in the late 1970s while the Federal Trade Commission was investigating licensing procedures within the professions.[5] The 1975 *Goldfarb* v. *Virginia Bar* case incited major changes in the interpretation of federal antitrust laws and their applicability to the learned professions (see Chapter 7). Because of this decision, other important Supreme Court cases, and pressures from the Federal Trade Commission, many practice acts were changed to provide for the appointment of lay people to the board as a means of assuring better representation for consumers. A concurrent trend in state practice acts during the 1970s was the adoption of mandatory continuing education requirements for professionals prior to the annual or biennial renewal of their professional licenses.

Definitions

Terms such as *animal, approved veterinary school, board, hearing, complainant, veterinarian,*

licensed doctor of veterinary medicine, animal health technician, direct supervision and others often fall within the definition section of a practice act. The most important of these definitions is that of *the practice of veterinary medicine.*

Defining the Practice of Veterinary Medicine

The most common definition of the *practice of veterinary medicine* seems to be something similar to that used in § 4826 of the California law. The key words in each section are italicized to provide emphasis.

Any person practices veterinary medicine, surgery, and dentistry, and the various branches thereof, when he or she does any one of the following:

(a) *represents him- or herself* as engaged in the practice of veterinary medicine, veterinary surgery, or veterinary dentistry in any of its branches.

(b) *diagnoses or prescribes* a drug, medicine, appliance, or application or treatment of whatever nature for the prevention, cure or relief of a wound, fracture, or bodily injury or disease of animals.

(c) *administers* a drug, medicine, appliance or application or treatment of whatever nature for the prevention, cure or relief of a wound, fracture, or bodily injury or disease of animals, *except* where such drug, medicine, appliance or application or treatment is administered at the direction of and under the *direct supervision* of a licensed veterinarian... However, no person other than a licensed veterinarian may induce anesthesia unless authorized by regulation of the board.

(d) *performs* a surgical or dental operation upon an animal.

(e) *performs* any manual procedure for the diagnosis of pregnancy, sterility, or infertility upon livestock.

(f) *uses* any words, letters or titles in such connection or under such circumstances as to induce the belief that the person using them is engaged in the practice of veterinary medicine, veterinary surgery or veterinary dentistry....

Section (c) above is a somewhat unique component of the practice act. It is this section that allows for the delineation of certain jobs that can be performed by registered or licensed AHTs under an established degree of supervision but not by nonregistered veterinary assistants. Furthermore, that section addresses the induction of anesthesia as a separate issue, rather than allowing it to be included within the general category of administration of any drug or medicine. If the induction of anesthesia is not specifically addressed by statute or by a regulation, it is unclear whether or not that procedure is limited to licensed veterinarians in the state.

An interesting alternative definition for the practice of veterinary medicine can be found in the Model Veterinary Practice Act, as set forth by the AVMA (see Appendix B).[6]

Practice of veterinary medicine means:

(a) to diagnose, treat, correct, change, relieve, or prevent animal disease, deformity, defect, injury, or other physical or mental conditions; including the prescription or administration of any drug, medicine, biologic, apparatus, application, anesthetic, or other therapeutic or diagnostic substance or technique; and the use of any manual or mechanical procedure for artificial insemination, for testing for pregnancy, or for correcting sterility or infertility, or to render advice or recommendation with regard to any of the above.

(b) to represent, directly or indirectly, publicly or privately, an ability and willingness to do an act described in subsection (a).

(c) to use any title, words, abbreviation, or letters in a manner or under circumstances which induce the belief that the person using them is qualified to do any act described in subsection (a).

(d) to apply principles of environmental sanitation, food inspection, environmental pollution control, animal nutrition, zoonotic disease control, and

disaster medicine in the promotion and protection of public health.

It is hard to imagine a statute with much broader coverage than that introduced in this Model Practice Act. One of the reasons for its breadth is to include new technological advances. Included would be procedures like embryo transplants, the diagnosis and treatment of mental conditions in animals, and the use of ultrasound or laser diagnostics or therapy. As technology continues to change, it is likely that most states will have to reevaluate what constitutes the practice of veterinary medicine, surgery, and dentistry in their states and revamp the wording in their practice acts accordingly.

Exemptions or Exclusions

Enforcing the broad definitions for the practice of veterinary medicine set forth in the average practice act would be virtually impossible. Thus, states commonly exempt particular acts or practices from coverage in the practice acts that would otherwise come under the definition of the practice of veterinary medicine. The following list enumerates those types of situations that are not prohibited by the state's practice act:

1. practicing veterinary medicine or administering to the ills and injuries of one's own animals

2. being assisted in the practice of veterinary medicine on one's own animals by an employee who is employed in the conduct of one's business

3. situations wherein lawfully qualified or regularly licensed veterinarians from other states are called to meet in consultation with licensed doctors of veterinary medicine within the licensing state

   According to a 1985 survey by the American Association of State Veterinary Boards (AASVB),[7] 29 out of 40 states responding to the survey allow licensed practitioners from another state to practice within their states without a state license. Although it appeared from the results that the consultation time in the majority of states was limited to specific cases, several states permitted consultation periods ranging from 3 to 90 days.

4. the practice of veterinary medicine by veterinarians in the performance of their official duties in the service of that state or the United States Government, either civil or military

5. students in schools or colleges of veterinary medicine who participate in the diagnosis, surgery, and treatment of animals assigned by their instructors or as part of their educational experience under the direct supervision of a licensed veterinarian appointed by the veterinary school

These examples represent activities commonly exempted; however, the wording of the exemptions varies significantly among states. In addition to these common areas, individual exemptions occur in different states. The following are a few of these exemptions:

1. the experimentation and research of a registered physician, dentist, osteopath, pharmacist, or veterinarian (Massachusetts)[8]

2. the gratuitous giving of aid or relief to an animal in an accident or emergency, provided the person giving the aid or relief does not represent himself as a registered veterinarian (Massachusetts)[8]

3. the performance of veterinary or surgical works or the giving of advice to one's neighbors, provided that residents do not hold themselves out as registered veterinarians or receive pecuniary consideration (Massachusetts)[8]

4. accredited schools, institutions, foundations, business corporations or associations, physicians licensed to practice medicine and surgery in all its branches, graduate doctors of veterinary medicine..., which or who conduct experiments, and scientific research on animals in the development of pharmaceuticals, biologicals, serums, or methods of treatment or techniques for the diagnosis or treatment of human ailments or when engaged in the study of...techniques directly or indirectly applicable to the problems and practice of veterinary medicine (Pennsylvania)[9]

5. any intern or resident who practices veterinary medicine for two years or less in any veterinary college within the state provided such practice is limited to those duties of an intern or resident and the person is under the supervision of a licensed veterinarian (New York)[10]

6. a professor of veterinary medicine who is a graduate of accredited schools of veterinary medicine and whose practice of veterinary medicine is incidental to his or her course of instruction while serving as a professor in a veterinary college (New York)[11]

7. farriers or people actively engaged in the art or profession of horseshoeing as long as their actions are limited to the art of horseshoeing (Maryland)[12]

8. any person who floats (files) equine teeth, removes caps, or scales or cleans animal teeth (Maryland)[12]

9. any nurse, attendant, technician, intern or other employee of a licensed and registered veterinarian who administers medications or renders auxiliary or supporting assistance under the responsible direct supervision of a licensed and registered veterinarian (Maryland)[12]

10. the administration of sodium pentobarbital for euthanasia of sick, injured, homeless, or unwanted domestic pets or animals, without the presence of a veterinarian when such person is an employee of a public pound or humane society and has received proper training in the administration of sodium pentobarbital for such purposes (California)[13]

11. the care, repair and rehabilitation of wildlife species by wildlife rehabilitators under the responsible supervision of a licensed veterinarian (New Jersey)[14]

The list goes on with special exemptions geared to the interests of the lawmakers or traditions of each state. Because the list is so varied and long, veterinarians should review their state practice acts before accusations are made that someone is practicing veterinary medicine without a license.

Defining Animal Health Technician

Although terminology varies, 30 of the 40 states responding to the AASVB questionnaire have some system for registering, certifying, or licensing veterinary paraprofessionals. The most common title used for these veterinary nurses is *animal health technician* (AHT), but the terms *animal technician* and *veterinary technician* are also employed. An example of how this term is defined by one state is as follows:[15]

- The person must be at least 18 years of age.
- The person must have provided satisfactory evidence of graduation from a two-year curriculum in animal health technology from a college or other institution approved by the board (if the school is accredited by the AVMA it will be approved by the state board) or be able to show that he or she has an equivalent education. People with bachelor of science degrees in a field or major related to animal health, including animal science, biology, chemistry, biochemistry, etc. also are eligible.
- The person must have passed a written and practical examination administered by the Board of Examiners in Veterinary Medicine and the Animal Health Technician Examining Committee and be registered by the board.

There are major variations among states regarding what tasks may be performed by AHTs but not by non-AHTs. Some states clearly define the differences, while others are very general, leaving considerable room for interpretation. The California statutes and regulations use the specific task approach.

AHT Tasks

The California regulatory approach treats registered AHTs as competent paraprofessionals with skills that are considerably more sophisticated than those of the non-AHT. Nonetheless, veterinarians are still responsible for determining the competency level of the paraprofessionals who are directed to perform animal health care tasks under their employment and supervision. Licensed veterinarians also are responsible for making all decisions relating to the diagnosis, treatment, management, and dispositions of animal patients.

Supervising veterinarians must examine animal patients prior to the delegation of any health care tasks to either an AHT or an unregistered assistant. Some states stipulate that veterinarians must do some type of examination prior to the performance of the health care task depending upon the degree of difficulty associated with the specific task.[16]

A major difference between California's law and that of many other states involves the delineation of certain health care tasks that only veterinarians or registered AHTs may perform. Included on this list are tasks such as

- inducing anesthesia by inhalation or intravenous injection,
- applying casts or splints,
- performing dental extractions, and
- suturing existing skin incisions.

A routine prohibition placed upon the activities of AHTs or non-AHTs in all states provides that they shall not perform surgery, diagnose or prognose animal diseases, or prescribe drugs, medicines, or appliances.[17]

Another unique component of the California regulations concerns the provision of emergency care in situations when the AHT's employer/veterinarian is not on the premises or readily available. Under California law, only licensed veterinarians and AHTs can perform the following life-saving or emergency treatments on an animal:[18]

- apply tourniquets and/or pressure bandages to control hemorrhage
- administer pharmacological agents to prevent or control shock, including parenteral fluids, provided that the AHT has had direct communication with a licensed veterinarian

  When direct communication cannot be established, AHTs may provide emergency care in accordance with written instructions established by their employer veterinarians.

- initiate resuscitative oxygen procedures
- establish open airways including intubation appliances but excluding surgery
- perform external cardiac resuscitation
- apply temporary splints or bandages to prevent further injury to bones or soft tissues
- apply wound dressings and external supportive treatment for severe burns
- provide external supportive treatment in heat prostration cases

Unless states adopt regulations or statutes differentiating health care tasks that can be performed by AHTs but not by non-AHTs, there is little motivation for these paraprofessionals to pass a state exam and become registered by the state.

Direct Supervision

A common term found in many veterinary practice acts is *direct supervision*. Although the definition of this term is more consistent among states than are those of many others, variations from state to state still exist. The most commonly accepted definition for *direct supervision* is that the presence of a licensed veterinarian on the premises in an animal hospital setting or in the same general area in a range setting is required.[19] Some states go even further, though, requiring that the supervising veterinarian be

> Quickly and easily available and that the animal be examined by a veterinarian at such time as good veterinary medical practice requires consistent with the particular delegated animal health care job task.[19]

Other states do not define direct supervision but discuss the need for supervision in the practice act's general information about animal technicians. One such state provides for a great deal of flexibility with the following limitation:[20]

> Each registered animal technician shall perform services only under the supervision and direction of a veterinarian...,but such supervision and direction shall not be construed to require the physical presence of the veterinarian at that place where services are rendered; however, the responsibility for proper performance of these duties shall be solely that of the employing or supervising veterinarian.

Indirect Supervision

Occasionally states establish another level of supervision to provide the board with additional flexibility. In one state, *indirect supervision* means that the supervisor is not on the premises but has given either written or oral instructions for treatment of the animal patient, the animal has been examined by a veterinarian at such time as good veterinary medical practice requires..., and it is not anesthetized.[21]

Additional Board Duties, Rights, Privileges, and Powers

The typical practice act adopted by a state legislature has an empowering section granting the board considerable power to fulfill its mission under the law. Laws of this type give boards the power to adopt, amend, or repeal such rules and regulations as are reasonably necessary to carry out their statutory duties.[22]

Most states require that any rules or regulations promulgated by examining boards must be subjected to the public hearing process. Thus the rights of all licensees as well as the public are protected because they have the opportunity to provide their input before ill-conceived regulatory policies are established by a board.

Veterinary Premise Inspections

As companion animal veterinary hospitals have proliferated, so have the states' needs to inspect those facilities for adherence to acceptable standards. In some states, as in California, the board may at any time inspect the premises in which veterinary medicine, dentistry, or surgery is being practiced.[23] Other states also allow for or require the inspection of licensed veterinary facilities.[24] As the public's expectations for quality veterinary care and hospital sanitation rise, additional inspection policies by state boards can be expected.

The Adoption of Minimum Standards

Traditionally, standards of care for veterinary practices have been established by the testimony of expert witnesses in the course of suits for malpractice or negligence. When lay people became active members of state veterinary boards during the 1970s, though, minimum standards of practice developed. The new state regulatory efforts aimed to ensure that no matter what veterinarian consumers saw, they would receive at least a minimum standard of care.

Virginia, Maryland, and California were among the first states, in 1978 and 1979, to adopt fairly stringent minimum standards of practice. The premise upon which the standards were based was that if the state could grant a monopoly to veterinarians to practice their profession, they could also demand that minimum standards of care be provided to all users of those professional services.

In general, minimum standards cover items such as:

- animal housing and care;
- construction standards for veterinary facilities;
- sanitation and instrument sterilization practices;
- feeding and caring for animals;
- facilities, equipment, sterile techniques, and supplies for animal surgery and postsurgical care;
- emergency services; and
- requirements for mobile clinics.

Appendix C shows the California minimum standards as of 1987, as well as proposed changes to the regulations. The proposals are the recommendations of a special committee of the California Veterinary Medical Association. Public hearings will be held and changes undoubtedly will be made before the final draft is adopted. Nevertheless, these proposed minimum standards represent the quality of care that California veterinarians believe consumers should be assured when they seek veterinary care within the state. The section for food animal practices may be the first set of minimum standards in the United States specifically covering that area of practice.

An additional set of recommended minimum standards relates to one aspect of food animal practice. In 1984 the AVMA House of Delegates approved a policy statement and guideline entitled *Recommended Minimal Standard of Performance for Practicing Veterinarians Who Offer Milk Quality Control Programs.*[25] This document outlines the standards that practitioners should be expected to meet if they provide a mastitis or milk quality control program. Any malpractice cases involving claims in the provision of this type of service to dairy farmers undoubtedly will be affected by the adoption of this document by individual states.

The "locale rule" that previously governed the standard of care for veterinary malpractice cases is obsolete and is no longer accepted by most state courts.[26] Consequently, the minimum standards adopted by one state's board of veterinary examiners theoretically could be introduced in a civil action for malpractice in another state as evidence showing the standard of care that should be exercised by veterinarians in that state and the United States in general.

Record Keeping Requirements

Many states have regulations stipulating what must be included in veterinary medical records. Chapter 14 covers the legal, business, and medical reasons for maintaining good medical records. Sometimes these requirements are a part of the minimum standards of practice, while in other cases they stand alone.[27] The most comprehensive regulations found to date are those appearing in Appendix C under the California Proposed Minimum Standards § 2031.

The Administration of Anesthetics

Because of the risks associated with the induction of anesthesia, some states regulate this aspect of veterinary practice more closely than others. Anesthetics are drugs, though, and treating them as such in some state practice acts can allow nonveterinarians to administer anesthetics (and therefore induce anesthesia). It is often unclear whether or not that is the intent of the state board and in many cases the issue may never

have been raised. When state law does not prohibit administration of anesthetics by nonveterinarians, the standard of care in veterinary medicine at large applies. The standard usually dictates that only qualified and competent veterinary paraprofessionals may administer induction doses of anesthesia. Whether or not that would include personnel who are not certified, registered, or licensed AHTs is questionable.

Because of the ambiguities surrounding this issue, at least one state (California) defines anesthesia and specifically directs which personnel may induce or monitor it. Anesthesia is defined as:

> A condition caused by the administration of a drug or combination of drugs sufficient to produce a state of unconsciousness or dissociation and blocked response to a given pain or alarming stimulus.[28]

In addition, California requires that every animal be given a preanesthetic examination by a licensed veterinarian within 12 hours of anesthesia and surgery. Furthermore, animals under general anesthesia must be continuously observed until at least the swallowing reflex has returned.[28] The specifics of California's minimum standards for anesthesia inform practitioners, paraprofessionals, and clients of what is expected with regard to this important medical procedure.

A significant addition to the proposed minimum standards in California is the requirement that there be effective means of exhausting inhalation anesthetic gases from hospitals. The inhalation of anesthetic gases by staff people has received considerable attention in recent years because of potential health hazards for humans. State boards probably will focus more attention on this issue in the future.

Issuance of Licenses

A key role of state boards is the issuance of licenses to practice veterinary medicine. The various duties involved in this task include:

1. developing a nondiscriminatory and secure method for processing applications to take the state examination;

2. issuing temporary permits allowing veterinarians to practice in the state until the next examination is offered (Approximately half of the states provide temporary permits);

3. evaluating applicants' qualifications to determine if they have fulfilled the requirements needed to sit for the state examination;

4. writing, developing, and justifying questions to be asked on the examination;

5. determining what knowledge and educational standards must be met in order to pass the examination; and

6. issuing licenses to professionals who have fulfilled the state requirements and passed the state board examination.

Processing License Applications

Application requirements vary considerably among states. The application usually is made on a form furnished by the board, and it must be accompanied by a copy of a diploma, a veterinary college transcript, or certification of graduation sent from the office of the dean of a veterinary college recognized by the board. Some states require notarized photographs of applicants and letters testifying to the person's moral character. The veterinary school from which the applicant graduated usually must be accredited by the AVMA for board approval. All schools in the United States and Canada are approved schools.

The best source of basic information about variations in state requirements is the annual *AVMA Directory*. This directory includes information such as when the state examinations are given, what credentials must be met, whether temporary licenses or permits are granted, the fee to take the examination, and the addresses of state board offices.

Foreign Veterinary Graduates

Veterinarians who receive professional veterinary medical degrees from schools that are not approved or accredited by the AVMA are treated differently than graduates of accredited schools. In most states it is required that such veterinarians complete the AVMA's Educational Commission for Foreign Veterinary Graduates Program (ECFVG) before they may sit for the state board exam. Significant changes in the AVMA's program were made in 1987. These are addressed herein. Additional information can be obtained by contacting personnel at the AVMA's ECFVG office.[29]

Candidates who wish to obtain an ECFVG certificate must first provide proof of graduation from an AVMA-listed college of veterinary medicine. Next they must demonstrate an ability to understand spoken English. Applicants whose native language is not English must pass the Test of English as a Foreign Language, the Test of Spoken English, and the Test of Written English. Applicants whose native language is English do not need to take these tests if they can document at least three years of full-time attendance at a high school where the language of instruction is English.

We realize, Doctor, that you are double board certified in small animal medicine and surgery, but to practice in this state you must be able to answer the large animal questions as well.

After these requirements have been fulfilled, foreign graduates must provide proof of having passed the National Board Examination (NBE) and the Clinical Competency Test (CCT). They must then complete a year of evaluated clinical experience at an AVMA-accredited or approved college of veterinary medicine in accordance with ECFVG-3 Guidelines. Prior to 1987, foreign graduates could fulfill their clinical experience requirements by completing a year as an intern in a state board–approved clinical practice. That option is no longer available in most states. When all of these demands have been met, foreign graduates will receive a certificate indicating that they have satisfactorily completed the ECFVG program.

An ECFVG certificate does not insure that a foreign graduate will receive a license to practice veterinary medicine. In a majority of states, an ECFVG certificate is merely a prerequisite to sitting for licensing examinations and meeting other requirements established by that state.

Various Examinations

Various types of examinations are utilized by state boards depending upon the candidate being examined. The 1985 AASVB survey provided the following information about types of examinations given in the 40 different states that responded:[7]

- NBE—39
- CCT—20
- State written examination—28
- State oral practical examination—19
- A participation clinical practical exam—7
- Other types of tests—3

If applicants do not have a veterinary license, the NBE and/or CCT is almost always required before they may take the state written or oral practical examination. Candidates who are licensed elsewhere may still be required to take the NBE or CCT before they can apply to take the individual state board.

In 1985, 21 of the 40 AASVB respondents allowed senior students to take the state exam in December of the year prior to the applicant's graduation, and 29 permitted them to take the exam in May. The rest of the states, presumably, did not allow students to take the state exam until after graduation.

The NBE

Most states require that veterinary graduates who have met their other requirements achieve a satisfactory score on the NBE before they are eligible to take the state's practical examination. The NBE is developed under the direction of the NBE Committee of the AVMA and the Professional Examination Service. Questions for the NBE are written exclusively by veterinarians who represent all aspects of the profession, including academicians, practitioners, members of AVMA-affiliated specialty boards, and the national practice associations.

The NBE is divided into 2 parts with a total of 400 questions. The scoring of the NBE is based on candidate responses to 360 questions derived from the content outline. Forty questions on each NBE are eliminated from the scoring because they are determined to be unclear, ambiguous, and/or potentially unfair based on answers and subsequent review.

Part I of the examination consists of 200 questions on the preclinical sciences. The subjects covered and number of questions in each section are as follows: anatomy (40), physiology (28), disease processes (32), etiologic agents (20), pharmacology (28), toxicology (15), and immunology (12). Other practice areas include public health, preventive medicine (32), and jurisprudence (8). Part II covers the clinical sciences and consists of diagnostics (48), therapeutics (40), medicine (48), surgery (40), and animal production (24). The numbers of questions on each organ system and the critical issues and diagnoses of the various species of animals can be obtained from an information guide available from the Professional Examination Service.[30]

The CCT

The CCT is a relatively new examination used by many states to test applicants' knowledge of clinical medicine. Some states require candidates to pass this examination before they may take the state's practical examination; others use it as a test for veterinarians who are already licensed in another state but are seeking licensure in a new state.

The CCT is a set of 14 animal patient management problems developed by the NBE Committee of the AVMA and the Professional Examination Service. The primary purposes of this exam are:

- to provide state veterinary licensing boards with information about a candidate's ability to solve problems and manage cases similar to those encountered in actual veterinary practice
- to assess the clinical competency of veterinarians at the entry level from a different perspective than that assessed by the NBE
- to provide state boards with an additional testing option

This examination is unique in that it utilizes a special marking pen and printing method called *latent-image printing*. Candidates presented with a case choose from many treatment options and learn the consequences of those choices by uncovering the latent-image printed responses. The candidate then decides the relevance of the information as it relates to the problem and makes further decisions as the simulated case progresses. Additional information regarding this examination is available from the Professional Examination Service.[30]

Reciprocity of Licensing

Reciprocity is difficult to evaluate because of different meanings associated with this term. Nine states allow reciprocity without examination, and another six states waive the state part of the examination for applicants licensed in other states.[7] The former treatment can be considered complete reciprocity, while the latter is limited reciprocity. An example of complete reciprocity is that of Kentucky, which assures practitioners

licensed there of licensure in Michigan, Missouri, and West Virginia.[25] Other states, like Kansas, provide for reciprocity with any state having equal standards and willing to return reciprocity, at the discretion of the board.

Many states provide for limited reciprocity. This means that if the applicant has practiced for a given period of time while licensed in another state, special, less-comprehensive examination procedures are created for that person. The California statute is a good example of how this provision might be applied.[31] Under that statute:

1. Applicants must be licensed in one or more other states where the board has determined that the licensing examinations are similar in scope and subject matter to the written and practical examinations last given in California. They must have achieved scores equal to those required to pass the examination in California.

2. Applicants must have been continuously engaged in the practice of veterinary medicine for four years or more in one or more states immediately preceding the application for licensure in California. (Many states require five years experience.)

3. Applicants must have graduated from a veterinary college accredited by the AVMA. (This is a distinct impedance to foreign graduates.)

4. The board must determine that no disciplinary action has been taken against the applicant by any public agency concerned with the practice of veterinary medicine. In addition, the applicant may not have been the subject of adverse judgments resulting from the practice of veterinary medicine which the board determines constitute evidence of a pattern of incompetence or negligence. (A court finding of liability for negligence in two or more instances, including small claims court holdings, might block licensure under this condition.)

5. Applicants must pass a practicing veterinarian examination administered by a committee authorized by the board. This can be oral, practical, or clinical, and full consideration is given to the duration and type of the applicant's prior practice experience. (If a person is involved only in small animal practice, the board might give minimal emphasis to the large animal portions of the exam.)

The Future of Reciprocity

The mobile nature of society in the 1980s, the trend toward specialization, and the rapid change of the veterinary profession from being a male-dominated vocation to one in which the predominance of new graduates are women are all causing changes in the current licensing procedures, particularly in respect to reciprocity. States have regarded licensure of professionals as an issue of states rights and will undoubtedly continue to do so. Nevertheless, justifying limited or nonexistent reciprocity as a means of protecting consumers is a difficult position to uphold. The chairman of the Federal Trade Commission stated in 1979 that when there is no reciprocity, state licensure reeks of professional protectionism.[31]

If consumer protection were truly the key state issue, then absolute reciprocity for a licensed Michigan practitioner with 15 years of experience in food animal practice who elects to move to Kentucky and set up a small animal practice without taking any examination does not make sense. Likewise, requiring a recently board–certified small animal surgeon licensed in New York to take the comprehensive multispecies state board exam in order to practice small animal surgery in New Jersey is equally nonsensical. The minimally qualified food animal practitioner from Michigan may readily become a small animal practitioner in Kentucky regardless of competence in small animal practice. Meanwhile, the competent small animal surgeon is denied access to practicing veterinary medicine in, for example, New Jersey

until he or she can pass an examination covering all species of animals. In reality, then, a questionably competent small animal practitioner is being foist upon the consumers in Kentucky, while a proven competent small animal surgeon is being denied consumers in New Jersey.

At the 1987 AVMA Convention, the House of Delegates took a big step toward the development of a national system for reciprocity. The House voted to urge each state to adopt a position qualifying any veterinarian for reciprocal licensure who has (1) graduated from an AVMA-accredited institution or fulfilled the requirements of the ECFVG program, (2) passed an entry-level examination (e.g., the NBE or CCT), and (3) practiced for at least five years and incurred no disciplinary action by any state or federal agency. If this recommendation is followed by state veterinary associations, state boards of examiners, and state legislatures, mobility for veterinarians will be greatly facilitated.[32]

Special Features of Practice Acts

The responsibilities and rights of veterinarians and AHTs regarding the provision of emergency care, and the reporting of animal cruelty and staged animal fights are areas of concern to state boards, the veterinary profession, and the public. Although there is generally no legal duty to provide emergency services except for cases already under the veterinarian's care, other things are at issue.

Good Samaritan Acts

In order to encourage veterinarians and AHTs to assist with emergency veterinary care, most states have adopted some type of good samaritan act. The following is an example of this type of act:

A veterinarian who on his own initiative, at the request of an owner, or at the request of someone other than the owner, renders emergency treatment to a sick or injured animal at the scene of an accident shall not be liable in damages to the owner of such animal in the absence of gross negligence.[33]

These laws can be found within the practice act itself[33] or in entirely different sections of a state's general statutes.[34] There usually are two consistent features: (1) the emergency care must be rendered at the scene of the emergency and (2) liability occurs only when gross negligence can be proven. Coverage for AHTs may be included under the good samaritan act discussing veterinarians, or it may be the subject of an entirely different statutory section.[35]

These statutes cover a veterinarian's or AHT's emergency care for animals. Liability concerning provision of medical care to human patients at the scene of an emergency is another matter. Again, variations among states are great. In some states no statutes address this issue, so the courts must rely on common law precedent within the jurisdiction. Liability can occur simply by proving that the person providing voluntary emergency assistance was negligent as opposed to grossly negligent. In other states, statutory good samaritan acts that speak directly to the issue of emergency care for humans are in effect. An example follows:

Any physician or any other practitioner of the healing arts or any registered nurse, licensed by any state, who happens by chance upon the scene of an emergency...shall not be liable for any civil damages as a result of any acts or omissions by such...practitioner..in rendering the emergency care, except any acts or omissions intentionally designed to harm or any grossly negligent acts or omissions which result in harm to the person receiving emergency care."[36]

If a state has no comprehensive statute encompassing all healing arts professionals, it may have one that covers the nonmedical

members of society. An example of this type states that:

Any person who renders emergency care, first aid or rescue at the scene of an emergency, or moves the person receiving such care, shall not be liable to such person for any civil damages as a result of any acts or omissions in rendering the emergency care...except any acts or omissions intentionally designed/to harm or any grossly negligent acts or omissions....[37]

This particular law goes on to say that the exemption from civil liability applies only to people who are holders of a current certificate documenting the successful completion of a course in first aid, advanced life saving, or basic life support sponsored by the American National Red Cross or the American Heart Association or an equivalent course of instruction approved by the state's department of health. It is very likely that a doctorate degree in veterinary medicine would be considered an equivalent course of instruction, but this is the type of ambiguity that often prevails when absolute answers are sought from any law.

Because of the immense variation among state laws, caution must be exercised when veterinarians provide emergency medical care for humans. Still, the law encourages good samaritans to come to the aid of others, and as long as veterinarians are not grossly negligent, it is unlikely that they would be held liable for providing emergency care for a person in need. Nevertheless, as soon as a registered nurse, physician, or trained paramedic arrives at the scene, veterinarians should defer to them.

Reporting Animal Cruelty Cases

A section of Chapter 2 focuses on the moral, ethical, and legal requirements in reporting animal cruelty cases to governmental or humane authorities. An example is given wherein a veterinary school decides that future cruelty cases must be reported regardless of breaches of confidentiality with clients. In the vast majority of situations, however, state laws cite no legal duty to report suspected animal cruelty cases.

The fact that there are no legal requirements to report animal cruelty incidents does not mean that veterinarians cannot use anti-cruelty laws as leverage to impress clients that they are responsible for their animals. Chapter 4 discusses ways in which these laws can be effectively used by veterinary practitioners.

Duties to Report Dogs Injured in Staged Animal Fights

An exception to the general rule that practitioners need not report suspected animal cruelty violations is with staged animal fights in some states. At least one state requires veterinarians who have "reasonable cause to believe that a dog has been injured or killed through participation in a staged animal fight" to promptly report that fact to appropriate law-enforcement authorities.[38] Practitioners who suspect that an animal is being subjected to staged animal fights should contact the state board to determine whether mandatory reporting of such incidents applies.

While dogfighting is illegal in all states, cock fights are not universally prohibited.[39] Bullfighting can be categorized as a staged animal fight and thus places some states at odds with others. Many states allow bullfights but some, like Rhode Island, prohibit all types of bullfights,[40] and other states allow only bloodless bullfights held in connection with religious celebrations or religious festivals.[41]

Licensing of Veterinary Premises

The need to hold one person responsible for the sanitation and cleanliness of premises where veterinary medicine, dentistry, or surgery is practiced has led some states to require that the premises be licensed. This procedure is a separate issue from the state licensing of veterinarians.[42] States that have adopted this approach may utilize a regular inspection system for veterinary premises, paid for from monies generated by the premise licensing fee. However, at least one state has granted its board the power to require routine inspections but has not provided its board with any way to fund the inspections.[43]

Premises can be defined to include mobile units, vehicles, buildings, and hospital kennels. Individual mobile units or vehicles can be exempted when they are operated from the licensee manager's principal place of business and the building is registered with the board.[44]

In California, if it is determined that the licensee manager has failed to keep the premises and all equipment in a clean and sanitary condition, the board may suspend or revoke the premise license or assess a fine of $50 to $500 per day until such violation has been rectified. The maximum fine is $5000.[45] In states where nonveterinarians are allowed to own veterinary practices, premise sanitation and cleanliness are especially important, because the statutes also authorize the board to suspend or revoke licensee managers' veterinary licenses whether or not they own the practice.

Ownership of Veterinary Hospitals

Many state boards have interpreted their practice acts to exclude the ownership of veterinary practices by anyone other than veterinarians. Nevertheless, there is a paucity of specific language addressing this issue in state practice acts and board regulations. The rationale often used is that since only licensed veterinarians may practice veterinary medicine, only licensed veterinarians may own a veterinary practice.

California has allowed ownership of veterinary practices by nonveterinarians for many years without experiencing any serious problems. As discussed previously, however, only veterinarians may apply for and hold a valid premise license for the practice. In addition, under the definition of *the practice of veterinary medicine*, decisions relating to the diagnosis, treatment, management, and disposition of the animal patient may be made only by the licensed veterinarian, not by the nonveterinary owner.

The *AVMA Principles of Veterinary Medical Ethics* addresses this issue in depth.[46] It is stated there that veterinarians working for nonveterinary corporations may render veterinary services to the public whenever it is permitted by state law. However, veterinarians who practice for such organizations must be especially vigilant in ensuring that their professional veterinary judgments and responsibilities are neither influenced nor controlled by such nonveterinary individuals to the detriment of the animal patient. Regardless of the setting in which veterinary medicine is practiced, practitioners must always maintain the quality of veterinary care at the level usually expected in the profession.

Dealing with Abuse of Alcohol and Other Drugs

Complaints filed with state boards frequently involve the negligence or incompetence of a licensee occurring secondary to drug or alcohol abuse. Many state practice acts allow boards only limited options for dealing with veterinarians who are convicted of crimes resulting from chemical dependency. The only avenues routinely available are the suspension or revocation of the person's license—not a very palatable response for most boards. A 1987 survey showed that 25 of the 39 states responding needed revisions in their practice acts in

order to establish a functional impairment program.[47]

Through the actions and perseverance of the American Medical Association, chemical impairment was recognized in the 1980s as a primary, progressive disease that leads to death of the affected individual unless the impairment is arrested.[48] Amendments to some practice acts and the establishment of state veterinary medical association committees to assist chemically impaired professionals have made it possible to treat veterinarians, AHTs, veterinary students, and their families with understanding and to provide needed help. At least 42 states now have committees to assist impaired professionals. Information is available upon request from the AVMA, including audiovisual materials and the *Impaired Veterinarian Resource Manual*. In addition, the *1987 AVMA Directory* contains the policy statements and guidelines for the AVMA's Model Program to Assist Chemically Impaired Professionals[49] as well as an address and phone listing of all state impairment committees.

In order for a program to be successful, several basic elements are needed:

1. There must be cooperation between the state veterinary association and the state board of examiners.

2. If the state's practice act does not allow for alternative ways to treat chemically impaired veterinarians, it should be amended. The Texas law is an example of a well-conceived approach including a method for funding impairment programs.[50] The legislative components of a peer-assistance program have been compiled for the AASVB and are reproduced in the AVMA's *Impaired Resource Manual*.

3. State boards should determine what constitutes an approved treatment program. These programs could be established by a state committee comprised of veterinarians or other professionals who follow the 12-step program developed by Alcoholics Anonymous or Narcotics Anonymous. Alternatively, an approved treatment

or rehabilitation program could be one run by an approved hospital drug or alcohol abuse center. A potential problem can occur if the approved rehabilitation center is not a hospital with the capacity to perform surgery and, therefore, is not an acceptable facility under the person's medical insurance policy.

4. A controversial but important component of a successful impairment program is a mandatory reporting requirement. Ideally it should be mandated that licensed veterinarians report a colleague's suspected chemical dependency if the person refuses to enter into some type of confidential treatment program. With such a legal requirement, practitioners need not fight the moral or ethical battles that have prevented them from reporting suspected addictions in the past. An example of such language was recently included as a footnote to the *Model Practice Act*:

> ...state licensing boards should adopt rules and regulations that will: (1) encourage treatment and rehabilitation centers, and (2) not interfere with a chemically impaired individual who is undergoing treatment and making satisfactory progress, or who is in a program of successful recovery. The identity of chemically impaired individuals should be treated with absolute confidentiality, unless treatment is refused or a previously treated individual refuses to reenter a treatment center following a relapse. Individuals refusing treatment should be subject to appropriate disciplinary procedures. State licensing boards should work closely with state veterinary medical association committees organized to assist chemically impaired individuals when questions of discipline relating to alcohol and other drugs are being considered.[51]

5. The state board must establish some type of comprehensive reporting and monitoring system to assure that impaired persons who have come to the licensing agency's attention are pursuing and progressing with treatment. In addition, if a mandatory reporting requirement is present in the state, an exemption must be provided for members of state impairment committees that refer individuals to treatment programs and monitor the impaired person's recovery so that they can protect that person's identity.

According to an AVMA report, between 6% and 15% of the United States population is affected by some type of chemical impairment. It is estimated that the prevalence among health professionals may be as high as 10% to 15% because of the ready access to alcohol and other drugs.[50] Information, mechanisms, and programs now exist to assist the profession and veterinary colleagues in dealing with these problems.

Penalties for Practice Act Violations

Nonveterinarians and unlicensed veterinarians as well as registered AHTs and licensed veterinarians can all be found guilty of practice act violations. A thorough discussion of some of the methods by which complaints against licensed professionals are handled can be found in Chapter 5.

Practitioners should realize, though, that state boards of examiners generally have no jurisdiction over the unlicensed practice of veterinary medicine. These cases may be investigated by staff people from the state's board of consumer affairs or a similar agency but usually must be sent to the local district attorney for adjudication. An exception to this is California's newly adopted citation and fine legislation, which is discussed later.

Penalties for Licensed Veterinarians

Until the mid 1970s, most practice acts allowed only for the suspension or revocation of practitioner's licenses. Both of these penalties were rather severe punishment, oftentimes not supported by the seriousness of the offense. Consequently, state boards would frequently admonish or reprimand offenders rather than suspend or revoke their licenses, which was often too lenient. Practice act modifications have occurred in recent years, giving boards a much wider and more practical choice of disciplinary actions. Included in these penalties are:

1. a dismissal of the complaint.

2. a reprimand of the licensee. This may or may not constitute disciplinary action for purposes of application for licensure in other jurisdictions, depending on the state's code.[52]

3. a fine not in excess of $5000 in California[53] or $10,000 in New York.[54]

4. the suspension of one's license wholly, for a fixed period of time; partially, until the licensee successfully completes a course of retraining in the area to which the suspension applies; or wholly, until the licensee successfully completes a course of therapy or treatment prescribed by the board.[54]

5. a judgment and penalty against the licensee but suspending the enforcement of that penalty and placing the licensee on probation. This tack is usually taken with a reservation by the court that if the licensee fails to comply with the terms of the judgment, the probationary order will be vacated and the original penalty will be enforced as stipulated.[55]

6. a requirement that the licensee complete a course of study or public service, or both, as prescribed by the board, and demonstrate renewed competence to the satisfaction of the board.[53]

7. a restriction or limitation on the extent, scope, or type of practice of the licensee.[53] (This section allows boards to prohibit licensees from performing surgery, practicing equine medicine, etc., until certain continuing education requirements have been fulfilled.)

8. the signing of a consent agreement. A consent agreement is the resolution of a complaint agreed upon by the board and licensee that contains conditions placed on the licensee's professional conduct by the board and that may include the voluntary surrender of a license by a licensee.[52]

9. the requirement that the licensee submit to a complete diagnostic examination by one or more physicians appointed by the board.[56]

State boards that lack the diversity of the broad scheme of disciplinary actions included herein might reconsider the penalty sections of their practice acts. The utilization of some of these alternatives allows for valuable constructive disciplinary actions rather than reprimands that are too lenient or license suspensions or revocations which may be too harsh.

Grounds for Disciplinary Action

The reasons given for disciplinary action by state boards are extremely diverse. Those most common are (1) the failure to keep one's premises and all equipment in a clean and sanitary condition, (2) conviction on charges of cruelty to animals, (3) conviction on charges based on violations of the federal or state statutes regulating narcotics and controlled drugs, (4) convictions of acts of fraud or dishonesty, (5) fraud or deceit in procuring or attempting to procure a license to practice veterinary medicine, and (6) false or misleading advertising having as its purpose or intent deception or fraud.

The terminology dealing with negligence and malpractice is probably one of the most important considerations in disciplinary actions. If the wording in this section of the practice act has not been amended in recent years, it is likely to require that the licensee be guilty of gross malpractice or gross negligence which has endangered the health or life of any person or animal.[57] With this type of wording, convictions for practice act violations for negligence or malpractice are nearly impossible. Wordings such as "habitually uses drugs or intoxicants,"[58] "professional incompetence,"[59] "incompetent as a practitioner,"[60] and "grossly negligent or deliberately cruel to an animal"[61] provide equally difficult burdens of proof to overcome.

Careful review of practice acts that utilize these types of descriptive phrases shows that the only disciplinary action usually available to boards in these states is either license suspension or revocation. The protectionism inherent in broad disciplinary standards like these stems from an urge not to deprive professionals of their means for making a living unless considerable proof of incompetence or malfeasance was present. A more liberal and constructive set of penalties, as discussed previously, allows boards to more realistically match their disciplinary action to the nature of the practice act violation. For a review of grounds for disciplinary action under the California Code, readers are referred to Appendix A.

Unprofessional Conduct

Some states classify all of their practice act violations as unprofessional conduct,[62] while others have established codes of professional conduct.[63] In New York, unprofessional conduct includes:

- fee splitting—defined as directly or indirectly offering, giving, soliciting, or receiving or agreeing to receive any fee or other consideration to or from a third party for the referral of a patient

or client or in connection with the performance of professional services.[64]

- failing to make available to a patient or client, upon request, copies of documents in the possession or under the control of the licensee that have been prepared for and paid for by the patient or client.[64]

- performing professional services that have not been duly authorized by clients or their legal representatives.[64]

- abandoning or neglecting an animal patient under and in need of immediate care without making reasonable arrangements for the continuation of such care.[65]

- excessive administering of treatment or use of treatment facilities not warranted by the condition of the patient.[65]

For the most inclusive code of professional conduct found to date, readers are referred to the newly adopted Massachusetts regulations found in Appendix F.

A New Method of Discipline

Because of the costs and excessive time involved in investigating complaints against licensed veterinarians or nonveterinarians, the California State Board decided to try something new. In 1986 the Cite and Fine legislation was passed.[66] Under this new regulatory process, the board of examiners can impose disciplinary action upon a licensed or unlicensed individual who is found to be in violation of the law. Unless contested, a citation does not typically involve the courts, the attorney general, district attorneys, or an administrative hearing.[67]

Benefits of Citation

It is expected that the citation program, which becomes operative in 1988, will increase the effectiveness of the board in the following ways:

- it establishes a method to address violations of the California Practice Act that would not normally warrant revocation or suspension of a license, an administrative hearing, or criminal prosecution.
- it provides the board with direct jurisdiction over improper conduct of licensed veterinarians and people engaged in unlicensed veterinary activities so that the board no longer needs to rely on the initiative of local district attorneys with more serious crimes to pursue than Practice Act violations.
- it allows for adjudication or abatement of violations in a relatively short period of time.
- it will reduce the number of complaints tried via the formal hearing process, thereby expediting the resolution process for cases that are considered minor offenses.
- it will reduce expenditures for legal fees.

The Citation Process

Violations by unlicensed people or licensed veterinarians that are classified as misdemeanors may (1) be investigated by the board, (2) be dealt with by establishing a reasonable time for such unlawful activity to be abated, or (3) contain an assessment of a civil penalty in the form of a fine. Before any citation may be issued, the executive officer of the board submits the alleged violation for review and investigation to at least one veterinarian designated by the board. The review includes attempts to contact the veterinarian or unlicensed person to discuss and resolve the alleged violation. When the designated veterinarians have concluded their review, they prepare a written finding of fact and issue a recommendation. If the designee concludes that probable cause exists that a Practice Act violation has occurred, a civil citation is issued to the veterinarian or unlicensed person.[66]

When licensed veterinarians or unlicensed individuals receive the citation, they have 10 business days to notify the executive officer of the board and request an informal conference with the executive officer or his or her designee. An informal conference must be held within 60 days after the request for one has been made. At the conclusion of this conference, the executive officer may affirm, modify, or dismiss the citation or proposed civil penalty and state with particularity the reasons for the action. A copy of that report is sent to the board, the veterinarian or unlicensed person, and the person who submitted the original complaint.

If people who have been cited wish to contest the decision, they must inform the executive officer in writing within five business days after receipt of the decision. If these parties fail to respond within the specified time, the citation and proposed penalty are deemed a final order of the board and cannot be subject to further administrative review. If the alleged violation is resolved by payment of the penalty or by agreement to comply with the order for abatement, the civil citation and any records relating thereto are kept confidential and are not subject to public disclosure. When veterinarians or unlicensed individuals notify the executive officer within the designated time frame that they intend to contest the decision, a hearing before an administrative law judge will be arranged in accordance with state law. After this hearing, the board and administrative law judge issue a decision based on findings of facts at that hearing.

Additional policies and procedures are described in a manual prepared by the California State Board.[67] All the administrative safeguards of the state have been met, and it is expected that this new disciplinary procedure will be implemented in 1988. Penalties vary from $50 to $500 for first-time and minor Practice Act violations to $501 to $1500 for repeated offenses. If a repeated offense results in an injury or death, the fine ranges from $1501 to $2000. Some violations are considered too serious to be dealt with by the cite and fine approach and must go through the state's administrative hearing process;

others can be dealt with through either avenue. Violations considered too serious for cite and fine include such things as convictions of charges related to controlled drugs, cruelty to animals, and crimes substantially related to a person's veterinary qualifications, functions, or duties.

References

1. California Business and Professions Code § 4875.2.
2. Soave O: *Veterinary Medicine and the Law.* Baltimore, Williams & Wilkins Co, 1981, p 60.
3. Pennsylvania Veterinary Medicine Practice Act § 2.
4. Hannah HW: Licensing—Some concepts old and new. *JAVMA* 174(11):1162, 1979.
5. Hannah HW: Professional licensing under siege. *JAVMA* 175(11):1162, 1979.
6. Model Veterinary Practice Act. *1987 AVMA Directory.* Schaumburg, IL, AVMA, Section 2 (7)(a), 1987, pp 629, 633-643.
7. Harrington B: *American Association of State Veterinary Boards Survey.* Raleigh, NC, AASVB, 1985.
8. Massachusetts General Laws, Chap 13, § 58 (2)(4)(7).
9. Pennsylvania Veterinary Medicine Practice Act § 485.32(5)(7), § 27(2).
10. New York Education Law § 6705.5
11. New York Education Law § 6705.6.
12. Annotated Code of Maryland § 2-301(g)(7)(8)(9)(10).
13. California Business and Professions Code § 4827(f).
14. New Jersey Professions and Occupations Code § 45:16—8.1.
15. California Business and Professions Code § 4839, 4841.5, and California Administrative Code Title 16, Chap 20, § 2066, 2067, 2068.
16. California Administrative Code, Title 16, Chap 20 § 2036.
17. California Business and Professions Code § 4840.2.
18. California Administrative Code § 2036.
19. California Administrative Code § 2034.
20. Rules and Regulations of the Pennsylvania State Board of Veterinary Medical Examiners § 31.31(2).
21. California Administrative Code § 2034(f).
22. California Business and Professions Code § 4808.
23. California Business and Professions Code § 4809.5.
24. Code of Virginia § 54-784.03(7).
25. *1987 AVMA Directory.* Schaumburg, IL, AVMA, pp 466, 633-643.
26. Hannah HW: Legal brief: The similar locality rule. *JAVMA* 173(5):489, 1978.
27. California Administrative Code § 2031; 256 Code of Massachusetts Regulations § 5.01; Virginia Board of Veterinary Medicine Regulations § 4.2.A.4.
28. California Administrative Code § 2032.
29. AVMA Educational Commission for Foreign Veterinary Graduates. *Guidelines for Graduates of Colleges of Veterinary Medicine Outside the United States and Canada.* Schaumburg, IL, AVMA, 1987.
30. Professional Examination Service, 475 Riverside Dr, New York, NY 10115.
31. California Business and Professions Code § 4848.
32. Displays and reciprocity emerge as key house issues. *JAVMA* 191(6):625, 1987.
33. California Business and Professions Code § 4826.1.
34. 42 Pennsylvania CSA § 8331.1.
35. California Business and Professions Code § 4840.5.
36. 42 Pennsylvania CSA § 8331.
37. 42 Pennsylvania CSA § 8332.
38. California Business and Professions Code § 4830.5.

39. Leavitt ES: *Animals and Their Legal Rights*. Washington, Animal Welfare Institute, 1978, p 124.

40. Rhode Island Statutes § 5-22-5.

41. California Penal Code § 597m.

42. California Business and Professions Code § 4853, 4853.5, 4853.6; Code of Virginia § 54-748.03(7); Rules and Regulations of the Virginia Board of Veterinary Medicine, Regulations 1.B., 9.C., 15.C.

43. 63 Pennsylvania Statues § 485.27.

44. California Business and Professions Code § 4853.

45. California Business and Professions Code § 4853.5.

46. *AVMA Principles of Veterinary Medical Ethics*. Schaumburg, IL, AVMA, 1987, p 5.

47. Shomer RS: Current status of the relationship of veterinary licensing boards with impairment/diversion/assistance programs. Paper presented at the World Veterinary Congress, Montreal, 1987. Copies available from the author, 10 Indian Field Ct, Mahwah, NJ 07430.

48. Gloyd JS: *The Impaired Veterinarian Newsletter*. Schaumburg, IL, AVMA, March 1987, p 3.

49. *1987 AVMA Directory*. Schaumburg, IL, AVMA, p 479.

50. State committees wage war against substance abuse. *JAVMA* 190(7):841, 1987.

51. Footnote to § 11—Discipline of Licensees, Item 3—Chronic inebriety or habitual use of drugs. *AVMA Model Veterinary Practice Act*. Schaumburg, IL, AVMA.

52. 256 Code of Massachusetts Regulations § 6.06:(1).

53. California Business and Professions Code § 4875, 4876.

54. New York Education Law § 6511.

55. 63 Pennsylvania Statutes § 485.24(4).

56. California Business and Professions Code § 4876(b).

57. New Jersey Statutes 45:16-6.I.

58. New Jersey Statutes 45:16-6.B.

59. 63 Pennsylvania Statutes § 485.21(20).

60. Annotated Code of Maryland § 2-310(10).

61. Annotated Code of Maryland § 2-310(9).

62. New York Education Law § 6506; Title 8 Education, Chap 1 Board of Regents, Part 29.1 (3) (7) (11).

63. 256 Code of Massachusetts Regulations § 7.01.

64. New York Education Law § 5606; Title 8 Education, Chap 1, Board of Regents, § 29.1.

65. New York Education Law § 5606; Title 8 Education, Chap 1, Board of Regents, § 29.6 (7) (8).

66. California Business and Professions Code § 4875.2.

67. *California Board of Examiners in Veterinary Medicine Citation Procedures Manual*. Sacramento, CA, 1987, p 1.

CHAPTER 4

Animals and the Law

Common law and statutory material are prolific on the subject of animals and the law. Many of the laws have been drafted or rewritten recently. Some stem from the animal rights movement of the 1980s, while others grew out of society's continuing demand for more stringent regulation of animal use and ownership. The more controversial issues include the (1) humane treatment and limited use of animals for research, (2) restrictions on the ownership of dangerous animals or dogs classified as fighting dogs, (3) restrictions on the numbers of animals that may be owned by people in urban environments, (4) preservation of endangered species of wild animals, (5) laws providing that veterinarians have a lien based upon possession of the animal for unpaid veterinary services, and (6) laws dealing with abandoned animals.

Those issues related to laboratory animal medicine and research are not covered herein. (An excellent bibliography of references on this topic can be found elsewhere.[1]) Laws relating to wildlife management are covered separately in Chapter 16. Only those aspects of the law that apply most frequently and directly to practicing veterinarians are discussed.

Terms and Categories

Defining Animals

The definition of the term *animal* is paramount in animal law. Some definitions for this word stem from court decisions, but most current definitions have a statutory basis. One of the older court cases held that animals are "those endowed with the power of voluntary motion."[2] Statutory definitions include such language as "every living creature except a human being,"[3] "any description of vertebrate excluding only *Homo sapiens*,"[4] and "every living warm-blooded creature except a human being."[5]

Clearly, the definition varies greatly. Some laws include only warm-blooded creatures, others include all vertebrates, and still others encompass all living creatures. The controversy most often faced by courts is not whether a particular entity is an animal, but what the legislative body intended when it used the term *animal*. The code sections of different states, counties, and cities vary greatly, and there is even variation within the code sections of any one jurisdiction. Therefore, a careful review of all statutory definitions is essential when reading any specific statutory law relating to animals. Some species of animals covered under the anticruelty laws, for example, may not be covered under the zoning laws of the same locale.

The Classification of Animals as Domestic or Wild

Animals are usually classified according to species and distinguished as either domestic or wild. Problems occur with simple classifications like this, because certain species or individual animals do not fall neatly into either category. Others fit into both categories based upon their use, for example, laboratory rats and mice, animals raised for fur production, and some of the newly domesticated exotic animal species like macaws, cockatoos, and ferrets. Additional difficulties are encountered with animals like reindeer, elephants, and water buffalo that might be considered to be domesticated in their native countries but are classified as wild in others.

Sharp differences occur in the application of laws depending upon the category wherein an animal is placed. Thus, careful review of the definitions provided by the statute may be critical to the issue at hand.

The AVMA Council on Public Health and Regulatory Veterinary Medicine has been working on a model definition for the terms *domestic* and *wild* whereby custody or ownership could be allowed or prohibited without the need for exhaustive lists of animals by species. Drafts of their attempts to define

identifiable differences probably are better than many of the statutory attempts currently used by various governments. An example of an exhaustive list by species can be found in § 416-2.016 of the Contra Costa County Animal Control Ordinance (see Appendix G). Under the AVMA proposals, a *domestic animal* is "any animal that has been traditionally bred and kept by people for agricultural purposes or as household pets." A *wild animal* would be defined as "any animal which is nondomestic (however tamed), fierce, dangerous, venomous, noxious, or naturally inclined to harm, in any place other than an approved zoological park, veterinary hospital or clinic, humane society shelter, circus, facility used for educational, scientific or medical purposes, or facility specifically permitted by the appropriate Health or Agricultural authority."

Knowing that not all animals fall readily into one category or another, the Council's proposal defines *exotic animal* as "any animal not considered domestic or wild, but which can be safely and humanely maintained in captivity."

Most state laws include among domestic animals livestock, dogs, and cats, and livestock is further defined as including horses, cows, sheep, goats, pigs, domestic rabbits, and domestic fowl (including game fowl raised in captivity).[6] By comparing a statute of this type with the model proposed by the AVMA, the problems in determining the category into which an animal falls are clear. Some individuals within the canine and feline species should probably be classified as wild animals, whereas certain tamed bison and ferrets might more realistically belong in the exotic or domesticated categories.

Ownership Rights and Duties According to Animal Status

Ownership of an animal entails duties and rights which vary greatly depending upon the category into which the animal falls. Some of the key differences in the ownership of wild animals versus domestic animals are listed in Tables 4.1 and 4.2.

Table 4.1   Rights of Ownership of Wild Animals

1. Owners have fewer rights and a higher level of tort (civil) liability.
2. Ownership is lost if the animal escapes.
3. The presence of scienter, i.e., a prior knowledge of the animal's vicious propensity (also known as the "first bite rule"), is not needed to bring about liability on the part of the owner.
4. Owners are usually held strictly liable for damages caused by animals belonging to them or kept under their custody.

Table 4.2   Rights of Ownership of Domestic Animals

1. Owners of domestic animals have more legal protection regarding their ownership rights but also more specific statutory responsibilities.
2. Ownership is not lost if the animal escapes.
3. In many states and with most species of animals, proof of scienter is needed before courts will invoke liability.
4. Injured parties must prove that negligence in the restraint or maintenance of an animal existed in order for owners to incur liability on behalf of animals belonging to them. (Exceptions to this generalization and the need for scienter exist in many jurisdictions regarding bite wounds by dogs).

The New Category Called Pets

For many years animals were classified either as wild or domestic. Animals in both categories were considered by law to be forms of personal property, in the same category as automobiles and appliances. The classification of animals as one form of property or another can be extremely important when courts determine the amount of damages that owners may collect for injuries suffered by those animals.

Pets are usually considered a subcategory of domestic animals. Although a specific definition for a pet might be difficult to formulate, the key to determining whether an animal is a pet or not focuses on evidence of the relationship between the animal and its owner. Just because people own companion animals does not mean that those animals will be classified as pets. In any given family, a father or mother might be the legal owner of an animal, but the daughter or son might be the person who has a relationship with the animal sufficient for it to be classified as a pet.

Recent research and writing on the subject of the human-animal bond continues to define the importance of pets in people's lives. In special capacities, animals serve as extensions of their master's senses, such as seeing eye dogs, hearing dogs for the deaf, and household pets that smell smoke in time to save their owners from fire. The use and immense value of animals in pet-facilitated psychotherapy programs are now common knowledge. Examples include horses for the handicapped; dogs and cats for the mentally ill; animals in prisons, convalescent hospitals, and nursing homes; and companion birds, dogs, and cats for the elderly or people who are housebound.

The concept that pets are different from and more important than other animals and distinct from other types of personal property is one that is gaining recognition in the courts. When asked to vitiate a no-pet provision in a lease, a New York court said:

> In today's troubled world and time, the need to communicate and reach out and care for other human beings and other forms of comforting animal life...should not be inhibited by stated but unmeant prohibitions. Instead, the courts should attempt to preserve decent and reasonable rules by which mankind and animals may live together in harmony.[7]

Pets have been recognized as a distinctly different form of animal property by the federal government's Department of Housing and Urban Development(HUD). Section 227 of the Housing and Urban-Rural Recovery Act of 1983 provided that no owner or manager of federally assisted rental housing for the elderly or handicapped may prohibit or prevent tenants from having common household pets living in the tenant's dwelling units. In 1987, after considering 4800 comments, HUD finally adopted guidelines to implement the rules allowing pets in public housing.[8] Part 243 of HUD's guidelines specifically enumerates a variety of animal species as *common household pets* including dogs, cats, birds, rodents (including rabbits), fish, and turtles traditionally kept in the home for pleasure rather than for commercial purposes.

Another New York court case often has been cited as evidence of the law's trend toward the identification of pets as a distinct form of property. In that case the court rejected the classification of a pet dog as a mere item of personal property by saying:

> This court now overrules prior precedent and holds that a pet is not just a thing but occupies a special place somewhere in between a person and a piece of personal property.[9]

As physicians, social workers, mental health professionals, courts, and governmental agencies recognize the unique status that pets have in the lives of their owners and keepers, the distinction between pets and other forms of animal property will very likely increase. This growing distinction probably will be most apparent in the form of increasing damage awards for the injury to or loss of people's pets. As Favre and Loring put it,

> It is conceivable that the legal system will completely reverse the nineteenth century position of pets having no intrinsic value, to one that gives full recognition and acceptance of the value of the pets to humans. The legal system may now be in the process of recognizing a new, third category of animals—pets.[10]

The Unique Position of Animals as a Form of Property

Although animals generally are considered by the legal system to be a form of personal property, the law repeatedly treats them as a unique form of property. In fact, the legal system is constantly struggling with precedents regarding how the actual and intrinsic value of animals should be differentiated and addressed. The legal position currently held by animals is not unlike that once held by slaves. Owners are expected to provide for animals differently than they would for inanimate property, but without the same legal duties that exist for human life.

In many ways the application of governmental regulations regarding the rights and duties of automobile ownership is analogous to that associated with some species of animals. For example, states require autos to be identified, licensed, and registered with a state agency so that they may be bought, sold, traded, ticketed, and insured.

Similar governmental demands are placed on dog ownership by requiring that this form of property be licensed and registered with local governments, be identified with a license tag so that it can be returned to the owner in case it is lost, and be ticketed if the animal is found in an illegal location (off leash and on property other than that of the owner). Some of the most recent legislation also requires that owners of dangerous dogs maintain in full force and effect a $50,000 surety bond or a $50,000 homeowner's liability insurance policy in case the dog injures a person or a person's animal.[11]

The analogy between animals as property and inanimate objects as property fails, however, when animals are treated cruelly. It is not a crime to treat one's auto in a cruel and inhumane manner, but cruelty to animals is a crime. Thus, animals are not merely property and cannot be subjected to all property law precedents. In addition, there are major differences in the application of the standard property law damage precedents to this different type of property.

Under standard property law principles, an auto worth $10,000 is considered "totaled" or "junked" if it is damaged and the cost for repairs exceeds its insured value. Owners always have the option of keeping the severely damaged vehicle and driving it as is or repairing it, but insurance companies responsible for reimbursing owners for the damage are required only to pay the maximum insured value.

If a responsible owner is walking his or her properly leashed pet poodle on a sidewalk and a reckless driver negligently drives onto the sidewalk, causing serious injury to the poodle and the owner, the driver's liability insurance will cover the injuries to the owner no matter how costly, up to the maximum benefit of the insurance policy. Agents for the same insurance carrier, however, often will try to argue that the company will only cover medical costs for the dog up to its market value. A major question arises, then, whether (1) the dog as a form of property can be considered "totaled" as soon as costs for repair exceed the purchase price paid by the owner to acquire the dog or the "Blue Book" depreciated value (as is done with autos), or (2) whether the insurance carrier can be required to pay all the costs for veterinary care regardless of the animal's value.

Under traditional personal property law, most forms of property with the exception of rare art, coins, and antiques become less valuable as they age. Should pets, then, be treated under the property law principles associated with autos and appliances that wear out in 10 to 15 years or as art and antiques?

Courts generally have held that full costs for medical services for pets are allowable. Two key questions arise associated with this situation: (1) Does this legal precedent indicate that animals are already considered a unique form of personal property with different legal principles? and (2) Would a case be decided differently if the injured animal was one that only had economic value (like a sheep or cow) rather than a pet?

Limitations on Ownership

Usually the law's impact on veterinary practice is a negative one involving an action for negligence, malpractice, breach of contract, etc. Sometimes, however, the impact can be positive. Legal limitations on animal ownership generally are intended to promote responsible animal care, but sometimes a knowledge of these laws can be used effectively by veterinarians to improve the welfare of animals and the quality of veterinary medicine practiced on those animals.

Animal Confinement Laws and Liability

Most states, counties, and cities have laws prohibiting animals from roaming freely. Some laws are written to include all domestic animals, some specifically apply only to dogs, and some to dogs and cats. Therefore, a close review of the statutory definition given to the word *animal* is again imperative. When laws exist that require the confinement of animals in a specific manner, owners who fail to do so can be cited and fined by local police or animal control officers and held financially accountable for damages caused by their unrestrained animals.

Both homeowner's and renter's insurance policies provide liability coverage for injuries or damages caused by animals belonging to an insured owner. Practitioners who know the local animal confinement laws and understand owner liability for the acts of their animals are in a position to help themselves and their clients. Such practitioners can encourage owners to pursue veterinary care based on their assessment of the likelihood that the injured animal's owner can recover the costs for those veterinary expenses.

If an owner's reimbursement of veterinary fees is possible, it may make the difference as to whether the injured animal receives the best medical treatment or the most economical treatment or maximal veterinary care versus euthanasia. The key to success in cases like this often, however, depends upon practitioners' knowledge of their local or state animal confinement laws.

My dog Bandit wouldn't hurt a flea – in fact, he loves everyone.

Types of Animal Confinement Laws

Some animal confinement laws are written as broad "running at large" laws. Statutes of this type generally require that police and/or animal control officers attempt to capture, restrain, and impound any dogs running at large. These same statutes typically define *running at large* to include any dog off the premises of its owner and not under the control of the owner or some other person.[12] Because most animal control agencies have found the enforcement of this type of law very difficult, many communities now have strict leash laws, especially for dogs. These statutes typically stipulate that dogs not under effective restraint by a leash are considered to be running at large.[13] An example of a complete running at large statute can be found in Appendix G.

State law is less restrictive than local law in many cases involving animal restraint. Cities or counties often have strict leash laws rather than laws that allow animals merely to be under the control of the owner. Additionally, local laws may include all animals, whereas the state laws may include only dogs. Thus, practitioners need to contact their local animal control agencies to ascertain which type of law governs their jurisdiction.

When clients are able to show that their animal was on their property or on a leash, and the animal causing the injury was not on its owner's property or on a leash, the law generally holds the other party liable for the injuries that occurred. Furthermore, this may hold true even without scienter (prior knowledge of any aggressive or vicious propensities).

It should be noted that some local ordinances are written to include confinement of cats as well as dogs. An interesting alteration to the standard confinement law is one stating that no cat owners shall permit their cats to damage public or private real or personal property, or to bite, scratch, or claw any person or animal that belongs to another person.[14] If that is the case, then owners whose cats venture into someone else's yard could find themselves liable just like dog owners even though the law did not require the cat to be on a leash.

Proving whose animal caused the damage and where the incident occurred is always extremely important and often difficult. A picture or videotape is the best evidence, but few owners are prepared to photograph such incidents. Therefore, veterinarians should advise owners to maintain some written documentation as to what happened and how, when, and where it occurred. Names of witnesses can be extremely helpful and important.

Whenever possible, the details of the altercation should be reported to the local animal control facility so that a second level of reporting, documentation, and investigation also exists. In addition, good medical documentation of wounds found and treatments rendered is essential so that the veterinarian's fee for repairing or attempting to repair the injuries is justified and defensible.

The Issue of Liability Insurance

Since the purpose of animal confinement laws is to prevent injuries and damages to people, other animals, and the property of others, animal owners who violate these laws can sometimes be held personally liable for injuries caused by their inadequately restrained animals. This could include the following:

- injuries to or death of a properly restrained or confined animal belonging to another person
- biting, scratching, kicking, or goring injuries suffered by a person
- injuries to the driver of an automobile or a motorcycle, a bicyclist, or a skateboarder, etc., who suffers an injury after running into or attempting to avoid an improperly restrained or confined dog, cat, or other animal while legally traveling on a highway or sidewalk.

Injured people and animal owners who are involved in these types of situations find it easier to recover their expenses when some form of liability insurance is present than when the animal owner is uninsured. However, when no insurance exists but ample proof is present, the small claims or municipal court system also can be a useful avenue for redress. The minimal filing fee for small claims court is usually less than $35, and most jurisdictions allow for suits up to $2500 in value. Attorneys may or may not be allowed to assist plaintiffs or defendants in small claims court during the courtroom hearing, depending upon the jurisdiction.

The veterinarian's advice to clients regarding their course of action is important when a third party might be financially responsible for the cost of veterinary fees incurred. In some cases an offer by the attending veterinarian to testify as to the medical treatments rendered and fees incurred may be all it takes to encourage a client to proceed with optimal treatment instead of giving up because of the expense.

Payment for Services Associated with Third-Party Liability

Whenever veterinary care is provided for a patient, the contract allowing for that care is between the veterinarian and the animal owner. Thus, practitioners should insist upon full payment directly from their clients for all services rendered. Owners of injured animals in turn must attempt to recover their losses from owners of the improperly confined animals or their liability insurance companies.

Depending upon the client's ability to pay for expensive veterinary care as it is rendered, practitioners may find themselves in the position of having to finance that care until the client can recover from the liable party. Veterinarians who are willing to extend credit under these circumstances will find that a thorough knowledge of the facts surrounding the case and of local confinement laws is essential. After all, the practitioner's chances of getting paid may depend on the client's ability to win a legal dispute regarding liability.

When practitioners are required to finance most of an animal's medical care, a phone call to an agent at the homeowner's or renter's insurance company is in order. That agent may be able to say whether or not the client's liability insurance policy will cover the estimated veterinary fees. Veterinarians should then explain what type of extensive and/or expensive care will be required to rehabilitate the patient. Direct discussions between the insurance agent or adjustor and the veterinarian early in the treatment process help avert problems with miscommunications or surprises later on.

If no insurance exists, it may help to talk with the potentially liable animal owner. Most owners without insurance, though, are not very cooperative unless they are concerned that an animal bite report will be filed with local authorities. If the animal is a dog with prior bite incidents on record, the owners are often much more cooperative because of their concerns about losing custody of the dog. In some jurisdictions, one serious bite incident can lead to the placement of the aggressor in the dangerous animal category.[15] It is for this reason that veterinarians should always encourage clients to report bite incidents to local authorities even though not all agencies are equipped to act upon or investigate such reports.

Licensing Requirements

In response to an increasing volume of complaints associated with animal ownership, most state or local governments have adopted laws requiring dogs (and occasionally cats) to be licensed. An example of such a law reads as follows:

> Every person owning, possessing, harboring, or having custody of any dog over four months old shall annually obtain a license and pay a license fee. Every person shall obtain a license within thirty days after a dog reaches the age of four months...or within thirty days after acquiring a dog over four months old.[16]

There are some exemptions to this law, most notably for nonresidents who are temporarily within the county for 30 days or less or for dogs brought into the county to participate in dog shows or field trials.

Difficulties with enforcement have been the primary obstacle to the adoption of laws requiring cat licensure. Some jurisdictions have adopted mandatory cat licensing laws in spite of this difficulty, while others have made it a voluntary decision.

Justification for Animal Licensing Laws

There are many reasons for dogs and cats to be licensed, and the consensus is that the benefits generally outweigh the nominal costs to owners. The reasons for licensing follow:

1. When animals have local licensing tags, enforcement agencies are better able to identify and reunite lost pets with their owners.

2. Income is generated to enforce laws requiring that dogs and/or cats be vaccinated for rabies. This is an important public health aspect of the licensing requirement.

3. Income is derived for local governments to pick up abandoned, stray, lost, or injured animals and maintain them in animal shelters until owners can claim them or until they can be humanely euthanatized.

4. Funding is made available to enforce leash laws and issue citations to owners whose animals are roaming freely and doing damage or creating a nuisance.

5. In some states, license fees provide income to pay for emergency veterinary care required by state law for all injured cats and dogs found without their owners in a public place.[17]

6. Some jurisdictions provide that licensing income is to be used for the reimbursement of livestock owners whose livestock have been injured or killed by dogs.[18]

7. License fees fund the investigation and recording of animal bite incidents and the quarantine of potential rabies suspects.

8. Complaints can be investigated and action taken against owners who allow their dogs to bark incessantly, thereby creating a nuisance.

9. In some localities, licensing fees fund efforts by animal control officials to provide elementary school education regarding responsible pet ownership.

Rabies Vaccination Requirements

Because of an increasing public and animal health threat, most states require that dogs over four to six months of age be vaccinated against rabies. Although the numbers of cats diagnosed with rabies in recent years has exceeded that of dogs, most states have not yet required that cats be vaccinated for rabies.

Although the legal onus is on the dog owner to have an animal vaccinated, practitioners are expected to recommend immunizations for rabies and administer vaccines at the animals' appropriate ages. This is usually after three or four months of age, followed by a booster immunization one year later, and thereafter every two to three years depending upon the jurisdiction.[19] Veterinarians also are expected to maintain adequate records of immunizations administered and fill out rabies certificates as required by state or local laws.

The Veterinarian's Role in Public Health Aspects of Rabies

Because of the fatal nature of rabies and the fact that veterinarians are considered to be public health authorities, there are several other concerns regarding the practitioner's duties in the detection of this disease. In some jurisdictions rabies is a reportable disease, and every veterinarian must immediately notify the county health department when rabies is suspected.[20] Whether or not the jurisdiction has a reporting requirement, any time that veterinarians have reason to believe that an animal could be rabid, both animal control and public health officials should be notified. If a known human exposure has occurred, veterinarians should notify or have their clients notify their physicians or public health authorities within the jurisdiction.

When animals die or are euthanatized and rabies is suspected or should have been suspected, veterinarians are responsible for properly preserving the head or brain of the animal in question so that it can be evaluated for the presence of the rabies virus. This duty becomes especially important if the animal owner or person bitten cannot be reached. Improper maintenance of the animal's brain tissue before it is decided whether to test for

rabies can result in people unnecessarily being subjected to rabies prophylaxis treatments. This, in turn, can lead to a veterinarian's professional liability for negligence.[21]

Other Rabies Law Requirements

Most jurisdictions require that veterinarians who vaccinate dogs for rabies also fill out vaccination certificates. In some locales practitioners must provide the appropriate animal control agency with a copy of every certificate.[20] This informs them of all vaccinated dogs and allows them to pursue licensing procedures with owners who might not otherwise have come to their attention. Other locations, however, are governed by statutes dictating that information contained in rabies vaccination records shall not be used for the purpose of licensing animals or for taxation of individuals who own animals.[22] Some areas require that veterinarians provide rabies tags for all vaccinated animals, while others rely on the license tag as evidence of rabies vaccination. Still other jurisdictions request that veterinarians sell dog licenses to clients who have had their animals vaccinated.

Liability for Animal Bites

Traditionally, animal law precedents have allowed dogs one bite before liability is imposed upon their owners. This doctrine, known as *scienter*, is consistently being replaced by statutes invoking a much stricter liability on the owners of biting dogs.

The law in California is explicit on this issue; those of other states and/or local governments vary. A typical dog bite liability law reads as follows:

> The owner of any dog is liable for the damages suffered by any person who is bitten by a dog while in a public place or lawfully in a private place, including the property of the owner of the dog, regardless of the former viciousness of the dog

or the owner's knowledge of such viciousness. A person is lawfully upon the private property of such owner within the meaning of this section when he is on such property in the performance of any duty imposed upon him by the laws of the state or by the laws or postal regulations of the United States, or when he is on such property upon the invitation, express or implied, of the owner.[23]

This statute clearly states that the strict liability standard is applied only when a person is bitten, and that the old scienter doctrine might still be valid with regard to bites suffered by animals. When an animal is bitten, this statute does not apply, and the courts look to the leash or confinement laws. If there are such laws, it is probable that owner liability will be upheld on the first bite even without a strict liability law like the one above.

From the above statute it appears that virtually no defenses to owner liability are acceptable if someone's dog bites a person in a location as stipulated. The courts are likely to allow several defenses, though. The first is that the person suffering the bite provoked the biting incident. If this occurred, provocation likely would be a full defense to liability.

A second avenue of defense would be that after being properly warned of the dangerous nature of the dog, or in a position or profession where the person knew or should have known about the risk, he or she was bitten. This defense is known as assumption of the risk. A California appeals court has held that although the California dog bite statute appears to impose strict liability on dog owners for damages suffered as the result of dog bites, the defense of voluntary assumption of a known risk is an applicable defense.[24]

A third defense would be that the person who was bitten did not provoke the bite but did do something that contributed to the bite. Proof of this would mean that the injured party was contributorily negligent; this can serve as either a partial or complete defense to liability, depending upon the jurisdiction.

In general, veterinarians who are bitten by their clients' dogs during the course of an examination are unable to recover damages. Courts usually hold that by the very nature of being a veterinarian a person has assumed the risk of being bitten. However, veterinarians and staff cannot assume risks that they do not know exist. Because of this, and especially when dog bite laws like the California one are in force, veterinary employees and veterinarians can recover from clients who fail to inform them that their dog has a history of prior bite incidents. Practitioners will have a difficult burden proving that, for example, other veterinarians or staff members had previously been bitten and the owner mentioned no such incidents prior to the occurrence. Nevertheless, if a veterinary staff person is severely bitten by a client's dog, cat, or other animal, some research into prior episodes of similar behavior at other veterinary practices could promote a successful legal action.

Reporting Bite Incidents

As previously mentioned, unless biting animals are reported to some central governmental or humane agency, it is difficult for their owners to be cited for improper restraint or confinement. Furthermore, if such dogs are to be dealt with as dangerous dogs, proof of prior bite incidents is usually essential. Thus, a valuable and useful local ordinance requires animals that have bitten any person or animal to be reported to the director of the local animal control agency. One such law reads as follows:

If the owner and/or keeper of any animal knows or learns from any source whatsoever, that their animal has bitten any person, any other animal, or has been bitten by another animal ...reasonably suspected of having rabies, such owner or keeper shall immediately confine the animal...notify the Animal Services Director, and shall make the animal available to the Animal Services Director for examination and/or confinement.

The victim of such biting shall report the incident to the Animal Services Director where the owner or keeper of the animal is unknown, or where the owner or keeper is unable to or refuses to make the required report.[25]

Not all local authorities have the manpower to investigate reported bites and may not have this type of mandatory bite report law. However, when this service does exist, a practitioner's knowledge thereof is important and appreciated by clients whose animals have been attacked. In addition, the investigation, documentation, and advice rendered by animal control officials often help clients in their efforts to be reimbursed by owners of biting dogs.

Dangerous Dogs

Because of a rash of human deaths brought about by pit bulls, many communities around the country are reassessing their laws relating to vicious or dangerous dogs. The cover of a recent *Sports Illustrated* magazine pictured a snarling pit bull, and the feature article of that issue dealt with "The Pit Bull Friend and Killer."[26] Clearly, the public's awareness and concern are heightened.

Many drafts of local ordinances have attempted to single out the pit bull as a breed and severely regulate ownership of these dogs. A recently proposed New York City ordinance defined a pit bull or pit bull terrier as any dog which at minimum contains at least 25% of any of the following breeds of dog: American Staffordshire terrier, Staffordshire bull terrier, and bull terrier.[27] That proposal required that all owners or persons in possession of a pit bull terrier register such animal with the New York City Department of Health. It established strict confinement standards for these dogs and required that they wear muzzles and be kept on leashes no longer than 6 ft. whenever they were not confined in their pens or owners' homes. Lastly, it required that persons under whose names the dogs are registered shall at all times maintain a liability insurance policy of at least $100,000.

Traditionally, the passage of laws limiting the rights of dog owners has been considered a constitutionally legitimate exercise of a city's police power to protect the public's safety and welfare.[28] The rash of ordinances that have attempted to single out the pit bull, however, have raised constitutional questions concerning the dog owners' fourteenth amendment rights of due process and equal protection. It is doubtful that these ordinances can classify effectively one breed of dog as inherently dangerous.

The primary issues raised by these breed-specific ordinances are: (1) because many breeds of dogs can cause serious harm to people, an ordinance that classifies only one breed as vicious appears to be underinclusive and in violation of the dog owners' equal protection rights under the constitution; and (2) because it is impossible to identify a breed of dog with the certainty required to impose criminal sanctions on the dog's owner, it appears that the ordinances are unconstitutionally vague, and therefore violate procedural due process.[28]

Veterinarians will likely be called upon to assist in drafting ordinances to regulate the ownership of pit bulls or other dangerous dogs. Any practitioners or others who become involved in this process are encouraged to procure a copy of *The Humane Society of the United States' Guidelines for Regulating Dangerous or Vicious Dogs* to use as a reference source.[29]

In 1987 the state of Washington adopted a dangerous dog law statute that has been accepted as a model for other jurisdictions to follow. It starts with a reasonable definition of a dangerous dog, that is, one that has (1) inflicted severe injury on a human being without provocation on public or private property; (2) has killed a domestic animal without provocation while off the owner's property; or (3) has been previously found to be potentially dangerous because the owner has received notice of such and the dog again aggressively bites, attacks, or endangers the safety of humans or domestic animals.[30]

The law then defines severe injury as "any physical injury that results in broken bones or disfiguring lacerations requiring multiple sutures or cosmetic surgery."[30]

An even broader definition of a dangerous dog law could read as the Contra Costa County, California ordinance does. It should be noted, however, that this is truly a *dangerous animal* ordinance, since it does not just cover dogs. Any animal except a dog assisting a police officer engaged in law-enforcement duties which demonstrates any of the following behavior is rebuttably presumed dangerous:

(a) an attack which requires a defensive action by any person to prevent bodily injury and/or property damage in a place where such person is conducting himself peacefully and lawfully.

(b) an attack on another animal or livestock which occurs off the property of the owner of the attacking animal.

(c) an attack that results in an injury to a person in a place where such person is conducting himself peacefully and lawfully.

(d) any behavior that constitutes a physical threat of bodily harm to a person in a place where such person is conducting himself peacefully and lawfully.[31]

The remainder of the Contra Costa dangerous animal ordinance can be found in Appendix G along with a full set of criteria for the issuance of dangerous animal permits.

The Washington statute provides for dangerous dog permits but leaves the issuance of certificates of registration up to the animal control authority of the city or county. One of the advantages of a state law like this is that it automatically establishes a standard for all parts of the state. Another advantage is that the law preserves the regulation of such dogs and adoption of restrictions placed on owners of potentially dangerous dogs for the local jurisdiction.[32] A disadvantage of the Washington statute is that the dog must have caused a broken bone or disfiguring injury to a person, killed a

domestic animal without provocation, or have been previously found to be potentially dangerous before the owner must obtain a dangerous dog registration certificate. This is a much narrower definition than the Contra Costa, California ordinance.

Like the proposed New York City pit bull law, the Washington State law requires that dangerous dogs be muzzled and restrained by substantial leashes when they are outside of their enclosures. It also requires proof of a homeowner's insurance policy or sufficient evidence of a surety bond issued by a surety insurer in the sum of at least $50,000, payable to any person injured by the vicious dog.[32] The Contra Costa law, on the other hand, does not require any proof of insurance.

To be effective, state statutes or local ordinances on the subject of dangerous animals should encompass many or all of the measures discussed above. Practitioners, animal control authorities, humane associations, and legislators should keep in mind, though, that any laws adopted must serve the interests of the animal, the animal owner, the community, and the animal owner's constitutional rights in order for them to be fair, valid, and effective.

Animal Noise as a Nuisance

Veterinarians often hear client complaints of neighbors' dogs, roosters, donkeys, etc. making an unreasonable amount of noise. In such cases, the clients are looking for more than just a sympathetic ear. All too often, by the time people complain, they are already on such bad terms with their neighbors that complaints and negotiation are impossible. On the other hand, clients often ask how they can deal with their own noisy animals, too. Animal behavior consultations can sometimes help provide ideas. Surgical removal of the vocal cords or tranquilization are other alternatives. In either case, though, veterinarians who know the local law can better appreciate the significance of the client's problem.

Many cities and counties recognize that animal noise is a serious problem and have adopted ordinances containing penalties for owners of animals who continue to allow their animals to make excessive noise. Thus, knowledge of local law is helpful when practitioners advise clients regarding what to do about a neighbor's or their own animal. In general, complaints registered by one or more neighbors will induce local animal control authorities to investigate and/or cite the offending party.

The following is an example of an ordinance covering the nuisance caused by animal noise:

> No person shall own, possess, harbor, control, or keep on any premises, any dog, fowl, or other animal, that barks, bays, cries, howls, or makes any other noise so continuously or incessantly as to unreasonably disturb the peace or quiet of any two persons living in different households within three hundred feet of the location of the disturbance.[33]

The type of noise that constitutes a nuisance is clearly defined. The more difficult aspects of noise problems, though, are things like (1) what kind of exceptions should be made for watchdogs; (2) has a violation occurred if the noise is generated only when the animal is provoked (as by the neighbor's dog, cat, or children playing or teasing the dog); or (3) should exceptions be made if people or other animals are trespassing or threatening to trespass? From a practical standpoint, the statutory language and enforcement difficulties pose almost insurmountable problems. One statutory attempt to deal with such issues can be found in § 416-12.202 of Appendix G.

Animal Waste Laws

As cities have grown, so has the amount of concrete and asphalt. Dense populations of people with pets living in those urban areas have created major animal excrement problems. Animals searching for places to void have produced serious aesthetic and public health problems on streets, sidewalks, public parks, sandboxes, pet owners' property, and neighbor's yards. Despite enforcement difficulties, many local governments have attempted to legislate responsible pet ownership by drafting and adopting what are affectionately known as "pooper scooper" laws. An example of an urban animal excrement law can be found in § 416-12.204 of Appendix G.

Rural area populations of this country have found that they are not immune from animal excrement problems. The wastes from feedlots, stables, dairy farms, and swine and poultry operations have been shown to be sources of serious pollution to our country's lakes, streams, and underground water reservoirs. The result of these ecological problems is the passage of laws controlling the disposal of large volumes of livestock excrement.

The state of Wisconsin has been a forerunner in this area. In 1984, Wisconsin's Department of Natural Resources (DNR) adopted an entire chapter of regulations dealing with animal waste management practices for large animal feeding operations.[34] Animal feeding operations are defined to include feedlots or facilities other than pastures where animals have been or will be fed and maintained or stabled for more than 45 consecutive days during any 12-month period.[34]

The state uses a system whereby owners or operators of large animal feeding operations must file permit applications with the DNR. Regulatory standards require owners or managers of feeding operations to install permanent rain water runoff control structures according to the maximum amount of rainfall generated by a 25-year rainfall table for each county in the state. When reviewing permit applications, such factors as soil permeability, drainage class, flooding hazards, and the potential impact of overapplication of animal wastes on state waterways are considered.

As this nation continues its attempts to improve the environment or maintain a clean one, more states will likely pass legislation regulating the disposal of large animal and companion animal excrement.

Limitations on Numbers of Animals Owned, Kept, or Harbored

Since the problems of noise pollution and animal excrement often stem from the presence of too many animals in a defined area, many communities have elected to strictly limit the numbers of animals that can be owned, and the location where they can be kept or harbored by individuals and businesses. These limitations usually appear in local zoning codes or animal control ordinances.

Animal Control Ordinances

An example of a typical animal control law can be found in § 416.200 of Appendix G. That law stipulates that anyone who keeps more than three dogs and five cats over six months of age in a single dwelling or business unit in an area not zoned for agricultural use must obtain a *multiple pet license*. Any person or business that keeps more than 20 dogs or cats in any single dwelling or business unit must have a *kennel license*. Terms such as *dog fancier, cat fancier, dog enthusiast, commercial kennel license, stable,* and others are used by local governments to define individuals or businesses who harbor multiple animals.

To acquire a permit, animal owners or businesses must show that many conditions can be met, including such items as satisfactory feeding, housing, immunization, licensing, and maintenance of the animals.[33] Veterinary hospitals are sometimes exempted from the requirements set forth in animal control ordinances because local zoning laws determine where they can or cannot operate.

Zoning Laws

Zoning is a means of establishing local control over the use of real estate within a certain jurisdiction. Via zoning, communities can ensure that their short- and long-range goals for development are met. Areas usually are clearly mapped and defined as residential, commercial, industrial, or agricultural. Numerous subdivisions may be included under these broad headings.[35] Variances, or use permits, may be granted for veterinary hospitals or to individual animal owners or ancillary businesses, provided that proprietors meet certain requirements and prove that neighboring properties will not be affected adversely.

Veterinarians or animal owners may find themselves in need of a special permit in order to build or maintain a kennel or hospital in a prohibited zone. If this is the case, the following tactics should be pursued prior to a hearing regarding a use permit:

1. Building and construction design plans that address the control of undesirable noises and odors should be presented. Testimony from other veterinary proprietors and some of their neighboring residents and businesses is extremely helpful to support the fact that these adverse effects of animal facilities can be controlled successfully.

2. A signed petition from nearby businesses and residents supporting the construction of and need for an animal care facility is invaluable. The concurrence of all adjacent property owners is frequently needed before a special permit will be issued. This may require considerable lobbying and persuasion of local residents. Testimony at hearings before the zoning or planning commission from key spokespeople representing surrounding property owners is also needed.

3. As many present or former clients as possible should be recruited to attend the zoning or planning commission hearing and attest to the integrity of the veterinary proprietor.

4. A full description of how the veterinary or kennel facility plans to deal

with the removal of animal wastes; prevent the attraction of flies, rodents, and pests; and eliminate the transmission of any communicable diseases is essential.

5. Drawings should be introduced showing that the exterior of the facility will be attractively landscaped and provided with a satisfactory sign. In addition, documents should be presented to provide financial assurance that the project will be completed as designed.

6. Automobile traffic flow patterns and parking needs must be addressed. In most cases, the need for parking can be established by assessing the daily utilization patterns of other similar-sized businesses.

Zoning and animal control ordinances can be difficult obstacles whenever an animal care facility is planned for an urban environment. Nevertheless, with proper planning these obstacles often can be overcome, enabling the diligent veterinarian to take advantage of a much better location than might otherwise be available.

Abandoned Animal Laws

The act of abandoning animals may leave them to face cruel death and often poses serious risks to humans, their property, and other animals. Moreover, society incurs considerable costs in the capture, care, and disposition of abandoned animals. To protect the interests of animals and society, many states directly prohibit the abandonment of animals.

Some states have simply worded statutes covering abandonment of all animals and others have different coverage depending upon the species of the animal. In addition, certain states have more complicated laws that differentiate between abandonment in different locations, that is, at a veterinary hospital, boarding kennel, or groomer versus on a street, road, or public place. Since practitioners can be held professionally liable for improper disposal of abandoned animals, the

safest thing to do is to find out what the local statutory requirement is concerning this issue before any action is taken.

Defining Abandonment

The first step in determining when an animal has been abandoned is to define the word *abandon*. Virginia, among other states, provides a statutory definition for the term *abandon*.[36] The Virginia law says that abandoning means deserting, forsaking, or intending to absolutely give up an animal without securing another owner or without providing the necessities of food and shelter.[37] Pennsylvania law holds that abandonment means to forsake entirely or to neglect or refuse to provide or perform the legal obligations for the care and support of an animal by its owner or agent.[38]

One of these statutes uses the phrase "intend to give up," whereas the other only talks about refusing to perform the legal obligations of care and support for the animal. This is a good example of the difficulties posed by slightly different wordings in otherwise similar laws. Proving that an intent to give up the animal was present is much more difficult than proving that an owner neglected or refused to meet the legal obligations of support.

If a state has no statutory definition, the court usually adopts some type of definition involving the inability of the animal to take care of itself coupled with a failure of the owner to make some type of provision for ongoing care. This could mean that the owner's failure to retrieve the animal in a timely manner from a veterinary hospital or other facility constitutes abandonment.

Another concern is whether the act of abandoning an animal is a violation of state or local law. A simple and all-inclusive law set forth in the Wisconsin statutes says, "No person may abandon any animal."[39] Anyone who does so is subject to a Class C forfeiture, that is, a fine not to exceed $500. Any person who intentionally or negligently abandons an animal is subject to a Class A misdemeanor and can be imprisoned for an amount of time not to exceed nine months or fined an amount not to exceed $10,000.[40]

Some state laws require that owners "cruelly," "unreasonably," or "willfully" abandon the animal before this offense is treated as a crime. Convictions under statutes like these are difficult.

Abandonment at Veterinary Hospitals or Kennels

The abandonment of animals is a universal problem. It is when animals are abandoned at veterinary hospitals, though, that practitioners become most involved in learning how to deal with this situation. The first place to request information concerning this type of abandonment is from the state veterinary association. Veterinarians practicing in states that do not have specific abandoned animal acts do not know how to handle these situations or what a court might hold if they destroy or dispose of an abandoned animal. Thus, it should be determined whether one's state has laws covering this topic and, if not, legislation should be proposed to deal with it.

The laws vary depending upon in whose custody a stray or abandoned animal is placed. Animals without license tags picked up by animal control facilities as strays or abandoned animals may be required to be held for 48 hours,[41] whereas animals delivered to any veterinary hospital, boarding facility, etc. and then abandoned by their owners may have to be held for up to 24 days.[42] There are significant differences in how veterinarians must deal with these animals depending upon whether the patient was admitted to the facility as a stray or whether it was brought in by a nonowner after having been abandoned by its owner. This is one good reason to know at the time of admission whether the person who brought the animal in for care is (1) legally the owner, (2) a good samaritan who agrees to accept full responsibility for costs of veterinary care (and thus, becomes the new owner), or (3) a concerned citizen who could not bear to see the animal suffer but who is unwilling to accept financial responsibility for the patient's medical care.

Stray Animals versus Abandoned Animals

At issue in abandonment cases are questions as to what activity and actions allow a person to be considered an owner. If someone found a dog and provided its food and shelter for two days and then sought veterinary care, could that person qualify as the owner? Would the "ownership" interest terminate if after seeking veterinary care the person refused to pay for it? Does a refusal to accept financial responsibility for veterinary care suddenly change the animal's status from that of abandoned to that of a stray, thereby permitting the veterinarian to call animal control and have them pick up the animal from the veterinary hospital as a stray? There are many questions but few answers in this fuzzy legal area. A 1979 Louisiana court case provides an excellent example of the application of statutory and common law principles to the issue of establishing ownership of an animal.[43]

Another variable in some abandoned animal laws is whether the animal was placed in the custody of the veterinary hospital, stable, or boarding kennel for a specified or unspecified period of time. In New York, if the time period is specified, the animal need only be retained for 10 days after a registered letter is mailed to the last known address. If the time period is unspecified, 20 days is required.[44]

Under most statutes, if the animal does not have an owner, it can be taken to the local animal control facility for them to maintain as soon as it has been determined that there is no owner. If, on the other hand, it was admitted to the hospital by an owner, the practice may have to retain the animal for a much longer statutory period before it may be disposed of. The method used for disposing of the abandoned animal can be another difficult legal issue. In New York, for example, after veterinarians or boarding kennel operators have kept the animal for the required time period, the animal is considered to be abandoned. At that time, it may be taken to a pound provided that:

> ...the person divesting himself of possession thereof, notifies the person who had placed such animal in his custody of the name and address of the animal society or pound to which the animal has been delivered...[44]

An assumption here is that if a new home was found for the animal or if it was euthanatized, this additional registered mail notice would not be required.

Problems with Statutory Language

Another common problem that veterinarians face concerns owners who say that they will come in to pick up their animals at a particular time and then fail to do so. In view of some statutes, it appears that cagey owners can postpone picking up their animals indefinitely simply by saying "I'll be in tomorrow." An example of a statute that could allow this is the California one. It says:

> Notwithstanding any other provision of law, whenever any animal is delivered to any veterinarian...kennel...animal hospital, or any other animal care facility pursuant to any written or oral agreement...and the owner of such animal does not pick up the animal within 14 calendar days after the day the animal was due to be picked up, the animal shall be deemed to be abandoned. The person into whose custody the animal was placed for care shall first try for a period of not less than 10 days to find a new owner for the animal, and, if unable to place the animal with a new owner, shall thereafter humanely destroy the animal so abandoned...

Notice that the time periods in this statute are quite long, and there is no duty to send any written notice to the owner regarding any disposition of the animal. In fact, under this statute, if the owner is contacted and

says, "I'll be in tomorrow," it appears that the 14-day period begins again, because that is the new date that the animal is due to be picked up. This is a good example of the type of statute that is detrimental to veterinarians.

Many statutes require that written notice be provided by registered mail to the owner's last known address with return receipt required before an abandoned animal may be disposed of. When this is the case, practitioners must check whether the statute allows them to dispose of the animal 10 days after registered return receipt mail is given[45] (meaning mailed) or a stated number of days after the receipt is returned. In states where no abandoned animal act exists, the safest policy is probably to wait 10 days after the registered mail notice was sent.

It appears that there is only one way to prevent the time periods in statutes like the California one and others like it from starting over again each time owners say they will pick up their animals. This requires that veterinarians and staff insist throughout all communications that, although they will allow the owner to pay the outstanding fees and pick up the animal in the near future, it was due to be picked up on the day it was originally scheduled to go home. Consequently, the statute's abandonment time period will continue to start with that date.

Charges for Veterinary Care During the Abandonment

When an owner appears to have abandoned an animal and then attempts to retrieve it, the question arises as to whether practitioners can charge for medical services rendered during the abandonment period. If the owner never attempts to reclaim the animal, can veterinarians sue for reimbursement of all costs incurred up until the time the animal was finally disposed of? How diligent must practitioners be in rendering treatment to animals that appear to have been abandoned? Are mere first aid and supportive care required for these patients, or must practitioners make valid attempts to cure them?

None of these questions have definitive answers. However, answers to the questions regarding the legality of charging for services rendered during the abandonment are probably the clearest. Whether or not practitioners can charge for services rendered during this period depends on the terms of the oral or written contract entered into between the animal's owner and the veterinarian when medical care was commenced. If all the elements of a contract were present when that care was initiated, the client would most likely be liable for hospitalization and medical services throughout the entire statutory abandonment period.

In the absence of any specific agreement as to the amount to be charged for such services, a contract would be implied for the client to pay a reasonable amount for services requested and/or rendered. Although chances for success may be limited by an owner's lack of financial resources, a lawsuit to recover fees assessed during an abandonment period would be in order. Practitioners who elect to pursue this route, though, must be certain that they have properly complied with the course of legal action set forth in the abandoned animal act.

Answering the questions regarding the extent and quality of medical care required during a period of apparent abandonment is more difficult. The only standard that can realistically be applied is to determine what type of action other reasonable veterinarians would have taken under similar circumstances. Supportive care without heroic efforts during the course of the abandonment should suffice, but court decisions can vary significantly depending on the facts presented in each case.

Humane Officer Assistance in Abandonment Cases

Since it is a crime in most states to abandon an animal, with severe penalties in some states, owners want to avoid facing legal charges filed by the local district attorney. Practitioners who are on good terms with their local animal control officers or humane association often can request that they go to an owner's home and issue a citation for abandoning an animal at their facility. The fact that most of these humane officials hate to see irresponsible owners abandon animals often makes them most willing to issue citations. Although this type of pressure may induce a rapid owner response, it will not provide any financial resources for owners to retrieve their animals, which most likely is why the animals were abandoned in the first place.

When the primary reason for the abandonment is the owner's lack of money, it is usually less expensive and generates less animosity to return the animal to the owner without requiring full payment than it is to deal with the legal requirements set forth in the statutes. Besides, veterinary staff members usually become attached to the animal before the 10 to 24 days is up, which means the practice will end up keeping the animal for whatever time it takes to find a new home, not just the time period set forth in the statute.

Liens for Veterinary Services

Veterinarians, owners of boarding kennels, trainers, and stable managers frequently seek counsel regarding their right to retain custody of an animal until the fees for services have been paid. The legality of this course of action is typically ruled by state law. Therefore, to answer this question, practitioners must seek additional information from legal counsel, their state boards of examiners, or state veterinary medical associations.

Until recently, courts have held under common law that people who had rendered service to personal property could retain possession of that property until the bill was paid.[46] Some courts still rule this way, while others are now more protective of debtors' rights. Consequently, in states without specific legislation regarding liens for veterinary service, it is never certain whether or not the court will uphold a common law lien based upon possession of the animal.

Another comparable but often unresolved legal issue involves a court's willingness to enforce a contract made via a consent form, signed by the client, which states that the veterinarian has the right to hold the animal if the bill has not been paid. At least one author maintains that veterinarians can provide for a lien by contract, either in the form of a hospital admission form or in an agreement signed by the client when the animal is treated.[46]

Many states have what is known as *agister's laws*. These laws state that people who keep, feed, board, stable, and provide care for animals belonging to other people may hold animals until payment is rendered. These states typically have concurrent laws allowing the custodians of such animals to sell them at public auction if the bill remains unpaid after proper notice is given. Such laws allow veterinarians to apply the proceeds of the sale to the outstanding bill and to pay costs encountered in executing the sale.[47] Any monies remaining after such a sale are to be returned to the owner. Practitioners should be aware, however, that sales based upon these lien laws are usually complicated legal matters and should not be commenced without the assistance of legal counsel.

Possession of the Animal and Fees for Medical Treatments

Lien laws must be read carefully to determine whether costs for veterinary medical care are included within the statutory language. If the state has a typical agister's law, it may allow veterinarians and other animal care businesses to retain custody of the animals and sell them at public auction. In this manner practitioners can at least recoup that portion of the outstanding fees related to the housing and feeding of the patient, even if they can not retain any money for medical treatments rendered.

Other issues involving statutory language focus on whether the animal custodian must

have possession of an animal in order to exercise the lien and whether veterinarians and veterinary services are specifically included under the statute. Both California and Minnesota laws apply directly to veterinary services and use the legal principle of possession in order to allow veterinarians to exercise their liens. The Minnesota law includes medical or surgical treatment or shoeing.[46] An excerpt from the California law follows:

> Every person, who while lawfully in possession of an article of personal property, renders any service to the owner thereof, by labor or skill...has a special lien thereon, dependent on possession, for the compensation...due to him from the owner for such service:...and veterinary proprietors and veterinary surgeons shall have a lien...for their compensation in caring for, boarding, feeding and medical treatment of animals.[48]

It should be noted that this law requires veterinarians to be "lawfully in possession" of the personal property. Such a clause means that practitioners cannot acquire possession through any form of entrapment or without the owner's permission.

Some states have adopted even more specific laws for veterinarians' liens. In Nebraska, for example, the lien law extends coverage to include veterinary care rendered to all types of livestock. It states that whenever animal owners have procured, contracted, or hired any licensed veterinarian to treat their livestock, the veterinarian shall have a first, paramount, and prior lien upon the animals so treated. If no price was agreed upon, the price will be established as that which would be the reasonable value for the biologics, medicines, and veterinary services rendered.[49] The law goes on to provide that this lien can be perfected by filing notice with a court within 90 days from the date that services were furnished. Although the language of the Nebraska statute is the exception and not the rule, in at least one state, possession of the animals is not required as long as the animals are classified as livestock.

While the law in an agricultural state like

Nebraska provides a lien for veterinary services rendered to livestock, other states, like consumer-oriented Massachusetts, take an opposite tack. The Code of Professional Conduct for Massachusetts says that veterinarians shall not refuse to return animals to their owners on the grounds that the owner has failed to fully pay for veterinary services.[50] On the other hand, Massachusetts does respect liens for boarding services based upon possession of the animal.[51]

Choosing Between Lien Laws and Abandoned Animal Statutes

Practitioners may want to exercise their lien right during the initial stages of an owner's failure to pay and then seek coverage under the state's abandoned animal law instead. The reason for changing options from one of these statutory courses to another is because under most abandonment laws veterinarians have the option of euthanatizing the animal if no home can be found. Under the lien laws, the only option is usually to sell the animal at public auction.

An opinion rendered by the legal counsel for the California State Board of Veterinary Examiners assesses the legal ramifications encountered in making such a change.

> If a veterinarian refuses to release an animal in order to protect a lien right authorized by the state's lien law, an animal would not be considered abandoned until: (1) the practitioner has given the owner of the animal express notice (or written notice with return receipt requested, if such notice is required by the state's abandoned animal law) that the lien right is being relinquished and the animal could be picked up on a specific date; and (2) the owner of the animal has not picked up the animal or otherwise contacted the veterinary facility to arrange for the animal to be picked up as required within the time frame specified in the state's abandoned animal act.[52]

As can be seen from the complexity of this action, legal counsel generally is needed when courses of action entail combinations of these two statutory directions.

The Practical Impact of Lien Laws

The existence of a state lien law ordinarily is of greater psychological than economic or legal value to veterinarians. Except in equine or food animal medicine, most animals are not of sufficient worth to merit pursuing their sale at public auction. Furthermore, the bad public relations generated by a veterinarian's retention or possession of an animal against the owner's wishes can easily result in greater detriment to the practitioner than any benefits gained by selling the animal.

Despite the potential for undesirable public relations, a knowledge of the state's lien law allows practitioners to inform clients of the legal right to retain an animal when that client has not paid in full. Even if the pressure applied is only temporary, it can be used to encourage owners to provide some form of payment before the animal is released.

Animal Cruelty Laws

Veterinarians' use of their knowledge of animal law as a means of improving the quality of life and veterinary care available to animals was discussed previously. Their knowledge of state or local anticruelty laws can serve the same function.

Animal cruelty takes on different meanings when it is considered in different contexts. For example, it can involve owners' neglect or cruelty toward their own animals, or a livestock owner intentionally killing a dog because it has caused or is about to cause serious harm to his livestock.

A General Analysis of Animal Cruelty Statutes

Anticruelty statutes can be found in many different formats. They vary greatly and can best be reviewed with several basic questions in mind:

1. Is the animal being considered included in the statute? (Some statutes include domestic animals but exclude wild animals from coverage.)

2. Is the person accused of cruelty within the scope of the law? (Some laws require that the person intended to cause an injury, while others omit any mention of intent.) Does the statute require any special level of human knowledge or intent in order for a violation to occur?

3. Is the act that supposedly occurred included in the statutory language?

4. Is the action inflicted on the animal exempted from coverage within the statute? (Docking tails, castrating livestock, and dehorning cattle without anesthesia may be exempted as animal husbandry practices, although these practices are often not addressed by the statutes. Medical research on animals properly conducted under the authority of the faculty of a medical college also may be exempted from coverage.)

5. Are there any defenses provided in the anticruelty statute or in other sections of the law in the jurisdiction? (Although not stated in the anticruelty statutes, it is presumed that self-defense is a proper defense to an allegation of cruelty.)

Sample Cruelty Laws

Anticruelty statutes are usually part of state law and generally appear in one of two different formats. Both types are rather archaic in their literary approach to this topic. One type, represented by a Mississippi statute, is classified as an "overdrive" type and says simply that any person who overdrives, overloads, tortures, torments, deprives of necessary sustenance, food or drink, or causes any of these items to be done to an animal shall be guilty of a misdemeanor.[53] No particular state of mind is mentioned as required for conviction—just the action that falls within the categories stated.

The other type, represented by a California statute, is an "intentional cruelty" type of statute. It requires proof of any of the above actions plus proof that a particular state of mind, usually malice, exists.[54] (For a thorough discussion of the issue of intent and many other aspects of anticruelty laws, see Reference 55.

It is considerably more difficult to sustain a court conviction if the statute includes proof of willful activity or malice. Nevertheless, for the purposes of the average veterinarian and the use of these statutes to encourage responsible animal ownership, either type of state law suffices.

Animal Cruelty Situations and the Veterinarian's Involvement

In most cases, veterinarians can rely on responsible, caring pet owners to follow their recommended courses of treatment. These people either pursue the suggested course of action because they believe in it, or they can be educated or persuaded to do so. Sometimes, though, practitioners see animals that they feel have been horribly neglected or mistreated. In these cases, it is natural to have serious doubts about the owner's ability to follow through on the doctor's recommendations. Animals with severely matted hair and infected skin, draining tumors, or maggots under the hair are examples. Pets whose choke chains or collars have cut through the neck and are buried in granulation tissue are another. The puppy or kitten presented with a concussion or fractured limb because it was thrown against the wall after whining or chewing too much is still another example.

The fact that the clients have sought veterinary advice puts veterinarians in an awkward position. If they are too judgmental and harsh, owners are unlikely to return because they will not want another lecture about animal cruelty. If, however, practitioners fail to let these clients know that their neglect or cruelty toward the animal is unacceptable behavior, clients will assume they can continue to get by with such activity and may very well not follow directions. The problem, then, is how to educate and reprimand clients without losing the opportunity to help the animal.

There is no simple way to accomplish this. Veterinarians have a duty to help animals and guard their welfare. Although clients may own the animals and pay the bills, the animals are, nonetheless, the veterinarian's patients, worthy of moral, ethical, and legal concern in and of their own right.

Pressures and Persuasions for Perpetrators of Animal Cruelty

In order to successfully utilize the subtle pressure technique discussed next, practitioners must be on good terms with at least one local humane officer. When that person is available and willing to act, a veterinarian's conversation with a client can take place as follows:

> Mr. Badowner, I am absolutely appalled that you could allow Sammie to become so horribly neglected. You may have all kinds of excuses for what has happened, but in my judgment the facts presented here indicate a possible case of cruelty to animals, which is a crime, you know. We cannot do anything today about what has happened in the past, but I want you to know that you are on trial. If you follow our directions and show us that you can take care of Sammie like a responsible owner, you may be able to regain my respect and you'll be off the hook. If you do not come back for the follow-up appointments that we will schedule for you today, and if you do not show us that you can provide proper care for Sammie, I will be compelled to report

you to my good friend Leslie at the SPCA.

Veterinarians who would like to make an even stronger impression, will take a picture of the animal.

This is what is called an *armtwister*, and it is amazing how powerful the effect of such a reprimand can be. When there is serious doubt about the intentions of the client, the following conversation can be added.

> You know, Mr. Badguy, your irresponsible attitude toward Sammie upsets me so much that I am going to call my friend Leslie at the SPCA today and tell her about what my staff and I have seen. As of this time your name will be kept confidential. The SPCA will be on notice not to take any action until we determine whether you can satisfactorily care for Sammie and follow our directions, but you are definitely on trial.

Establishing the Ground Rules

Once clients are aware of their veterinarians' evaluation of the situation, which they surely are by this time, certain rules should be presented. This can be done very politely and with considerable seriousness by saying,

> I am expecting you to follow our entire recommended course of treatment for Sammie. If you cannot afford everything that needs to be done, we will establish some type of payment plan. However, if you do not show up next Tuesday when I want to see Sammie again, and if you fail to follow through with his medical care or the payment plan we work out, we will report your absence to the SPCA and ask that they begin an investigation of this matter. Do you understand our concern regarding this matter?

This entire behavior modification technique for clients can be done in a forceful, yet very tactful manner, letting them know that the veterinarian's primary concern is for the welfare of the animal. It puts the client on notice that this situation is viewed as a serious matter and, although payment for service is important, it is less important than the doctor's concern about the patient. It also can be good for business because, if done effectively, it can convert basically nonserious pet owners into good clients.

Ignorance is often the culprit in these cases. Clients who, as children, saw animals treated with neglect and indifference will continue to treat animals in this way unless they are educated to a different standard, much akin to what is reported with child abuse passed on from generation to generation.

As of 1987, there is no legal duty to report animal cruelty cases to any authority except, in many states, in cases of staged animal fights. However, when veterinarians see animals that have been or are being mistreated, they have a deep moral duty to intervene on the animal's behalf. The SPCAs, humane associations, and animal control facilities consistently look to veterinarians for guidance and examples as responsible leaders in animal welfare. They can be great allies when it comes to situations like those described here and usually welcome an invitation to get involved.

The Need for Proper Documentation

Since the pursuit of animal cruelty cases requires legal action, veterinarians who suspect cruelty must pay special attention to proper medical record documentation. In addition, animal control or humane association officers who have been trained in investigative work should be called to assist with this process.

All evidence found in, on, and around the animal should be saved and carefully stored. Photographs or videotapes of the animal and, when possible, its environment, should be taken by humane authorities or veterinary staff people. Emaciated or dehydrated animals should be weighed, and PCVs and total protein levels should be run to help determine the severity of their condition. For starving large animals that cannot be

weighed, girth measurements should be recorded so that they can be compared with later ones made after the animal has regained its normal weight.

Undersized collars that have cut into or through the skin of an animal's neck should be cut and removed but saved as evidence. The inside circumference of such a collar should be measured and compared with that of the animal's neck.

In general, veterinarians must think like detectives when animal cruelty cases are suspected, preserving all evidence that is found and generating additional information that will help establish the seriousness of the offense. Many district attorney offices do not place animal cruelty cases as high priority items because they have so many crimes against people to deal with. However, when veterinarians have assisted in the evaluation of a case, helped with the provision of credible evidence, and expressed a willingness to testify as expert witnesses, the likelihood that the district attorney will pursue legal action will be increased significantly.

Rights of Animal Owners

An important point regarding animal ownership is that the animals themselves have no legal rights, responsibilities, or obligations. Thus, in addition to numerous limitations placed on the ownership of animals, the law grants owners many rights that are tied to that ownership.

Legal status for animals is obtained through their owners and, therefore, if the owner does not assert a right, no one else will be able to do so. The following list establishes the most important rights of animal owners under traditional legal principles:[56]

1. The owner may convey the animal, i.e., sell, loan, rent, or give it away.

2. The owner may use the animal as collateral, i.e., as a legal commodity that allows financial institutions to lend

money to the animal owner. Agreements of this nature generally provide that legal title to such animals is pledged to the institution in case the borrower defaults on the loan.

3. The owner has the right to obtain the natural dividends of the animal, i.e., the offspring and/or marketable materials produced by the animal such as wool, milk, and eggs.

4. The owner may consume or destroy the animal. Although this right pertains most directly to animals used for food, it also extends to pets. Limitations on what owners can do to their animals, however, are governed by the anticruelty laws. The right also extends to the owner's property interest in the animal after its death, a matter which will be discussed in depth later in the chapter.

5. The owner may exclude others. This multifaceted right includes the right to use force to protect one's property from outside threats.[57] It also provides owners with methods of regaining possession of the animal or obtaining financial reimbursement for the loss or damage to an animal when someone has improperly interfered with the owner's possession. Furthermore, society, through its criminal law system, furnishes additional protection to animal owners by punishing people who interfere with the lawful possession of animals.

In order to limit the volume of material on this topic, further discussion covers only the rights that veterinarians are most apt to deal with. It is not an exhaustive analysis of all rights of animal owners.

Rights Embodied in Wills and Trusts

Since animals are a form of personal property, they may be conveyed, used, consumed, and even destroyed unless the law intervenes. Yet, there is a paucity of legislation and legal discussion dealing with bequeaths for animals or destruction of animals by provisions in wills. Since veterinarians may find themselves in the middle of either of these types of disputes, a basic understanding of the law in each area is worthwhile.

Will Provisions for the Benefit of Animals

Animals cannot be beneficiaries of wills, and courts will not uphold bequeaths of money directly to animals. The author of a will may, however, name a person and provide that party with the legal capacity to own or hold property for the benefit of the animal.[58]

The least complex legal way for people to accomplish the goal of providing for their animals after their death is to give an outright gift of money to another person with instructions for that person to provide for the food, housing, and medical care of the animal(s) for as long as the animal(s) shall live. This requires faith in the named person's willingness to spend money wisely on the deceased person's animals, but it is a simple solution.

Another method that can be used is an *honorary trust*.[59] An honorary trust is a noncharitable trust without any ascertained or ascertainable beneficiaries, but wherein the court permits the trustee to carry out the purposes of the trust in spite of the fact that it is unenforceable.[60] This may be a better method to provide for the benefit of a deceased person's animals than an outright gift of money to another person, because it can be overseen by a court and it will be upheld as long as the trustee acts in accordance with the terms of the trust.

For at least 140 years courts have upheld provisions in wills providing for the care of a deceased person's animals.[61] The drafting of an honorary trust should be done with the assistance of legal counsel, but it can be effectuated by a caring owner and a willing trustee.

Destruction of Animals by Will

A 1980 California case entitled *Smith* v. *Avanzino*[62] drew attention to a provision in a will calling for the destruction of an animal at the time of the owner's death. In that case the San Francisco SPCA gained custody of the animal after the owner died and refused to release it, thereby preventing implementation of the terms of the will. After a great deal of publicity, the state legislature passed a special law saving the dog's life.[63] Although the statute made judicial action unnecessary, the San Francisco Superior Court still elected to render a decision invalidating the provision in the will in order to ensure that a valid legal precedent would exist for future references.

An excellent law review article has been published outlining the legal bases for invalidating destruction of pets by provisions in wills.[64] Included among these bases are such grounds as: (1) the destruction of property in

estates violates public policy, (2) the existence of animal protection statutes indicates a policy against the summary killing of animals, and (3) the interpretations of testators' true intents would most likely be to provide for the future of their animals if they had known that a good home was available.

Two solutions are available to prohibit the implementation of pet destruction provisions in wills. The first involves legislation passed by states stating that

> A provision in any will whereby the testator seeks to compel or requires the destruction of a healthy pet animal shall not be implemented unless the court so orders upon a showing that a suitable adoptive home could not be found after reasonable attempts to find such home were made by the executor.[64]

Until legislation is passed, provisions such as those in Figure 4.1 in a will would be superior to an unconditional provision to have a pet killed after the death of a caring owner.

My _____ *(description of animal)* _____

shall be delivered to —————————

or to —————————

for temporary holding. The executor shall determine the amount from the estate to go with the animal for its care and feeding. The executor shall advertise and otherwise make diligent efforts to find a good home for the animal, taking a reasonable amount of money for these purposes from the estate. If no home can be found after _____ weeks, the animal shall be taken to

_____ *(name and address of veterinarian)* _____

to be killed by the most humane method the doctor has competency to use.[64]

Figure 4.1 A model will provision providing for the disposition of animals.

The Right of Stray Animals to Receive Emergency Care

In most jurisdictions, if an injured animal is found without its owner in a public place, its potential for receiving emergency care depends upon several factors: (1) a good samaritan agreeing to transport the animal to a veterinary office and to accept the responsibility for the costs of such care, (2) a veterinarian agreeing to provide emergency care even though no owner has accepted financial responsibility therefore, or (3) the availability of treatment at the rare animal control or humane association that has the capability of offering veterinary services.

Another avenue exists, however, in states where residents believe that all dogs and cats deserve some type of emergency care. The source of income used to foster this treatment comes from effective licensing procedures as well as subsidies from local governments. The only statute found to date addressing this issue is one in California.[17]

A Statutory Right to Emergency Care

Under California law, it is the duty of officers of pounds, humane societies, and animal regulation departments to convey injured cats and dogs found without their owners in a public place directly to a veterinarian who ordinarily treats such animals.[17] In addition, it is the duty of all police and sheriff departments to see to it that such injured dogs and cats are conveyed to a veterinarian. Veterinarians who examine these injured animals are required to determine whether they should be immediately and humanely destroyed or hospitalized and given proper care and emergency treatment. Any practitioner who determines that an animal has been severely injured or is incurably crippled is legally authorized by this law to humanely euthanatize such animal.

This California law was passed in 1971. It has provided an effective way for veterinarians to render emergency care to injured and unclaimed animals yet be assured of a modest payment for their services. The limited financial resources of local authorities generally require that only basic emergency care or first aid be rendered unless the animal possesses some form of identification. In addition, in order for practitioners to come under the legal authority of this section, an agent at a local humane society or animal control department must authorize the treatment before it is undertaken.

Legal research has not turned up any other states that establish a statutory right for animals to receive emergency care. The language of this California statute is discussed in more depth later in this chapter, whereas the legal requirements for veterinarians to provide emergency care are discussed in Chapter 6.

The Requirement to Stop at the Scene of an Accident

A comment often heard from clients whose animals have been hit by a moving vehicle is "They didn't even stop." However, in their concern and dismay for their animals, clients tend to forget that this is one of the reasons local confinement laws require animals to be leashed or under their owners' control. Veterinary staff members know quite well that animals are not usually hit by moving vehicles unless they are improperly confined. They also can empathize, though, with the client's anger toward a hit-and-run driver. Pointing out to such owners that they are most likely responsible for their animal's injuries may be accurate but may be interpreted by clients as a lack of compassion. One wonders, then, if there is anything that can be said in a situation like this to ease the owner's pain and allow a staff person to understand and agree with the client's point of view.

Obviously, drivers of vehicles can be held liable for the injuries or death of animals if their vehicles were negligently driven. Otherwise, though, owners of improperly restrained animals should be more concerned about their own potential liability for injuries suffered by the drivers of the vehicles. At least some states have laws requiring drivers of motor vehicles to stop at the scene of an accident even if they were not the party responsible for the accident. A familiarity with such a law allows a veterinarian to empathize with a client's anger.

An example of this type of law is found in § 20002 of the California Vehicle Code. That code states that the driver of a vehicle involved in an accident resulting in damage to any property, including motor vehicles, is required to stop the vehicle immediately and do one of two things: (1) locate and notify the owner or person in charge of such property of their name and address and present a driver's license and vehicle registration to the property owner, or (2) leave a written note in a conspicuous place on the property which was damaged giving their name and address and a statement of the circumstances surrounding the accident.

This type of statute is geared primarily toward owners of other vehicles or owners of real property, but animals also are a form of property and, as such, they are covered by this law. Under the California law, anyone who fails to comply with all the requirements of the statute is guilty of a misdemeanor and can be fined up to $1000 or punished by up to six months in jail.

It is unlikely that owners of injured or dead animals will be able to locate a hit-and-run driver. Unless it is possible to prove that the vehicle had been operated in a negligent manner, the owner of the animal also is unlikely to be able to recover any of the costs for remedial veterinary care. Still, it can be a valuable public relations gesture for veterinary staff people to be able to inform the animal owner that even though they were in the wrong for ineffectively controlling their animal, the driver of the other vehicle was also wrong for not stopping. In these cases offering some form of reassurance is better than offering none at all, especially when owner's are seeking to clear their consciences of self-guilt.

Property Rights Pertaining to Animal Cadavers

From time to time veterinarians are confronted with the death of an animal in their custody and they are unable to contact the owner to arrange for disposal of the body. Courses of action available to practitioners who face this predicament vary depending upon the size of the animal, outside climatic conditions, the availability of refrigerators or freezers, state laws, and the reason for the animal's death. Practitioners should be aware that serious problems of liability can occur if the owner's property rights to the animal's body are not respected.

In general, owners have the sole right to determine how they wish to dispose of an animal's body. If the animal has died of a reportable zoonotic disease (like anthrax, tuberculosis, or brucellosis), practitioners may refuse the owner's demands for the body and make separate arrangements under the direction of public health or agricultural authorities.[65] In all other situations, however, the animal's body should not be disposed of

without an owner's authorization if it is at all possible to store it until contact has been made.

There are many reasons for this rule. First, since animals are a form of property, only the owner of that property (or the owner's agent) can determine what should be done with it. The fact that the animal died does not terminate the property rights to the body. Owners may want to bury the animal on their property, have it cremated (with the ashes returned to them), or arrange for a funeral and a burial at a pet cemetery. A deprivation of the right to dispose of a body could result in a legal cause of action. In a New York case, the errant exchange of a dog's body for that of a cat resulted in an award of $700 for the owner's emotional distress.[66]

The second reason for respecting an owner's property right over an animal's dead body is because the intentional, arbitrary, or negligent disposal of a patient that had been undergoing veterinary care is likely to produce serious questions regarding its cause of death. This issue exists even if the animal was expected to die, but it is much worse if the animal was expected to live. If the body was negligently or intentionally disposed of, such action could be held to be the destruction of evidence, because the unavailability of a body for necropsy denies the owner a right to attempt to determine the cause of death. At least one legal action resulting in damages for the owner's emotional distress has stemmed from this situation.[67]

A third reason for not disposing of a body without an owner's authorization is because some states specifically address how veterinarians should handle bodies of deceased animals under the practice act regulations. California's Minimum Standards of Practice, for example, require that when the owners of deceased animals have not given veterinarians authorization to dispose of their animals, practitioners must retain the carcass in a freezer for at least 14 days. Because of the size of large-animal patients, this requirement does not apply to food animal or equine practitioners. Nevertheless, a failure to comply with this requirement regarding small animals would automatically mean that a practitioner had performed below the standard of care.

In states with no regulations on this subject, courts would most likely require the testimony of expert witnesses to establish the standard of care within the profession concerning disposal of bodies without an owner's consent. They could, however, look at the California Minimum Standard as representative of the profession at large.

It is clear that practitioners must make legitimate attempts to preserve the body until the owner can be contacted. Nevertheless, some unanswered and difficult legal questions remain:

1. How extensive should a veterinarian's efforts be to preserve the body for necropsy? Must veterinarians rent freezer or refrigerator space elsewhere if such space is unavailable at their practice? If any chance exists that the animal's cause of death could be related to or will appear to the owner to have been caused by the veterinarian's negligence, maximal efforts should be made to retain and preserve the body.

2. Should a dead body be refrigerated, or is freezing a preferable course of action? The answer to this question may depend on how long the practitioner expects it will take to reach the owner. When it is likely to require more than one to two days, veterinarians should seek guidance from pathologists as to which course they ought to pursue.

3. If the owner cannot be contacted and veterinarians feel confident that their medical care had nothing to do with the animal's death, should they make their own arrangements for a necropsy before the body decomposes in order to protect themselves? Would this be satisfactory justification for pursuing a necropsy without the owner's authorization? The answers to both of these questions depend significantly on the facts in each case. Each question, however, probably could be answered in the affirmative under certain circumstances.

4. Should veterinarians who provided the medical or boarding care prior to the animals' death perform the necropsy themselves, or should they locate another practitioner or pathologist to do it? Because necropsies rendered by veterinarians who provided medical care prior to death will always appear self-serving, other practitioners should be called upon to execute or at least assist with this procedure. Again, the answer depends upon the facts of each case. In certain situations the performance of a necropsy by anyone other than a board-certified pathologist would be a grave mistake.

Postmortem changes occur rapidly, especially in unrefrigerated bodies. If an animal dies and the owner cannot be reached, it is often wise for practitioners to contact their insurance carriers, legal counsel, diagnostic laboratories, or other experienced veterinarians to decide what course of action should be taken and what standard of care would apply to these serious legal quandaries.

Consent Forms for Disposing of Bodies

Occasionally major misunderstandings and even lawsuits will occur because veterinarians have disposed of a body in a method other than that chosen by the owner. In other cases practitioners or staff members simply fail to inform owners of the variety of disposal options available for companion animals. The emotionally charged moments just before or after animals have died or been euthanatized are not conducive to discussions regarding disposal of the animal's body. Owners who are unaware of their disposal options sometimes feel guilty about quickly made decisions and wish they had had more information, even though these discussions are always awkward for veterinarians and clients.

The form shown in Figure 4.2 has been used at one veterinary school to provide owners with a written discussion of their available options. This form is given to owners at the time that their decision is being made, so that they can either read it in the reception area before they leave or take it home. If a decision about disposal of the body is being made via telephone, the information on this form can be read to an owner verbatim so that veterinarians or employees always present their discussion of this topic in a sensitive manner. This is especially valuable for inexperienced clinicians or staff members.

The first page of a form like that presented in Figure 4.3 can be given to owners so that they have a record of their choice of disposal options. A second page of this form can have computerized billing codes or fees in the appropriate locations and is retained for the medical record.

Performing Necropsies Without the Owner's Permission

It often seems awkward and insensitive to request authorization for a necropsy at the time that owners are informed of their animal's death. Still, because of the property right to an animal's body, necropsies should not be performed without the owner's approval. What, then, are the risks of performing an unauthorized necropsy, and are there ways that practitioners can approach the subject of a postmortem that will prevent them from exposure to liability?

The Risks

The risks of liability center on causes of action defined as (1) the tort of outrageous conduct[68] or (2) the right not to have one's sensibilities shocked.[69] Both of these principles stem from common law concepts that may or may not be codified in the statutory law of a given state.

An example of a legal action involving outrageous conduct occurred when a husband and wife discovered that the body of their premature child that died shortly after birth had not been buried but had been preserved by the hospital in a jar of formaldehyde. The jar, with the fetus floating inside, was exhibited to the mother and, as a result, she suffered emotional shock. In this 1975 Tennessee case, the husband and wife were awarded $100,000 in compensatory damages because of the emotional distress they suffered.[69]

Veterinarians should know that permitting owners to see the body of their decapitated or dismembered animal after it has been necropsied will shock them. Because of the unsightly nature of an animal that has been properly necropsied, owners can be shocked even when they have authorized the necropsy beforehand. However, if owners authorize disposal of the body but do not authorize a necropsy and then request that the body be returned to them so that it can be disposed of, the shock to their sensibilities will be even greater. Likewise, a veterinarian's retention and use of an animal's body for medical or research purposes after having previously agreed to dispose of it can provide the grounds for a legal action.

Obtaining Consents for Necropsies

One of the best ways to obtain authorization for an animal's necropsy is to discuss the issue with the owner prior to its death or euthanasia. This is likely to be a less emotional, less sensitive, and more rational time to address the educational merits of this procedure. If the owner consents, a notation in the medical record is signed by the client, and the client will probably be amenable to a necropsy at the time of the patient's death. A section of Figure 4.3 provides the language for a written necropsy consent.

If a consent like this was signed within several days before the patient died or was euthanatized, it would most likely be adequate authorization to proceed with the necropsy. If, however, a necropsy consent is provided several weeks or months before the animal dies, during which time owners

OPTIONS CONCERNING DISPOSAL OF DECEASED PETS
Veterinary Hospital of the
University of Pennsylvania

The loss of a family pet is never easy to accept. The staff at VHUP understands this, and most of us have gone through the same experience that you are facing.

As veterinarians we are trained to diagnose and treat illnesses in animals and prefer to pursue this route whenever possible. However, there are times when painless euthanasia is the kindest thing we can offer to ease an animal's suffering. Pet owners generally feel the same way. A four-year follow-up study of about 500 older animals examined at VHUP showed that most of them (59%) were eventually euthanatized when they could no longer be helped medically or surgically. Euthanasia at this hospital is performed by administering a lethal overdose of anesthesia intravenously (into the vein). This allows your pet to die painlessly and peacefully in a matter of seconds.

What happens to the body depends upon the owner's wishes and circumstances.

AVAILABLE OPTIONS

1. Diagnostic autopsy followed by cremation.

Most owners recognize that our ability to diagnose, treat, and make accurate prognoses is based upon the willingness of other owners to let us perform diagnostic autopsies on animals that have died or were euthanatized. Information gained from autopsies is extremely valuable in determining what happened to your animal and how we might treat other animals. This is especially important in the case of breeding animals in order to detect and characterize hereditary defects that might be passed on to their offspring. In addition, it may be reassuring for owners to have more information about problems that were present in their pets so that they do not have to wonder later about what truly happened. Since this information is frequently helpful in gaining new knowledge and assists in teaching, we do not charge for diagnostic autopsies followed by cremation. Results of microscopic examinations of these tissues are not available for several months and will be provided only if your doctor at VHUP has received a written request from the owners.

2. Diagnostic autopsy followed by individual cremation with ashes returned to owner.

If an owner wishes to have a patient cremated and the ashes returned after a diagnostic autopsy has been performed, a charge of $50 to $100 is made depending upon the size of the animal. Arrangements must be made in advance with the business office regarding payment of this fee (phone 215-898-8884). Owners will be notified by mail when the ashes are ready to be picked up, usually within 2 to 3 weeks.

3. Home burial without autopsy.

Owners who wish to bury their animal at home must arrange to pick up the body within three days. We will place the body in a plastic bag inside a cardboard box and maintain it under refrigeration in order to prevent decomposition of the body. The body can be picked up between the hours of 10 AM and 3 PM Monday through Friday. There is no charge for this service.

4. Pet cemetery burial.

A list of pet cemetery services is available at the business office or appointment desk. Owners need to contact the pet cemetery and make arrangements for them to handle the body or owners must pick up the body themselves for delivery to the cemetery.

5. Disposal without autopsy.

This cremation is restricted to animals that are patients of VHUP. If an owner does not allow an autopsy and does not wish to have the body buried, we will arrange to have the body cremated at the owner's expense. The fee for this service is $25.

6. Individual cremation without autopsy but with ashes returned to owner.

For owners who wish to have their pet's body cremated without an autopsy and the ashes returned to them, the fee is $75 to $125 depending on the size of the animal. Arrangements for payment of this fee are made through the Business Office (phone 215-898-8884). Owners will be notified by mail when the ashes are ready to be picked up, usually within 2 to 3 weeks.

Figure 4.2   A sample form for clients regarding options for disposal of deceased pets.

might change their minds, a new consent should be sought at the time of death.

Many owners are not averse to a necropsy; however, when the animal dies they fail to consider the value of this diagnostic procedure or are afraid to request it because they think it will add an additional fee to their bill. In cases like this, a gentle inquiry and an offer to perform the service at no charge will generally foster a willing consent.

An option given at one school of veterinary medicine, where necropsies are of immense research and educational value, involves the offer of both the necropsy and the standard disposal of the body at no charge if the postmortem is approved. Option No.1 of Figure 4.2 alludes to such an arrangement.

Owners' Rights to Destroy Their Animals

Because animals have traditionally been defined as property, common law has allowed owners to treat them as they would other forms of property. An increasingly controversial right of animal ownership, however, is an owner's right to kill or have his or her animal humanely killed.

Livestock owners probably will always have the right to kill their animals to provide food. However, the right of pet owners to have their pets killed without good reason is already being challenged by many veterinarians on moral grounds and most likely will be questioned even more frequently in the future.

An interesting, though perhaps archaic law is one requiring that owners have certain animals put to death. A California statute provides as follows:

> Every animal which is unfit, by reason of its physical condition, for the purpose for which such animals are usually employed, and when there is no reasonable probability of such animal ever becoming fit...shall be by the owner or lawful

possessor...deprived of life within 12 hours after being notified by any peace officer...or employee of a...public agency who is a veterinarian to kill the same, and such owner, possessor, or person omitting or refusing to comply with the provisions of this section shall, upon conviction be deemed guilty of a misdemeanor; provided, that this shall not apply to such owner keeping any old or diseased animal belonging to him on his own premises with proper care.[70]

The fact that owners and possessors of animals not only have the right to end their animals' lives but also may be required under certain circumstances to do so is amazing. This entire issue becomes even more morally, ethically, and philosophically confusing, however, when one considers the following: Under the above statute and various anticruelty statutes, the failure to end a suffering animal's life is a misdemeanor. Under legal principles pertaining to human beings, intentionally ending the life of an incurably ill and suffering person is considered murder.

Rights of Livestock Owners

The rights of various types of animal owners are in serious conflict when it comes to the injury or destruction of livestock by other domestic animals. Most damages of this type involve dogs chasing, worrying, injuring, and/or killing sheep, goats, poultry, pigs and, occasionally, cattle. Although usually only veterinarians in rural and suburban environments have to deal with this, all veterinarians should be aware that livestock owners have considerable statutory authority to protect the well-being of their livestock.

As with other aspects of animals and the law, the statutes vary significantly among states. Consequently, only a few states' laws are evaluated herein. For practitioners to become knowledgeable regarding the law in their own jurisdiction, it is essential that they

Date ————————————————

Doctor ————————————————

DECEASED PATIENT DISPOSITION FORM

I hereby certify that I have received a copy or have been informed of VHUP's "Options Concerning Disposal of Deceased Pets."

————————————————Owner's Signature (Veterinarian signs here, as owner's agent, for telephone authorizations)

A.   I am unable to make a decision today but will call Dr.————————
at 898-————————— before 9:30 tomorrow.

B.   I request the option circled and/or initialed below:

1. Diagnostic autopsy followed by cremation. ————————————
   No VHUP charge   initials

2. Diagnostic autopsy followed by individual cremation; ashes
   returned

   $65.00 $85.00 $105.00
   0-20 lbs.   21-70 lbs.   Over 70 lbs.   ————————————
                                               initials

3. Home burial without autopsy.
   No VHUP charge
                                               ————————————
                                               initials

4. Pet cemetery burial.
   No VHUP charge
                                               ————————————
                                               initials

5. Disposal without autopsy.
   <50 lbs.--$25.00, > 50 lbs.--$35.00
                                               ————————————
                                               initials

6. Individual cremation without autopsy but with ashes returned.

   $75.00 $95.00 $120.00   ————————————
   0-20 lbs.   21-50 lbs.   Over 70 lbs.   initials

I hereby authorize that an autopsy and microscopic analysis of tissue samples be performed for diagnostic purposes on my animal named ————————————————.

————————————————————   ————————————————
Owner or agent signature   Date
(Veterinarian signs here, as agent, for telephone authorizations)

————————————————————   ————————————————
Witness   Date

Figure 4.3   A sample form for obtaining owners' authorization of the method of disposition of their deceased pets.

contact the animal control facility, humane society, or clerk of court in their jurisdiction for information about applicable laws.

Examples of Statutory Language

California law splits the state into two types of areas: the more urban setting and the more rural area. Each county may adopt one set of codes or the other for the county or specific areas of the county. Section 31102 of the California Agriculture Code says the following:

> ...any person may kill any dog in any of the following cases,
>
> (a) the dog is found in the act of killing, wounding, or persistently pursuing or worrying livestock or poultry on land or premises which are not owned or possessed by the owner of the dog.
>
> (b) the person has such proof as conclusively shows that the dog has been recently engaged in killing or wounding livestock or poultry on land or premises which are not owned or possessed by the dog's owner. No action, civil or criminal, shall be maintained for the killing of any such dog.

This type of statute provides livestock owners with an extremely strong right to protect their livestock. In addition to being authorized to kill the offending dogs, they are immune from legal actions brought by the dog's owner.

It may be difficult for livestock owners to provide sufficient evidence to prove that a dog was truly worrying the livestock. However, if a wounded dog's blood trail originated on the livestock owner's land or if the dog's dead body was found on the rancher's land, it will be even more difficult proving that the dog was not worrying or chasing the stock. Furthermore, very few dog owners are present when this type of activity occurs to be able to provide any direct evidence for a valid defense.

It is important that practitioners know the rights of livestock owners so that they can educate their clients regarding the strong rights that livestock owners have and the tenuous position their clients are in if their dogs are found worrying, wounding, or persistently pursuing someone's livestock. In fact, even if the dogs are not seen in the act, under a state law like Section (b) above, ranchers who are able to show "conclusive proof" in the form of tracks in the mud or snow or blood on the dog have the right to take action.

Based upon a statute like this, it seems doubtful that the livestock owner could come onto the property of the dog owner and kill the dog, because that would constitute trespassing. Yet, the law is unclear on that point. Note that this particular statute allows "any person" witnessing this situation to take action—not just the owner of the livestock.

Under Texas law, the tax-paying voters of any county have the option of adopting a state statute much like the county governments do in California. This law says:

> Any dog...found attacking any...domestic animals or fowls, or which has recently made or is about to make such attack...may be killed by anyone present and witnessing or having knowledge of such attack without liability in damage to the owner of the dog. Any dog known to have attacked, killed or injured any...domestic animal or fowl shall be killed by the owner...and upon failure of such owner to to so, any sheriff...is authorized to kill such dog and such officer is further authorized to go onto the premises of the owner of such dog for such purpose."[71]

One wonders what kind of proof is needed to allow a sheriff to enter someone's property and kill a dog. Whatever the case, this state law also provides livestock owners with powerful rights when it comes to protecting their livestock from marauding dogs.

Potential for Liability

Since most statutes are intended to protect the livestock owner's livelihood, and since a dog that created this type of damage would have been "running at large," in most states the dog owner very likely might be found liable for the value of the injured or dead livestock whether the law specifically addressed that issue or not. In both Texas and Wisconsin, laws specifically provide that the dog owner is liable to pay all damages to the livestock owner.

In addition to dog owner liability, some states, like Wisconsin, have statutes that provide an additional remedy for the livestock owner in cases in which the owner of the dog causing the damages cannot be found. In these cases, monies for reimbursement come from local dog license taxes or from township tax funds. California and Pennsylvania allow for reimbursement from dog license tax sources, but not local taxes. A knowledge of these facts is extremely valuable for practitioners; when such a monetary source exists, it can be used to help finance the veterinary services incurred for treatment of the injured livestock. The fact that this money exists may make the difference between euthanasia and thorough medical care for the injured livestock.

Another interesting facet of state law exists in the Wisconsin statute. If dog owners are aware of a prior livestock attack by their dog, they can be held liable for two times the full amount of damages and fined up to $500.[72] Furthermore, under the same Wisconsin law, fines can be assessed against dog owners for injuries to deer, game birds, or nests or eggs of game birds.

Statutory Defenses to Liability

State laws that require the licensing of dogs usually apply to dogs belonging to livestock owners as well as those owned by their urban or suburban neighbors.

One purpose of licensing laws is the generation of revenues to help compensate people whose property is damaged by unidentified dogs running at large. Because of the economic importance of their property, livestock owners are identified as a particular category of people who can recover money from dog licensing fees or local gov-

ernments when their animals are injured or killed.

Several states have statutory language that prohibits reimbursement of livestock owners whose dogs are not licensed.[73] Therefore, it behooves veterinarians to point out this exemption to livestock owners when they notice that the livestock owner's dog(s) is unlicensed. Also, they should ascertain the licensure status of the livestock owner's dogs before undertaking extensive medical care for injured livestock and expecting reimbursement from governmental sources.

Bailments

A bailment is defined as a delivery of something of a personal nature by one party to another to be held according to the purpose or object of the delivery and to be returned or delivered over when the purpose is accomplished.[74] Whenever veterinarians assume custody of clients' animals, a bailment takes place.

Bailments arising from express agreements may be written or oral. Statements that are part of written boarding agreements are examples of written bailments. Announcements like "Don't worry, we'll take good care of your Rover," as a client hands possession of the animal over to a veterinary staff person support the creation of an oral bailment.

Bailments also may be implied by the circumstances. When someone rents a horse, for example, a bailment is established as a matter of law, even in the absence of any agreement or discussion between the parties. The same is true whenever clients leave their animals in the care and custody of their veterinarians without clearly defining what the veterinarian is supposed to do for the patient. Clearly, considerable overlap occurs between the law of contracts, negligence, and bailment.

Two elements are essential for the creation of a bailment. First, there must be physical delivery of the property to the bailee (the party accepting custody of the animal) from the bailor (the party handing over custody of the animal). Second, there must be a knowing acceptance of possession of the property by the bailee. Some examples follow:

- Mr. A wishes to borrow a Columbia ram to use for breeding his five ewes. Ms. B agrees to lend him a ram named *Humdinger* for one month in return for the choice of one lamb. As Ms. B unloads Humdinger from her truck at Mr. A's farm, the ram is injured. Even though there is an agreement, no bailment exists because physical possession has not been transferred. If, on the other hand, Mr. A had loaded Humdinger into his truck at Ms. B's farm and an accident occurred while Ms. B was riding with him in his truck en route to his farm, physical possession would have been transferred, and a bailment would have existed.

- Ms. P, a long-standing client of Dr. B, left for work early one morning so that she could drop her bulldog Phoebe off at Dr. B's veterinary hospital. Dr. B's receptionist was late for work that day, so when Ms. P arrived, the hospital was locked. She carefully tied Phoebe to a clamp provided by Dr. B next to the side door and left a note reminding Dr. B that the dog was there to be treated for her itching. At the point that Ms. P left the hospital there is no bailment, because there has been no knowing acceptance by Dr. B, the bailee. If, however, when the receptionist arrives and reads the note she takes Phoebe into the hospital for treatment, a bailment immediately commences.

Several different categories of bailments can be distinguished. The most common types are of a commercial nature, but others also exist. A bailee may rent an animal to another person for personal pleasure or to use for stud, a bailor may lend an animal to a friend or client without charge, a bailee may

Mindy will be right up with Spot.

keep an animal as a favor or for the convenience of the bailor without compensation, or a bailee may transfer possession to a veterinarian or trainer for some form of treatment or special training.

Duties of Bailors and Bailees

Since bailors are transferring possession of the animals, their duties are fairly limited. Nevertheless, they must inform the bailee of such things as the animal's aggressive nature; its inherent fear of or dislike for women, men, cats, other dogs, etc.; a known ability and affinity for trying to escape; its allergies to certain foods or other agents; its need for special medication; and anything else pertaining to its unusual or exceptional need for special care.

As might be expected, bailees who accept possession of animals have more numerous and detailed duties. The primary duty is to return the animal either at a set time or on demand to the bailor or that person's agent in at least as good condition as it was in when it was received. The greatest number of problems that arise concern the duty of care required on behalf of the bailed animal. Like the law of negligence, the law of bailment requires that the bailee provide a level of care appropriate to the circumstances. This is generally a jury question, also known as a question of fact, decided on a case-by-case basis. That means that the duty to provide care and the quality of care will be assessed by the reasonable-man standard, i.e., that degree of care that would have been rendered by a reasonable bailee under the same or similar circumstances.

As a minimum, bailees must meet the standard of humane care and provide adequate food, water, and shelter. If unusual or extraordinary events occur, the bailee must contact or at least attempt to contact the bailor to get further instructions. If an animal is being boarded, often the bailee's duties will be spelled out by the bailment agreement and will include decisions regarding the pursuit and payment of veterinary services. In the absence of any agreement, if an unusual illness or accident occurs, the bailee may not have a duty to incur large veterinary expenses.[75] Bailees who are confronted with this situation are urged to contact the animal's owner or agent as discussed in Chapter 8.

For additional discussion on such things as distinguishing bailments from leases, sales, joint ventures or gifts; recoveries allowed for the loss or injury of bailed animals; injuries to the bailees by the bailed animal; liability for injuries to third parties by bailed animals; and liens associated with bailments, readers are referred to the chapter on bailments found in Reference 1.

Emergency Care and Euthanasia

Since the relationship of veterinarians to clients is a contractual one, current legal precedents do not require that veterinarians render emergency care to animals until an offer has been made and accepted and a contract formed.[76] This rule of American law

may seem very clear, but it poses repeated problems for veterinarians who are asked by good samaritans to provide emergency care for sick or injured stray or abandoned animals. Ethically and morally, veterinarians often want to help. However, if they initiate care for a patient, they could be held liable for their failure to provide adequate care. Furthermore, they usually must undertake such care without any assurance of payment for their services.

California recognized this animal welfare/veterinary medical dilemma. Since 1970, it has had a state statute, Section 597f in the Penal Code, that deals with the issue of injured stray dogs and cats as follows:

> It shall be the duty of all officers of pounds or humane societies, and animal regulation departments of public agencies to convey, and for police and sheriff departments, to cause to be conveyed all injured cats and dogs found without their owners in a public place directly to a veterinarian known by such officer or agency to be a veterinarian that ordinarily treats dogs and cats for a determination of whether the animals shall be immediately and humanely destroyed or shall be hospitalized under proper care and given emergency treatment. Any such veterinarian who agrees to make such a determination, shall himself perform euthanasia on an animal if the owner does not redeem the animal within the locally prescribed waiting period or if he determines that such animal is incurably crippled. If any such veterinarian determines that the animal shall be hospitalized under proper care and given emergency treatment, the costs of any such services which are provided pending the owner's inquiry to such agency, department, or society shall be paid from the dog license fees, fines, and fees for impounding dogs in the city, county, or city and county in which the animal is licensed or if the animal is unlicensed the jurisdiction in which the animal was found, subject to the provision that this cost be repaid by the animal's

owner. No such veterinarian shall be criminally or civilly liable for any decision which he makes or services which he provides pursuant to the provisions of this section.

This statute has worked extremely well to provide emergency medical care for seriously injured stray cats and dogs. It allows veterinarians to be reimbursed for rendering such care regardless of whether an owner is ever located. In addition, veterinarians are permitted under the statute to render a lower standard of emergency care than they otherwise might be willing to provide without fear of civil or criminal liability. If the animal has an identification tag, animal regulation authorities generally authorize considerable emergency care because there is a reasonable likelihood of reuniting the animal with an owner and holding the owner responsible for the fees incurred. If no identification is present, usually only observation or emergency first aid is authorized. The only requirement to come under the purview of the statute is to obtain authorization for treatment from local authorities before treatment is initiated.

Unless careful control is exercised over the payment of emergency veterinary fees for unidentified stray or abandoned animals, animal regulation authorities have found that the expenses of this care can be exorbitant. Therefore, for a program to be effective, everyone must compromise. Veterinarians who participate receive relatively low fees for their efforts but are assured of payment; animal control agencies experience additional costs to run their programs but know that the animals are receiving some emergency care; and animals receive at least some emergency care.

When good samaritans bring injured cats and dogs directly to veterinarians for emergency care but do not accept responsiblity for any of the fees associated with that care, practitioners must telephone someone at the local animal regulation agency and request authorization for treatment. If animals are not seriously injured, these agencies may request that practitioners simply hold the animals until

they can be picked up. If they are seriously injured and authorization to render emergency care is given, it dramatically speeds up the process.

Additional benefits from cooperation between veterinarians and local animal regulation authorities where statutes like this exist include the following:

1. The removal of injured stray animals by caring citizens from locations where their presence could cause accidents is expedited because veterinarians encourage people to bring such animals directly to them instead of suggesting that they call the local police department or animal control facility and wait for them to arrive.

2. When animal emergency clinics are present, the volume of off-hours calls to which animal regulation employees must respond is reduced because citizens are able to bring injured strays directly to the emergency facilities and veterinarians there are willing to receive them.

3. It assures veterinarians that they will be provided some remuneration for rendering emergency first aid and acting as a temporary holding facility for these animals.

4. Veterinarians who comply with the statute by requesting authorization for treatments from animal control authorities are granted immunity from criminal and civil liability for any decisions they make or services they render. This can be of immense psychological value for veterinarians who want to provide assistance but do not want to be held liable for making decisions that might result in lawsuits.

5. Veterinarians do have a legal right to humanely euthanatize seriously injured or incurably crippled stray or abandoned animals under such a law. Many states have good samaritan acts for veterinarians, but these usually provide immunity only from gross negligence and, in most cases, pertain

only to the rendering of emergency treatment at the scene of an accident, not in the veterinarian's hospital or clinic (see Chapter 3).

If all states had laws patterned after the California statute, the rights and responsibilities of veterinarians who provide emergency care for injured stray and abandoned animals would be more clearly defined. By exercising reasonable judgment regarding the extent of emergency care required and the fees for such care, police departments and animal control agencies, animal owners, animals, and veterinarians all benefit. A law like this should be promoted by veterinary political action committees, veterinary associations, SPCAs, humane associations, animal control agencies, and pet-loving citizens and submitted for adoption by their state legislatures.

References

1. Favre DS, Loring M: *Animal Law*. Westport, CT, Quorum Books, 1983, p 3.
2. *Holcomb v Van Zylen*, 174 Mich 274, 140 NW 521 (1913).
3. New York Education Law § 6701.
4. The Philadelphia Code § 10-101.
5. Wisconsin Statutes § 947.01(1).
6. Wisconsin Statutes § 174.001.
7. *New York Life Insurance Co v Dick*, 71 Misc 2d 52 N.Y.S.2d 802-811 (1972).
8. Guidelines for pets in housing projects published. *Calif Vet* 41(2):27, 1987.
9. *Corso v Crawford Dog and Cat Hospital, Inc*, 415 N.Y.S.2d 182-183, 97 Misc 2d 530 (1979).
10. Favre & Loring, *supra* note 1 at 14.
11. Washington Statutes, Chap 16.08 § 2.(2)(b)(c).
12. Wisconsin Statutes § 174.042.
13. Contra Costa County, Calif Revised Animal Control Ordinance § 416-4.402 (b)(1).
14. Yolo County, Calif Animal Control Ordinance § 6-1.420.
15. Contra Costa County, Calif Revised Animal Control Ordinance § 416-12.402(b), 416-12.406, 416-12.408.
16. Contra Costa County, Calif Revised Animal Control Ordinance § 416-6.002.
17. California Penal Code § 597(f).
18. Wisconsin Statutes § 174.11.
19. 3 Pennsylvania Statutes 455.8 (a).
20. Contra Costa County, Calif Revised Animal Control Ordinance § 416-10.010.
21. Hannah HW: Veterinarians and rabies laws. *JAVMA* 173(1):26, 1978.
22. 3 Pennsylvania Statutes 455.8 (c).
23. California Civil Code § 3342.
24. *Nelson v Hall*, 165 Cal App 3d 709, 211 Cal Rptr 668 (1985 3d Dist).
25. Contra Costa County, Calif Revised Animal Control Ordinance § 416-10.008(a).
26. Swift BM: The pit bull friend and killer. *Sports Illus* (July 27):72-84, 1987.
27. The Council, City of New York, Int No 881, July 14, 1987, § 17-343(a), 17-346(a),(d),(e).
28. Marmer M: The new breed of municipal dog control laws: Are they constitutional? *Cincin Law Rev*: footnote 17, 1075, 1984.
29. *Guidelines for Regulating Dangerous or Vicious Dogs*. Washington, DC, The Humane Society of the United States, 1987.
30. Washington Statutes § 16.08.
31. Contra Costa County, Calif Revised Animal Control Ordinance § 416-12.4.
32. 16.08 Regulatory Code of Washington § 3.(1),(2),(3).
33. Contra Costa County, Calif Revised Animal Control Ordinance § 416-12.202.
34. Wisconsin Department of Natural Resources 194-1, Chap NR 243.
35. Hannah HW: Legal brief: Zoning laws and the veterinarian. *JAVMA* (Sept 1): 1969.

36. Favre & Loring, *supra* note 1 at 153.

37. Virginia Code § 3.1-796.50.

38. 3 Pennsylvania Statutes § 459-1201(c).

39. Wisconsin Statutes § 948.15(1).

40. Wisconsin Statutes § 948.18(1). 41. 3 Pennsylvania Statutes 459-303.

42. California Civil Code § 1834.5.

43. *Peloquin v Calcasieu Parish Police, Jury et al*, 367 So2d 1246 (1979).

44. New York Agriculture and Markets Law § 331.

45. 3 Pennsylvania Statutes § 459-1202.

46. Hannah HW: Legal brief: Liens for veterinary service. *JAVMA* 187(1):24, 1985.

47. California Civil Code § 3052: If the person entitled to the lien...is not paid the amount due...within 10 days after the same shall have become due, then such lienholder may proceed to sell...such property...at public auction, and by giving at least...10 days' but not more than...20 days' previous notice of such sale by advertising in some newspaper published in the county in which...such property is situated...; provided, however, that...within 20 days after such sale, the legal owner may redeem any such property so sold to satisfy...such lien..., upon payment of the amount thereof, all costs and expenses of...such sale, together with interest on...such sum at the rate of 12 per cent per annum... The proceeds of the sale must be applied to the discharge of the lien and the cost of keeping and selling the property; the remainder, if any, must be paid over to the legal owner thereof.

48. California Civil Code § 3051.

49. Nebraska Statutes § 52-701.

50. 256 Code of Massachusetts 7.01.

51. Massachusetts General Laws § 255.24.

52. Effects of the lien and abandonment laws upon veterinarians in California. *Calif Vet* (Oct):26, 1980.

53. Mississippi Statutes § 98-41-1.

54. California Penal Code § 597.

55. Favre & Loring, *supra* note 1 at 121-166.

56. Favre & Loring, *supra* note 1 at 47-52.

57. *People v Wicker*, 357 NYS2d 597, 1974. The defendant was justified in killing a dog to protect his dog. *Ford v Glennon*, 74 Conn 6, 49 A 189, 1901. The defendant used unnecessary force to protect his cat, therefore he is liable to the owner of the dog that was killed.

58. Favre and Loring, *supra* note 1 at 103.

59. Favre and Loring, *supra* note 1 at 105.

60. Bogert GG, Bogert GT: *The Law of Trusts and Trustees*, ed 2 (revised). St. Paul, West Publishing Co, l979, § 166, p 163.

61. Hannah HW: Legal brief: Bequests for animals. *JAVMA* 188(11):1234, 1986.

62. No. 225698, (Superior Court, San Francisco County, June 17, 1980).

63. California Senate Bill 2509 passed unanimously and was signed into law on June 16, 1980. It states in part: The legislature hereby finds that under the facts meeting the description set forth in Section I of this act, the testator, having the best interests of her pet dog in mind, would not wish her instructions for the destruction of the pet dog carried out were she cognizant of the present circumstances assuring the well being and happy future for the dog, occurring as the result of unexpected developments following her death. In order to prevent the unnecessary and undesirable killing of animals, pursuant to the requirements of decedents' will, it is necessary that this act go into immediate effect.

64. Carlisle F: Destruction of pets by will provision. *Real Property, Probate, & Trust J* 16(4):894-903, 1981.

65. Hannah HW: Legal brief: Euthanasia—Property rights in bodies—necropsies. *JAVMA* 163(12):1352, 1973.

66   *Curso v Crawford Dog and Cat Hospital, Inc*, 415 NYS2d 182, 183, 97 Misc 2d 530 (1979).

67. *Levine v Knowles*, 218 So2d 217 (Fla 1969).

68. Hannah HW: Legal brief: Abusive language—The tort of outrage. *JAVMA* 190(5):521-522, 1987.

69. Hannah HW: Legal brief: Shocking the sensibilities. *JAVMA* 169(9):874-875, 1976.

70. California Penal Code § 599e.

71. Texas Civil Statutes 192-3.

72. Wisconsin Statutes § 174.02.

73. Wisconsin Statutes § 174.11(4); 3 Pennsylvania Statutes § 459-705.

74. Hannah HW: Legal brief: The veterinarian as bailee. *JAVMA* 185(11):1278, 1984.

75. Favre & Loring, *supra* note 1 at 73.

76. Hannah HW: Legal brief: Refusal to treat and refusal to continue treatment. *JAVMA* 186(7):666, 1985.

CHAPTER 5

Minimizing Complaints and Settling Disputes

No matter how competent veterinarians are and how diligently they communicate with clients, complaints will occur. These complaints can stem from the actions of veterinary assistants, receptionists, kennel assistants, stable attendants, associate veterinarians, or practice owners themselves. Problems can evolve from difficulties involving animal restraint; communication mixups at the receptionist's desk, the business office, or the pharmacy; communication shortcomings on the part of the veterinarian; and alleged negligence in the practice of veterinary medicine.

This chapter addresses the types of situations that are most likely to lead to client grievances. Veterinarians who understand a complaint's origin will be less likely to become entrapped in the overall complaint process.

Complaints against any employees or associates in a practice comprise grievances against the veterinary practice itself. Therefore, the practice owner is usually the party who must answer to a client, even though the problem may have been with an employee. When peer review complaints, ethics grievances, state board administrative actions, civil lawsuits, or simply angry clients are involved, the offending employee may be party to the suit, but the ultimate responsibility always lies with the practice owner.

Causes for Complaints

Breakdowns in Communications About Medical Care

Breakdowns in communication are at the root of most grievances. Unfortunately, courses in communication skills have not been offered routinely in the preveterinary or veterinary school curricula. An education heavy on the sciences may help create great doctors, but without a good grasp of the art of communication, many veterinarians can find themselves in trouble with client relations.

111

Client Misconceptions

During veterinary school, students are taught to communicate using medical terminology, which is international and a more accurate descriptive form of communication than everyday language. Most clients, however, are unfamiliar with most medical terms and will not fully understand the situation if explanations are provided in medical terms.

For example, a dental prophylaxis may mean a teeth cleaning to a client, but to a veterinarian it may mean cleaning and polishing the teeth, plus extracting any number of teeth with serious periodontal disease or infected roots. If a veterinarian, then, announces to a client after completing a dental prophylaxis that 12 teeth were extracted because they were rotten, clients may respond with horror and concern and claim that they had no idea this was going to happen. Sometimes even the best possible explanation will not win back the client's trust and confidence, because what transpired was beyond the owner's expectations.

A personal experience illustrating a communication breakdown between the author and a client by the name of Mr. Smith follows. At the time of a routine visit, Mr. Smith pointed out a 6-cm-diameter lipomatous mass in his 30-lb poodle Hector's left inguinal area. An aspiration biopsy confirmed that it was nothing but fatty tissue. Mr. Smith was notoriously difficult to please and extremely concerned about Hector's comfort. When he was informed that postsurgical healing in this area can be slow due to seroma formation, that lipomas are rarely malignant, and that Hector might have to wear an Elizabethan collar for 10 days if the surgery was performed, it was agreed that observation would be the better course of action.

About one month later Mr. Smith returned with Hector because he had noticed three other small lumps. Aspiration biopsies of these were not performed because an oral examination showed that it was time for a dental prophylaxis, and there was now ample justification for an anesthetic. Surgery was scheduled to remove the lumps and clean the teeth the following week.

Mr. Smith arrived for the surgery appointment and was hurriedly assured by the author that everything should go well because the period of anesthesia would be relatively short. That day Hector was anesthetized, the three lumps—all sebaceous gland cysts—were surgically removed, and the dental work was performed without any difficulties.

When Mr. Smith returned that afternoon, the hospital was busy. Mr. Smith was very excited to see his dog, so an assistant brought Hector up before the author had an opportunity to discuss the benign nature of the three small lumps. By the time Mr. Smith's patient-release appointment arrived, he was infuriated. "Why didn't you remove the big tumor in his groin like you were supposed to?" was his greeting.

The author's response was, "Don't you recall that we knew what that mass was but we didn't know what the other firm lumps were and so we were only planning to remove the three small ones, not that great big one?"

"You never told me that," retorted the unhappy Mr. Smith. "I brought him in here to get his teeth cleaned and to get rid of that ugly lump down by his private parts."

This embarrassed doctor responded, "Mr. Smith, don't you recall our discussion about the need for an Elizabethan collar and the fact that because of seromas and friction, surgical incisions do not heal well in that location? We were only supposed to remove the three small lumps, not that one."

There we were—a total communication breakdown about what was going to be done and what was not going to be done. The conversations from a month prior never resurfaced when the dental prophylaxis and surgery were scheduled. No discussion of the surgical plan took place at the time of the hurried presurgical admit appointment. The groundwork was laid for a major communications mixup and, sure enough, it occurred. Mr. Smith was incensed.

The problem was satisfactorily resolved via compromise, and Mr. Smith was retained as a client. The compromise included the surgical removal of the lipoma two weeks later with no charge for anesthesia or hospitalization, since those fees had already been paid once. The only charge Mr. Smith had to bear was the cost for the time involved to remove the lipomatous mass.

Most veterinarians in practice can tell similar stories. The issue, though, is whether anything was learned by the experience. Discussions regarding what procedures will or will not be performed must occur beforehand if time-consuming, emotional exercises like this are to be avoided.

Mistaken Perceptions of Client Expectations

Another mistake that veterinarians make is prejudging clients' wants and needs for veterinary care as well as their willingness and ability to pay for that care. Some practitioners assume that clients want everything done as cheaply as possible. To these veterinarians, owners' inquiries about fees are evidence that cost is the most important factor, when in reality the clients simply want to know what the price will be.

One former member of a state board has written several humorous but true synopses of what goes wrong prior to the filing of a complaint. One of these, a case of mistaken perceptions, is illustrated in the following story extracted from the *California Veterinarian*:

> This case involves a dog that recently had a litter of puppies. Mrs. Concerned called Doctor Invisible's office and told the receptionist she wanted to make an appointment to have her dog "spayed." The receptionist instructed Mrs. Concerned to bring her dog in at 8:00 a.m. the following day and to pick her up at 5:00 p.m. The owner suggested to the receptionist that the doctor should examine her dog first because her dog was very thin. The receptionist reassured her that the doctor would check the dog thoroughly before surgery was performed. (The time bomb fuse is set.)

You castrated Ralph?! But I only brought him in to have his toenails trimmed!

> The next morning Mrs. Concerned left her dog at the hospital. Shortly thereafter the receptionist telephoned and informed the owner that the doctor found her dog to be very thin, but otherwise seemed fine. She explained to Mrs. Concerned that the doctor attributed the dog's loss of weight to her recent litter of puppies, but it was possible there could be other causes for her loss of weight. However, the doctor felt it was alright to schedule her for surgery. (The bomb continues to tick.)

> The surgery was performed the same morning and, unfortunately, the dog died during the immediate postoperative period. (Boom!) The hospital's receptionist called and informed Mrs. Concerned of this development. When the client questioned the receptionist as to the possible cause of death, she responded by commenting, "I don't really know, but it was possibly due to giving a little too much anesthetic and the dog was allergic to it."

> The grief-stricken owner picked up the body and took it to be checked by another veterinarian. The postmortem examination revealed that the dog had a

heavy infestation of ascarids associated with a secondary enteritis.

The following is a summary of the client's letter to the California State Board:

I took my dog 'Sadie' to Doctor Invisible's hospital to be `spayed.' She had had a litter of puppies about two months previously. I was concerned about the fact that she was quite thin so I tried to make an appointment to have her examined by the doctor. The receptionist told me that it wasn't necessary because the doctor would check the dog thoroughly before doing surgery. They didn't seem to be too worried about her physical condition so I agreed to have the surgery done.

I assumed at the time that the doctor would not have done the surgery if there had been any risk involved because of her weakened condition. I feel this doctor is guilty of malpractice. How can your Board allow this kind of doctor to prey on the unsuspecting public? He doesn't care about animals; all he is interested in is the money. The doctor never talked to me personally, and he didn't even have the courtesy to call me after he killed 'Sadie.

The state board requested that the veterinarian supply them with a copy of the medical record as well as an explanation of what had happened. The following is a summary of the veterinarian's comments.

I performed an ovariohysterectomy on Mrs. Concerned's dog. The operation was uneventful, but during the postsurgical period she developed respiratory problems and died. The cause of death was due to cardiac arrest brought on by an allergic reaction to the amount of anesthetic agent used. I can assure I did everything possible to save her, including oxygen administration and intensive care therapy.

The dog was thin, but I thought this was due to her recent pregnancy. The client was warned, however, that the dog's underweight condition could have

been due to other causes. I did not do any presurgical workup because I was trying to save the client some money. (Remember the client's comment, "He's only interested in the money." In my area I am regarded as a good practitioner. The Board should not waste their time investigating veterinarians like me. Instead, you should go after the bad guys in our profession...[1]

This type of story is frequent. Veterinarians create difficulties for themselves because they tend to undersell quality with the justification that they did not think the client would have wanted to do all of the things that could have been offered.

Convincing clients that more complete work-ups are desirable or necessary can be difficult. Furthermore, it requires time to examine these patients and convince clients that fecals need to be run, heartworm tests performed, radiographs taken, or blood work evaluated. Time adds cost to the performance of veterinary care, but it also reduces complaints. Each diagnostic test must be medically justified, properly performed, and accurately interpreted in order to be within the standard of care for the profession. Clients have every right to become angry when they find out from another veterinarian that more complete care was available than was ever offered to them by their own veterinarian.

Just as breakdowns in communications about medical care precipitate complaints, failures to communicate effectively about fees can do the same.

Some clients raise the issue of fees every step of the way, while others are not comfortable discussing this topic at all. Chapter 8 on contract law and Chapter 13 covering debt collection present more details about estimates as integral components of the contract.

Client Failure to Request an Estimate

Clients do not request estimates for a variety of reasons. Sometimes it is because they do not care how much it costs to help their animals. Occasionally, it is because they are afraid that raising the fee issue will lessen their esteem in the eyes of their veterinarians. Other times it is because they simply underestimate how much it costs to perform a basic diagnostic work-up.

Another type of person who may not request an estimate is the client who comes rushing in with an emergency, demanding that medical care be provided immediately. When the issue of fees is broached, the categoric response is "Go ahead and do everything possible, Doc. Money is no object." These words should raise doubts immediately about the client's financial responsibility. A statement like this should also prompt the veterinarian to obtain a significant deposit or prepayment of fees from this client.

Often people who make these statements will not allow an estimate to be presented. Subconsciously, they are troubled because they have not provided proper care for the injured animal and they have not set aside money for emergencies. The only way that they can deal with their own shortcomings is to transfer the problem to the veterinarian. The veterinarian is angrily criticized by such clients for placing concerns about money before the patient's need for medical care.

Cases like this are real challenges. A failure to provide minimal first aid legitimizes the client's contention that the veterinarian is thinking only of money. Yet, proceeding quickly with all essential medical care and failing to force the client to consider the financial consequences, as presented in an estimate, leaves the practice vulnerable to large unpaid and usually uncollectable veterinary bills.

The Failure to Offer Estimates

Excuses can always be found for not presenting an estimate to a client. It can be because the emotion of the moment would have made discussing finances improper. It can be because the client was unavailable for a discussion of fees at the time the procedures needed to be authorized. Other times

numerous clients are waiting to be seen, and there is not sufficient time to develop an itemized written estimate.

If a new graduate is involved, it is sometimes due to a lack of understanding as to the difficulty of the case and the length of time it will take to perform the required procedures. Many new graduates question their abilities and self-worth to the point that they are embarrassed or uncomfortable giving estimates that coincide with those of the practice owner. When well-established practitioners provide care for long-time clients they often feel they know their clients so well that those clients do not need or care about receiving an estimate.

The list of excuses is endless, but the end result is often the same. There is a major difference between how difficult and expensive the client thought the veterinary care would be and how much it actually costs after the care has been rendered.

In most cases, clients do not expect estimates to be exact, but they would like to know the approximate cost. Complaints can be avoided if practitioners simply provide estimates for veterinary care whether or not clients ask for them. Estimates can be tabulated with computers in minutes, so there is virtually no reason why they cannot be supplied routinely, at least for the first 24 hours of medical care. Owners can always be advised that a more complete estimate of total costs will be provided as soon as all the diagnostic information has been evaluated.

The Failure to Inform Clients of Estimate Changes

During the course of a surgical or anesthetic procedure, or while rendering emergency care, practitioners sometimes discover that a case is much more serious than they had expected. Under traditional contract law theory, there is no agreement to perform or charge for additional care. Under the law of negligence and malpractice, however, veterinarians may not allow a patient to die because they are about to exceed the fees agreed to by the owner.

Providing medical care that exceeds the veterinarian's estimate without first notifying the owner makes clients skeptical. Practitioners will find it difficult, after the fact, to convince owners that no alternative existed except to proceed with additional care.

This type of situation becomes even more serious when the owners were readily available at home or at work during the time such a decision had to be made. Clients cannot be expected to pay for extra medical care without knowing the approximate costs as well as the prognosis with or without the additional care.

In general, there are very few acceptable excuses for failing to seek authorization for additional medical care before it is rendered. A truly life-threatening situation would be one satisfactory justification. A second exception that might be acceptable, depending upon all the facts, involves proceeding with the additional care after an attempt has been made to contact the owner by telephone. In most cases, if someone can be located, approval for the extra expense and care is granted. If no one can be located to provide an authorization, the phone number(s) called and time of day should be documented on the medical record. When owners come to pick up their animals, they can be informed that an attempt was made to contact them at a specific time and place. The veterinarian can then explain that since no one could be reached, the staff went ahead and did what they thought the clients would have wanted.

Whether or not this extra treatment and the additional charges are acceptable, veterinarians who have followed these steps will have done their best to satisfy the client. Very few critics will find fault with practitioners who have followed these guidelines. Readers should review the discussion of quasi–contract law found in Chapter 8 for more information on this topic.

The Failure to Compromise on Fees

Occasionally, cases do not proceed the way they were expected to because of prob-

lems brought on by veterinarians, their staffs, the patients, the clients, or fate. If the problems originate from the owner's lack of attention or inability, practitioners should feel minimal need to make any adjustments in the fees charged. If the care and treatment by the staff or veterinarian are responsible for the failure of a case, care must be exercised when compromises are considered so that a fee adjustment is not viewed as an admission of negligence, malpractice, or wrongdoing.

Sometimes, even with the best of home supervision, patients destroy their splints, chew their bandages off, lick and chew their sutures out, or are so hyperactive that their injuries cannot heal. When circumstances like these are beyond the control of the veterinarian or owner, compromises regarding fees can help minimize the repercussions.

Some problem cases are simply no-win situations. Clients are disgruntled because they must pay for additional veterinary care, and veterinarians are annoyed because they must continue providing care, usually at reduced rates. The patients also lose because they continue to suffer discomfort, receive medication, wear Elizabethan collars, etc. Clients are willing to pay for many setbacks, but as costs escalate they often look for ways to prove that the extra fees are related to incompetent veterinary care.

Many disagreements about fees can be resolved through oral negotiation. Sometimes compromises arrived at in this manner leave practitioners wary about admissions of negligence or malpractice. The following disclaimer was designed to encourage the settlement of at least some cases.

This reduction in the fee owed by (Mr./Ms.) _____ for the care of _____ to _____ Veterinary Hospital is purely a gesture of goodwill. It is understood and agreed that this reduced-fee settlement is a compromise, and that such fee reduction is not to be construed as an admission of any negligence or liability on the part of_____ Veterinary Hospital.

The author's "disclaimer" to this disclaimer is to say that this is not a legal document but a way that veterinarians can attempt to settle fee disputes on their own. Legal counsel should be consulted in cases wherein any potential for claims of malpractice, contract breach, or client retribution exist.

The Failure to Provide Satisfactory Quantity and Quality of Veterinary Care

The most serious complaints derive from dissatisfaction with the quantity and/or quality of veterinary care. When grievances stem from allegations of negligence, incompetence, fraud, or deception in the practice of veterinary medicine, practitioners usually need attorneys to provide legal counsel.

Often, cases in this category are initiated via lawsuits or through the administrative hearing process. The state boards of examiners are the recipients of the complaints in the administrative hearing process and are the initiators of case reviews or investigations. Local veterinary association ethics committees have avoided these more serious complaints, saying that an evaluation of medical care is beyond their jurisdiction. Some local ethics committees will deal with grievances involving fee disputes, while others will not. The recently established local veterinary association peer review committees, on the other hand, do have the procedural jurisdiction to review appropriateness of care and quality of treatment in addition to fees.

There are many examples of cases involving substandard veterinary care. The following illustrates some important points on the subject. It is extracted from a file of the California Board of Examiners in Veterinary Medicine.[2]

> I want to lodge a complaint against Doctor Wingit. On 4/20 (Monday) I took my dog Zelda to the doctor because she had been vomiting for two days and was acting very listless. I was particularly con-

cerned because I thought there was blood in the vomited material. When I called the hospital, the receptionist suggested that Zelda was probably suffering from an upset stomach and advised me to give her some Kaopectate. I told her I felt it was more serious than that and insisted she schedule an appointment for me with the doctor.

When I arrived at the hospital, the receptionist at the counter did not seem in any hurry to get us in to see the doctor. She asked me to be seated and told me the doctor would see me 'in a few minutes.' There was no one in the waiting room at the time. I patiently waited for 20 minutes and then asked how much longer would it be before the doctor could see us? The receptionist assured me that I would be seeing the doctor 'in a few minutes.' All during this period, the receptionist was busy chatting with another girl in the office. About ten minutes later, a young man struggled through the front door with two large pizzas in his arms. The receptionist rushed to the front door to help him in. He was ushered immediately to the back of the hospital. I then heard a lot of laughing and giggling. I couldn't help thinking to myself that a pizza received more immediate attention in this hospital than sick dogs. After waiting over 45 minutes, I finally was ushered into the examination room.

Ten minutes later, Doctor Wingit came in. I told the doctor that I thought I saw some blood in the vomited material. The doctor was also informed that Zelda had a tendency to eat foreign material. Zelda was given a shot and some capsule medication (ed. note: chloramphenicol) that was sent home for her. The doctor asked me to call him in a few days if Zelda wasn't improved.

The case was diagnosed by Dr. Wingit as "garbage gastritis." An interesting story unfolds as the case developed further. In summary, after eight days of treatment under Dr. Wingit's care, including the misinterpretation of laboratory results, the client removed Zelda from Dr. Wingit's care and sought attention elsewhere. Upon exploratory laparotomy, it turned out that Zelda had ingested a golf ball and had an intestinal obstruction. She died postsurgically after an attempt was made to perform an anastomosis.

A brief summary of Dr. Wingit's comments includes the following statements:

> I am truly sorry that the dog died but in reviewing this case, I do not feel that it was handled improperly. This is my eleventh year in practice, so I feel quite confident that I deliver a good level of medical care to my clients. In cases like this, I usually do not recommend x-rays or a medical work up because it is my desire to keep medical expenses down whenever possible....
>
> This type of situation, I am sure, happens to many veterinarians. It is just the nature of private practice. Sometimes you lose animals when you don't routinely do a complete work up on all cases. I hope your decision will be in my favor because I would hate to think I will be forced to practice defensive medicine in order to protect myself.[2]

The medical records associated with the care in this case were almost nonexistent. This example shows how often complaints focus on one or more of the items listed in this chapter. In this partial synopsis, three significant problems can be identified: (1) negligent practice of medicine, (2) office chatter and frivolity, and (3) the assumption that cheaper medical care is what clients want.

Grievances that center around inadequate quality and/or quantity of medical care may be unresolvable through compromise. Client allegations of malpractice or negligence should be referred to practitioners' insurance companies as soon as they occur.

Other charges of unsatisfactory quality and quantity of veterinary care can involve claims of fraud or deception. In these cases, criminal charges could possibly be filed separately or in addition to a state board action for a license suspension or revocation.

Examples of fraud and deception include the routine use of outdated pharmaceutical or biological products, telling clients that certain laboratory procedures have been performed when they have not, and predating or postdating health or insurance certificates.

Client complaints of this type need the most immediate and careful attention. The advice of professional liability carriers and attorneys should be sought before any action is taken to resolve grievances when criminal court action is a possibility.

The Failure to Offer Referrals

The legal doctrine that will have an increasing impact on veterinary medicine is the duty to refer. It is unclear at this point whether the law will impose an actual duty to refer cases requiring specialty care or whether the duty will be merely to offer a referral. For simplicity, it is assumed that veterinarians have a duty only to inform clients of the availability of specialty care and offer referrals, not a strict duty to refer.

There are two common reasons for complaints regarding veterinary referrals. The first is a failure to mention the availability of specialty care. The second is procrastinating until it is so late in the treatment process that specialists cannot help the patient. Compounding each of these situations is the problem that if clients finally do seek specialty care, it is impossible for the specialist to say anything that will make the regular veterinarian look competent. If a diagnosis is arrived at too quickly and easily, clients become skeptical about the competency of the prior care that they received. Doubts like this precipitate grievances.

The duty to offer referrals includes referrals to board-certified specialists, veterinary schools, and veterinarians with special interests (like cage bird specialists). When finances, distances, and client reluctance or inconvenience hinder referrals, a valuable alternative is for the veterinarian in charge of the case to consult by telephone or in person with a specialist. More current medical information can be obtained and notations can be made on the patient's medical record to substantiate one's efforts to provide the best possible medical care.

When intensive care is needed at night, on weekends, or during holidays, and veterinary emergency clinics are readily available, clients need to be apprised of this fact. If an emergency care facility is not convenient or is too expensive, clients can elect not to use it. If they were never informed that this specialty care was available, however, the failure to inform them is potentially the source of a complaint and a lawsuit for negligence.

In the past, deaths that occurred while a veterinary facility was closed for the night or weekend were explained by merely expressing regrets at the animal's loss. This tack is becoming less and less acceptable to clients who are aware of and willing to pay for 24-hour care for their animals.

The Failure to Show Adequate Compassion

The ability to convey a caring attitude and to show compassion can do more to quiet a complaint than any other effort. Veterinarians deal with death more frequently than any other healing arts profession. According to sources at the California State Board, approximately 50–70% of all grievances are associated with the death of an animal.[3] Many of these complaints could have been avoided if an explanation of what happened had been provided along with a healthy dose of compassion.

Fortunately, considerable educational emphasis has been placed on this topic in recent years. Excellent continuing education seminars and valuable written resources have been offered.[4] Opportunities exist for veterinarians and staff people to improve their awareness and skill in dealing with this aspect of human relations. A failure to provide adequate compassion is manifested in several different ways.

The Veterinarian's Failure to Become Emotionally Involved

For many reasons, some veterinarians fail to personally express compassion. In some cases, it is because they are emotionally unable to do so. In other cases it is because they lack the education or experience to be confident and comfortable dealing with people who are crying or distraught. Other veterinarians do not recognize the overwhelming importance of this aspect of practice.

Doctors must show compassion and empathy to clients who are experiencing grief over the loss of a beloved animal. The grief can be from the loss of a pet dog, cat, chicken, rabbit, horse, cow, or other animal. Some veterinarians who may not be highly skilled members of their profession manage to minimize client complaints by portraying a kindly bedside manner which includes the generous administration of compassion.

The Failure of Staff Members to Offer Compassion

Although it may be most important for the doctor to demonstrate compassion, an awareness of its importance by staff people is also critical.

Laughter, joking, or distracting office chatter by employees while a patient is dying or during the performance of euthanasia can leave a lasting bad impression on a client. If any other aspect of a patient's veterinary care has angered the client, incidents like these will add fuel to the fire. Staff people must be made aware that their behavior can have a dramatic influence on cases in which the potential for trouble already exists.

Little things such as removing patients from reminder lists are extremely important. Nothing is more upsetting to a client than receiving an examination and booster vaccination notice shortly after the patient died or was euthanatized.

Another irritant for a grievance involves an uninformed staff person cheerfully inquiring about a patient when the owner comes in to pay the veterinary bill a few days after the animal died while under care at that facility. There are ways to avoid such an embarrassing situation. One technique is to place a magic marker board out of client view but in a location employees can readily see on which the names of patients who have just died are listed. In this manner, everyone at the facility is made aware of the death of a patient and is better prepared to say something comforting to the client. The heading "In Memoriam" printed atop the board adds a caring touch in case a client should see it.

Many other ideas are currently being touted as ways for turning the death of a patient into a tolerable experience for the client and the practice. Sympathy cards or letters can be sent. Handwritten notes seem to be most effective, although a form letter is probably better than none at all. One of the very best expressions of sympathy is a donation by the veterinarian to a companion animal memorial research fund in the name of the client's deceased pet. These foundations, in turn, acknowledge the receipt of the veterinarian's monetary gift in the pet's name by sending their own sympathy notes. Clients are impressed and grateful, veterinarians will have done their part, and the nonprofit foundations can provide research money to continue improving veterinary medicine.

In general, recognition of client grief coupled with thoughtful actions by veterinarians and staff people can do wonders to help avert complaints that are linked to an animal's death.

Aggravating the Potential for Complaints

Aside from the gamut of reasons for complaints just cited, still another source of grievances exists. Comments that one veterinarian makes about the care rendered by another are an invitation for trouble.

Four groups of veterinarians are most likely to make statements about other practitioners that can stimulate clients to file complaints. These groups are (1) veterinarians working at emergency clinics, (2) veterinarians providing specialty referral services, (3) veterinarians attending cases at veterinary schools, and (4) egotistical veterinarians who maintain they could have saved any animal if they had just seen it several days earlier.

Emergency Clinic Personnel

Emergency clinic personnel consistently see clients who are unhappy because they cannot reach their regular daytime practitioners. As a result of that unavailability, some clients arrive at an emergency clinic angry and critical of their personal veterinarian. In addition, they are often convinced that the visit is going to be expensive, and they want to blame someone for the cost and inconvenience.

A significant number of cases seen at emergency clinics have been treated previously by another veterinarian, yet emergency clinic staff people have no access to the medical records describing that care. Because of the emergency nature of the visit, it is often impossible to reach the regular veterinarian or anyone at the practice to obtain important information. This is one problem that specialists and university personnel seeing cases during the normal workday are less likely to face.

Experienced practitioners know that clients frequently forget what diagnostic tests have been run, what diagnoses were made, and what treatments were rendered by prior veterinarians. Thus, emergency clinic personnel often receive brief, disorganized, and inaccurate reports of the patient's prior medical care. The result is that it is often difficult not to make critical comments about the medical efforts of veterinarians who have rendered previous veterinary care. Simple questions like, "You mean to say Dr. A did not run a blood sugar test or a urinalysis on Rover?" (when Rover is a polydipsic, polyuric, polyphagic, 12-year-old dog that has has been vomiting for two days) can make Dr. A look incompetent.

The client may answer, "No, he didn't," thereby fulfilling the emergency veterinarian's belief that Dr. A is truly incompetent. If all the facts were known, however, it might be shown that Dr. A recommended blood tests and a urinalysis, but the client refused to spend the extra money for laboratory tests that would have facilitated a diagnosis. In other words, the real answer was "No, Dr. A did not run any lab tests, but it wasn't for not asking."

There will always be cases in which the care rendered by other veterinarians looks negligent or incompetent. These present moral and ethical dilemmas for other practitioners who may feel that a client and an animal have been maligned. The cardinal rule to remember is that there are two sides to every story. Making any comments regarding veterinary care rendered to a patient without all of the facts helps no one and may lead to the filing of an unfair complaint.

Specialists

Veterinary specialists also treat many cases wherein their comments can incite retributive actions against other veterinarians. Specialists (especially surgeons) are often placed in the unfortunate position of having to repair something after a previous veterinarian has chosen an errant course of treatment. In numerous situations, their hands are tied because there are no normal tissues left with which to work.

Specialists are a step ahead of emergency clinicians, though, because they usually have some form of medical history from previous veterinarians. If clients do not bring written records with them, the specialists have the option of calling the prior veterinarian during the normal workday.

Self-referred clients or clients from veterinarians who never refer patients are the most difficult for specialists to handle from both a medical and a professional standpoint. These cases may have been so mishandled prior to arriving that nothing positive can be said or done. It is the specialists' difficult task to rectify the medical problem and remain as neutral as possible.

Veterinary School Personnel

The third group of veterinarians who must exercise considerable caution regarding statements about prior veterinary care are veterinary medical school personnel. For many reasons these people have greater opportunities and, perhaps, propensities, to make comments that might be interpreted as critical than veterinarians in general practice. Some of these reasons are as follows:

1. Clients who are dissatisfied with veterinary care received elsewhere tend to seek doctors at veterinary schools because they believe university veterinarians are the ultimate authorities on veterinary medical care. Consequently, university clinicians have more invitations and demands placed on them for comments and opinions than the private practitioner. Many clients will ask outright if the previous treatment is the way they would have handled the problem.

2. Most schools are represented by veterinarians from nearly every specialty discipline. These doctors and their residents often see clinical cases only within their particular discipline. In order to teach, they must acquire and maintain a high level of scientific knowledge. However, due to their teaching, research, and writing commitments, many of these people often see clinical cases only one day per week. The result is that their case load exposure, and thus their practical knowledge, may be more limited than that of specialists in private practice or some general practitioners. Additionally, faculty personnel are not

pressured to produce an hourly income sufficient to pay a staff and themselves. The combination of these factors unwittingly predisposes university clinicians to situations wherein their comments might unintentionally impugn the quality of medicine provided by previous veterinarians.

3. The average client who has been referred to a veterinary school is usually much less concerned about the costs for veterinary care than about the competence and quality of that care. This frequently gives university clinicians a significant advantage over private practitioners regarding the extent to which diagnostic procedures can be utilized. In addition, diagnostic procedures at schools are generally more readily available. Unless these factors are considered by faculty members and pointed out to clients, subtle comments about prior care could provoke a complaint against the generalist.

4. Experienced veterinary school clinicians know that there are always two sides to a story. They are not apt to be trapped by clients who are fishing for critical comments. Residents and interns, however, have less experience and, as a result, may be more inclined to make questionable comments about previous care. Inexperienced students are the group most likely to make inappropriate comments that they may regret later. They hear all the private comments of staff people and are often familiar only with the procedures and standards available at the university.

These factors, and probably others, emphasize the need for university administrators and service chiefs to provide guidance and supervision for each new rotation of residents, interns, and students.

Egotistical Veterinarians

The last group that can be readily identi-

fied as aggravators of client complaints are egotistical veterinarians or those people who think that omissions, mistakes, and failures never happen to them. When prior care by another veterinarian was unsuccessful, some veterinarians feel compelled to place themselves above their colleagues in the eyes of their clients. For example, these doctors are inclined to indicate that they could have saved an animal if it were brought to them first: "If I had just seen Fido a few days ago (weeks ago, hours ago), I think we could have saved him." Such comments are certainly inflammatory, even if they were not intended to be.

When clients question someone else's approach to a case, the following tack is more truthful and apropos: "Yes, I might have handled this case differently than Dr. A did, but I have the advantage of hindsight, knowing that what he tried did not work." An additional comment could be, "Your animal's care today is what is most important to me at the moment, not what has transpired previously. My policy is not to comment on prior care until I have the facts from all parties involved in the case. Let's get on with today's care."

Some veterinarians of this type preface their examinations with comments similar to those in the Fido example. Others mask their own failures by casting aspersions on previous treatment by other veterinarians. They, like most human beings, prefer to place the blame on someone else when things do not go as planned. The statement, "I'm sure we could have saved Fido" requires minimal thought and is easy to make. Discovering the facts and arriving at a rational judgment which includes an analysis of everyone's participation in the course of events is much more difficult and time consuming.

Some derogatory comments are made inadvertently and unintentionally. Other times, the statements are meant for colleagues or "competitors" with whom the veterinarian wants to find fault. The recipient of intentional comments or innuendos may be a former employee who left and set up a practice nearby; someone who never attends veterinary association functions; a veterinarian who advertises in every available newspaper, coupon book, and telephone book; or a practitioner who is notorious for low standards of practice.

There are two considerations that most practitioners who are anxious to denigrate others fail to remember. The first is that the facts always look and sound considerably different when heard from the previous veterinarian as well as from the client. The second is that no practitioner is perfect. Clients come and go, but bad will directed toward colleagues usually results in likewise treatment from them when the shoe is on the other foot.

When Criticism Is Appropriate

Sometimes it is obvious that previous care was below the standard of care and, in these cases, both the client and the veterinary profession deserve the support of veterinarians who have witnessed a problem. This is the only time that criticism is appropriate, however. At all levels of practice, unnecessary and uninformed comments and inferences critical of the veterinary care provided by others must be strictly avoided.

During the course of student training, professor-led discussions regarding cases like this must occur. This should be accomplished in a formal classroom setting as well as in informal rounds presentations where diagnostic and therapeutic plans are decided. In this manner, students, faculty, residents, interns, referring veterinarians, and the profession at large would all benefit. Additional ideas and materials concerning this topic can be found in the AVMA *Principles of Veterinary Medical Ethics*[5] and in materials on ethics in Chapters 1 and 2 of this text.

Avenues for Addressing Grievances

At some point in the complaint process, it must be recognized that a grievance is likely to be filed. When that happens, there are several common avenues available for attempting to resolve complaints.

Personal Contact

When practitioners receive referred cases, many are reluctant to telephone colleagues when either criticism or skepticism surfaces regarding prior medical care or when it is apparent that a client is upset about that care. Still, this is often the best possible time to discover the facts, clear the air, and possibly inform colleagues of an impending problem.

Because it is human nature to be defensive of one's actions, extremely tactful communications with colleagues are essential. When calls are placed to other practitioners, no comments about the clients' attitudes should be made until after the prior veterinarians have been invited to tell their stories regarding the case. If they question the reason for the inquiry, they can be told that the client is describing previous care in a manner that raises serious doubts about accuracy. Once colleagues have had a chance to present their information, they can be informed that the client has registered dissatisfaction with their care. Criticisms about someone else's care are inappropriate at this time if the avenues for positive discussions are to be kept open.

Spending the time needed to ascertain what has transpired is worth the effort whether clients want or request it. Most clients are impressed with the thoroughness of veterinarians who seek out information regarding prior veterinary care. Other clients refuse to even state the name of the person or hospital that provided the care. The veterinarian's justification for efforts to discover medical information is because it may prevent the duplication of expensive diagnostic procedures and avoid the repetition of unsuccessful courses of therapy.

Other valuable information also may emerge. The practitioner may discover that the client's memory does not concur with the medical records and recollection of the prior veterinarian. When this happens and a more complete version of what occurred is revealed, it may change the entire medical, ethical, and legal picture in the eyes of the follow-up veterinarian.

Also, clients tend to become less critical of the actions of others and more accurate in their recollections of facts if they know their story will be verified. Finally, it may be discovered via the phone call that the client is chronically slow in making payments and, in fact, still owes considerable money. This is often a significant part of the client's unhappiness.

It may be necessary to assess a fee for the time it takes to pursue this research, but most clients are quite willing to pay for the effort in order to avoid duplication of treatments. The bonus for caring practitioners who put forth this effort is that they can be instrumental in resolving otherwise volatile situations.

If prior veterinarians are defensive, callers should reassure them that there are two altruistic reasons for the call. The first is that the best possible follow-up care can be provided with minimal duplication of services, expense, complications, or further client anger. The second reason is a matter of courtesy. Colleagues deserve to know about upset clients so that they can attempt to resolve problems before they go any further.

Traditional Ethics Committees

For many years local and state veterinary associations have appointed ethics committees to review client complaints involving violations of the association's code of ethics. The power placed in these committees to resolve grievances is limited. There are some things they can do and some things they cannot. The following is a list of some of their functions:

- They act as a sounding board, which is what many protesting clients need most.

- The presence and efforts of these

committees demonstrate to the public that local veterinary leaders are concerned with the activities of their peers.

- They act as mediators and encourage communication, negotiation, and compromise between the complaining party and the veterinarians.

- They answer questions regarding standard procedures within the veterinary industry.

And below are those functions the committees cannot perform.

- They have no jurisdiction over practitioners who are not members of the local veterinary association, unless those veterinarians volunteer to participate in the complaint review process established by the veterinary association.

- They cannot require that the veterinarian perform or refrain from any particular action.

- They cannot impose penalties other than to recommend that an association member be suspended or dismissed from the veterinary association.

- In most cases they cannot comment on the fairness of a fee charged for a veterinary service. The marketplace determines veterinarians' fees, and most local ethics committees will not accept complaints concerning excessive fees.

These limitations do not mean that the efforts of ethics committees are not worthwhile. The limits must be explained to clients at the time of their initial complaint, though.

During the past 10 years, the AVMA *Principles of Veterinary Medical Ethics* have been updated and expanded dramatically. They now provide considerably more guidance for ethics committees, although some key issues still have not been addressed.

The author's membership on an ethics committee for Contra Costa County, California, allowed for considerable first-hand experience. At that time (early 1980s), only a few complaints were brought to the committee each year. Complaint review was limited to client grievances pertaining to the assessment of fees or interpretations of the AVMA's Code of Ethics. If quality of veterinary care was a factor in a fee dispute, that topic also could be considered. No punitive actions could be levied against veterinarians other than suspensions or expulsions from the association. Clients who were relentless with their demands were provided with the address and phone number of the California Board of Examiners in Veterinary Medicine. The activities of the committee were well received by both veterinarians and clients.

In other locations, such as Broward County, Florida (Fort Lauderdale area), the local association's ethics committee is very active. From 25 to 40 grievances per year are considered by committee members, most of which are resolved with a telephone call opening up avenues of communication between the client and the veterinarian.[6] The ethics committee in Broward County is comprised of the past president, president, and secretary of the county veterinary association. This committee reviews client protests dealing with interpretations of the AVMA Code of Ethics, the Florida State Veterinary Practice Act, negligence, fraud, incompetence and almost anything relating to the practice of veterinary medicine. The local association reviews all cases first and refers to the state association for advice as needed. Although it is called an ethics committee, it follows many of the guidelines established in the peer review process.

Veterinary associations and ethics committees vary greatly from state to state and from one local association to another. Many local associations have neither ethics nor peer review committees. The total unavailability or exorbitant costs associated with veterinary association liability insurance has placed a damper on committee activities of this type in recent years. In Broward County, Florida, however, the association decided that the benefits of maintaining an active ethics committee exceeded the risks of a lawsuit by such a large margin that the committee has been maintained without insurance coverage. When committee members feel that their review of a case exposes the association or themselves to liability, they inform the complainant of their inability to accept the case and refer the case to the state association. If caution and common sense are exercised, the risks of lawsuits are minimal. Thus, this factor alone should not keep associations from recognizing the benefits of an ethics committee.

The time required to be an active participant on a committee of this type can be considerable. Because of the immense opportunity to learn from others' mistakes, however, participation on such a committee can be an excellent service activity for young practitioners.

Efforts at self-regulation within the veterinary profession are beneficial to maintaining its integrity and reputation. This form of control is viewed by most leaders in the profession to be far superior to regulation from governmental agencies. Legislative activity dealing with potential liability problems should be pursued so that these committees and the following ones can be maintained.

Peer Review Committees

"It is essential not only that justice be done: it must be perceived to have been done."[7] That is the opening sentence in the preface of the AVMA's *Peer Review Procedure Manual*.

In the early 1980s, with examples from other healing arts professions, the wheels were put in motion to establish peer review committees within every local veterinary association in the United States. On July 13, 1983 the AVMA House of Delegates adopted the Policy Statements and Guidelines prepared by the AVMA's Council on Veterinary Services.

As the process of forming peer review committees was getting under way, the liability insurance crisis hit. This predicament has had dramatic financial impact on cities, boards of directors of corporations, officers, directors and committees of nonprofit professional associations, and many other organizations. The evolution of peer review has been dramatically retarded by concerns of liability and, with it, one of this profession's most sincere efforts at self-regulation.

In time, state legislatures probably will develop statutes exempting members of peer review committees from liability for their activities and decisions associated with the peer review process. Until the legal, legislative, and insurance worlds resolve the issue of liability, it is expected that the development of the peer review process will continue to be retarded. A brief discussion of this complaint-resolving mechanism is still in order, however, because within a few years it may be reactivated. In the meantime, the guidelines set forth in the AVMA *Peer Review Procedure Manual* can be followed by any associations with committees or individuals involved in any of the complaint-resolution processes.

The AVMA manual establishes a step-by-step method for mediating differences between clients and veterinarians and between veterinarians. The services of the committee can be requested by clients, or by veterinarians who are trying to reconcile complaints with clients. It provides a credible system for effectively and expeditiously resolving disagreements without involving attorneys, courts, administrative hearings, the state board of examiners, and many other components of a formal hearing.

These committees are empowered by the guidelines set forth in individual associations to review various types of matters. Among these are:

- appropriateness of care—including the professional acceptability of planned or completed diagnostic procedures and treatments.
- quality of treatment—This includes an evaluation of the skill with which treatments were provided as determined by the standards that generally prevail within the profession.
- fees—This includes whether the fee in question was the veterinarian's usual

fee for a given procedure. If it appears that the fee was unusual, the committee can then determine whether the fee is reasonable considering the degree of difficulty or complexity of the case.

Committees should be comprised of licensed veterinarians representing a cross section of the profession in age, species expertise, and experience. Well-respected nonveterinarians also should be appointed. When a specialist is the subject of a complaint, specialists should be included on the committee.

All grievances within the geographic boundaries of the association should be referred to the chairperson of the committee. When phone calls to appropriate parties can possibly resolve complaints, they should be attempted first. Simply listening to the aggrieved party's story and agreeing that something should be done or explaining that normal standards of practice have been met often helps resolve the dispute.

To initiate the review process, complainants must submit a written request explaining the circumstances of the grievance. Supporting records, pertinent information, and specific questions should be included. This requirement alone tends to reduce the numbers of requests for review. Written requests are critical because, without them, the problem may be too vague to evaluate.

Upon receipt of the written request, the chairman appoints one committee member as a mediator. If the complaint is resolved, the mediator submits a written report to the chairperson, and the case is closed.[7] Complaints not resolved through the mediation process are heard by the full committee. Mediators present their reports to committees and then leave. Each party to the grievance is then interviewed separately by the committee. Since peer review proceedings are aimed at mediation and conciliation, the participation of attorneys is discouraged. When enough information has been presented to satisfy the committee, a closed-session discussion occurs, and a report is written. Clients and veterinarians are informed of the decision via letter.

The panel's action, for example, might be rejection of the complaint and full defense of the veterinarian, a recommendation to the executive committee of the local association that the member be expelled from the association, a recommendation that the veterinarian attend continuing education seminars on a particular subject, or a recommendation that some form of adjustment occur regarding the fees charged. If evidence of illegal activity, incompetence, or malpractice surfaces, the complaint can be referred to the state board for investigation and disciplinary action. If either party wishes to appeal the findings, they may request that the state veterinary association peer review committee hear the case.

The materials presented here are a brief summary of the peer review guidelines. Many sample letters and report forms are included in the AVMA materials along with considerable information regarding documentation of the efforts to mediate these disputes. The procedures in the manual are easy to follow and, if adhered to closely, will stand up well to legal challenge.

Two major obstacles have prevented the widespread use of the peer review process. One is the concern of committee members about personal liability for their decisions. Although some risk is present in veterinary medicine, it is not nearly as great as the risk that physicians take, in that their privileges to practice at a particular hospital can be revoked by a peer review committee. This type of action is tantamount to depriving a physician of his or her livelihood. Because nearly all veterinarians work at privately owned hospitals, though, the likelihood of a peer review decision causing any major financial detriment to a veterinarian is not a significant concern.

The second obstacle is a more serious one for veterinary medicine. This concerns whether or not the minutes and findings of the peer review committee are protected from discovery by a plaintiff in an action for negligence or malpractice based on the same facts. If no state law protects these records from discovery, clients could wait until a peer review committee reaches a decision about their complaint and then request a copy of that decision to support a finding of negligence in a civil action.

In 1985 the Supreme Court of Missouri held that no privilege existed to protect information gathered by a peer review committee from discovery. The defendant argued that the protection of the peer review committee report from discovery was essential to ensure that the peer review system would be productive. However, the court found that public policy for allowing discovery outweighed the defendant's interest. The court's rationale was that the purpose of peer review is to evaluate the quality of medical care for the benefit of the public and those committed to the care of animals. While the majority of jurisdictions afford peer review records a qualified immunity from discovery, this case demonstrates that courts may balance the competing interests involved.[8] Until the issues of liability and discovery have been clarified by each state, it appears that the development of the peer review process will be stymied.

Peer review is not a court of law, it is not an adversary proceeding, and it is not a punitive expedition. At its best, it works to educate, adjudicate, clarify, and rectify when necessary. Most important, it demonstrates to the public the profession's commitment to quality care and the orderly and inexpensive resolution of complaints. Leaders of this profession should pursue legislatively the immunity needed to make this process a viable way to solve disputes. Once this hurdle has been overcome, constituent associations must be encouraged to create peer review committees and educate members regarding its use.

State Boards of Examiners Review

According to one source who has recently served on the California Board of Examiners in Veterinary Medicine, "A major problem confronting the veterinary profession in

California today is veterinary consumer complaints."[9] Whether this problem affects all of the states as dramatically as it has a consumer-oriented state like California is not readily known.

Procedural differences certainly exist in the way various state boards of examiners review complaints. There are also similarities, though. For the sake of brevity, the procedures used by the California Board will be the primary ones discussed herein.

The types of complaints handled by the California Board's review process generally involve issues like fraud, deception, negligence, incompetence, fraudulent advertising, and drug and alcohol abuse. Consumer complaints regarding fees are not subject to board review. They are referred to local association ethics and peer review committees.

Similar to the peer review process, consumers who wish to lodge complaints must do so in writing, explaining in detail the nature of the complaint. After the complaint is reviewed by the Board's executive director and determined to be within the Board's jurisdiction, the veterinarian is asked to submit medical records, radiographs, and a summary of the case. When applicable, consulting veterinarians are also asked to submit case summaries and medical records. The owner's complaint, the veterinarian's response, and all medical records are then sent to the Complaint Review Committee, comprised of two people from the southern part of the state and two from the north. In order to minimize the chances of conflicts of interest, all complaints from the southern half of the state are reviewed by the committee members from the north and vice versa.

Committee members are experienced, dedicated volunteers who review the cases before any of the Board members do and recommend one of the following courses of action:

- Close the case—They may close the case if it is without merit.

- Seek additional information—Committee members may ask for additional information from the veterinarian, the

consumer, a specialist, or any other appropriate source before making a decision.

- Recommend admonishment—If the complaint has some merit but is not serious enough for the board to pursue legal action against the veterinarian, they can request that a letter of admonishment be sent. This letter may include specific suggestions for improvements in medical, office, or communication procedures.

- Request investigation—If the complaint is determined to be serious, they may recommend that a formal investigation be undertaken by the Board.

- Recommend a citation and fine—Under newly passed legislation and regulations, the Board can issue citations and assess fines for violations of the Practice Act. This remedy may be utilized in cases in which veterinary misconduct is serious enough to merit a penalty but not serious enough to merit a full administrative hearing for license suspension or revocation (see Chapter 3).

If the two members who were assigned to review the case cannot agree, the complaint is reviewed by a third member of the committee. Once a majority of committee members are in agreement, the case and the committee's recommendations are returned to the executive director. If the complaint review committee decides admonishment or dismissal of the case is in order, the executive director implements that recommendation.

If a decision is made to investigate the complaint, the case is referred to the California Department of Investigation and assigned to a special investigator. Investigators interview the consumers lodging the complaint, the doctors involved, and other appropriate parties.

After evaluating the data, the California Department of Investigation recommends a course of action to the executive director of the Board. If legal action is to be pursued, the case is referred to the California Attorney

General's Office. If no settlement occurs, a court trial is held with an administrative law judge presiding. There is no jury at these hearings.

Administrative law judges who find practitioners guilty of alleged charges submit their recommendations for appropriate disciplinary action to the full Board. Members of the Board may vote to accept, reject, or modify the administrative law judge's recommendation. Board members have no knowledge of the complaint and are uninvolved in the complaint review process prior to this stage of the procedure.

A helpful review of the legal principles that have led to this procedural course of action in California is provided by Dr. Joseph Marasco in a *California Veterinarian* article:

> The legal argument put forth by the Attorney General's Office supporting this dilemma involves the legal principle of maintaining "impartiality," which means that if Board members have prior knowledge of a consumer complaint before the case goes to court, the opposing attorney representing the veterinarian can legally charge the Board members with being biased. This would "handcuff" the Board and force all of the members to disqualify themselves from participating in the final decision. Since only a small percentage of cases go to trial, this legal principle excludes the Board from becoming directly involved in approximately 98% of all consumer complaints.[9]

In some states, board members are involved in reviewing consumer complaints against veterinarians as well as investigating the cases, hearing evidence, arriving at judgments and deciding penalties.[10] Until the early 1980s this was also the case in California; however, when major due process arguments were raised with this "system of justice," California altered its procedures.

The state of Virginia recognized the potential for a legal challenge and in 1986 changed its complaint review process from one of total review by the Board to one more like that in California. Written complaints against

veterinarians are received now by a central investigative arm representing many licensing boards and assigned to an investigator. After the investigation, a report is submitted to the executive director of the Board and the case is assigned to two Board members for review. These Board members have the option of dismissing the case, reprimanding the veterinarian, determining some form of punishment if they feel it is needed, or pursuing the case through an informal or formal administrative hearing process.

One of the biggest legal concerns regarding bias is the involvement of the same arm of the veterinary licensing system in investigating, hearing, deciding, and sentencing for individual cases. Whether or not partiality exists, boards are vulnerable to attack. Inferior fact-finding procedures predispose them to errant decisions in their subsequent role as judge and jury. Complicating matters are decisions involving:

- evidence—Which will be heard and which will be voluntarily or involuntarily excluded?
- forms of evidence—What will be allowed, e.g., direct evidence, hearsay evidence, circumstantial evidence?
- importance—How much weight will be given to each form of evidence?
- quantity—Is there enough evidence to decide a case?

It appears to be only a matter of time until changes are made to include a separate investigatory arm for all veterinary complaint review procedures in the hearing processes in other states.

Courts of Law

The final forum for resolution of client grievances is the court of law. Some clients elect to start in a courtroom. This should be the last resort. The legal procedures associated with this form of complaint resolution are documented in Chapter 1.

In some cases, the only reasonable solution to a client-veterinarian dispute is to allow the judicial system to decide who is right and who is wrong. Legal proceedings are generally excellent fact-finding missions. The major difficulties are the costs incurred for legal counsel, the lost work time, the emotional drain on the parties involved, and the delays incurred in resolving the dispute. The courts should be reserved for cases involving significant legal or financial consequences.

References

1. Marasco JV: A second look: The stealth bomber syndrome (the case of the invisible doctor). *Calif Vet* (March/April):39-40, 1985.
2. Marasco JV: Rediscovering history. *Calif Vet* (July/Aug):64-65, 1985.
3. Hill G: Personal communication, California Board of Examiners in Veterinary Medicine, 1987.
4. Nerghberg H, Fisher E: *Pet Loss—A Thoughtful Guide for Adults and Children*. New York, Harper & Row, 1982.
5. Professional relations with new clients. A *VMA Principles of Veterinary Medical Ethics*. Schaumberg, IL, American Veterinary Medical Assoc, p 6, 1987.
6. Bellows JE, Dee JD: Personal communication, Broward County Ethics Committee, 1987.
7. *1987 AVMA Directory*. Schaumberg, IL, American Veterinary Medical Assoc, pp 471, 475.
8. Shemonsky NK: Missouri Supreme Court holds peer review committee records are discoverable. *Legal Aspects Med Pract* 13(10):6-7, 1985.
9. Marasco JV: A second look...the consumer complaint review process. *Calif Vet* (Jan/Feb):21-22, 1985.
10. Mewshaw J: Personal communication, Maryland State Board of Veterinary Medical Examiners, 1987.

CHAPTER 6

Professional Liability

In a time when million dollar liabilities involving medical malpractice, auto accidents, and consumer products are prevalent, the veterinary profession has managed to avoid such litigious awards. Veterinarians thus have been spared the high cost of professional liability insurance and, with it, the continuous need to practice defensive medicine. In large part such liability has been spared the profession because animals are treated as personal property and, as such, they have no legal rights and possess finite economic value. Also, under current legal doctrines, major financial recoveries for losses of animals have been limited.

Times are changing, though, and a handful of recent precedent-changing legal cases indicate that the courts are willing to expand the law's recognition of damages relating to the injury or loss of animals. If this trend continues, the boundaries of a veterinarian's professional liability may well be extended.

Numerous areas of veterinary professional wrongdoing and potential liability are discussed in other chapters of this book. This chapter focuses on the most common causes of action experienced in tort law: negligence, malpractice, libel, slander, wrongful discharge of employees, false imprisonment, and assault.

The Magnitude of the Professional Liability Problem

The AVMA Professional Liability Insurance Trust insures 65 to 70% of the practicing veterinarians in the United States. In an attempt to analyze various risks and allocate them properly among the different types of veterinary practices, the Trust has been maintaining claims statistics since 1976. During this time, the following trends have emerged: (1) The greatest share of liability lies in the area of equine practice, with mixed-animal practices next, (2) costs for legal fees have been mounting rapidly, to the point that with some species they nearly equal the costs for claims paid, and (3) claims for human injuries comprise a significant portion of all claims paid under the Trust program.[1]

Between 1976 and 1985, 16% of the Trust's claims were paid for injuries involving humans. This amounted to a total of $1,636,768, of which 70% or $1,156,107, could be directly attributed to injuries caused by horses. Cats, dogs, and cattle were a distant second, third, and fourth, respectively, as sources of claims for human injuries.

The other 84% of the Trust's expenses for claims were related to claims for clients' animals. Statistics covering animal losses are available from 1976 through 1986. During that time, the Trust paid out $9,044,819 for losses involving animals and an additional $4,528,256 in legal fees to settle or defend those cases, for a total of $13,573,075. Other insurance companies also provide professional liability insurance but have not published any data regarding their insurance claims experience.

The following breakdown has been provided by the AVMA Professional Liability Insurance Trust for the 1976 to 1986 time period in order to help practitioners ascertain risks according to species:

1. Horses—claims, $4,586,457; legal fees, $2,209,316; total $6,795,773

2. Cattle—claims, $2,356,348; legal fees, $906,914; total $3,263,262

3. Dogs—claims, $993,277; legal fees, $886,906; total $1,880,183

4. Cats—claims, $312,161; legal fees, $155,473; total $467,634

5. Swine—claims, $325,474; legal fees, $97,087; total $422,561

6. Sheep—claims, $138,473; legal fees, $7,346; total $145,819

7. Other—claims, $332,629; legal fees, $265,214; total $597,843.[2] Valuable cage birds are increasingly a source of liability and are grouped in the "other" category.

As seen in this statistical report, the dollar value of claims in large animal practice is approximately double the cost for legal counsel, whereas in small animal practice, costs for claims paid and legal expenses are almost equal. This represents the disparity between the market values of horses and food animals and that of companion animals, as well as the fact that claims in large animal medicine sometimes involve entire herds or flocks rather than individual animals, as in the companion animal area.

The Law of Negligence and Malpractice

Of all the types of legal actions in tort law, practitioners are most likely to incur some degree of professional liability from the law of negligence. The law of malpractice is an extension of the law of negligence. Thus to understand the risks involved under the malpractice laws, a thorough knowledge of negligence law is necessary.

Under current law, a veterinarian's greatest risk for liability involves an injury to a client. Such a personal injury usually falls under the basic law of negligence. Most cases involving veterinary professional liability originate under the law of malpractice, though, and result from injuries, deaths, or escape of clients' animals.

In either case, to maintain the veterinary profession's integrity and to minimize the high costs associated with practicing defensive medicine, practitioners must learn to avoid malpractice suits. (See the discussion on minimizing complaints and settling disputes, Chapter 5.) Many veterinary clients cannot afford and are not willing to pay the high costs of defensive medicine. Therefore, a veterinary malpractice crisis of the magnitude in human medicine would be a crisis for the future of the veterinary profession itself.

Negligence Defined

Black's Law Dictionary defines negligence as the doing of some act that a person of ordinary prudence would not have done under similar circumstances or the failure to do what a person of ordinary prudence would have done under the same or similar circumstances.[3]

The legal system imposes a duty on all people to act carefully, so as not to create unreasonable risks of danger to others. Some conduct can be classified as negligent even if a person is anxiously concerned for the safety of others. A person's state of mind is material only in determining whether his or her conduct was reasonable in light of what he or she knew. However, whether the person's actions were truly reasonable will be judged by a jury and not by what the person believed at the time that the act was performed.

If a defendant's conduct did not pose an unreasonable threat of harm to a plaintiff, the defendant is not negligent, even if he or she intended to act in total disregard for the safety of the plaintiff. The test applied in negligence cases is to determine if other reasonable people would conclude that the defendant acted unreasonably.

If an accident occurs despite the exercise of due care, the issue of negligence is not involved. For example, a driver who loses control of a car because of a blowout in a defective tire may have caused an accident but will not be found to be negligent if he did not know about the defective tire. However, a driver who has an accident and knew that the car had a badly worn tire would be liable for negligence.

Relating the Law of Contracts, Negligence, and Malpractice

The law of negligence pertains to the way people run their personal lives and the way that professionals run their businesses, while the law of malpractice applies only to the way that professionals practice their profession. Since it is through the formation of contracts that veterinarians generally begin the medical care of their patients, an understanding of contract law also is required to better understand the law of malpractice.

Chapter 8 discusses contract law, including the importance of preliminary discussions and estimates in establishing the terms of the contract for veterinary care. Because much of the law of malpractice relates closely to the contract for veterinary services agreed upon, practitioners are urged to review contract law principles in conjunction with information regarding malpractice.

The law of negligence applies as soon as a client or any invitee walks onto the premises of a veterinary practice. The law of malpractice generally applies only after the client and the veterinarian have entered into a contractual relationship for the care of an animal. Exceptions to these situations include the rendering of emergency care, when there is inadequate time to make a contract, or while owners are assisting with the restraint of their animals before an agreement for treatment is reached.

The Elements of a Cause of Action for Negligence

The law of negligence requires proof of four essential elements:

* establishing that the defendant had a duty to prevent an injury from occurring to the plaintiff or the plaintiff's property

* establishing that the defendant violated that duty by failing to act in accordance with the standard of care expected of other veterinarians under the same or similar circumstances

* showing that a reasonably close causal connection existed between the defendant veterinarian's conduct or lack of conduct and the resulting injury. This is known as the *doctrine of proximate cause.*

- proving that actual damage or harm occurred to the interests of another person

Duty

The law of negligence places a duty on all individuals at all times to exercise reasonable care for the physical safety of other people and for their property. Differences can occur regarding the extent of that duty depending upon whether the case is based upon negligence or malpractice. The broad concept of a person's duty is limited according to whether the party's conduct creates a foreseeable risk of harm to others. However, whether a person has any legal duty toward an injured party in the first place is a question of law to be decided by the court and not by the jury.

Under malpractice law, the duty placed on veterinarians is to practice medicine in a manner that meets the standards expected in the profession. In negligence law, the duty is to maintain one's premises in a manner that reasonable people would expect would prevent injuries from occurring to people entering upon those premises.

It is easier to prove the presence of a duty in malpractice cases, because whenever veterinarians enter into agreements to treat patients, the law implies that they have a duty to provide care equal to that extended to similar cases by other practitioners within the profession. The duty requirement is slightly different in negligence cases, in which clients or invitees may be filing personal injury lawsuits. In these cases, for example, if a person is bitten or scratched by an animal in a reception room or someone slips on urine in a hallway, the duty is a general one that applies to the public at large rather than to a particular client or patient.

Whether a person who fails to assist another person in need can be held liable for an injury suffered by that person depends upon the relationship that exists between the parties. For example, under the law of malpractice, veterinarians who see injured animals lying on highways (or who are presented with injured animals to treat at their places of business) and who have no preexisting relationship with the animal's owner are not required to help those animals. However, when there is a preexisting veterinarian-client-patient relationship that might lead the animal owner to reasonably expect some aid, there can be a duty to provide medical care.

Preexisting relationships also can impose duties to act under the law of negligence. Examples include the duties of automobile drivers to assist their passengers, employers to assist their employees, and hosts to aid their guests.

Courts hold that people who voluntarily provide assistance to injured parties must act reasonably, and cannot escape responsibility by relinquishing the duty that was assumed when the aid was initiated. Therefore, people cannot begin to help accident victims and then suddenly leave them unattended. Liability also is imposed if people increase injured peoples' dangers, mislead them by creating a false sense of security, or deprive them of possible assistance from others. Conversely, people who elect not to assist other people in need of help are not liable for their failure to provide assistance.[4]

The Veterinarian's Duty to Provide Emergency Care

The subject of emergency care has long been of great interest to medical professionals, attorneys, sociologists, and philosophers. Although a refusal to provide emergency veterinary care may cause considerable moral indignation and bad public relations, there currently is no legal duty in the United States for veterinarians in private practice to provide emergency care to animals.[5] Veterinarians employed by the government, however, often have a contract with their employing agency to perform certain services for the public. In these cases, the agencies they work for can set the rules and policies for their public service.

In the only veterinary case wherein a private practitioner's duty to provide emergency care has been subjected to judicial review, the court sidestepped the issue. In that case, the court held that there was insufficient evidence to prove that the veterinarian had refused to serve the client or that the veterinarian did not allow his employees to examine or treat a kitten in need of emergency care.[6]

A caveat to consider, though, concerns veterinarians' duties to continue providing medical care for patients already under their supervision. Once clients are accepted and a contract to render veterinary care has been made, there is an implication that the veterinarian will continue to render service until (1) the animal recovers from its illness or injury, (2) the veterinarian has completed all of the care contracted for, (3) the animal dies, or (4) the client terminates the contract.[5] A veterinarian's right to terminate a contract for medical care is limited more than a client's right. Clients need not accept professional services from anyone, and they may dismiss themselves as patients or clients, but health professionals must continue service until the treatment has been completed or until the care can be terminated without injury to clients or their animals.

Practitioners who do not comply with their agreements to provide medical care can be held liable for abandoning their patients. Under standard legal principles, professionals who wish to discontinue medical services should not do so during any critical phase of the patient's care and must give clients sufficient time to find another veterinarian so that no harm occurs to the animal. (See Chapter 14 for language that can be used to terminate a veterinarian's responsibility for ongoing care.)

Once a contract for medical care is terminated by the veterinarian's completion of the agreed-upon treatment, by the patient's death or recovery, or by the client, the owner is no longer legally a client. Thus, if veterinarians want to pursue or clients request additional routine or emergency treatment for their animal(s), a new contract must be created. In such cases there is no legal duty to provide future emergency care for problems unrelated to past treatments just because a client's animal has been a previous patient. Issues like this always involve professional judgment, and if questions arise, a veterinarian's conduct will be compared with that of other veterinarians in similar circumstances.

Limiting Duties Through the Passage of Good Samaritan Acts

The potential liability for allegedly causing harm while voluntarily assisting at the scene of an accident has increased the reluctance of many medical professionals to stop and help injured people. In order to minimize the liability associated with these voluntary acts of assistance where no duty to provide such help existed, many states have adopted good samaritan acts. Under these laws, people coming to the aid of others are not held liable for any injuries that occur to the victims unless gross negligence is proved. Many states also have good samaritan acts that apply to veterinarians and animal health technicians who assist injured animals (see Chapter 3).

The Standard of Care

The second essential element to prove in negligence cases is the defendant's failure to act in accordance with the required standard of care.

The Standard Under Negligence Law

Although there is no universal standard, most states require that veterinarians provide a standard of care equal to that provided by other business owners and other veterinary practice owners. This requires that practitioners keep their facilities free of hazards that could cause injury to anyone entering those premises. It means that there is a duty to foresee and eliminate icy sidewalks, faulty parking lots, puddles of urine, and unrestrained animals. It also means keeping doors, windows, and gates secured to prevent the escape of any animals on the premises. Because of the risks of escape, veterinary proprietors must be constantly concerned about entrances left open by clients, employees, and delivery people.

The Standard Under Malpractice

Under malpractice law, the standard of care requires veterinarians to "exercise the care and diligence as is ordinarily exercised by skilled veterinarians."[7] This is the realm of the *reasonable man* theory; the basis of the law of negligence and malpractice.

This standard is not intended to make veterinarians guarantors of the recovery of their patients, provided they do not offer such assurances to clients. Similarly, veterinarians are not presumed negligent if injuries or deaths occur during or after treatment. It does not mean that practitioners must conform to the highest standard of skill nor use extraordinary diligence. It also does not mean that one's surgical technique or treatment cannot vary from that provided by average veterinarians, so long as it is not unreasonably or blatantly inferior or outdated. The law says that reasonable practitioners, not the best or the most highly skilled professionals, set the standard.[8] Of course, defining the word *reasonable* can sometimes be a difficult matter requiring the testimony of one or more expert witnesses.

The Similar Locality Rule

The results of the reasonable veterinarian principle can vary depending upon the group of veterinary peers with which a defendant is compared. In past years, when dissemination of information was much slower and more limited, professional people usually were judged by the actions of other professionals in their own locale or in a similar locale.

Today's extraordinary supply of books, journals, audio and video tapes, and continuing education seminars makes application of the locale rule by a court less likely. Courts also are reluctant to apply the locale rule because it is often difficult to convince local veterinarians to testify against colleagues whom they know personally. If the locality rule is applied, only local veterinarians qualify as expert witnesses, and legal actions can fail because of an inability to find willing experts. Therefore, most jurisdictions currently use a standard of care applicable to professionals generally, rather than applying the traditional locality rule. Variations do exist, however, and the law of each state will control this issue.

According to Favre and Loring's *Animal Law* book,[8] Utah and Louisiana have qualified their standard with the phrase "in the community,"[9] North Carolina has taken a middle ground with the phrase "similarly situated,"[10] and Iowa has rejected the "in the community" rule in favor of a very general standard.[11] Much of the legal literature indicates that the locality rule is obsolete and generally inapplicable to negligence cases. Cases involving physicians in Montana and Upper Michigan, however, indicate that the courts have subscribed to the premise that the locality rule is still alive.[12]

Notably, all of the cases cited herein supporting some form of the locality rule were decided prior to 1981. Today's courts may be unwilling to continue to support those precedents. When questions about the locality rule arise and no veterinary medical cases exist to establish a precedent, it is reasonable to expect that whatever rule the jurisdiction currently employs for medical malpractice also will be applied to cases involving veterinary malpractice.

Omissions and Commissions

When the standard of care for malpractice cases is applied, the omission of a medically indicated diagnostic procedure or treatment may be just as serious as the commission of an act that produces an adverse and undesired result. The following omissions are examples of grounds for malpractice suits:

- the failure to do a simple dip stick urinalysis or blood glucose on a polydipsic, polyuric dog that dies within a few hours because therapy for diabetes was not initiated

- the failure to use a cardiac monitor when high-anesthetic-risk animals are anesthetized

- the failure to institute massive intravenous fluid therapy and administer corticosteroids and/or blood transfusions to treat patients in hypovolemic or endotoxic shock

- the failure to do vaginal cultures and sensitivities on a herd of cattle experiencing abortions

- the failure to adequately identify animals being examined for health certificates, note the identities on the health certificate, and assure that the transporter of the animals accepts custody of those animals

Each of these easily could be considered an omission that constitutes a failure to meet the accepted standard of care.

A healthy fear of omitting an important medical procedure improves the practice of medicine but also drives up the costs for medical care if too much is done. Questions regarding how much is enough are critical as the legal system ponders veterinarians' omissions, because veterinary medicine is affected so greatly by clients' economic concerns and options to euthanatize their animals. Practitioners' decisions in this area always will be questions of fact for juries to determine.

Considerable expert testimony often is required to determine what constitutes a sufficient cross section of diagnostic tests to assure that practitioners did not miss uncommon or obscure diagnoses or complications. This is one of the greatest areas of disagreement in malpractice cases and the area where the views and competence of experts are critically important in helping juries reach decisions.

Omissions also can occur in the realm of negligence. Some examples include:

- a failure to muzzle a dog after owners have informed the veterinarian that they are afraid the animal might bite (and an owner is bitten while assisting the practitioner in restraining the patient),

- the failure to insist that all animals brought into a hospital be properly restrained (with the resultant injury to a frail client who is knocked down and seriously injured by a golden retriever running loose in the reception area), and

- the failure to properly label and package potentially harmful drugs dispensed to clients for their animal's use (and the subsequent fatal ingestion of the drug by a child in the family).

Expert testimony also is required in negligence cases to prove a veterinarian's compliance or noncompliance with the standard of care. Since these cases involve injuries to the person, they are the type most likely to provoke lawsuits and result in major financial settlements. Some commissions are so blatantly presumptive of negligence that a special doctrine called *res ipsa loquitur* has been formulated to deal with them.

Generally it is easier to prove medical malpractice with commissions of medically improper treatments than with omissions. Omissions, however, occur more frequently than commissions. Common examples of medical acts that could be considered to be commissions include:

- administering the right dosage of an incorrect drug or the wrong dosage of the correct drug,

- performing surgery on the wrong limb or patient,

- applying a bandage or splint in a manner that impairs circulation and necessitates the amputation of a limb,

- leaving a sponge or instrument inside a patient's body cavity,

- performing a rectal examination on a horse and tearing the rectum or colon during the examination, and failing to advise the owner of the injury,

- placing an anesthetized or debilitated animal on an inexpensive nonmedical-quality electric heating pad and causing severe burns to the animal.[13]

Some examples of commissions involving negligence include the following:

- attempting to administer an injection to an animal but accidentally injecting the animal's owner while that person is restraining the patient, and

- disposing of the body of an animal that had shown bizarre neurological signs symptomatic of rabies without advising an owner who had been bitten by the animal of the need to test the animal for the presence of rabies.

Continuing Education and the Standard of Care

The failure to continue one's education is another example of a failure to meet the standard of care. Prompted by society's concerns and recognition of the rapid advances in scientific knowledge, many states have adopted legislation that requires 5 to 20 hours of continuing education each year in order for professionals to renew their licenses. Thus, the failure of practitioners to continue their education can easily support a finding that they were negligent before they even began treating a patient.

A recent law review article examines applicable legal cases to further support the contention that in the human health care field, hospitals and physicians are expected to stay abreast with advances in medicine. The article says,

> ...it is unquestionable that a hospital that permits staff members to practice when they have failed to stay abreast of recent developments in the fields in which they treat patients, will likely become involved and liable if a patient suffers harm attributable to that fact.[14]

The Changing Standard of Care

As new technological and scientific breakthroughs occur in veterinary medicine, the standard of care changes. Therefore, the standard of five years ago often will not be the accepted standard for today's "reasonable veterinarian." This is especially true regarding advances in diagnostic testing procedures.

An example is found in the changing standard for the diagnosis of Addison's disease (hypoadrenocorticism) in dogs. For years the basis for diagnosing this life-threatening malady depended primarily upon the animal's symptoms, an elevated BUN, a radiographically smaller-than-normal heart shadow, and a high blood potassium. No significant changes in diagnostic methodology appeared in veterinary textbooks between the 1980 edition of *Current Veterinary Therapy VII*[15] and *Current Veterinary Therapy VIII* (1983).[15]

During this time period, though, advances were being reported in journals regarding radioimmunoassay techniques for measuring body hormones. By 1986, veterinary textbooks had caught up with these changing times, and the section on Addison's disease in *Current Veterinary Therapy IX* said, "Definitive diagnosis of hypoadrenocorticism requires the demonstration of inadequate cortisol response to exogenous ACTH."[15] Even though the symptoms previously discussed are still important clues, the entire diagnosis portion of that section discusses only the use of ACTH stimulation tests to diagnose this disease. Thus, sometime during the mid 1980s, the diagnostic standard of care for Addison's disease underwent a significant change. The point at which such changes are applied to general practitioners always will be a question of fact for juries to decide based upon expert testimony.

An example of a currently changing standard of care involves the development of transtelephonic electrocardiography. For a modest initial expenditure and a reasonable fee per telephone transmission, practitioners can readily offer this diagnostic service to their clients.[16] This means that general practitioners no longer need attempt to accurately interpret an occasional ECG when a telephone consultation with a cardiologist who has read the ECG is available, often within minutes.

In a related development, the sudden death of 1984 Kentucky Derby and Belmont Stakes winner Swale has resulted in a new focus on equine cardiac disease. Journal publications have begun to recognize the fatal syndromes known as exercise-induced pulmonary hemorrhage and exercise-associated ventricular fibrillation.[17] With advances in equine electrocardiography, serious ventricular arrhythmias that can result in poor performance and even sudden death may be detected. Auscultation of heart sounds alone usually will not allow equine practitioners to detect the cardiac abnormalities associated with this syndrome.

In the past it has been impractical to run ECGs at the side of the racetrack or at a stable. But there is now an affordable, portable, solid-state ECG transmitter-recorder which allows veterinarians to record a horse's ECG anywhere (for example, on the track or in the stall) and transmit it over the telephone at a later time.[18] Arrhythmias that develop with moderate or maximal exercise can be recorded at the track or work location using this unit and interpreted later with the assistance of telephonic transmissions and consultations.

In general, standards of care change as basic research leads to the diagnoses of previously unrecognized medical problems, e.g., exercise-induced pulmonary hemorrhage. Continuing education seminars and journal publications apprise practitioners of the condition's existence.[15] Next, a new diagnostic test or piece of diagnostic equipment is produced and marketed.[16] Finally, various segments of the veterinary industry apply the new system or the new information.

In the equine mortality insurance business, for example, the Rhulen Insurance Agency of New York was the first insurance company to see the need to have better control over the sudden death risk of insured horses. In January 1987, this agency requested that ECGs be performed prior to insuring valued horses for mortality insurance policies. Within a few more years, this new technology could well be standard in the entire insurance and equine industry.

Standards Expected of Specialists

The standard of care for veterinary practitioners can vary significantly depending upon whether the defendant is a generalist or a specialist. The *1987 AVMA Directory* lists at least 35 different veterinary medical specialties, some focusing on medical disciplines and others relating to different animal species. Specialty groups based upon medical disciplines include veterinary allergy, cardiology, dermatology, immunology, internal medicine, ophthalmology, pathology, radiology, surgery, and many more. The specialty associations related to species include veterinarians whose primary interests focus on cattle, cats, horses, sheep, goats, swine, avian species, exotic and zoo animals, and laboratory animals.

Although general practitioners can belong to many of these associations at will, membership in others is restricted to an elite group of veterinarians who have passed a board-certification examination. These practitioners are referred to as *board-certified specialists*, and they usually restrict their professional activity to that aspect of practice in which they are boarded.

When the standard of care for cases involving alleged veterinary malpractice is being assessed, general practitioners usually are compared with generalists, and specialists are compared with similar specialists. However, a further breakdown in terminology regarding the word *specialist* should be noted. This is because some generalists have special interests in particular aspects of veterinary medicine but are not board certified therein. Depending upon their training and experience, the competence of these veterinarians may be equal to, higher, or lower than that of board-certified specialists.

General practitioners can be considered specialists even if they are not board certified if their practices have developed along particular lines. This is especially true when they let it be known that they consider themselves to be specialists and represent themselves to the public as specialists. All of these factors are important, because practitioners who are considered by the courts to be specialists will be held to a higher standard of care than that of the general practitioner.[19]

Considerable expert witness testimony may be needed to determine which standard of care defendant veterinarians are required to meet. Additional inquiries may be required to evaluate factors such as the proximity of other specialists with similar abilities and the willingness of general practitioners with special interests to offer and accept referrals.

Another standard of care problem can occur when a generalist undertakes a difficult procedure normally performed by a specialist. For example, a small animal practitioner named Dr. A elects to perform a laminectomy on a dachshund with rear leg paralysis. The extent of Dr. A's training involves attendance at a continuing education seminar presented by a well-known veterinary surgeon where this procedure was described with the use of slides and video tape. Dr. A has performed three similar surgeries in the two years since he attended this seminar. In order to keep costs low, he does not perform myelograms before surgery, relying instead on high-quality noncontrast radiographs. Of his three patients, two have experienced considerable improvement, and one remained paralyzed.

In a city 20 miles away, Dr. B, a board-certified veterinary surgeon, is part of a specialty group practice. She has completed a residency program, has passed her surgery boards, and has practiced at this location for five years. She routinely performs myelograms before doing laminectomies to ensure that she has an accurate diagnosis and is operating on the correct intervertebral spaces. She does over 50 myelograms and 30 laminectomies per year and receives referrals

from veterinarians practicing in a radius of approximately 75 miles.

If Dr. A proceeds with the laminectomy and is eventually sued by his client because the case shows no improvement, will his surgery be judged by the standard of care expected of other generalists or that of the surgical specialist? As with most legal cases, the answer to this question depends on many factors. No veterinary court cases have been found that address this question. However, it is generally accepted that generalists who undertake difficult procedures will be held to the standards of care of the specialist.

An exception to this rule could occur in situations where specialists are not readily accessible to clients whose animals need specialty care. Although the facts of each case will differ, most clients would not be expected to travel several hundred miles to seek specialty care. In cases like this, generalists may have no choice except to do the best they can performing procedures normally reserved for specialists. If results are unsatisfactory, their efforts would probably be compared with those of other generalists similarly situated rather than with a specialist's performance.

Whether generalists can be relieved of the duty to meet the standard of care expected of specialists because of a client's inability to afford the higher fees charged by the specialists is an unanswered and serious issue affecting veterinary medicine. The primary question to be asked in cases like this is the following one: Was the client adequately informed so that he or she could make an educated choice between the two different levels of veterinary care before a decision was made? A parallel question that the court system will also need to adjudicate is whether veterinarians will be allowed to continue offering different levels of veterinary care based upon their clients' willingness and abilities to pay.

Malpractice Liability of Referring Veterinarians

According to a recent law review article, when a lawsuit for malpractice in the human health care industry involves more than one defendant, the plaintiff's likelihood of success almost doubles.[20] However, in most cases "[a] referral of a patient by one physician to another competent physician, absent partnership, employment, or agency, does not impose...liability on the referring physician."[21]

The tendency of courts seems to be that (1) if a referring physician's participation in a surgical procedure is only casual, and another doctor assumes decision-making responsibility, the referring physician is not responsible for the receiving doctor's negligence, and (2) if referring physicians only provide information to the receiving doctor and do not participate in any medical procedures, the referring doctors will most likely not be held liable for negligence.[20] If, however, a referring professional remains in active charge of a case or actively assists a specialist in establishing a diagnosis, performing surgeries, or rendering treatments, a court may reason differently.

When a professional's involvement with a case terminates at the time the case is referred to another doctor, courts are reluctant to hold the professional liable. This appears to be true even though the general rule is that a professional who recommends another professional must exercise due care in making such a recommendation. Therefore, veterinarians who refer cases to emergency clinics, veterinary schools, or specialists probably have little risk of liability for their referrals unless they possess information indicating that the referral facility or doctor lacks competence or has engaged in fraudulent activities.

Statutory Standards of Care

When veterinarians are sued for malpractice, the courts must determine whether or not they met accepted standards. As already discussed, in most states this means that a practitioner's diagnostic efforts and treatment will be compared with those of other veterinarians generally, rather than with practitioners in the same locality.

In making a judgment, however, the court

can be expected to ask for evidence from at least three additional places besides the expert witness testimony of other similar practitioners, these being (1) the state's veterinary practice act, (2) rules and regulations adopted by the state board of veterinary examiners, and (3) standards that have been established by state or national veterinary associations like the AVMA and AAHA.[22]

In states that already have regulations establishing a minimum standard of practice, those standards can be used to help define that state's minimum standard of practice to a judge or jury. (See Chapter 3 and Appendix C for examples.) It is unclear whether a judge or jury will accept such minimum standards as the reasonable standard of care for the jurisdiction or the minimum standard. The trend toward a national standard of care rather than a local one also may allow the minimum standards established in one state to be introduced in another state's court to show what the standard is or should be. In this fashion, the extensive minimum standards of practice already adopted in California (and soon to be expanded) may influence the standards for veterinary practice elsewhere.

Practitioners who are members of the AAHA might be held to the higher standards of medical record keeping and practice adopted by their association. In addition, since AAHA is an organization with national membership, its standards may be applied more readily to member veterinarians in the future than the minimum standards of an individual state like California.

The adoption of minimum standards of practice by state boards of examiners has its pros and cons. One major benefit is that regulations of this type are subject to the public hearing process and, thus, veterinarians have input in their creation. A supporter of this approach writes:

> The tendency of courts to promulgate medical standards which exceed the professional's technical ability to comply or which significantly exceed the current standard of practice has resulted in the necessity of remedial legislation to

restore to the medical profession a sphere in which judgment may be exercised without fear of incurring unfortunate legal liability...Reliance on ad hoc court decisions is not only confusing and frustrating to patients...but also has the potential of overburdening the judicial system. If the medical profession receives confusing and contradictory messages from the judiciary as to the boundaries in which its practice is sanctioned by law, the medical profession will lose confidence in its ability to exercise judgment in the best interest of patients and will instead exercise judgment in the interest of avoiding litigation...[23]

The primary detriment is that medical professionals traditionally have expressed apprehension about standards of practice being established by legislative or regulatory fiat. Most professionals are opposed to any bureaucratic intervention in the way that they render professional care. They generally wish to leave the practice of their profession to the judgment of individual licensees who best understand the nature of each case they see rather than allow this judgment to be made via bureaucratic process.

Each of these arguments has some validity. However, the fact that states are adopting more specific minimum standards of practice indicates that many professionals would rather trust the judgments set forth by their state board's regulatory process than those established through the judicial system.

Standards Regarding Animal Restraint

Because of the risk of human injury, caution and foresight are necessary when asking owners or agents to restrain their animals. While veterinarians are always regarded as experts in the diagnosis and treatment of animals, they also are expected to be experts in the restraint of those patients. Traditionally, the standard of care has allowed owners to restrain their own ani-

mals. If, however, owner restraint becomes such a major human injury liability that veterinarians must provide trained assistants to restrain all animals, it will significantly increase the costs of providing veterinary care.

Therefore, it is in the profession's best interest to discourage or prohibit owner restraint of animals in the following situations:

- whenever clients present new animals with which they are unfamiliar for veterinarians to examine and it is apparent that the animals are not under the owners' control,

- whenever clients specifically request assistance from veterinarians or employees in restraining their animals,

- when clients exhibit considerable fear, inexperience, inability, or incompetence in the restraint of their animals,

- when the small size or stature of a client makes it unlikely that he or she will be able to safely and effectively restrain a much larger animal, and

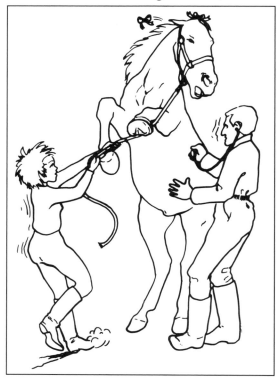

Whoa Boy George! This doctor won't hurt you!

- when veterinarians undertake diagnostic procedures or treatments that are known to cause pain to the patient.

Because of their size, the restraint of horses probably poses the most serious concerns for liability, although cats and dogs also can create serious hazards. As mentioned previously, 16% of all AVMA Professional Liability Insurance Trust payments involves claims for injuries suffered by people. According to information provided by the AVMA Insurance Trust, many of these are related to situations in which owners and friends or agents of the owner were restraining animals. Thus, the standard of care could change in the area of owner restraint, and great caution should be exercised.

Informed Consent and the Standard of Care

In order to understand the *informed consent* doctrine as it applies to veterinary medicine, practitioners must first understand this doctrine in human health care.

The Doctrine Defined

In general, the physician has a right to treat a patient, absent emergencies or unanticipated conditions, when there is mutual consent of both the patient and doctor. In order for this consent to be valid, there must be *true consent*,[24] that is, some affirmative decision by the individual receiving the treatment. The underlying foundation for this concept is embodied in the belief that human beings of adult years and mind have a right to determine what should be done with their bodies. Accordingly, "true consent to what happens to one's self can be defined as the informed exercise of choice to receive treatment which entails an opportunity to evaluate knowledgeably the options available and the predictable risks attendant upon each option. In short, patient comprehension is the keystone of true and viable informed consent."[25]

The Three Tests for Informed Consent

The majority of jurisdictions have adopted the position that physicians must "disclose facts which a reasonable medical practitioner in a similar community and of the same school of medical thought would have disclosed regarding the proposed treatment."[25] In these jurisdictions, only doctors are competent to testify about standard medical customs. Furthermore, only doctors who fail to inform patients of the nature and hazards of the procedure and who deviate from the standard of performance of other reasonable physicians in a similar area fall below the standard of care.

Veterinarians who are sued in jurisdictions using this test can rely on the testimony of their colleagues to set the standard for the amount of risk discussion required before medical procedures are undertaken.

The second "objective minority view," also known as the *reasonable man view*, requires that physicians disclose all risks that would be material to a reasonable, prudent person in the patient's position. This standard is not subjective; it remains objective with due regard for the patient's informational needs and with suitable leeway for the physician's situation.[24]

Veterinarians in jurisdictions employing this standard are required to consider the needs of reasonable clients along with the amount of risk discussion generally employed by their veterinary colleagues.

The third view of informed consent is the "subjective minority view." A 1979 Oklahoma court decision rejected the medical paternalism of the reasonable physician rule as well as the reasonable man or patient view and instead opted for a full disclosure standard. Under this test, the jury "determines what risks were or were not material to the *particular* plaintiff-patient's decision with respect to treatment received or not received."[26]

This is a much more stringent view of informed consent, placing the needs of the individual person above those of the medical profession or other reasonable people.

Whether a court would be willing to apply this test to a veterinary malpractice case in which an injury occurred to a client's animal rather than to the person is yet to be seen.

According to the interpretation of these views in the *South Texas Law Journal*:

> All three views hold that a physician, absent a privilege not to disclose, has an affirmative duty to inform the patient in order that the latter may make an informed and knowledgeable treatment choice. There seems to be a consensus also, that there is no need to advise a patient of dangers or risks of which he is already aware, or those of which the physician is unaware. Additionally, there is no need to give the patient a mini-medical course, but rather, only reasonable explanations "in non-technical terms as to what is at stake: the therapeutic alternatives open to him, the goals expected to be achieved and the risks that may ensue from particular treatment or no treatment."[25]

In comparing these three views of informed consent, only the full-disclosure requirement of the subjective minority view protects each individual patient (or, in the veterinary world, each client). Some people might think this form of true consent will improve the delivery of medical care, while others think it will hinder significantly the efficient delivery of such care. On the other hand, the majority view, that of the reasonable physician or veterinarian, will most likely be overly protective of health care professionals. Although the objective minority view weighs the needs of both physicians and reasonable patients, it disregards the differences between one person's need for information and that of another. Because of all these variances, the standard applied to the doctrine of informed consent will undoubtedly remain uncertain for many years to come.

Veterinarians and Informed Consent

Although the informed consent doctrine is

based primarily upon precedents involving human medical care, one of the three views presented almost certainly will be applied to medical care involving animals. Veterinarians are not expected to perfect a cure in every patient as long as they do not guarantee a result before treatment is begun. Likewise, they need not discuss every risk of performing or not performing a procedure or treatment. This means, however, that practitioners should learn to temper all prognoses in language that does not assure owners that a medical recovery, surgical success, or absence of risk is 100% certain. The use of percentages for success, complications, side effects, and failures based upon personal experience or the research of others often helps accomplish this goal.

Because of the informed consent doctrine, a modicum of discussion regarding risks and complications should occur prior to undertaking some procedures so that clients can provide an educated consent. Examples of situations in which risk discussion is essential follow:

- explaining the risks of seizures or fatalities in the performance of myelograms,

- acquainting horse owners with the risk of rectal tears in performing rectal or pregnancy exams,

- discussing the possibilities of peritonitis after intestinal anastomoses and other major gastrointestinal surgeries,

- explaining the potentials for disseminated intravascular coagulopathy, cardiac arrhythmias, endotoxic shock, gastric wall necrosis, pulmonary emboli, and recurrence of a torsion even after performing surgery on dogs that have gastric torsions, and

- mentioning the likelihood of self-inflicted trauma, nonunions, and infections after repairing compound, contaminated long-bone fractures in large dogs and livestock.

If the hazards inherent in certain procedures, including the risk of anesthetic deaths, are not discussed, owners will be unable to provide their informed consent. The extent of the discussion required is always a question of fact for the jury. The amount of discussion necessary can vary depending upon the seriousness and frequency of the risk; the age, breed, and size of the patient; the attachment of owners to their animals; the prognosis and success of the procedure; the experience or inexperience of the clinician; and the numbers of questions asked by the client.

To fulfill the requirements for both the law of negligence and malpractice, a certain amount of risk discussion is required. Contract law also requires risk discussion to be able to prove that a valid contract was formed.

Proximate Causation

The third element that plaintiffs must prove in negligence or malpractice cases is the one entitled *proximate cause*. This element requires proof that a reasonably close causal connection exists between the conduct of the defendant veterinarian and the occurrence of the injury. Some courts use the rule that the defendant's conduct is a proximate cause of the event if it was a "material element and a substantial factor" in bringing about the type of injury or result that occurred. Others ask the jury to try to determine "what in fact" caused the injury?

The element of proximate cause also requires a close look at foreseeability. Generally, courts do not hold defendants liable unless their negligent conduct affects people or property within a foreseeable zone of danger. This usually requires that the harm that occurred be of a type that is reasonably expected to occur as a result of the defendant's actions. The exact manner in which the harm occurs need not be foreseeable as long as the injured person or property is within the foreseeable zone of danger.[4] For example, an injury to a pedestrian is a foreseeable risk of a large animal practitioner's negligent driving whether the practitioner strikes the pedestrian directly or collides with a sign and causes it to fall upon the pedestrian.

An example involving a veterinary malpractice situation follows: A veterinarian fails to ensure that food was withheld before surgery or fails to provide close postoperative attention to a dog that died subsequent to surgery as a result of aspirating some vomitus. This is most likely considered to be the proximate cause of death in that it is a substantial factor in bringing about death by a foreseeable risk which close postoperative care and good preoperative instructions (withholding food) might have avoided.

If, however, the dog had died from a ruptured aneurism or a pulmonary embolism during a postoperative recovery period, and sufficient supervision had not been present, the negligence in not providing diligent postoperative care would most likely not be the proximate cause of the animal's death. In such a case, the cause of death by an embolism or ruptured aneurism would most likely not have been a foreseeable risk from the surgery performed; and, secondly, the inadequate postoperative care would not have been a substantial factor in preventing or causing the death of the patient. As a result, there is no proximate cause and no valid lawsuit.

The last principle applicable to proximate cause is the "thinskulled" or "eggshell skull" plaintiff rule. This refers to the fact that negligent defendants are stuck with plaintiffs as they are, that is, with any and all frailties they might have as part of their physical makeup. Thus, if a veterinarian performs a simple procedure in a negligent manner on a von Willebrand's-positive Doberman (where clotting problems are likely), and the dog suffers severe hemorrhage or death due to what would have been a minor problem for most other dogs, the veterinarian is still liable for the full extent of the dog's injuries.

Damages

The fourth and final element needed for a cause of action in negligence or malpractice law is proof that the plaintiff suffered some measure of damage. Three basic types of damages can be awarded: nominal, compensatory, and punitive.

In negligence cases, damages usually are not a major obstacle, since these cases generally involve clients' personal injuries. In veterinary malpractice cases, however, proving large-dollar damages can be more difficult. Although many horses and purebred livestock have considerable market value, most courts have not allowed recoveries for injuries to pets to exceed the market value for the animal. Despite the fact that consequential damages are awarded to owners of pets and livestock, limitations on market value have helped spare the veterinary profession from the malpractice crisis faced by physicians.

Nominal Damages

Nominal damages are awarded when judges or juries recognize that (1) plaintiffs have filed valid causes of action and (2) they have fulfilled their burden of proof to support a verdict in their favor. In these cases a damage award of $1 is usually granted because there is insufficient proof of actual damages to support any further monetary recovery.

Compensatory Damages

A second type of damages is known as *compensatory damages*. The theory behind this measure of damages is that plaintiffs should be compensated for their injuries, and the legal system should attempt to restore them as closely as possible to the position they were in before the wrong occurred.

With most forms of property, the calculation used to determine the fair market value of the damaged goods is a standard commercial procedure. Difficulties develop, however, when attempts are made to equate animals with property. Establishing value is not clear-cut, because unique issues exist, such as whether the law allows the cost of repairing the animal to exceed the animal's market value and whether the owner's mental pain and suffering can be considered.

Animals pose another unusual problem which the legal system has not yet addressed. Compensatory damages are intended to compensate some "being" for harm that has occurred to itself or its property. Because animals lack standing as a "being" to appear in court on their own behalf when they are injured or suffer pain and anguish, the legal system is unable to address these wrongs directly. Instead, it focuses solely on the harm to the human owner even though the pain, injury, or death occurred to the animal. As long as compensatory damages are measurable, as defined by the rules of *special damages*, the legal system has a reasonable method for handling most situations. It is when an owner's emotions and mental health are injured and the rules of *general damages* are applied that great disparities among jurisdictions develop.

Special Damages

The special damage type of compensatory damage is routinely applied to losses involving animals. Under this legal doctrine, damage awards involve establishing the animal's fair market value. Depositions from or testimony of expert witnesses familiar with the market for the type and species of animal involved in the legal action are required to establish this value. When possible, the difference between the animal's fair market value before and after the injury is the measure allowed.

The largest veterinary malpractice claim to date involved the destruction of over 100 seed-stock cows, 2 prize bulls, and numerous other cattle in Oklahoma in 1977 and 1978 because of brucellosis.[27] The cattle had been moved from Florida within the year prior to the outbreak. Evidence introduced at trial indicated that the veterinarian failed to individually tag or identify each animal inspected on the health certificate or to watch the loading of the cattle being shipped before they left Florida. It also was shown that the veterinarian did not write the truck tag number on each certificate for the cattle loader, give the certificate directly to the truck driver, inquire about the health or source of the cattle being certified, or test individual cattle over six months of age for brucellosis, as required by law. The veterinarian retained no records or files of the transaction and had destroyed his copies of the interstate certificates for the cattle he had inspected.

After a trial that lasted seven days, the jury awarded damages of $988,000 to the plaintiffs, most of it in the form of special damages for the value of the animals that had to be destroyed. By the time appeals had ended, another $200,000 in interest had accumulated. These components, coupled with expenses for legal defense, brought the total costs to $1.2 million.

As part of the animal's fair market value, special damages include considerations based upon the animal's unique value to the owner. Specific characteristics of the animal are taken into account, such as its age and general health, pedigree, special breeding qualities, milk production, show record, hunting ability, and prize winnings or awards. In addition, its costs of training for use as a police patrol horse or patrol dog, guard dog, seeing eye dog, tracking dog, or hearing dog for the deaf can be considered.

The Unique Property Theory of Establishing Damages

A Massachusetts rule of law exists allowing plaintiffs who have lost property that has no market value to recover, as the measure of damages, "the actual value of the property to its owner."[28] It is clear from an 1880 Massachusetts case that this precedent is longstanding. That case held that the fair market value rule

> does not apply when the article sued for is not marketable property. To instruct a jury that the measure of damages for the ...loss of a family portrait is its market value would be merely delusive. It cannot with any propriety be said to have any market value. The just role of damages is the actual value to him who owns it, taking into account its cost, the practicability and expense of replacing it, and such other considerations as in the particular case affect its value to the owner.[29]

Other Massachusetts cases support this precedent.[30] In affirming a jury verdict of $7,500 for the loss of family movies, a 1979

Washington case has adopted an identical precedent.[31] In that case, the court held that "if the destroyed property has no market value and cannot be replaced or reproduced, then the value to the owner is the proper measure of damages...." (See also *Jankowski* vs *Preiser Animal Hospital*, 157 Ill. App. 3d 818, 1987.)

Consequential Damages

When the property of another is damaged, the liable party also can be held responsible for any normal and foreseeable consequential damages that arise from the injury.[32] These can be in the form of:

- expenses incurred in attempting to prevent the death or permanent disability of the animals (including veterinary fees),
- lost income while the animals are out of production,
- loss of use of the animal (e.g., as a stud or dam), or
- costs incurred searching for a lost animal (e.g., expenses related to attempts to find an animal that escaped from a veterinary hospital or boarding facility including posters, classified ads, owner's trips to the pound, lost work time, and telephone expenses).

To recover consequential expenses, animal owners must show that their expenditures are related directly to the defendant's negligence and would not have been incurred if it had not been for the animal's injury, escape, or death.

Veterinary Expenses

The most common type of damages sought in this category are the veterinary bills resulting from the animal owner's efforts to repair the animal and to minimize or mitigate damages. A West Virginia court was unwilling to award veterinary fees for the death of a dog when no evidence was presented at trial to prove the animal's market value.[33] This decision was based partially on a state statute that said, "...Any person whose dog shall be killed or injured wrongfully or unlawfully by any other person shall have a right of action against the person who shall so kill or injure such dog, but in no case can recovery be had in excess of the assessed value of such dog."

According to a member of the insurance industry, most insurance carriers will pay the costs for veterinary fees even if they exceed the animal's fair market value.[34] It may be, however, that the reason insurance companies take this tack is to avoid large expenditures for legal counsel rather than because of court precedents.

Favre and Loring's *Animal Law* book addresses this issue as follows:

> If an individual injures a pet, it is certainly foreseeable that professional care will be obtained to care for the animal. The consequential damages of veterinary fees should be allowed, if reasonable. A charge would be recoverable if (a) the charge for service rendered is reasonable, and (b) the service rendered was appropriate under the circumstances. As long as the veterinarian's efforts did not constitute heroic attempts without a chance of success then the fees should be awarded as consequential damages.[32]

Defining what constitutes reasonable fees or heroic efforts is a major problem for judges or juries. Should treatment for shock and a fractured leg be classified as nonheroic in nature while thoracic surgery to remove a traumatized lung lobe and repair a ruptured diaphragm be termed heroic?

An even greater problem occurs when expensive fees are added to the equation. Costs for veterinary care can range from a few hundred dollars to several thousand dollars depending upon the nature of the injury, species, and available specialty care. Can legitimate decisions be made as to what is reasonable or what is heroic based solely upon the costs for repair? Should it make any difference whether the injured animal was acquired as a gift or at no cost, or whether it had a purchase price of $100, $500, or $1,000?

Many animals adopted free of charge are loved and cherished as much as or more than expensive ones. Should the rules applied to these pets deny their owners any recovery because the animals have no market value? Can an animal be considered "totalled," as an auto would, just because it has a low economic value due to its heritage, age, or the fact that it has been neutered?

Because of veterinary medicine's increasing knowledge and sophisticated technology, it is extremely common for fees to exceed the fair market value of an injured animal. A major issue arises, therefore, concerning whether a liable insurance carrier, boarding facility, veterinarian, or other person should ever be allowed to claim that the fees are so reasonable and the care so heroic that they will no longer accept financial responsibility for such care.

Many questions akin to this are still unresolved by the legal system. Until better legal precedents are established, veterinarians and animal owners alike will continue to operate without a great deal of legal guidance when attempts are made to estimate maximum allowable recoveries for treatments rendered to animals with minimal market values.

Lost Use, Lost Income, and Lost Profits

In addition to consequential damages in the form of veterinary fees, animal owners may be able to recover damages resulting from lost use of the animal or lost profits. The generally accepted rule is that (1) where the loss of profits is shown to be the natural and probable consequence of the injurious act or omission, and (2) where the amount of damage is shown with reasonable certainty, the owner may be able to recover the lost profits.[32] Such damages must not be speculative, contingent, or uncertain, and there must be reasonable proof of the value of the loss.

One interesting case involved a Georgia dairy farmer who received 100 lb bag of arsenic instead of bicarbonate of soda due to the negligence of a local feed store.[35] Testimony showed that 21 cows and 3 heifers eventually died, milk production was drastically reduced, and the abortion rate increased. In this case, the court found that where the type of business and history of profits make calculation of profits ascertainable, a reasonable method for estimating a prospective profit is acceptable. Evidence of previous production records, valuation and production comparisons between the exposed and unexposed portions of the herd, the price of milk per pound, business expenses, lack of change of management or personnel, and the anticipated lost profits were sufficient for the court to uphold the jury's verdict for $275,000.

In commercial activities, the animals represent the business's capital investment, and the fair market value of the animal includes its potential for producing income. Therefore, when attempts are made to substantiate lost profits, it is important to distinguish between the animal's value and the business's loss of income. When the animal produces a product like milk, wool, or eggs, an owner may be inadequately compensated unless some allowance is made for lost profits on these commodities. Many cases involve a mixture of losses for the animals' fair market value (special damages), as well as lost income and profits (consequential damages).

Lost income should be allowed for such period of time as is reasonably necessary for the owner to replace or treat the animals and have them return to full production. In a case in which a defendant's contaminated feed injured the plaintiff's chickens, the Georgia court awarded damages equal to the full loss of revenues for the period of time during which the chickens stopped laying eggs.[36]

If an animal has a proven value as a stud (or perhaps as an embryo donor), its stud (or dam) services may become a factor in determining the fair market value of the animal. In cases in which owners have ongoing businesses and stud or embryo fee contracts have been arranged before a stud or dam was injured or killed, lost profits can be awarded if owners are unable to provide a suitable substitute in the time available.[37] In general, though, loss of profits deals with fixed contract obligations and not

with general liability for the lifetime of a stud or dam.

General Damages

General damages are those caused by and flowing naturally from the negligence of the defendant, like damages in the form of pain and suffering or emotional distress. To date, this type of recovery has been upheld by appellate courts in only a few states. However, the fact that out-of-court settlements for deaths or injuries suffered by pets often exceed the market value of those animals indicates some recognition by insurance companies of a client's emotional distress as well as an election to settle cases rather than incur major legal expenses and take their chances in court.[38] The growing volume of scientific evidence proving the social, emotional, and psychological value of pets is expected to encourage the continuation of this trend.

The following appellate court decisions already support emotional distress or pain and suffering awards to pet owners in four different jurisdictions.

1. In 1963, a Texas Court of Civil Appeals upheld a $200 award for an owner's mental pain and suffering when a dog was shot twice with a shotgun by police officers in the owner's garage as the owner-plaintiff was having lunch in an adjacent room.[39] Although it was not specifically identified by the court as a case of negligent infliction of emotional distress, the facts support such a finding.

2. Florida has three cases that consider the owner's emotional distress when making damage awards for the loss of a pet. The first involved the intentional killing of a dog by a garbageman who threw a trash can at a feisty dachshund and killed it while the owner was watching.[40] The second case involved the cremation of a dog that died while it was under care at the defendant veterinary hospital, even though the

owner had requested that the dog's body be retained by the veterinarian for the owner to pick up.[41] The third case involved the postsurgical placement of a small dog on an electric heating pad, resulting in burns to the animal that purportedly contributed to its death.[42]

In each of these cases the court took the owner's mental anguish into consideration when it awarded damages against the defendants for the intentional infliction of emotional distress. (These cases are discussed in more depth under Punitive Damages.)

3. Louisiana also has had three cases upholding the precedent that owners and possessors of animals may recover damages for mental anguish in addition to special or actual damages. The first case involved a mare,[43] the second a dog,[44] and the third a cat.[45]

4. The most far-reaching of all the cases involving injuries or deaths of animals is the Hawaii case wherein the state Supreme Court upheld a damage award for mental distress suffered by five members of a family.[46] In this case, the family dog was being transported by a state agency from a quarantine station to a veterinary hospital on a hot day in an unventilated van. The dog died of heat prostration after arriving at the pet hospital. The court upheld a $1000 award for emotional distress even though the family had not witnessed the death of the animal or seen the body after the animal's death. They learned of its death by phone, and did not require psychiatric or medical assistance. In allowing a recovery, the court eliminated the preconditions of time, place, relationship, and physical injury or impact that are required in most other jurisdictions. Instead, the court used a test of foreseeability and applied the preconditions as factors to be con-

sidered in determining the level of damages.[32]

Some Generalizations About Pain and Suffering Damages

Damages for pain and suffering or infliction of emotional distress vary considerably by jurisdiction. Some jurisdictions require proof that the defendant intentionally inflicted emotional distress, whereas others allow recoveries when the emotional distress was negligently inflicted. Some courts will not award damages for pain and suffering unless plaintiffs suffer an impact on their body, while others require plaintiffs to witness the injury suffered by a family member and experience mental or physical ill effects.[47] Some courts, such as Hawaii's, allow for recoveries absent bodily impact, the need for medical or psychiatric assistance, or the witnessing of the negligent action.[46]

The precedents in each jurisdiction vary, and the law determining recoveries for these types of human injuries often controls the court's direction concerning the award of emotional distress damages for the loss of pets. The trend, though, has been toward increasing victims' rights for compensation rather than decreasing them.

Favre and Loring contend that recoveries for mental distress is a new area of the law, and thus, courts have not yet established many precedents regarding criteria that might be used for judging the appropriate damages for situations involving the death or injury of a pet. Favre and Loring cite the subjective jury instruction in the Hawaii case[48] as an example of the fact that it is the common experience of the jury that will ultimately set the appropriate compensation.[32] Instead of giving such a subjective instruction to a jury, it seems reasonable for courts to provide juries with many objective factors to consider. Included would be considerations such as:

- how long the animal had been a pet,
- any special training or endearing qualities the pet had that made it an

exceptionally important part of the family,

- whether the death or injury occurred in a manner that made it particularly difficult for the owner to cope,

- whether the pet's death or injury required the owner to change his or her pattern of living, and

- whether the owners needed medical or psychiatric assistance.

A widow who experiences the unexpected death of a beloved eight-year-old schnauzer which sleeps on her bed, does not go outside without its sweater, has its own pet health insurance policy, and eats sauteed mushrooms and scrambled eggs for breakfast and broiled ground round for dinner clearly endures pain and suffering. It is also quite likely that the loss of a seeing eye dog, a hearing dog for the deaf, a horse belonging to a sensitive, psychologically disturbed 11-year-old girl who communicates better with her horse than her peers and parents, or even a highly trained police dog will produce emotional distress for the owner.

This is especially true if the mental anguish occurs because of some negligence on the part of a veterinarian. A recent law review article concludes that, "If the pet owner is to have a realistic remedy for veterinary malpractice, and if the veterinary profession is to be effectively regulated, the archaic views found in the case law (classifying animals only as personal property, thus prohibiting pain and suffering recoveries) must be discarded...."[49]

The California courts have looked carefully at the negligent infliction of emotional distress theories and established some realistic requirements to allow recoveries. One of the interesting precedent-setting cases there involved a complaint by a husband against a hospital and doctor. The husband sued for damages because the defendant had diagnosed his wife as having syphilis during a routine physical examination.[50] Six months later, when the syphilis test was finally repeated, it was determined that the wife did not have this disease. The court held that

where the risk of harm to the plaintiff was reasonably foreseeable, the hospital and doctor owed the plaintiff a duty to exercise due care in diagnosing the physical condition of his wife. Thus, a recovery was allowed for the negligent infliction of emotional distress.

Another pertinent case in California involved a home owner whose property was damaged when a tractor was negligently allowed to roll away from the place it was parked and through the children's playroom of the plaintiff's house.[51] No one was home at the time, but the plaintiff suffered headaches, intestinal disorders, and stress afterwards that affected her emotionally and physically. In this case the court held that:

> While the courts have expanded the scope of the tort of negligent infliction of emotional distress, reasonable limitations on the extent and remoteness of a defendant's liability must be maintained. Although emotional distress arising out of loss of property evokes a sentimental loss, recovery is limited to cases where, at a minimum, a duty of care exists by virtue of a preexisting relationship between the parties or where the damage arises out of an intentional tort.[51]

It appears to be a short judicial step from allowing recoveries for the intentional infliction of emotional distress for the loss of animals, as seen in the Florida cases, to the allowance of recoveries for the negligent infliction of emotional distress in cases in which a preexisting relationship between the parties is present as discussed under the California cases. The dramatic willingness to extend the law's coverage for these types of emotional distress damages by some courts, however, is best illustrated by the example found in the Hawaii case discussed previously.[46]

Comparisons Between Pets and Heirlooms

A good argument can be made supporting the fact that since emotional distress recoveries are allowed for losses of heirlooms, similar recoveries should be allowed for losses of or injuries to pets.[49] In fact, there are some legal precedents allowing recoveries for lost items of sentimental value or emotional distress for the loss of heirlooms.

In one of those cases, the Texas court stated the rationale for allowing such recoveries as follows:

> Items which have their primary value in sentiment...generally have no market value which would adequately compensate their owner for their loss or destruction. Such property is not susceptible of supply and reproduction in kind, and their greater value is in the sentiment and not in the market place. In such cases the most fundamental rule of damages that every wrongful injury or loss to persons or property should be adequately and reasonably compensated requires the allowance of damages in compensation for the reasonable special value of such articles to their owner taking into consideration the feelings of the owner for such property.[52]

A California court upheld a $4,000 damage award for emotional and physical injuries for the loss of six rings with sentimental value.[53] In this case, the court supported the plaintiff's right to recover by establishing that:

> ...at the time the bailment was created, plaintiff made known to defendant that the rings were cherished mementos of her husband and were old family rings which, because of their sentimental value, she wished to have made into an heirloom for her daughter. This was a special circumstance known to both of the parties at the time the contract was entered into. Since that contract was one whose terms related to matters directly concerning the happiness and comfort of plaintiff, and were such as to move her affection and tender feelings, the jury was entitled, under the rule we are discussing, to include in the damages recoverable for the loss of the rings by reason of defendant's negligence, damages for physical suffering or illness proximately resulting from such loss, in addition to the damages sustained because of the actual loss.[53]

Since courts are willing to award emotional distress damages for heirlooms, it is likely that they will extend that coverage to include emotional distress suffered in the loss of companion animals. After all, animate, loving, protective, humorous, dedicated, and/or subservient animals certainly have equal or more sentimental value than heirlooms.

Punitive Damages

The last type of damages recoverable are those called *punitive* or *exemplary* damages. These are awarded in addition to compensatory damages. Recoveries in this category are awarded only for willful, malicious, intentional, or fraudulent acts or for gross and wanton acts of negligence.[54] Because the award of these damages is intended to punish defendants, recoveries are not limited to the market value or special value of the animal involved, and they are not covered by professional liability insurance.

Under this rule of law, damages may be assessed without consideration of the compensatory damages awarded. Thus, the most likely way to obtain large-damage recoveries against veterinarians, boarding kennels, groomers, or any other animal handlers would be to show that they acted maliciously, fraudulently, intentionally, or with gross negligence. Of course, proving any of these is difficult.

In determining an appropriate dollar award for punitive damages, juries will be asked to consider:

- the degree of malice present,
- the nature of the property interest invaded,
- the dollar award needed to punish the defendant and deter such future conduct,
- the cost of bringing the suit, and

- the annual income and net worth of the defendant.[32]

An example of punitive damages being awarded for the death of an animal is found in a 1980 Minnesota case.[55] In that case, a local animal warden received a phone call from the owner of a day care center complaining that a cat was being a nuisance in her yard. By the time the warden arrived, the cat had returned across the street to a patio of the apartment complex in which the cat's owner resided. The warden captured the cat and put it in a cage. After a brief conversation with the tenant living in the adjacent unit and a cursory search for the owner, the warden returned to the city hall with the lawfully impounded cat.

Because the city had no facilities to care for the cat and had no contract or arrangement with any kennel or agency to care for impounded cats, the warden attempted to find a city employee who would volunteer to care for the cat for the five days the city was required to hold the animal. He was unsuccessful. Thereafter, the warden called and met with the deputy chief of police that same afternoon, and they agreed that the cat should be killed. After attempts to asphyxiate the cat failed, the warden and the police officer took the cat to a rifle range and shot it three times with a shotgun.

The Supreme Court of Minnesota held that: (1) punitive damages against municipal officers and employees are not precluded by statutes that impose limits on monetary awards against municipalities and their employees, and (2) the award of punitive damages of $500 against the city's warden who intentionally killed the plaintiff's pet cat in violation of an ordinance and statute requiring that an impounded animal be held for five business days before it could be destroyed was appropriate. The court concluded that the animal warden did not act with malice toward the cat's owner and did not know who was the cat's owner, but it went on to say:

> Nevertheless, the award of punitive damages was appropriate because Larson's conduct in killing the cat within

hours of its impoundment evinces a willful disregard for both the law and the property rights of private citizens.[55]

Additional examples of cases invoking punitive damages can be found in the three Florida cases mentioned previously under general damages. The first of these involved a garbage collector who, without any reason, threw a garbage can at a dachshund and killed it. The owner was present in her kitchen and rushed out in time to hear the collector laugh and depart. The Florida Court of Appeals upheld a $1000 verdict for punitive damages and, without engaging in a discussion of emotional distress damages separate from the issue of punitive damages, made the following statement:

> The restriction of the loss of a pet to its intrinsic value in circumstances such as the one before us is a principle we cannot accept. Without indulging in a discussion of the affinity between "sentimental value" and "mental suffering," we feel that the affection of a master for his dog is a very real thing and that the malicious destruction of the pet provides an element of damage for which the owner should recover irrespective of the value of the animal.[40]

The second and third cases involved punitive damages and emotional distress in cases where veterinary care was involved. In *Levine* v. *Knowles*, the Florida Appellate Court ruled that the owner of a dog that died while undergoing apparently routine treatment for a skin condition could consider seeking an award for punitive damages.[41] In this case, the owner requested that the veterinarian retain the animal's body. Unfortunately, unknown employees of the veterinarian cremated the dog's body before it could be reclaimed. The veterinarian admitted receiving the owner's instructions and had no adequate explanation for the animal's cremation. The court said that if compensatory damages "...are too lenient for admonitory purposes or if the payment of compensatory damages only would not handicap the defendant sufficiently to discourage such conduct in the future...," punitive damages could be awarded. The court went on to say that if the conduct was "...willful, wanton, reckless, malicious, or oppressive...," punitive damages could be awarded.

The third Florida case involved a dog that was placed on a heating pad in its cage following an operation and left unattended for more than one day of a weekend. Burns from the electric heating pad compounded other problems, and eventually the animal had to be euthanatized. The appellate court upheld a judgment of $1000 compensatory and $12,000 punitive damages, saying:

> ...on the evidence the jury could and no doubt did view the neglectful conduct which resulted in the burn injury to the dog to have been of a character amounting to great indifference to the property of the plaintiff such as to justify the jury award.[42]

As seen from these cases, if the actions of veterinarians are sufficiently reprehensible, juries will allow and courts will uphold punitive damage awards for the loss of animals. The potential for bad public relations and the financial and emotional demands associated with a legal charge serious enough to evoke such a judgment should convince veterinarians to avoid conduct that could possibly provoke a punitive damage recovery.

The Duty to Refer

Advancements in medical knowledge and technology have led to the evolution of specialists and subspecialists. Concurrent with this trend, the law has recognized that general practitioners should call upon experts to aid in the diagnosis and treatment of complicated illnesses and diseases. The legal doctrine upon which this duty is based is known as the duty to refer to a specialist.

Although no veterinary cases dealing directly with this issue have been found to date, the rules governing the duty and liability of physicians and surgeons in the performance of their professional services are applicable to veterinarians as well.[56]

Damages are awarded when physicians are deemed negligent in not calling in specialists and a patient's life or health is endangered by such decisions.[19]

Hirsh made the following observations about the legal ramifications of consultations and referrals:

> From a professional and legal viewpoint there is no accepted standard of care regarding consultations and referrals. Neither lays down a specific rule, except that the responsibility lies with the physician to know when he needs help or the patient's care is beyond his immediate abilities. In other words, the physician must examine his own competence and capabilities, then make a decision....He is not required to be a jack of all trades, but neither is he required to be a "traffic cop," directing patients to specialists.
>
> As a practical matter, it is better to be safe and seek consultation or refer the patient than be sorry for not doing so. It must be remembered that our actions are always viewed retrospectively. Unfortunately, it may be that hindsight is better than foresight in the eyes of the jury.[57]

Practitioners can only be held liable for the failure to refer to specialists if the evidence is clear that the veterinarian deviated from the usual standards of care.[58] Because of the growing numbers of specialists practicing at the 27 veterinary schools in the United States, and the increasing numbers of specialists practicing in the private sector, the standard of care regarding referrals is changing dramatically.

How Expert Are the Experts?

Several factors apply to the duty to refer to a specialist. The first is to determine how well qualified the experts are. It is well accepted that board-certified specialists have demonstrated their advanced knowledge and skills by passing a specialty board examination. Other practitioners, though, may be regarded as specialists even if they lack board certification. This can occur, for example, if they have developed special interests in areas of practice coinciding with those of their board-certified counterparts. This form of specialization is affirmed if practitioners convey to the public via the telephone book or by accepting referrals from colleagues that they consider themselves to be specialists. In either case, specialists will be held to a higher standard of care than practitioners who make no such claims.[19]

Experts in new specialty areas like veterinary oncology, animal behavior, cage bird medicine, and emergency medicine and critical care undoubtedly will continue to become more widely accepted and available. With this trend, the standard of care for the specialist will rise, and general practitioners will be expected to refer clients or at least offer them the option of a referral when they realize that a particular problem is beyond their expertise.

How Available Are the Experts?

A second factor regarding the duty to refer to a specialist is the availability of the experts. In the 1950s and 1960s, nearly all veterinary specialists practiced at veterinary schools. In the early 1970s, specialists began to open practices in densely populated areas, making specialty care much more readily available. This trend has continued and will undoubtedly be a part of the profession's future as the volume of medical and technical knowledge increases.

As specialists become more readily available, general practitioners will be expected to consult with them regarding their difficult medical patients earlier and with increasing regularity. Because the specialists are closer, practitioners also should assume that their clients will be more willing to utilize specialty services and, thus, be more amenable to accepting a referral.

Emergency Clinics as Sources of Specialty Care

Companion animal emergency care is another expanding area of veterinary medicine. At one time, the standard for practitioners was to accept their own emergency calls or share this duty with a group of nearby colleagues. Today, fully staffed emergency hospitals are open nights, weekends, and holidays in almost every metropolitan area of the United States. In many cases, emergency practices are corporations owned by 10 to 35 practitioners in the surrounding area. Their availability in a 'crisis, ability to provide constant medical attention during off hours, and greater expertise in dealing with critically ill or trauma patients increase the general practitioner's duty to refer cases to them.

The trend toward specialization in veterinary medicine will probably continue. As it does, referring to specialists or emergency centers or at least informing clients of the availability of such specialty care will become an increasingly important duty for general practitioners. If an animal dies during the night, and the owners subsequently discover that all-night emergency care was available a few blocks or miles away, they certainly will have a valid cause of action if the practice that admitted their critically ill animal at 9:30 p.m. one night failed to inform them of the availability of this type of expertise and care nearby. The same would be true if the owners of an animal with congestive heart failure or cancer were informed by a general practitioner that the only remaining option was euthanasia and they discovered later that a nearby specialty practice employs a cardiologist, an oncologist, and an internal medicine specialist.

When Should Cases Be Referred?

The generally accepted rule regarding when physicians (and thus veterinarians) are expected to make a referral is stated best as follows:

> One of the requirements that the law exacts of the general practitioner...is that if (he) discovers, or should know or discover, that the patient's ailment is beyond his knowledge or technical skill,

ability or capacity to treat with a likelihood of reasonable success, he is under a duty to advise his patient to consult a specialist or one qualified in a method of treatment which the physician is not qualified to give, and the physician failing to so advise his patient has been liable for malpractice.[58]

Clearly, when a patient's problem is beyond the general practitioner's expertise but a client does not inquire about specialty care, practitioners should proceed with the case only after the client is apprised of the existence and availability of specialty care. Written notations of such discussions should be made on the patient's record to document that the client was adequately informed.

Res Ipsa Loquitur

In actions for negligence or malpractice, plaintiffs have the burden of proof to show that the preponderance of evidence supports their contention that the defendant failed to comply with the standard of medical care. A much heavier burden, that of proof beyond a reasonable doubt, is necessary in criminal cases. In some civil cases, however, courts have held that the mere fact that an accident occurred indicates that a negligent act was probably present. The legal theory underlying this doctrine is known by its Latin name *res ipsa loquitur* which means "it speaks for itself."

Credit for initiating the res ipsa loquitur doctrine goes back to 1863 when Judge Pollock, an English judge said, "There are certain cases of which it may be said `res ipsa loquitur' and this seems to be one of them. In some cases the courts have held that the mere fact of the accident having occurred is evidence of negligence...."[59] In this case a barrel of flour rolled out of a warehouse and struck a pedestrian walking in front of the building. Judge Pollock was of the opinion that a barrel could not roll out of a warehouse but for the negligence of someone employed by that business. Why then, he said, should a plaintiff have to call witnesses

to prove the defendant's negligence? Why not, instead, provide plaintiffs with a presumption of negligence and require that defendants produce evidence proving that they are not negligent?

Much has been written about res ipsa loquitur and the circumstances under which this doctrine will be applied to the facts at hand.[60] One of the better definitions can be found in a 1926 Illinois case wherein the court said:

> [Res ipsa loquitur] asserts that whenever a thing which produced injury is shown to have been under control and management of the defendant and the occurrence is such as in the ordinary course of events does not happen if due care had been exercised, the fact of injury itself will be deemed to afford sufficient evidence to support recovery in the absence of any explanation by the defendant tending to show that the injury was not due to his want of care.[61]

The application of the res ipsa loquitur doctrine changes the course of a legal proceeding. In most jurisdictions, if the court invokes this doctrine, it allows plaintiffs to stop producing evidence proving the defendant's negligence and forces defendants to go forward with evidence proving that they were not negligent. In a few jurisdictions, its application to the case shifts the entire burden of proof (as opposed to the burden of going forward with evidence) from the plaintiff to the defendant.[60] The plaintiff's value of employing the res ipsa loquitur doctrine is that the burden of proving that practitioners are not negligent often can be a difficult burden to overcome.

A veterinary medical example of the application of the res ipsa loquitur theory could involve a case wherein a cast or splint was applied to a patient's rear leg in such a manner that circulation was impaired, requiring amputation. A plaintiff's argument would be, "But for the negligence of the attending veterinarian, this result would never have developed."

If the judge agrees that the res ipsa loquitur doctrine applies to the facts at hand, the defendant veterinarian is required to produce evidence proving that no negligence occurred. This might require, for example, expert testimony from a pathologist who examined the amputated leg showing that the patient's circulatory failure was due to a blood clot occurring in the femoral artery at the time of the injury and not a splint or cast applied too tightly.

According to Prosser, some specific conditions must exist before res ipsa loquitur will arise: (1) the accident must have been one that does not ordinarily occur unless there is negligence, (2) the agent or instrumentality causing the injury complained of must have been within the control of the defendant, and (3) the injury must not have been due to any voluntary action or contribution on the part of the plaintiff.[62]

Since veterinarians' patients cannot speak for themselves, and since few ancillary personnel are usually in attendance when veterinary care is being provided, it seems that the res ipsa loquitur doctrine has more application to negligence in this profession than in human medicine. However, in considering its application to veterinary medicine, Hannah sets forth some relevant observations:

1. The mere fact that an animal was injured by a veterinarian or his employees or agents does not support application of the doctrine.

2. A presumption created by application of res ipsa loquitur yields to any contrary proof and is thus destroyed.

3. There may be an inference of negligence on the part of the veterinarian without the res ipsa loquitur doctrine applying. [An inference requires less likelihood of something having happened than does a presumption.]

4. An admission by the veterinarian that his act caused the injury complained of may create a presumption in favor of the plaintiff but does not justify application of the res ipsa loquitur theory if the defendant disclaims fault (unless, of course, it would otherwise apply).

5. Application of res ipsa loquitur does not depend on a contractual relation. It could be applied to a veterinarian rendering gratuitous service, to... emergency cases and to other situations in which there is no privity of contract.[60]

Other examples of negligence cases in veterinary medicine to which res ipsa loquitur might apply include:

- if a surgical procedure is performed on the wrong patient,

- leaving a surgical instrument or sponge inside a patient's body cavity,

- if a patient awakens from an anesthetic or surgical procedure with some form of nerve injury that was not present before the procedure was performed,

- allowing a patient to hang itself from its collar while hospitalized,

- if an animal is released with burns on its body after it had been placed on an electric heating pad or had been given a medicated bath,

- if a group of animals show signs of a drug intoxication several hours after they were treated, and

- euthanatizing the wrong animal.

Legal Defenses to Negligence Actions

Even when defendants have acted or performed services in a negligent manner, it does not automatically follow that they will be held liable for their negligence. A series of defenses have been established by the courts to provide either a complete or partial defense to a legal action for malpractice or negligence.

Contributory Negligence

The most common defense employed by defendants is the one known as *contributory negligence*. In defining this term, *Black's Law*

Dictionary cites the following language from a court case:

> Conduct by a plaintiff which is below the standard to which he is legally required to conform for his own protection and which is a contributing cause which co-operates with the negligence of the defendant in causing the plaintiff's harm.[3]

The thrust of this defense is that, although defendant veterinarians may have been negligent, the plaintiffs also were negligent. Just as the defendant's negligent act must have been (1) below the standard of care for veterinarians, and (2) the proximate cause of the plaintiff's injury, the plaintiff's contributory negligence must have been (a) the proximate cause of the injury that occurred to their person or to their animal and (b) below the standard of care expected of reasonable clients. Some common examples include clients' failures to:

- return for timely reexaminations to check casts, splints, or bandages,

- confine their animals as instructed,

- exercise animals as directed,

- give medications as prescribed, and

- provide proper food and shelter.

The most critical factor in the defense of contributory negligence is documentation in a written medical record of exactly what the owner was instructed to do or refrain from doing after the patient was released. Copies of hospital handouts provided at the time of a patient's discharge; reexamination dates written directly on splints, casts, or bandages; and appointments made at the time patients are released all are corroborative evidence of the information clients were provided when their animals were released. Without such written evidence, the jury simply hears the self-serving word of the defendant veterinarian and counters that with the self-serving word of the plaintiff, and whoever has the most believable story wins.

The Comparative Negligence Standard

In jurisdictions that apply the traditional contributory negligence doctrine, plaintiffs who are contributorily negligent are denied recoveries even if they prove that defendants were negligent. Because this often has produced unfair results, many jurisdictions have adopted a comparative negligence standard. Under comparative negligence statutes or doctrines, negligence is measured in percentages, and damages allowed by juries are diminished in proportion to the amount of negligence attributable to the plaintiffs.

Juries are asked to weigh the severity of the plaintiff's contributory negligence against the negligence of the defendant. Even though this is often an imperfect way to measure damages, most jurisdictions find that it is superior to the old method of allowing a minimal amount of contributory negligence to completely bar a plaintiff's recovery. Some jurisdictions using a comparative negligence standard allow plaintiffs to recover even if they are found to be more than 50% at fault. In most jurisdictions, however, plaintiffs can recover only if they are less than 50% at fault.[63]

Assumption of Risk

Another defense to negligence cases is entitled *assumption of the risk*. Under this doctrine, when a defendant is able to prove that a plaintiff voluntarily encountered a known risk, the plaintiff may be barred from recovering even if the defendant was negligent. Assumption of the risk differs from contributory negligence in that contributory negligence usually does not involve the plaintiff's or defendant's awareness of any risk.

Two different situations exist wherein this defense is frequently raised. The first involves owners or agents who are injured while restraining their animals during the course of a veterinarian's examination or treatment. When veterinarians foresee or should have foreseen that an animal might injure its owner, they have a duty to warn clients of the impending risk.

The justification for this is that restraining animals safely is assumed to be part of a veterinarian's training and expertise and, therefore, practitioners have a duty to foresee animal-induced injuries and prevent clients from being subjected to them. However, when clients are aware that their animals are often unmanageable during veterinary exams but insist that they restrain them anyway, they can be held to have assumed the risk of being injured and may be barred from recovering. If they simply agree to restrain the animal(s) as opposed to insisting on doing so, there is a higher likelihood that a court will not find that they assumed the inherent risks. The outcomes of cases like this vary considerably depending on the specific facts and evidence presented.

The second-most-likely situation in which this defense is employed involves suits by veterinarians or veterinary staff members who are injured by clients' animals. When a veterinary professional becomes a plaintiff in a legal action against an animal's owner to recover for a personal injury, the defendant will usually raise the assumption of risk defense. The contention will be that the nature of veterinary practice requires that its professionals consistently assume risks of injuries of this type. Therefore, they should be barred from recovering for injuries incurred while they are performing their duties as veterinary professionals.

A 1940 Missouri Appellate Court case held, however, that while veterinarians assume certain risks because of the nature of their profession, they do not assume all risks.[64] Since they only can assume risks they are informed of, their knowledge of the risk is a question of fact to be determined by a jury on a case-by-case basis. Because of this rule of law, duties are imposed on clients to inform veterinary staff of known aggressive or vicious propensities of their animals. The failure by clients to comply with this duty can lead to liability even with veterinarians

who are held to be experts in animal restraint.

Statutes of Limitation

Another somewhat different approach occasionally can be used to defend against suits for negligence, malpractice, or any other tort. This involves proof that a plaintiff's legal action was not commenced within the state's statutes of limitation.

In order to eliminate claims based upon stale evidence, courts have recognized that lawsuits must be filed within some reasonable and ascertainable time after negligent acts occur. In addition, time limitations provide defendants a fair opportunity to investigate claims unimpaired by the loss of evidence through the disappearance of documents or witnesses or inaccurate recall. Statutes that govern the length of time within which lawsuits must be filed are known as *statutes of limitation*.

Most statutes mandate that suits for malpractice must be filed within one to two years of the date that plaintiffs know or reasonably should know of the injury. However, it is rare for states to have statutes of limitations that specifically apply to veterinary malpractice. In veterinary cases, courts may hold that the statutes encompassing other health professions also were intended to apply to veterinary medicine, or they may decide that the longer statutes of limitation covering general negligence are appropriate.

In medical malpractice cases, the time at which the statute of limitations begins often depends upon the nature of the injury or illness. Two distinct lines of cases have developed. In the first type, called *traumatic injury cases*, the injury itself alerts plaintiffs to its wrongful causation, so statutes begin to run at the time plaintiffs learn of the injury. In the second type, known as *disease cases*, the wrongful causation may not be apparent immediately, and thus sufficient notice has not been provided. Consequently, the limitations period begins only after plaintiffs know or reasonably should know of the injury and know or reasonably should know or discover that it was caused by the defendant's wrongful conduct.[65] In some cases, this is years after the negligent act was committed.

Although both of these types of cases traditionally apply to medical malpractice, the same line of reasoning can be applied to cases involving other professionals such as attorneys, accountants, and veterinarians.

Essential Types of Liability Insurance

Professional liability insurance is an attempt by a group of professional people to pool their resources so that funds are available to protect any individual in the event of legal action. Professional liability can stem from practitioners' actions as business people, as veterinarians, as officers in veterinary medical associations, and as boarders (bailees) of animals; thus, many different types of insurance coverage are needed.

Professional Liability Insurance

Professional liability insurance covers liabilities arising from one's practice of veterinary medicine. Generally, the policy covers the insured entity, which in most cases is the hospital owner or corporation and partners. Employed veterinarians are not parties to the contract and normally would not be individually insured by the practice's policy. This means that if any employees are sued individually or separate from the practice, the practice's professional liability insurance will not cover them.

This is often misunderstood, because insurance companies sometimes charge practices an extra premium fee for employed veterinarians. This additional coverage only protects practice owners from liability for the acts of their employees, though; it does not

protect the employed veterinarians from their own personal liability. Therefore, under most professional liability insurance policies, individual veterinarians must have their own policies, separate from and in addition to that of the employer. Unless employed veterinarians are working part time in other practices, it makes good business sense for employers to pay the premium for this added protection just to assure employees that they are adequately covered while working in the practice.

Liability insurance is not meant to be used as a public relations vehicle by which veterinarians purchase the continued goodwill of clients and have their insurers pay for damages that are not proximately caused by the insured veterinarian's negligence. Veterinarians cannot personally pay clients for injuries to their animals and then request reimbursement from their insurance carriers. Most policies clearly state that insured professionals shall not, except at their own cost, make any payments, assume any obligations, or incur any expenses under their professional liability insurance policies. Payment of claims may be determined to be an admission of negligence by practitioners and can be authorized under the insurance policy only when a claim is meritorious as to the cause and amount of damages.[66]

When evaluating professional liability insurance policies, it is important to consider the company's procedure regarding settlements of claims with or without the consent of the insured veterinarian.[67] Such factors as the future effect on the veterinarian's practice and reputation, the chances of successfully defending the case, the dollar costs of settling versus the legal costs of defending, and the likelihood of a large jury award or undesirable legal precedent are all items that must be jointly considered by defendants, legal counsel, and insurance carriers. Veterinarians should never allow themselves to be left out of this process simply because their insurance policy allows the company to settle a claim without their approval.

Most professional liability insurance policies require insured veterinarians to notify the company immediately upon receipt of a summons involving a legal action that could provoke liability under the policy. In these cases, a failure to inform the insurance company of an outstanding legal action in a timely fashion can occasionally void one's coverage under the policy. Likewise, when insurance companies contact veterinarians to assist in their defense, practitioners are required to cooperate with the company.

In most cases it is wise to contact one's professional liability insurance carrier for advice at the time that a serious complaint is lodged and before any legal action is commenced. Because of their experience in dealing with such situations, insurance company personnel may be able to take action or provide suggestions that will allow for an orderly settlement of a case before the costs of legal action are initiated.

Directors' and Officers' Liability Insurance

Veterinarians also can be held liable in a professional capacity as a member of a board of directors or officer of a veterinary association. Liability in this area could stem from legal action by a disgruntled member or perhaps even from an injured client at an association-sponsored vaccination clinic.

Standard professional liability insurance does not cover legal actions arising from a practitioner's activities as a member of a professional association. Therefore, veterinarians who serve as officers or board members are encouraged to ensure that the association provides liability coverage for their activities on behalf of the association.

Comprehensive General Liability Policies

A comprehensive general liability policy is another type of essential coverage and generally is part of a broad business package of public liability and property damage insur-

ance. These policies cover veterinarians' business-related liabilities as opposed to their malpractice liability. It is this type of coverage that provides protection for clients' personal injury actions that are unrelated to the veterinarian's practice of medicine. Examples include a client's concussion suffered after slipping on an icy sidewalk at the entrance to the practice or a bite from another client's dog while waiting in an office reception room.

This coverage also includes protection against (1) liability suits for contracts entered into, (2) damages occurring to leased property, and (3) liability for fire damage to other people's property that resulted from negligence or events occurring on properties controlled by the insured person. In addition, it covers product liability cases, i.e., suits arising from the sale, manufacture, or distribution of any products in the course of one's business. Product liability suits are currently very popular, because a strict liability standard is usually enforced.

Coverage also should be included here for risks of personal liability for slander, libel, defamation of character, invasion of privacy, and wrongful eviction. An excellent addition to one's coverage is a rider that pays the medical bills of any guests injured on the premises up to a specified dollar value without regard to liability or negligence on the part of the owner.

Bailment Coverage

Another type of essential insurance coverage for veterinarians is an inexpensive extension to the professional liability policy to cover bailments. These policies cover a practitioner's negligence involving clients' animals that die, are destroyed, are lost, or are injured while they are in the custody of the veterinarian. Liability also is covered from such external causes as:

- fire and lightning
- windstorm, cyclone, tornado, hail, explosion, water damage, vandalism, and earthquake

- being accidentally hit or run down by a motor vehicle while in a practitioner's care, custody, or control
- collision, upset, or overturn of a vehicle in which veterinarians or their employees are transporting animals
- theft of animals from the veterinarian's premises
- escape of the animal
- monetary loss that veterinarians would suffer if accrued but unpaid charges became uncollectible as a result of loss or damage to the client's animal
- direct physical loss of or damage to animal accessories that are in the custody of the veterinarian but are the property of the client[68]

Veterinarian Countersuits

In the early 1970s, the number of medical malpractice suits involving physicians and dollar awards granted by courts and insurance companies for those actions rose to what many people considered a crisis level. Numerous physicians have maintained that the majority of these malpractice claims are frivolous; however, there is little objective proof of this charge.[69]

Because of lost work time, legal fees, loss of professional reputation, emotional distress, and increased malpractice insurance premiums, physicians who have successfully defended or settled malpractice suits often find little satisfaction in having won. For the most part, veterinarians have been able to avoid these draining experiences, but many questions remain regarding the courses of action that professional people can take against clients and attorneys who file baseless and frivolous malpractice actions.

Searching for a way to recoup their losses and punish the patients and attorneys who initiated these suits, physicians have pursued the gamut of legal theories. Among those theories are malicious prosecution, abuse of process, negligence, barratry (the offense of frequently exciting or stirring up suits and quarrels between others), defamation, infliction of emotional distress, invasion of privacy, and prima facie tort.[70] Despite the wide variety of legal theories employed, physicians have consistently failed in their efforts to countersue, and courts have overwhelmingly cited the policy of open access to the judicial system as outweighing a doctor's right to recover for what was thought to be a frivolous lawsuit. According to one source, only three state appellate courts have upheld judgments for physicians in countersuits against patients and attorneys.[70]

Malicious Prosecution

The most common legal theory employed in countersuits is malicious prosecution. Under this legal cause of action, four elements must be proved: (1) termination of the malpractice action in the defendant's favor, (2) lack of probable cause in bringing the malpractice action, (3) malice in initiating the malpractice suit, and (4) damages.[71]

Only court judgments in their favor, not settlements, allow doctors to meet the first element that must be proven. As for the probable cause element, doctors must prove that considering only those facts known at the time the malpractice suit was filed, plaintiffs and their attorneys did not have probable cause to warrant a reasonable person's filing a malpractice action. The difficulty in proving a lack of probable cause has been a difficult requirement to meet against patients and even more so against their attorneys.

The third element, malice, also has been most difficult to prove. In one case, the court held that "at its most obvious, malice includes proof of an intentional or willful act which attempts to bring about a wrongful result."[72] The best and often only way for doctors to prove malice is first to prove that probable cause for a legal action did not exist. That element, though, also is hard to prove.

Two different views have emerged regarding the fourth element—damages. Twenty-seven states have ruled that doctors can recover damages that are common to someone who has been sued for malpractice. Such damages include those for loss of reputation, loss of income during the malpractice proceedings, and trial costs. Seventeen states adhere to various interpretations of the English rule. Under this rule and its interpretations, proof of damages varies from the demonstration of special injuries, like actual interference with one's person (arrest) or property (seizure), to proof of lost future income. In jurisdictions adopting this rule, the following types of damages generally will not satisfy the special injury requirement: loss of income during the malpractice action, transportation costs, mental anguish, reputational damage, increased malpractice premiums, loss of consortium, legal fees, and being forced to change the way one practices medicine.[70]

Overcoming these burdens is a monumental task for professional people who would like to countersue clients, patients, and their attorneys.

Abuse of Process

The second countersuit theory employed is that entitled *abuse of process*. This cause of action involves allegations that the malpractice plaintiff brought the suit with an ulterior motive. The elements that must be proved in this category are that (1) patients (or their attorneys) made improper and unauthorized use of legal process, (2) malpractice plaintiffs had ulterior purposes or motives for bringing suit, and (3) doctors have incurred damages resulting from the abuse of process.[71]

This appears to be a more likely avenue for success than malicious prosecution, since there is no need to prove lack of probable cause. However, courts consistently have held that the mere institution of a groundless civil suit is not sufficient by itself to state a cause of action under this theory, because "process" does not include a civil complaint and summons to appear in court.

In a Nevada case, the court found evidence sufficient to support the jury's conclusion that a plaintiff's malpractice suit had been brought for the ulterior purpose of coercing a nuisance settlement.[73] The finding in this case was supported by the attorney's failure to adequately investigate the case and the total absence of essential medical expert advice or testimony.

Negligence

A completely unsuccessful claim to date has been that the plaintiff's attorney was negligent in bringing an unfounded lawsuit against the defendant. Courts have consistently found that attorneys owe no duties to avoid claims of negligence to third parties unless those parties were intended to benefit from the attorney's actions.[74] Additionally, courts have supported the policy that attorneys who file unfounded suits are not negligent, because under our adversary system of justice, they must zealously represent their clients.

Charges of negligence against attorneys for breaching the Code of Professional Responsibility for Lawyers also have failed. The most common sections under which actions are alleged are: (1) "A lawyer shall not handle a legal matter without preparation adequate in the circumstances,"[75] and (2) "In his representation of a client, a lawyer shall not file a suit, assert a position, conduct a defense, delay a trial, or take other action on behalf of his client when he knows or when it is obvious that such action would serve merely to harass or maliciously injure another."[75] To date, courts have refused to grant individuals a cause of action when these ethical codes have been violated, suggesting instead that the proper remedy for such violations is to institute disciplinary proceedings against the attorneys.

Barratry, Defamation, Emotional Distress, Invasion of Privacy, and Prima Facie Tort

Neither barratry, defamation, emotional distress, invasion of privacy, nor prima facie tort have been successful causes of action in veterinary medicine. Under the barratry allegation, multiple acts of stirring up suits must be proved, which is highly uncommon. When actions for defamation (libel or slander) are pursued, the biggest obstacle is that demeaning or critical statements made about doctors in judicial proceedings for malpractice, including allegations found in the pleadings, are immune from defamation suits.

When damages are sought under the negligent or intentional infliction of emotional distress theory, plaintiffs must prove that they were damaged by conduct so outrageous as to shock one's conscience. It seems unlikely that frivolous lawsuits would provoke emotional distress sufficient to meet this standard.

Under invasion of privacy countersuits, there must be either an intrusion upon the plaintiff's solitude or seclusion, public disclosure of private facts, or publicity that places the doctor in a false light in the eyes of the public. These claims, too, are extremely difficult to prove.

The prima facie tort theory of damages is the last and newest approach suggested for countersuits. It evolves from English law, in which system the court made the statement, "Now intentionally to do that which is calculated in the ordinary course of events to damage, and which does in fact damage another in that person's property or trade is actionable if done without just cause or excuse."[76]

The outlook for success in professional countersuits based on the prima facie tort theory is new enough that most jurisdictions have not yet ruled on this theory.[70] Further research into this cause of action must be pursued before it can be discarded or developed to assist health care professionals in their countersuits against frivolous lawsuits.

Assault and Battery

It is unlikely that veterinarians will find themselves in situations in which they can be held liable for assaulting another person. However, anger is an unpredictable emotion, and the frustrations of dealing with irate, belittling, ungrateful, badgering, and nonpaying clients are very real. Incidents of assault and battery occur nearly every year involving professional athletes, and they can occur as well through the activities of veterinarians. Charges can provoke criminal actions as well as suits for civil liabilities, and they may or may not be covered by one's business or liability insurance.

Defining Assault and Battery

An assault is an act that creates apprehension in another person of an imminent, harmful, or offensive contact. A battery is unlawful, unpermitted, harmful, or offensive touching of another person. Sometimes assault is defined loosely to include battery; thus, the expression *assault and battery* usually means battery.

A good definition and group of examples of what constitutes an assault can be found in an old English Common Pleas case from 1853, in which the court held:

> An assault is an attempt, with force or violence, to do a corporal injury to another, as by holding up a fist in a menacing manner; striking at another with a cane or stick, though the party striking may miss his aim; drawing a sword or bayonet; throwing a bottle or glass with intent to wound or strike; presenting a gun at a person who is within the distance to which the gun will carry; pointing a pitchfork at a person who is within

reach; or by other similar act, accompanied with such circumstances as denote at the time an intention, coupled with a present ability of using actual violence against the person of another.[77]

Under common law, both offenses were misdemeanors. Today, under virtually all criminal codes, they are either misdemeanors or felonies. They are characterized as felonies when they are accompanied by a criminal intent, such as an intent to kill, rob, or rape, or when they are committed with a dangerous weapon.

Intent is an integral element of both offenses, and it is generally only essential that defendants have an intent and present ability to do the act that caused the harm or unauthorized touching. Although an intent to cause harm to a victim also may have been present, defendants need not actually intend to cause harm to be held liable for an assault or battery.

Defenses

Just as in negligence law, the fact that an assault or battery occurred does not mean that the case is lost. Several defenses must be considered.

Consent

In almost all states, consent voluntarily given by the victim constitutes a valid defense. In determining the presence or absence of consent, courts consider the victim's behavior as well as any words that were stated. Thus, in some cases courts will imply consent based upon the person's actions. Consent may not, though, be obtained by fraud or duress.

When parties engage in mutual combat, each is civilly liable to the other for any physical injury inflicted during the fight. The fact that they voluntarily engaged in combat is no defense to an action by either of them to recover damages for their individual personal injuries. Thus, a person who participates in a contact sport impliedly consents to a certain amount of physical contact. Participants, however, are not deemed to consent to contact beyond that which is commonly permitted in the sport. [78]

Self-Defense

In general, courts allow people to use whatever degree of force is reasonably necessary for them to protect themselves from bodily harm. Whether or not self-defense is a valid defense is usually determined by a jury after hearing all the facts. The usual test is one similar to that applied in negligence law, i.e., whether a reasonable person under similar circumstances would have responded with a similar amount of force. A person who initiates a fight, however, cannot claim self-defense unless the opponent responded with a greater and unforeseeable degree of force.

Deadly force may be justified if the situation is such that reasonable people would fear for their lives. In some states, courts require people to retreat prior to using deadly force if the individual can do so in complete safety. A majority of states, however, allow people to stand their ground even though there is a means of safe escape.

Defense of Others

Going to the aid of another person in distress also is a valid defense, provided that the defender is free from fault. In some states, defenders are treated as though they stand in the shoes of the person being protected. Therefore, the defender's right to claim defense of another depends upon whether the person protected had a justified claim of self-defense. In a minority of jurisdictions, this defense may be asserted if the defender believed, or a reasonable person would have believed, that the third party was in need of aid.

Defense of Property

People may use a reasonable amount of force to protect their property from damage, but they may not use deadly force. This is because society and the courts have placed a lesser value on property than they have on human life. An owner of real property or a tenant may use force against a trespasser. Generally, a request to leave the property must be made before any force is applied, unless a request would be futile. Additionally, the amount of force must be reasonable and, unless it is necessary for self-defense, the infliction of bodily harm upon an intruder is prohibited. The old saying "A man's home is his castle," which he can protect under all circumstances no longer applies in modern society.

It is because of this attitude of reason that spring guns or vicious guard dogs may not be used against trespassers or intruders on unoccupied premises. By the use of a guard dog, landowners or tenants are substituting the judgment of an animal for their own and may well be bound by the animal's indiscretion.[79] Part of the rationale for this precedent is that firefighters, law enforcement officers, public utility employees, or postal workers might need to enter the property and would have a legal right to be there. In addition, children might enter the premises. A spring gun or a dog would be unable to distinguish between actual trespassers and other such people.

False Imprisonment

Another tort or crime that veterinarians could unwittingly perpetrate is that of false imprisonment. In order to be subjected to the tort of false imprisonment, individuals must be confined to a substantial degree, that is, their liberty of movement must be restrained. No evidence of physical force is needed. False imprisonment claims have occurred in veterinary hospitals when practitioners insisted that clients could not leave an examination room or exit the premises until they had made some type of payment or financial arrangements for the care of their animal.

The mere interference or obstruction of an individual's freedom to go where he or she wishes does not constitute false imprisonment if some type of alternative egress is present. Restraint sufficient to provoke liability can stem from fear or apprehension of physical force even though such force may never actually be exercised or expressly threatened by the accused. The circumstances surrounding each case determine whether or not fear of physical injury may be considered to have been an element of the defendant's restraint.

Voluntary submission by a plaintiff to restraint of movement negates false imprisonment, since it is essential that the restraint be contrary to the plaintiff's will and without legal justification. Similarly, accidental or incidental confinement of a person by a defendant does not constitute false imprisonment, because liability for this tort requires proof that the defendant intended to cause the plaintiff's confinement.

Libel and Slander

Libel and slander involve the communication of false information about individuals, causing injuries to their good name or reputation. Libel is a type of defamation that can be seen. It includes writings, paintings, printings, effigies, motion pictures, or statues. Slander is a defamation that is spoken and heard. Considerable overlap occurs between these torts, because many defamations are both seen and heard.

Many situations occur in practice that can lead practitioners to make slanderous comments. Some examples include (1) recurrent evidence of negligent or incompetent veterinary care rendered by other veterinary practices; (2) boarding or grooming facilities that perform shoddy work; (3) pet shops, breeders, kennels, or stables that sell animals with hereditary defects or infectious diseases; and (4) trainers who perform services in a manner that is rough or cruel toward the animals.

Although the United States Constitution protects citizens' freedom of expression and speech, libel and slander are not protected by its First and Fourteenth Amendments. This is because the public's interest in order and morality outweighs the constitutional value of protecting libelous or slanderous statements. Criticism and defamation can be distinguished on the basis that criticism is an expression of opinion on facts that provide the grounds for differences of opinion. Furthermore, criticism does not attack people's private or personal affairs but relates only to the quality of their work or public conduct. Libel and slander, on the other hand, attack the personal qualities of individuals with untrue statements that harm their reputation.

The Elements

There are four essential elements that must be proved to succeed with a legal action for libel or slander. These include:

- the making of a defamatory statement by the defendant,

- publication of such statement to an individual other than the plaintiff,

- identification of the plaintiff as the individual defamed in some manner, and

- injury or damage to the reputation of the plaintiff.

The Defamatory Statement

The statement or publication that is the source of the complaint must cause injury to the reputation of a living individual or an existing organization. Libelous or slanderous statements about dead people constitute crimes in a number of states where statutes exist to preserve the memory of the deceased person and the public interest. Civil actions for damages usually cannot be brought by surviving relatives.

Before legal actions for defamation can be submitted to juries, courts must decide as a *question of law* whether the language used could reasonably be construed as defamatory. Only if courts decide this question in the affirmative can cases be submitted to juries to determine whether as a *question of fact*, the language used was interpreted and understood by the listeners as defaming the plaintiff. Different words might be interpreted differently by different people under different circumstances and, thus, courts permit juries to determine whether the words constitute defamation against a particular plaintiff.

For example, an editorial published in a small town newspaper by local government officials accusing a local group veterinary practice of charging outrageously high fees for treating and boarding six neglected cats brought to them by local animal control officials could be considered defamatory.

Such a statement might be regarded as libelous, since it would cause prospective clients or those who ordinarily patronize the veterinarians at that practice to form a negative opinion about them and stop seeking veterinary care there. Depending upon the actual language used, this could likely be a question of fact for a jury to consider. The fact that no complaint or discussion with any veterinarians in the practice was registered prior to the publication of the editorial in the newspaper also would be a consideration for the jury.

Plaintiffs must prove that, regardless of the manner in which it is presented, the communication complained of could be understood by others who saw or heard it as having a defamatory meaning, irrespective of whether they personally believe it to be true. Likewise, plaintiffs must establish that someone other than themselves understood the words or image as an attack on their reputation. Defendants, conversely, can show that the communication had at least one nondefamatory meaning that others understood, or that the communication was made in a joking manner and could not reasonably be taken seriously.

Publication

Publication refers to the communication of the libelous or slanderous statement to someone other than the individual who was defamed. Publication might occur in front of a group of people or simply when one individual makes a defamatory statement in a clearly audible voice, in a public place, directly to one person, and such statement is overheard by others. In such situations, the communicators either intend that others overhear the accusation, or they are not concerned with whether it is overheard, and their conduct is thereby regarded as reckless. An example of a costly slanderous statement occurred in front of a local veterinary association meeting in California a few years ago when, in the opinion of one member, the views of another member "should be discounted because everyone knows his son is queer."[80]

No libel or slander can take place if the victim is the one who reveals the communication to others, since the defamer must intentionally or recklessly promote publication. Republication by people other than the victim can provoke liability on the part of the defamer if the republication is a foreseeable consequence.

Identification of the Defamed Person

Plaintiffs must establish that they were the specific persons being defamed to prove a case of libel or slander. In many instances, the target of a defamatory communication is not clearly named, and identifying to a jury that the plaintiff was the subject of the defamatory statement can be a difficult proposition.

Injury or Damages

By their very definition, defamatory statements have the effect of tarnishing the reputation of the victim. Thus, the law recognizes that victims are entitled to compensation in the form of damages for any injuries sustained as a result of the libelous or slanderous statements.

In some cases, plaintiffs must plead and prove special damages, showing that they

. . . so I tol' Miz Sewall that the surgery Hackenslash did on her dog wuz the worst mess I'd ever seen . . .

have suffered actual and identifiable financial losses as a result of the defamatory statements. In other cases, *slander per se* and *libel per se*, general damages for mental distress, embarrassment, and loss of reputation can be awarded without the need to plead and prove special damages. Jurisdictions vary with regard to damage awards, but in general, words or statements such as the following do not require proof of special damages: (1) accusations that plaintiffs have loathsome and communicable diseases (such as a venereal disease and AIDS), (2) statements imputing unchastity (such as statements that victims are prostitutes), (3) slanderous statements about a plaintiff's calling, business, profession, or office (such as statements that certain veterinarians are quacks or are cruel to animals), and (4) statements imputing heinous crimes to plaintiffs (such as murder or any crime involving moral turpitude).

Legal precedents in the area of damages vary significantly and must be researched on a jurisdictional basis before veterinarians can determine whether or not they have a legitimate claim to pursue a libel or slander case.

Defenses

Just as there are four basic elements to prove a libel or slander case, there are four basic defenses.

Truth

The best defense to a defamation case is to prove that the statement or words are true. This rule is based on the rationale that people are not entitled to a greater reputation than they deserve and that the public benefits by knowing as much as possible about people in their community with whom they might need to deal. The motives of these communications are not relevant if truth is used as a defense.

Consent

Consent to publication of the defamatory statement by people who are libeled or slandered is another defense. This defense is a little more complex. As an example, Dr. A says to Dr. Q, "You know, Dr. Q, you are a no good, lousy, dishonest veterinarian and a disgrace to the veterinary profession." Shortly thereafter, Dr. G joins the vehement discussion. Dr. Q says to Dr. A, "Okay, Dr. A, repeat what you just said about me again in front of Dr. G." If Dr. A repeats this statement, and subsequently Dr. Q sues Dr. A for slander, the suit will be unsuccessful, since Dr. Q consented to publication of the slanderous statement to Dr. G.

Accident

If there was no negligence or intent to publish a defamatory statement, and it was truly an accident, this can serve as a valid defense to a suit for libel or slander. This can be a difficult position to support, but incidents can occur wherein a defamatory statement is heard about someone, and an error in the pronunciation or spelling of the name occurred.

Privilege

Some compelling interests of society justify an absolute privilege conferred on people who are directly involved in the furtherance of the public's business. Statements made during judicial proceedings by attorneys, judges, jurors, or witnesses are absolutely privileged on public policy grounds. Statements made during legislative proceedings are privileged as long as the words used are used in the person's role as a legislator and they pertain to legislative business.

Fair Comment About Public Officials and Public Figures

The traditional rule was that fair comment was the honest expression of the communicator's opinion on a matter of public interest based upon facts correctly stated in the communication. This general defense permitted political and artistic criticism by the media. Courts slowly expanded the scope of fair comment to include commentaries that contained exaggeration, sarcasm, ridicule, and even viciousness if justified by the underlying facts. The rationale for this expansion was that the public interest required that media professionals who furnish information about public servants should not be deterred from doing so by fear of potential lawsuits that would require proving the truth of their statements in court.

The United States Supreme Court voiced an opinion on the constitutionality of the fair comment privilege defense in the landmark case *New York Times Co.* v. *Sullivan*, when they held that defamatory communications concerning the official conduct of public officers were privileged under the First Amendment guarantee of freedom of the press.[81] Most importantly, the Court established the principle that public officials cannot recover damages for defamatory falsehoods relating to official conduct unless the officials prove with convincing clarity or reckless disregard of its genuineness that the statement is made with actual malice.[82] This requires proof of knowledge that the statement in question is false. Clearly, libel and slander recoveries by public officials are very difficult.

Subsequent legal decisions have extended the public official rule to cases involving public figures, where public figures include people who, through accomplishments, fame, mode of living, or adoption of a profession give the public a legitimate interest in their lives. People in this category include public officers, famous inventors and explorers, war heroes, athletes, musicians, and child prodigies. Any people who have positions such that public attention is focused upon them, regardless of whether they thrust themselves into the public's eye voluntarily or involuntarily, can qualify for inclusion in this category. Once they qualify as public figures or officers, defamatory material about them published without malice carries with it a qualified privilege of fair comment.

The area of libel and slander is constantly changing because of ethical, legal, and moral battles between an individual's right to privacy and the constitutional guarantees of freedom of speech. Because of this, expert legal counsel is essential if any legal action for libel or slander is to be undertaken or defended.

Wrongful Discharge

In recent years, the courts have created a new area of liability called *wrongful discharge*. Some of the legal decisions of wrongful discharge are based on standard tort law principles, while others arise from contract law. In either case, employers can be held liable for general, special, and punitive damages if courts hold that they have wrongfully terminated employees.

In the absence of an employment contract, most states historically have allowed employees to leave their employment at any time for any reason. At the same time, employers have been free to terminate employees without cause, or *at will*. An example of this concept codified by state law can be found in the California Labor Code § 2992, which reads in part: "An employment relationship, having no specified term, may

be terminated at the will of either party or on notice to the other." This precedent is known in legal circles as the *at will employment law doctrine*.

This concept has eroded recently in numerous courts in various states. In the California case of *Tamemy v. Atlantic Richfield Company*, an employee was fired for allegedly refusing to participate in a gas price fixing scheme.[83] In that case, the California Supreme Court held that there is a *public policy exception* to the at will doctrine. It ruled that the employee could recover general, special, and punitive damages for a wrongful termination even though the employment was for an unspecified term and was therefore technically at will.[84] It was held that termination for a reason that offends public policy, like not agreeing to support company action that could be held to violate antitrust laws, was unfair and improper.

The same year, another California case resulted in an even broader exception. In a case entitled *Cleary v. American Airlines*, Cleary, the plaintiff, had been employed by American Airlines for 18 years prior to the date he was fired for allegedly organizing union activities.[85] The employer failed to provide Cleary with a hearing prior to termination, as required by the company's own employee policy manual. The court held that, because of the longevity of service and the violation of the company's employee manual, Cleary was fired without just cause. Under these circumstances, the court decided that American Airlines had violated an implied covenant of good faith and fair dealing that was present in every employment contract. This is a good example of court-made law, adopted to provide fairness and compensation to what the public would otherwise consider to be unfair behavior on the part of an employer.

In a third major California case, *Pugh v. See's Candies*, the court found that an employer had breached an implied promise of continued employment.[86] The Court ruled that because of the employee's 31 years of successful employment, commendations, and promotions, the lack of direct criticism of the employee's work, and the employer's well-known policy of retaining "loyal" employees, the employee was entitled to an implied promise of continued employment. Thus, the at will doctrine suffered further erosion into what is rapidly becoming the "at will with adequate justification" doctrine.

One other interesting case involved a Michigan employee who sued his employer for age discrimination, wrongful discharge, and negligence. In that case, a 22-year-old employee claimed that he had been fired because he was "burned out" and because he and his employer did not get along. The court found that none of these reasons amounted to age discrimination. Moreover, due to the employee's repeated insubordination, the court found that there was just cause for discharge. However, the court ruled that the company was negligent because the employee was not advised in his annual evaluation that a failure to improve his performance would mean his dismissal. The court awarded $360,906 in damages, which was reduced to $61,354, because the employee was 83% responsible for his own termination.[87]

Avoiding Liability

New trends in the area of employment law have put employers on guard to develop techniques for improving employee/employer relations and avoid liability. The following is a list of measures that can be taken to minimize potential liability:

1. If written contracts exist with employees, or if there is a hospital employment policy manual, specify in either or both documents that employment of employees may be terminated by the employer on two weeks' notice with or without cause.

2. When internal procedures exist to deal with excessive tardiness, absenteeism, use of telephones for personal calls, etc., employees should be told in advance what conduct is considered excessive, and then hospital policies should be applied to all employees.

3. If termination policies are going to be changed or implemented for the first time, copies of those policies should be posted in a conspicuous spot or brought to the employees' attention in the form of a written handout or individual discussions.

4. Written employee performance evaluations should be completed on a regular basis (semiannually or annually). If there are no evaluations, accurate written records of reprimands or discussions about job performance should be kept for each employee.

5. When an employee's work is unsatisfactory, regular wage increases should be withheld until performance improves sufficiently to justify a raise. Policies that give automatic raises based solely on employment for specified amounts of time should be avoided.

6. When employees are performing work in an unsatisfactory manner, they should be told about it, allowed an opportunity to respond, and given a specified period of time to improve their performance.

7. If employees who are performing unsatisfactorily are under some type of short-term stress (pregnancy, family death or illness, personal problems, etc.), employers should advise them of their dissatisfaction with the performance and inform them that were it not for these problems they would be asked to leave. They should be given an opportunity to improve once the short-term problems are resolved, at which time they can be reevaluated or terminated.

8. Employees should never be denied employment or fired for reasons related to race, religion, color, national origin, ancestry, handicap, medical condition, marital status, age, sex, or pregnancy.

With these policies as guidelines, most employers will be able to avoid legal entanglements with employment law precedents whether or not they have a full understanding of all the labor law principles.

References

1. Dinsmore JR: Injuries to people. *Professional Liability. AVMA Prof Liability Trust Rep* 6(4):3, 1987.
2. AVMA Professional Liability Insurance Trust, PO Box 74221, Chicago, IL 60690-8221 (1988).
3. *Black's Law Dictionary*, ed 5. St. Paul, MN, West Publishing Co, 1979, p 931.
4. *The Guide to American Law*, vol 8. St. Paul, MN, West Publishing Co, 1984, pp 5-6.
5. Hannah HW: Legal brief. Refusal to treat and refusal to continue treatment. *JAVMA* 186(7):666, 1985.
6. *Matter of Kerlin*, 367 A2d 939 (NJ 1977).
7. *Posnien v Rogers*, 533 P2d 120 (UT 1975); *Ruden v Hansen*, 206 NW2d 713 (IA 1973); *Brockett v Abbe*, 206 A2d 447 (Conn 1964).
8. Favre DS, Loring M: *Animal Law*. Westport, CT, Quorum Books, 1983, p 115.
9. *Posnien v Rogers*, 533 P2d 120 (UT 1975); *Dyess v Caraway*, 190 So2d 666 (La 1966).
10. *Williams v Reynolds*, 263 SE2d 853 (NC 1980).
11. *Ruden v Hansen*, 206 NW2d 713 (IA 1973).
12. Hannah HW: Legal brief: The similar locality rule. *JAVMA* 173(5):458, 1978.
13. Dinsmore J: AVMA Professional Liability Insurance Trust. Personal communication: Electric heating pad burns are common, and such devices should not be used unless they are the water blanket type or have specially built controls designed to prevent burns from occurring to patients in contact with them.
14. Weintraub A: Physician's duty to stay abreast of current medical developments. *Med Trial Tech Quart*: 331, 1985.
15. Kirk RW: *Current Veterinary Therapy VII*. Philadelphia, WB Saunders Co, 1980, p 984; Kirk RW: *Current Veterinary Therapy VIII*. Philadelphia, WB Saunders Co, 1983, pp 857-858; Kirk RW: *Current Veterinary Therapy IX*. Philadelphia, WB Saunders Co, 1986, p 974.
16. Cardiopet Division of Animed, Inc, 25 Lumber Rd, Roslyn, NY 11576-2105; 800-652-2700.
17. Miller MS, Gertsen KE, Dawson H: Paroxysmal atrial fibrillation: A case report. *Equine Vet Sci* 7(2):95, 1987; Tobin T: Sudden death in racing horses: The "Swale" syndrome? *Equine Vet Sci* 7(3):184-185, 1987; Gelberg HB, Zachary JF, Everitt JI, et al: Sudden death in training and racing thoroughbred horses. *JAVMA* 187(12):1354-1356, 1985.
18. Cardiopet Division of Animed, Inc. A recorder-transmitter costs $650, and resting and postexercise ECGs cost $50. See *supra*, note 16.
19. Hannah HW: Legal brief: The general practitioner and the specialist. *JAVMA* 174(5):462, 1979.
20. Stevens GE: Malpractice liability of a referring physician. *Med Trial Tech Quart* (Fall):121, 124-125, 1985.
21. 61 Am Jur 2d 612, Physicians Surgeons and Other Healers, § 295, 1981.
22. Hannah HW: Legal brief: Practice standards and the standard of skill and care. *JAVMA* 188(5):497, 1986.
23. Greenbaum H: *West State Law Rev* 7:3, 1979.
24. *Canterbury v Spence*, 464 F. 2d 780, 786 (DC Cir 1972).
25. Trichter GJ, Lewis PW: Informed consent: The three tests and a modest proposal for the reality of the patient as an individual. *So Texas Law J* 21:155-156, 159, 161, 1981.
26. *Scott v Bradford*, 606 P2d 554, 558 (Okla 1979).
27. Insurance notes: Anatomy of AVMA's largest malpractice insurance claim. *JAVMA* 188(1):26-27, 1986.
28. *Sarkesian v Cedric Chase Photographic Laboratories, Inc*, 324 Mass 620, 87 NE2d 745-746 (1949) (lost roll of film).
29. *Green v Boston* and *Lowell Railroad*, 128 Mass 221, 226-227, 1880.
30. *Accord, Hall v Paine*, 224 Mass 62, 68 (1916) ("In general when exceptional circumstances appear which demonstrate that the rule of fair market value would not afford compensation, then the usual principle becomes no longer applicable and inquiry is made as to the real damages sustained..."); *Weston v Boston* and *Maine Railroad*, 190 Mass 298, 300 (1906) ("[W]here the property...has no market value but has a special damage to the plaintiff he can recover that value"); *Wall v Platt*, 169 Mass 398, 406-407 (1897) ("In some cases there is no market value, properly speaking, and in others, if there is, it plainly would not of itself afford full indemnity...[F]air market value...would have nothing to do with the real value of the articles, or with their actual worth to the owner...[T]he damages should be assessed according to the actual worth of the articles to her...at the time of the fire.")
31. *Mieske v Bartell Drug Company*, 92 Wash 2d 40, 593 P2d 1308,1310 (1979).
32. Favre DS, Loring M: *Animal Law*. Westport, CT, Quorum Books, 1983, pp 55-57, 61.

33. *Julian v De Vincent*, 184 SE2d 535 (WV 1971).

34. O'Brien J: Personal communication, President, Mason McDuffie Insurance Services, Inc, Pleasant Hill, CA, 1987.

35. *Moultrie Farm Center, Inc.* v *Sparkman*, 320 SE2d 863-864 (Ga App 1984).

36. *Bennett v Smith*, 245 Ga 725, 267 SE2d 19 (1980).

37. *MacPhail v Sagner*, 266 Md 318, 293 A2d 257 (1972).

38. Dinsmore J: AVMA Professional Liability Insurance Trust. Personal communications, 1987.

39. *City of Garland et al* v *White*, 368 SW2d 12 (1963).

40. *LaPorte v Associated Independents, Inc*, 163 So 2d 267 (Fla 1964).

41. *Levine v Knowles*, 197 So2d 329 (Fla 1967), same case 218 So2d 217 (1969), 228 So2d 308 (1969).

42. *Knowles Animal Hospital, Inc v Wills*, 360 So2d 37 (Fla 1978).

43. *Brown v Crocker*, 139 So2d 779 (La App 2 Cir 1962).

44. *Lincecum v Smith*, 287 So2d 625 (La 1973).

45. *Peloquin v Calcasieu Parish Police Jury*, 367 So2d 1246 (La 1979).

46. *Campbell v Animal Quarantine Station*, 632 P2d 1066 (Hawaii 1981).

47. *Dillon v Legg*, 69 Cal Rptr 72, 441 P2d 912 (1968).

48. The Hawaii Court approved the following jury instruction: Plaintiffs have a right to recover all damages which they have suffered and which the defendants or a reasonable person in the defendants' position should have foreseen would result from their acts or omissions. Such damages may include reasonable compensation for emotional distress and disappointment, if any....There is no precise standard by which to place a monetary value on emotional distress and disappointment, nor is the opinion of any witness required to fix a reasonable amount. In making an award of damages for emotional distress and disappointment, you should determine an amount which your own experience and reason indicate would be sufficient in light of all of the evidence. Campbell, *supra* note 46 at p 1070.

49. Mazor D: Veterinarians at fault—Rare breed of malpractitioners. *UC Davis Law Rev* 7:400, 408, 1978.

50. *Molien v Kaiser Foundation Hospitals*, 27 Cal3d 916; 616 P2d 813 (1980).

51. *Cooper v The Superior Court of Los Angeles County* and *Lomita Trenching and Excavating Inc*, 153 Cal App3d 1008, 1009; 200 Cal Rptr 746 (1984).

52. *Brown v Frontier Theaters*, 369 SW2d 299, 304, 305 (1963).

53. *Windeler v Scheers Jewelers*, 8 CA3d 844, 852; 88 Cal Rptr 39 (1970).

54. *Hannah HW: Legal brief: Pet owners and punitive damages. JAVMA* 179(3):224, 1971.

55. *Wilson v City of Eagan*, 297 NW2d 146, 151 (1980).

56. Strobel MJ: Malpractice by veterinarians. *15 Clev-Mar Law Rev* 2:277, 1966.

57. Hirsh HL: Legal ramifications of consultation and referrals. *Legal Aspects Med Pract* 13(12):2, 1985.

58. Hannah HW: Legal brief: Malpractice—The veterinarian's duty to call in a specialist. *JAVMA* 165(5):400, l974.

59. *Byrne v Boadle*, 2 H & C 722, 159 Eng Rep 299 (Exch 1863).

60. Hannah HW: Is res ipsa for the dogs? *3 Val Law Rev* 3: 183-185, 195, 1969.

61. *Johnson v Marshall*, 241 Ill App 80, 89 (1926).

62. Prosser WL: *Cases and Materials on Torts*, ed 3. St. Paul, MN, West Publishing Co, l964, p 295.

63. Hannah HW: Legal brief: Comparative negligence and the veterinarian. *JAVMA* 184(3):259, 1984.

64. Hannah HW: Legal brief: The client's contributory negligence. *JAVMA* 175(3):264, 1979.

65. Torts/Statute of Limitations. *Ill Bar J* 70:661, 1982.

66. Insurance note: Professional liability insurance: What it is and what it is not. *JAVMA* 180 (11):1291, 1982.

67. Hannah HW: Legal brief: Settlement without consent. *JAVMA* 180(1):31, 1982.

68. Bailment coverage offered with AVMA liability insurance. *JAVMA* 188(3):229, 1986.

69. Birnbaum SL: Physicians counterattack: Liability of lawyers for instituting unjustified medical malpractice actions. *Fordham Law Rev* 45:1003, 1977.

70. Logan S: Physicians countersuits: An eye for an eye, a tooth for a tooth, etc. *Med Trial Tech Quart* 32:153, 154, 156, 162, 1985.

71. Janzer: Countersuits to legal and medical malpractice actions: Any chance for success? *Marq Law Rev* 65:93, 1981.

72. Greenbaum H: Physician countersuits: A cause without action. *Pac Law J* 12:745, 1981.

73. *Bull v McCuskey*, 615 P2d 957 (1980).

74. *Brody v Ruby*, 267 NW2d 902 (IA 1978).

75. Code of Professional R. for Lawyers. DR6-101[A][2], DR7-102[A][2].

76. *Mogul S.S. Co v McGregor & Co, Med Trial TechQuart* (fall):endnote 20, 121, l985.

77. *Read v Coker*, 13 CB 850, 138 Eng Rep 1437 (Common Pleas, 1853).

78. *Condict v Hewitt*, 369 P2d 278 (Wyo 1962).

79. Sox J: Beware of unguarded guard dogs. *Calif Vet* 3:37, 1979.
80. O'Brien J: Personal communication. (President, Mason McDuffie Insurance Services, Inc, Pleasant Hill, CA). This case was settled out of court by payment of $10,000 to the complaining veterinarian.
81. 376 U.S. 254, 84 S Ct 710 (1964).
82. *Guide to American Law*. St. Paul, MN, West Publishing Co, 1984, vol 7, p 173.
83. 27 Cal3d 167 (1980).
84. Wheelwright KW: Wrongful termination of employees—Let the boss beware! *Calif Vet* 3:75, 1984.
85. 111 Cal App 3d 433 (1980).
86. 16 Cal App 3d 311 (1981).
87. Schachter V: Update on current developments in employment law for veterinary practitioner. *Calif Vet* 3:72, 1984.

CHAPTER 7

Antitrust and Advertising

In 1975 the United States Supreme Court handed down a landmark antitrust decision that is continuing to have an impact on the veterinary profession today. The case known as *Goldfarb* v. *Virginia Bar*[1] held that the learned professions (medical, legal, veterinary, accounting, architecture, etc.) are not exempt from the federal antitrust laws. The *Goldfarb* case involved minimum fee schedules established by attorneys, but its holding indicated that none of the professions is exempt from the Sherman Antitrust Act.

Antitrust Among the Professions Prior to 1975

Changes in the American way of life since World War II have caused professional operations to evolve from a manufacturing-oriented to a service-oriented economy. The nation has become very consumer oriented, requiring high standards of performance from industry and the professions.

Advances in science, medicine, and technology have brought to Americans extensive medical, dental, and veterinary care. The costs of human health care outranked the consumer price index year after year as scientific advances in such areas as angiography, CT scanning, ultrasound diagnostics, magnetic resonance imaging, and cardiac bypass surgery became common.

Consumer advocates like Ralph Nader began making headlines in the 1960s. Consumer advocacy became a popular political campaign issue by the early 1970s. The American public including professionals rallied behind those consumer advocates and governmental agencies as they exposed price fixing in the oil industry, the pharmaceutical business, and the big grain dealers. Everything was fine as long as no one disturbed the status quo of the professions.

During this time and prior to it, professional associations were utilizing minimum fee schedules. Some veterinary association codes of ethics contained covenants that "No member shall endeavor to build up a practice by undercharging another practitioner."[2] Many had prohibitions against advertising of professional services. Professional people failed to recognize that, through the licensing process, the states grant them a limited form of monopoly on the practice of their professions.

These measures were permitted under the guise of maintaining high standards of medical care. In 1975, however, the American public (and the courts) decided that some of those strict measures were neither justified nor effective.

This was the backdrop to the 1975 Supreme Court case that changed the law.

The Goldfarb v. Virginia Bar Case

In 1922 a United States Supreme Court case held that attorneys traveling interstate performing professional duties were not engaged in commerce.[3] A 1931 case established that the practice of medicine was a profession and not a trade.[4] Other Supreme Court cases between 1922 and 1950 mentioned the issue of whether people practicing a profession were in trade or commerce, but the Supreme Court held that in those cases the references to trade or commerce were "passing references in cases concerned with other issues."[5] The court said that until it chose to hear the *Goldfarb* case, it had never attempted to decide whether the practice of a learned profession fell within the Sherman Act. The reason that the trade or commerce issue is so important is because, without it, the Sherman Act has no jurisdiction over professional activities.

The law in this area began to change in 1971 when a husband and wife, the Goldfarbs, contracted to purchase a house in Fairfax County, Virginia. The financing agency required the couple to secure title insurance, and this required a title examination. When they contacted a lawyer to perform that service, the attorney quoted a fee of 1% of the property value for performing the title search. The couple wrote to 36 other lawyers in Fairfax County requesting fee quotations for title searches. Nineteen

lawyers responded, all quoting the couple the same 1% fee which was the fee published in the Fairfax County Bar minimum fee schedule. Several respondents stated that they knew of no attorney who would charge less than the 1% minimum fee.

The couple had the real estate title examined and then filed a class action lawsuit against the County Bar for maintaining a fee schedule and against the Virginia State Bar because only a member of the State Bar could do title searches. The District Court held that the fee schedule violated the Sherman Act and that the learned professions were not exempt from coverage. The Court of Appeals reversed that decision, stating that the practice of law was not trade or commerce under the Sherman Antitrust Act.

On June 16, 1975, the United States Supreme Court decided the *Goldfarb* case by supporting the trial court's view that "suggested minimum fee schedules" constituted a classic illustration of price fixing. They also found that the other elements required for a Sherman Antitrust Act violation (like interstate trade or commerce) were present. The precedent still stands today.

The Sherman Antitrust Act

The Objective

All federal and state antitrust legislation preserves the underlying principle that our nation shall function under a competitive business economy. The basic unifying principle of these statutes is to ensure economic freedom for competitors and consumers.[6] A 1972 United States Supreme Court case says it well:

> Antitrust laws in general, and the Sherman Act in particular, are the Magna Carta of free-enterprise. They are as important to the preservation of economic freedom and our free-enterprise system

as the Bill of Rights is to the protection of our fundamental personal freedoms. And the freedom guaranteed each and every business, no matter how small, is the freedom to compete—to assert with vigor, imagination, devotion, and ingenuity whatever economic muscle it can muster.[7]

Delegation of Administration

The second unifying principle of the antitrust laws is the decision of Congress, exemplified in each of the four statutes, to place a wide degree of discretion in the interpretation and application of the laws into the hands of the Department of Justice, the Federal Trade Commission (FTC), and the courts.

Arms of Government as the Enforcer

The Antitrust Division of the Department of Justice initiates most legal proceedings under the federal laws. The first antitrust cases brought against the veterinary profession after the *Goldfarb* case occurred in the spring of 1976 when the Alameda and San Diego County Veterinary Medical Associations in California were indicted. Members of these associations were accused of violating federal antitrust laws because of the following actions: (1) conducting fee surveys; (2) publishing results of fee schedules; (3) adopting minimum fee schedules; (4) adopting minimum suggested fee schedules; (5) publishing, circulating, and utilizing minimum and suggested fee schedules; and (6) prohibiting members from accepting referrals from animal welfare agencies for spay and neuter operations at reduced fees. Both cases were settled with the signing of consent decrees stating that members would no longer engage in such activities. Legal fees for the two actions totaled more than $30,000.

A similar case against the Arizona Veteri-nary Medical Association was filed by the Arizona Attorney General under state antitrust statutes in the spring of 1976. This suit alleged that the association circulated minimum fee schedules, that members conspired not to solicit or compete for each other's customers, and that members agreed not to advertise medical services and products.[2] The result, according to the allegations, was that the prices of veterinary services and products were maintained and stabilized at artificial and noncompetitive levels, and purchasers of those services were deprived of the benefits of a free and open marketplace. After considerable legal expense, this case, too, was settled out of court (with intervention by the governor) on the day before it was to go to trial. Changes in Arizona's Code of Ethics were made to reflect the new legal precedents involving minimum-fee schedules and advertising of routine professional services.

Private Litigants as the Enforcer

Actions under federal antitrust statutes can also be initiated by private litigants. Sections of the laws allowing courts to award treble damages and attorneys' fees have encouraged such suits. A good example of the effectiveness of this type of litigation occurred in California, where a legal action was filed based on antitrust violations and slander. The case involved a company engaged in low-cost mobile vaccination clinics filing a suit against numerous veterinarians and two veterinary associations. Similar to the Justice Department cases and the Arizona VMA case before it, this case concluded with an out-of-court settlement. Settlement costs in excess of $400,000 awakened the profession to the risks of antitrust violations.[8]

Another example of private litigation as a means of attempting to enforce the Sherman Act began in 1979 when four veterinarians filed an antitrust action against the AVMA, the American College of Veterinary Ophthalmologists (ACVO), the Canine Eye Registration Foundation (CERF), and 11 veterinarians who were members or officers of ACVO.[9] This attempt failed and, in fact, backfired with countersuits successfully filed against them.

CERF is a nonprofit, tax-exempt, charitable organization. Its purpose is to collect, collate, and disseminate information concerning hereditary eye diseases in dogs by establishing a registry listing purebred dogs of those breeds that are susceptible to hereditary eye diseases. CERF's procedures required that dogs be examined by veterinarians certified by the ACVO before listing them in its registry. ACVO veterinarians evaluated the dogs using forms provided by CERF and returned copies of the form to CERF. When owners remitted the originals to CERF with a $5 registration fee, CERF issued certificates to the dog owners.

The four plaintiffs, all veterinarians, claimed that they were denied the opportunity to participate in CERF-sponsored canine eye-evaluation clinics because they were not board-certified veterinary ophthalmologists. They also alleged that CERF and ACVO engaged in a group boycott, an illegal tie-in arrangement, and price fixing, since all ACVO members charged between $5 to $7.50 per animal for the eye examination. The plaintiffs asked for monetary damages in the form of lost income, because of the restrictions against their performance of these special eye examinations and damage to their reputations. Their allegations were based on several legal theories. They also asked that both ACVO and CERF be disbanded permanently.

The case was tried in the Federal District Court in San Francisco. The veterinarians lost on all counts; the ruling was appealed and the judgment of the trial court was upheld on every legal point. The veterinary plaintiffs failed to prove any of their allegations. The appellate court decision subsequently was upheld by the United States Supreme Court, when it denied certiorari (the right to be heard).

This case is possibly the only veterinary-related antitrust case that has gone to trial and has had appellate decisions published.

Some of the language of the court is included herein to provide guidelines for other veterinary organizations confronted with similar tie-in arrangements. The court held that even though there was evidence of a series of discussions and committee activities between ACVO and CERF, there was insufficient evidence of a contract, combination, or conspiracy to meet the requirements for that element of the Sherman Act. The discussion goes on to say that:

> Even if there were sufficient evidence of an agreement, the record before us demonstrates that the 'agreement' amounts to nothing more than a type of exclusive dealership agreement: CERF provided examination forms only to ACVO members and would accept no other type of form for inclusion in its registry. The reason justifying this CERF-ACVO relationship is valid. ACVO members are the only veterinarians who have objectively demonstrated that they are qualified to perform the hereditary eye examination. Obviously, examination reliability is of utmost concern to CERF.[10]

The court also said that this type of exclusive dealership arrangement is not violative of Section 1 of the Sherman Act. In reviewing this issue, the appellate court cited several other cases and said:

> We must begin with the well-settled proposition that a trader has the right to deal or refuse to deal with whomever he pleases for reasons sufficient to himself. A refusal to deal is not unlawful unless it implements an arrangement to restrain trade by, for example, enforcing price maintenance, barring a competitor from a market, or maintaining a dominant market position.[11]

The entire decision in the *Rickards* v. *CERF* case should be read by veterinarians or their legal counsel whenever any relationships with other organizations could lead to claims of antitrust violations. These organizations did many things right, and therefore antitrust allegations against them could not be upheld. If the court had determined that this type of discriminatory activity by board-certified specialists and private organizations violated antitrust laws, it would have been a tremendous blow to the entire array of exclusive-dealing privileges that go along with the status accorded board-certified specialists in all of the healing arts professions.

During the evolution of this case, with encouragement from the court, CERF filed a counterclaim against the four veterinarians. In that counterclaim, CERF alleged that the four veterinarians had violated Sections 1 and 2 of the Sherman Act, filed a vexatious complaint for an improper purpose, wrongfully interfered with CERF's present and prospective business relationships, and violated California antitrust laws and the California Unfair Trade Practices Act.[12] They also contended that the actions of the defendants amounted to malicious prosecution and abuse of the legal process—allegations that are usually very difficult to prove.

On March 1, 1984, the federal court magistrate signed an order for partial final judgment and held that:

> the Rickards group had (1) violated Section 1 of the Sherman Act under both the rule of reason and per se standards; (2) violated Section 2 of the Sherman Act by engaging in a conspiracy to monopolize and an attempt to monopolize trade or commerce; and (3) "brought a lawsuit which was baseless and a sham, and in furtherance of their overall scheme to violate the antitrust laws.[13]

The court awarded CERF $416,894 in damages and trebled that amount ($1,256,682) pursuant to 15 U.S.C. § 15. In June 1985 that decision was appealed to the United States Court of Appeals. On February 27, 1986, the appeals court upheld the trial court's judgment. This decision, too, was appealed to the United States Supreme Court and that court again refused to hear the case, thus upholding the district court's judgment.

In November 1986 the United States District Court for the Northern District of California granted a partial summary judg-

ment in favor of CERF on the issue of the veterinarians' liability for malicious prosecution. On February 6, 1987, the same court also granted CERF's motion for partial summary judgment on the issue of abuse of process.

To date, CERF and its founders have not recouped any of the approximately $500,000 expended in legal fees. The four veterinarians have liens against their assets in excess of $1.25 million, and CERF now has sought to recover damages from the insurance companies of the veterinarians. Some valuable legal precedents were established for veterinarians, but not without great personal and financial cost to many people.

The FTC and the Courts as Interpreter of the Law

The FTC and the courts are responsible for the interpretation and application of the competitive objectives of the antitrust laws. Because Congress granted a great deal of interpretative leeway to these branches of government, considerable confusion and inconsistency exists. With respect to the Sherman Act, it has been pointed out that:

> The prohibitions of the Sherman Act were not stated in terms of precision or of crystal clarity and the Act itself did not define them. In consequence of the vagueness of its language...the courts have been left to give content to the statute...[13]

The same basic philosophy exists regarding the Federal Trade Commission Act, where decisions about what constitutes unfair methods of competition are also without specific statutory definition.

Language of the Sherman Antitrust Act

The Sherman Antitrust Act was enacted in 1890. Sections 1 and 2 of this act provide

Every contract, combination in the form

of trust or otherwise, or conspiracy, in restraint of trade or commerce among the several States, or with foreign nations, is declared to be illegal. Every person who shall make any contract or engage in any combination or conspiracy hereby declared to be illegal shall be deemed guilty of a felony and, on conviction thereof, shall be punished by fine not exceeding one million dollars if a corporation, or, if any other person, one hundred thousand dollars, or by imprisonment not exceeding three years, or by both said punishments, in the discretion of the court.[14]

The only changes of substance to this section in the past 100 years are those substantially increasing the criminal penalties.

Combinations, Contracts, and Conspiracies

Section 1 applies only if three conditions are met. The first is proof of a contract, combination, or conspiracy. A contract is an agreement between two or more parties in which each party is bound to do or refrain from doing some act. A combination is the union of two or more previously independent persons. A conspiracy is a combination of two or more people planning and acting together secretly, especially for an unlawful or harmful purpose. In this case that purpose is to restrain trade.

Each of these terms also requires proof of *intent* as an element. In a conspiracy, two different types of intent are generally required. The first is a basic intent to agree. The second is the more traditional intent to effectuate the object of the conspiracy.[15] Proof of one of the initial three elements of the Sherman Act and an intent to commit an act in restraint of trade satisfy the first requirement under the federal antitrust laws.

In veterinary terms, it is likely that a discussion between two or more practitioners from different businesses to raise, maintain, or lower fees could be viewed as a contract, combination, or conspiracy.

Whether or not an inquiry by one practitioner to another regarding a fee charged for a given service, without any additional discussion, constitutes an illegal act is questionable. Also of concern are discussions or agreements among colleagues to share emergency calls or to arrange for identical hours of business.

Whether or not these acts are illegal depends on the facts ancillary to the inquiries, discussions, or agreements. Absolute answers may not exist because the issues have not been tested in court.

Trade or Commerce

Section 1 of the Sherman Act is applicable only if the contract, combination, or conspiracy restrains interstate trade or commerce. The terms *trade* or *commerce* have been interpreted by specific court decisions to include the transportation of goods and passengers, the sale of commodities, dealings in intangibles, commercial services and, as in the *Goldfarb* case, the practice of law.[6]

While it is advantageous to be able to prove the existence of an explicit agreement, the existence of an agreement can be proved with circumstantial evidence.[16] Attendance at meetings of competitors, such as trade or professional meetings, followed by uniform prices or other business conduct may be sufficient to show agreement. A tacit understanding suffices and a "knowing wink can mean more than words."[17] The agreement may be inferred from admissions in correspondence, from the existence and content of telephone conversations with competitors or colleagues, or from the bylaws or minutes of a trade or professional association. The FTC investigation of the veterinary profession from 1978 through 1980 required the American Veterinary Medical Association, the California Veterinary Medical Association and numerous other state and local associations to expend considerable time and effort retrieving and photocopying minutes from board and committee meetings in order to comply with the FTC's request for information.

Overall, the court has considerable leeway to determine what conduct meets the statutory requirements. Consequently, great restraint must be exercised in any forum when practitioners start discussing fees with colleagues.

The Interstate Commerce Requirement

In order for contracts, combinations, or conspiracies to fall within the jurisdiction of the Sherman Act, the interstate commerce element also must be satisfied. This requirement is met if the challenged activity occurs or is part of the flow of commerce among various states. In the *Goldfarb* case, title examinations by attorneys were held to be an integral part of interstate transactions. If that nexus is not found, a second standard can be used to satisfy this element. Even if the activity is purely local in character, the interstate jurisdictional requirement is met if the activity affects interstate commerce.

In an Oklahoma case, the defendant was an electric utility company whose service area was limited to the State of Oklahoma.[18] The plaintiff, an outdoor lighting business in Tulsa, alleged that the Public Service Company had attempted to monopolize the outdoor lighting business in the Tulsa metropolitan area. The court found that the supplying of illumination in and around the Tulsa area, although local in nature, had a substantial impact on interstate commerce because of the repeated, ongoing interstate purchase of lights and lighting components by both the plaintiff and defendant. This impact on interstate commerce was sufficient to meet the interstate commerce requirement of the Sherman Act.

When the Justice Department filed the antitrust actions against the Alameda and San Diego County Veterinary Medical Associations, the Justice Department contended that substantially all anesthetics, drugs, antibiotics, vaccines, and surgical supplies used by association members were manufactured in states other than California.

We've got to come to some 'understanding' about these fees or we'll all go broke.

Additionally, they stated that health certificates written by members for animals traveling interstate affected interstate commerce. The issue of whether this was truly sufficient interstate commerce to come under the umbrella of the Sherman Act was never judicially resolved, because the cases were eventually settled out of court. However, other cases like the Oklahoma case indicate that courts have very broad powers in determining what constitutes an effect on interstate commerce.

Restraints of Trade

Section 1 of the Sherman Act provides that *every* contract that restrains trade is illegal. If this were to be interpreted literally, many business agreements would be banned. To prevent this from happening, the Supreme Court held that the term *every* means only those contracts, combinations, and conspiracies that *unreasonably* restrain trade are prohibited.[19] It was this judicial limitation that led to what is known as the *rule of reason*. Under this rule, courts evaluating the legality of a restraint will consider a variety of market factors such as the nature of the restraint and its effect, market conditions, and the history of the restraint.[20]

The Per Se Rule

A major corollary of the rule of reason is the *per se rule*. The court has held that certain practices were so plainly anticompetitive that they are conclusively presumed illegal without the examination of any market factors or business reason for their existence.[21] Per se illegality is limited to those practices that lack any redeeming virtue and have no purpose except to stifle competition. Included in the per se category are agreements between competitors whose only purpose is to (1) fix prices (upward, downward, or remaining the same), (2) allocate territory or divide markets, (3) limit production, and (4) boycott third parties.[6]

In the *Goldfarb* case, the court said the following about price fixing and professional association involvement therein:

> A professional association cannot separate itself far enough from its members or work in a sufficient vacuum so as not to influence its members if it publishes such information. Therefore, mere guidelines, though not price fixing per se, could easily be utilized by members in setting their fees and, thus, still violate the Sherman Act.[22]

Since this ruling, any association participating in the pricing of professional fees runs the risk of being accused of price fixing even if it is purely advisory in nature.

Average fee schedules published by individual nonveterinary association entities, e.g.,*Veterinary Economics* journal or practice management newsletters, have not been challenged. Likewise, fee schedules established for emergency clinics by a board of directors, where the board is comprised of practitioners from competing practices, have not been challenged either. A key reason is that in these examples, there is no contract, combination, or conspiracy among individual business entities.

The Rule of Reason

If a business practice is held not to be a per se restraint of trade, it does not necessarily mean that the practice is legal. The court must still determine the reasonableness of any restraint in which the business is involved. The burden of proof in such cases is on plaintiffs to show that the challenged business practice is unreasonable, and defendants are not required to prove that their business practices are reasonable.[17] Consequently, there are no ready answers about the legality or illegality of business practices that are not classified as illegal per se. Instead, the courts interpret cases on an individual basis as they arise.

Examples of veterinary business practices that could fall under the rule of reason include (1) agreements by colleagues (competitors) to close for a particular holiday and send all their cases to an emergency clinic, (2) agreements to close on Saturdays or in the evening at a particular hour of the day, and (3) agreements between members of a professional association or a group of nonaffiliated practitioners to rotate emergency calls from one hospital to another and set the after-hours emergency fee at a specified high cost at all involved hospitals.

All of these business practices could be considered restraints of trade in one form or another, yet all of them seem reasonable to the average practitioner who is trying to make a living and still preserve a satisfactory home life. How the court would view these restraints is an unresolved issue.

The only basis for deciding the legality of these practices in veterinary medicine is found in the now famous footnote 17 of the *Goldfarb* case. That note said:

> The public service aspect, and other features of the professions, may require that a particular practice, which could be viewed as a violation of the Sherman Act in another context, be treated differently.

The public service aspects of veterinary medicine, and the need to provide rational agreements pertaining to emergency care and office hours may allow a court to find that agreements like these are not illegal restraints of trade. Until the issues in these examples are adjudicated, though, answers will not be definitive.

A Hypothetical Example

An example of a situation in which a court might find that the activity of a group of veterinarians violates the antitrust laws can be hypothesized. A business that operates low-cost mobile vaccination clinics begins advertising and holding monthly clinics in the local supermarket parking lot. Several local veterinarians are angry because the mobile clinic does not pay local property taxes or other city taxes. They feel this is unfair competition. After several months have passed, they agree to establish their own low-cost vaccination clinics across the street at the identical time the others are held. This occurs for two consecutive months whereupon they discover that the newcomer has ceased all activities in their city. They are thrilled and celebrate their success by holding a third and last low-cost clinic.

Six months later these local practitioners are hit with a lawsuit by the owner of the mobile clinics. The suit claims that the actions of the group constituted a violation of the antitrust laws.

What is their potential liability? Is interstate commerce involved? Is this a per se violation, or would the rule of reason apply? These are tough questions—ones that would likely be decided in a court of law.

Would the situation be any different if the local practitioners had contacted the supermarket store manager and convinced him not to rent space to this mobile clinic instead of their setting up a competing clinic?

Both of these examples reek of antitrust violations and should be avoided at all costs. If local veterinarians form a separate business entity for the purpose of holding low-cost vaccine clinics, operate it as a separate business entity, and continue holding regular low-cost clinics for a few years after the initial business ceases to hold its own clinics, a strong case can be made that an antitrust violation has not occurred. Also, if practitioners approach their city governments requesting public hearings on the public health, unfair competition, and liability aspects of low-cost vaccine clinics instead of *conspiring* with the supermarket manager not to allow the mobile clinics, they will have a much better defense if any antitrust action is filed.

The potential for private litigation for antitrust violations is endless. Most states have their own antitrust laws wherein proof of an effect on interstate commerce is not needed. Therefore, practitioners should not engage in any communal activities that could be viewed as a restraint of trade without first seeking the advice of legal counsel.

Sherman Act Exemptions

There are exemptions to the Sherman Act that allow certain industries to avoid violations of the antitrust laws. The activities of labor unions establishing wages for entire industries clearly fall under the per se category of restraints of trade. The insurance industry is another one that appears to consistently violate the law in this area.

The reason some industries are not covered by the antitrust laws is because they were legislatively exempted from coverage. The insurance business, labor unions, and professional sports are examples of industries that need not be concerned about restraints of trade because of their exemptions.

The Statutory Basis for Penalties

Section 2 of the Sherman Act establishes the penalties for people convicted of federal antitrust violations. If a corporation is involved, a fine of up to $1 million can be imposed. When a person is convicted, the fine may be as high as $100,000. The court may also sentence the individual to three years in prison instead of issuing the fine, or it may enforce both the fine and imprisonment.

Section 4 of the Clayton Act[23] creates a private right of action for damages under the federal antitrust laws. This section provides that:

> ...any person who shall be injured in his business or property by reason of any-

thing forbidden in the antitrust laws may sue thereafter in any district court of the United States in the district in which the defendant resides or is found or has an agent, without respect to the amount in controversy, and shall recover threefold the damages by him sustained, and the cost of suit, including a reasonable attorney's fee.

Attorney's fees can include the recovery of nontaxable expenses like travel expenses as part of the fee, and at least one circuit court now allows costs and fees to draw interest.[24]

Even more important, if a private individual has filed an antitrust action, the filing of a federal antitrust action by the Department of Justice stops the statute of limitations from running on the private action. Thus, private litigants can wait for the outcome of the federal action before pursuing their own lawsuits for treble damages and use the judgment in the federal case to prove the presence of a violation.

Professional Liability Insurance and Antitrust Suits

A careful reading of professional liability insurance policies shows an absence of insurance coverage for suits founded upon violations of antitrust laws. This is another major reason for practitioners to avoid any type of professional activity that could be considered a restraint of trade.

Some plaintiffs will file suits based partly on antitrust violations and partly on actions in tort law, involving claims for libel or slander. This requires insurance carriers to defend their insured veterinarians and provides for greater financial resources than are available from individual veterinarians. When causes of action that are covered by the policy are alleged in the suit, the insurance company must defend the insured veterinarians. This was precisely what happened in the $400,000 California suit discussed earlier.

Although professional liability insurance companies may be forced to defend these cases, they are not held liable for damages that stem from an antitrust violation. The veterinarians named as defendants in the suit are personally at risk for payment of those damages.

If the lawsuit was based purely on an antitrust violation, these practitioners would discover that their professional liability insurance would probably afford them little or no coverage. Only if the suit alleged a cause of action like libel, slander, or some other covered form of liability would an insurance company provide a defense for a case based on an antitrust violation.

The FTC Act

The FTC Act originally enacted in 1914 is the second statute that contains the competitive objective of the country's antitrust laws. As one author states:

> Just as the Sherman Act is the great and first commandment in this field of law, so the Federal Trade Commission Act is the second...with one significant administrative variation. This difference lies in the fact that Congress sought, by its enactment, to supplement judicial enforcement of the antitrust laws through the administrative process of a bipartisan Federal Trade Commission staffed by experts experienced in the field of trade regulation.[6]

Because appointments to the FTC are political, significant variations in philosophy, budget, and direction for this agency occur as the political and economic climate changes.

Unfair Methods of Competition

The statutory provisions of Section 5 of the FTC Act declare that:

Unfair methods of competition in or affecting commerce, and unfair or deceptive acts or practices in or affecting commerce, are declared unlawful.[25]

This section, while not technically an antitrust law, overlaps the Sherman Act because its prohibition of unfair methods of competition encompasses unreasonable restraints on interstate commerce. The "unfair methods of competition" clause has been interpreted by courts to give the FTC adequate power to deal with restraints of trade and monopolistic practices prohibited by both the Sherman and Clayton Acts. Thus the FTC has the authority to restrain horizontal price fixing, boycotts, and resale price maintenance agreements.[6]

Furthermore, it has been held that Section 5 of the Act goes even deeper than the Sherman or Clayton Acts in that it allows the Commission to proceed against any unfair method of competition at a very early stage. In other words, it allows the FTC "to stop in their incipiency acts and practices which, when full blown, would violate those Acts."[26]

Investigations by the FTC

Under the Sherman Act, regulatory action occurs only after a restraint of trade has occurred. The FTC Act allows the FTC to investigate unfair or deceptive acts or practices in or affecting commerce early in their evolution, before restraints of trade have occurred. It was because of this very broad jurisdiction that the FTC could investigate national, state, and local veterinary associations in the late 1970s to see if antitrust violations were occurring, rather than wait until they had happened and then file suit to prohibit them.

Changes in the Law Regarding Advertising

Prior to the late 1970s, advertising of professional services was considered unethi-

cal professional conduct. It did not take long after the *Goldfarb* case was decided, though, before the law in this area began to change.

The Beginning of Change

Following the *Goldfarb* case, another case involving activities of professionals came to the forefront. This time the plaintiffs were two nonprofit organizations and a Virginia resident who suffered from diseases that required her to take prescription drugs daily.[27] Their claim was that the First Amendment entitled people who used prescription drugs to receive information concerning the prices of such drugs. Meanwhile, a state law declared that pharmacists licensed in Virginia were guilty of unprofessional conduct if they published, advertised, or promoted, directly or indirectly, any price, discount, or rebate for drugs that only could be dispensed by prescription.[28]

On May 24, 1976, in the case known as *Virginia Board of Pharmacy* v. *Virginia Consumer Council*, the Supreme Court held that the free flow of commercial information is indispensable and that commercial speech, like other varieties, is protected. They did not hold that the advertising of professional products like prescription drugs could never be regulated in any way. What they did say, though, was that states may not completely suppress the dissemination of truthful information about entirely lawful activity.[29] Footnote 25 of this decision left the door open to consider the issue of advertising professional services by other members of the learned professions at a later date.

Major Changes Occur

The consumer movement was well entrenched by the mid 1970s, and the Supreme Court seemed receptive to changing the rules under which the learned professions operated. The next major case began in 1976 when two attorneys, Bates and O'Steen, decided to advertise routine legal services such as uncontested divorces, uncontested adoptions, simple personal bankruptcies, and changes of name in a Phoenix, Arizona daily newspaper. This activity was in direct violation of a disciplinary rule of the Supreme Court of Arizona. That rule held that lawyers shall not publicize themselves, their partners, associates, or firms through newspaper or magazine advertisements, radio or television announcements, or display advertisements in the telephone directories, nor shall they permit others to do so in their behalf.[30]

After hearings before the state bar, a one-week suspension from the practice of law was recommended. The attorneys, as permitted by the Supreme Court's Disciplinary Rules, sought review of this ruling in the Supreme Court of Arizona. They argued that such a ban on advertising violated the Sherman Antitrust Act and the First Amendment guarantees of freedom of speech. When the Supreme Court of Arizona rejected both of these claims, Bates and O'Steen appealed to the United States Supreme Court.

For the third consecutive year, the Supreme Court cut a broad swath through existing rules of professional conduct. In the case entitled *Bates and O'Steen* v. *State Bar of Arizona*, the court put the finishing touches on complete prohibitions on advertising by professionals. They rejected the antitrust arguments, determining instead that the state government of Arizona "as sovereign, imposed this restraint on advertising as an `act of government' which the Sherman Act does not prohibit." In other words, a prohibition on advertising by professionals that is invoked by an arm of the state is not a violation of antitrust laws. The court went on, however, to decide that a total ban on truthful advertising concerning the availability and terms of routine legal services was a violation of the First Amendment freedom of speech.

When presented with arguments that attorney advertising is inherently misleading due to the highly individualized nature of legal services, the court said it was not persuaded that "restrained professional advertising" by lawyers will inevitably be

misleading. In an effort to interpret its definition of restrained professional advertising, the court said, "The only services that lend themselves to advertising are the routine ones; the uncontested divorce, the simple adoption, the uncontested personal bankruptcy, the change of name, and the like....[31] The court did not go on to define what "the like" meant, but in the 10 years since this decision was rendered, those words have provoked minimal controversy.

An article in the *JAVMA* is an excellent reference regarding the subject of professional advertising.[32] The following is a summary of the key points discussed therein which were produced by the *Bates* decision:

1. Since it serves individual and societal interests in assuring informed and reliable decision making, commercial speech is entitled to First Amendment protection.

2. The *Bates* case does not specifically address the advertising of quality of services, although the Court stated that advertising of quality might be seen as false, deceptive, or misleading and could warrant restriction.

3. In-person solicitations of clients might pose dangers of overreaching and misrepresentation and might warrant restraints.

4. The First Amendment protects, among other things, basic factual content of advertising such as information as to name, address, telephone, office hours, and "the like."

5. Advertising that is false, deceptive, or misleading or that concerns illegal transactions may be restrained.

6. There may be reasonable restrictions on the time, place, and manner of advertising.

When this list is compared with the advertising regulations adopted in the AVMA's *Principles of Veterinary Medical Ethics*, it becomes apparent that many of these permissible limitations have been included. Although this case involved attorneys practicing law, the Justice Department and the FTC agree that *Bates* applies to all learned professions including veterinarians.[32]

The Veterinary Profession Has Its Day in Court

About the same time as the *Bates* case was winding its way through the Supreme Court, a case involving advertising in veterinary medicine was being tried and appealed. This case began in Florida and was known as *Society for the Welfare of Animals, Inc.* v. *Walwrath.* It involved the right of a nonprofit, low-cost spay and neuter clinic to advertise its services. Dr. Walwrath's action was based on § 474 of the Florida Practice Act, which prohibited the advertising of veterinary services.

Both the trial court and the state court of appeals rendered decisions in favor of Dr. Walwrath, the veterinarian who was seeking court action to prohibit the advertising of low-cost veterinary services. The United States Supreme Court accepted the case but did not write an opinion on the subject of veterinary advertising. Instead, in October 1978, it issued an order vacating the lower court's decision and sent the case back for the state court of appeals to reconsider in light of the 1977 *Bates* decision, decided a few months after the court of appeals had rendered a verdict for Dr. Walwrath. This action was an exercise of common judicial courtesy, allowing the Florida court to modify its decision to conform to later developments. The summary disposition by the Supreme Court indicated that a majority of the justices thought that the principles of the Bates case applied to veterinary medical advertising.[33]

The Final Outcome

Shortly after the *Bates* decision was handed down, the AVMA completely revamped its Principles of Ethics to correspond with the Supreme Court's rulings.

Advertising is without a doubt considered legal in veterinary medicine as long as it is within the restraints outlined by the Code of Ethics.

Since the *Bates* case, some states have elected to statutorily define false or misleading advertising. One example is found in California's Business and Professions Code:

> It is unlawful for any person...with intent...to perform services, professional or otherwise,...to induce the public to enter into any obligation relating thereto, to make or disseminate...in any newspaper...or any advertising device...any statement concerning such...services... which is untrue or misleading, and which is known, or which by the exercise of reasonable care should be known, to be untrue or misleading...with the intent not to sell such...services...so advertised at the price stated therein, or as so advertised. Any violation of the provisions of this section is a misdemeanor punishable by imprisonment in the county jail not exceeding six months, or by a fine not exceeding two thousand five hundred dollars ($2,500) or by both.[34]

An additional attempt at legally defining what can be said about some veterinary services and what cannot be said can be found in a regulation in the California Business and Professions Code. This one relates to the advertising of emergency services:

> A veterinarian who advertises a veterinary hospital or clinic shall include in all such emergency hospital or clinic advertisements the hours during which such emergency services are provided and the availability of the veterinarian who is to provide the emergency service. The availability of the veterinarian who is to provide emergency service shall be specified as either 'veterinarian on premises' or 'veterinarian on call.' The phrase 'veterinarian on premises' shall mean that there is a veterinarian actually present at the hospital who is prepared to render emergency veterinary services. The phrase 'veterinarian on call' shall

mean that a veterinarian is not present at the hospital, but is able to respond within a reasonable time to requests for emergency services and has been designated to so respond.[35]

Certainly, other states have statutes and regulations governing professional advertising. In view of the *Virginia Board of Pharmacy* and *Bates* cases, state definitions restricting

advertising by professionals are still constitutional providing the court's guidelines have been met. Principles of ethics will always have merit as a means of attempting to define what services may be advertised and how associations may attempt to regulate such activity. However, another method is through the legislative process, as has been done with these California laws.

References

1. 421 U.S. 773 (1975).
2. *Arizona Attorney General* v *Arizona Veterinary Medical Association* (1976).
3. *Federal Baseball Club* v *National League*, 259 U.S. 200, 209 (1922). ("a firm of lawyers sending out a member to argue a case...does not engage in... commerce because the lawyer...goes to another state").
4. *FTC* v *Raladam Co*, 283 U.S. 643, 653 (1931). ("medical practitioners...follow a profession and not a trade...").
5. *Goldfarb* v *Virginia Bar*, 421 U.S. 773, 790, footnote 15 (1975).
6. Van Cise JG, Lifland WT, Sorkin LT: *Understanding the Antitrust Laws*, ed 9. New York, Practising Law Institute, 1986, pp 26, 31, 33-34, 42, 45.
7. *United States* v *Topco Assoc Inc*, 405 U.S. 596, 610 (1972).
8. *Giammattei et al* v *Blaine et al* (1981). Settled before trial in the Superior Court of the State of California in and for the County of Sacramento, involved 13 named veterinarians and 2 local veterinary associations. See also Price DA: Editorial: Mobile vaccination clinics. *JAVMA* 183(2):178-179, 1983.
9. Veterinary ophthalmologists sue veterinary ophthalmologists and AVMA. *JAVMA* 175(12):1242, 1979.
10. *Rickards* v *Canine Eye Registration Foundation*, 704 F. 2d 1449, 1454 (1983).
11. *Bushie* v *Stenocord*, 460 F. 2d 116, 119 (9th Cir 1972).
12. *Rickards* v *Canine Eye Registration Foundation*, 783 F. 2d 1329 (9th Cir 1986).
13. *Apex Hosiery Co* v *Leader*, 310 U.S. 469, 489 (1940).
14. 15 USC 1.
15. *United States* v *United States Gypsum Co*, 438 U.S. 422, 443 (1978).
16. *American Tobacco Co* v *United States*, 328 U.S. 781, 810 (1946).
17. Hills CA: *Antitrust Adviser*, ed 3. Colorado Springs, CO, Shepard's McGraw-Hill, pp 7, 8, 1985.
18. *Lease Lights, Inc* v *Public Service Co*, 701 F. 2d 794 (10th Cir 1983).
19. *Standard Oil Co* v *United States*, 221 U.S. 1 (1911).
20. *Board of Trade* v *United States*, 246 U.S. 231, 238 (1918).
21. *Arizona* v *Maricopa County Medical Society*, 457 U.S. 332 (1982).
22. *Goldfarb* v *Virginia Bar*, 421 U.S. 773, 790 (1975).
23. 15 USC 13.
24. *Copper Liquor, Inc* v *Adolph Coors Co*, 701 F. 2d 542 (5th Cir 1983).
25. 15 USC 45(a) (1982).
26. *FTC* v *Motion Picture Adv Service Co*, 344 U.S. 392, 394-395 (1953).
27. *Virginia Board of Pharmacy* v *Virginia Consumer Council*, 425 U.S. 341 (1976).
28. Virginia Code § 54-524.35 (1974).
29. 96 S.Ct. 1817, 1830-1831.
30. Disciplinary Rule 2-101(B), embodied in Rule 29(a), 17A Arizona Rev Stat (1976 Suppl), p 26.

31. Hannah HW: Legal briefs. Advertising. *JAVMA* 171 (10):11, 1977.

32. Rankin JW: Veterinarian advertising. *JAVMA* 172(9):1014-1016, 1978.

33. U.S. Supreme Court rules in Florida veterinary advertising case. *AVMA News from Washington*. Washington, DC, AVMA (Feb 15) l979.

34. California Business and Professions Code § 17500.

35. California, Title 16, Professional and Vocational Regulations, Chap 20, Board of Examiners in Veterinary Medicine, § 2030.5.

CHAPTER 8

Contract Law

The types of contracts that veterinarians most often encounter involve the sale of goods, the performance of professional services, employment, and real estate. These different types of contracts are controlled by varying statutory laws as well as different common law precedents.

Veterinarians very often are unaware of the legal requirements and interpretations surrounding contract law until disagreements or misunderstandings occur. It is then that the importance of the legal doctrines associated with contract law becomes evident. This chapter presents basic contract law terminology and principles to help practitioners determine their rights and responsibilities under oral and written agreements. Contract law, however, is often complex and vague, and legal counsel is recommended whenever veterinarians are about to enter into major agreements.

Formation of the Contract

The Contract

The term *contract* generally refers to an agreement between two or more parties. This agreement consists of a promise or mutual promises that the law will enforce or the performance of which the law recognizes as a duty.[1] Simply stated, a contract is an agreement that creates an obligation.[2]

Traditional Contract Law

Traditional common law precedents of contract law evaluated agreements for the presence of five elements essential to the formation of a contract. These included three objective elements: (1) an offer, (2) an acceptance, and (3) consideration; as well as the subjective elements, (4) an intent to contract, and (5) a meeting of the minds. Current contract law emphasizes only the three objective elements of an agreement.

The Uniform Commercial Code

Modern consumer law is a mixture of old and new law. Unfair or fraudulent business practices that were more prevalent in the first half of this century forced state legislatures and the courts to put consumers on a more equal basis with sellers. That led to the creation of a code of law called the *Uniform Commercial Code (UCC)*, which applies to the sale of goods. This code protects buyers from unfair business practices by requiring sellers to disclose certain relevant information that was not offered during the "buyer beware" era.

The UCC was created during the 1960s to make consumer transactions involving the sale of goods consistent among states. The UCC has been adopted as statutory law in all states but Louisiana. It defines goods as:

> All things (including specially manufactured goods) which are movable at the time of identification to the contract of sale....[3]

The language in the UCC and the court interpretations thereof provide the primary sources of legal information and precedents covering the sales of goods. When the UCC does not specifically address an issue, traditional common law precedents apply.

Determining Which Law Covers a Transaction

Common law principles apply to contracts for labor, services, or the sale of land. Contracts for veterinary services, however, often include sales of both goods and services. In order to determine which body of law applies, it must be determined whether goods or services comprised the predominant thrust and purpose of the sale. When the predominant effort was the sale of goods, the UCC applies; if the principal purpose was the rendering of services, traditional contract law applies.[1]

Throughout this chapter, references are made to the *Restatement of Contracts, Second* as a source of information about contract law. This reference is published by the American Law Institute to inform lawyers and scholars of the law in a general area, how it is changing, and what direction the authors think that change should take. Although the *Restatement of Contracts, Second* is a valuable reference, it is a private legal publication and is not always followed by the courts; thus, contract law precedents vary from one jurisdiction to another.

Offer Under Common Law

The first element required for the creation of a contract is an offer. An offer is a promise or a commitment made in reasonably certain terms to do or refrain from doing some specified thing in the future.[4] When one person demonstrates a willingness to enter into an agreement involving certain definite terms and invites the other party in the bargaining transaction to agree to the same terms, a legally sufficient offer has been made.

Another element that is considered essential for the formation of a contract is known as the *meeting of the minds*. The mere statement of a price, standing alone, may be held to be a legally unenforceable offer because it omits many terms necessary to the making of a contract.[5] In order for the offer to be considered legally sufficient, it must contain enough information so that reasonable people would understand what it was they were agreeing to.

Most offers leading to the performance of veterinary services for clients' animals are presented orally. However, contract offers can also be presented in a formal written document, as with sales involving the purchase of real estate or an expensive piece of hospital equipment. In addition, offers are sometimes written informally and placed in the classified section of a newspaper or professional journal. If words of commitment are used or there is an invitation to take action without further communication, this form of advertising to the general public can also constitute a valid offer.

It is in the advertising of merchandise or services via newspapers, direct-mail flyers, radio messages, television commercials, or other means that problems can occur regarding the presence or absence of an operative offer. For example, does a newspaper announcement from a particular veterinary hospital advertising low-cost spays allow any owner of a female dog or cat to walk into that office and say, "I accept your offer to spay my obese bulldog (or pregnant cat or 12-year-old dog with a draining pyometra) for the price advertised on this flyer. Here is the cash. When shall I pick her up?"

In such a situation, what looks like an offer may not be a legally operative offer. Instead, it may be only a preliminary invitation for prospective clients or buyers to consider when negotiating the purchase of the advertised service. The *Restatement of Contracts, Second* § 26 addresses this issue:

> A manifestation of a willingness to enter into a bargain is not an offer if the person to whom it is addressed knows or has reason to know that the person making it does not intend to conclude a bargain until he has made a further manifestation of assent.

Most reasonable animal owners, and especially bulldog owners who are aware of the additional anesthetic risks associated with that breed, should know that such an offer could depend on many medical factors. They should recognize that a further manifestation of assent on the part of the veterinarian might be essential before the low-cost service offer was extended to them. Conversely, an all-inclusive advertisement like this should not be made unless veterinarians are willing to offer the service to owners of all healthy, young, non-anesthetic-risk breeds of dogs. One does not know what the courts would say if a reasonable person accepted this offer only to find that the veterinarian wanted to charge more than quoted. As is always the case with the law, decisions are based on an analysis of all the facts as well as the legal precedents.

Some states have consumer laws and regulations that address the issue of operative offers in advertising. Massachusetts[6] and California are two such states. Section 17500 of the California Business and Professions Code says the following about offers for services:

> It is unlawful for any person...with intent directly or indirectly...to perform services, professional or otherwise...to induce the public to enter into any obligation relating thereto, to make or disseminate...in any newspaper or other publication...any statement concerning such...services...which is untrue or misleading, and which is known, or which by the exercise of reasonable care should be known, to be untrue or misleading...with the intent not to sell such...services...so advertised at the price stated therein, or as so advertised. Any violation of the provisions of this section is a misdemeanor punishable by imprisonment in the county jail not exceeding six months, or by a fine not exceeding...$2500, or both.

Offers that do not state a time within which another party must accept or reject the offer pose another legal hurdle associated with the offer component of a contract. In general, an offer may be accepted or rejected within a reasonable time. Just what would be deemed reasonable is open to legal review, so it is extremely unwise for any business to make an offer without an expiration date. With certain exceptions, offers without expiration dates can be revoked or withdrawn at any time before they are accepted. Offers that have expiration dates may not be withdrawn before that date.

Offers may originate from sellers or consumers. The consumer who places an order for specific goods or services and mails or leaves a deposit for such items will be held to have made a valid offer. However, that same consumer may be able to withdraw the offer if action is taken before the seller communicates an acceptance. If no acceptance is ever communicated by the seller, no contract will have been formed, and the consumer is entitled to a refund of the deposit.[6]

The Common Law Acceptance

Once a valid offer has been made, the next essential element in the establishment of an enforceable contract is proof of an acceptance. An acceptance occurs when the party to whom the offer is made makes the return requested in the offer.[7] Under common law, the acceptance must conform precisely to the terms of the offer. If it varies from those terms, it fails as an acceptance[8] and instead becomes a counteroffer.[9]

It is through this traditional common law process that practitioners can find themselves faced with offers and counteroffers to the point that they no longer know whether they are the offeror or the offeree. They may offer to perform specified veterinary services for a stated fee and then find that they are being asked to accept a client's offer to pay for those veterinary services under entirely different payment terms than they had originally intended. At this point veterinarians may elect to counter that offer with a different payment plan or a less-expensive treatment plan.

It is through this offer and counteroffer bargaining process that misunderstandings occur which lead to disputes. When veterinarians realize that this is happening, they should be reminded that it is time to produce a written estimate. Only if this is done can facts be drawn upon to show that sufficient common ground existed to find that a valid acceptance was present.

The Acceptance in Implied versus Express Contracts

It would seem that proof of an acceptance would be a fairly straightforward component of a contract, free of much legal wrangling. If the words "I accept" are uttered, it is a simple matter. Words to this effect indicate a willingness to provide the consideration requested (usually to pay the bill). This form of acceptance is called an *express acceptance* and establishes an *express contract*.

In many cases, however, no words or signatures on a document are provided, and then the process is more complicated. If no express acceptance can be proved, courts still may find that an acceptance can be inferred from the actions of the parties. In such situations, the acceptance may be an *implied acceptance* and the agreement is then called an *implied contract*. Even if a contract can be implied, though, the terms agreed upon and whether the entire agreement or only parts of it were accepted may still be called into question.

An acceptance by a client for veterinary care is implied, for example, if an animal with a medical problem is dropped off at a veterinary hospital with information about its symptoms, but with no direct communication between the doctor and the animal's owner. An equivalent example in large animal practice would be if a client left a cow in a stanchion with a note attached to an adjacent post describing some symptoms. If the farmer is off working and is unavailable for consultation, an acceptance of the care rendered could be implied. The extent of the medical care that a court might allow in cases like this may be in question, but an implied contract for some medical care certainly exists.

In both of these examples the presence of an implied acceptance would be enhanced if similar transactions had occurred previously between the client and the doctor and full payment for the veterinary services had been made. The theory is that ratification of prior treatments by payment without any challenge is grounds for implying an acceptance for similar requests in the future. Clients who do not wish to make such an implied acceptance need to inform their veterinarians that no diagnostic procedures or treatments are to be performed until further discussions are held and an express authorization for those services is given.

Offer and Acceptance Under the UCC

Most contracts between veterinarians and clients are for combinations of services and goods. Practitioners provide services in the form of professional time for examinations, surgery, dentistry, and diagnostic procedures. Sometimes, though, they also dispense large dollar volumes of goods in the form of medications, pet food, and supplies. The cost of these goods in many cases exceeds the cost of veterinary services.

As previously discussed, the type of contract law governing such transactions varies. If sales of services predominate, the contract will be regulated by common law principles. If the major portion of the agreement consists of the sale of goods, it will be regulated by the UCC.

Unlike common law, the UCC makes no attempt to define an offer and, under its principles, a valid contract may be present even in the absence of certain traditional contract terms or elements. If it can be found that the parties intended to make a contract and that an agreement existed based upon language used by the parties or by implication from other circumstances, such as a "course of dealing," a "usage of trade," or "a course of performance," a contract for the sale of goods will be enforced.[10] However, the more terms that are left open, the less likely it is that the parties intended to have a contract and the less likely it is that a court will find in favor of the existence of a contract.[11]

Meeting of the Minds

One of the traditional subjective elements associated with the creation of a contract is called a *meeting of the minds*. It can be seen from the new legal concepts embodied in the UCC that the precise language of the contractual agreement is less important than the intent of the parties as illustrated by their actions. Thus, in contemporary thinking, it is less critical to subjectively establish what each party was actually thinking than it is to objectively show what a reasonable person in the position of the other party would have concluded from the course of events.

It is under the element entitled *meeting of the minds* that written fee estimates become critically important. Without their formal use, it is difficult for veterinarians to organize and set forth the various diagnostic and treatment options available. If this is not accomplished, clients often fail to comprehend total costs and cannot become knowledgeable participants in helping to determine which diagnostic procedures or courses of therapy should be pursued. Thus, the formal estimate becomes a valuable medical decision-making tool as well as a memorandum supporting the parties' agreement regarding which services are to be rendered and how much those efforts will cost. Consequently, when written estimates are provided, the likelihood for disputes decreases, and the probability of the courts finding a valid contract increases.

Intent

The more traditional subjective view of contract law required the presence of a fourth element for the formation of a contract, i.e., an intent to contract. The rationale for this element was that a valid contract could not be formed if the parties did not intend to form one. However, proving to a court what the parties to a contract intended or did not intend is difficult, especially when the parties themselves may not have known precisely what they intended at the time.

Although practitioners may still find this subjective element to be under legal discussion, the newer trend, as seen in the UCC, is to approach the law of contracts objectively. Under this theory of contracts, less importance is placed upon a party's intent and more emphasis is placed on what a reasonable person in the position of one party would conclude from the conduct of the other person.

Standard Form Contracts, or Contracts of Adhesion

The world of commerce could not function without the use of standardized printed contract forms. Anyone who has purchased a car, appliance, or house is familiar with them. It is commonplace for such forms to be accepted and signed whether or not they are read or understood.

These printed forms are frequently referred to as *adhesion contracts* or *contracts of adhesion*. An adhesion contract may be defined as a contract written exclusively by one party (the *dominant party*) and presented to the other party (the *adhering party*) under circumstances in which there is no realistic opportunity to negotiate.[4] The consequences of signing an agreement vary under the UCC as compared with common law precedents. In practice, even if people are able to read and understand these contracts, they are still helpless to vary them in any way. The only recourse usually offered is to sign the form just as it is.

The common law rule was that "one who signs a contract which he had an opportunity to read and understand is bound by its provisions."[12] That rule is formulated on the rationale that signed contracts would not be very reliable if parties were allowed to claim at a later time that since they did not read or understand the contracts, they should not be bound by them.

The unfairness of this rule was dealt with in 1960 with the famous case of *Henningsen* v. *Bloomfield Motors, Inc.*[13] In that case the court refused to enforce a warranty disclaimer found in fine print on the reverse side of a purchase order for a car. The theory invoked was that a disclaimer that forced buyers to accept an unalterable contract on an unconditional basis was against public policy.

The UCC takes the same approach by including in the code what it calls the *doctrine of unconscionability*. This legal precept affords consumers who have little or no bargaining power and who accept form contracts that are procedurally or substantively unconscionable the right to resist their enforcement.

There are several types of situations for which provisions within adhesion contracts are not enforced by the courts. These include situations in which

- provisions protecting the dominant party, like disclaimers of warranties, are buried in fine print on the back side of the form or in the middle of a long paragraph.

- written provisions are legible but are presented in such a way as to make it unlikely that they would come to the attention of the other party.

- the dominant party represents to another party what is contained in the document. The other party signs the document without reading it and then later discovers that the representations were false. In this type of situation, one party is negligent and the other is fraudulent.

There is a trend away from strict enforcement of the duty-to-read rule with adhesion contracts.[14] The theories differ, but the result is that provisions that operate unfairly or oppressively will not be enforced against an uninformed party or someone who could not reasonably have been expected to know of it.[14]

Consideration

The fifth and final element required to form a contract is consideration (sometimes called *legal detriment*). This is the factor that justifies the enforcement of a promise or the thing bargained for or given in exchange for the promise. Consideration means that someone does or promises to do something that he or she was not already legally obligated to do, or refrains or promises to refrain from doing something that he/she had a legal right to do.[4]

In simple terms, consideration is a benefit conferred to the promisor and a detriment incurred by the promisee. In most transactions the promise to pay money to obtain goods or services constitutes consideration.

An issue occasionally encountered under this contract law element involves how much benefit or detriment must exist in order to establish or modify a contract. Historically, the courts have held that if a contract was freely made by competent parties, the fact that it was not supported by sufficient consideration was not a satisfactory reason to refuse to enforce it.[15] More recently though, as discussed previously, courts have refused to enforce a contract, or particular clauses within the contract, if they have found the terms to be unconscionable under the circumstances. Agreements that exceed the limits of any reasonable claim or expectation can be classified by courts as unconscionable. Whereas under common law this doctrine can vary from one jurisdiction to another, the UCC gives it explicit recognition.[16]

There are several other issues regarding the subject of consideration. Two of them that have particular application to running a veterinary business are discussed below.

The Preexisting Duty Rule

There is a well-established rule of contract law that a promise to do what one is already legally bound to do is not binding for lack of consideration. The rationale given is because no legal detriment exists.

This rule comes into play, for example, if veterinarians elect to accept less than full payment as payment in full for a debt owed them by a client (see discussions under "the failure to compromise" in Chapter 5). The general rule is that partial payment of an amount that is admitted to be due is insufficient consideration to support a promise by the creditor to discharge the rest of the debt. For example, a client has owed Dr. Jones $200 for the past two months and does not dispute the amount owed. Dr. Jones is tired of waiting for the money so she calls the client and is in the process of getting put off for another month when she decides to offer a compromise. Dr. Jones says, "If you will pay me $100 within the next two days, I will accept that as payment in full for the entire debt."

If the client pays the $100 within the two-day time limit, does it mean that Dr. Jones cannot collect the remaining $100? In most jurisdictions, the parties to a contract can agree to an arrangement like this, and the creditor can promise to accept the lesser amount as payment in full. However, because the debtor is already under a legal duty to pay the full amount, there is a lack of consideration to be able to enforce this new agreement. As a result, Dr. Jones can accept the lesser amount and still sue for the balance.[17] It is certainly not recommended that this course of action be pursued, but under the preexisting duty rule, the law would support it.

Sometimes a dispute exists as to the amount of a debt. If the debtor sends an amount less than that which is claimed to be due and clearly indicates that the payment being sent represents full payment, the creditor's acceptance of the lesser amount is a full discharge of the remainder of the unpaid account.

Promissory Estoppel, or Action in Reliance

Another doctrine of contract law that can have an impact on veterinarians involves *promissory estoppel* or *action in reliance*. The *Restatement of Contracts, Second* defines this doctrine as follows:

> A promise which the promisor shall reasonably expect to induce action or forbearance on the part of the promisee or a third person and which does induce such action or forbearance is binding if injustice can be avoided only by enforcement of the promise....[18]

In nonlegal language this means that, although there may have been no agreement

B-but doctor, how will I find another job out here in Timbuctoo?

ironed out by the parties, justice requires the enforcement of one's promise when another party has justifiably relied upon that promise and changed its position, incurring substantial detriment.

An example of the application of this doctrine to veterinary medicine is a one-year offer of employment to a graduating veterinary student starting a month after graduation. The student relies on the offer, which includes a salary of $2,000/month, and tells the employer, "I will be there on July 1st." A number of details concerning the term of the contract and benefits are vague, and no contract is ever signed.

The student rejects one other job opportunity and stops looking for employment. After graduating, she drives 400 miles to the town where the job is located and finds a place to live. The prospective employer is out of town at a seminar but knows she is in town searching for an apartment. Three days before the new veterinarian is to start work, the intended employer contacts the new graduate and informs her that he cannot hire anyone due to a slowdown in the business.

Did a contract exist? Is the student entitled to damages because of a breach of contract? In analyzing the facts of this hypothetical situation, the new graduate incurred considerable debt and personal expense looking for a place to live and turned down another offer because she thought she had a job. The employer knew of the prospective employee's efforts to find a place to live and said nothing to discourage that effort. Based on these facts, a court would very likely find that a contract had been formed. This is precisely the type of setting in which the doctrine of promissory estoppel could come into play to support the existence of consideration.

Capacity to Contract

There are three basic situations wherein questions regarding the capacity to make a valid contract would be entertained. These are minority, mental disability, and intoxication.

Minority

Under the common law rules, people lacked the legal capacity to enter into contracts until the age of 21. Most states now have statutes setting the age of majority at 18, although a few require people to be 19.

The law does not say that minors cannot enter into contracts and uphold them. The law does, however, grant people the right to avoid or disaffirm any contracts made while they were minors. Specific state statutes do allow minors to enter into some types of valid contracts and have them enforced against them. Two of the more common types are contracts for motor vehicle liability insurance and contracts with institutions of higher learning for the purpose of financing an education.

If minors enter into contracts, only they—not the adults with whom they contracted—may disaffirm or void the contracts. This is true in the majority of jurisdictions even if the minors misrepresent their ages at the time they entered into the contract. Surprisingly, minors who disaffirm contracts are not required to return property they obtained and no longer have. If they do have the property contracted for, they are required to return it, but they are entitled to recover any consideration paid. Contracts entered into during the age of minority may be disaffirmed at any time during that minority or within a reasonable time after reaching the age of majority.

The law carves out a separate niche for items classified as "necessaries" of life. Minors may be held liable for the fair market value of necessaries, but the party claiming against them has the burden of proving that the items furnished were necessaries that a legally responsible parent was unwilling or unable to supply.[19] It is very doubtful that veterinary services would ever be classified in this narrow group.

It is not uncommon for veterinarians to be approached by minors seeking medical care for their animals. The best way to effect an enforceable contract with these individuals is to contact a parent or guardian and have them provide the required acceptance. If parents have ratified contracts initiated by their minor children in the past by paying for services on a timely basis, the argument can be made that the parents have appointed them as their agents. It may be a satisfactory policy for practitioners to depend on this course of dealing with the children of parents who have reliably paid in the past if the costs for services to be rendered are reasonably low. The safest course always will be, however, to ask youthful-looking people how old they are and, if they are minors, to proceed with veterinary care only after contacting a parent or guardian for authorization to render services.

Mental Disability

People who lack the required mental capacity to make a contract can avoid or disaffirm contracts just as minors can. Mental illness, retardation, and senility are the most common reasons for releasing these people from their contractual obligations or decisions. The test is whether the party seeking to avoid the contract was capable of comprehending the nature and quality of the transaction entered into and its probable consequences. Also at issue is how heavy a duty is placed on the other party to foresee and comprehend the extent of the mentally disabled person's mental capacity. Contracting parties cannot be held to a rigid standard to foresee at what point a person slips from a mentally competent state to incompetence. Obvious mental disorders, however, must be recognized.

Because of the large population of elderly people, senility is the incapacity that veterinarians are most likely to face. Watching clients' memories and health fail is difficult. The concurrent failure of their animals' health because of their inability to properly care for them is disheartening. Sometimes, the only morally and contractually acceptable way to deal with these situations is for veterinarians to seek out another family member who can make decisions for the client.

In a contract setting, senility becomes important in at least two primary matters: (1) contracts for expensive care in which, because of a mental disability, clients cannot remember what they agreed to (and they refuse to pay for those services), and (2) when agreements are being made to euthanatize patients belonging to senile or mentally ill owners. The former of these is the less serious one because it may simply mean that veterinarians will have trouble collecting debts owed. The latter constitutes a worse hazard, because euthanasia cannot be reversed. Extra precautions are needed when the mental competence of owners to make decisions about euthanasia is in question.

In order to prevent either the unnecessary

death of an animal or a major family feud, animals should not be euthanatized until practitioners are certain that this is what a concurring family member wishes to do. Practitioners may need to wait until the next day before performing the act of euthanasia in order to provide sufficient time to contact someone else in the family or the client's legal guardian.

Intoxication

In most cases the courts do not look favorably upon intoxication as an incapacity. If the state of intoxication is extreme, however, the affected person is not unlike the mentally disabled person who cannot understand the nature and consequences of the contract and, thus, cannot assent to the agreement.

The modern view of voluntary intoxication as a grounds for avoiding contracts focuses considerable attention on whether the sober party or a reasonably sober party in a similar position should have been aware of the intoxication. A side issue that is also considered by the courts is whether the sober party took unfair advantage of the other party's intoxicated state.

If a contract is voidable because of intoxication, when intoxicated people become sober, they can either ratify or disaffirm the agreement in much the same manner as minors can. If they disaffirm the contract, they must return the consideration received. If the consideration has been used or wasted before the intoxicated people become sober, they do not need to make restitution.[19]

Intoxicated clients are not uncommon in veterinary medicine. When alcohol is the culprit, the outward evidence of intoxication is reasonably obvious. When drug abuse is the cause of the intoxication, the mentally disabled state may not be as noticeable. Any time that there is serious doubt about intoxication, the same concerns regarding euthanasia or incurring major expenses for medical services discussed under mental disability should be considered.

Statute of Frauds

Many people are surprised to learn that the majority of oral contracts are valid and enforceable. History has shown that the larger the value or the longer the term of a contract, the more likelihood there is for fraud to be associated with it. Because of this concern, in the 1600s the English enacted a statute known as the *Statute of Frauds*. This law required the production of a written memorandum before the courts would enforce certain kinds of contracts. The basic tenets set forth in that law are still applicable today.

Types of Contracts Covered

Most American jurisdictions have retained the original wording of the English statute. The most common types of contracts that must be in writing are (1) contracts for the sale of real estate, (2) leases for longer than one year, (3) contracts not to be performed within one year, (4) contracts to answer for the debts of another, and (5) contracts for the sale of goods over a specified price. The law says that these types of contracts are "within the Statute of Frauds" and are therefore unenforceable without a written document.

Although each of these types of contracts has a body of law interpreting the Statute of Fraud's application to it, one which needs some further explanation is that pertaining to the sale of goods. Where written contracts are required, the UCC separates sales of goods into different categories. Those categories with special significance to consumers are sales of goods valued at greater than $500,[20] contracts involving securities,[21] security agreements,[22] and sales of other types of personal property.

Under the UCC section covering the sale of goods valued at greater than $500, two of the rules are that the written agreement must be signed by the party to be charged, and it must specify the quantity of goods sold.[23] As for the sale of personal property, the Code requires a writing for the enforceability of contracts involving the sale of personal property where the value exceeds $5,000.

Remedies for a Failure to Comply

Most courts hold that an oral contract that falls within the Statute of Frauds is unenforceable if no sufficient written memorandum exists, but it is not void or ineffective. This is an important consideration, because it means that the courts will uphold oral contracts that have been fully performed. For example, an oral contract that required more than one year for performance is enforceable if one party has fulfilled the term and has fully performed the other requirements of the agreement.

The doctrine of promissory estoppel reappears under the Statute of Frauds. If one party has detrimentally relied on a promise or acted in reliance and in doing so has substantially performed the requirements of an oral contract, those actions will take the case out of the Statute of Frauds. In other words, under the Statute of Frauds, an oral contract that should have had a writing in order to be enforceable becomes enforceable in order to avoid injustice to the injured party.[24]

Parol Evidence

The parol (oral) evidence rule is another complex legal doctrine worthy of discussion because it is often referred to in contract law and in the context of a claim for breach of contract. When two parties have made and signed a written contract, and included in the agreement a clause stating that the writing represents the entirety of the contract, oral testimony aimed at altering or contradicting the terms of the writing will not be permitted.

Strict enforcement of a rule like this would create numerous hardships because it is impossible for most written agreements to clearly include everything to which the par-

ties are agreeing. As usual, the law has provided some exceptions to strict application of the parol evidence rule. Parol (oral) evidence is admissible to explain ambiguous language in a written contract and to prove fraud, duress, and mistakes. Fraud in this context can be misrepresentations in the written contract that do not reflect an accurate prior oral understanding of the parties. This can include contracts where the writing omits terms agreed upon or includes terms not agreed upon.

In sum, parties to contracts should not be allowed to lie and thereby win their lawsuits; but neither should they be allowed to win because the rules of evidence keep the court from hearing additional information about the agreement they thought they were entering into. Although written documents are often the most credible evidence regarding the terms of a contract, additional evidence that would help a court decide the merits of the case should be allowed. The parol evidence rule and its exceptions blend the merits of the written word with the need for some oral explanation to provide a better form of justice for all concerned parties.

Remedies for Breaches of Contract

When a party to a contract fails to perform a contractual duty and has no legal excuse for that failure, a breach of contract has occurred. In most cases, it is impossible for the courts to require specific performance of the contract as it was written or agreed upon. Consequently, an attempt is usually made to assess the damages and award monetary compensation to the party who suffered a loss because of the breach.

Damages

Whenever a breach of contract has been proven, the nonbreaching party is entitled to a verdict for at least some damages. It is easy for a jury to say, "Yes, there was a broken promise, a breach of contract, an injustice, but we cannot see where any significant damage was incurred because of that." It is because of situations like this that attorneys are often forced to inform clients that the legal costs incurred to pursue a case will probably be greater than the damages likely to be awarded. Unless the legal principle is extremely important, what is otherwise a legitimate case will not be worth pursuing. If the court decides a breach occurred but damages were minimal, an award of *nominal damages* is made. A sum of $1 is common for cases awarding nominal damages.

Compensatory damages are awarded when the plaintiff is found to have sustained considerable financial detriment. This can be one of the most serious and difficult elements of a legal action to prove.

When considering compensatory damages, courts have many possible approaches for arriving at an amount. The following situations are but a few examples of the many approaches:

- Where there is a failure to perform labor or services required under a contract, as in building or construction cases, plaintiffs may recover the reasonable costs for completing the contract.

- Where a defendant's performance under the contract is completed but defective, the measure of damages is the reasonable cost of repairing the defect.

- When it is too impracticable to repair or remedy the defect, the damages can be the difference between the value of the work as completed and the value it would have had if the contract had been properly fulfilled.

- Where specific damages for a failure to fully perform under the contract have been established in advance and stated in the contract, those damages are called *liquidated damages*. The purpose for this type of damage determination must be to compensate and not to punish. If a breach occurs and the amount of damage is reasonable in light of the

anticipated or actual loss incurred, the measure of damages allowed will be the preset amount established by the contract.

Many other methods exist to determine the value or extent of damages or to fit the injustices created by various types of contract breaches. Only competent legal counsel can help evaluate and advise practitioners who need additional help in such matters.

Specific Performance

The emphasis of law generally is not to compel people to perform precisely what was promised in a valid contract. Instead, courts try to establish a monetary value for the damages incurred. This is because it is virtually impossible to force people to get along or perform an agreement that will meet the exact expectations and requirements of each party.

There are, however, some circumstances wherein damages are simply inadequate to compensate the nonbreaching party. It is in these situations where the remedy entitled *specific performance* can be utilized.

When the court elects to grant a request for specific performance, the breaching party is ordered to comply with the precise terms of the contract. This remedy is granted most frequently in breaches of contract involving real estate sales. The rationale is that real estate is unique and money alone cannot adequately compensate the plaintiff.

Specific performance is never allowed with breaches of employment contracts because of the impossibility of forcing people to work together without discord. With contracts pertaining to personal property, specific performance can be invoked by the court if it can be shown that the property is unique or of limited supply. Heirlooms are a common example, but champion or unique animals also can be the subject of a plea for specific performance. For example, if someone purchases a champion ram at the National Columbia Show and Sale and the seller refuses to transfer title to that ram to the buyer, offering a substitute animal of equal or higher quality instead, a plea for specific performance may be the most equitable solution. It is well known that national champions are unique and that they provide owners with special breeding and marketing capabilities. It is likely that in such a case, a court would order the breaching seller to transfer title of this specific champion rather than try to arrive at monetary damages.

Restitution

Restitution is a contract remedy that can be requested as an alternative to monetary damages or specific performance. Restitution is appropriate if the breaching party has been unfairly enriched by the acts of the nonbreaching party. The purpose of this remedy is to require breaching parties to give up their unfair gains. Damages in these cases are measured by valuing the defendant's unfair gains—not simply by compensating plaintiffs for their provable losses.[25] This remedy is similar to the unjust enrichment or quasi contract doctrine (discussed later in this chapter).

An example wherein restitution could be employed as a remedy follows:

> Dr. Able agrees with the seller of some real estate to buy one acre of land upon which a veterinary hospital will be built. The seller assures Dr. Able that the city will allow the construction of a veterinary facility at that location. Relying upon this assurance, Dr. Able accepts the seller's offer and leaves a $10,000 deposit with the seller, who agrees to hold that amount in escrow until the sale is completed.
>
> After six months of research and haggling with city planners, Dr. Able is informed that obtaining a use permit for a full-service veterinary hospital is virtually impossible. Dr. Able contacts the seller, informs him of the situation, and demands that the $10,000 be returned along with six month's worth of interest and $1,000 for time and expenses. The

seller informs Dr. Able that he cannot do this because he used the money to buy stock in a new biological engineering company and the sale or transfer of that stock is restricted for a period of two years.

> Dr. Able sues for breach of contract, and the suit drags on for a year and a half. At the time of trial, Dr. Able lists his damages as (1) the $10,000 downpayment, (2) $1000 for his time and effort, and (3) $2000 for 2 year's interest on the $10,000 at 10%. Meanwhile, the bioengineering company hits the jackpot with an FDA approval, and the stock is now worth $40,000.
>
> Dr. Able has a cause of action for damages for breach of contract that amounts to $13,000 (the sum of the above figures). Dr. Able also has a claim in restitution for $40,000 (the current value of the downpayment that the seller invested in the stock). Under the restitutionary remedy for determining damages from this breach of contract, Dr. Able can recover the full value of the investment made by the seller with the $10,000, because he breached the contract and misused Dr. Able's money.

An entire body of law exists on the subject of restitution as a means of measuring damages. Veterinarians should be aware of this alternative type of remedy for breaches of contracts that focus on the defendant's gains and not the plaintiff's losses.

The Duty to Mitigate Damages

When a contract is breached, severe hardship can be created if a nonbreaching party relies only on lawsuits to recoup damages and does nothing to limit the damages caused by the breach. To prevent injustices, the court established a requirement that the party suffering the breach must attempt to mitigate or minimize any damages incurred.[26]

The earlier illustration in the section on promissory estoppel wherein the new graduate acted in reliance on the contract offer from the veterinarian 400 miles away is a good example wherein the duty to mitigate damages might come into play. (For the purposes of this example, it is assumed that the court would find in favor of the existence of a contract in that case.)

To mitigate damages, the new graduate could try to find another job in the area where she had made arrangements to live (if, for example, she signed a lease for a one-year term) so as not to incur damages for breaking that lease. Alternatively, she could break the lease, taking the loss on that item, and attempt to find a job elsewhere so that she did not lose the $2000 per month salary for an indefinite period of time. She would not have to take the first job that came along but could hold out for a reasonable time to find a job similar to the one offered by the veterinarian who breached the agreement. Costs of job searching might also be recoverable if she could show that those expenses were incurred in a diligent attempt to mitigate the damages. This is not a complete analysis of all damages recoverable but should suffice to illustrate this point of law.

The Law of Quasi Contract, or Unjust Enrichment

The law of quasi contracts, or unjust enrichment, is a valuable doctrine of contract law with which practitioners should be familiar. This is a portion of the law of restitution created to fill a void between contract law and tort law (the law of negligence). Under this theory, defendants are required to repay money or restore property because it would be wrong and against public policy for them to retain any benefit or value.

During their practice of veterinary medicine, practitioners are called upon repeatedly to render veterinary services without the authorization or consent of an animal's owner. The petition for care can come in an emergency or nonemergency situation and often occurs without any assurance of payment for services. The request might be made by a friend, relative, or neighbor caring for someone's horse, dog, or cat; by a boarding kennel acting as a bailee; or by a helpful person who picks up an injured animal for someone who does not have a regular veterinarian. Although the law imposes no legal duty to be a good samaritan, there is a logical expectation that doctors and nurses will assist injured people and veterinarians will assist injured animals, and the law does not discourage that expectation. The law of quasi contract further recognizes that average people seek to have such care administered if they are around to request it, and that veterinarians and other health professionals are in the business of providing medical services for pay, not gratuitously.[25]

Quasi contract law was established by the courts to deal with situations in which any of the above situations occurred. The basic philosophy is that the law should not allow one person to be unjustly enriched at the expense of another. So that justice is exercised only in those cases where it legitimately applies, there are certain limitations placed on this doctrine. The following are critical factors that are considered by the legal system before it applies the law of unjust enrichment or quasi contract:

1. The more valuable the animal is, either from its visual appearance or from statements made about the animal by a minor, a friend, a neighbor, a secretary, a boarding facility, or anyone else who knows about the animal, the better is the chance that a court will allow a recovery.

2. The more emergent the animal's needs are, the more leeway exists to provide the required emergency medical care. In such cases radiographs, blood work, good medical records, photographs,

the presence of witnesses, and anything else that helps document the life-threatening situation become important. Most owners do not balk at minor fees for services rendered without their knowledge; however, convincing evidence that the patient's life was in danger must be presented in order to justify major expenditures for emergency care.

3. The veterinarian's attempt to reach the owner prior to rendering medical care is evaluated. Documentation of efforts made to reach an accountable person must be shown and must be believable. Notations on the medical record as to who attempted to call the owner, what number(s) were called, what time of day it was, and how many attempts were made to reach the owner are all important facts to list.

4. Lastly, the extent of emergency care required to stabilize the patient is considered. If at all possible, once a patient is stable, it is best not to proceed with in-depth care until the owner has been contacted. For example, if a dog had a fracture of the tibia and fibula that was serious but not compounded, the court might well allow recovery for the costs incurred in applying a Robert Jones bandage and treating the concomitant shock. The court would probably balk, however, at a claim for reimbursement for emergency compression plating or pinning unless extenuating circumstances were present.

In short, the legal system encourages good samaritans to render life-saving medical care without authorization from the owner when certain circumstances exist. The law frowns on the unjust enrichment of one party at the expense of another person who has shown that he or she is reasonable, practical, and well meaning.

Personal Service Contracts

Contracts to purchase veterinary supplies or to provide veterinary services are the contracts most frequently encountered by practitioners. The next most common type is a contract with employees. Disputes over the terms of an employment agreement are not uncommon and may require considerable management time to reconcile. The disagreements may be merely disagreements; they may result in major misunderstandings and hard feelings; or they may result in lawsuits.

Reasons Why Practitioners Avoid Employment Contracts

Many practices do not utilize employment contracts. The most frequent reasons that practitioners cite for having no contracts are that

- they believe that such business formalities are time-consuming, and they simply do not want to afford the time.
- they do not wish to spend money hiring an attorney to draft a contract.
- they have never determined the terms they want in an employment contract. They prefer, instead, to have the flexibility to decide employment issues as the need arises.
- they feel that a modicum of distrust would be generated by their suggesting that a formal written agreement be created, especially for employees who have been with the practice for several years.

Problems with Recollection

Most new employees come from a pool of applicants. Thus, employers often have discussions regarding salary and benefits with many different people before one is ultimately hired. Practitioners should be concerned about the information provided during the employee-selection process, because things said initially can be interpreted and remembered quite differently by the prospective employee than they are by the employer.

Once new employees are working and have been paid for their services, it is apparent that some type of contract must have been formed. This is so even if the terms of an oral agreement are unclear. If the agreement exceeds one year in length, it is unenforceable under the statute of frauds unless a written memorandum exists. Since most employment contracts are for less than one year, the oral agreements are perfectly valid. Unless some written agreement exists, though, the terms of the contract are still open for interpretation.

Contract Terms

Employment contracts can be lengthy or short documents. Determining which components are the most critical is futile, because different people will find different elements more important. Some of the major ingredients that should be in a written contract or that should at least be discussed in an oral agreement include the following:

- term of employment
- compensation
- emergency calls
- vacation time
- sick leave
- continuing education
- holidays
- medical insurance
- pension plans
- bonuses
- profit sharing plans
- work schedule
- duties

- restrictive covenants
- uniform allowances
- whether a pager will be provided for on-call service
- covenants not to compete (restrictive covenants)
- professional liability insurance
- options to buy into the practice

Sample Contracts

Two sample written contracts are provided herein (Figures 8.1 and 8.2). These contracts are clear and easily comprehensible, so that veterinarians and employees should have no trouble in their use. Alterations can be made to fit individual needs, and the revised contract can be submitted to a local attorney for final review if necessary. Figure 8.1 is designed for use with a veterinarian who is employed at a specified salary, as opposed to a percentage of income generated. Figure 8.2 is a basic contract for use with nonveterinarians. The section on duties would need to be altered in order to apply to someone other than a receptionist.

Another even simpler fill-in-the-blank-type employment contract can be found in Figure 8.3.

Covenants Not to Compete

Each year many veterinarians seek employment with established practices. It is not uncommon for these professionals to encounter clauses in agreements presented for them to sign containing promises not to compete with their employers after they leave the practice. These contract clauses go by several interchangeable titles, including *covenants not to compete*, *restrictive covenants*, and *noncompetition clauses*.

Agreement dated _____ between _____, hereinafter called the Employer, and _____, of _____ (address), hereinafter called the Employee.

1. Employment. The Employer hereby employs the Employee and the Employee hereby accepts employment upon the terms and conditions set forth in this agreement.
2. Term. This agreement shall be for _____ months commencing on _____ provided, however, that the Employer may terminate the Employee at any time for cause. A Formal Employee evaluation will be provided by the Employer at the conclusion of _____ weeks of employment and again after _____ weeks of employment, which shall be considered a probationary period. At the conclusion of that time either the employee or the employer may terminate the remainder of this agreement by submitting such decision in writing to the opposite party. The failure to submit such written intention to terminate this agreement by the end of _____ weeks shall be conclusive evidence of an intent to fulfill this agreement as written.
3. Compensation. The Employer shall pay the Employee a salary of $_____ per month payable in equal installments on the first and fifteenth day of each month.
4. Emergency Calls. The Employee accepts the responsibility for emergency calls on behalf of the Employer for _____ nights and _____ weekends per month. An emergency call schedule shall be established by the Employer _____ weeks prior to the Employee's on-call service. Compensation for emergency cases seen by the Employee at the Employer's practice shall be at the rate of $_____ for each after-hours emergency case he/she attends plus _____% of any charges for emergency surgery and anesthesia fees generated in conjunction with these emergency cases. The Employee will receive no compensation for emergency cases unless the Employer receives payment for at least one-half of the total fee charged for the emergency call.

5. Vacation Time. The Employer shall provide vacation time at the rate of _____ days per year, provided that the Employee's vacation time will not vest until one full year of employment has been completed. Vacation time will be paid at the daily salary rate in force at the time such vacation is taken. Once the Employee's vacation time has vested, time earned but not taken shall be paid to the Employee by the Employer at the termination of this agreement.
6. Sick Leave. The Employee shall accrue sick leave at the rate of _____ days per year payable at the daily salary rate in force at the time such leave is taken. The Employee will be eligible to take sick leave for legitimate illnesses after the completion of six months of full-time employment.
7. Continuing Education. Commencing after the completion of _____ months of full-time employment, the Employee shall be entitled to _____ days of time off per year without pay for participation in veterinary medical continuing education seminars. The Employer will provide $_____ per year to help offset travel and registration costs associated with the Employee's scientific or practice management continuing education.
8. Holidays. Paid holidays will include a full day's pay for New Year's Day, Memorial Day, Fourth of July, Labor Day, Thanksgiving, and Christmas whether the Employee was scheduled to work those days or not. The Employee will be required to attend hospitalized cases and take emergency calls on one-half of these specified holidays. The Employee's holiday emergency call schedule shall be established six months prior to any holiday upon which he/she will be on call.
9. Medical Insurance. _____ months after commencing full time employment, the Employee shall be eligible for participation in the Employer's group hospital and medical insurance plan. The premiums for the Employee's $_____ deductible health insurance plan will be fully paid by the Employer.
10. Pension Plan. The Employee shall be enrolled in the Employer's pension plan upon commencement of employment but will not qualify for any Employer contributions until he/she has completed _____ years of full-time (greater than 50%) employment.

Figure 8.1   A sample contract for veterinarians on salary.

Professionals have entered into agreements containing restrictive covenants for years. In the past, the law of supply and demand seems to have favored an employee's freedom to contract without being bound by noncompetition clauses. In recent years, however, the supply and demand of veterinarians and job opportunities in the United States have changed, so that the AVMA has forecast a continuing surplus of private practitioners on a national level through the year 2000.[27]

Because of the increase in the supply of veterinarians, it cannot be assumed that an existing practice will continue to grow and prosper even if a former employed veterinarian opens a practice nearby. For this reason, veterinary practice owners are more likely to insist on noncompetition clauses in employment contracts in the future than they were in the past.

Legal Precedents

Both contract and antitrust laws apply to

11. Professional Liability Insurance. The Employer will ensure that the Employee is named on the business's professional liability policy and will pay any additional premiums required for such coverage. If the Employer's insurance carrier requires that the Employee have his/her own policy, the Employee shall obtain a professional liability insurance policy satisfactory to the Employer. The Employee will pay the premiums for such coverage and be reimbursed by the Employer.

12. Work Schedule. The Employee's regular work schedule shall be from _____ until _____ on _____, from _____ until _____ on _____, and from _____ until _____ on alternate Saturdays. Changes in this schedule may be encountered occasionally when other veterinarians are unable to work. The Employer will make reasonable attempts to provide the Employee with one week's notice prior to changes in the work schedule.

13. Duties. The Employee shall devote his/her entire time, attention, and energies to the business of the Employer during working hours, and shall not during the term of this agreement be engaged in any other veterinary business activity without the approval of the Employer. The Employee will be employed as a small-animal veterinarian and will have approximately _____ hours of his/her weekly work schedule set aside for elective surgery beginning _____ months after the commencement of this agreement. The Employee shall take one-half of all emergency calls.

14. Restrictive Covenant. The parties agree that the Employer's business is local in scope and that the Employer would suffer serious damage and loss of goodwill if, upon termination of this agreement, the Employee competed with the Employer by providing veterinary services for the clients who are currently regular clients of the Employer. The Employee, therefore, agrees that for a period of two years after the termination of this agreement, he/she will not within 5 miles of the employer's current business address directly or indirectly own, manage, operate, control, be employed by, participate in, or be connected in any manner with the ownership, management, operation, or control of any business similar to the type of small animal veterinary practice conducted by the Employer at the time of termination of this agreement.

15. Option to Purchase. At the conclusion of _____ months of this agreement, the Employer shall formally discuss options with the Employee for the Employee's purchase of not less than a _____ % interest in the _____ Employer's veterinary practice.

16. Invalid Provision. If any term, provision, covenant, or condition of this agreement is held by a court of competent jurisdiction to be invalid, void, or unenforceable, the rest of the provisions shall remain in full force and effect and shall in no way be affected, impaired, or invalidated.

17. Contract Terms to Be Exclusive. This agreement supercedes any and all other agreements, whether written or oral, between the parties hereto with respect to this employment agreement and contains all of the promises and agreements between the parties. Each party acknowledges that no representations, inducements, promises, or agreements have been made, orally or otherwise, by any party, or anyone acting on behalf of any party, that are not embodied herein. All other agreements, statements, or promises not contained in this agreement shall be invalid.

18. Waiver or Modification Ineffective Unless in Writing. It is further agreed that no waiver or modification of this agreement or of any covenant, condition, or limitation herein contained shall be valid unless in writing and duly executed by the party to be charged therewith and that no evidence of any waiver or modification shall be offered or received in evidence in any proceeding, arbitration, or litigation between the parties hereto arising out of or affecting this agreement, or the rights or obligations of any party hereunder, unless such waiver or modification is in writing, duly executed as aforesaid.

Date_____ Signed _____(Employer)

Date_____ Signed_____(Employee)

restrictive covenants, although most causes of action stem from contract law principles.[28] The materials and precedents in the ensuing discussion relate to employment contracts. States that prohibit covenants not to compete in employment contracts, without exception, uphold restrictive covenants as long as a sale of goodwill has occurred as part of the purchase or sale of a business.[29] This variation on the enforceability of restrictive covenants is discussed under the heading "State Laws." Since violations of antitrust laws may preclude enforcement of restrictive covenants, a brief review of antitrust law follows.

The Sherman Antitrust Act

Antitrust laws originate from both federal and state sources. Four basic requirements must be met in order to successfully litigate a claim under Section One of the Sherman Act:

- There must be at least two people acting in concert.

AGREEMENT

Agreement dated _____ between _____, hereinafter called the Employer and _____, of _____ (address), hereinafter called the Employee.

1. Employment. The Employer hereby employs the Employee, and the Employee hereby accepts employment upon the terms and conditions set forth in this agreement.

2. Term. The term of this agreement shall begin on _____ and shall terminate on _____. The first two months of employment shall be considered a probationary period. A formal Employee evaluation will be held after the first and second months of employment, at which time a salary increase will be considered. Prior to or at the conclusion of the two-month probationary period, either the Employer or the Employee may terminate the remainder of this agreement upon one week's notice by submitting such decision in writing to the opposite party. The failure to provide this notice before the end of the second month shall be conclusive evidence of an intent to fulfill the agreement as written. After completing the probationary period, one month's notice shall be provided by either party prior to the termination of the agreement.

3. Compensation. The Employer shall pay the Employee a salary of _____ per hour payable every two weeks commencing on _____.

4. Raises. An annual salary evaluation will occur within two months after the completion of each successive year of employment. Merit pay raises and cost-of-living increases will be considered at that time.

5. Uniforms. The Employer will provide the Employee with a uniform allowance of $_____ per year so that the Employee can purchase and wear appropriate uniforms to work each day.

6. Vacation Pay and Sick Leave. The Employee will qualify for sick leave and vacation pay if he/she works more than 20 hours per week. The Employer will provide _____ days of sick leave and _____ days of vacation pay each year for employees working 40 hours per week. Part-time employees working greater than 20 hours per week will receive sick leave and vacation pay based upon whatever percent of a 40-hour work week they routinely work. For example, if the work week averages 36 hours, 90% of vacation and sick pay will be provided. If the average is 30 hours per week, a 75% factor will be used. Neither sick leave nor vacation time will vest until one full year of employment has been completed. Unused sick leave which accumulates in excess of 10 days will be paid to the Employee as a good health bonus at a time mutually agreed upon by the parties. After one full year of employment has been completed, the Employer agrees to pay any unused sick leave or vacation pay to the Employee at the termination of employment.

7. Holidays. Paid holidays will include 8 hours pay for New Year's Day, Memorial Day, July 4th, Labor Day, Thanksgiving, and Christmas. If the Employee is normally working more than 36 hours per week, he/she will be paid a full day's pay for each of these holidays whether or not he/she was scheduled to have worked on the holiday. If the Employee works more than 20 hours but less than 36 hours per week, he/she will receive holiday pay based upon the same formula as that employed for vacation pay/sick leave in Part 6 of this agreement.

8. Medical Insurance. _____ months after commencing employment, the Employee will qualify for the Employer's medical and hospitalization plan, fully paid by the Employer if the Employee is working more than 32 hours per week. If the Employee is covered by another medical insurance policy and does not desire additional coverage, the Employer will increase the Employee's monthly compensation by an amount equal to the cost of medical insurance that would have been paid if the Employee had been included in the hospital medical plan.

9. Veterinary Care. The Employer will provide medical care for Employee's companion animals at 25% of retail cost, except for radiographs, which will be charged at 40% of retail cost, and outside lab work, drugs, and pet food, which shall be charged at the employer's actual cost.

10. Pension Plans. The Employee shall become eligible for enrollment in the Employer's pension plan upon the commencement of employment but must remain employed more than 50% of full time for _____ years before any contributions can be made to the plan by the Employer.

11. Bonuses. Bonuses may be paid from time to time by the Employer, but only Employees who have been employed more than six months will be eligible. These bonuses will be prorated for part-time Employees in the same manner as illustrated in Part 6 of this agreement.

12. Duties. The Employee shall serve as a receptionist/animal health technician/veterinary assistant (circle one or more). Primary duties (using receptionist as an example) will include answering the telephone, scheduling appointments, attending to the needs of clients and patients, maintaining medical records, receiving monies paid on accounts, balancing the day sheet and cash drawers, and limited amounts of typing.

13. Work Schedule. The employee's regular work schedule shall be from_____ until _____ and _____ until_____ on the following days: _____. Additional work days may be required occasionally if staff turnover occurs or when other employees are unable to work.

14. Overtime. The Employee will be paid one and one-half times his/her base pay for time worked in excess of 40 hours per work week. The Employee shall have the option of accepting one and one-half times the number of hours worked in excess of 40 hours per work week as compensatory time off in lieu of overtime pay.

15. Contract Terms to Be Exclusive. This written agreement represents the sole and entire agreement between the parties.

Date_____ Signed_____
(Employee)

Date_____ Signed_____
(Employer)

Figure 8.2 A veterinary practice employee contract.

Name_____

Date_____

Address_____

Zip_____

SS #_____

Telephone_____

Job Title_____

Full/Part Time_____

Duties and Responsibilities_____

1. Probationary Period: The first _____ weeks of this agreement shall be considered a probationary period, during which time the Employee may leave or be dismissed with 24 hours notice. An employee evaluation will be conducted at or before the end of the first and the second months of employment.

2. Work Schedule: From _____to_____ and_____ to_____the following days: S_____M_____Tu_____We_____Th_____F_____Sa_____

3. Salary and Benefits: Starting rate of pay: _____ Pay days will be as follows: _____Vacation time of _____ days per year will not vest and may not be taken until one full year of employment has been completed. Sick leave amounting to _____ days per year will not vest or be paid until 6 months of employment have been completed. Other benefits_____

4. Uniform Requirements: The employer will provide the employee with a uniform allowance of $_____ per year. The uniform requirement includes _____ _____

5. Termination: After the probation period, the Employee is expected to give _____ weeks notice before resigning from this job. If dismissed by the employer after the probationary period, the employee will receive _____ weeks notice or the equivalent in severance pay. In the event of fraud, theft, or unprofessional conduct, the employee may be dismissed without notice or severance pay.

Date _____

Signed _____(Employer)

Date _____

Signed _____(Employee)

Figure 8.3   A simple fill-in employment agreement.

- The restraint must involve trade or commerce.
- The restraint must involve interstate commerce.
- The restraint must be unreasonable.[29]

A Contract

The first element of a Sherman Act violation requires the presence of a contract, a combination, or a conspiracy. This requirement is easily met in cases of a restrictive covenant because a formal contract is already in existence.

Trade or Commerce

The second element, trade or commerce, is also fairly easy to prove. The landmark *Goldfarb* v. *Virginia Bar*[30] case held that the practice of a profession was indeed trade or commerce and, therefore, for at least some purposes, federal antitrust laws will be applied to members of the "learned" professions.

Interstate Commerce

The third element, interstate commerce, may be harder to prove because the practice of veterinary medicine is basically a local activity.[31] The two key requirements under the Sherman Act are that either the actual effect or potential effect of the restraint must be both adverse and substantial.

In many cases it is difficult to prove that a veterinary practice has a substantial effect on interstate commerce. Among the factors the courts review is the amount of revenue that flows to the veterinary practice from interstate transactions. There is no specific amount of money that the courts rely upon; instead, cases are decided on an individual basis. Practitioners near state borders or at racetracks where many horses move interstate could possibly affect interstate commerce sufficiently to satisfy this requirement.

Another relevant, and often significant, factor concerns the volume of supplies and equipment shipped to the practice from out of state. Since most biologicals, drugs, hospital supplies, and veterinary equipment are part of interstate commerce, practitioners are always at risk of a court holding that that activity alone substantially involves interstate commerce.

A third consideration involves the volume of patients practitioners treat that have moved or that will be moving interstate. Ancillary to this question are two more concerns: (1) whether the practitioner has a practice that serves more than one state, and (2) whether the veterinarian spends money on interstate travel for purposes related to the practice. Receiving referrals from adjacent states, issuing health certificates for interstate movement of animals, and making farm calls in more than one state could be of importance here. To determine what types of factors have been judged to be an insufficient nexus with interstate commerce, see Reference 28.

The issue of interstate commerce is a particularly cogent issue whenever a practice is located close to a state border or when major cities are in close proximity with others in adjacent states, as is the case in the northeastern portion of the United States. This element, like the others, though, is only one of the factors to be evaluated in deciding whether there is substantial effect on interstate commerce.

An Unreasonable Restraint

The fourth and final element that must be present in order to successfully challenge a violation under Section One of the Sherman Act is the presence of an unreasonable restraint of trade or commerce.

Since convenants not to compete do not fall under the United States Supreme Court's definition of an unreasonable restraint of trade (like price fixing), they must be analyzed under the court's "rule of reason." This rule requires courts to fully evaluate the reasonableness of a covenant not to compete. Although the immediate discussion herein involves federal law interpretations of the rule of reason, state law interpretations closely parallel the federal precedents.

Three factors are considered to be important in determining whether a restrictive covenant is reasonable. These include an evaluation of the need for protection of the practitioner-employer; an evaluation of undue hardship on the employee; and an evaluation of the effect of the restraint on the public's interest.

Employer's Interests

One of the key issues upon which many cases turn involves the breadth of the restrictive covenant. If the restrictive covenant is broader than needed to protect the employer, it can be struck down or reduced. Courts frequently point out that the employed doctor was "fresh from training when he moved as a stranger into the established practitioner's community, solely for the purpose of association with him."[32] Language like this illustrates the court's concerns with fairness toward established employers when efforts are made to enforce a restrictive covenant.

Limitations on the Practice of One's Profession

The extent to which the medical practice of an employed physician can be limited by a restrictive covenant was examined in *Karpinski* v. *Ingrasci*.[33] In that case the plaintiff was an established oral surgeon in solo practice. He hired a person who had just completed his training in oral surgery. As part of the contract, a clause was included which restricted the defendant from practicing "dentistry and/or oral surgery" within a five-county region. The New York Court of Appeals found that a restriction against the practice of "dentistry and oral surgery" was impermissibly broad.

A similar Wisconsin case found that a covenant to refrain from practicing medicine and surgery for nine months following termination of employment was also unreasonably broad.[34] In that case a surgical group offered no proof to establish that if the plaintiff-employee practiced only medicine, he would still compete with the defendant's surgery practice.

The Nevada Supreme Court evaluated a covenant in a physician's contract restricting him from practicing "medicine" within five miles of the employer's business for two years after termination of the employment contract. Six months after beginning work as an employee, the physician notified the clinic of his decision to terminate the agreement and practice orthopedic surgery in the area.[35]

In this case the court found the restraint to be unreasonable. The court said the restraint was beyond any legitimate protectable interest of the clinic where the physician had been working, because none of the associates at that practice were orthopedic specialists. The public's interest in the outcome of the case was another key issue. If the employee was prohibited from practicing orthopedic surgery, residents of Elko would be forced to travel long distances to Reno or Salt Lake City for specialty surgical care. When the court balanced all the factors, it determined that the loss suffered by the employee and the public would be greater than the loss incurred by the employer if the employee was allowed to practice orthopedic surgery. The Nevada Supreme Court resolved this case by modifying the restrictive covenant, allowing the physician to practice orthopedic surgery but not general medicine within the two-year time period.

These cases illustrate that, even in jurisdictions where restrictive covenants are upheld (a vast majority of the states), the restriction must be reasonably narrow in scope. If an employee was practicing in an exclusively small animal practice but a covenant prohibited that person from practicing veterinary medicine within a five-mile radius, it could be attacked as overly broad if the employee terminated the contract and opened an exclusively large animal practice nearby. Practitioners who seek to include restrictive covenants in employment contracts should be cautious in making clauses any broader than necessary to protect their financial interests.

Geographic Limitations

Geographic limitations placed upon veterinary employees also will be considered by the courts. Acceptable radii could vary considerably from small animal practice, for which five miles might be reasonable, to large animal practice, for which a 20-mile radius might be considered satisfactory. Because of the nature of a specialist's referral practice, a radius of 50 to 100 miles might be acceptable.

In an Ohio case, a 30-mile radius for a physician in general practice was held to be unduly burdensome.[36] An Idaho case, however, held a 25-mile restraint against an obstetrician reasonable.[37] In Illinois, the Supreme Court upheld a covenant not to compete in a case involving an employed veterinarian but changed the radius from 30 to 20 miles.[38]

Time Limitations

Significant variations in the length of time before opening a competing practice have been upheld by the courts, but the thrust is always that the time must be reasonable. In order to avoid an overly broad covenant that may be struck down or altered by the court, it is advisable to keep the time frame within two to five years.

The Employee's Interests

The second major factor that courts consider to evaluate reasonableness is whether the restriction causes undue hardship for the employee. Overall, courts are very reluctant to find undue hardship. More often they find that the professional doctor is competent enough in age and intelligence to realize the extent of the terms of the contract. The court expects doctors to seek legal advice prior to signing a contract with a restrictive covenant.

Effect on the Public

The final factor that courts consider in determining the reasonableness of a covenant not to compete is the effect of that covenant on the public. The earlier case involving the only orthopedic surgeon in Elko, Nevada is an example of a situation wherein the interests of the public were important to the court.[39] The question that the courts entertain is whether other professionals in the area could provide the same type of services as those offered by the restrained employee.

Given the fact that there are fewer veterinarians than physicians in the United States, there may be more legitimate reasons to protect the public's interest when veterinarians are involved in restrictive covenant disputes than when physicians are involved. One reason might be the need for a food animal veterinarian in a rural area not serviced by any other practitioner within 20 to 50 miles. Another might be the public's need of a veterinary radiologist, surgeon, neurologist, or other specialist in a densely populated area of the country where there are no similar specialists.

Other Invalidations of Restrictive Covenants

Another way that restrictive covenants can be invalidated is if an employee shows that the employer breached the terms of the employment contract. In a New Hampshire case, an employer's substantial financial difficulty due to mismanagement was an important issue. The court noted that an employment contract carries with it an implied obligation on the "part of the employer to afford a certain degree of financial security to the contracting employee...."[40] Since the employer's financial problems amounted to a breach of the employment contract, the court was unwilling to allow the employer to enforce a restrictive covenant.

State Laws

Most states have antitrust laws similar to the Sherman Act. Some have statutory language related directly to restrictive covenants. The common law and statutory law in this area is in a constant state of flux, so changes can occur that require veterinarians to check with local attorneys before including these covenants in their employment contract.

Some state statutes prohibit virtually all restrictive covenants associated with employment contracts. California's law on this subject says:

> Except as provided in this chapter, every contract by which anyone is restrained from engaging in a lawful profession, trade or business of any kind is to that extent void.[41]

The rest of the "chapter" referred to in this statutory section allows restrictive covenants to be enforced provided that the covenant is ancillary to the sale of the goodwill and all of a person's share of a business.[42] This approach is standard in most states that have statutes covering restrictive covenants.

An interesting exception is found in Colorado, where restrictive covenants for physicians are illegal per se.[43] Since the section refers only to physicians, though, Colorado law relating to veterinarians would be the same as in California, i.e., restrictive covenants in employment contracts are void unless coupled with a contract for the purchase or sale of a business or the assets of a business.[43]

Other states take a somewhat different statutory tack. The Wisconsin law, for example, reads as follows:

> A covenant by an assistant, servant or agent not to compete with his employer... during the term of the employment..., or thereafter, within a specified territory and during a specified time is lawful and enforceable only if the restrictions imposed are reasonably necessary for the protection of the employer.... Any such restrictive covenant imposing an unreasonable restraint is illegal, void and unenforceable even as to so much of the covenant or performance as would be a reasonable restraint.[44]

This statute is basically a codification of the principles discussed under the antitrust heading. A caveat regarding the Wisconsin law, though, is that if the covenant is held to be unreasonably broad, the court will not simply reform it and make it enforceable—it will hold that the entire covenant is void and unenforceable.

Falling in between California's complete prohibition on restrictive covenants in employment contracts and the states that have no statutory law on this issue is the South Dakota law. It states,

> An employee may agree with an employer at the time of employment or at any time during his employment not to engage directly or indirectly in the same business or profession as that of his employer for any period not exceeding two years from the date of termination of the agreement and not to solicit existing customers of the employer within a specified county, city or other specified area for any period not exceeding two years from the date of termination of the agreement, if the employer continues to carry on a like business therein.

This is not unlike the Wisconsin law. Except for the vagueness of the terms "city or other specified area" (which may not be of concern in a sparsely populated state like South Dakota), it gives a clear indication of what is probably acceptable in most states.

Summary

Contract law is a vital part of the veterinarian's daily business existence. The more that practitioners know about contracts, the less likely it is that they will be subject to time-consuming controversies which detract from their primary professional goal—the delivery of veterinary services.

References

1. Restatement, Second, Contracts § 1; p 1.
2. *Black's Law Dictionary*, ed 5. St. Paul, West Publishing Co, 1979, pp 291-292.
3. UCC § 2-105(1).
4. Schaber, Rohwer: *Contracts in a Nutshell*, ed 2. St. Paul, West Publishing Co, 1984, § 7; § 131, p 232; § 48, 49.
5. Calamari, Perillo: *Law of Contracts*, ed 2. St. Paul, West Publishing Co, 1977, § 2-10, pp 39-40.
6. Alperin HJ, Chase RF: *Consumer Law*. St. Paul, West Publishing Co, 1986, § 3, pp 4-5.
7. Restatement, Second, Contracts, § 50(1).
8. Restatement, Second, Contracts, § 58.
9. Restatement, Second, Contracts § 59.
10. UCC § 1-205(1), (2) and 1-201(3).
11. Alperin HJ, Chase RF: *Consumer Law*. St. Paul, West Publishing Co, 1986, § 4, p 7.
12. *Paterson* v *Reeves*, 304 F. 2d 950, 951 (D.C.Cir.1962).
13. 32 NJ 358, 161 A.2d 69 (1960).
14. Alperin HJ, Chase RF: *Consumer Law*. St. Paul, West Publishing Co, 1986, pp 10-11.
15. Restatement, Second, Contracts § 79.
16. UCC § 2-302(1).
17. *Voight & McMakin Air Conditioning, Inc* v *Property Redevelopment Corp*, 276 A.2d 239 (D.C.App. 1971).
18. Restatement, Second, Contracts § 90(1).
19. Alperin HJ, Chase RF: *Consumer Law*. St. Paul, West Publishing Co, 1986, § 23, p 40; § 26, p 43.
20. UCC § 2-201.
21. UCC § 8-319.
22. UCC § 9-203.
23. UCC § 2-201 [1].
24. Alperin HJ, Chase RF: *Consumer Law*. St. Paul, West Publishing Co, 1986, § 12, p 25.

25. Hunter HO: *Modern Law of Contracts, Breaches and Remedies*. Boston, Warren, Gorham, and Lamont; § 7.02 (4), pp 7-8; § 9.01(4) pp 6-9.

26. Restatement, Second, Contracts § 347, 350.

27. Wise KJ, Kushman JE: US veterinary medical manpower study: Demand and supply from 1980 to 2000. *JAVMA* 187: 4,358–361 (1985).

28. Mayo JM: The antitrust ramifications of noncompetition clauses in the partnership and employment agreements of doctors. *Loyola Law Rev.* 313, 1984.

29. Florida Statutes § 542.33, Colorado Statutes § 8-2-113, California Bus and Prof Code § 16601.

30. 421 U.S. 773 (1975).

31. *Williams* v *St. Joseph Hospital* 629 F.2d 448, 7th Cir (1980).

32. *Foltz* v *Struxness* 168 Kan. 714, 215 P.2d 133, 139 (1950).

33. *Karpinski* v *Ingrasci* 23 NY 2d 45, 268 NE 2d 751 (NY 1971).

34. *Georcaris* v *Surgical Consultants, Ltd* 100 Wis. 2d 387, 302 NW 2d 76 (Wisc Ct App 1981).

35. *Ellis* v *McDaniel* 95 Nev 455, 596 P.2d 222 (1979).

36. *Droba* v *Berry*, 2 Ohio Ap.2d 50, 139 NE 2d 124 (Ohio Ct of C P 1955).

37. *Marshall* v *Covington*, 81 Idaho 199, 339 P. 2d 504 (1959).

38. Hannah HW: More about restrictive covenants: *Legal Briefs. JAVMA* 182:11, 1162 (1983).

39. *Ellis* v *McDaniel*, 95 Nev 455, 596 P.2d 222 (Nev 1979).

40. *Laconia Clinic, Inc.* v *Cullen*, 119 NH 804, 408 A.2d 412 (1979).

41. California Business and Professions Code § 16600.

42. California Business and Professions Code § 16601.

43. Colorado Statutes § 8-2-113 (3); § 8-2-113 (2) (a).

44. Wisconsin Employment Regulations § 103.465.

CHAPTER 9

The Legal Use of Veterinary Drugs

The creation and marketing of a vast array of pharmaceuticals and biologicals during the past three decades have improved the quality of care in veterinary medicine dramatically. Vaccines, hormones, antibiotics, enzymes, chemotherapeutic drugs, insecticides, sedatives, anesthetics, and analgesics are among the many types of drugs and products currently available. This growth has in turn greatly altered and expanded the responsibilities of both federal and state agencies in this area, so that the system and body of regulation are now quite complex.

The Regulatory System

Federal Regulatory Agencies and Legislation

Although it may seem that the government sometimes overregulates certain areas and underregulates others, there really is an overall scheme to the drug, pesticide, and biologicals regulatory process.

The Food and Drug Administration

The Food and Drug Administration (FDA) Center for Veterinary Medicine (CVM) is responsible for regulating animal foods/feeds and most animal health products. Veterinary drugs, medicated animal feeds, and pet foods are examples of specific items that are subject to the requirements of the Food, Drug and Cosmetic Act (FD&C Act). Some items receive more attention than others, and some are concurrently governed by state laws.

The United States Department of Agriculture

The United States Department of Agriculture (USDA) has authority over the regulation of the entire biological products market. Within that department, the veterinary biologics staff

215

at the Animal and Plant Health Inspection Service has jurisdiction over all viruses, serums, toxins, and analogous products of natural or synthetic origin. The Virus-Serum-Toxin Act of 1913 is the federal legislation that allows the USDA to regulate such products as antitoxins, vaccines, live microorganisms, and the antigenic or immunizing components of microorganisms intended for use in the diagnosis, treatment, or prevention of disease in animals. Contrary to common belief, the FDA has nothing to do with the regulation of products in the veterinary vaccine market. The regulation of biologicals is covered in Chapter 10.

The Environmental Protection Agency

Another group of products falls within the drugs category but outside the FDA's powers. These are preparations used as rodenticides, insecticides, and germicidal preparations topically on animals or systemically and topically on inanimate objects. If any product in this group is to be administered systemically, such as cythioate or fenthion for fleas, the FDA has jurisdiction. Otherwise, the Environmental Protection Agency (EPA) possesses the regulatory powers as provided by the Federal Insecticide, Fungicide and Rodenticide Act. The original version of this law was enacted in 1947, but it was amended and updated in 1972. An analysis of the statutes and laws in this area is found in Chapter 10.

The Drug Enforcement Agency

Most practitioners are familiar with the regulatory actions exerted by another arm of the federal government, the Drug Enforcement Agency (DEA). This agency enforces the federal Controlled Substances Act. The Controlled Substances Act, enacted in 1970, is the major federal law regulating the manufacture, distribution, dispensing, and delivery of certain drugs or substances that are subject to or have the potential for abuse, physical dependence, or psychological dependence. This is an area of drug control in which state governments may have administrative counterparts to the DEA and in some cases have stricter standards regarding controlled drugs. The use of drugs falling into this category is controlled by the FDA and the DEA. Chapter 11 focuses on the DEA's regulation of these drugs.

State Government Regulations

State governments become involved in some issues affecting the utilization of veterinary drugs and biologicals. Some states have adopted specific policies that define what is needed for the existence of a valid veterinarian-client-patient relationship; other states use the definition created by the FDA. Most states have laws or regulations that establish what must appear on the labels of drugs being dispensed. The majority of those laws are written with human medical care in mind, but the labeling laws usually apply to veterinary drugs as well. On a related topic, practitioners also need to know what the law says about the packaging and dispensing of drugs in child-proof containers.

The FD&C Act

Under Title 21 of the United States Code, also known as the the FD&C Act, the FDA CVM has been given the authority to govern the manufacture, distribution, and use of veterinary drugs that are distributed between states. The federal code also gives the FDA the authority to write regulations on how it will enforce the FD&C Act. Those regulations are contained in the Code of Federal Regulations Title 21.

Trying to understand all the intricacies of the FD&C Act and the Code of Federal Regulations is an overwhelming task which most practitioners hopefully will never need to face. Veterinarians should have a reasonable understanding of the law in this area, however, in order to abide by it and avoid legal actions related to the use or misuse of veterinary drugs. In addition, knowing the controls and safeguards comprising this complex system will help practitioners understand why new pharmaceutical products are expensive.

Drugs in Interstate Commerce

The FD&C Act has very broad jurisdiction concerning drugs in interstate commerce. The Act states that drugs may be considered to be in interstate commerce if at any time in their history they or any of their components have been delivered in interstate commerce and held for sale.[1] According to sources at the FDA, several years ago a federal court held that even if the only thing moving interstate was the bottle in which a drug was packaged, there would still be sufficient contact with interstate commerce to apply federal law to the case. It is clear, therefore, that most drugs come under FDA regulation unless extreme precautions are taken to keep all activities and materials within the state of origin. The enormous limitations this puts on the size of the market for such a product render it impractical for most companies to create non-FDA-approved drugs in any except the largest states.

Obtaining FDA Approval: New Animal Drug Applications

Section 512 of the FD&C Act outlines the rules that govern the safety and efficacy of new animal drugs.[2] According to a special commentary written by the FDA, the following best describes what constitutes a new animal drug:

> An animal drug is defined as "new" under the Act because, among other things,

it is not recognized generally, among qualified experts, as safe and effective for use under the conditions prescribed, recommended, or suggested in its labeling. Section 512(d)(2) specifically sets forth factors that are to be considered, among others, in determining whether a new animal drug will be safe under its proposed conditions of use. Among the enumerated factors are: (A) the probable consumption of such drug and any substance formed in or on food because of the use of such drug, (B) the cumulative effect on man or animal of such drug, taking into account any chemically or pharmacologically related substances, (C) safety factors which, in the opinion of experts qualified by scientific training and experience to evaluate the safety of such drugs, are appropriate for the use of animal experimentation data, and (D) whether the conditions of use prescribed, recommended, or suggested in the proposed labeling are reasonably certain to be followed in practice.[3]

Although this seems fairly uncomplicated so far, the same Section 512 regarding new animal drugs goes on to discuss many other details including materials needed to file an application for the use of a new animal drug (eight items), grounds for refusing an application (eight items including such things as a contention that the drug causes cancer when ingested by humans or animals), the criteria for withdrawal of approval of a drug (eight items), methods for appealing an FDA finding, exemptions of drugs for research, and much more.

This is only the beginning. Section 514 of Title 21 of the Code of Federal Regulations sets forth in depth the requirements for evidence that must be submitted to demonstrate the safety and efficacy of a drug before approval can be granted. The new animal drug approval (NADA) process is extremely complicated and a very effective safeguard.

Once a new animal drug has cleared this process and gained FDA approval, the FD&C Act provides for publishing notice of approval in the *Federal Register*.[4] This approval identifies the specific conditions for which the drug has been shown to be safe and effective as well as any restrictions for use.

Although the same drug may be effective and safe for other uses or perhaps other species, the economics of a limited marketplace often prohibit a pharmaceutical company from performing additional research sufficient to seek wider approval. This fact and others often result in "extra-label" uses for drugs, a topic that is discussed in more detail later in this chapter.

Drug Categories

Products Not Subject to Federal Regulation

The FD&C Act does cover cosmetics, as its title indicates, but only as they pertain to human use. Therefore, grooming products that are used only for cleansing or promoting the attractiveness of animals do not fall within the FDA's regulatory control. If any of these products are intended and marketed as therapeutic aids or contain an active drug ingredient, they could be governed by the FDA. If, instead of a drug, they have an insecticide as an active ingredient, they generally fall within the purview of the EPA.

Adulterated Drugs

Under Section 301 of the FD&C Act, the introduction or delivery for introduction into interstate commerce of any food, drug, device, or cosmetic that is adulterated is prohibited.[5] Section 501 of Title 21 defines what constitutes an adulterated drug. Simply stated, drugs that contain unsanitary components, lack adequate control in manufacture, differ in strength from that recognized in the official compendium, or that are mixed with another substance to reduce their quality or strength are considered to have been adulterated.

A frequent violation of the adulteration section of the FD&C Act involves a drug being offered for sale without a NADA. Under current law an unapproved drug is, in itself, adulterated.[6]

A common example of the creation of an adulterated drug occurs when practitioners take two or more FDA-approved drugs and mix them in one syringe or one dispensing bottle. In doing this, the drugs have been adulterated, and administering such a drug combination constitutes a violation of the FD&C Act. The creation of such home concoctions is discouraged by the FDA because generally no safety, efficacy, or stability tests have been performed or evaluated on this type of "new drug." In addition, tests to determine depletion of residues from edible products of food-producing animals have not been completed.

Veterinarians do have some leeway under current legal standards to use drugs in manners other than as directed on the labels, provided that sufficient corroborative evidence indicates safety. (These rules are discussed later in this chapter under the heading "Veterinarians' Rights to Use Nonstandard Treatments.") Nevertheless, when veterinarians create a new drug in this fashion, they have become the manufacturers of that new drug and can be held liable for deleterious side effects and illegal tissue residues.

Misbranded Drugs

The other type of drug prohibited for introduction into interstate commerce by § 301 of the FD&C Act is any drug that has been misbranded. Section 502(a) of the FD&C Act (21 USC 352[a]) states that misbranded drugs include drugs on which the labeling is false or misleading in any particular. Section 502(b) goes on to state that a drug or device is deemed to be misbranded if it is in a package form and does not bear a label that contains the name and place of business of the manufacturer, packer, or distributor and an accurate statement of the quantity of the contents in terms of weight, measure, and numerical count.

Although numerous other definitions of misbranding exist in § 502, one of the most important ones is § 502(f)(1).[7] This section says that a drug is misbranded unless its labeling bears adequate directions for use. The regulations contained in 21 CFR 201.5 define adequate directions as directions by which a lay person can use a drug safely and for the purpose for which it was intended.

Unless exempted by regulation, all drug products are required to bear directions adequate for use. If no requirement of adequate directions for use is necessary for the protection of the public health, the Secretary shall promulgate regulations exempting such drug or device from the requirement.

Over-the-Counter Drugs

Rules have been created to determine which drugs can be labeled and allowed to be sold as over-the-counter (OTC) drugs.[8] The type of drug most easily classified as such is that for which directions for use can be readily understood and followed by the ordinary individual.[9] Probably the best known human drug classified as OTC is aspirin, for which directions can be written for ordinary uses. Some other drugs such as certain antihistamines and topical corticosteroids have, in recent years, been reclassified by the FDA from prescription drugs to OTC drugs due in part to long-term familiarity by the general public. Over the years, veterinary drugs such as penicillin, tetracycline, and even gentamicin have changed from prescription to OTC status for many uses in livestock after sufficient familiarity by the consumer was established.

Distinguishing Prescription from OTC Drugs

Identifying drugs as prescription or OTC can be confusing. By reading the label and understanding some basic terminology, practitioners can determine whether or not a product is a prescription drug.

Prescription or Legend Drugs

Many drugs may be used only by or under the supervision of a veterinarian. These are called *prescription*, or *legend* drugs. (Legally, these terms mean the same thing. For clarity and simplicity, this text will refer to them as prescription drugs.) The FD&C Act does not specify that the FDA can restrict drugs to a veterinary prescription status; however, the FD&C Act has been interpreted to allow the FDA to do so. The Code of Federal Regulations describes the conditions for restricting drugs to prescription status, and these have been upheld by the courts.[10] This allowance is important because, without it, drugs could not be marketed unless adequate directions for use by lay persons could be written. It is through the court cases cited and this circuitous approach that veterinary prescription drugs come into existence.

Label Requirements for Prescription Drugs

Section 201.105 of the Code of Federal Regulations requires that the following conditions be met for a drug to qualify as a veterinary prescription drug:

The drug is

- in the possession of a person (or his/her agents or employees) regularly and lawfully engaged in the manufacture, transportation, storage, or wholesale or retail distribution of veterinary drugs and is to be sold only to or on the prescription or order of a licensed veterinarian for use in the course of professional practice; or

- in the possession of a licensed veterinarian for use in the course of professional practice.

In addition, the CFR requires that the label of the drug bear:

- the statement "Caution: Federal law restricts this drug to use by or on the order of a licensed veterinarian";

- the recommended or usual dosage;

- the route of administration, if it is not for oral use;

- the quantity or proportion of each active ingredient;

- the names of all inactive ingredients if the drug is for other than oral use; and

- an identifying lot or control number from which it is possible to determine the complete manufacturing history of the drug.

Occasionally, labels of veterinary drugs bear notations such as "sold only to licensed veterinarians" or "for veterinary use only." Statements like these merely represent sales policies established by the drug manufacturer and have no legal basis. In fact, any drug with this label is an OTC drug. Only drugs with the FDA's "Caution" legend are prescription drugs.

Certain veterinary drug companies, called "ethical" companies, take pride in the fact that they routinely sell only to veterinarians even though many of their products qualify as OTC drugs. They contend that the products they manufacture are the highest quality available and are better than their generic counterparts. Some of their products, however, have somehow turned up in wholesale drug order houses for sale as standard OTC products without the companies' knowledge. Because of the veterinary-use-only-type labels, this has exacerbated the confusion about identification of drugs as prescription or OTC.

Extra-Label Drug Use

Because economic realities often limit the scope of the FDA approval for a given drug, there is considerable temptation among veterinarians to use veterinary drugs other than as approved by the FDA on the label. In addition, information gained from observations, lectures, and published accounts of drugs approved for use in humans, for whom a much broader array of drugs exists, provides a continuing incentive to apply those drugs to veterinary medical uses.

These factors, coupled with innovative minds and veterinarians' access to both human and veterinary drugs, have created the current environment wherein veterinarians use numerous FDA-approved drugs in manners other than approved on their labels. This is called *extra-label use*.

Extra-Label Drug Use in Food-Producing Animals

Veterinarians historically are accustomed to free reign in the selection and use of drugs on animals as long as they inform livestock producers of the appropriate drug withdrawal times for food-producing animals. Although the FDA attempted to restrict antibiotic use in food-producing animals as early as 1977, the first formal policy on the extra-label use of drugs in food-producing animals was not instituted until August 1983. At that time the FDA declared that food animal veterinarians could use drugs only in the exact manner stated on the label. This policy is based upon the strict prohibition of the use of a new animal drug in any manner not in accord with the approved label.[11]

Through the cooperation of animal producer groups and the FDA, the AVMA was able to negotiate a compromise under which the FDA would use its regulatory discretion when veterinarians use FDA-approved drugs in an extra-label manner under defined circumstances.[12] The FDA policy has been modified slightly on several occasions, most recently in November 1986.

In order to inform the profession about changing specifications with regard to the use of veterinary drugs, the AVMA published its "Guidelines for Supervising Use and Distribution of Veterinary Drugs" in the Oct. 1, 1988 *JAVMA* (see Appendix N).

In the past the FDA has refrained from instituting action against licensed veterinarians for administering or prescribing any drugs they could legally obtain. The FDA has, however, maintained that legal action will be pursued against veterinarians who are responsible for creating violative drug tissue residues in the human food supply, especially if these residues are the result of drugs used contrary to label instructions. In addition, the FDA asserts that regulatory action will be taken against anyone (including farmers treating their own animals) whose extra-label use of drugs results in illegal drug residues in the food chain.[13]

In the FDA policy guide on the use of drugs in food animals, it says, "A finding of illegal drug residues no longer will be a prerequisite for initiating regulatory action based on extra-label drug use of drugs in food-producing animals."[13] The guidelines continue with a statement of the new policy:

> The use or intended use of new animal drugs in treating food-producing animals in any manner other than in accord with the approved labeling causes the drugs to be adulterated under the Federal Food, Drug and Cosmetic Act (the Act) (sections 501[a][5] and [6], 512[a][1][A] and [B], 512[a][2]). The agency will consider regulatory action when such use or intended use is found, whether by a veterinarian, producer, or other person. Regulatory actions will also be considered against distributors and others who might cause adulteration of approved new animal drugs. Nevertheless, extra-label drug use in treating food-producing animals may be considered by a veterinarian when the health of animals is immediately threatened and suffering or death would result from failure to treat the affected animals. In instances of this nature, regulatory action would not ordinarily be considered provided all of the following criteria are met and precautions observed:
>
> 1. a careful medical diagnosis is made by an attending veterinarian within the context of a valid veterinarian-client-patient relationship;
>
> 2. a determination is made that, (a) there is no marketed drug specifically labeled to treat the condition diagnosed, or (b) drug therapy at the dosage recommended by the labeling has been found clinically ineffective in the animals to be

> treated;
>
> 3. procedures are instituted to assure that identity of the treated animals is carefully maintained; and
>
> 4. a significantly extended time period is assigned for drug withdrawal prior to marketing meat, milk, or eggs; steps are taken to assure that the assigned time frames are met, and no illegal residues occur.
>
> Therefore, extra-label use of drugs in treating food-producing animals may be considered only in special circumstances. The exempting criteria do not include drug use in treating food-producing animals by laypeople. Laypeople cannot be expected to have sufficient knowledge and understanding concerning animal diseases, pharmacology, toxicology, drug interactions, drug withdrawal times, and other scientific parameters to use drugs in treating food-producing animals in any way other than as labeled.[14]

The FDA's observation and control of drugs in the food animal sector is continuing to become more stringent. Because of increasing consumer pressures to establish an unadulterated source of human food, it is expected that this trend will continue.

Drugs Prohibited for Use in Food-Producing Animals

There are basically two ways that drugs can be placed in the FDA's category of drugs prohibited for use in food-producing animals. The first arises under § 355(e) of Title 21. If the FDA determines based on new information that an approved new animal drug is no longer safe and effective, it has the authority to initiate proceedings to withdraw approval of that drug and prohibit its use in animals. When it became known that the FDA-approved drug diethylstilbestrol, a known carcinogen, was resulting in residues in beef and no adequate analytical method for monitoring meat existed, its use in animals was considered to be a health hazard. On November 1, 1979, the approvals of all veterinary drugs containing diethylstilbestrol were withdrawn and legal use of diethylstilbestrol was terminated. The use of unapproved diethylstilbestrol products has continued in small animal medicine, but since this does not produce a food residue problem, that use has not prompted FDA regulatory actions.

The second reason that drugs are prohibited is because they are either unapproved or used in extra-label manners. The drug dimetridazole falls into the prohibited category partially because it is a carcinogen and partially because it is an extra-label-use drug. Its use was approved by the FDA only for the treatment of "blackhead" in turkeys. Over the years, though, it became commonly used as an effective extra-label treatment for swine dysentery. Initially the FDA listed this extra-label use for priority regulatory attention. Then, in December 1986, the FDA conducted a hearing on a proposal to withdraw the use of dimetridazole in food-producing animals because (1) it is a known carcinogen, (2) no means for determining tissue residues existed, and (3) it was being used in an extra-label manner. During these hearings it was determined that other FDA-approved drugs are readily available for the treatment of swine dysentery. Initially, the FDA simply placed dimetridazole on the prohibited list, but on July 6, 1987 the FDA withdrew approval for the use of this drug in any species. Part of the rationale for this withdrawal was that the directions for use printed on the label have not been followed in practice and are not likely to be followed in the future.[15]

Chloramphenicol is another extra-label-use drug in the prohibited category. A type of blood dyscrasia that is usually fatal to a significant number of people with an apparent predisposed sensitivity to chloramphenicol has been associated with extremely low-level exposure to this drug. Because of the serious threat to human health by even small quantities of chloramphenicol, the drug has never been approved for food animal use.

For economic reasons, many veterinarians had been using a small animal oral-solution chloramphenicol in food animals for years, administering it both intramuscularly and intravenously. When rumors and investigations indicated that veterinarians were purchasing this small animal product in larger quantities than could be used in dogs and cats, the FDA was forced to take action. To minimize the temptation to continue administering or prescribing this prohibited small animal oral solution to food animals, on January 23, 1986 the FDA withdrew its approval. In addition, food animal practitioners were emphatically warned that the use of this or any other form of chloramphenicol was prohibited in food-producing animals.

In the past few years, the FDA has been conducting investigations of veterinary facilities pertaining to chloramphenicol use in food-producing animals, and numerous practitioners have found themselves in violation of the law. In general, the veterinarian's livestock chloramphenicol inventories have been confiscated or returned to the supplier/manufacturer. In one instance, two California veterinarians were indicted on misdemeanor criminal violations of the FD&C Act; one of the two on a felony violation. The indictments were based on purported false statements made during a July 1984 FDA investigation. The hospital owners supposedly told the investigator that they had no chloramphenicol powder or solution on hand and that chloramphenicol was being dispensed for use only in dogs and cats.[16]

That case went to trial in Fresno, California in February 1987 and was abruptly dismissed because one of the FDA's investigators could not find a necessary document while making his presentation during a redirect examination on the witness stand. The judge dismissed the trial on grounds of misconduct by the government counsel. Within a minute the FDA witness found the missing document, but it was too late. Since that time the veterinarians involved as defendants in the lawsuit have filed a civil suit against the FDA for damages.[17]

According to one of the FDA prosecuting attorneys, the FDA does not regard the case closed. He went on to say that veterinarians

You'd think they'd a taught us something in vet school about the FDA, the DEA, the USDA, the PPPA . . .

can expect a number of new animal drug criminal cases filed against them soon. In addition, on March 24, 1987, the FDA filed notice of its intent to appeal the United States District Courts' dismissal.[18] Dr. Joe Gloyd, Assistant Director of the AVMA's Division of Scientific Activities, says, "My advice to veterinarians who are continuing to use chloramphenicol in food-producing animals is: quit unless you want to destroy your practice."

It seems certain that additional drugs will be prohibited in the future. Under scrutiny at this time is the use of subtherapeutic levels of sulfamethazine in swine. According to USDA statistics, in 1986 over 6% of slaughtered swine had illegal tissue residues of sulfamethazine. By mid 1987 that level had dropped to 4 to 5%. However, the FDA has said that if the swine industry is unable to reduce violative tissue levels of this drug to under 1% of the slaughtered pork, approval of this drug may be withdrawn.[19]

Unapproved Drugs

It is important to differentiate extra-label use of approved drugs from the use of unapproved drugs. The key difference between

these two is that extra-label drugs have been approved by the FDA for at least one purpose but have not been approved for the specific use or for the manner employed by the veterinarian. Unapproved drugs, on the other hand, are drugs that are not generally recognized as safe and effective by experts and never have been subjected to the FDA approval process.

The FDA takes a strong stance opposing the use of unapproved drugs. Dr. Gerald Guest, Director of the FDA's CVM, speaking at the AVMA Annual Meeting in Atlanta, Georgia, in 1986, explained why:

> You can be assured that when you order something out of a catalog as a bulk product, not labeled or with any claims on it, that it is an unapproved product. When that happens you have lost any assurance that you are buying what in fact it is you think you are buying, and that the potency is anywhere near what it ought to be. You do not really know when you mix one of those powders whether you are getting the product that you think you are getting, you do not know if the pH is okay, you do not know whether the thing is still going to be potent a week from now, you do not know if you have to keep it in the refrigerator or not, you do not know what the withdrawal time is prior to slaughter. Those kinds of things are the assurances that you lose when you buy the unapproved product. Nobody has inspected that particular plant to see if what they are making is in fact a good drug, and if in fact they are following good manufacturing practices.[20]

The question of whether the use of unapproved drugs by veterinarians is illegal arises repeatedly. Veterinarians have assumed since the mid 1960s that they have the right to use any drug they have access to; that it is a professional judgment decision, not an FDA-directed one. Dr. Guest maintains, however, that an unapproved drug is an illegal drug, according to the FD&C Act.[20]

Most often, unapproved drugs are generic

copies of drugs that are legally approved and on the market. Unless these generics have a NADA, they are illegal under the FD&C Act. This does not place them in the same class as Schedule I controlled drugs like heroin and cocaine, however.

All new animal drugs (and copies) must be approved by the FDA to be sold legally. If an application to the FDA has been made but not approved, the drug is either an unapproved new animal drug or it falls under some separate legal category. New animal drugs that are marketed without NADAs violate the FD&C Act, and that violation can carry civil and criminal penalties.[20]

To date, the law does not get more specific than this regarding the legality of prescribing or administering unapproved drugs. One is left to wonder, then, what stance the FDA or a court of law would take with regard to the use of a drug like Saffon, which is an unapproved drug commonly used by veterinarians in the United States as an anesthetic for exotic animals. Various anesthetic/analgesic and dissociative drugs have been approved by the FDA for use in food animals and pets, but no anesthetics have been approved for use in exotic animals. In fact, it is unlikely that any drugs will ever be approved for use on exotic animals or zoo animals because the market is too small. The question arises, then, whether the statutes will be applied differently for some species of animals for which few if any drugs are approved than for other species for which many drugs have FDA approval.

The FDA's current position is that a high degree of regulatory discretion is and will continue to be allowed when drugs are used extra-labelly in non-food-producing animals. This is because the FDA's principal concern relates to the safety of food products of animal origin.

Identifying Unapproved and Bulk Drugs

Many unapproved drug labels create the impression that the product inside is the generic equivalent of a commonly available drug.[21] It is often very difficult, therefore, to differentiate an approved from an unapproved drug via the label. There are approximately 10,000 to 12,000 products in the marketplace, including preparations by different manufacturers of the same drug. Of those, about 2,000 have gone through the FDA approval process. To help sort things out, the CVM recently urged manufacturers to voluntarily print the NADA number and the fact they are FDA approved on their labels. Some have begun to do this, and it should help considerably to differentiate approved from unapproved drugs.

There are other ways to identify unapproved drugs as well. Usually drugs bought in bulk, such as tetracycline, sulfonamides, or gentamicin, packaged in tubs as a powder, with very little labeling other than, for example, sulfanilamide USP, do not have NADAs. Almost no bulk products have gone through the approval process.

Products that are specifically labeled and that have an insert detailing the product's stability under different conditions as well as claims and cautions are likely to have gone through the approval process. In contrast, a product with purely foreign labeling, containing little mention of either United States manufacturers or terminology, is probably from outside the country and is unapproved, with the exception of some products with Spanish-language-labeling marketed in Puerto Rico.[21]

The FDA and the AVMA have been working for the past seven years on a satisfactory policy for the prescription and use of bulk drugs (mostly antibiotics). In view of consumer concerns about tissue residues from bulk antibiotics in the human food supply, a satisfactory policy for the use of bulk drugs may never be issued. Until approved drugs in bulk form are available, practitioners should think of the consequences before purchasing, selling, or distributing bulk drugs.[22] In an attempt to help practitioners differentiate approved drugs from unapproved drugs, the FDA is publishing a list of approved veterinary drugs. The list will identify currently marketed animal drug products approved by the FDA on the basis of safety and effectiveness. Entries on this list will contain at least the following elements:

- chemical name (name of primary active ingredient[s] of the drug)
- trade name
- sponsor name
- NADA number
- availability (prescription or OTC)
- approval date
- species for which it is approved[23]

Generic versus Brand Name Drugs

When new drugs are approved by the FDA, manufacturers establish brand names for the products. At some later point, either when the patent expires at 17 years or when the manufacturer sells production rights to someone else, generic copies of the brand name drug appear.

A NADA application is required for all generic drugs. Once a drug's patent expires, another potential manufacturer of the same material must submit its drug to the NADA process before the drug can be sold legally as a generic product.[20] The reason for this requirement is that often the generic drug is chemically similar but not identical. Minor differences in drug preparations can result in great discrepancies in the therapeutic effect of some of these agents. The application to the FDA for a generic drug does not necessarily require the full complement of safety and efficacy studies of a new drug, but the FDA does need to review the chemistry data; the quality, consistency, and manufacturing data; the bioequivalency data; stability tests; and tissue residue data before determining that the generic drug is equal to the brand name product that was originally granted a NADA.

Drugs for Minor Use

The NADA system of the FDA has always made the costs of producing a new drug high. This has rendered it impractical for companies to introduce new drugs for use in species of animals with small numbers. The practice of veterinary medicine involving pheasants, quail, mink, rabbits, etc. was being hindered significantly because of the economics of the pharmaceutical marketplace. In addition, some of the major species, e.g., cattle, horses, sheep, hogs, goats, and poultry, have medical problems of minor incidence for which the economics of the marketplace would not allow the introduction of new drugs. Consequently, veterinarians who were called upon to treat these species had no choice except to use drugs in an extra-label manner if they were to have any drugs at all at their disposal. Since this is exactly what the FDA wanted to discourage, especially in food-producing animals, it was contributing to a serious problem.

The FDA has published regulations that provide that data used in support of a drug approved for a major species also may be used to support an application for the same or similar indication in a closely related minor species.[24]

It is now possible for the FDA's CVM to approve new drugs for use in minor species or for minor uses in major species in an economically viable manner. Consequently, several drugs have been created and marketed successfully in recent years to serve precisely these markets.

FDA Regulatory Efforts– A Changing Scene

The FDA is increasingly publicizing its requirements and enforcing its rules for prescription drug use in recent years. The misuse of veterinary drugs is seen as a problem mainly due to (1) a misinformed veterinary profession, (2) the enforcement difficulties by the FDA, (3) the economic pressures placed on the pharmaceutical industry by unfair competition from the sale of unapproved drugs, and (4) the economic hardship incurred by veterinarians from the sale of drugs by nonveterinary sources.

The biggest impact on the drug-use issue in veterinary medicine has been in the area of food animal medicine. One of the main reasons for this is the vocal concerns of consumer groups alarmed about what they perceive to be increasing adulteration of food for human consumption. Two groups in particular, the Center for Science and Public Interest and Americans for Safe Food, have actively lobbied Congress on this issue.

Antibiotics in the Food Chain

Recently published materials from the Centers for Disease Control support the concerns of scientists and consumers about the antibiotics used in food-producing animals. A report in the *New England Journal of Medicine* in March 1987 provides some interesting insights:[25]

> The number of *Salmonella newport* isolates from humans identified at the Los Angeles County Public Health Laboratory rose from 69 in 1984 to 298 in 1985. Two patients from whom chloramphenicol-resistant strains were isolated died. An increase in *newport* isolates was noted statewide ...; at the California State Microbial Diseases Laboratory, the proportion of *newport* rose from 40 percent (60 of 149) in 1984 to 87 percent (675 of 776) in 1985. A single, identical, approximately 25-megadalton plasmid was found in 99 percent of the isolates (137 of 139) tested ...;

The report continued:

> In May 1985, the Los Angeles County Health Department laboratory received a markedly increased number of *newport* strains. Most were resistant to chloramphenicol and had a single, identical plasmid. Resistance to chloramphenicol is unusual in salmonella. Using the antimicrobial-resistance pattern and plasmid profile of the multiply resistant *newport* strain, we epidemiologically and micro-

biologically incriminated hamburger as the vehicle of transmission and traced the strain back to the dairy farms of origin, identifying a major, persistent reservoir for drug-resistant salmonellae in California.[25]

It was concluded that food animals are a major source of antimicrobial-resistant *Salmonella* infections in humans and that these infections are associated with antimicrobial use on farms. In view of this information, it seems likely that more discussion and action on this issue will take place in the near future.

Changes in the Political Climate

Whether due to the cries of consumer groups or just because the time had come, in 1985 Representative Ted Weiss (D-NY), Chairman of the House Government Operations Subcommittee, conducted hearings and an investigation into pesticides, animal drugs, and pathogenic bacteria in our food sources.

In October of 1986 Senator John H. Chafee, Republican of Rhode Island, introduced a bill that would have sharply restricted the feeding of antibiotics to animals. It was not acted upon by Congress, but Senator Chafee plans to reintroduce a similar bill in the future.

To illustrate the seriousness of the concerns of scientists and consumers regarding adulterated food, from October 27 to 31, 1986, the United States hosted 175 international specialists representing 40 nations at the first meeting of the Codex Committee on Residues of Veterinary Drugs in Food. This committee's goal was to promote international food standards that will protect public health and to eliminate trade barriers.

The committee attracted great interest by tentatively establishing international maximum tissue residue levels and safety evaluations for seven priority veterinary drugs. Some of the drugs on this list are chloramphenicol, anabolic steroids, sulfonamides, and the nitroimidazoles.[26]

The magnitude of the concern about drug residues becomes especially pertinent in light of the fact that the European Economic Community is expected to impose a ban in the near future on importation of meat from countries using anabolic hormone growth promotants.[26]

The concern of meat producers about drug residues is demonstrated by a program being designed by the Nebraska Feedlot Council in concert with the USDA. This Council is proposing a very comprehensive Beef Quality Assurance Program to ensure that cattle shipped from participating Nebraska feedlots are healthy, wholesome, and meet FDA, USDA, and EPA standards. This voluntary program would include, among other things, keeping records of all feed sources and ingredients fed to beef cattle and random sampling of carcasses for drug and pesticide tissue residues at packing plants.

It is interesting that much of the emphasis and action in this area has occurred since political activists entered the arena. Because of growing national and, now, international consumer and scientific concern, much more activity concerning drugs in food-producing animals is anticipated in the years to come. Regardless of what the future holds, though, things have already changed dramatically in the past few years, and veterinarians must continue to be aware of these changes.

The Veterinarian-Client-Patient Relationship and the FDA

Concerns regarding veterinarian-client-patient relationships have evolved recently for several reasons. First, the mushrooming availability of low-cost dog and cat vaccinations provided via clinics held in parking lots, SPCA and Humane Association clinics, animal control facilities, and veterinary clinics has focused attention on this topic in the small animal realm. Most of the attention, however, has stemmed from concerns about drug residues in food animals. A strict policy

has been established for the use of drugs in food-producing animals, and that policy extends to the use of drugs in companion animals. The issue of the veterinarian-client-patient relationship as it pertains to the use of biologicals in both food-producing animals and companion animals is discussed in Chapter 10.

The AVMA's Definition of the Veterinarian-Client-Patient Relationship

Because of these increasing concerns, the AVMA Counsel on Biologicals and Therapeutic Agents wrestled with some policy positions a few years ago. Out of this came a definition of the veterinarian-client-patient relationship which was approved in July 1986 to be included in the AVMA Model Practice Act. It is as follows:

"Veterinarian-Client-Patient relationship" means that:

A. The veterinarian has assumed the responsibility for making medical judgments regarding the health of the animal(s) and the need for medical treatment, and the client (owner or other caretaker) has agreed to follow the instruction of the veterinarian.

B. There is sufficient knowledge of the animal(s) by the veterinarian to initiate at least a general or preliminary diagnosis of the medical condition of the animal(s). This means that the veterinarian has recently seen and is personally acquainted with the keeping and care of the animal(s) by virtue of an examination of the animal(s), and/or by medically appropriate and timely visits to the premises where the animal(s) is(are) kept.

C. The practicing veterinarian is readily available for follow-up in case of adverse reactions or failure of the regimen of therapy.[27]

California's Definition of the Veterinarian-Client-Patient Relationship

Although the Model Practice Act is worthwhile, it has no significant meaning unless it has been adopted by a State Board of Examiners. The practice of veterinary medicine is regulated at the state level by statutes, regulations, and policies under the jurisdiction of each state's board of examiners in veterinary medicine. At least one state became involved in the doctor-client-patient issue quite early. In 1984, the California Board of Examiners in Veterinary Medicine working with the California Veterinary Medical Association defined a doctor-client-patient relationship in that state. That board uses the following definition:

> For a Doctor/Client/Patient relationship to exist, and for a veterinarian to exercise properly the rights granted by the veterinary license, the following must be present:
>
> 1. a. An examination of the animal, herd or flock.
>
>   b. Or, under certain circumstances such as with large herds or flocks, adequate prior familiarity on the part of the veterinarian of the client and the operation to enable proper evaluation of reported signs.
>
> 2. A diagnosis, which must be entered in the veterinarian's permanent records. The method of arriving at a diagnosis is to be consistent with that considered "normal" or "accepted" for a given practice type or field (see footnote).
>
> 3. A treatment plan, to include all recommendations and medications. The veterinarian in charge is responsible for assuring that any drugs prescribed are properly administered, for maintaining accurate records to include strength, dosage and quantity of all medications

prescribed, for proper instructions to clients on the administration of drugs when the veterinarian will not be providing direct supervision, and for informing clients of potential drug residues and proper withdrawal times.

> 4. A follow up to determine the effectiveness of the treatment plan.

Footnote: Because methods of practice vary among the species, and what is considered to be proper practice in one practice type may not be proper practice in another, grievances will be brought before a review committee of the practitioner's peers to determine if good veterinary medicine has been practiced in a particular case.

Example: If a poultry practitioner diagnoses via client input and general knowledge of client's animals, without an actual exam, and a review committee of poultry practitioners states that this method is customary for this practice type, then the method of diagnosis would be considered correct.

Currently, "Anyone who fails to establish a doctor-client-patient relationship could be in jeopardy of violating the California Practice Act, e.g., unprofessional conduct or negligence."[28]

Even if a state board had not adopted a policy on the veterinarian-client-patient relationship, veterinarians who were found to be in violation of the federal FD&C Act could be convicted of a federal crime. Such violations could have an impact on practitioners' state veterinary licenses because, under most state practice acts, conviction of a crime involving the practice of veterinary medicine can be grounds for license revocations, suspensions, or other administrative actions.

As one can see, the rigorous enforcement of this policy by the FDA and by state veterinary boards is certain to have a major impact on the ways practitioners utilize drugs today and in the future.

Priorities for FDA Regulatory Attention

With any regulatory effort, a set of priorities must be established to determine which violations are the most serious or far reaching. As of November 1, 1986, the situations with the highest priority for FDA attention included the following:

- instances in which illegal residues of drugs were found in food products
- situations in which the prohibited drugs chloramphenicol, dimetridazole and other nitroimidazoles, or diethylstilbestrol have been found or are being used in food-producing animals
- manufacturers and distributors who promote extra-label use of drugs
- the mixing of extra-label drugs into medicated feeds
- extra-label use of drugs by laymen at their own initiative[29]

The FDA's Investigations and Penalties

The FDA has the authority to inspect veterinary clinics when there is any question regarding the improper use of veterinary drugs. In one state, investigators attempted and were allowed to purchase prescription drugs over the counter from 40 of 43 veterinary clinics approached.[30] According to the *Pennsylvania Veterinary Medical Association News*, FDA investigators entered 10 Pennsylvania veterinary practices in the fall/winter of 1986-1987 and in 100% of the clinics were able to buy veterinary drugs without a prescription and with no existent veterinarian-client-patient relationship.[31]

In order to inform all veterinarians licensed in Pennsylvania of the FDA's intent to enforce the veterinarian-client-patient relationship requirements, in June of 1987 a letter

from the FDA and Pennsylvania State Board was sent to all licensed Pennsylvania veterinarians. In that letter, the FDA reiterated that the sale of prescription veterinary drugs without a valid veterinarian-client-patient relationship was illegal. Any further violative sales may result in regulatory sanctions in the form of drug seizures, injunctions, or prosecution.[32]

FDA Inspections

The authority for inspections of veterinary establishments comes from Section 704 of the FD&C Act.[33] As with everything else relating to drug regulatory policies, the inspection procedures are somewhat controversial.

The FDA investigators are employees of the 21 district FDA offices around the United States. These investigators have a science background most often in life science, chemistry, or pharmacy. The investigators frequently do many different types of inspections (e.g., food, drug, and medical device firms) and are not restricted to animal health issues.[34]

The reasons that an FDA investigator might check on a veterinarian are as follows:

- to follow up on reports of adverse reactions to drug therapy,
- to determine the effectiveness of drug recalls,
- to obtain detailed information from veterinarians attending or consulting on incidents of livestock illnesses or deaths,
- to follow up on reports of illegal tissue residues in edible products of treated food-producing animals,
- to collect samples and shipment documentation of marketed drugs,
- to see how a practitioner conducts clinical trials done in support of clinical investigations by drug sponsors under investigational exemption,
- to inspect drug formulation procedures of products sold to customers

outside the confines of a usual practice,

- to investigate reports of drugs prescribed or sold to livestock producers outside a valid veterinarian-client-patient relationship, and
- to investigate reports of extra-label use of animal drugs outside the intent of the FDA's previously announced extra-label use policy.[34]

Many veterinarians will never be confronted by an FDA investigator. With the recent enforcement efforts regarding veterinarian-client-patient relationships as well as the prohibitions from using specific drugs in food-producing animals, though, the presence of such investigators may increase in the years ahead.

The Inspection Procedure

What can a veterinarian expect if an FDA investigator comes? Investigators usually arrive unannounced. They may act as clients to find out whether the practice will sell prescription drugs without the satisfactory veterinarian-client-patient relationship, in which case the veterinarian might not even learn about the investigation.

If the investigator is there to perform an inspection, though, the course of events is as follows: The investigator identifies him- or herself and asks either for the person in charge or the individual to be interviewed. The investigator presents FDA credentials including a photograph, the authorizing documentation, and the government seal. Depending on the assignment, the investigator may produce a "Notice of Inspection" form, which is required by law if an inspection is to be conducted. Section 704 of the FD&C Act provides the following:

> After presentation of appropriate credentials and a written notice to the owner, operator, or agent in charge, FDA investigators are authorized to enter and inspect, at reasonable times and within reasonable limits, in a reasonable manner, the factory, warehouse, establishment, or vehicle and all pertinent equipment, finished and unfinished materials, containers, and labeling where food, drugs, devices, or cosmetics are manufactured, processed, packed, or held.[34]

Controversial Issues

It appears that a search warrant is not essential for the FDA investigation to proceed. If agents do not intend to conduct an inspection, they need not present any Notice of Inspection. Thus, opportunities for entrapment seem possible when all the agent is trying to investigate is the hospital's policy for applying the veterinarian-client-patient relationship to the sale of drugs.

Some controversy surrounds whether a warrant is or is not legally required for an inspection. Harold Hannah, LLB, states that only "pervasively regulated" businesses can be inspected without a warrant. To support his contention that veterinary offices are not pervasively regulated businesses, he cites *United States* v *Article of Device...Therametic*, 641 F2d 1289 (9th Cir 1981).[35] Mr. Hannah then goes on to say that receptionists and veterinarians have a right to deny FDA investigators access to important records unless there is a warrant.

Contending this, Lester Crawford, DVM, PhD, previously Director of the FDA's CVM, says, "With respect to inspections, veterinarians and other practitioners are part of an industry that is 'pervasively regulated' under the act and, therefore, inspections can be made without warrants."[36]

To differentiate his opinion regarding warrants from that of Mr. Hannah, Dr. Crawford refers to a further court opinion in the *Therametic* case (*Therametic*, 1983), where the ninth circuit court recognizes the fact that its earlier opinion applied in only very specific and limited situations involving seizures of medical devices. He also said "Therametic does not apply to inspections in the home or office." Although Dr. Crawford insists that the regulation of veterinary practice is best accomplished under the authority of state veterinary medical boards, it is his opinion that search warrants for FDA inspections are not needed, and a refusal to permit an inspection could constitute a violation of section 301(e) or (f) of the FD&C Act.[36]

In conclusion, the FDA has considerable authority to delve into a veterinarian's inventories, dispensing practices, and records regarding veterinary drugs. In addition, if practitioners find themselves confronted by this type of situation, they may very well need the information in this chapter, the cited references, and legal counsel. Adherence to FDA guidelines is a much simpler course of action.

Penalties for Illegally Selling or Dispensing Drugs

It is a difficult concept to grasp that veterinarians dispensing or selling prescription drugs without a valid veterinarian-client-patient relationship have violated the FDA's misbranding laws. Prescription drugs that are not dispensed within the strict confines of a professional relationship lose their exemption from the "adequate directions for use" provisions of the law and are considered to be misbranded. The reason that prescription drugs were initially permitted to enter the marketplace even though adequate directions for use by laymen could not be written was because the FDA declared that they could be used only if they were dispensed by prescription. Any sales of these drugs without a valid veterinarian-client-patient relationship violates the prescription-only requirement and, therefore, is considered to be unsatisfactory professional conduct. Where the regulations exist, a state board of veterinary examiners has the jurisdiction to take action in the form of a citation, reprimand, fine, or license suspension or revocation for this type of unprofessional conduct.

To emphasize its seriousness regarding violations of the FD&C Act, the federal government recently passed a law known as the *Criminal Fines Act of 1984*. This new law provides for the following fines:

- a fine of up to $100,000 for a misdemeanor by a corporation or an individual not resulting in death
- a fine of up to $250,000 for a misdemeanor perpetrated by an individual that results in a death, or for a felony.
- a fine of up to $500,000 for a misdemeanor perpetrated by a corporation that results in a death, or for a felony[30]

In addition, a veterinarian who dispenses a prescription drug with the intent to mislead or defraud can be fined a maximum of $250,000.

From the magnitude of these fines, it is apparent that the FDA and federal government are serious about the veterinarian's duty to assure that prescription drugs are used and dispensed properly.

Managing Veterinary Drugs

How can veterinarians practice effectively and responsibly with all of the foregoing regulations in mind? What kinds of legal risks pose the biggest hazards, and how can practitioners minimize these risks?

The first priority for practitioners is to protect their licenses, themselves, and their practices. If clients request or demand that their veterinarians provide medical treatments that would violate the FD&C Act, they should be refused. Humorous—but serious—comments regarding the client's willingness to pay tens of thousands of dollars worth of legal costs that might be incurred because of a violation can sometimes provide an easy way to escape these difficult demands.

Distributor Assurances Regarding Product Liability

Before veterinarians buy unapproved drugs for use in their practices, they should ask drug suppliers if they will assist in the defense of a civil action brought by an animal owner in the event that an adverse drug reaction occurs. A written statement indicating that the company will support the veterinarian is a valid request. Most distributors or manufacturers will not comply with such a request if it is for an unapproved drug. Only by asking these hard questions, though, will they be made aware that the veterinary profession is concerned about their unapproved product as well as professional and product liability.

Veterinary Liability for Drug Residues in Food

Veterinarians are sometimes asked by clients or voluntarily elect to use unapproved or extra-label drugs in manners that could cause illegal tissue residue problems in food-producing animals. If a shipment of milk, poultry, or other meat is condemned because the veterinarian treating those animals failed to inform the owner of the proper drug withholding period, a major professional liability incident can occur. Such negligence by the veterinarian may or may not be covered by insurance depending upon the circumstances. Conversations with Dr. Jack Dinsmore from the AVMA Professional Liability Insurance Trust have indicated that the Trust will cover claims arising from the extra-label use of veterinary drugs but may not cover claims associated with the use of unapproved drugs since their use is not legal under the FD&C Act. If problems with tissue residues of drugs used in an extra-label manner occur with any frequency, however, professional liability insurance rates will certainly rise dramatically.

Concerns about drug residue problems and withdrawal of drugs prior to slaughter prompted an in-depth publication in 1985 on this topic.[37] In addition, several papers on this subject were presented at the 10th Annual Food Animal Medicine Conference in 1984. The focus of that conference was drug use in food animal medicine. An espe-

cially cogent presentation entitled "Residue Avoidance: Withdrawal Times for Drugs Not Labelled for Food Animals" can be reviewed for ideas on minimizing risks for adulteration of foods and the liability involved.[38] The Nebraska Veterinary Medical Association has developed and published an elementary and readily usable National Drug Withdrawal Residue Guide that can be found in Appendix E.

Separating Prescription Drugs from OTC Drugs

A good way of avoiding liability problems is for veterinarians to take an inventory of drugs on hand and separate the OTC from prescription drugs. Employees and associates should be carefully informed that prescription drugs are not to be sold outside of a proper veterinarian-client-patient relationship. Telephone consultations alone in all likelihood do not sufficiently establish the required relationship. In addition, some form of medical record should be kept of all prescription drugs dispensed, showing who received the drugs, for what purpose, and which doctor ordered the drugs dispensed.

Hospital Policies Regarding Prescription Drug Sales

Veterinary practices are encouraged to establish policies prohibiting clients from purchasing prescription drugs if the animals to be treated have not been seen recently by the veterinarian. If someone who is not a familiar client requests that a prescription from another veterinarian be refilled, the refill should not be granted without first calling the previous veterinarian. If nonclients attempt to purchase prescription drugs for regular clients, the regular clients should be called to assure that they have knowledge of the situation. If persons attempting to make drug purchases are not who they claim to be or do not have proper agency authority, these people should be reported to the state board of veterinary examiners and local law enforcement officials.

Veterinarians or staff members who discover clients, nonclients, or local retail suppliers who are obtaining or selling prescription drugs without any evidence of veterinarian-client-patient relationships should write or call the Office of the Associate Director for Surveillance and Compliance, 5600 Fishers Lane, Rockville, MD 20857; 301-443-3400.

Keeping Abreast of the Changing Times

Changes over the past few years have drastically altered the way veterinary drugs may be used, prescribed, and dispensed. Many of these changes are in the form of federal regulatory actions taken by the FDA. While these regulations are being changed frequently, veterinarians are expected to keep current and to abide by these laws and regulations. As Dr. Joe Gloyd aptly put it, "The profession's reputation for integrity as well as the livestock and poultry industries' reputation for providing wholesome food products may well depend on sound advice rendered by veterinarians."[39] In the future, these new regulatory directives and efforts must become part of the veterinary profession's continuing education programs.

Labeling and Packaging

Adequate labeling and packaging of veterinary dispensed drugs should be a major concern of practitioners. According to studies by the Consumer Products Safety Commission, most veterinary drugs for small animals are generic equivalents of orally administered human drugs. Approximately 95% of veterinary prescriptions are for small animals and are kept in or around

the home. Furthermore, approximately 90% of those drugs have been dispensed by veterinarians.[40]

Many veterinary practices still use little white envelopes to dispense medication. A large number of practices do not place all the required information on the label. Although most state laws do not require veterinary drugs to be in child-resistant containers, both the Consumer Products Safety Commission and the AVMA Council on Therapeutic and Biologic Agents encourage veterinarians to use them. On the other hand, proper labeling of dispensed drugs is required by law.

In the event that a poisoning occurs, it is vitally important for the veterinarian, physician, or poison control center to be able to determine the identity and quantity of the substance ingested. Whether all states have laws requiring full labeling of veterinary drugs or not is almost irrelevant, because common sense alone is probably sufficient for a court to place full liability on a veterinary practitioner who fails to meet the minimum standards for drug labeling and packaging.

Label Requirements

The basic label requirements set forth by the California Business and Professions Code are cited here as a good example of the scope of state requirements. Included are the following:

- Name of the prescriber
- Name and address of the dispenser of drug
- Name of the patient
- Date dispensed
- Name of the drug
- Unit strength of the product dispensed
- Volume or quantity of the drug dispensed
- Clear directions for product use
- Expiration date (if required on the original label of the drug manufacturer)

The simple policy of never dispensing any medication without at least the majority of the above information on the label seems morally right even if it might not be legally required in all states. When veterinarians see incomplete labels from other veterinary hospitals, they should encourage clients not to accept drugs with label omissions in the future. If the life of only one child or one animal is saved by this minimal professional effort, the modest cost and inconvenience are worth the effort.

Poison Prevention Packaging Act

The issue of child-resistant dispensing containers is presented here in moderate depth because of the federal laws covering this subject and the possibilities for veterinary liability in this area of the law. Drugs, as a group, account for the vast majority of serious accidental poisoning cases that occur each year.[41] In 1970, the United States Congress passed the Poison Prevention Packaging Act. This law requires that prescription drugs and certain nonprescription drugs be dispensed in containers with safety caps.

One of the things that the Poison Prevention Packaging Act (Title 15, § 1471) did was create the Consumer Products Safety Commission in order to administer the laws and regulations pertaining to packaging of "household substances." Section 1471 (2) of the act defines this term as follows:

> The term "household substance" means any substance which is customarily produced or distributed for sale for consumption or use, or customarily stored, by individuals in or about the household and which is termed a hazardous substance under the federal Hazardous Substances Act; an economic poison under the federal Insecticide, Fungicide and Rodenticide Act; a food, drug, or cosmetic under the FD&C Act; or a household fuel when stored in a portable container.

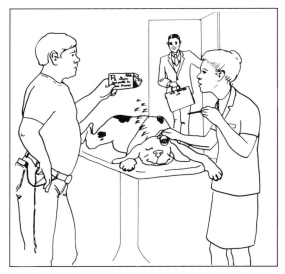

We taped the pills to the dog food bag like Dr. Duzwell said, so we wouldn't forget them, but the poor baby ate all the pills AND ten pounds of dogfood!

Clearly, a wide range of normal household products, drugs, and toxic chemicals are covered by the safe packaging laws.

Implementation of the Poison Prevention Packaging Act

The Poison Prevention Packaging Act requires that substances posing hazards to children by reason of their packaging be contained in special packages. Section 1471 (4) of the Act says:

> The term special packaging means packaging that is designed or constructed to be significantly difficult for children under five years of age to open or obtain a toxic or harmful amount of the substance contained therein within a reasonable time and not difficult for normal adults to use properly, but does not mean packaging which all such children cannot open or obtain a toxic or harmful amount within a reasonable time.

The Code of Federal Regulations § 1700.15 (b)(1) defines what is required even more specifically. Currently only substances like aspirin, furniture polish, turpentine, antifreeze, paint solvents, prescription and controlled drugs for human use, and several others are specifically covered by the regulations. The only veterinary drugs included are iron-containing products.

It should be noted that there are variations by state, and that veterinary drugs are included under some state laws. Virginia is one state where all repackaged tablets and capsules dispensed for companion animals must be in approved safety enclosure containers. Safety caps are not required if a person requests that the medication not have a cap or when the medication is of such size that it cannot reasonably be dispensed in such containers (e.g. topical ophthalmic and otic medications).[42]

According to one source, states are enacting laws based on the Model State Poison Prevention Packaging Act that was adopted by the National Drug Trade Conference in 1972. The Model State Act is based on the federal law but varies from state to state.[43] Because the potential for poisonings from veterinary drugs is just as great as that of human-use drugs, however, drugs dispensed by veterinarians may well be included in both state and federal laws or state board regulations in the future.

Caveats Regarding Drug Dispensing

One of the safest rules to abide by if veterinarians elect not to dispense all drugs in child-resistant containers is to dispense medication in such containers if any of the following circumstances exist:

- there are small children in the family
- the drug to be dispensed is a relatively or severely toxic drug like digoxin, cyclophosphamide, chloramphenicol (for a companion animal), or an organophosphate insecticide
- the owner requests a child-resistant container
- the pet chews and/or ingests foreign material
- the substance dispensed is one of the iron-containing products included in

the Poison Prevention Packaging Act list.

To accommodate these situations, it is suggested that veterinarians maintain a supply of medium-sized child-resistant dispensing vials in their pharmacies at all times.

Adverse Drug Reactions

An adverse drug reaction is an unexpected side effect or unintended change in the structure, function, and chemistry of the body including injury, toxicity, sensitivity reaction, or lack of efficacy associated with the clinical use of the drug.[44]

Information about adverse drug reactions is extremely important to the FDA as well as to the manufacturer of the product. Although major safety and efficacy data are required prior to the granting of FDA approval, sometimes the volume of cases submitted for justification is not large enough to demonstrate idiosyncratic adverse drug reactions or sensitivities peculiar to certain ages, breeds, or species. A good example occurred in the mid 1970s when a new endoparasite wormer, Sansalid® (uredofos), was approved. Within several months it became apparent that a modest percentage of dogs, especially the large breeds, were becoming seriously ill or dying as a result of this medication. Rapid verification of this situation, notification to the veterinary profession, and withdrawal of this drug from the market saved many canine lives—and lawsuits, too.

Documenting Drug Reactions

Information about adverse drug reactions is critical to the CVM's ongoing surveillance of animal drugs to assure their continued safety and effectiveness. Personnel at the FDA analyze this information to determine if any modifications are needed in a drug's labeling, dosage level, or instructions for use.[44] In a very few cases, the adverse reactions may be so severe that the FDA will withdraw its approval of a drug.

Reports also should be made to the drug manufacturer when adverse reactions occur. Manufacturers of new animal drugs are responsible for maintaining records of all reported side effects and adverse reactions and submitting this information to the FDA. The first contact, therefore, following a veterinarian's observation of an adverse reaction should be to the manufacturer. Depending upon the manufacturer's response, veterinarians also may wish to report the incident to the FDA.

Reporting Adverse Drug Reactions to the FDA

Adverse reactions may be reported by telephone between 8:00 a.m. and 4:30 p.m. by calling 301-594-1751 collect or 301-594-0797 after hours. In lieu of a telephone report, veterinarians may photocopy the form FDA 1932a, Veterinary Adverse Reaction, Lack of Effectiveness or Product Defect Report (Figure 9.1).

The FDA's CVM actively solicits these reports from veterinarians and depends on them to keep apprised of potential adverse effects. All names are held in strictest confidence by the CVM.

Product Liability and the Veterinarian

As more and more products for consumers have been marketed, the potential for harm from those products has increased. Ever since Justice Cardozo wrote about the defective wheel on the Buick motor car and defined the law of product liability in 1916, the courts have been developing the law in this area.[45] Courts have been asked repeatedly to place legal blame or liability on manufacturers or sellers of all types of products for causing injuries. As the product liability precedents have expanded, manufacturers and distributors of pharmaceuticals, pesticides, and biologicals have been held liable just as auto manufacturers and heavy industry have.

At one time, only a person who had a contractual relationship with the seller of a product could file a suit for an injury related to that product. The legal theory behind this precedent was called "privity of contract." The privity theory, however, was overthrown years ago, and courts now allow an injured party to seek redress regardless of any contractual relationship with the manufacturer or seller.

Implied Warranties

The other legal development impacting on product liability has been the implied warranties embodied in the Uniform Commercial Code. There are two types of implied warranties: (1) an implied warranty of merchantability, and (2) an implied warranty of fitness for a particular purpose.[46] Because of limitations inherent in the implied warranty of fitness for a particular purpose, the implied warranty of merchantability is more likely to apply to product liability cases involving drugs.

Implied warranties are warranties created by operation of law, not by agreement of the parties. Under the Uniform Commercial Code, there is an implied warranty of merchantability in every sale of goods as long as two conditions are met: (1) The seller is one who ordinarily sells such goods, and (2) the warranty has not been validly excluded or modified. "Merchantability" means that the goods are of average, acceptable quality in the trade, fit for their ordinary purposes. An implied warranty entitles consumers to some protection from manufacturers and sellers of products even though no express contract or warranty is present.

Concurrently, manufacturers and sellers have a duty to foresee potential harm and to assure that consumer products are safe for

VETERINARY ADVERSE REACTION, LACK OF EFFECTIVENESS OR PRODUCT DEFECT REPORT	DATE REPORTED	Form Approved: OMB No. 0910-0012 Expiration Date: **May 31, 1987**

NOTE: This report is authorized by 21 U.S.C. 352(a) and (f). While you are not required to report, your cooperation is needed to assure comprehensive and timely assessment of product labeling.

SOURCE OF REPORT AND OWNER'S NAME ARE HELD IN CONFIDENCE

1. VETERINARIAN'S NAME AND ADDRESS

TELEPHONE (Include Area Code) ___ __ __ · __ __ __ · __ __ __

2. OWNER'S NAME OR CASE ID

3. SUSPECTED DRUG AND DOSAGE FORM

4. MANUFACTURER'S NAME

5. DIAGNOSIS AND/OR REASON FOR USE OF DRUG

6. ADMINISTERED BY
☐ VETERINARIAN
☐ OWNER

7. DOSAGE REGIMEN AND ROUTE (Ex. 250 mg, q 12h, 5 days, orally)

8. DATE(S) OF ADMINISTRATION

9. SPECIES	10. BREED	11. AGE	12. SEX	13. WEIGHT _____ LBS.

14. CONCURRENT CLINICAL PROBLEMS
☐ NONE

OVERALL STATE OF HEALTH WHEN SUSPECTED DRUG GIVEN:
☐ GOOD   ☐ FAIR   ☐ POOR   ☐ CRITICAL

15. CONCURRENT DRUGS ADMINISTERED
☐ NONE

16. REACTION INFORMATION

a. TIME BETWEEN INITIATION OF THERAPY WITH SUSPECTED DRUG AND ONSET OF REACTION WAS _____.

b. TIME BETWEEN LAST ADMINISTRATION OF SUSPECTED DRUG AND ONSET OF REACTION WAS _____.

c. OUTCOME: ☐ RECOVERED FROM REACTION   ☐ DIED FROM REACTION   ☐ OTHER (Comment Below)

d. WAS THE REACTION TREATED?   ☐ NO   ☐ YES (Comment Below)

e. WHEN THE REACTION APPEARED, TREATMENT WITH SUSPECTED DRUG:
☐ HAD ALREADY BEEN COMPLETED
☐ WAS DISCONTINUED DUE TO REACTION
☐ WAS DISCONTINUED AND REPLACED WITH ANOTHER DRUG
☐ WAS DISCONTINUED AND REINTRODUCED LATER
☐ WAS CONTINUED AT ALTERED DOSE
☐ OTHER (Comment Below)

AND THE REACTION →

☐ CONTINUED
☐ STOPPED
☐ RECURRED
☐ OTHER (Comment Below)

f. LEVEL OF SUSPICION THAT DRUG CAUSED THE REACTION: ☐ HIGH   ☐ MEDIUM   ☐ LOW

17. DESCRIBE THE REACTION, ADD DETAILS ABOUT CASE HISTORY AND OUTCOME (Include numbers if group of animals involved). GIVE COMMENT ON POSSIBLE CONTRIBUTING FACTORS. DESCRIBE LACK OF EFFECTIVENESS OR PRODUCT DEFECT (Include Expiration Date and Lot No.).

NOTE: Triple fold as marked, seal with tape, no postage required. Additional space on back, if needed.

FORM FDA 1932a (1/86)

Dk: 7m

Figure 9.1   A form for reporting adverse reactions.

anyone who might reasonably be expected to use them or be affected by them.

In many jurisdictions, the courts have invoked a "strict liability" standard against manufacturers. This means that there is no need to prove negligence on the part of the defendant. Instead, the basic elements to be proved are those of an action for breach of warranty. These include proof of the existence of a warranty (often implied by the courts), proof that the warranty was breached, and a showing that a failure covered by the warranty was the proximate cause of the injury.

The Restatement of Torts View of Strict Liability

Where strict liability exists for product liability cases, the Restatement of Torts, Second is often cited. It provides the following comments:

> § 402A. Special Liability of Seller of Product for Physical Harm to User or Consumer
>
> 1. One who sells any product in a defective condition unreasonably dangerous to the user or consumer or to his property is subject to liability for physical harm thereby caused to the ultimate user or consumer, or to his property, if
>
>   a. the seller is engaged in the business of selling such a product, and
>
>   b. it is expected to and does reach the user or consumer without substantial change in the condition in which it is sold.
>
> 2. The rule stated in Subsection (1) applies although a. the seller has exercised all possible care in the preparation and sale of his product, and b. the user or consumer has not bought the product from or entered into any contractual relation with the seller.
>
> Caveat:
>
> The Institute expresses no opinion as to

whether the rules stated in the Section may not apply:

> 1. to harm to persons other than users or consumers;
>
> 2. to the seller of a product expected to be processed or otherwise substantially changed before it reaches the user or consumer; or
>
> 3. to the seller of a component part of a product to be assembled.
>
> Comment:
>
> c. ...[T]he justification for the strict liability has been that the seller, by marketing his product for use and consumption, has undertaken and assumed a special responsibility toward any member of the consuming public who may be injured by it; that the public has the right to and does expect, in the case of products which it needs and for which it is forced to rely upon the seller, that reputable sellers will stand behind their goods; that public policy demands that the burden of accidental injuries caused by products intended for consumption be placed upon those who market them, and be treated as a cost of production against which liability insurance can be obtained; and that the consumer of such products is entitled to the maximum of protection at the hands of someone, and the proper persons to afford it are those who market the products.[47]

Under section (1)(b), the product liability doctrine requires that the product "reach the user or consumer without a substantial change in the condition in which it is sold." Veterinarians must therefore be sensitive to the repackaging of drugs in their offices or to the mixing of home concoctions. Any time the product or drug has been substantially changed, veterinarians may find that they will be classified as the manufacturers. Under this theory it is possible that merely relabeling or mislabeling could be adjudicated as a substantial change in condition. If that occurs, veterinarians may find that they can no longer look to the manufacturer to help defend a product liability legal action. States have varying precedents regarding product liability law, so if a veterinarian is involved in a case in which this doctrine could be invoked, good legal counsel is essential.

Foreseeability as a Part of Product Liability

A 1986 Legal Brief article by Harold Hannah provides some additional insight into the philosophy of foreseeability in the following veterinary case:

> For manufacturers, this move toward protection of the consumer means that more testing must be done and that the issue of "foreseeability" assumes great importance. A good illustration is afforded by a Missouri Appellate Court case in which the plaintiff, a cattle owner, recovered damages from the manufacturer of a herbicide, though he was in no way involved with the purchase or use of the product. The herbicide had been used by drainage commissioners to spray their ditch banks and to control vegetation. The product's reaction with willow leaves produced nitrates and nitrites harmful to the plaintiff's cattle. Though the product was labeled as not harmful to animals, the court allowed the plaintiff to recover, saying that this was an occurrence the manufacturer might have foreseen.

The willingness of courts to hold liable anyone in the chain of distribution, all the way from the manufacturer to the seller or user, means that veterinarians are more vulnerable now than they were even twenty years ago. Coupled with this is a move by many veterinarians to make more over-the-counter sales and to actively engage in the retailing of veterinary and veterinary-related products. Though veterinarians may in some cases be able to turn to the manufacturer when

liability is imposed upon them, the increased threat of product liability is not a comfortable prospect.[48]

Foreseeability is always a primary element of concern with product liability cases. Mr. Hannah offers additional thoughts on this topic:

> Lawsuits arising from unsatisfactory results in the use of drugs often times involve a question of foreseeability, i.e., should the manufacturer have known, or should the veterinarian have known that the undesirable reaction might occur and therefore have issued proper warnings or dissuaded the client from using the product? Ultimately it is up to the court to decide whether the manufacturer has gone far enough in its investigation to determine whether the bad result should have been contemplated or whether the veterinarian was as well informed about the possibility as he or she should have been. The "foreseeability" test emphasizes the importance to veterinarians of "keeping up" and understanding all they possibly can about the drugs they use.[49]

Product Recalls

A good example of the change in thinking regarding the issue of manufacturer's foreseeability can be viewed in today's auto manufacturer's policies for recalling vehicles. Automobile recalls became more accepted and much more common after the multimillion dollar award in the Ford Pinto product liability case in the mid 1970s.

Auto and other manufacturers now understand the need to recall products when they discover a defect that might result in harm to the users. A failure to do so can enhance a product liability claim based on the theory that once a defect is discovered, the manufacturer has a duty to warn its buyers.

The FDA has caused the pharmaceutical industry to recognize the need to recall its products whenever a drug-tampering discovery is made by a retailer or the medical profession. It is assumed that the same concerns about foreseeability are valid pertaining to the distribution of veterinary drugs. A manufacturer's failure to warn veterinarians, or the public, could add considerable fuel to any product liability suit. Whether the veterinarian has a duty to warn clients separate from that of the manufacturer still appears to be an open legal question.

Avoiding Liability Problems

One of the primary issues in most product liability cases involving veterinarians focuses on the quality and quantity of communication with the client. An excellent set of questions was raised by Mr. Hannah in a 1980 *Legal Brief* applicable to this issue where he asks, "Were there adequate directions, warnings, listing of antidotes, indications of possible side effects, or other information which either the manufacturer or the professional man should have revealed to a user?"[50]

In situations involving the administration of drugs, the veterinarian is clearly the player between the animal owner and the drug manufacturer. Both the manufacturer and the animal owner rely on the veterinarian to communicate the manufacturer's product information and warnings to the client. Veterinarians who are negligent in informing themselves or their clients about potential adverse drug reactions or side effects can find themselves individually liable for such negligence or jointly liable with the manufacturer in the event a product liability case occurs.

Precautionary Measures

Precautionary measures can be taken by veterinarians to minimize their potential legal risks in the product liability arena just as they can in other areas.

- Veterinarians and staff people should know as much as possible about the products they use, prescribe, and sell. The more dangerous the product is, the more time must be taken educating staff members and clients regarding its use. A simple, inexpensive reference system can be created by placing clear plastic page shields in a loose-leaf notebook and then alphabetically filing the package inserts that come with each drug used in the practice in shields. This way relief veterinarians and the entire hospital staff can readily find and review a pertinent source of information when they need it or a client inquires about a particular product. The *Veterinary Pharmaceuticals and Biologicals* reference book[51] is a more professional means of retrieving product information than a loose-leaf notebook and costs only $34.45. Not all products used in veterinary medicine are in that book, though, so it may still be wise to have a notebook available for storing extraneous drug inserts.

- Be aware of how purchasers intend to use the product. If clients indicate that the product will be used for a purpose other than that intended or approved by the manufacturer, veterinarians should caution clients that this may void the manufacturer's liability for any adverse effects that occur. A 1980 *Legal Brief* article discusses this point in the context of the use of an anaplasmosis vaccine on a herd of pregnant cattle.[50] Practitioners should keep in mind that they can be held professionally liable if they are aware that a client's use of a product is contrary to the manufacturer's recommendations and they fail to caution the client against such use.

- Be sure that new employees check with a veterinarian before a product is dispensed to a client. Whenever staff turnover occurs, the risk of dispensing the wrong drug, the wrong dosage of a drug, the wrong quantity of a drug, and the risk of placing the wrong instructions on the label increases.

Unless employees have worked in a veterinary hospital for a while, they cannot be expected to have any understanding of the toxicity of some veterinary drugs. Products that might be safe in one species can be lethal to another, e.g., organophosphates and chlorinated hydrocarbons in cats. Many new employees cannot appreciate the overwhelming toxicity of something as simple as a double dose of digoxin. Maximal supervision and moderate employee education are critical for veterinarians to avoid liability problems. The following are situations in which supervision and education are recommended:

- Labels, instructions, and warning signs on products should be adequate and placed where they are readily seen. This is especially true when practitioners repackage products after receipt from the manufacturer. Insecticides pose some of the greatest risks because of their inherent toxicities.

- Whenever possible, informational literature from the manufacturer or practitioner should be included with the product being dispensed. Do not remove the manufacturer's inserts from these products prior to sale. Veterinarians have traditionally been reluctant to provide clients with any more information than absolutely necessary. When it comes to self-defense and product liability, however, one of the best defenses is to show that the injured party had ample access to information about the product in question.

- Communicate with clients. Establishing a proper veterinarian-client-patient relationship is impossible without communication. When that relationship is present and the client has been apprised of the risks and benefits of products that a veterinarian uses and dispenses, the risk of a product liability suit diminishes.

- Lastly, whenever possible use drugs and products that have been approved by the FDA. One of the major concerns

in product liability involves the premarketing research and documentation for the drug that is the subject of a lawsuit. When products have been approved, it generally can be assumed that there are sufficient safety and efficacy data so that product liability precedents can be applied to the manufacturer. However, if product liability suits are initiated concerning drugs used in extra-label manners, or involving unapproved drugs, it is much more difficult, if not impossible, for veterinarians to refer liability back to the manufacturer.

Defenses to Product Liability Actions

When product liability suits occur, veterinarians, manufacturers, and distributors have some defenses. Ideally these defendants are able to show that they were not negligent with respect to the use or sale of the product in question. Veterinarians who can show proper documentation regarding drug doses, volumes, and precautionary discussions with owners improve their chances of mustering a successful defense. Such defenses will not prevent strict liability from being enforced against the manufacturer but should help prevent practitioners from being held liable.

Contributory Negligence

Negligence on the part of the client in the use, administration, storage, or mixing of the drug is considered contributory negligence. In some states contributory negligence can be a complete defense to a legal action. However, in product liability law, comment "n" to § 402A of the Second Restatement of Torts reads:

> Contributory negligence of the plaintiff is not a defense when such negligence consists merely in a failure to discover the defect in the product, or to guard against the possibility of its existence. On

the other hand the form of contributory negligence which consists in voluntarily and unreasonably proceeding to encounter a known danger, and commonly passes under the name of assumption of risk, is a defense under this Section as in other cases of strict liability. If the user or consumer discovers the defect and is aware of the danger, and nevertheless proceeds unreasonably to make use of the product and is injured by it, he is barred from recovery.

In states where a comparative negligence standard exists (and it appears that this now includes a large majority of the states) the court will assess the contributory negligence or assumption of risk by the client (plaintiff) and offset the liability of the defendant accordingly.

Veterinarians' Rights to Render Nonstandard Treatment

Chapter 6 discussed the law of negligence and malpractice. A key part of the information on that topic revolves around the standard of care to be exercised by professionals. Practitioners who deviate from the standards of their fellow veterinarians run the risk of being held liable for departures from the norm.

FDA Policies

Concerns in the area of drug utilization by veterinarians are especially pertinent because of the recent development of specific FDA policies. With respect to the use of drugs in food-producing animals, practitioners' opportunities for innovation definitely have been curtailed. In order to comply with the FDA's policy covering extra-label use of drugs on food animals, the health of the animals must be immediately threatened, and suffering or death must be likely to

occur if the animals are not treated before a drug may be considered for use in an extra-label manner. This does not mean that the use of an extra-label drug is legal but that the FDA would normally not consider legal action provided these guidelines have been followed.

Because there is no concern about tissue residues in companion animal medicine, the FDA is willing to grant considerably more leeway with respect to companion animal drug therapy innovation than there is in food-producing animals. How willing the courts will be, however, to allow novel approaches to therapy is an open question.

Extra-Label or Unapproved Drug Use

Some of the criteria to be considered with respect to the use of unapproved drugs or extra-label use of drugs in an attempt to be innovative follows.

As the condition of the animal becomes more hopeless and all known procedures or remedies are likely to fail, veterinarians have increasing opportunities to use unorthodox approaches to treatment. This concept is particularly applicable to the use of chemotherapeutic drugs for treating animals with cancer. According to FDA authorities, there are no animal drugs approved for treating cancer in animals, just human drugs. Thus, these drugs may be used extra-labelly provided the owners are aware of the risks to the patient.

Articles in reviewed veterinary journals or textbooks about the use of unapproved drugs or the effective extra-label use of certain drugs can provide practitioners with good justification for using such drugs in their practices. The more references one has, the better the defense. Although reviewed journal articles lend more credibility to the case than do nonreviewed articles, any and all publications discussing drug usages are worthwhile when defending one's actions.

Notes taken from veterinary school classes or continuing education seminars presented by veterinarians who are recognized experts in their fields can provide good support for the use of novel approaches to drug therapy, too. In this respect it helps if speakers have some type of advanced training in their particular specialty or are associated with a university or veterinary school.

Another acceptable avenue to show that an extra-label use or unapproved drug is acceptable is to demonstrate that the product is in common use within the profession. For example, neither ketamine nor valium are approved for use in dogs. That combination, though, after a preanesthetic dose of acepromazine, has been in such common use as an induction anesthetic for dogs in some areas of the country that it would most likely be found to be within the standard of care and thus acceptable. The same could be said about the extra-label use of megestrol to treat numerous medical problems in cats.

Depending upon the circumstances, it is even possible that a particular protocol of drug therapy employed after years of successful experience by an individual practitioner could be found to be acceptable. For example, a veterinarian who has worked for years with a particular disease in cattle may have generated ideas about successful treatment that are not documented in texts or by fellow veterinarians. Courts have protected such deviation in malpractice cases if the veterinarian can show that he or she had substantial reason for using the method of treatment and especially if it is demonstrated that it was used in the past with success.[52] (For additional guidelines on the extra-label use of drugs see Appendix N.)

Client Consent Considerations for Drug Use

It cannot be assumed that clients have consented to a veterinarian's use of drugs in animals belonging to them unless those clients have some information about the potential effects of the drug in question. It is difficult to say how serious the risks from a particular drug must be or how likely side effects are before veterinarians have an affirmative duty to inform the client. Common sense, standard procedures within the profession, and previous experiences with the drug should all influence practitioners' decisions regarding this area of potential liability.

Side Effects: The Owner's Right to Know

Veterinarians must routinely weigh the apprehensions they will create in owners by emphasizing drug risks against the potential for liability if a drug-induced reaction occurs. Too much risk discussion can result in the failure of a client to administer a medication or pursue an effective course of therapy, resulting in more damage to the animal from not medicating than there would have been if a drug had been used. Too little information prevents the client from giving an informed consent to the use of the drug, and this can potentiate a lawsuit.

Drugs of Special Concern

Some drugs need more discussion prior to their use than others. The following drugs require greater client discussion.

Anesthetics

Since one of the known adverse effects associated with anesthetics is death, these drugs need more discussion than other drugs.

Psychotropic Drugs

Owners who are experiencing undesirable behavior in their animals often seek the assistance of a veterinarian to prescribe a drug that will improve the animal's behavior. Drugs used for these purposes pose a unique set of liability concerns.

Owners of hyperactive animals often request tranquilizers. Those who own aggressive animals want drugs that will decrease aggression. People who have pets that show fear (of thunderstorms, fireworks, guns, people, other dogs, etc.) may request antianxiety drugs.

Sometimes these requests come from owners; sometimes practitioners themselves prescribe the drugs; and other times the requests originate with animal trainers or nonveterinarian animal behaviorists who advise people to obtain specific drugs from their veterinarians. Considerable caution should be exercised with the employment of these drugs, but special precautions should be observed when the selection and dosage of psychotropic drugs are outside of the standard veterinarian-client-patient relationship.

Unless veterinarians agree with the diagnosis, understand the rationale behind the use of the drug, have confidence that the individual who recommended the drug therapy is a qualified expert in animal behavior, and are willing to be responsible for monitoring responses to those drugs, the situation is an invitation for legal trouble. A better policy may be to refer clients directly to veterinarians with special expertise in animal-behavior disorders.

The most common drugs prescribed as behavior modifiers are:[53]

- aceepromazine in dogs, cats, and horses for tranquilization purposes

- diazepam (Valium®) for noise phobias in dogs and urine marking in cats,

- megestrol acetate (Ovaban®) for dominance aggression directed toward people, urine marking, intermale aggression, mounting, and roaming in dogs; and urine marking and intermale aggression in cats,

- amitriptyline (Elavil®) for separation anxiety and excessive grooming related to distress in dogs and excessive grooming related to distress in cats,

- chlordiazepoxide (Tranxene®) in dogs for noise phobias in cases in which a longer-acting drug than valium is needed, and

- chlorpheniramine for antianxiety effects in cats.

None of these drugs is FDA approved for any psychogenic or psychotropic indications in animals except aceepromazine, which is approved as a tranquilizer. Thus use of any of the other drugs referred to above is an extra-label use.

Owners should always be cautioned that animals may continue to display the undesirable behavior that is being treated while they are under the effect of these drugs. However, since these patients already have behavior problems for which a drug has been prescribed, it may be difficult to ascertain whether an undesired behavioral episode occurred as a result of the medication or in spite of it. Animals can bite, scratch, buck, attack, kick, or fall while under the effect of one of these drugs, and it is difficult to determine whether the prescribed drug was responsible for that behavior or not.

The assumption most owners will make is that the medication caused the injury (which could be to the animal, the owner, or a third party). Disproving this assumption may be difficult, and testimony from experienced veterinary animal behaviorists is essential. Because of these issues and the fact that so few of the drugs in this group have been approved for administration to animals, additional measures to obtain proper consent for their use is advisable.

Chemotherapeutic Drugs

To be effective, most chemotherapeutic drugs must kill rapidly growing cancer cells, which means they also can be toxic to healthy tissues. When some of the serious side effects from these drugs occur, the costs for supportive medical care may be exorbitant and an unpleasant surprise for owners. These considerations coupled with the fact that most of the products in this group have never been approved for use in animals make them candidates for legal action.

Medical Factors Influencing the Need for Consent

Differences in the medical aspects of each case should prompt different types of discussion before drugs or biologicals are used. Various types of consent may be needed depending upon several factors:

1. The age and physical condition of the animal are the first of these considerations. Owners of young, healthy animals generally need less discussion of anesthetic risks prior to anesthesia than do owners of older, more compromised patients, unless the client seems especially nervous or specifically asks if an anesthetic risk exists. In this case, an honest analysis is in order. As patients age and develop higher anesthetic risks, it may be wise for veterinarians to initiate some discussion even if the clients do not inquire. A blend of sound medical judgment, good client relations, and proper anesthetic protocols will help considerably as practitioners decide what to say regarding anesthetic risks and when to say it.

2. The likelihood of an undesired side effect is another factor affecting the type of consent needed. For example, a modest percentage of dogs treated with glucocorticoids (cortisone) will drink more water, urinate more often, and sometimes have urinary accidents. These side effects are not generally medically serious, but they can become financially serious if the treated patient urinates profusely on the owner's carpets, drapes, or furniture. Monetary settlements by professional liability carriers have occurred in cases in which cortisone was dispensed without adequate warnings of the side effects.[54]

3. The seriousness of the side effect must be considered. Some side effects are common but are not life threatening. A good example is the vomiting associated with the administration of some antibiotics or anthelmintics. Practitioners commonly fail to caution owners about this adverse effect because it is not particularly serious. Still, veterinarians should consider the possibility of things like damage to hardwood floors, carpeting, or expensive bedspreads from a patient vomiting in the client's home as well as harm to the patient.

4. Other side effects are rare but, when they do occur, can be fatal. Sudden mortalities have, for example, been reported in conjunction with the use of mitotane for the treatment of Cushing's syndrome in dogs. Although this is a rare complication, the fact that it is life threatening should prompt some discussion of it before therapy is initiated.

5. Finally, different consents for drug use may be necessary if the animal is pregnant. There are data for most drugs from tests performed on pregnant animals prior to the granting of FDA, EPA, or USDA approval. If the directions on the package insert are followed regarding the use of the product during pregnancies, practitioners can generally rely on a manufacturer's product liability responsibility to support them in the event of a lawsuit. If, however, veterinarians administer drugs extra-labelly or use unapproved drugs on pregnant animals and abortions, fetal deaths, or birth defects occur, it is unlikely that the manufacturer will be interested in defending any legal actions.

Various Types of Client Consent

Oral Information and Oral Consent

When prior experiences with a drug, potentially serious drug-induced side effects, or client nervousness suggests a need for some form of additional consent, several alternatives exist. First, an oral explanation without any written documentation can be given. From a legal defense viewpoint, this is not a very valuable approach. Proving that any discussion took place or that the client heard the information that was supposedly conveyed makes defending this situation difficult. It is, nevertheless, better than no discussion at all.

Practitioners also can attempt to establish that it is standard business policy to discuss the side effects of certain commonly dispensed drugs with all clients at the time the drug is dispensed. An example would be that all clients who receive the oral flea product cythioate are instructed orally not to use any choline esterase–type flea collars, sprays, or dips in conjunction with that product. Instead, they are routinely counseled that only pyrethrin-based insecticides can be used simultaneously with cythioate. This standard operating procedure could be proved ultimately because staff and many clients have heard the discussion. It is not a very wise approach, however, if the drug has a particularly frequent or dangerous side effect.

As the use of computers increases in veterinary medicine, the ability to key specific written instructions to any risky drug becomes more realistic. This advanced technology, already available from some veterinary computer software vendors, may rapidly improve the standard of care in terms of written warnings on the labels of dangerous drugs.

Oral Information and Written Notes

The second form of consent involves a higher level of attention on the part of the veterinarian. A written note is made by the veterinarian or a staff member in the medical record pertaining to an oral discussion with the client. A sample notation in the patient's medical record discussing the side effects of a chemotherapeutic drug like cyclophosphamide (Cytoxan®) could read as follows:

> Disp. 30 Cytoxan 50 mg tabs, give 1 tab daily for 1 wk., will do exam and CBC weekly during course of therapy. Owner cautioned about possible hem. cystitis, bone marrow suppression, and susc. to infect. O. to call if abnormal symptoms develop.

This documentation is not as good as a written consent with an owner's signature, but it is much better than nothing at all or simply an oral discussion. The fact that this note is present on the medical record is not absolute proof that the owner was properly informed, but it lends considerable support to a veterinarian's defense.

Oral Information, Written Notes, and Owner's Initials

The third approach is a minor modification of the second one. In addition to a veterinarian's or a staff member's handwritten notation in the record, a request is made for the client to sign or initial the note in the record. The presence of a legible client signature can increase the likelihood that a jury will believe the doctor if a legal question is raised.

Signed Written Consent Forms

The fourth alternative involves a formal document for the owner to sign. This has its pros and cons. Presenting the owner with a typewritten document increases the owner's anxiety and can necessitate taking considerable time explaining the risks and benefits of using the drug. If the risks are serious, the value of this procedure easily outweighs the costs incurred. If, however, the risks are negligible and considerable time is required to convince the owner to sign the consent form, this procedure may be economically impractical. Although no form of consent is foolproof, a formal written one is much more difficult for a client or attorney to successfully attack than the oral approaches discussed previously.

Written Consent Forms for Psychotropic Drugs

The more highly specialized a practitioner is, the higher is the standard of care required to avoid problems with professional liability. It seems justifiable, then, for clients to expect to receive more information about an experimental drug from an animal behaviorist at a veterinary school than they would get from a general practitioner. For this reason, well-conceived, written consent forms are needed more in specialized veterinary care situations than in routine practice. General practitioners who lack depth of experience with the use of psychotropic drugs to alter behavior but elect to use them also should be concerned about proper client consent as well as careful monitoring of the patient's response to therapy. Figure 9.2 is a form for use with the prescription of drugs in this category.

As mentioned earlier, no consent form can be written so well that it cannot be challenged in court. However, the value of such a signed form is twofold. First, clients have a much heavier burden of proof to overcome if they have signed a document like this than if no form existed at all. Second, the fact that a signature exists has considerable psychological value and, therefore, can help dissuade clients from suing.

Informed Consent for Cancer Therapy

Nearly all of the cancer treatment protocols for veterinary medicine involve the use of non-FDA approved drugs, radiation

---

I, the undersigned, certify that I am the owner or duly authorized agent for the owner of a _____ year-old _____ (species) named _____. I understand that a psychotropic (behavior-modifying) drug will be used under the direction of Dr. _____ in an attempt to alter the following undesirable behavioral characteristics currently present in this animal: _____

_____ .

I understand that the drug being prescribed has been used in other animals with similar problems but is not approved by the Food and Drug Administration for this use in my animal. I am aware that this drug could cause possible side effects such as _____

_____ ,

that this drug may not alter the course of the behavioral problem, and that my animal may continue engaging in the problem behavior or injure itself, other animals, or people. I hereby give my informed consent to Dr. _____ for the administration of this drug to my animal and personally accept both legal and financial responsibility for any actions that may occur from the use of such drug.

_____   _____
Client's signature   Date

_____   _____
Veterinarian's signature   Date

Figure 9.2   Informed consent for use of psychotropic drugs.

therapy, immunotherapy, or aggressive surgery, with the increased potential for serious, if not fatal, side effects. Fortunately, many of the clients who pursue oncological treatment protocols for their pets also develop very close veterinarian-client-patient relationships. It is probably because of the closeness of this relationship that few lawsuits evolve from these types of cases in spite of the severity and frequency of adverse effects created by the drugs involved.

Nevertheless, the risks are notable, the undesirable drug side effects frequent, and the human-animal bond very strong. If sufficient time is not allotted to educate these clients, discussing the risks and benefits of various treatment protocols versus no treatment, the opportunity for lawsuits is significant.

The use of signed informed consent forms is recommended in these situations. Practitioners who are exposed to the highest risks are:

- general practitioners who undertake aggressive chemotherapy treatments on patients without much prior experience or knowledge of the risks involved.

- private practice specialists engaging in specialty care where the standard of care exceeds that of the general practitioner.

- board-certified specialists or residents at veterinary university hospitals where the most advanced (and often the most experimental) forms of oncological therapy are being attempted.

Concerns about these risks have led to the development of a sample consent form at a leading United States veterinary school (Figure 9.3).

Consent forms like these are not for everybody and hopefully will never be universally needed in veterinary medicine. The cost of completing this time-consuming task each time a drug is administered does not fit well into the routine practice of veterinary medicine. Nevertheless, written consent

forms are extremely valuable as aids to preventing or defending legal actions. In selected cases, the time required to obtain this consent may be well worth the effort. Veterinarians are encouraged to retain legal counsel as needed to modify and adapt the sample forms included here to fit their needs.

Administering Drugs to Show and Racehorses

American Horse Show Association Rules

Equine practitioners should be aware of certain significant rules affecting the administration of drugs to horses entered in American Horse Show Association (AHSA) shows. If any of numerous listed prohibited drugs are administered, horses must be withdrawn from competition for at least 24 hours.

Although AHSA rules only require owners or trainers to comply with association rules regarding drugs, veterinarians have a responsibility to inform those people that forbidden drugs have been used.[55]

Horses that are treated with forbidden drugs and that test positive via blood or urine samples are subject to disqualification. Trainers and owners can be penalized for showing horses in this condition and may be forced to forfeit trophies, ribbons, and prize money. In addition, they could be fined or suspended by the AHSA.

Two groups of drugs are of concern. The first group includes any substances that could have the main or side effect of a stimulant, depressant, tranquilizer, or local anesthetic. The second group consists of those that have a potential to interfere significantly with drug detection procedures. They are called *masking drugs* and include such products as furosemide, sulfa drugs, dipyrone, benzimidazole anthelmintics, and many others.

Informed Consent for Cancer Therapy Using Experimental Methods or Non-FDA-Approved Drugs

The goals of the "_____ Veterinary Oncology Group" are to effectively manage cancer in pets while minimizing discomfort. In order to treat cancer, various procedures must be used including: 1) surgery, 2) radiation, 3) chemotherapy, 4) immunotherapy, and 5) combinations of two or more treatment modalities. Some patients will be placed on clinical protocols for specific tumors where the most effective type of treatment is yet to be determined.

1. I hereby grant my informed consent to the veterinarian named below, and/or such assistants as may be selected by him or her, to undertake one or more of the above procedures on my pet.

2. The possible risks, side effects, benefits, and consequences of the procedures have been explained to me including cosmetic changes and anesthetic risks. I understand that vomiting, diarrhea, depressed blood cell counts, fever and even death are possible sequela to these treatments.

3. I authorize the lab tests, x-rays and biopsies required by the veterinarian(s) to diagnose and properly treat my pet.

4. I authorize the taking and use of photographs for treatment and teaching purposes.

5. I understand that the treatment of cancer in animals is an investigational branch of veterinary medicine. I am aware that most of the chemotherapy drugs which will be used on my animal have been used in other animal patients, but that they have not been approved by the FDA for use in animals. Many treatments are of unproven benefit, and I acknowledge that no guarantees have been made to me as to the results of this treatment.

6. I understand that in some cases complications from this cancer therapy may require additional hospitalization and nursing care which could result in further financial responsibility on my behalf. I will be informed of the estimated fees for these services before services are rendered.

7. I am aware that cancer treatments are administered on strict time schedules and will do my best to cooperate with the schedules presented to me. I understand that I may withdraw my pet from the treatment protocol at any time.

8. I have been given an opportunity to ask any questions I have concerning this treatment, and all such questions have been answered to my satisfaction.

_____   _____   _____
Owner's Signature   Date   Pet's Name

_____   _____
Veterinarian's Signature   Date

Figure 9.3   An informed consent for cancer therapy form.

Although compliance is the responsibility of the owner or trainer, a potential for liability exists if veterinarians use those drugs and fail to properly inform the owners and trainers. Practitioners who plan to serve as show veterinarians or treat horses competing in AHSA shows should be familiar with AHSA rules. Additional information on this subject can be obtained from the AHSA.[56]

State Laws On Drugs Used for Horses

California (and perhaps other states) has a state program directed toward the control of substances that will affect the performance of horses entered in public horse shows, horse competitions, or horse sales.[57] The California Director of Food and Agriculture has defined classes of prohibited drugs to include (1) stimulants, (2) depressants, (3) anesthetics, (4) masking agents, (5) steroids, and (6) carrying agents such as propylene glycol. Racehorses are exempt from the California Horse Drugging Law unless they are participating in a competition, show, or sale covered by the state law.[58] In California, racehorses are covered by a separate statute similar in scope to the Horse Drugging Law.[59]

Any person who administers, attempts to administer, instructs, aids, or conspires with another to administer, or attempt to administer, prohibited drugs is subject to the penalties. Thus, in California veterinarians can be prosecuted for administering forbidden drugs to show horses. California veterinarians who are in a position to be treating show horses are urged to become familiar with these laws by contacting the California Department of Food and Agriculture.[60]

National Association of State Racing Commission Rules

All 28 racing jurisdictions in North America with pari-mutuel betting test for illegal medications in the blood or urine of horses. Usually this is done after races, but in some cases, it is performed before and after races. This area of drug testing and drug regulation is probably the most highly developed and oldest, having been in place for about 50 years.[61] The amount of information on this subject is so voluminous that only cursory coverage is provided here. The reference materials on this topic are excellent.

The drugs that appear in the AHSA rules are also regulated under the National Association of State Racing Commission rules. The complexity of the rules, drug interactions, testing procedures, testing inadequacies, and legal aspects of rule enforcement are the subject of an entire book.[62]

Four basic types of racehorse drugging rules are used today. The simplest is the "no detectable level" rule. This requires that no trace of any drug can be present in any body fluid. Canada, Australia, England, and New York operate with this rigid rule.[63, 64]

The second type of rule, just beginning to be used, is the "tolerance level" rule, which provides for a small amount of leeway in detectable drug levels. Although it is not without problems, it seems to be the most equitable approach, because it allows for at least some differences between laboratories, sampling techniques, and the individual physiology of various horses.

The third rule is one like that employed by the AHSA. It is a time rule, which states that drugs shall not be administered within a specified time before a competitive event. Although these rules are easy to write and understand, they are difficult to enforce and thus are not widely used in the racehorse business.

The fourth option is to have no rule at all. This has been advocated by at least one authority because of the inherent enforcement difficulties and costs associated with drug testing procedures. The best-known example of a no-rule-drug is dimethyl sulfoxide (DMSO), a topical anti-inflammatory agent that aids drug penetration.[63]

Although blood testing is on the increase, the primary source of body fluid for postrace testing today is urine. Urine is superior to blood because it is available in relatively large amounts. Additionally, because of the kidney's ability to concentrate and excrete drugs, urine tends to contain more concentrated amounts of drugs that can be more easily detected. A major drawback is that it is slow and difficult to collect, and urine concentrations may not correlate well with blood levels.

Blood samples are easy to collect and, once a drug is identified, the amount of drug present can be accurately quantified. The drawback with blood is that sample volumes are generally small (compared to urine), and concentrations of drugs and drug metabolites are low, exacerbating chances for mechanical or human error. The best monitoring system for accurate drug detection seems to be a combination of both blood and urine.[65]

Summary

The law surrounding the administration, dispensing, and prescribing of veterinary drugs is the most volatile and fastest-changing area of law affecting veterinarians. The penalties for failing to follow the rules can be serious, including significant professional liability and the loss of one's veterinary license. Because of the inherent dangers associated with the use of drugs, the trend toward tighter regulatory controls over their use is expected to continue. Practitioners owe it to themselves to gain at least a minimal amount of knowledge of the law on this subject in order to avoid serious legal problems.

References

1. Soave O, Ballitch E: FDA veterinary notes: Selling prescription drugs over the counter. *JAVMA* 188(11):1986.

2. 21 USC 360(b).

3. Stefan G, et al: Special commentary: FDA regulations of veterinary prescription drugs. *JAVMA* 189(5):513,1986.

4. § 512(i) of the FD&C Act.

5. 21 USC 331(a).

6. Gushec J: FDA veterinary notes: Bulk drugs and chemical substances. *JAVMA* 189:878,1986.

7. § 502(f)(1); 21 USC 3606.

8. 21 CFR 201.

9. 21 CFR 201.5.

10. *Federation of Homemakers* v *Schmidt*, 593F.2d740 (CADC,1976), *Udall* v *Jerry J. Colahan*, et al: *US* v *IBA, Inc* et al, (DC 6, 1985), and *National Nutritional Foods Assoc* v *Weinberger*, 512F.2d699 (CA 2,1975).

11. § 512(a) of the FD&C Act.

12. Gloyd JS: Editorial: Protecting your practice and the food animal industry. *JAVMA* 190(1):33,1987.

13. Food and Drug Administration Compliance Policy Guides, Chap 25. *Animal Drugs, Guide 7123.06.* Office of Enforcement, Division of Compliance Policy, Associate Commissioner for Regulatory Affairs, Food and Drug Administration, Rockville, MD 20857.

14. Stefan G: FDA and the practice of veterinary medicine. *FDA Vet* I(1):4,1986.

15. Approvals withdrawn, dimetridazole appeal cancelled. *Veterinary Medicine News From Washington* 11(5), Aug 1987, Governmental Regulations Division, AVMA, 1522 K St. NW, Suite 828, Washington, DC 20005.

16. Dols P: Regulatory highlights. *FDA Vet* I(1):6,1986.

17. Waltersheid E: FDA vs. DVM: Profession scores TKO against regulation.*Vet Econ* 34 (April): 1987.

18. Veterinarian files suit against FDA. *JAVMA* 190(9):1081,1987.

19. VM & NPPC talk about sulphur residues in swine. *FDA Vet* I(II):3,1986.

20. *The Use of Unapproved Drugs in Domestic Animals, Proceedings of a Symposium.* Lawrenceville, NJ, Veterinary Learning Systems Co, Inc, l986, p 14. Available from Dr. James Walsh, Solvay Veterinary, Inc, PO Box 7348, Princeton, NJ 08543-7348.

21. Overflow crowd attends drug symposium. *JAVMA* 189(6):610,1986.

22. Gloyd JS: Editorial: Protecting your practice and the food animal industry. *JAVMA* 190(1):33,1987.

23. Sink B: Listing of FDA-approved veterinary drugs available soon. *FDA Vet* I(II):7,1986.

24. 21 CFR 514.1

25. Spika JS, et al: Chloramphenicol-resistant *Salmonella newport* traced through hamburger to dairy farms. *Engl J Med* 316(10):565-566,1987.

26. Codex veterinary drug residue committee holds first meeting. *JAVMA* 190(3):251,1987.

27. Model Practice Act. *AVMA 87 Directory*. Schaumburg, IL, AVMA, 1987, p 629.

28. *California Board of Examiners in Veterinary Medicine Newsletter*, Winter 1984, 1420 Howe Ave, Suite 6, Sacramento, CA 95825.

29. *FDA Compliance Policy Guides*, No. 7123.06, Aug 1, 1986,p 3. Dept. of Health and Human Services, Food and Drug Administration, Center for Veterinary Medicine, Rockville, MD 20857.

30. Soave O: FDA veterinary notes. Selling veterinary prescription drugs over the counter. *JAVMA* 188(11):1236,1237, 1986.

31. Thompson R: Don't sell veterinary drugs illegally. *Penn Vet Med Assoc News* (Jan/Feb):5,1987.

32. Johnson LY: Letter from Department of Health and Human Services, Public Health Service, Food and Drug Administration to all licensed PA veterinarians. Philadelphia, PA, June 26, 1987.

33. 21 USC 374.

34. Ballitch EJ: FDA veterinary notes. Veterinarians and FDA investigators: A case of human relations and the law. *JAVMA* 184(12):1456-1457, 1984.

35. Hannah HW: Legal brief: The right to inspect a veterinary practice. *JAVMA* 185(5):498,1984.

36. Crawford LM: Comments on "legal brief," Letters to the editor. *JAVMA* 186(1):4-5, 1985.

37. Sundlof S: *Food Animal Drug Manual*. College of Veterinary Medicine, University of Florida, Box J 137 JHMHC Gainesville, FL 32610-01370.

38. Powers JD, Powers TE: *Proceedings of Tenth Annual Food Animal Medicine Conference, The Use of Drugs in Food Animal Medicine*. Columbus, OH, Ohio State University Press, 1984.

39. Gloyd JS: Editorial: Protecting your practice and the food animal industry. *JAVMA* 190(1):34,1987.

40. Voluntary use of child-resistant containers urged. *JAVMA* 190(6):643,1987.

41. Manoguerra AS: Safety packaging and full labeling of prescription drugs...why? *Calif Vet* 10, 1981.

42. Virginia Board of Veterinary Medicine Regulation § 4.2,3.a.

43. De Marco CT: *Pharmacy and the Law*. Aspen Publications, Aspen Systems Corp, Rockville, MD p 224.

44. Dols P: Veterinary drug adverse reaction reporting. *FDA Vet* I(II):9,1986.

45. *Mac Pherson v Buick Motor Co.* 217 N.Y. 382, 111 N.E.1050.

46. Uniform Commercial Code § 314 and § 315.

47. Keeton RE: *Tort and Accident Law*. 50 W Kellogg Blvd, St Paul, MN 55165, West Publishing Co, p 700-701, 1983.

48. Hannah HW: Legal brief. Product liability and the veterinarian. *JAVMA* 189(7):754,1986.

49. Hannah HW: Legal brief. Drugs—Client information and foreseeability. *JAVMA* 189(11):1403,1986.

50. Hannah HW: Legal brief. Product liability—Veterinarians in the middle. *JAVMA* 177(7):607, 1980.

51. *Veterinary Pharmaceuticals and Biologicals*, ed 5. Lenexa, KS, Veterinary Medicine Publishing Co, 1987/1988.

52. Hannah HW: Legal brief. The right to use nonstandard materials or methods. *JAVMA* 184(1):29,1984.

53. Voith V: Personal communication, Veterinary Hospital, University of Pennsylvania, 1987.

54. Dinsmore J: Personal communication, AVMA Professional Liability Insurance Trust, PO Box 74221, Chicago, IL 60690-8211, 1987.

55. Lengel JG: Treating show horses: AHSA rules. *Equine Pract* 8(5):36,1986.

56. American Horse Show Association, Inc, 220 E 42nd St, 4th Floor, New York, NY 10017-9998.

57. California Agriculture Code § 24008.

58. Berry LJ: California's law unique in nation. *Calif Vet* 41(May/June):3,1987.

59. California Penal Code § 337 f.

60. California Department of Food and Agriculture, Animal Health Branch, Horse Drugging Program, 1220 N St, Sacramento, CA.

61. Woods WE, Chay S, Houston T: Efficacy of testing for illegal medication in horses. *JAVMA* 187(9):927-930,1985.

62. Tobin T: *Drugs and the performance horse*. Springfield, IL, Charles C Thomas, 1981.

63. Tobin T: Medication control: Rules. *Equine Vet Sci* 6(4):191-193, 1985.

64. Tobin T: Medication control: The efficacy and cost of drug testing. *Equine Vet Sci* 6(6):334, 1985.

65. Blake JW, Tobin T: Testing for drugs in horses. *Equine Vet Sci* 6(2): 93-94, 1985

CHAPTER 10

The Law on Veterinary Biologicals and Pesticides

Regulation of Veterinary Biologicals

The federal government is the primary regulator of vaccines and biologicals, although individual states may have their own statutory control over the manufacture and sale of these products. The regulatory agency presiding over this segment of the animal health industry is the Veterinary Services division of the Animal and Plant Health Inspection Service (APHIS) of the United States Department of Agriculture (USDA).

The Virus-Serum-Toxin Act of 1913

The law that originally established control over veterinary biologicals is known as the *Virus-Serum-Toxin Act of 1913*. The backbone of this act is a section that makes it unlawful to:

> prepare, sell, barter, or exchange...in any place under the jurisdiction of the United States...any worthless, contaminated, dangerous, or harmful virus, serum, toxin, or analogous product intended for use in the treatment of domestic animals and no person, firm, or corporation shall prepare, sell, barter, exchange or ship as aforesaid any virus, serum, toxin, or analogous product manufactured within the United States and intended for use in the treatment of domestic animals, unless and until the said virus, serum, toxin, or analogous product shall have been prepared, under and in compliance with regulations prescribed by the Secretary of Agriculture, at an establishment holding an unsuspended and unrevoked license issued by the Secretary of Agriculture...[1]

Interestingly, this section of the act refers only to biologicals for use in the treatment of domestic animals. Under traditional property law definitions, domestic animals only include horses, cows, sheep, goats, pigs, and dogs. In the Virus-Serum-Toxin Act, though, domestic animals means "all animals other than man, including poultry."[2]

Defining Biologicals

To more fully understand the volume and scope of products under the jurisdiction of the *Virus-Serum-Toxin Act of 1913*, one must turn to the Code of Federal Regulations, where the term *biological products* is defined as follows:

> The term biological products, sometimes referred to as biologics, biologicals, or products, shall mean all viruses, serums, toxins, and analogous products of natural or synthetic origin, such as diagnostics, antitoxins, vaccines, live microorganisms and the antigenic or immunizing components of microorganisms intended for use in the diagnosis, treatment, or prevention of diseases of animals.[3]

Although most practitioners only think of vaccines and bacterins in relation to USDA regulations, the various immunologic testing kits for animal diseases are also included. Diagnostic products such as bovine leukemia test kits, canine distemper virus antibody test kits, equine infectious anemia ELISA antibody test kits, intradermal skin-testing antigens, feline leukemia virus test kits, and pseudorabies virus antibody test kits are within the jurisdiction of USDA regulation.

Interstate Commerce, Intrastate Shipments, and Exports

The preparation and sale of products in interstate commerce have always been covered by the Virus-Serum-Toxin Act. The way the act was worded, however, left some doubt as to whether intrastate or export products were also covered. The Food Security Act, passed on December 23, 1985, clarified this by legislatively placing both intrastate and export biologicals within the USDA's jurisdiction. Manufacturers who were selling products on an intrastate basis prior to December 23, 1985 and who did not have prior USDA approvals for those products have been granted until January 1, 1990 to accumulate data and seek USDA approval for their products.

Testing Procedures

Much of the regulation of biologicals is similar to that of drugs. When treating diseases with drugs, efficacy requires that specific blood or tissue residues be achieved in order to kill the offending infective agent. The goal of a biological product, however, is to supply sufficient antigen to the body so that its immune system is primed to protect it from infection. A successful response minimizes the need for drugs to treat the disease at any future time and thus reduces the potential for drug residues. Because of this, much of the regulation in the biologicals area deals with efficacy, packaging, and labeling, and not worrisome tissue residues.

Testing the Products

Jurisdiction over testing comes from the Code of Federal Regulation, wherein the Deputy Administrator of Agriculture has authority to require that all veterinary biological products manufactured in or imported into the United States be examined and tested for purity, safety, potency, or efficacy.[4] These regulations require that the products yield the results intended with reasonable certainty when used as recommended on their labels prior to the expiration date.

Licensed products may not be shipped to consumers until release for marketing is authorized by the USDA. This authorization is not given until all applicable tests required by the "Standard Requirements" or by the approved "Outline of Production" have been completed and the product has been found to be satisfactory.[5] Test results for each batch or serial number are reviewed by the USDA before release is authorized.

Although it may sound like the approval process is dramatically easier for a biological than for a drug, the Code of Federal Regulations does contain 150 pages of regulatory material on this subject. As might be expected, the approval process has many checks and balances. According to USDA authorities, from the time that a completed application is submitted, the approval process usually requires from three to six months on a diagnostic product, six to eight months on a killed bacterin or vaccine product that has been produced before, six to nine months for a modified-live virus product that has been produced previously, and approximately one year for approval on an entirely new product. Significant variations do occur. New vaccine products for which an initial outline of production must be developed can require three to six years to pass from the product-development stage through the testing and research stages to ultimate USDA approval.

Packaging and Labeling Requirements

As with drugs and pesticides, there are stringent rules governing the labeling and packaging of biological products.[6] No false or misleading information may appear on any label or carton containing a biological product. In addition, the regulations require that the following items appear on the label:

- The principal part of the true name of the biological product.
- If the biological is prepared in the United States, the name and address of the producer.
- The license or permit number assigned by the USDA.
- Storage temperature recommendations for the product.
- Full instructions for the proper use of the product (these can appear in an insert if the final product container is too small for all this information to be included).
- In the case of a product recommended for use in food-producing animals, a withholding statement of not less than 21 days that reads: "Do not vaccinate food-producing animals within (insert number ___) days before slaughter."
- The expiration date of the product.

- A serial number by which the product can be identified.
- Statements about the addition of an antibiotic if such drug was added as a preservative during production.
- Several other items of lesser importance than these are also required.

Questions About Product Efficacy

Veterinary consumers occasionally have questions about unsatisfactory product performance, adverse patient reactions, or the arrival of vaccines in an unrefrigerated state. The first action should be to document information like the name of the manufacturer and/or distributor; the batch, lot, or serial number; and any important clinical signs of adverse effects. If the product arrived unrefrigerated, practitioners should attempt to ascertain how hot it became and approximately how long it was unrefrigerated. In general, modified live products are more stable at high temperatures than killed products because they are protected by stabilizers. Killed products will deteriorate more rapidly because of protein coagulation.[7]

Although many vaccines are received from distributors, employees at these establishments may not possess enough knowledge to give advice on the efficacy of unrefrigerated products. Therefore, once all relevant information about any of the above problems has been accumulated, practitioners should notify the manufacturer and request instructions regarding use of the product. Manufacturers are required by law to keep track of any adverse reactions (including reports of ineffective products, but not shipment errors) and report them to the USDA.

No matter how trustworthy people are, veterinarians may wonder if employees of the manufacturers or distributors will provide truly unbiased answers to questions about the efficacy of their products. Although the USDA does not have any formal reporting procedure for adverse reactions or consumer complaints, governmental employees can be called for information. The Veterinary Biologics Field Office in Ames, Iowa (phone 515-232-5785) can be called to obtain information or report an adverse reaction or ineffective product. An alternative regulatory center to call with any remaining unanswered questions is the USDA APHIS VS, Federal Bldg. #835, 6505 Bellcrest Rd., Hyattsville, Maryland 20782 (phone 301-436-8245).

Extra-Label Use of Biologicals

The extra-label use of biologicals does not worry consumers or regulatory agencies nearly as much as the extra-label use of drugs. There are several reasons for this. First, unlike with drugs, wherein positive, negative, or neutral effects are often observed within a few days, evaluating the efficacy of vaccines and bacterins usually requires several months. Because of this time delay, most practitioners are not as likely to experiment with biologicals as they are with drugs.

Three exceptions to this general rule have occurred in recent years. One involved the use of killed and modified-live-virus feline enteritis vaccine in dogs when the parvovirus outbreak occurred in 1979, before any canine vaccine had been manufactured. The second extra-label use involved fairly widespread administration of the feline *Chlamydia* vaccine to prevent abortions and reproductive disorders in mid-western dairy cattle. The third situation deals with the increased ownership of some species of exotic animals like ferrets and raccoons. Since no vaccines have been approved for small markets, extra-label use of biologicals will continue to be fairly common in the exotic species.

Second, different species of animals generally have different infectious diseases. Therefore, the bacterins or vaccines for one species often have no value in another species. This fact, too, creates fewer incentives to use these products in an extra-label manner.

Third, since these products are unlikely to produce or leave behind any dangerous residues in the food supply, there is little reason for consumer-advocate groups to expend resources and/or energy calling for strict regulation of these products.

Perhaps due to the lesser dangers, the USDA has never had any written policy on the extra-label use of biologicals. Its position consistently has been that any product legally obtained by licensed veterinary practitioners may be used in any manner deemed to be effective. By this philosophy, only concerns about malpractice or state regulations govern any extra-label uses.

The Veterinarian-Client-Patient Relationship

The USDA has no specific policies or regulations governing the need for a veterinarian-client-patient relationship with regard to the use of biologicals by veterinarians. Instead, USDA officials rely on state practice acts to regulate this phase of the utilization of biologicals.

It appears from this, then, that if individual states do not have a formal definition for the veterinarian-client-patient relationship, biologicals may be used by veterinarians in any manner that would be considered to be in conformance with the standards of practice for that state. If, however, the state does have a specific definition of the existence of a veterinarian-client-patient relationship, the biological products are governed by that definition in the same manner as are veterinary drugs (see Chapter 9).

The only area in which USDA regulations would apply the veterinarian-client-patient doctrine is in the 1985 amendment to the Virus-Serum-Toxin Act. If veterinarians elect to develop and produce a biological product for use only by their clients, they need not obtain federal approval for that product. In such cases, however, they must be able to demonstrate the existence of a valid veterinarian-client-patient relationship or they will be in violation of the federal law.

Administration of Rabies Vaccines

Veterinarians have long assumed that only a veterinarian may give a rabies vaccination to an animal. According to the USDA, however, the laws that stipulate who may administer rabies vaccines have to be state laws, not federal laws or regulations.[8] Thus, in the absence of state laws or policies to the contrary, it appears that veterinarians may allow personnel in their hospitals to immunize animals for rabies without a prior examination. Additionally, they may sell rabies vaccine to clients so that they can vaccinate their animals at home.

Most state veterinary practice acts do not address the issue of rabies vaccines being administered by nonveterinarians. Some state practice acts, such as California's, require "that the animal has been examined by a veterinarian at such time as good veterinary medical practice requires"[9] prior to the administration of any drug or biological.

What "good veterinary medical practice requires" is always open to challenge, but veterinarians in California have consistently allowed competent staff members to administer these vaccines as long as the animal has been examined previously by a veterinarian in the practice and there is a doctor on the premises and within reach. The biggest question for debate has focused on whether a nonveterinarian may administer the very first rabies vaccine an animal receives without an examination by a veterinarian in the practice. It appears that good veterinary practice will always require that the first rabies vaccine be preceded by a veterinarian's exam. Subsequent vaccines, though, can be administered without an examination as long as the good veterinary medical practice requirement was fulfilled.

Sometimes laws or regulations pertaining to rabies vaccines can be found in the state public health and safety codes or other state legislative codes. Therefore, to be absolutely certain that nonveterinarians can legally administer rabies vaccines, practitioners are urged to have their state boards of veterinary examiners publish a statement on the issue.

Some Concluding Thoughts

The relative uncertainty surrounding federal regulations dealing with biologicals often leaves veterinarians unsure of what they can or cannot legally do. A lack of any significant federal attention to this area seems to indicate that not much is likely to change in the near future. Therefore, when questions arise regarding the proper administration of biologicals, veterinarians are urged to contact their state boards of examiners for the policies, laws, and interpretations that apply to the use of these products in their jurisdictions.

The EPA and Veterinary Responsibilities for the Use of Pesticides

The use of pesticides is a whole other area of regulation in which different issues arise.

The Federal Insecticide, Fungicide, and Rodenticide Act

As mentioned at the beginning of this chapter, the FDA has no authority over pesticides unless they are administered orally or parenterally. That leaves all of the environmental and topical pesticides, the fungicides, and the rodenticides to be covered by a different set of statutes known as the *Federal Insecticide, Fungicide, and Rodenticide Act (FIFRA)*. These statutes designate the Environmental Protection Agency as the federal agency with jurisdiction over this group of compounds.[10]

Basic Concerns About Veterinarians' Use of Pesticides

Considerable material has been presented on the subject of extra-label use of FDA-approved drugs. The extra-label use of pesticides is another type of situation. If, for example, a veterinarian recommends the use of a topical flea product every other day and the label approves it for use once weekly, does the practitioner have any potential liability? Are risks of litigation and liability so great that veterinarians should refrain from recommending the best or most effective medical treatment for fleas (or any other pest) in order to conform to label directions?

Active versus Inert Ingredients

When reviewing the FIFRA, the first task is to establish some definitions. The drug compounds of pesticides are always separated into active components and inert ingredients. FIFRA defines active ingredient as follows:

> (1) in the case of a pesticide other than a plant regulator, defoliant, or desiccant, an ingredient which will prevent, destroy, repel, or mitigate any pest;...[11]

Other sections of FIFRA discuss plant regulators, defoliants, and desiccants, but since they are not used by veterinarians, no discussion of them is presented here.

When it comes to inert ingredients, the act takes an interesting, though disheartening, approach. It defines inert simply as any ingredient that is not active.[12]

Such a definition does not mean that these ingredients correspond with the average person's understanding of inert, whereby those ingredients contain few or no active properties or are neutral. In fact, according to consumer groups like The National Coalition Against the Misuse of Pesticides, some of the inert ingredients may be equally or more toxic than some of the active ingredients. For example, the inert ingredient isopropyl alcohol is very toxic when inhaled—especially by cats. However, since the inert component does not have any intended effect on the pest, no disclosure of inert components is required on the label.

Labels and Labeling

It is in the area of product labeling that veterinarians may have difficulty with the law. FIFRA defines label as the written, printed, or graphic matter on or attached to the pesticide or device or any of its containers or wrappers.[13] It goes on to define labeling as:

> ..all labels and all other written, printed, or graphic matter (A) accompanying the pesticide or device at any time; or (B) to which reference is made on the label or in literature accompanying the pesticide or device....

The reason that definitions of labels and labeling are important is because of the act's policy regarding products that have been misbranded.

Misbranding

Chapter 9 discussed at length the Food, Drug and Cosmetic Act's definitions and complicated problems surrounding the definition of misbranding. FIFRA says that a pesticide is misbranded if:

> (A) its labeling bears any statement, design, or graphic representation relative thereto or to its ingredients which is false or misleading in any particular; (B) it is contained in a package or other container or wrapping which does not conform to the standards established by the Administrator...; (D) its label does not bear the registration number...; (E) any word, statement, or other information required by or under the authority of this Act...to appear on the label or labeling is not prominently placed thereon with such conspicuousness...and in such terms as to render it likely to be read and understood by the ordinary individual under customary conditions of purchase and use;...[14]

In short, the message is that no pesticide should be dispensed or sold by practitioners in any container other than the original one.

Risks of Liability and Uses Inconsistent with the Labeling

Aside from misbranding, there are still other legalities to consider. Another section of the FIFRA declares that it is unlawful for any person to detach, alter, deface, or destroy, in whole or in part, any labeling required under the act.[15] This indicates that it would be a violation of the FIFRA for a veterinarian to repackage and resell a pesticide without the manufacturer's label.

The biggest concern for practitioners is that FIFRA states that it is unlawful "to use any registered pesticide in a manner inconsistent with its labeling."[16]

A commentary in the *JAVMA* illustrates the relevance of this section when it says,

> Any other use of a pesticide contrary to the labeling is illegal, whether the user is a layperson or veterinarian. A veterinarian advising or employing the inconsistent use faces prosecution with civil penalties (assessed by EPA) of up to $5,000 and criminal penalties (imposed by federal court) of up to $25,000 and one year in prison. Advising a client to employ an unauthorized use could get the client in trouble. Prosecution of violations is, of course, within the discretion of EPA enforcement officials and, in the case of criminal charges, US attorneys.[17]

State Law Application to Pesticide Uses

Federal law may be the primary concern in the area of pesticides, but state law precedents also must be considered. Since very little if any state law exists regarding the control of pesticides, the primary state law that can be applied is that of veterinary malpractice and professional conduct.

If a veterinarian uses a pesticide as specified on the product's labeling, minimal anxiety about professional liability should exist as long as clients have been apprised of any serious risks. On the other hand, if the recommended use of the pesticide is inconsistent with its labeling, veterinarians bear a significant legal burden with regard to negligence because their recommendations have been in violation of the FIFRA.

Minimizing and Avoiding Problems

Anyone who has engaged in small animal practice in the flea-infested areas of the United States knows that to use flea products only as indicated on the label would frequently result in failure. What course can be taken, then, if the only successful approach to pest control involves an extra-label use?

To date there is no good answer to this problem. The only recommendations that can be made are to

- use these products with great discretion.
- never remove the labeling from any pesticides dispensed.
- repackage these products only if great care is extended toward assuring proper relabeling. Better yet, do not repackage at all.

If the only use that is effective is contrary to that approved on the label, be sure that ample corroborative recommendations from veterinarians with special expertise on this topic are available to help defend any type of lawsuit regarding the use of these products that might occur.

Be ready to bring in expert witnesses in the form of other veterinarians to testify that the standard of care for veterinary practice currently requires that pesticides be used in manners inconsistent with their labels in order to preserve the health of the animals and to successfully treat the cases at hand.

References

1. 21 USC 151.
2. 9 CFR 101.
3. 9 CFR 101.2(w).
4. 9 CFR 113.6(a).
5. 9 CFR 113.5.
6. 9 CFR 112.
7. Appelgate J: Personal communication, Solvay Veterinary Inc, Princeton, NJ, 1987.
8. Espeseth DA: Personal communication, Agriculture and Plant Health Inspection Service, Hyattsville, MD, 1987.
9. Title 16, California Administrative Code § 2034.
10. 7 USCS 136.
11. 7 USCS 136(a).
12. 7 USCS 136(m).
13. 7 USCS 136(p).
14. 7 USCS 136(q).
15. 7 USCS 136(j) (a)(2).
16. 7 USCS 136(j) (a)(2) (G).
17. Special commentary. Veterinary responsibilities for use of pesticides *JAVMA* 183(4):418, 1983.

CHAPTER 11

Controlled Substances

The Importance of Laws Governing Controlled Substances

Controlled substances are those drugs that are subject to abuse by staff members, clients, veterinarians, and people who rob or burglarize veterinary hospitals in search of them. Knowledge regarding the ordering, receipt, storage, record keeping, administering, dispensing, and prescribing of these compounds is particularly important because of the potential for civil and criminal actions.

Veterinarians who unwittingly violate these laws are subject to police investigations, action by state boards of examiners, and civil penalties up to $25,000. Violations of controlled substance laws committed with knowledge or intent incur criminal penalties of up to 15 years in prison, a fine of up to $25,000, or both[1] for the first offense, and possibly veterinary license suspension or revocation.

Federal Regulation of Controlled Substances

Prior to 1970, the federal laws governing controlled drugs were scattered throughout the United States Code. Because of increasing enforcement and abuse problems associated with controlled drugs, in 1970 Congress completely revamped the laws governing these substances by passing the Comprehensive Drug Abuse Prevention and Control Act.

This major federal law regulates the manufacture, distribution, dispensing, and delivery of certain drugs or substances that have the potential for abuse or for physical or psychological dependence and have been classified as controlled substances or controlled drugs.

Title 1 of the Comprehensive Drug Abuse and Prevention Act establishes rehabilitation programs for drug abusers. Title 3 regulates the import and export of controlled drugs. Title 2, the section that is the most applicable to the practicing veterinarian, is known as the *Controlled Substances Act (CSA)*. It regulates, by way of federal registration, all persons involved in the legitimate chain of manufacture, distribution, or dispensing of controlled drugs.

The United States Congress enacted more than 50 pieces of legislation regulating and controlling the diversion of dangerous drugs between 1914 and 1970. The CSA of 1970 became effective May 1, 1971. It collected and tailored most of the diverse laws into one piece of legislation. The CSA was designed to provide a "closed" system for legitimate handlers of controlled drugs and reduce the opportunities for diversion of controlled drugs from lawful channels into the illicit drug market. The Drug Enforcement Administration (DEA) is the primary federal law enforcement agency charged with the responsibility of combating the abuse of controlled substances.

The DEA was established July 1, 1973 under the Presidential Reorganization Plan No. 2 of 1973. It resulted from the merger of the Bureau of Narcotics and Dangerous Drugs (BNDD), the Office for Drug Abuse Law Enforcement, the Office of National Narcotic Intelligence, those elements of the Bureau of Customs that had drug investigative responsibilities, and those functions of the Office of Science and Technology that were drug-enforcement related. The DEA was established to more effectively control narcotic and dangerous drug abuse through a nationally organized enforcement and prevention system. In carrying out its mission, the DEA cooperates with other federal agencies, as well as state and local governments, private industry, and other organizations.

State Drug Control

Most states had adopted some version of the Uniform Narcotic Drug Act and the Drug Abuse Control Amendments of 1965 before the CSA was passed in 1970. Since passage of the CSA, most states have been replacing their old laws with adaptations of the Uniform Controlled Substances Act. This law, based on the CSA, was created as a model for states to use in writing their own laws. In addition to these state statutes, some state boards of examiners have added their own regulations regarding controlled substances.[2]

Veterinarians must be aware of their state laws, because when state law record keeping and inventory requirements are more stringent than federal requirements, the state regulations take precedence. In addition, state laws dealing with prescriptions for controlled substances may differ from those set forth by the federal regulations. New York, for example, requires the use of prescription blanks printed and numbered by the state. Practitioners should contact their state boards of examiners or state veterinary associations for information regarding individual state requirements.

Classification of Controlled Substances

Section 812 (b) of the CSA divides controlled substances into five schedules primarily according to their potential for abuse.

Schedule I

The drugs in Schedule I have a high potential for abuse and no currently accepted medical use in treatment in the United States. Furthermore, there is a lack of accepted safety for use of the drug or substance under medical supervision. Examples of substances in this schedule are the opium derivatives such as heroin and codeine methylbromide, plus the hallucinogenic substances marijuana, LSD, THC, peyote, mescaline, and others.

Schedule II

The drugs classified under Schedule II have a currently accepted medical use in treatment in the United States but a high potential for abuse which may lead to severe psychological or physical dependence.

Some of the substances in this category are opium, morphine, codeine, etorphine hydrochloride (used only to restrain wild animals and zoo animals), hydromorphone (Dilaudid®), methadone, meperidine (Demerol®), cocaine, oxycodone (Percodan®) and oxymorphone (Numorphan®). Also included are some of the stimulants like amphetamine (Dexedrine®) and methamphetamine (Desoxyn®) as well as methylphenidate (Ritalin®), pentobarbital (Nembutal®), secobarbital (Seconal®), and phencyclidine (angel dust).

Schedule III

Schedule III substances have less of a potential for abuse than the drugs or other substances in Schedules I and II. These drugs have a currently accepted medical use in treatment in the United States, and their abuse may lead to moderate or low physical dependence or high psychological dependence.

Some drugs in Schedule III are compounds containing limited quantities of narcotic drugs along with nonnarcotic drugs. Examples include Hycodan®, Empirin® with codeine, Tylenol® with codeine, and Phenaphen® with codeine. A drug commonly used by veterinarians to reverse the effect of a narcotic in animals, nalorphine hydrochloride (Nalline®), also falls into this category.

Schedule IV

The substances in Schedule IV have a low potential for abuse relative to the drugs in Schedule III. These drugs have a currently accepted medical use in treatment in the United States, but consumption may lead to limited physical or psychological dependence. Included are products such as chloral hydrate, meprobamate (Equanil® and Miltown®), chlordiazepoxide (Librium®), diazepam (Valium®), pentazocine (Talwin®), and propoxyphene (Darvon®).

Schedule V

Schedule V drugs have a low potential for abuse and a currently accepted medical use in the United States. Abuse of these drugs, though, may lead to limited physical or psychological dependence. Schedule V drugs must not contain more than specified concentrations of narcotic drugs plus nonnarcotic active ingredients, and they generally have antitussive and antidiarrheal indications. Diphenoxylate hydrochloride with atropine sulfate (Lomotil®), Robitussin A-C® syrup, Phenergan® with codeine, and Actifed-C® expectorant are examples of drugs in this schedule.

Rescheduling of Controlled Substances

As times change and uses or abuses of drugs wax or wane, it occasionally becomes necessary for the DEA to alter classifications for various controlled drugs. Under Section 811 of the CSA, the attorney general and the administrator of the DEA have broad powers to reschedule a drug, bring an unscheduled drug under control, or remove the controls on a drug. This process is undertaken generally after scientific and medical data have been evaluated and after public hearings have been held.

One example of such a change involved moving some of the amphetamines from Schedule III to the more rigidly controlled Schedule II group. Another change occurred in 1973 when chlordiazepoxide and diazepam were changed from noncontrolled status to Schedule IV.

Registration

The DEA's regulations have been written primarily to cover physicians, pharmacists, and human hospitals. Physicians generally prescribe controlled drugs, pharmacists dispense them, and hospital personnel administer them. Veterinarians, however, perform all of these functions. Because of this, it often appears questionable whether the regulations apply to veterinarians in exactly the same manner as they do to physicians and pharmacists.

In general, DEA regulations are written to cover all medical practitioners, and veterinary practitioners are treated no differently than professionals from any other medical field. It is difficult for the DEA to provide interpretative opinions on questions involving the statutes and their regulations unless they know all the facts surrounding the situation. Practitioners who have questions regarding registration that are not answered herein should contact the appropriate DEA office (Appendix L) in order to ensure that they are complying with the pertinent federal or state controlled substance laws in their jurisdiction.

Who Must Register

One of the primary requirements of the CSA is that anyone who manufactures, distributes, or dispenses a controlled substance must register with the DEA annually unless exempted by law.[3] According to Section 802 (10) of the CSA:

> The term "dispense" means to deliver a controlled substance to an ultimate user or research subject by, or pursuant to the lawful order of, a practitioner, including the prescribing and administering of a controlled substance and the packaging, labeling, or compounding necessary to prepare the substance for such delivery. The term "dispenser" means a practitioner who so delivers a controlled substance to an ultimate user or research subject.

It is apparent from this definition that the administration of drugs is also included in the dispensing of drugs. Section 802 (2), however, specifically defines the term *administer*. According to that definition, administer means the direct application of a controlled substance to the body of a patient or research subject by practitioners (or, in their presence, by their authorized agents) by injection, inhalation, ingestion, or any other method.

Defining Practitioners

The impact of these definitions is more readily apparent when the CSA's definition of practitioner is considered.

> A physician, dentist, veterinarian, scientific investigator, pharmacy, hospital, or other person licensed, or otherwise permitted, by the United States or the jurisdiction in which he practices or does research, to distribute, dispense, conduct research with respect to, administer, or use in teaching or chemical analysis, a controlled substance in the course of professional practice or research....[4]

Veterinarians Working at Multiple Locations

The regulations dealing with DEA registration are particularly important to veterinarians who work at more than one veterinary establishment. Research on this topic has produced considerable confusion within both the profession and various regulatory agencies.

The language employed by many boards may imply or require that veterinarians who wish to administer or dispense controlled drugs at more than one location have a valid registration for each employment site. Consultations with DEA officials in Washington, D.C. refute this implication. The DEA regulations provide a specific exemption for agents and employees in multiple-employment situations. The following statements in the Code of Federal Regulation can be relied upon when veterinarians are working part time or in a relief capacity at various hospitals:

> (a) The requirement of registration is waived for any agent or employee of a person who is registered to engage in any group of independent activities, if such agent or employee is acting in the usual

course of his business or employment. (b) An individual practitioner, as defined in § 1304.02 of this chapter...who is an agent or employee of another practitioner registered to dispense controlled substances may, when acting in the usual course of his employment, administer and dispense (other than by issuance of a prescription) controlled substances if and to the extent that such individual practitioner is authorized or permitted to do so by the jurisdiction in which he practices, under the registration of the employer or principal practitioner in lieu of being registered himself.[5]

It is apparent from part (b) of this section that individual practitioners may prescribe controlled drugs if they are registered at some principal place of business. To administer or dispense, however, they must either be classified as an agent or employee of a registrant or they must be registered at each facility where they are employed.

California's "Practitioner's Guide to Controlled Substance Regulations,"[6] which interprets the Uniform Controlled Substances Act, and discussions with officials at the California Bureau of Narcotic Enforcement indicate that the same policy is true at the state level.

Although variations could exist in other states, it appears that if practitioners hold a valid DEA registration at one location they can legally prescribe controlled drugs at additional locations. California officials maintain that this can be done even in states where multiple prescription forms are required in order to prescribe Schedule II drugs. This is the rule under federal law, and it appears this is probably the case under most state laws. At least one person in authority at each veterinary facility, however, must have a valid registration in order for the practice to maintain an inventory of controlled drugs. When that registrant exists, an agency relationship may be established to allow other people to administer or dispense controlled drugs. At least one state board of examiners is confused on the issue of registration. Board regulations there require that each licensed veterinarian administering, prescribing, or dispensing Schedule II-V drugs shall obtain and maintain on the premises a controlled substances registration certificate.[7] Meanwhile, the Drug Control Act in that state clearly indicates that the same agency and direct supervision language which appears in § 1304.24 of the CFR apply within the jurisdiction.[8] It would appear, therefore, that in this state practitioners who are registering at every facility where they work are doing so unnecessarily. This inconsistency may well exist in other states also. Practitioners who wish to clarify the issue in their states should request that legal counsel for their state boards research applicable state statutes.

This "agency" type exemption dramatically simplifies the situation for part-time or relief veterinarians who work at multiple hospitals and would like to administer, dispense, or prescribe controlled drugs. It enables them to administer or dispense controlled substances without registering at each site as long as the registrants are willing to grant the part-time veterinarians agency status and authorize them to use the registrant's inventory of controlled drugs. It is extremely important, however, that registrants in this situation demand strict adherence to all storage and record keeping requirements, because they will be held accountable if any controlled drug law violations occur.

Administration of Controlled Drugs by Nonveterinary Staff Members

Animal health technicians and other veterinary practice employees cannot legally prescribe drugs under state practice act laws; thus, they can never legally prescribe controlled drugs. Most state practice acts do, however, allow these employees to administer drugs at the direction of and under the direct supervision of a licensed veterinarian. Under the authority granted in the CFR where the term *administer* is defined,[5] animal health technicians or other veterinary practice employees may administer or dispense controlled drugs provided that they are (1) agents or employees of the registered practitioner, (2) performing this task in the usual course of business, (3) acting under the direction of a licensed veterinarian, and (4) under the direct supervision (veterinarian on the premises) of a licensed veterinarian. It is possible that there are some state law variations on this issue, but this is the interpretation of the federal law provided by the DEA.

Independent Contractors

For tax reasons, specialists or other people who work at particular veterinary facilities might be treated by practice owners as "independent contractors" rather than employees. If these people are paid as independent contractors (without any taxes withheld), they might not be considered to be agents or employees and, therefore, might not be covered by this exemption.

Practitioners seeking opinions as to whether or not a person treated as an independent contractor for tax purposes would still be covered by the agency or employee exemption found in CFR § 1301.2 are urged to contact the appropriate DEA divisional office for an interpretation. If any doubt exists, it is best to require that independent contractor veterinarians maintain separate registrations. The minimal cost incurred assures compliance with the CSA while also helping to substantiate the independent contractor status to any tax authorities who might challenge such a relationship.

Applications, Renewals, and Address Changes

Newly licensed veterinarians who will be entering practice or who will be in positions in which they may be administering controlled drugs in a research environment should apply for DEA registration immediately after they become licensed to practice. New application registration forms (Figure 11.1) can be obtained from the United States Department of Justice, DEA.[9]

Practitioners generally check all of the boxes representing the various schedules. The boxes for Schedule II drugs and the box in number 4 must be checked in order to receive the triplicate order forms required to obtain Schedule II drugs from various drug distributors.

Renewal forms (Figure 11.2) will be generated by and sent out from the DEA's computer application facility in Atlanta, Georgia. In the past, registrations have been granted and renewed annually at a cost of $20. Starting in July 1987, $60 three-year registrations were phased in. Each year for three years one third of the annual renewals will be converted to the three-year type.

Veterinarians who change employment locations within the same state should request modification of their registrations by contacting the Registration Section of the DEA.[10]

Registration of Animal Shelters

The DEA's registration of animal shelters may be handled differently than the registration of individual practitioners, depending upon variations in state law. Some state controlled drug laws allow for the registration of animal shelters as separate entities. If this is the case, the DEA will issue a registration in the name of the animal shelter and not require that an individual practitioner be named. The registration certificates in these cases will read "Hospital-Clinic-A.S."

Under these circumstances, individual veterinarians are not held accountable for directing the use of controlled drugs. Instead, personnel managing the shelter are responsible for ordering the drugs, keeping records, and providing security. Employees and agents of these shelters performing duties in their usual course of employment may administer or dispense controlled drugs as allowed by state law and as directed by shelter management. States that do not address animal shelters as separate entities must follow the rules established by the DEA. A limited quantity of controlled

Form **DEA** — 224
(Jul, 1987)   OMB No. 1117-0014

NEW
APPLICATION FOR REGISTRATION
UNDER
CONTROLLED SUBSTANCES ACT OF 1970

Please PRINT or TYPE all entries.

No registration may be issued unless a completed
application form has been received (21 CFR 1301.21).

RETAIN Copy 3. Mail Orig. and 1 copy with FEE to:

UNITED STATES DEPARTMENT OF JUSTICE
DRUG ENFORCEMENT ADMINISTRATION
P.O. Box 28083
CENTRAL STATION
WASHINGTON, D.C. 20005
For INFORMATION, Call: 202 254 8255

See "Privacy Act" Information on reverse

CITY   STATE   ZIP CODE

THIS BLOCK
FOR DEA
USE ONLY

REGISTRATION CLASSIFICATION: Submit Check or Money Order Payable to the **DRUG ENFORCEMENT ADMINISTRATION** in the Amount of $ 60.00.

1. **BUSINESS ACTIVITY:** *(Check ☑ ONE only)*   *(Specify Medical Degree, e.g.,*
   DDS, DO, DVM, MD, etc.)

   A ☐ RETAIL PHARMACY   B ☐ HOSPITAL/CLINIC   C ☐ PRACTITIONER   D ☐ TEACHING INSTITUTION
   (Instructional purposes only)

   ● FEE MUST
   ACCOMPANY
   APPLICATION

2. SCHEDULES: *(Check ☑ all applicable schedules in which you intend to handle controlled substances. See Schedules on Reverse of Instruction Sheet.)*

SCHEDULE II NARCOTIC	SCHEDULE II NONNARCOTIC	SCHEDULE III NARCOTIC	SCHEDULE III NONNARCOTIC	SCHEDULE IV	SCHEDULE V
☐	☐	☐	☐	☐	☐

3. ☐ CHECK HERE IF YOU REQUIRE ORDER FORMS.

4. **ALL APPLICANTS MUST ANSWER THE FOLLOWING:**

   (a) Are you currently authorized to prescribe, distribute, dispense, conduct research, or
   otherwise handle the controlled substances in the schedules for which you are
   applying, under the laws of the **State** or jurisdiction in which you are operating
   or propose to operate?

   ☐ YES **State** License Number(s) _____

   ☐ NOT APPLICABLE   ☐ PENDING

   (b) Has the applicant ever been convicted of a crime in connection with controlled substances
   under State or Federal law, or ever surrendered or had a DEA registration revoked,
   suspended or denied, or ever had a State professional license or controlled substance
   registration revoked, suspended, denied, restricted or placed on probation?
   ☐ YES ☐ NO

   (c) If the applicant is a corporation, association, partnership, or pharmacy, has any officer,
   partner, stockholder or proprietor been convicted of a crime in connection with
   controlled substances under State or Federal law, or ever surrendered or had a DEA
   registration revoked, suspended or denied, or ever had a State professional license or
   controlled substance registration revoked, suspended, denied, restricted or placed on
   probation? ☐ YES ☐ NO ☐ NOT APPLICABLE

   IF THE ANSWER TO QUESTIONS 4(b) or (c) is YES, include a statement using the space
   provided on the REVERSE of this part.

● ATTACH CHECK HERE ●

Print or Type Name Here - Sign Below   *Applicants Business Phone No.*

**SIGN
HERE** ▶

Signature of applicant or authorized individual   *Date*

*Title (If the applicant is a corporation, institution, or other entity, enter the TITLE
of the person signing on behalf of the applicant ((e.g., President, Dean, Procurement
Officer, etc....))*

5. **CERTIFICATION FOR FEE EXEMPTION**

   ☐ CHECK THIS BLOCK IF INDIVIDUAL NAMED HEREON IS A FEDERAL,
   STATE, OR LOCAL OFFICIAL.

   The Undersigned hereby certifies that the applicant herein is an officer or employee of a Federal,
   State or local agency who, in the course of such employment, is authorized to obtain, dispense,
   or prescribe controlled substances or is authorized to conduct research, instructional activity or
   chemical analysis with controlled substances, and is exempt from the payment of this application
   fee.

   Signature of Certifying Official   *Date*

   Print or Type Name

   Print or Type Title

   Name of Institution or Agency

   **WARNING: SECTION 843(a)(4) OF TITLE 21, UNITED STATES CODE, STATES THAT
   ANY PERSON WHO KNOWINGLY OR INTENTIONALLY FURNISHES FALSE
   OR FRAUDULENT INFORMATION IN THIS APPLICATION IS SUBJECT TO
   IMPRISONMENT FOR NOT MORE THAN FOUR YEARS, A FINE OF NOT
   MORE THAN $30,000.00 OR BOTH.**

   Mail the Original and 1 copy with FEE to the above address. Retain 3rd copy for your records.

Figure 11.1   A new application for DEA registration.

substances may be maintained by veterinarians at animal shelters provided that a valid registration in the veterinarian's name is in force at that location. Practitioners holding registrations are responsible for all of the shelter's controlled substance activities. Employees or agents of the shelter may administer controlled drugs (usually euthanasia drugs) without the veterinarian's presence provided that there is no conflict with state law. Practitioners who are in this position, however, should create strict guidelines and verify that employees are conforming to them.

Veterinarians who are asked to serve as the registered practitioner for an animal shelter and who do not know how animal shelter registration is handled in their states can contact the appropriate state bureau of narcotic enforcement, state veterinary association, or state board of examiners.

Termination of Registration

If a registrant dies, goes out of business, discontinues in professional practice or, in the case of a corporation or partnership, ceases legal existence, the DEA must be notified immediately so that the registration can be terminated.[11] Any unused drug order forms must be returned to the nearest DEA office.[12]

Practitioners or representatives of their estates having controlled substances in their possession at the time the practice is discontinued should contact their regional DEA office to determine how to dispose of unused controlled substances. These substances should not be sent to the DEA unless specific instructions have been received to do so. DEA Form 41 (Figure 11.3) is used to fulfill this requirement.

Figure 11.2   A renewal application for DEA registration.

Ordering Controlled Substances

Practitioners must be licensed in the states where they are practicing and have a valid DEA registration to order controlled substances from distributors. No special form is needed for orders of drugs in Schedules III, IV, and V. All controlled substances in Schedule II, however, must be ordered with the Federal Triplicate Order Form DEA-222 (Figure 11.4).

Obtaining Order Forms

The DEA Triplicate Order Forms 222 are sent out by the DEA at no charge when new registrations are granted or renewals are issued provided that the applicant has checked the appropriate box on the application. More forms may be ordered whenever necessary from the Registration Section of the DEA.

Whenever any used or unused order forms are stolen from or lost by a registered veterinarian, the DEA should be notified immediately.[13] Such notification should include the serial numbers of the missing forms and should be made to the Registration Unit of the DEA.[9] If the serial numbers are not known or an entire book is missing, the DEA should be contacted for instructions.

Completing Order Forms

Since it is often months between the ordering of Schedule II drugs, practitioners are

OMB Approval No. 1117-0007	DEPARTMENT OF JUSTICE / DRUG ENFORCEMENT ADMINISTRATION **REGISTRANTS INVENTORY OF DRUGS SURRENDERED**	PACKAGE No.

The following schedule is an inventory of controlled substances which is hereby surrendered to you for proper disposition.

FROM: *(Include Name, Street, City, State and ZIP Code in space provided below).*

Signature of applicant or authorized agent

Registrant's DEA Number

Registrant's Telephone Number

NOTE: REGISTERED MAIL IS REQUIRED FOR SHIPMENTS OF DRUGS VIA US POSTAL SERVICE (see instructions on reverse of form)

NAME OF DRUG OR PREPARATION (Registrants will fill in Columns 1, 2, 3, AND 4 Only.)	Number of Con-tainers	CONTENTS (Number of grams, tablets, ounces or other units per con-tainer)	Con-trolled Sub-stance Con-tent. (Each Unit)	DISPOSITION	QUANTITY GMS.	QUANTITY MGS.
1						
2						
3						
4						
5						
6						
7						
8						
9						
10						
11						
12						
13						
14						
15						
16						

DEA Form (Jul. 1984) **-41**   Previous edition may be used   *See instructions on reverse side*

Figure 11.3   A form for disposal of unused controlled substances, sides 1 and 2.

NAME OF DRUG OR PREPARATION	Number of Con- tainers	CONTENTS (Number of grams, tablets, ounces or other units per con- tainer)	Con- trolled Sub- stance Con- tent (Each Unit)	FOR DEA USE ONLY		
				DISPOSITION	QUANTITY	
					GMS.	MGS.
	2	*3*	*4*	*5*	*6*	*7*
17						
18						
19						
20						
21						
22						
23						
24						

The controlled substances surrendered in accordance with Title 21 of the Code of Federal Regulations, Section 1307.21, have been received
in _____ packages purporting to contain the drugs listed on this inventory and have been: **(1) Forwarded tape-sealed without opening;
(2) Destroyed as indicated and the remainder forwarded tape-sealed after verifying contents; (3) Forwarded tape-sealed after verifying contents.

DATE _____ 19 ____   DESTROYED BY: _____

** *Strike out lines not applicable.*   WITNESSED BY: _____

INSTRUCTIONS

1. List the name of the drug in column 1, the number of containers in column 2, the size of each container in column 3, and in column 4 the controlled substance content of each unit described in column 3; e.g., morphine sulfate tabs., 3 pkgs., 100 tabs., 1/4 gr. (16 mg.) or morphine sulfate tabs., 1 pkg., 83 tabs., 1/2 gr. (32 mg.), etc.

2. All packages included on a single line should be identical in name, content and controlled substance strength.

3. Prepare this form in quadruplicate. Mail two (2) copies of this form to the Special Agent in Charge, under separate cover. Enclose one additional copy in the shipment with the drugs. Retain one copy for your records. One copy will be returned to you as a receipt. No further receipt will be furnished to you unless specifically requested. Any furhter inquiries concerning these drugs should be addressed to the DEA District Office which serves your area.

4. There is no provision for payment for drugs surrendered. This is merely a service rendered to registrants enabling them to clear their stocks and records of unwanted items.

5. Drugs should be shipped tape-sealed via prepaid express or registered mail to Special Agent In Charge, Drug Enforcement Administration, of the DEA District Office which serves your area.

PRIVACY ACT INFORMATION

AUTHORITY: Section 307 of the Controlled Substances Act of 1970 (P.L. 91-513).

PURPOSE: To document the surrender of controlled substances which have been forwarded by registrants to DEA for disposal.

ROUTINE USES: This form is required by Federal Regulations for the surrender of unwanted Controlled Substances. Disclosures of information from this system are made to the following categories of users for the purposes stated.

   A. Other Federal law enforcement and regulatory agencies for law enforcement and regulatory purposes.

   B. State and local law enforcement and regulatory agencies for law enforcement and regulatory purposes.

EFFECT: Failure to document the surrender of unwanted Controlled Substances may result in prosecution for violation of the Controlled Substances Act.

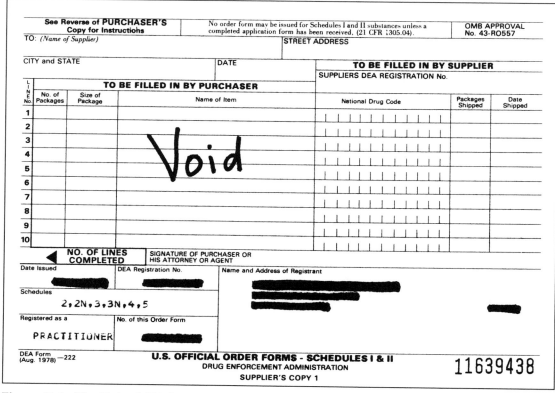

Figure 11.4 The Federal Triplicate Order Form DEA-222 for purchase of controlled substances on Schedule II.

encouraged to have their drug detail representative assist them in properly filling out the order forms. These people perform this task regularly and are generally familiar with the requirements. Forms that are completed incorrectly will be rejected, resulting in considerable shipment delays. Only a registered veterinarian or a person with a valid power of attorney may legally sign the order forms.

Federal regulations require that Copies 1 and 2 of the triplicate forms be submitted to the supplier. Copy 3 is retained by the registrant. The supplier retains Copy 1 and sends Copy 2 to the DEA.[14] Schedule II substances will be shipped only to the location printed on DEA Form 222. When these drug shipments arrive from the distributor, the date of receipt and the number of containers of each drug received should be recorded on Copy 3 of the order form that was originally retained by the registrant. The packing slip invoice and the Copy 3 forms then are stored with other inventory forms in a

manner described under the section on record keeping.

Veterinarians may cancel part or all of an order that appears on the order form by notifying the supplier in writing of the cancellation. The supplier or sales representative indicates the cancellation by drawing a line through the cancelled items and printing "cancelled" in the space provided for the number of items shipped.[15]

Powers of Attorney to Order Controlled Drugs

Another problem that can arise concerns ordering controlled substances when the principal registered veterinarian is away from the business. Section 1305.07 provides for the creation of a power of attorney to deal with this situation. Once this document has been executed, veterinarians who are agents of the principal veterinarian may order controlled substances under the registration of the principal. Since the power of attorney does not apply to prescribing, agents must still have their own DEA registration number at some location in order to perform this service. In addition, even with a power of attorney, the people ordering must be agents or employees of the registrant in order to administer or dispense controlled drugs.

The forms to execute a power of attorney are available from the regional offices of the DEA. Although the use of this document may be restricted to a specific time frame, it can be written in such a way as to provide for an extended period. The only caution is that the registrants are still the responsible parties. As such, they must carefully supervise the record keeping and the use of their inventory of controlled drugs.

Record Keeping

It is in the area of incomplete record keeping where veterinarians can easily find themselves at odds with the law. An example of why one never wants to be under investigation for a controlled drug violation can be found in an article published several years ago in the *California Veterinarian*.[16]

This article cites the case of a Northern California veterinarian who used Demerol as his routine preanesthetic. When a local pharmacist reported that the practitioner was ordering too much Demerol for the average veterinarian, an investigation ensued. The veterinarian was asked to show with proper records where all of the Demerol he had purchased in the past two years had been used. He had not maintained a running log of the hospital's usage and so was required to go through each individual patient's medical record to try to account for this controlled drug. After two months' effort, his records still showed that the hospital was 500 cc short. Several months later he was arrested, handcuffed, escorted to an awaiting police car, fingerprinted, photographed, and jailed! He was able to post bail, and ultimately the case was dismissed, but not without significant embarrassment, emotional distress, and legal fees.

The Rationale for Records

The basic rationale for maintaining records regarding drugs received from suppliers and drugs dispensed to patients is to complete the DEA's "closed system" for monitoring possibilities of diversion into illicit channels. With the strict record keeping requirements established by the DEA, controlled substances can be accounted for from the time raw materials are imported or manufactured through distribution to suppliers and practitioners and ultimately to the patient receiving the drug. Since most veterinary practitioners do not administer or dispense large quantities of controlled substances, their activities generally are not under close governmental scrutiny.

Nevertheless, any medical facility is a good target for a drug addict needing cash or drugs. If a theft or break-in occurs, a police investigation is likely to follow. Any kind of police investigation, state board inspection, or American Animal Hospital Association accreditation inspection will require that the registered practitioner account for all of the controlled substances as required by state or federal laws. The forms in Figures 11.5 and 11.6 are examples of records used to keep track of controlled drugs. The format in Figure 11.5 allows for running totals of drugs to be maintained but requires a separate record for each drug. The form in Figure 11.6 minimizes the numbers of separate record forms but makes it more difficult to produce running totals of controlled drug inventories.

Familiarity with and adherence to the regulations formulated by the DEA, therefore, is worth the effort.

Record Keeping Rules

The regulations covering record keeping for controlled substances are sometimes difficult to interpret and fully understand. Several

NARCOTICS LOG
VETERINARY CONTROLLED DRUG DISPOSITION RECORD

NAME OF DRUG ————————— FORM ——— STRENGTH ———— SIZE ——

Date	Time	Full Name and Address of Animal's Owner	Species of Animal	Signature of Person Using	Initial Amount	Amount Used	Balance

Figure 11.5   One type of form for monitoring use of controlled drugs.

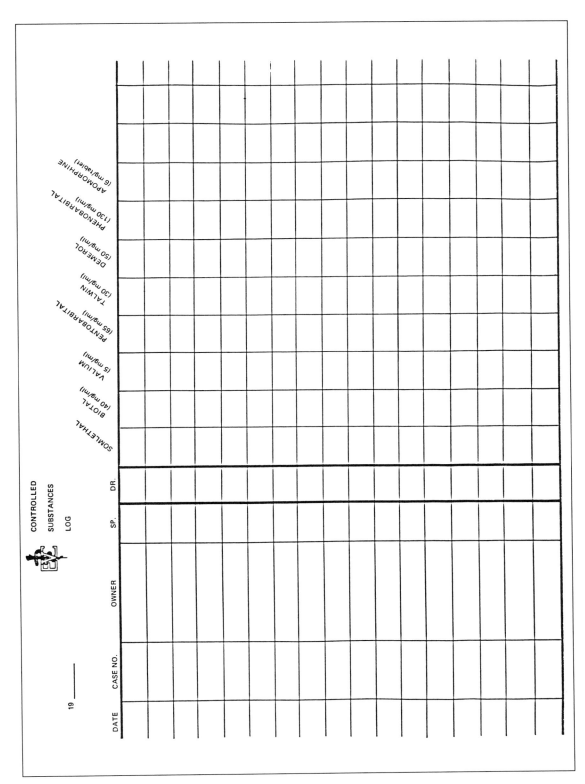

Figure 11.6 Another type of log sheet for monitoring controlled drug use.

sections in the Code of Federal Regulations pertain to record keeping.

In general, any practitioner who regularly dispenses or administers controlled substances and charges a fee to patients, either separately or along with charges for other professional services, must keep records on each transaction.[17] Veterinary practitioners are not, however, required to keep any records pertaining to prescriptions rendered. The pharmacies ultimately filling these prescriptions are the parties responsible for maintaining records of the transactions.

Although some practitioners have routinely kept track of their controlled drugs only on the patient's medical record, this does not meet DEA requirements. Records of transactions involving Schedule II drugs, particularly, must be stored separately from other files, i.e., separate from the medical record.[18] The rules are slightly different with regard to Schedule III, IV, and V drugs, though the end result may be the same. Inventories and records of drugs in these categories shall be maintained either separately from all other records of the registrant or in such form that the information required is readily retrievable from the ordinary business records of the registrant.[19]

Theoretically, the required information associated with the administration or dispensing of Schedule III, IV, and V drugs can be obtained from the medical record of the individual patient. It is not likely, though, that this information can be readily retrieved, which is what is required by the law. The practical result, therefore, is that records indicating the usage of controlled drugs must be maintained separate from the medical record. Such a rule makes the dispensing of common drugs like Lomotil, Hycodan, and Valium more trouble than it is worth for most veterinarians. Consequently, many practitioners elect to maintain minimal stocks of controlled substances, while others stock them but are consistently at risk because of inadequate record keeping.

Lending Controlled Drugs to Other Practitioners

It is not uncommon for practitioners to run out of essential controlled substances and want to borrow them from a neighboring clinic. Frequently, this loan is granted and the drugs are later returned. This activity is in violation of federal law.

There is, however, a way to accomplish the transaction legally. Section 1304.03(b) of the Code of Federal Regulations says that registered practitioners must keep records of controlled substances that are dispensed other than by prescribing or administering. Nowhere does the code say that an individual practitioner cannot simply deliver or transfer a controlled drug to another registrant, as long as records are kept of the transaction.

Thus, for Schedule III, IV, and V drugs, a practitioner can simply transfer a quantity of drugs to another registrant and obtain a receipt signed by the registered veterinarian who received the drug. This invoice is then stored with the other inventory records.

Veterinarians who receive the controlled substance in this manner should keep copies of the receipts showing that the drug was received from another veterinarian instead of the usual supplier. Drugs can be returned to the veterinarian from whom they were borrowed as long as the return is carried out with these same record keeping methods.

If the transfer involves Schedule II drugs, the same type of record keeping should be performed except that a DEA order form 222(c) also must be filled out. Copy 3 stays with the veterinarian receiving the drug, Copy 1 is retained by the registered practitioner supplying the drug to the neighboring registrant, and Copy 2 is sent to the DEA.

As can be seen from this transferring method, the DEA does not want to make transfers illegal or impossible, but they need a proper accounting so that the flow of these drugs can be traced.

Other Systems for Record Retrieval

Computer technology is currently available from some of the veterinary computer system vendors that enables practitioners to track all patients receiving controlled drugs. This superb computer-age by-product can eliminate the need for maintaining separate inventory accounts of controlled drugs within the veterinary pharmacy itself. Any such computer system must provide on-line retrieval via CRT display or hard-copy printout of the name, strength, dosage form, and quantity of controlled substance.[20]

Practitioners with computers may find that their systems can adequately record and retrieve information about drugs that have been dispensed so that a separate inventory tracking system for these drugs is unnecessary. Without specifically inputting information regarding controlled substances administered to patients in the hospital, though, records of these drug transactions would still have to be maintained manually. If, however, each dose of a controlled substance administered to a hospitalized patient were entered on the computer medical record for that patient, then all controlled drug records could be maintained and retrieved by computer.

Inventory of Controlled Substances

New Businesses or Change of Registrant

Under the CSA, when veterinarians start a new business or acquire an existing one, an initial inventory of controlled substances must be taken. DEA regulations require that this be done as of the date practitioners first engage in dispensing or administering controlled substances.[21]

State law requirements are frequently more stringent and worth following. They often state that an inventory must be taken coincidental with any change of business ownership or registration, not on the first date a controlled drug is used.[22] Inventories taken at this time assure practitioners who are assuming responsibility that an accurate accounting exists. When such transfers occur, practitioners transferring responsibility should prepare an invoice of all drugs being delivered as described earlier in this chapter. The invoice should be dated and signed by both the transferor and the recipient and should indicate whether it was taken at the beginning or close of the business day.

An exact count of all Schedule II substances is required.[23] Estimated counts for substances in Schedules III, IV, and V are permitted unless the container holds more than 1000 tablets or capsules, in which case an exact count is needed. Records showing all receipts of controlled drugs from distributors must be maintained along with these inventory records.

Biennial Inventories

Every two years following the initial inventory date, the registrant must take a new inventory of all controlled substances on hand.[24] The records of these inventories are to be kept with other DEA records at the registrant's business location and retained for two years. Again, variations from federal to state regulations and from state to state may exist. Some states, like California, require that inventories be retained for three years. Schedule II inventory records must be stored separately from other files. Schedules III, IV, and V inventory sheets may be stored separately from other files or so that they are readily retrievable from the practitioner's other business and professional records.

Security of Stored Controlled Drugs

The Securely Locked, Substantially Constructed Cabinet Rule

In general, practitioners who store controlled drugs and substances within their offices, hospitals, or clinics must keep these drugs in securely locked, substantially constructed cabinets or safes.[25] Drug stocks should be kept to a minimum. If any substantial quantity of controlled substances is stored at the facility, additional security measures should be taken beyond those ordinarily required, e.g., an alarm system. Access to the storage area should be restricted to an absolute minimum number of employees.

A commonly discussed exception in the regulations that does not apply to veterinary practitioners but which has continually caused confusion says,

> (b) Controlled substances listed in Schedules II, III, IV, and V shall be stored in a securely locked, substantially constructed cabinet. However, pharmacies and institutional practitioners...may disperse such substances throughout the stock of noncontrolled substances in such a manner as to obstruct the theft or diversion of the controlled substances.[25]

Although veterinary facilities usually have pharmacies, individually registered veterinarians do not fit the definition of either a pharmacy or an institutional practitioner. Therefore, controlled drugs in veterinary facilities may not be dispersed legally throughout the stock of noncontrolled substances but must be kept in locked cabinets.

Strict enforcement of this regulation would place all of the controlled drugs at one site within the hospital. The result of this policy is that if thieves gained access to the site, the drugs would be more vulnerable to theft than

if they were dispersed among the noncontrolled drugs. Because of this and general interpretations of § 1301.75, the DEA has said that veterinary practitioners may disperse their stocks of controlled drugs throughout the noncontrolled drugs in such a manner as to obstruct a theft provided that those cabinets can be locked.

This means that practitioners may store controlled substances in Schedules II through V in any substantially constructed, securely locked cabinet. The drugs do not have to be placed in a safe or vault. In fact, they can be stored with the antibiotics, hormones, steroids, etc., as long as clients and nonstaff people do not have ready access to them. It is probably worth some extra effort, however, to place the Schedule II drugs in a relatively inaccessible and more secure location than the other controlled substances. A policy like this formalizes the controlled nature of these drugs and makes their access more difficult for all hospital personnel.

Security for Potent Drugs Used on Exotic and Wild Animals

The most rigidly controlled drugs in veterinary medicine are etorphine hydrochloride (M-99) and its antagonist diprenorphine (M 50-50). These compounds are delivered from dart guns for restraining and immobilizing wild animals. The use of these drugs is restricted to veterinarians engaged in zoo and exotic animal practice, wildlife management programs, and/or research. Suppliers may not fill orders for these drugs unless the administrator of the DEA has specifically authorized the registered veterinarian to handle the substances.[26]

Due to the extreme potency of etorphine hydrochloride, special security and special record keeping provisions are required for its use.[27] Etorphine hydrochloride and diprenorphine may be shipped only to the purchaser at the location printed by the DEA and even then only under secure conditions using substantial packaging material with no markings on the outside that would indicate the content. Storage must be in a United States Government Class V security container, i.e., a safe or vault.

Thefts or Losses of Controlled Drugs

Registrants are required to notify the Regional Office of the DEA of the theft or significant loss of any controlled substances upon discovery of such loss or theft.[28] DEA Form 106 (Figure 11.7) is to be filled out at the time such notification takes place.

If a burglary, theft, or robbery involves controlled drugs, the local police department also should be notified. Because of the possibility of such events and subsequent police investigations, practitioners cannot afford to take risks with regard to the record keeping of controlled drugs. Since the record keeping associated with the use of controlled substances is so involved and the drugs themselves a temptation for staff people and thieves, many practitioners elect to keep the variety and volume of controlled drugs to an absolute minimum.

In addition to any thefts, breakages resulting in losses of controlled drugs also must be reported. Breakage of a partial bottle of Demerol, for example, with "a significant loss of controlled substances" would merit filing a notice with the DEA.[29] Since the term *significant* is not defined, the wisest course is to file a Form 106 (Figure 11.7) with the DEA's divisional office whenever any quantity of controlled drug is lost or stolen. If this is done at the time such loss occurs, it will save an inordinate amount of time and energy later explaining what happened to that quantity of drug.

Prescriptions

Prescriptions for controlled substances may be issued only by veterinarians who are prop-

erly licensed by the state and registered with the DEA. All prescriptions must be dated and signed on the date the prescription was issued.

Prescriptions for Schedule II drugs must be written and must bear the full name and address of the patient, plus the name, address, and registration number of the practitioner. These prescriptions shall be typed or written in ink or indelible pencil and must be manually signed by the practitioner.[30] Refilling of Schedule II prescriptions is prohibited.[31]

Approximately 35% of all licensed medical practitioners in the United States (veterinarians, dentists, physicians, etc.) are practicing in states that currently require multiple-copy prescriptions for any Schedule II substances. California, Texas, Illinois, and New York are included among these states. Since veterinarians do not commonly write prescriptions for Schedule II drugs, this does not pose any major problems. The trend, however, is in the direction of more states requiring multiple-copy prescriptions of controlled substances.

Prescription orders for substances in Schedules III, IV, and V may be provided in writing or they may be issued to pharmacists orally.[32] These prescriptions may be refilled up to five times within six months after the date of issue. Since pharmacists are required to record DEA numbers when receiving orders for controlled drugs by phone, veterinarians are advised to place that number on the written prescription or have their DEA numbers readily available whenever phoning prescriptions to pharmacists.

Schemes and Shams

Veterinary clients have been known to seek access to controlled drugs by requesting that their veterinarians provide them with prescriptions of sleeping pills, tranquilizers, diet pills, or sedatives for their pets. When clients continually request refills in shorter time periods than originally prescribed, veterinarians should become suspicious that maybe the client, not the animal, is taking the drug.

Some states have laws that prohibit anyone from providing controlled substances under

---

U.S. DEPARTMENT OF JUSTICE / DRUG ENFORCEMENT ADMINISTRATION

REPORT OF THEFT OR LOSS OF CONTROLLED SUBSTANCES

OMB APPROVAL
No. 43 - RO464

Federal Regulations require registrants to submit a detailed report of any theft or loss of Controlled Substances to the Drug Enforcement Administration.
Complete this form in triplicate. Forward the original and duplicate copies to the nearest DEA Regional Office. Retain the triplicate copy for your records.

1. NAME AND ADDRESS OF REGISTRANT (Include ZIP Code)

ZIP Code

2. PRINCIPAL BUSINESS OF REGISTRANT *(Check one)*
1 ☐ Pharmacy   3 ☐ Manufacturer/Distributor
2 ☐ Practitioner   4 ☐ Other _____

3. DEA REGISTRATION NUMBER
2 ltr. prefix   7 digit suffix

4. COUNTY IN WHICH REGISTRANT IS LOCATED

5. DATE OF THEFT OR LOSS

6. NUMBER OF THEFTS OR LOSSES REGISTRANT EXPERIENCED IN LAST 12 MONTHS

7. WAS THEFT OR LOSS REPORTED TO POLICE   ☐ YES   ☐ NO

8. NAME AND ADDRESS OF POLICE DEPARTMENT

9. TYPE OF THEFT OR LOSS (Check one)
1 ☐ Night Break-In (complete Item 10 below)
2 ☐ Armed Robbery (complete Item 11 below)
3 ☐ Employee Theft
4 ☐ Customer Pilferage
5 ☐ Other (specify) _____
6 ☐ Lost in Transit (complete Item 12 below)

10. IF NIGHT BREAK-IN, WHAT WAS THE POINT OF ENTRY?

11. IF ARMED ROBBERY, WAS ANYONE INJURED?   ☐ NO   ☐ YES (If Yes, HOW?)

12. IF LOST IN TRANSIT, COMPLETE THE FOLLOWING:

A. Name of Common Carrier	B. Name of Consignee	C. Consignee's DEA Registration Number

13. IF OFFICIAL CONTROLLED SUBSTANCES ORDER FORMS WERE STOLEN, GIVE NUMBERS.

14. WHAT IDENTIFYING MARKS, SYMBOLS OR PRICE CODES WERE ON THE LABELS OF THESE CONTAINERS? (Insert your pricing codes)

15.a. IF CASH WAS TAKEN, WHAT AMOUNT?

15b. IF MERCHANDISE WAS TAKEN, VALUE?

16. WHAT SECURITY MEASURES HAVE BEEN TAKEN TO PREVENT FUTURE THEFTS OR LOSSES?

PRIVACY ACT INFORMATION

AUTHORITY: Section 301 of the Controlled Substances Act of 1970 (PL 91-513)

PURPOSE: Report theft or loss of Controlled Substances

ROUTINE USES: The Controlled Substances Act Registration Records produces special reports as required for statistical analytical purposes. Disclosures of information from this system are made to the following categories of users for the purposes stated:

A. Other Federal law enforcement and regulatory agencies for law enforcement and regulatory purposes

B. State and local law enforcement and regulatory agencies for law enforcement and regulatory purposes

C. Persons registered under the Controlled Substances Act (Public Law 91-513) for the purpose of verifying the registration of customers and practitioners

EFFECT: Failure to report theft or loss of controlled substances may result in penalties under Section 402 and 403 of the Controlled Substances Act.

DEA Form — **106** (Apr. 1976)   Previous edition dated 9/75 is Obsolete.

Figure 11.7   The DEA Form 106 to report the theft or loss of any significant amount of controlled substance, sides 1 and 2.

LIST OF CONTROLLED SUBSTANCES LOST

NAME OF SUBSTANCE OR PREPARATION (Include Manufacturer)	NAME OF CONTROLLED SUBSTANCE IN PREP.	DOSAGE FORM AND STRENGTH	QUANTITY	TOTAL NET WT. (Gms.) OF CONTROLLED INGREDIENT
EX: EMPIRIN ++ 3	CODEINE	½ GR TAB.	100	3,200
1.				
2.				
3.				
4.				
5.				
6.				
7.				
8.				
9.				
10.				
11.				
12.				
13.				
14.				
15.				
16.				
17.				
18.				
19.				
20.				
21.				
22.				
23.				
24.				
25.				
26.				
27.				
28.				
29.				
30.				
31.				
32.				
33.				
34.				
35.				
36.				
37.				

FOR DEA REGIONAL USE ONLY	GRAMS
AMPHETAMINES	
BARBITURATES	
COCAINE	
CODEINE	
DIHYDROCODEINONE	
DILAUDID	
METHADONE	
METHAMPHETAMINE	
MORPHINE	
NUMORPHAN	
OPIUM	
OXYCODONE	
PETHIDINE	
OTHERS (List)	

I certify that the foregoing information is correct to the best of my knowledge and belief.

Signature _____

Title _____

Date _____

GPO : 1976 O - 204-310

certain circumstances. The California Health and Safety Code § 11154 says the following:

> (a) Except in the regular practice of his or her profession, no person shall knowingly prescribe, administer, dispense, or furnish a controlled substance to or for any person or animal which is not under his or her treatment for a pathology or condition other than addiction to a controlled substance,...(b) No person shall knowingly solicit, direct, induce and or encourage a practitioner authorized to write a prescription to unlawfully prescribe, administer, dispense, or furnish a controlled substance.

Here again is the requirement of a veterinarian-client-patient relationship that has recently gained much exposure under new FDA regulatory efforts.

An example where a veterinarian might unknowingly be providing controlled drugs to an improper recipient can be found in the following scam, reported in the Southern California Veterinary Medical Association's monthly newsletter *Pulse:*

> Your receptionist receives a phone call from someone who identifies himself as a technician from Dr. X's office (a doctor whose practice is in the same general vicinity as yours). The caller states that Dr. X has just run out of phenobarbital and would like to borrow a bottle until his shipment arrives. Being the good neighboring veterinarian, you help out.[33]

The article goes on to point out that a controlled substance has just been furnished to a person (and not an animal) who was not under your treatment. The penalty under a law like the California Code could be one year in prison or $20,000 or both. The DEA has indicated that even if state laws like this do not exist in every state, providing a controlled drug to someone outside of the veterinarian-client-patient relationship is a violation of federal law.

Chemically Impaired Veterinarian Programs

For many reasons, the veterinary profession has had increasing reports of members with chemical dependencies. In years past, alcohol was the primary culprit. More recently, controlled substances are being abused also.

Since these drugs are readily available to veterinarians and veterinary staff members, there is always a potential for drug abuse problems. Good record keeping and frequent evaluations of the records by the registered veterinarian in a practice can help detect staff abuses. Once detected, the difficult job of dealing with the personnel involved must be faced. Employers can simply fire these employees, be more strict about security of the controlled drugs, or seek counseling to help those involved overcome their dependencies.

This approach may work for chemical-dependent staff employees. The drug-dependent practice owner or staff veterinarian, however, may also need help. Because of pressures brought to bear by state boards of examiners and association members, the American Veterinary Medical Association (AVMA) has developed the Model Program to Assist Chemically Impaired Veterinarians, Veterinary Students, Animal Health Technicians, and Their Families. A copy of this program can be found in the reference section of any current *AVMA Directory.*[34]

The problems of chemical dependency are very real, resulting in distraught families, shattered interpersonal relations, financial crises, suicides, and the practice of inferior veterinary medicine—endangering lives of animal patients. Through efforts of the AVMA and with the cooperation of state veterinary associations, 37 states now have their own impaired-veterinarian programs.[35] Veterinarians needing personal assistance or help for employed personnel are urged to contact the appropriate state veterinary medical associations or review the list of state committees provided in the April 1, 1987 *Journal of the AVMA.*

Summary

Tremendous opportunities for legal violations exist within the menagerie of laws and regulations directing the use of controlled drugs. Good record keeping and strict security are required when practitioners plan to use these drugs, or they should not be used at all. Practitioners who have further questions about controlled drugs are encouraged to write to the DEA in Washington, D.C. for additional information. Two booklets, *The Physician's Manual: An Information Outline of the Controlled Substances Act of 1970* and *A Pharmacist's Manual* are available from the United States Department of Justice, DEA, Washington, D.C. 20537. For specific questions not answered anywhere else, veterinarians should contact the DEA Divisional Office serving their locale listing in Appendix L.

References

1. 21 USC 841 and 842.
2. Virginia Board of Veterinary Medicine Regulations § 4.2 (4) (e) and (f).
3. 21 CFR 1301.21.
4. 1 CFR 1304.02.
5. 21 CFR 1301.24.
6. *A Practitioner's Guide to Controlled Substance Regulations.* Sacramento, CA, Bureau of Narcotic Enforcement, 1984.
7. Virginia Board of Veterinary Medicine Regulations § 1.8.A.2.
8. Virginia Drug Control Act § 54-524.47:2.(c) (1); § 54-524.66—A veterinarian...may administer drugs, and he may cause them to be administered by an assistant or orderly under his direction and supervision.
9. U.S. Dept of Justice, DEA, PO Box 28083, Central Station, Washington, DC 20005; 202-254-8255.
10. DEA, Registration Section, 1405 "I" St, NW, Washington, DC 20537.
11. 21 CFR 1301.62.
12. 21 CFR 1305.14.
13. 21 CFR 1305.12.
14. 21 CFR 1305.05, 1305.06, 1305.09.
15. 21 CFR 1305.15.
16. Collinson RL: AAHA tip of the month. *Calif Vet* (Nov):36, 1980.
17. 21 CFR 1304.03.
18. 21 CFR 1304.04(f)(1)(g).
19. 21 CFR 1304.04(f)(2).
20. 21 CFR 1306.22(b).
21. 21 CFR 1304.12.
22. Virginia Board of Veterinary Medical Regulations § 4.1 (B)(1)(d).
23. 21 CFR 1304.17.
24. 21 CFR 1304.13.
25. 21 CFR 1301.75.
26. 21 CFR 1305.16 (b).
27. 21 CFR 1301.75(d), 1301.74(g); 21 CFR 1305.16(b)(1).
28. 21 CFR 1301.76.
29. 21 CFR 1301.76(b).
30. 21 CFR 1306.05(a).
31. 21 CFR 1306.11.
32. 21 CFR 1306.21.
33. Roberts JF: Caution regarding disbursing of controlled substances. *Pulse* (monthly journal of Southern California VMA Pico Rivera, CA) (Aug): 23, 1983.
34. 1987 *AVMA Directory.* Schaumburg, IL, American Veterinary Medical Assoc, 1987, p 479.
35. News from the AVMA. State committees wage war against substance abuse. *JAVMA* 190:842, 1987.

CHAPTER 12

The Veterinarian as an Expert Witness

It is not uncommon for veterinarians to be called upon at some time during their careers to participate in the American legal system. Occasionally this is as the defendant in a lawsuit. At other times it is to provide expert witness testimony regarding the medical facts associated with the care of or injury to an animal that is the subject of someone else's lawsuit. Whatever the case, any time that veterinarians are asked to render medical opinions concerning animals, they must be prepared to face the judicial process.

Defining an Expert

Black's Law Dictionary defines an expert witness as "One who by reason of education or specialized experience possesses superior knowledge respecting a subject about which persons having no particular training are incapable of forming an accurate opinion or deducing correct opinions." With this in mind, veterinarians can be classified as experts with regard to animal medical care, restraint, production, animal welfare, or any other subject whereupon four or more years of advanced veterinary education plus specialized experience set them apart from the average person.

The Duty

Veterinarians can act as expert witnesses voluntarily when their involvement is requested by legal counsel for a plaintiff or defendant, or on a compulsory basis, i.e., via the subpoena process. Generally, veterinarians are subpoenaed only if they were personally involved with the care of or diagnostic efforts directly related to a case. The court can require them to testify in such situations, because their testimony may be crucial to the outcome. Given such a court requirement, a request for a change in the court appearance time may be granted, but a refusal to appear at all can result in being found in contempt of court. In such a case, one is subject to arrest, the posting of bond, a fine or, in some cases, imprisonment.

In the voluntary situation, a practitioner may elect not to testify as an expert witness. Such reasons as a conflict of interest or insufficient expertise regarding the specific case would be acceptable. Since testimony by expert witnesses is usually crucial to the outcome of cases involving care for animals, it is the author's opinion that members of the veterinary profession have a moral, professional, and ethical duty to provide expert consultations or testimony whenever possible if they are called upon to do so.

Type of Expert

There generally are two types of participation by experts. The first involves testimony based upon the expert's personal involvement. An example is the pathologist who acquires knowledge of the case by performing a necropsy on a dog that died from a suspected poisoning by a neighborhood crank. Another example of a practitioner's personal involvement could arise where a malnourished and mistreated animal was presented to the veterinarian by a humane officer. Because of the veterinarian's assessment of the case coupled with information gathered during the humane officer's investigation, charges of cruelty to animals are filed against the owner. When the veterinarian testifies regarding the findings on this case, he or she will be speaking as a witness who saw the animal and as an expert witness who is rendering an opinion about evidence of owner cruelty towards the animal.

The second type of participation by veterinarians as experts is where no personal knowledge of the case is present. Instead, hypothetical questions are presented containing a series of facts that are assumed to have been proven. (They are not proven until the jury decides the case.) In those situations, the facts outline the case and will have been prepared by whichever legal counsel called the expert to testify. The expert's knowledge allows an opinion to be given regarding the care rendered in the particular case. Experts must be prepared to explain and defend their opinions just as they

would if their testimony were derived from personal observations. An example would be the rendering of an opinion regarding whether the preanesthetic workup and anesthetic protocol employed in a case were within the *standard of care* for similar patients under the same or similar circumstances.

The Constitution of Evidence

The *Common Law* system of justice depends upon the use of only the most reliable sources of information. Legal counsel for both the plaintiff and the defendant try to introduce into the judicial process all relevant evidence that helps prove their contentions in the case. Items that can serve as evidence include such things as personal observations, writings, radiographs, material objects, and anything that helps prove the existence or nonexistence of a fact.

Evidence includes information about events that occurred (acts of commission) as well as events that did not or may not have occurred (acts of omission). In malpractice cases (cases involving negligence in the practice of medicine), medical records frequently are the only or the most credible evidence of what did or did not happen in a case. Because of this, medical records generally are a critical ingredient in the commentary by the expert witness. In straight negligence cases, however, records may not be a factor at all. Such cases might include injuries to clients while they were on a veterinarian's property, injuries to owners who were restraining their own animals, the escape of an animal under veterinary care, or the improper restraint of an animal by a veterinarian. The outcome then could depend entirely upon the expert's opinion as to whether the defendant's actions were within the standard of care for operating a veterinary practice.

Types of Evidence

The primary types of evidence are direct and hearsay evidence. Direct evidence is that information provided by persons who witnessed an occurrence with their own ears, eyes, noses, and other senses. Rules of evidence recognize this as the best source of information, because people who are directly involved can be questioned and cross-examined about their own perceptions before the judge or jury.

The judicial system has recognized that trials often occur long after the event they concern. A big risk associated with this, of course, is the witnesses' loss of memory over that time. To overcome this, the rules of evidence permit writings to be introduced that will help to refresh a witness's memory as long as those writings are relevant and authenticated.[1] This is one of two ways that a medical record can be introduced into the legal process. The other possible method for introducing the medical record will be discussed later, under the Hearsay Rule.

The medical records may have been created by the experts at the time of their personal observations or by another person, e.g., the defendant, and be introduced for the expert's analysis and comments. The quality and quantity of medical care as indicated by the record are subjects for review and critique. Another topic for question, though, is the believability of the medical record. Records that are too perfect can create doubts about whether they originated at the time the care was provided or were recreated for the purposes of the legal action. Records that are too succinct or sloppy may indicate a general lack of quality in the medical care provided.

It must always be kept in mind that trials are games of proof as well as truth. It is quite likely that the truth will convince a jury about the occurrence or nonoccurrence of a given fact. Without adequate proof, however, i.e., in the form of written medical records, it may be impossible to convince anyone that what was remembered actually did take place.

The verbiage of a medical record does not guarantee that what was written did in fact occur, however. Records can provide either side of a case with a presumption that if something was supposedly said or done and was written on a credible medical record, there is a higher likelihood that it actually was done than if no written record of that fact exists.

The second type of evidence is hearsay evidence. This is evidence of a statement that was made other than by a witness testifying at the hearing and that is offered to prove the truth of the matter.[2] A medical record created by a veterinarian who is not testifying at the trial is an example of hearsay evidence.

Hearsay evidence generally is inadmissible because the person who made the statement is not present and cannot be cross-examined. Rigid enforcement of this rule frequently would prevent very important information from surfacing, however, so courts and legislatures have defined certain exceptions that allow some hearsay evidence to be admitted. The following are three of fourteen common exceptions to the Hearsay Rule:

1. Spontaneous statements.[3] Spontaneous statements are those that were made spontaneously while the declarant was under the stress of excitement.

2. Declaration of a person who is dying.[4] These are statements made by dying people respecting the cause of and circumstances of their death, if the statements were made under a sense of immediate impending death. Such declarations are assumed to be reliable statements since there is minimal reason for such a person to lie.

3. The business records exception.[5] This exception allows another avenue for the introduction of the medical record even if the veterinarian who made the entry is not at the trial. It should be noted here that computer-generated records can also be introduced in trial under this rule. Thus, records need not be hand written to be admissible evidence (See Chapter 14, Medical Records and Their Legal Implications). For this exception to apply, however, several criteria must be met:

   a. the writing must have been made in the usual course of business,

   b. it must have been made at or near the time of the event in question,

   c. the custodian of the records or someone who can authenticate the record must testify as to the identity of the entry on the record, and

   d. the source of information and method and time of preparation must have been such as to indicate its trustworthiness.

Because of the business records exemption, it is quite possible that experts will be asked to comment on evidence with which they have no personal involvement (e.g., records made by others). In such cases, advance preparation and careful review of any such documents are essential.

Preparation

Veterinarians who are contemplating serving as expert witnesses should meet with the involved attorneys before an agreement to participate is formalized. This allows them to fully evaluate their ability to work with the people on the case before committing themselves.

Legal counsel often provides a biased summary of the facts surrounding the case during the recruitment of an expert. In truth, the case may not be as clear-cut as it first appears. The personal meeting with counsel is a time for the expert to ask questions and determine that the case truly has merit. Since the veterinary community is a remarkably small one and often the most important asset veterinarians have is their reputation, it is important to be certain that the case is meritorious. It is unwise to allow monetary remuneration or ego flattery to affect one's decision whether to testify.

After agreeing to participate, the next step in the legal process is the deposition stage of pretrial discovery. Experts are required to answer a myriad of questions about themselves and the case at this time. All questions and answers are recorded by a court reporter in a written transcript, so answers must be carefully considered.

Veterinarians will usually find that attorneys know little about veterinary medicine or cases involving animals. Consequently, expert witnesses often must help educate counsel regarding the facts and issues crucial to the medical aspects of the case. To ensure that all important data will be admitted into evidence, it is valuable for experts to submit a list of questions they want to be asked prior to the presentation of any testimony. This assures that all the relevant opinions and thoughts

provided by the expert are heard, and that the testimony is presented in the correct chronological sequence for optimal jury comprehension.

If the case actually goes to trial, the experts must consider closely what they plan to say to the jury and how they will say it. The jury usually is comprised of people with an assortment of educational backgrounds, so it must be assumed that the jurors will have minimal knowledge about animal care and veterinary issues relating to the litigation. Also, an expert should assume that the jury will be ignorant of complex medical terminology. Because of this, any testimony should be presented as though one is teaching a class to laymen. Pictures drawn on blackboards, photographs, videotapes, and slides are useful teaching aids.

If the case is rather complex, and many are, experts should encourage counsel to hold a rehearsal prior to the appearance in court. During such a session, attorneys should ask all questions that can arise on cross-examination as well as during the direct exam. This can increase the cost of proceeding with the case, but it greatly enhances the expert's chances of performing well when testifying.

Usually the opposing side will also have experts testifying. If this is the case, one can offer to assist counsel in the creation of questions or at least in reviewing the line of questions to be asked of those witnesses. Since many legal cases are won or lost based primarily upon the testimony of the experts, the side with the best experts and pretrial preparation generally wins.

Once veterinarians have agreed to become involved in a case, it behooves them to consult with colleagues to broaden their knowledge and solidify their stance regarding the correctness or incorrectness of the opposing party's actions. In conferring with colleagues, however, the names of any parties involved in the litigation must not be divulged. This is important to avoid any opportunity for a libel or slander suit to arise due to pretrial comments made about the facts or parties involved in the case.

The better educated the experts are and the more sure they are that their colleagues agree with their feelings about the case, the more confident they will be on the witness stand. When asked how they arrived at their opinions, they can cite discussions with these partners, colleagues, and specialists to support their opinions. If, on the other hand, none of their sources agree with their assessment of the situation, they may elect to extricate themselves from the case.

Important Papers

Prospective experts should request a complete list of parties and participants in the litigation. This should include names of all witnesses and attorneys just in case an expert has serious trepidations about opposing or dealing with any particular person.

A veterinarian who serves as an expert witness should have copies of all pleadings in the case. The pleading is a statement by the plaintiff's counsel comprising the plaintiff's grounds for the lawsuit and a demand for compensation. One finds that the pleadings often dramatically overstate the plaintiff's case, but that is simply the way the system works.

In addition to copies of the pleadings, experts should request all relevant medical records; lab reports; radiographs; and depositions and letters from the plaintiff and/or defendant to a state board, peer review committee, or ethics committee. After reviewing these materials, the expert can develop a list of appropriate books, journals, and lecture notes for the attorney to peruse to become better educated about the issues of the case.

The Overly Modest Expert

Opposing counsel will almost always challenge the expert witness's degree of expertise. Thus, veterinarians who plan to participate as experts must be prepared to defend their abilities as experts at the deposition stage of the case as well as when they become witnesses at the trial. Experts must be able and willing to uphold their opinions throughout what is frequently a difficult cross-examination process, unless it is proved that the facts they relied upon were incorrect.

A potentially serious problem can occur when, because of excessive modesty, experts admit on the stand that they are not the *true expert* on the issue at stake. It should be kept in mind that a person can be an expert without being the foremost authority in the world. If during cross-examination experts are surprised by questions in this vein and suddenly claim not to be expert, their credibility with the jury can plummet. Thus, modesty is encouraged, but expert witnesses should not concede that because someone else is an authority, they are not also valid authorities.[6]

Taking Sides

Experts also should be apprised of a variety of problems that can occur regarding a position they take on a particular issue. Some people develop a stance on a specific drug, treatment, surgical procedure, etc. and never waver from it. Others may never have held a position on the issue being litigated. Still other people may have had an opinion and then have changed it.

Each of these types of witnesses must understand their vulnerability to effective cross-examination. The first of these three types may be vulnerable to accusations that they are extremely close-minded individuals unwilling to change positions. The second type can be subjected to criticism based upon the premise that the jury cannot really expect them to be expert if they have never thought about the issue being litigated. The third group is open for attack because they vacillate from one position to another. Any of these tactics may be used by opposing counsel during the questioning and are therefore worth consideration by prospective experts prior to presenting opinions about a case.

Payment for Testimony

In most legal proceedings experts must answer a line of questioning by an opposing attorney regarding the payment they are to receive for their testimony. The expert's response should be reviewed by counsel and the expert before trial. In some cases, the expert witness's rationale for testifying is based upon strong principles. In others, it is because the expert has a close friendship with one of the parties. Occasionally, experts like to testify in order to develop a name for themselves or because of a hefty expert witness fee. Any of these reasons can be attacked.

A close friendship promotes a willingness to provide testimony without compensation, which can provoke a charge of bias. An interest in developing one's reputation or an acknowledgement that one is being paid a fee for testifying allows the innuendo that the expert is simply willing to sell opinions on the open market.

According to one author on the topic of experts:[6]

> Experience shows that even if the expert has a close relationship with the litigant, and is willing to testify gratis, it is probably best for the litigant to pay the witness a fee anyhow so that the witness can properly say that he is testifying for a fee (or at least his travel and other related expenses) rather than gratuitously, as a favor just to help the litigant.

Clearly, juries expect expert witnesses to be paid for their time; thus, it is best that the expert charge a fee for the testimony. Although there is no established precedent for fees, it seems that veterinarians should receive at least the equivalent of what they earn hourly as teachers or working in their practices. With this in mind, a variation of from $40 to $200 per hour can be easily justified. Travel or telephone expense can be added to that figure. Travel time and time expended in the research of colleagues' opinions also is frequently in-

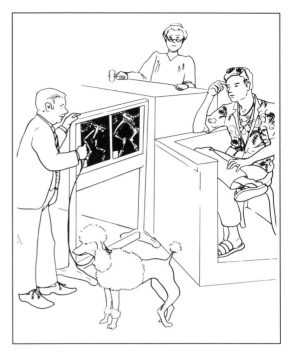

. . . and in your expert opinion, Dr. Surfer, was the repair of the femur of Mrs. K's poodle executed according to the standard of care in the state of California?"

volved. If monetary concerns are an obstacle, experts may elect to charge a lower hourly rate for services rendered preparing for and traveling to and from the hearings than the rate they charge for time spent testifying at the deposition or the trial.[7]

Lastly, despite strong support in legal circles for the contention that a fee of some kind should always be charged, there are times when gratis testimony is appropriate. One example might be a trial in which the allegation is one of cruelty to animals and the veterinarian is testifying on behalf of the animal world in general. Another is when a veterinarian simply wants to speak out on a particular principle at issue in the case and when no finding of bias could ever be established.

Qualifying as an Expert

A careful examination of the qualifications of any veterinarian testifying as an expert generally occurs at the deposition stage and/

or at the trial. In most cases, the attorney soliciting a practitioner's presence as an expert will request that a copy of a resume or a curriculum vitae be provided. Questions regarding continuing education seminars attended, advanced training in specific areas, knowledge of current books and journals, and expertise associated with cases like the one under litigation are asked. On cross-examination, the legal counsel for the opposing side may vigorously attempt to impeach the credibility or credentials of the expert. During this process, anything is fair game. Embarrassing information like a fact that the witness had the lowest academic record in his or her graduating class could be an item for impeachment. Experts also should be aware that if they have had any problems with a state board of examiners, peer review committee, ethics committee, or a bankruptcy proceeding, questions relating to these situations may be asked during cross-examination, too.

People who will serve as expert witnesses must go through a period of self-scrutiny prior to trial and be prepared to convince the jury of their credibility. Since some attorneys thoroughly enjoy impeaching any witness, especially expert witnesses, veterinarians with fragile egos or hot tempers might best refrain from subjecting themselves to the rigors of serving as an expert.

The Questioning Process

Once the preliminary questioning about an expert's qualifications is over, questions about the pending case are posed. The first line of questions concerns the disease, condition, or factual situation in general. With these questions, attorneys try to establish what constitutes the standard of care applicable to the diagnosis, treatment, or handling of cases like the one before the court.

Witnesses are expected and required to answer all questions put to them unless they do not know or cannot recall the answer. They may not ask questions and cannot initiate discussions about various aspects of the case. Generally, answers to questions should be as short as possible. Long answers give opposing counsel additional time to gather their thoughts and may contain seeds for other lines of questioning. Lengthy answers can be beneficial, however, when witnesses are trying to assist friendly counsel with comprehensive coverage of all the important aspects of the case. When employed with opposing counsel, however, lengthy answers may educate the examining attorneys and eventually allow them to hit upon some points useful to their side of the case.

After utilizing the expert to inform the jury or judge of the standard medical approach to the case, the next line of questions varies according to the side of the case for which the expert is testifying. If the expert witness is on the plaintiff's side, the questions are geared toward showing how the veterinarian's care failed to meet standards. If, on the other hand, the expert is on the defendant veterinarian's side, the questions will attempt to establish that the handling of the case was within the standard of care.

It is essential that the expert speak in terms that the judge or jury can understand when answering questions. Good attorneys will rephrase questions if it appears that the jury cannot understand the expert, but they cannot be expected to do this repeatedly. Only with practice can experts avoid this common pitfall.

Sometimes during the questioning process attorneys ask leading questions in an attempt to trap witnesses into saying something they did not want to say. Attorneys who have recruited those experts should object to such questioning. If counsel does not do so and the expert does not want to answer the question, it is best simply to ask that the question be repeated. Such a tactic, coupled with eye contact with the witness's "friendly" counsel, allows the attorney a second chance to object to the wording of the question.

Good experts are constantly alert for attempts by opposing counsel to entice them into making statements that will conflict with their prior testimony or impeach their credibility. It should be borne in mind that this is what attorneys are trained to do. It can be very damaging to a case and personally embarrassing as well when the expert gets caught in one of these situations, so experts must be constantly on guard.

Appearance in Court

A problem that faces many experts who are enthusiastic and active speakers is the requirement that they testify from a sitting position with the lower half of their body shielded from the jury by the witness box. This precludes them from the use of body language, but allows examining attorneys to move around freely. Some of the detriment produced by this unfairness can be overcome by proper planning that requires the expert to stand before the jury and draw diagrams on a magic marker board, blackboard, or overhead projector. The use of a slide presentation so that the expert can stand in front of a screen and point out various facts also enhances opportunities to use body language.

Witnesses should keep in mind the importance of the jury's impression of them during testimony. Juries react more favorably to a congenial and pleasant witness than they do to someone who is argumentative or pompous. Clothing worn should reflect a serious business approach to the case and the courtroom setting. A well-prepared, professional appearance on the witness stand, undivided attention, and direct answering of questions help the witness give a favorable impression.

One of the biggest faults of witnesses is their use of indefinite terminology. Phrases such as "I believe," "I suppose," "I guess," "maybe," and "that could be" will not convey confidence or knowledge. Furthermore, they will not be permitted by opposing counsel to stand, because these phrases do not indicate a definitness conveying the certainty of fact which the law requires. Some witnesses are prone to slip into such colloquial phrases as "to tell the truth...," or "honestly." This might convey to the jury that witnesses were not honest

during their other testimony or that they were not telling the truth on some prior occasion.

A common fault of witnesses is speaking too softly or letting their voices drop at the end of sentences. Jurors and the court are interested in everything expert witnesses have to say, and if they cannot hear everything, they may miss some statements crucial to the outcome of the case.[7]

Opinion Evidence and Hypothetical Questions

Routine witnesses at a trial or in the deposition stage of a trial cannot be asked any questions that require stating an opinion regarding the case; they may only testify as to what they believe are the facts. This rule changes once a witness qualifies as an expert. Because an expert is a person who has special skill or knowledge beyond that possessed by the average person, only expert witnesses are allowed to express opinions.

Questions requiring an opinion usually are posed in the hypothetical form. These questions normally are lengthy statements of the facts in the case created by counsel for whichever side the expert is testifying. Since only facts that are proven can be used in hypothetical questions, it is counsel's duty to actually prove that those facts are true.

If during pretrial preparation, an expert does not believe that all of the facts in the attorney's hypothetical can be verified, he or she should advise counsel to omit those facts that are in question. Also, counsel should be cautioning their experts that they are likely to be questioned on each of the assumed facts contained in the hypothetical. During such interrogation, the opposing counsel will very likely ask whether the expert's opinion would change if one or more of the facts were different or if additional facts were present. If such information would change their opinion, experts should concede this in order to maintain credibility. There is nothing wrong, however, with the expert taking issue with such facts and pointing out that they either do not exist or are irrelevant to the case at hand.[8]

Attributes of Good Expert Witnesses

The following are general pointers to bear in mind when testifying as an expert witness.

1. Good experts must know their subject. They should have done their homework and have reviewed all pertinent materials the day before the trial. They must understand the weaknesses of the case and be ready to present defenses in these areas.

2. Good experts are confident, cooperative, courteous, and calm. Nothing is worse than a cocky, overly confident, antagonistic expert witness. On grueling cross-examination it often is difficult maintaining composure and not becoming antagonistic. That is exactly the type of behavior that the opposing counsel tries to elicit, because it impeaches the credibility of the witness's testimony.

3. Some questions should be answered in a manner that leaves the expert with an out. Nothing in medicine is 100%. Answers should be phrased in a manner such as, "It appears from the facts presented here that this was not the best choice of treatment" rather than in absolute terms like, "There is no way that that medication should have been given."

4. Be honest. Experts should admit when they do not know an answer. They are not expected to know everything. Good experts do not overextend themselves to support their side of the case unless they are adamant that their contentions are true. Statements that are detrimental should be admitted, with explanations, if they are true. It is the duty of legal counsel to bring out the nature of the differences and show why the overall expert's testimony does not weaken the case, even if some of the assertions made were detrimental.

5. Experienced experts address the jury, not just the attorney, when answering questions, and do so using terminology that laymen can understand. Although it may be necessary to watch the attorney when the question is being asked, it is the jury that must comprehend the answer. Unless the jury's response to an answer is observed, experts will not know if the jury has understood.

6. When notes are needed for experts to refresh their memories, they should be brought to court and utilized. Opposing counsel will want to review the content of these notes, but reliance on memory alone, particularly under the stresses experienced during deposition or trial, is an invitation to trouble.

7. Beware of statements from books or journals. Attorneys often quote statements from books or journals as the ultimate authority on a subject. Witnesses have the right to inspect documents being quoted as sources of information, and this right should always be exercised. Review the material for date of publication and demand to see the entire article or book. Sometimes only a single page will have been photocopied because the complete article or book contains material detrimental to the examining attorney's opinion. Be especially cognizant of material in the text immediately prior to or after the section upon which one is being asked to comment.[9] Properly prepared experts should be aware of many of the current publications and be prepared to testify as to why they agree or disagree with them.

8. A commonly asked question is whether or not payment for expert testimony is being provided. Answers

should be addressed according to what was decided with counsel prior to the presentation of testimony.

9. Do not try to match wits with opposing counsel. Attorneys have been trained to interrogate witnesses and challenge their testimony. Since very few experts will win contests with opposing counsel it is best not to try. Nevertheless, experts should attempt to anticipate which direction each line of questioning is going in order to avoid being led astray and trapped.

10. Good experts do not serve on cases they do not believe in. If the facts of the case make it difficult to strongly support or oppose what appears to have transpired, it is best to decline serving as an expert.

11. If at all possible, experts should arrange in advance with friendly counsel for an opportunity to summarize their position, in the same manner as classroom lectures or journal articles. Comments should be brief and should reiterate the three or four major points the expert wants the jury to remember.

12. Above all, be an expert! The expert witness should act like, dress like, speak like, and behave as such.

References

1. California Evidence Code § 771.
2. California Evidence Code § 1200.
3. California Evidence Code § 1240.
4. California Evidence Code § 1242.
5. California Evidence Code § 1271.
6. Kraft MD: *Using Experts in Civil Cases*. New York, Practising Law Institute, 1982, pp 11, 23-51.
7. Liebenson HA: *You, The Expert Witness*. Mundelein, IL, Callaghan & Co, 1962.
8. On the direct examination of an expert witness in state court, the hypothetical question must be based upon facts in evidence. On cross-examination, however, a greater latitude may be permitted, and a fact germane to the issue, whether testified to or not, may in the sound discretion of the court be used for testing the expert. *Livingston* v *New Haven*, 125 Conn 123, 3 A.2d 836 (1939).

    On cross-examination, any fact may be assumed as hypothetical to test the skill, learning or accuracy of experts or to ascertain the reasonableness or expose the unreasonableness of their opinions. See *Cecio Bros Inc* v *Feldmann*, 161 Conn 265, 287 A.2d 374 (1971); *Floyd* v *Fruit Industries*, 144 Conn. 659, 136 A.2d 918, 63 A.L.R. 2d 1378 (1957).
9. Tobin T: Experiences as an expert witness: Educating people while under oath. *Equine Vet Sci* 6(3):129-133, 1986.

CHAPTER 13

Credit Management and Debt Collection

Most veterinary practitioners need more training or experience to guide them in the credit-management and debt-collection processes. Ideas are presented herein to assist veterinarians in performing these functions in a manner that will help avert trouble with the law or with their clients and improve their cash flow.

Since the maximum credit allowed in most veterinary practices is between twenty and several hundred dollars, this chapter focuses on debts in this range. Debts considerably higher than this commonly occur in equine and food animal practices and may require more planning as well as further advice from legal counsel. By limiting the scope of this material to debts that fall within the maximum limits established by the small claims court system, the information can be geared toward methods for dealing with client debt on one's own. Small claims court limits vary from $750 in some states to $4,000 in others, with the majority of states in the $1,500 range.

Most veterinarians expect that they will provide services for clients and that those clients will provide full payment upon the completion of the veterinary care. Unfortunately, it does not always work that way. When full payment is not made at the time of treatment, veterinarians have little choice other than to extend credit.

A well-planned system of credit extension provides for the collection of the vast majority of client debt. It also allows for the delivery of a higher quality and larger quantity of veterinary care because full payment at the time a patient is released is no longer a major factor limiting the provision of veterinary services. There will, nevertheless, always be some clients who fail to make payments as promised for a variety of reasons. Although veterinarians would often benefit from some legal assistance in collecting on these accounts, most practitioners attempt to resolve them on their own.

Debt Avoidance Techniques

There are a variety of techniques that clients try to avoid or postpone payment of a veterinary bill. Some clients may claim that they owe nothing because no contract for services ever existed.

Others will file a countersuit to the doctor's suit for payment, claiming that they suffered extraordinary damages because the veterinarian did not perform under the contract in a satisfactory manner. The more vigorously practitioners pursue collection of the debt, the more likely they are to witness aggressive avoidance tactics.

Another avenue for debt avoidance is the countersuit for negligence or malpractice. This tactic generally brings the veterinarian's professional liability insurance carrier into the picture along with major legal efforts. It postpones the possibility of a court judgment and can also remove the suit from the small claims court system.

It is because of these possibilities of negative client action that veterinarians should always consider the strengths and weaknesses of their cases before attempting collection via collection agencies or small claims courts. If the potential for a countersuit exists, the wiser course may be to forget about the debt altogether.

. . . and then the dog had diarrhea on your checks and you can't get any more for two more weeks?

Contracts

Most debts incurred by clients evolve through the formation of a contract for veterinary services. A brief review, therefore, of some contract law principles is presented here. See Chapter 8 for details on contract law.

Implied Contracts

Contracts are created with varying amounts of preliminary discussion. In some situations courts hold that a contract was implied by the actions of the parties. The performance of veterinary services in an emergency, when no time exists for prior discussions and negotiations, is one example of an implied contract. Another type would be if an owner dropped a pet off at a veterinary hospital for an examination and treatment but could not stay for the examination.

In the large animal setting, a contract could be implied if a practitioner answered a call to treat a farmer's sick animal but, because of other duties, the farmer was not present when the treatment was rendered.

The inability to discuss diagnoses, recommend courses of therapy, provide prognoses, or quote fees and arrange for their payment in such cases provides significant ground for misunderstandings. Debts incurred in these situations are among the most common types that become delinquent and necessitate further collection activity. When attempts to negotiate and settle these rifts fail, the legal system becomes involved in determining a reasonable resolution.

Oral Contracts

The vast majority of contracts for veterinary care or for the supplying of veterinary practice inventory needs are oral contracts. As long as the contract does not involve leases longer than a year, the sale of real estate, or agreements that cannot be performed within a year (items covered by statutes of fraud[1]), an oral contract is completely enforceable.

The risks of mistaken recollections or misunderstandings are lower with oral contracts, in which at least some discussion transpired, than with implied contracts, in which no discussion occurred. The potential for difficulties is likely to be higher with oral agreements than with written agreements, however.

Written Contracts and Estimates

Detailed written contracts are uncommon in the veterinary care business. Occasionally they are used by veterinary emergency clinics, specialty veterinary practices, and with first-time clients at some small animal practices. They are recommended for situations in which limited or no previous business relation exists between the practitioner and client.

Practices that use written estimates tend to have fewer disagreements regarding fees as well as less frequent need for extraordinary debt-collection measures. Written estimates can be computer generated or handwritten on specific forms. They can be double copy documents, with or without the owner's signature, with owners receiving a copy. These estimates can also be single-copy documents left in the medical record or simply notations written on the medical record. Each of these forms of written documentation helps identify the contract terms and forms the basis for the existence of a contract. Signed, written estimates are better than oral discussions, although the added formality occasionally evokes resistance from established clients.

Credit Management

An explicit credit-management policy is imperative to avoid debt-collection problems. Practice-management consultants' opinions vary regarding the wisdom of providing credit. Some consultants advise the acceptance of cash, credit card payments, or personal checks only. Veterinarians know, however, how impractical a rigid policy like this is to implement, so providing some credit is inevitable. A well-conceived and carefully managed credit policy can increase a practice's growth and dramatically expand its goodwill. A thorough analysis of credit extension is provided elsewhere.[2] Whatever the case, four major questions should be asked when credit is being requested by a client or offered by the veterinary practice:

1. Is this client a good credit risk?
2. What limit should be placed on this client's credit?
3. What terms will be extended?
4. What controls should be enacted to ensure that collection of the debt is possible?

Managing Client Debt

Although most veterinarians would prefer having no unpaid client accounts, it is virtually impossible to maintain an accounts receivable level at zero and still be able to offer a desirable quality and quantity of medicine. Decisions must be made, therefore, regarding the amount of credit that will be extended in order to practice high-quality, intensive medicine. Encouraging euthanasia or mediocre medicine might insure timely full payment, but this type of care is often not in the animal's best interest.

A rigid no-credit policy frequently retards the economic expansion of the practice's gross income. A credit policy that is too lenient places a practice in financial jeopardy, because too many clients will be overextended and unable to repay their debts to the practice. The following is a list of credit-management pointers to help practitioners formulate a controlled and healthy credit management policy.

1. Display a prominent sign informing clients of the practice's policy regarding payment. A sign posted at the receptionist's office stating "Payment required at time of treatment unless other arrangements are made in advance" clarifies this issue. It alerts clients that they should discuss payment if they are unable to pay in full.

2. Display small wall placards in exam rooms that help clients feel comfortable discussing fees. Such statements can read "Please feel free to discuss fees before services are rendered."

3. Provide a formal estimate of the fees. Since it is extremely difficult to accurately estimate fees until all the diagnostic evidence is in hand, wide ranges should be given. Clients understand that it is impossible to predict exactly how much the fees will be before a definitive diagnosis is reached. They do, however, want to know whether it will be around $150 or closer to $350.

4. Clarify that clients must apply for credit. Keep in mind that when clients are requesting that the veterinary practice extend credit, they really are asking that the owner(s) lend them money. Clients should not be allowed to demand credit. Make it clear that they must apply for credit and that credit will be granted only after the business office has had time to evaluate the application and determine if they qualify. Since decisions about the patient's care and future may depend on credit being extended, the office may have to arrive at a decision quickly.

5. Create a credit application form and have clients complete it before credit is extended. This form should include the owner's full name, address, and phone number; the name of the party's personal bank and account number; driver's license number; and two personal credit references with phone numbers and addresses (Figure 13.1).

6. Verify the credit worthiness of the client with two of the best and simplest tests: (1) call the client's home phone number to assure that it is in service and accurate and (2) call the client's employer to verify employment and length of employment. If the request for credit is made at a time when most businesses are closed, the Yellow Pages should be consulted to see if the stated employer exists. When either one of these does not check out, only minimal credit should be extended.

7. Credit decisions and limits should remain with the doctor or authorized staff member. Some veterinarians and/or staff members seem willing to extend credit without sufficient client information and without proper authorization. When this is a problem, these people should be asked if they would be willing to lend an equivalent amount of their own money to the client. If they say no (and they usually do) remind them that since they just lent the practice's money, management would like for them to personally guarantee that loan. It is amazing how differently staff people look at extending credit when they are asked to lend their own instead of the business's money.

8. Exercise extreme care when expensive pathology, blood chemistry, radiology, microbiology, or pharmaceutical fees are part of the medical costs for which credit is being arranged. If a client fails to pay for a practitioner's in-house time and services, the lost income can be most disheartening. If, however, a client fails to pay for expensive lab fees, drugs, and x-ray film that actually cost the practice money in addition to the veterinarian's time and services, the costs of a bad credit risk can be devastating. Collect a deposit to cover the out-of-pocket costs so that practitioners' only exposure to loss is the value of their time.

9. Extend credit on an individual-need basis only after a client has paid cash for $300 (or any other comfortable amount) of veterinary services within a given period of time. Although this is a helpful policy, a client's financial situation can change rapidly. This should not, therefore, be the only factor considered when credit decisions are made.

10. Create the terms of the credit by formulating a payment plan. Ask clients to explain what type of repayment schedule is financially feasible for them. Offers dramatically below those that

FOUR CORNERS VETERINARY HOSPITAL

CREDIT APPLICATION FOR VETERINARY SERVICES

OWNER'S NAME _____ PHONE ( ) _____
ADDRESS _____
DRIVER LICENSE # _____ PET'S NAME _____
SPOUSE'S OR CO-OWNER'S NAME_____
OWNER'S PERSONAL REFERENCE: NAME _____
ADDRESS _____ PHONE ( ) _____
OWNER'S NEAREST RELATIVE (not at same address):
NAME _____ PHONE ( ) _____
ADDRESS _____
OWNER'S BANK AND BRANCH _____ ACCOUNT NO. _____

EMPLOYER'S NAME_____ PHONE ( ) _____
(If unemployed, state last employer and date of termination)
ADDRESS _____
SPOUSE'S OR CO-OWNER'S EMPLOYER _____ PHONE ( ) _____
ADDRESS _____
LENGTH OF EMPLOYMENT: OWNER _____SPOUSE _____

AMOUNT PAID AS A DEPOSIT _____
AMOUNT TO BE PAID UPON RELEASE OF ANIMAL _____
AMOUNT REMAINING TO BE PAID_____

I, the undersigned owner or agent for _____ (name of animal)
hereby agree to pay the remaining balance of $ _____ on a schedule of
$_____ every_____ weeks commencing on _____ , 19___ (date.)
I promise to have the above balance paid off by_____ , 19 ___ (date.)
[Please set a date that you feel confident you will be able to meet.] I understand that
interest will be charged on this account at a rate of 1 1/2% of the unpaid balance per
month.

_____   _____
              Date   Signature

Member American Animal Hospital Association Since 1956

Figure 13.1   A credit application form.

would be considered adequate indicate a poor credit risk. On the other hand, sometimes a client's offer for repayment will be much more generous than that proposed by the practice. Room for negotiation exists, but proceed with caution.

11. Request that a parent, relative, or friend who has some financial assets cosign the loan statement on the bottom of the credit application (Figure 13.1). This is especially important when the owner is a minor.

12. Accept Visa and MasterCard payments. The 2.5% to 3.5% service charge transfers the credit risk to a bank and is the most inexpensive line of credit any business can provide.

Credit management policy deserves considerable thought and constant attention. Making credit extension too easy for clients is tantamount to suggesting that they treat the privilege lightly. However, making credit impossible to obtain has its drawbacks as mentioned above, namely, impeding good medical practice. Too often this aspect of practice simply evolves without any detailed planning. One well-known practice-management consultant suggests that if small animal practices do not maintain accounts receivable equal to 25% of one month's gross income, they will not expand as rapidly or as dramatically as they could otherwise.[3] It is paramount, therefore, for practitioners to recognize that credit can be beneficial to the practice as long as well-defined techniques have been developed regarding credit extension.

The Billing System

A monthly billing service is a necessity to veterinary practice. Billing techniques can be employed that will significantly increase timely payments.

Billing Statements

The first item to consider when establishing a billing policy is that most people receive their paychecks at the end of each month. It is thus advisable to mail monthly invoices before the 25th of the month. This way, the bills arrive at the same time people receive a primary paycheck.

Less client resistance is incurred with itemized bills than with simple photocopies of statements showing the total amount due. This type of bill requires additional staff time, however, so perhaps it is best used selectively to accompany only the larger bills.

Computer systems are extremely efficient for maintaining account receivables, preparing timely billing statements, and generating the necessary reports of aged accounts receivables and ensuring timely action. Without a computer, monies owed should be listed on detailed ledger cards for each client. These records must be reconciled with the accounts shown on the day sheet at the end of each business day. In addition, medical record files should be clearly flagged and segregated to show which clients have outstanding balances. When these procedures are followed, the ledger card can be photocopied to serve as a monthly statement.

Practitioners must be assured that payments on accounts have been properly recorded before any type of collection activity is initiated via telephone or letter. All information acquired by staff members regarding delayed payments must be recorded either on the medical record or on a note page attached to the ledger card. Nothing is more embarrassing than calling a client with what is purported to be an overdue account and discovering that the real problem is an inefficient bookkeeping system within the practice.

Interest Charges and Billing Fees

Types of Consumer Credit

There are two basic types of consumer credit: sales credit and loan credit. In the case of sales credit, the consumer purchases goods or services from a seller who supplies the product or performs the service and permits the consumer to pay for it in the future, with or without a finance charge. Loan credit, on the other hand, occurs when the consumer borrows money from a bank or finance company in order to pay for goods or services received from a third party. The Federal Truth in Lending Act (15 U.S.C.A. § 1601) applies to these latter credit agreements, not to the type of consumer credit that is provided by professionals rendering services and making credit arrangements with clients.

Although there is considerable variation from state to state, interest rates on sales credit transactions are generally regulated by special state usury laws known as *retail installment sales acts* or by the state's version of the Uniform Consumer Credit Code. A retail installment sales contract is an agreement between a buyer and a seller for the purchase of goods or services for consumer purposes. Under the terms of the agreement, the buyer agrees to pay a price for the goods or services plus a credit charge in installments over a specified period of time.[4]

States have established several statutory categories for the finance charges associated with these installment sales and set maximum finance charges based upon the category. Some establish rates only on credit sales of motor vehicles, others have rates for motor vehicles as well as rates for all goods other than motor vehicles, and still others have comprehensive "all goods" types of laws applying to both. Many states, however, impose no limits on finance charges that retail sellers of goods or sellers of motor vehicles may add. In these states, the finance rate is regulated only by the agreement between the parties.

Interest, Finance Charges, and Usury

The cost of credit is the price charged by the cash lender for the use of money or by the credit seller for the deferment of payment. Historically, this price is called *interest* when it is charged for a cash loan and a *finance charge* when it is associated with a credit sale.

The law has traditionally imposed limitations on the amount of interest that can be charged for a loan of money. Usury is the act or practice of lending money at a rate of interest

higher than that allowed by the state in which the transaction occurred. The maximum limits allowed vary considerably from one state to another, ranging from 10% in some states to 21% in others. In some states the rate can be whatever was agreed upon in the contract.[5] Practitioners should find out from their accountants, attorneys, or Better Business Bureau what rate applies in their state before adding finance charges to outstanding accounts.

Extending Credit

Traditionally, veterinarians have provided credit without any assessment for finance charges. In fact, many veterinarians are uncomfortable charging interest on past-due accounts, thinking that it will provoke too many client complaints. Credit without finance charges, however, encourages clients to pay other bills first and postpone payment to the veterinarian.

In recent years, increasing numbers of practices have been assessing finance charges. In addition, many practices have been charging a separate fee that covers billing costs. A cost accounting of the expenses involved in sending a bill to a client can easily justify a fee of $3 to $5 per client. Whether this would be classified as usury if such a charge were assessed on, for example, a $10 veterinary bill depends on the agreement one has with the client and the law of each state. Whatever the case, no such charge should ever be made unless the client has prior notice.

Defining Interest and Finance Charge

It is necessary to establish which charges in a transaction are for services and which are for finance or interest to determine if a violation of state usury laws has occurred. The general rule is that any compensation or benefit received by the creditor is considered interest or a finance charge unless the charge is made to reimburse the creditor for a specific expense or service other than the extension of credit.[4]

To decide whether a billing fee or service charge is a finance charge or a legitimate fee for professional service, it helps to look at supplemental charges made by lenders that are not considered to be interest or finance charges. These include:

- closing charges such as fees for appraisals, credit reports, title searches, attorney's fees, and recording fees,
- independent broker's fees for placing a loan,
- commitment fees for giving borrowers the option to take a loan,
- late charges or delinquency fees (nearly all states allow a 5% delinquency charge when payments on accounts owed are 10 or more days late),[5]
- prepayment penalties, and
- required insurance, at the usual rates, to protect the creditor.[4]

Regardless of what it may be called, any benefit extracted by the creditor as a condition of extending credit is considered interest or a finance charge, excluding those listed above. Thus, charges for a monthly billing service, when coupled with the interest being charged, may subject the creditor to state usury laws.

Most states allow finance charges to be billed for unpaid accounts as long as clients are informed beforehand that this fee will be assessed. This holds true even if the client has not signed a written credit agreement.

If all credit transactions were handled in a forthright manner, finance charges would not be billed unless a client had previously signed a formal credit agreement authorizing those fees. This is often not practical, especially when clients assure the practitioner that they will make a payment within the next few days but then are not heard from for a month.

A simple credit agreement is found at the bottom of the form illustrated in Figure 13.1. If clients have signed such an agreement and the interest rate charged is within the state's allowable limits, no legal challenges are likely. If no written agreement or oral credit arrangements were discussed between a client and the veterinary practice, caution must be exercised before any finance charges are included on the monthly statement.

The following is an example of an announcement establishing a billing fee for accounts that have not been paid on a timely basis:

> Due to the escalating cost of interest, stamps, and processing billing statements, a $3.00 per month charge will be made for accounts being billed on a monthly basis. Please save the hospital and yourself this expense by paying fees in full before _____.

As mentioned previously, this service charge would most likely be considered a finance charge and, depending on the size of the debt owed, could create problems with state usury laws. Veterinarians seeking definitive answers regarding this matter should contact their local legal counsel.

A different type of policy statement, covering both the billing fee and finance charge, could be added to the written credit agreement or printed on monthly billing statements as follows:

> Please be informed that due to the increased costs of providing a client billing service, we will be required to institute a monthly billing fee of $3.00 for any account less than $150.00. A monthly billing and financing fee of 1 1/2% of the unpaid balance will be applied to accounts greater than $150.00. This policy becomes effective with your next monthly statement.

Avoiding Usury

Practitioners may decide to use a formal written agreement with finance charges properly set forth whenever they provide any credit. This can be awkward, difficult, and time consuming.

Alternatively, practitioners may elect to notify clients on their billing statements that a finance charge will be imposed on overdue accounts commencing with the next monthly statement. No service charge should be assessed as long as clients pay the bills before the practice sends out the second monthly billing statement. Minimal legal risks are incurred if these policies are implemented. To be properly protected, however, legal counsel should be consulted to ascertain the state's allowable interest rates and to review the language used.

Penalties for Usury

Practitioners are at risk of breaking the law if they establish a monthly billing fee without legal counsel. They must question what the consequences are if their finance charges plus their billing fee result in a finding that they have violated state usury laws.

In the normal course of events, consumers do not carefully check the accuracy of interest or finance charge computations. When an account is turned over to a collection agency or a doctor sues to collect a debt, however, clients frequently will analyze their bills. It is not uncommon, then, for clients to invoke usury as a defense to the creditor's action. This is when monthly billing fees of $3 to $5 for small accounts receivable may be found to be usurious.

Debtor's who successfully raise usury as a defense will find a variety of remedies available depending upon the state in which they reside. Included are the following:

- Forfeiture of all interest and finance charges, lawful as well as usurious, is the most common remedy. Creditors are still entitled to the principal.

- Penalty clauses in some states provide that a multiple of the usurious interest be subtracted from the account. In Delaware, for example, three times the amount of interest collected in excess of that permitted by law can be subtracted from the bill.

- Multiples of all the interest are forfeited by the doctor in some states, e.g., in Illinois it is twice the amount.

- There are various specific penalties in different states, e.g., North Dakota allows twice the amount of the interest plus 25% of the principal, and Texas allows recovery of three times the illegally excessive interest but not less than $2000 or 20% of the principal, whichever is smaller.

- Deprivation of all principal and interest (Ohio, Connecticut, and Nebraska have invoked this severe penalty).

Serious pitfalls exist whenever service-oriented businesses become lenders. Practitio-

ners are urged to proceed with caution in this area. However, credit without finance charges is no longer given in many segments of the American economy. Unless this profession joins the trend, veterinary accounts will always be the last ones to be paid.

For further detailed information on this subject, the reader is referred to Reference 2.

Aging Accounts

The longer that unpaid accounts go without full payment or without activity, the less is the chance for recovering fees. A reporting system for aging accounts receivables by date, time past due (30, 60, 90 days), and amount (ranging from the highest to the lowest amount) should be prepared on a monthly basis.

In some cases inactive accounts should be turned over to a collection agency after the first 30 days; in other cases, it is advisable to wait until three months have passed without any payment. These decisions depend on factors like (1) how well the client is known, (2) the size of the debt, (3) the excuse that the debtor has provided for the delay in payment, (4) the abilities of veterinarians or staff people to function as collection agents, and (5) the degree of effort already expended by the veterinary business to contact the debtor.

A formula often used by businesses to monitor activity on accounts receivable is called *the average collection period*. First, the average daily practice income is established by dividing the annual gross income by 365:

$$\text{Daily income} = \frac{\text{gross income (\$365,000)}}{365 \text{ days per year}} = \$1,000$$

The average collection period is then established by dividing the accounts receivable by the daily income figure:

$$\text{ACP} = \frac{\text{total accounts receivable (\$15,000)}}{\text{daily income (\$1,000)}} = 15$$

According to one source, an average collection period of less than 30 days shows an effective credit and collection policy.[6]

Another practice management consultant evaluates the level of credit being extended by a practice by comparing the total accounts receivable with the monthly gross income. This person maintains that practices without accounts receivable equal to 25% to 50% of one month's gross income will not be expanding services or volume as rapidly as they could otherwise.[3] Finance charges must be collected in this case, however, to help offset additional administrative costs and nonpayment by some clients.

The basic premise to bear in mind regarding aging accounts is that some activity on the part of the practice or the client is essential within three months after the debt was incurred or further action must be taken immediately.

In-House Collection Techniques

Many veterinarians are unsuccessful at collecting debts. Firmness, a quick wit, patience, and self-confidence are all important attributes for this job. These traits can be developed or improved in order to deal with the task at hand.

Since it is easier for clients to ignore mailed communications, the telephone is an invaluable tool in debt collection. Some employees become very adept at this chore if they are given a percentage of whatever they are able to collect. Veterinarians should do the telephoning when sizable accounts are involved. It is much harder for a client to say no to the doctor who took care of the patient than it is to refuse a staff person who was not involved in prior communications.

Sometimes handwritten notes on the billing statement from the veterinarian who provided the care will yield positive results. This may or may not be more cost effective than a collection agency. It depends on how valuable the doctor's time is, how big the bills are, and what type of collection agency is being used. Handwritten notes may not be as effective as telephoning but may be worth trying.

Employees and staff people who are involved in telephoning clients about overdue accounts should be trained in the following manner:

- Be firm yet always polite.
- Refrain from acting angry no matter how clients respond.
- Keep the conversation on the subject of how the client intends to deal with the overdue bill. Ask why they have not made a payment as they promised.
- Ask clients when they will be making a payment on the outstanding bill and give them time to outline a new payment plan. Their plans may be more generous than the ones presented by the veterinary practice. Also, clients who formulate their own plans are more likely to follow through with payments according to that plan.

Once payment plans have been established, a successful outcome is more likely if someone at the practice calls the client when payment has not been received within a day of the time it was due. A separate calendar in the business office maintained specifically for this purpose is helpful. An alternative is to write the names and phone numbers of accounts needing special reminder attention in red ink at the top or bottom of the appointment book on the day they are to be called. It may seem ridiculous to put forth this much effort for overdue accounts, but the techniques described here are considerably less costly than the 40% to 50% of the outstanding balance that is charged by most collection agencies. Furthermore, practices do not want to establish a reputation for being an easy target for deadbeats.

In practices in which no one is good at collecting overdue accounts, a collection agency should be used as soon as a payment is six weeks past due. Sometimes particular overdue accounts provoke the ire of the veterinarian who provided special care. This can have a negative effect on the way that practitioner deals with other people each time the issue comes to the fore. If this occurs, it is best to remove the account receivable from the monthly billing file and turn it over to the collection agency. This makes the offending account less visible and thus less irritating. On the other hand, if numerous accounts are overdue, it is important for veterinarians to see all of them in order to recognize that the entire credit policy needs revision.

Fair Debt Collection Statutes

State statutes on debt collection vary. Some states have specific statutes addressing the collection process, and others do not. The California Fair Debt Collection Practices Act (CA Civil Code § 1788) and the New York statute (NY General Business § 600) are somewhat unusual in that they regulate collections both by collection agencies and businesses. The federal Fair Debt Collection Act[7,] after which most of the California statute is patterned, covers only collection agencies, not businesses collecting debts on their own behalf.

Most of the requirements set forth in both the federal and California statutes are based on extensions of common sense and fair business practices. Practitioners should check with their veterinary associations for specific information about their state regulations. If the information is not readily available, abiding by the principles set forth in the California law would be prudent.

Transactions Not Covered By the California Act

Under the California statute, debts owed to veterinarians by corporations, partnerships, or people operating animal-related businesses, including breeders or ranchers, are not included within the purview of the act. To be covered by the act, the debt must be owed by a "natural person" and incurred for personal, family, or household purposes.[8] More aggressive collection procedures are allowed when businesses are the delinquent parties than when natural persons are the offenders. This varies by state depending upon how consumer oriented the legislature is in that particular state.

Personnel Who Are Covered by the Act

Under the California Civil Code, any veterinarian or staff person who "...in the ordinary course of business, regularly, on behalf of himself or others, engages in debt collection" must abide by the state statute.[8] Although worded quite differently, the New York law includes veterinary staff members who attempt to collect "consumer claims" just as California law does.[9]

Employers are responsible for the acts of their employees performed within the scope of their employment. Thus, it behooves veterinarians whose employees are involved in the debt-collection process to be sure the staff is familiar with the principles set forth below.

Communications Regarding the Debt

Communications with Employers

The actions prohibited under § 1788.12 of the California act are really extensions of those just discussed. The only difference is that these prohibitions have to do with communications to persons other than the debtor.

Communication with the debtor's employer regarding the debt is permitted only under very limited circumstances. Creditors may write an employer in order to verify a place of employment, locate the person, or arrange for an attachment of wages after a court judgment. Under the California law, oral communications with the employer are limited to three situations:

- Verification of the debtor's employment at that location,
- Oral discussions with the employer if after 15 days there has been no response to the written request for information, and
- Unrestricted communications provided the client has consented in writing.

If a state does not have a fair debt collection law, adherence to these strict standards may not be essential. Whatever the case, though, prior to a court judgment in the veterinarian's favor, discussions with a debtor's employer must be limited to information verifying employment and locating the debtor. Nothing that could be construed as harassment or a conspiracy against the debtor should be discussed. After a judgment, however, discussions regarding garnishment of the debtor's wages are permissible.

Communications with a Debtor's Family

Communications with a debtor's family also have some limitations under the California law.[10] Prior to obtaining a court judgment, communications are limited to the debtor's spouse or the parents or guardians of a minor unless the request is simply for information as to how the debtor may be located. Information provided on the initial credit application form should be most helpful to assist in locating people with overdue balances. Communications with references listed on the credit application regarding the debtor's whereabouts are permitted.

Impermissible Threats

Certain verbal or written threats are prohibited by § 1788.10 of the California Civil Code. These include, among others:

- Threats to physically harm clients or their animals or the reputation or property of any person,
- Threats that falsely accuse clients of crimes,
- Threats to spread false information about the client, and
- Threats that include false representations as to what will become of the client or the client's property if the action being threatened is not actually contemplated or is not legally permitted.

In other words, if the practitioner says that nonpayment of the bill by a certain date will result in the filing of a small claims court action,

that action must be taken if the client does not pay as stipulated. The same holds true of threats to turn accounts over to collection agencies by specified dates unless a payment has been received. No threats should be made by veterinary staff members that are not truly contemplated or legally possible to fulfill.

Prohibited Behavior

The behavioral principles set forth below are best followed even if a veterinarian's state does not have a statute like the California law. Section 1788.11 of the California Civil Code lists examples of language and telephone behavior that are prohibited:

- The use of obscene or profane language.
- Attempts to entice the client into a telephone conversation by misrepresenting the identity of the caller.
- Causing expense to any person for long-distance telephone calls, telegram fees, or charges for other similar communications by misrepresenting to such person the purpose of such telephone call, telegram, or similar communication.
- Any use of the telephone to annoy or harass a client. Techniques such as calling every 10 minutes, calling every night at midnight (because that is when the delinquent client came to the veterinary hospital seeking emergency veterinary care), or allowing the telephone to ring repeatedly are prohibited.

Prohibitions Against Notations on Written Correspondence

The California Fair Debt Collection Act prohibits any attempt to embarrass a client by sending letters with information about the debt written on the envelope. Statements such as "Notice Long Overdue Debt" on the envelope could be interpreted as offensive and libelous by a litigious client and should never be used.

Other Prohibited Practices

Another type of prohibited practice is misrepresentations in communications. California Civil Code § 1788.13 lists several important examples that are forbidden:

- Communications with the debtor other than in the name of the business to which the debt is owed or the collection agency. Veterinary staff people may not write or call the debtor and represent that they are from a collection agency or an attorney's office.

- Sending letters that are designed to look like or which purport to be official documents from a court or any other governmental agency.

- The false representation that the debt may be increased by the addition of attorneys' fees, investigation fees, service fees, finance charges, or any other charges if, in fact, such fees or charges may not be added legally to the existing obligation.

- A false statement that information concerning a debtor's failure to pay has been or is about to be referred to a consumer reporting agency.

The basic principle surrounding this group of prohibitions is that businesses may not communicate in any way that misleads the debtor or threaten to do things that are illegal or that will not actually be carried out.

Prohibitions Against Deadbeat Lists

Any selling or giving of a debtor's name to the creators of a "deadbeat" list is prohibited.[10] An interesting and important exception to this provision is found in § 1788.12 (e). That section permits the disclosure of information about the consumer debt or the debtor to any other person reasonably believed to have a legitimate business need for such information.

In simple language, this means that telephone calls from or to other veterinary practices inquiring about the status of a client's account receivable are permissible provided that a legitimate business purpose exists and no deadbeat file is being compiled by local veterinarians. Therefore, under this exemption, prudent practitioners may, for example, call the veterinary practice that rendered emergency care to ascertain the status of a client's account at that facility before rendering additional medical care or credit at their own practice.

Since this procedure is allowed by the strict California law, it should then apply to other states without any debt collection statutes. This valuable business tool can and should be utilized whenever a general veterinary practice or specialty practice is about to engage in extensive follow-up care and considers rendering credit.

Debtors' Responsibilities

From the foregoing material it appears that debtors have all the rights and that businesses lending money have incredible obligations to be amenable. Some additional components of the California Fair Debt Collection Act, however, often overlooked or forgotten by both debtors and creditors, can be found in the Civil Code, § 1788.20-1788.22.

Firstly, no person may request or apply for credit at a time when that person knows there is no reasonable probability of being able to repay the obligation within the terms and conditions to which he or she agrees. The veterinarian's awareness of this statute does not help the destitute repay the debt. It does, however, at least allow the staff collector who is communicating with debtors to inform them that their false statements about repaying the loan were illegal acts. This reminder may reduce a client's attempts to stall payment by filing a counterclaim.

Another fact worth knowing is that consumers who initiate any consumer credit are required to notify their creditors of any change in name, address, or employment within a reasonable time after such change occurs. Businesses may inform debtors that their failure to keep the business apprised of these important changes is a violation of state law.

This can provide some clout when debtors are asked firmly, but politely, to keep the practice informed of all future name, address, or employment changes.

Collection Agencies

When efforts to collect accounts receivable have met with total or partial failure, it may be time to call upon the experts for assistance. Collection agencies specialize in extracting money from people who have not paid their bills.

Pros and Cons of Collection Agency Use

After veterinary practices have made fairly diligent but unsuccessful efforts to collect unpaid accounts, they have little to lose and potentially something to gain by transferring these accounts to a collection agency. Care must be exercised in the choice of an agency so that the agency's tactics or personnel do not alienate clients.

Most clients whose accounts are assigned to a collection agency will not create significant bad will for a practice unless they are extremely upset about the quality of veterinary care or the level of communication they received from that practice. In fact, many veterinarians are amazed when clients want to return for additional veterinary services after their accounts were transferred to collection and subsequently paid off. For these clients, collection agencies are just part of life and are not considered to be evidence of frustration or anger on the part of their veterinarian.

Caution must be exercised, however, regarding the assignment of accounts to collection agencies if the outcome of the case or a disagreement with an animal owner could provoke aggressive action by the client. This concern is no different for cases assigned to collection agencies than it is for cases where veterinarians are considering small claims court actions.

Practice managers are urged to review all form letters used by the agency being considered and speak with at least one reference before they select a collection service to represent their practices. State veterinary associations should be contacted before choosing a company, because they sometimes have enough information and experience to actively support a particular collection service. A call to the Better Business Bureau can also be worthwhile to evaluate a local collection agency's reputation.

Types of Collection Services

There are two basic types of collection agencies. One provides a series of letters sent by them on a timely basis to people with unpaid accounts. Each letter is more demanding, although all of the correspondence is very professional. The last letter is generally sent out on the stationery of an attorney who works for these agencies. With this type of service, practitioners generally purchase blocks of application forms from the agency, fill them out with all pertinent information regarding the debtor, and send them with the accounts as they are turned over to the agency. The cost of this type of service is approximately $7.50 to $10.00 per client, depending on how many forms are purchased. This is a flat fee no matter how large or small the account. At the conclusion of the series of written correspondence to clients by these agencies, the account is returned to the veterinary business. Since this type of collection service does not employ telephone communications with debtors, it is imperative that the practice supply current names and addresses to the agencies.

Collection agencies generally encourage businesses to submit all accounts that are six weeks or more overdue in making payments. The agencies send monthly reports to the businesses showing the status of each account plus totals illustrating how much money has been collected by their service in relation to the cost of purchasing the application forms.

The second type of collection agency assumes full responsibility for the account as soon as it is assigned to it, but charges 40% to 50% of the balance collected as the fee for services rendered. There are no initial costs. Any payments made to the veterinary business on assigned accounts after the accounts have been transferred must be submitted to the agency and shared according to the agreement.

These businesses tend to be less interested in the smaller accounts than the larger ones. They do, however, assign each account to an individual who may investigate the account via telephone. Since these agencies use the telephone, accounts without addresses but with valid telephone numbers will receive action at this type of agency. Often an agency represents various business accounts and can pool information. By accumulating several unpaid accounts of the same person, it is worthwhile for them to seek redress via intensive telephone negotiations or in small claims court. Thus, they will usually accept small accounts as well as large ones.

No type of collection agency can be expected to collect any more than 10% to 40% of the business transferred to it. Perhaps the best reason then to utilize their services is simply to remove an irritating unpaid account from the receivables file.

Small Claims Court

Small claims courts are part of the judicial system, but they utilize special procedures to simplify the disposition of claims. These courts, often called *people courts*, are intended to help people recover small sums of money without necessarily hiring an attorney. Maximum damage claims permitted by these courts vary from $500 to $4,000, depending upon state law.

The small claims court system allows consumers the opportunity to present their complaint, in person, before an impartial judge who may order the offending person or business to pay money owed. Trials are usually held within 30 to 60 days of the filing date, and verdicts are declared within a few weeks after the trial. The rules of evidence are very liberal, and court procedures are generally simple, informal, and inexpensive. Filing costs are usually less than $25 and can be recovered by the prevailing party. The mere filing of a small claims court action has a strong enough psychological impact to prompt some debtors to pay off the balance due before a trial date is ever set.

Types of Complaints

Most states allow suits whenever it can be shown that a person or business has been harmed and the offending party has refused to pay for the damages. The majority of these complaints center on breaches of contracts or negligence claims. Some examples are

- a veterinarian suing a floor-covering contractor for damages to a medical records cabinet that occurred at the time a new floor was installed.

- a client suing a veterinarian for negligently spaying a cat, i.e., leaving part of an ovary and thus necessitating a second surgery by another veterinary hospital to find the remaining ovarian tissue.

- a poodle owner suing a groomer for veterinary costs incurred when the groomer caused a severe clipper burn to the client's dog, necessitating veterinary care.

- clients suing a neighbor (and thus, involving the homeowner's insurance company) to recoup $1500 in veterinary costs incurred for their dog after it was attacked on their front lawn by the neighbor's off-leash German shepherd.

Drawbacks to Small Claims Courts

The only remedy provided by the small claims court is that of monetary damages, in most cases. Specific property or merchandise seldom can be recovered.

Considerable time can be spent preparing for trial and waiting at the courthouse for the trial to take place. Often the trial time is postponed because of something completely outside the control of the complaining party, and the value of all the lost work time is not recoverable. In some situations, where the veterinarian is the complaining party, it may be more effective to retain an attorney or to seek assistance from another source, such as a consumer affairs office or governmental agency.

Other drawbacks to the small claims court form of legal redress include the following:

- In most states, winning the case is the easy part. Collecting the money is a separate process and often the most difficult task. It is particularly difficult to collect money from fly-by-night business operators, companies no longer in business, and clients who have no assets.

- Small claims court actions are often ineffective in resolving disputes with firms or people who do not do business or have property located in the area where the suit originated. In such cases, they may be outside the court's jurisdiction. It is especially difficult if the defendant is located in another state.

- Veterinary businesses that win their cases often discover that the verdict is a compromise which is less than satisfactory to either side. The offending party will not be sent to jail or required to pay fines because those are not remedies that are within the jurisdiction of the small claims court system.

- Delays are a common and frustrating part of this system of justice. When these delays change the day set for the hearing or defer the remainder of the hearing until a future date, they are called *continuances*. Judges are generally fairly liberal in granting these requests, and considerable time can be wasted.

Factors to Consider Before Filing

The filing of a small claims court lawsuit is a serious matter. All efforts to resolve a dispute should be exhausted before practitioners file a claim. If the complaint involves a nonpayment for veterinary services and no resolution is possible, the strengths and weaknesses of the case should be weighed. The possibility of a countersuit should be evaluated before any action is initiated. When the suit involves a substantial sum of money, an attorney's advice should be sought. In a few states, attorneys are not allowed to appear in the small claims court, but their advice can be invaluable whether they assist at the trial or not.

The following additional pointers are worth consideration before action is taken:

- The complaint should be clearly communicated to the person or business involved. If the case involves a business, a manager, owner, or official as high in status as possible should be spoken to. The complaint should be clearly and concisely stated in a letter to that person. Notices should be sent via registered mail in order to demonstrate one's seriousness.

- If veterinarians are contemplating legal action against another business, sometimes the Better Business Bureau, consumer action division of a talk radio station, Automotive Consumer Action Panel, local board of realtors, state licensing board, or similar agencies can help resolve the case faster than the small claims court. Complete records should be kept of all conversations or correspondence pertaining to the dispute including dates, times, and phone numbers. If the case ends up in court, the judge may ask what steps have been pursued to resolve the problem before the court appearance. Documentation is essential.

- Serious consideration should be given to any compromises that might help settle the matter. A compromise in which even half of what is owed is offered might be preferable to all the effort required in going to court. Furthermore, a court action does not guarantee a verdict for the full amount of the debt owed. The principle of the case might not be worth all the effort. For first-time small claims filers, a trip to the court clerk's office to gather information is worthwhile. Many courts have brochures available, and some have clerks or counselors who are trained to assist consumers.

- A visit to a small claims court session as a spectator is a valuable training tool prior to the trial date. This can be done by the veterinarian or by an office manager, receptionist, or bookkeeper employed by the veterinary practice. In fact, the entire claim filing and trial preparation process can be delegated to a mature employee willing to handle claims of this nature.

- As soon as a decision has been made to proceed, the complaint should be filed immediately. The older the claim gets, the more difficult it is for people to remember what happened and the harder it is to locate parties essential to the case. State statutes of limitations may dictate that the claim be filed within a year or two of the time that the debt was incurred.

Filing the Claim

The plaintiff usually needs to appear before the clerk of the small claims court to file a claim. Some states will mail claim forms to a plaintiff. Often, however, helpful information can be gleaned from a personal conversation with the clerk, making a trip to the office worth the effort. A *Claim of Plaintiff and Order* form is the document that must be filed. In states without a standard form, the clerk can advise on how to file.

The plaintiff veterinarian frequently needs to determine the filing costs, take the forms

back to the practice to be filled out, and then return or mail them with a check. Filing costs are usually less than $25 to $35, and these can be sought as part of the claim for damages. When the forms have been submitted, the clerk will assign a case number and schedule a trial date. If a good reason can be established, defendants may have the right to ask that a different date be set.

When a claim is filed, a cause of action should be clearly and simply stated. The claim must state the following:

- Who is being sued.

- The grounds for the suit.

- A full list of all damages claimed. If the case involves fees for veterinary services, the list should include the costs for all veterinary care, additional costs incurred to board or hospitalize the animal before it was picked up by the owner, costs for euthanasia and disposal of the body if those services were rendered, court costs (including the costs for service of process by the marshall), some collection agency costs, and any unpaid interest or finance charges that were legally assessed.

If a business is being sued, its correct legal name must be used when filing the complaint. A business known as *Aardvark Linoleum* may actually operate under a different legal name. Suits can be carried out only against correctly named defendants. Plaintiffs who are unsure of the correct business name should look for licenses posted on the premises, such as sales tax licenses, for accurate determination of the legal name.

Service of Process

Serving defendants with a summons that notifies them of the legal action is called *service of process*. This can be done by the plaintiff, an agent for the plaintiff, a sheriff, a marshall of the court, or by private process servers. Personal service is accomplished by handing the claim of plaintiff and order form to the defendant or, if the defendant refuses to take the paper, by merely touching him or her and letting the form fall. Force should never be used when serving a defendant with any legal papers.

Other methods of service of process include service to the defendant's residence or usual place of business or using registered mail. Nevertheless, service by the sheriff, marshall or an officer of the court is probably the best method.

It usually costs an extra $10 to $30 to have an officer of the court serve the defendant, but the time savings, knowledge that this task will be performed properly, and psychological impact on the defendant make the use of such officials worth the added cost. Plaintiffs who win can recoup this cost just as they do with filing fees.

Answers to Small Claims Court Actions

Defendants do not have to file any document to defend a case filed in small claims court. They need only be in court on the hearing date and present their evidence and defenses.

Counterclaims

Defendants who feel that they have been wronged by the plaintiff in a case may file their own claim, called a *claim of defendant* against the plaintiff. These claims, also called *counterclaims*, must arise from the same transaction or situation that formed the basis of the plaintiff's action. Defendants usually must make arrangements for their counterclaims to be served upon the plaintiff at least five days before the hearing. Each claim must be for an amount within the limits of the court and is heard on the same hearing date. If the defendant's counterclaim exceeds the small claims court maximum, the case cannot be pursued within the small claims court system.

As mentioned earlier, this is one of the methods sometimes used by obdurate debtors to postpone or confound the debt-collection process.

Venue

Before a suit is filed, a determination must be made that proper *venue* exists. This means that claims must be filed in the judicial district where at least one of the following is true:

- The defendant currently resides or does business there.
- The injury to a person or damage to personal property occurred there.
- The defendant entered into or signed a contract there.

The filing of an action in the wrong court will cause the case to be dismissed without prejudice. This means that it can be refiled or transferred to the right court at the request of the defendant or upon the court's initiative. A request for change of venue can be made orally at the time of trial or by letter anytime prior to the date of trial. No fee is charged for the transfer.

Another reason to request a change of venue can be because another court would be more convenient for key witnesses. The party making a motion for this type of venue change must show that justice would be better served by the change despite extra expenses or inconveniences to the parties of the lawsuit.

Preparation for Trial

One of the most valuable things that a plaintiff or defendant can do to prepare for trial is to attend a session of small claims court as a spectator. The dos and don'ts can be quickly learned after a few hours as an observer.

As mentioned earlier, documentation is important in proving a case. Copies of medical records, appointment books, billing statements, telephone messages, letters, client registration forms, cancelled checks, receipts, and estimate sheets should be brought to court and organized in such a way that individual documents can be easily located. When cases involve damaged property, photographs of the damaged items or the actual goods should be presented. If the case involves a claim that the veterinarian should be liable for malpractice or negligence, textbooks, journal articles, and continuing education or veterinary school notes can be important and should be available.

Be sure to arrive at the court 15 minutes early on the day of the hearing and know how to find the correct courtroom. Nothing is worse than having a default judgment filed for the defendant because the plaintiff veterinarian forgot the date or could not find the courtroom. Defendants quite often fail to show, allowing plaintiffs to obtain default judgments.

A rehearsal of the case is well worth the effort. Any witnesses to be called should be familiar with their roles at the hearing and able to provide their information quickly. Small claims courts rarely devote more than 15 or 20 minutes to a case, so the presentation must be concise.

Testimony at the Trial

The court should be called the day beforehand to ensure that the trial is still scheduled. If, on the day of trial, the opponent requests a postponement, object and make it clear that any cancellation will create a costly inconvenience because of lost work time. When witnesses are present, good arguments can be made that it will be difficult for them to be asked to take off another day from work. If the judge grants a postponement, ask that the next trial date be final.

If the opposing party does not arrive at the time the case is called, a request should be made for the court to enter a default judgment. Some judges do this automatically, but others may be willing to wait until later in the day to see if the party appears. If this happens, and the opposing party still fails to show, a request for a default judgment should be reentered.

Plaintiffs present their evidence first and should stand when speaking. Judges are ad-

dressed with the title "Your Honor." The court docket is usually packed, so judges try to resolve each claim as quickly as possible. People who are disorganized try the judge's patience and, consequently, may be unable to present all of their evidence. Judges generally control the course of the hearing and often the line of questions. They can be very tough on unprepared participants.

Testimony should always be presented in a straightforward manner. The hearing is no place for nastiness or an argumentative approach toward the judge or adversary party. Do not interrupt the opponent or any of the witnesses no matter how outrageous their testimony.

Witnesses may be critical to the case. The testimony of fellow veterinarians can be quite valuable in cases in which practitioners have been accused of negligence or malpractice. No subpoena is needed if witnesses will appear on a voluntary basis. They should be called and reminded about the place and time of the hearing the day before it occurs. If essential witnesses will not voluntarily appear or cannot be trusted to attend the trial, the clerk of court will, upon the request of a party to the lawsuit, issue subpoenas ordering them to appear. A failure to appear means that the subpoenaed witness can be held in contempt of court, and an arrest warrant can be issued.

Witnesses should be chosen and subpoenaed with great caution. If they are unfriendly or not well versed on the case, their testimony can hurt more than it will help.

Cases are presented thoroughly but selectively, starting with evidence showing why a legitimate cause of action exists. If the suit is based upon a breach of contract, the terms and existence of the contract should be presented first.

Any claim asserted should be substantial and defensible or it should not be made. Parties on either side of the case should be prepared for arguments that opponents are likely to present and have answers well thought out. Knowing what one wants to present and how the facts supporting it will be presented builds confidence. Trying to marshall a case on the spur of the moment is a recipe for disaster.

The Decision and Appeals

Judges may decide the case at the conclusion of the trial. More often, however, a written judgment stating the monetary damages awarded is mailed to the parties a few weeks later.

Appeal provisions vary greatly from state to state. Some states do not permit any appeals; some allow only the defendant to appeal; and others provide for appeals by either party. In jurisdictions where attorneys are not admitted at the small claims court hearing, they are allowed in the court receiving the appeal. Clerks of court can provide advice about the appealability of cases within that jurisdiction.

As mentioned previously, failures to appear at the hearing result in default judgments for the opposing parties. No appeals from default judgments are allowed until a *motion to vacate the default judgment* has been submitted to the small claims court and accepted by the court. These motions must be submitted to the court within approximately 30 days after the clerk has mailed the *notice of entry of judgment*. Convincing arguments of hardships are usually needed in order to convince the court that default judgments should be set aside.

Judicial Collection Devices

If all informal collection efforts have failed and legal action is being contemplated, practitioners should be aware of some remedies that can be initiated prior to the trial of the case. The first of these is called *attachment*.

Attachment

The term *attachment* refers to a statutory procedure that authorizes the taking into legal custody of real estate and personal property owned by defendants and in their possession and control for the purpose of affording plaintiffs security for any judgments they may be awarded at trial.[11] The pursuit of this remedy usually requires the assistance of an attorney. Practitioners should be aware of this action for cases in which large debts are owed them by clients or if debts are owed by the practitioner to someone else.

When properly employed, this procedure can take place before a trial ever begins. The goal of attachment is to prevent prospective defendants from transferring, concealing, or removing their property in order to avoid satisfaction of judgments against them. Prior to 1970 creditors could use this tactic as an intimidating device that was designed to coerce payment from debtors before a lawsuit was filed. They could seize, tie up, or place a lien on a consumer's home, car, or other property without the consumer even knowing that such action was being pursued.[4]

In 1969 a landmark United States Supreme Court case was decided that forever changed the law regarding both attachment and garnishment. In *Sniadach* v. *Family Finance Corp. of Bay View* (395 U.S. 337) the Supreme Court held that attachment and garnishment by creditors prior to the imposition of notice and a hearing was a violation of the constitutional guarantee of due process of law. As a result, to secure a pretrial attachment of assets, creditors must now file a complaint commencing a lawsuit and then file an affidavit in which grounds for an attachment are set forth. If the judge in a hearing on the attachment issue alone orders the attachment, a writ is issued and a sheriff or other official takes action. If the attachment is for personal property, the sheriff may seize the property and keep it until the final disposition of the lawsuit. If the attachment is for real property, the sheriff causes a notice to be recorded on the public record at the local office where real estate titles are kept. Real property subjected to an attachment cannot be disposed of by the owner until the attachment is lifted.

If the plaintiff succeeds at trial and is granted a judgment, the debtor must pay that judgment from some other source of income or assets or the attached property will be sold at public auction.

Garnishment

Garnishment is a statutory procedure that makes property and credits belonging or owed to a debtor but in possession of a third party available as security for a potential judgment.[11] Most garnishment proceedings involve banks holding a debtor's money on deposit or employers who owe wages to the debtor. The garnishee is the party holding the debtor's asset, i.e., the bank or employer. When a *writ of garnishment* is granted by the court, the garnishee is, in effect, warned that the creditor is claiming a right to have any judgment satisfied from property belonging to the defendant but being held by the garnishee. Garnishees who do not hold the property described in the attachment until final disposition of the lawsuit will be held liable.

In some ways garnishment is similar to attachment. It differs, however, in two major respects. First, garnishment can be employed both as a prejudgment and postjudgment remedy. Second, the property garnished is not physically seized by the officer serving the process on the garnishee but is left in that person's hands until a final disposition in the case occurs. Garnishees must file an answer to the court indicating that the property, funds, or earnings of the debtor will be held as demanded by the garnishment notice.

To the consumer debtor, garnishment usually has more severe consequences than attachment. If debtors' homes are attached they can still live there until the case has been resolved. If some personal property is seized, they can generally find a way to get along without that property. If, on the other hand, debtors' wages or bank accounts are frozen, they may be forced to file for bankruptcy or find a new job about which the creditor does not know.

Significant limitations are imposed by Title III of the Federal Consumer Protection Act on what assets may be garnished. This law limits the amount of wages or salary that may be garnished to approximately 25% of the person's disposable earnings for a week or 30 times the federal minimum hourly wage in effect at the time the weekly earnings are payable, whichever is less.[12] In addition, it prohibits employers from discharging employees whose wages have been garnished as the result of one indebtedness incident.[12]

The counsel of an attorney familiar with consumer credit law is required if garnishment proceedings are being pursued against a debtor client.

Legal Recourses After a Judgment Has Been Rendered

The prevailing party is entitled to collect the amount awarded once the time for appeal has expired. Ideally, the loser already has arranged for payment before that time arrives.

If the amount is not paid, the clerk of court should be asked what recourse is available. This is the point in the debt-collection process at which pursuit of an overdue account via the small claims court is the most disappointing. If the debtor has a job or an active bank account, the best postjudgment action may be to ask the court for a writ of garnishment. Some states, like Pennsylvania, however, do not allow garnishment of wages.

A second approach is to request a *writ of execution* from the court. This is a court order to a sheriff to levy upon or seize the property of the debtor, sell it at public auction, and turn over the proceeds less the costs of the sale to the creditor.[13]

The consumer facing a writ of execution has come to the end of the line. Any valuable assets may now be reached to satisfy the judgment. Tremendous variations exist among state laws exempting specific property or categories of property from the judgment creditor's grasp. The best-known exemption is the homestead exemption for one's house, so long as that residence is the principal dwelling of a debtor who is the head of a family. Other modern-day exemptions include personal property up to specific dollar amounts or categories such as household furnishings and appliances, or public assistance benefits.

Writs of execution are generally difficult actions to pursue. The difficulties involved in an attempt to execute on a judgment will most likely require the retention of legal counsel. When that happens, the costs to collect on the debt owed may exceed the benefits produced by a sale of the debtor's assets.

Summary

It is clear from this discussion why veterinarians are reluctant to get into the business of lending money. The information presented here, though, is not intended to discourage practitioners from providing credit when they have properly evaluated the client and the client's potential to pay off a loan. The intention is to help practitioners understand the entire credit-management and debt-collection process so that they can better decide what actions to take when problems arise.

In food animal and equine practices, sometimes the only way practitioners have any chance of being paid for huge volumes of services rendered to businesses that are failing is to continue providing more service in hopes that the livestock owner can get things turned around. If this is the case, these practitioners should understand what types of legal remedies they might have before they render any more services on credit.

The myriad differences that exist among states frequently necessitate the assistance of legal counsel. Because of the small size of most debts owed to veterinarians, attachment, garnishment, and writs of execution are utilized only rarely. These remedies might, though, be perfectly valid courses for large animal practitioners to consider, where larger bad debts are likely to occur. Collection agencies and small claims court actions may be used frequently and should be thoroughly understood.

Just as veterinarians should never prejudge how much a client can afford to pay for veterinary services, neither should they assume that collection agency costs or legal fees will make recovering unpaid accounts financially unfeasible. Questions should always be asked first, and only then can wise business decisions regarding debt collection be made.

References

1. California Civil Code § 1624.
2. Sarner H: *The Business Management of a Small Animal Practice*. Philadelphia, WB Saunders Co, 1967, pp 20-23.
3. Clark RD: Personal communications: contributing editor,*Vet Econ*, 1986.
4. Alperin HJ, Chase RF: *Consumer Law: Sales Practices and Credit Regulation*. St. Paul, MN, West Publishing Co, 1986; § 502, p 198; § 488 pp 176-177; § 660 p 401.
5. *Consumer Credit Guide*. Commerce Clearing House, Inc, para 520.
6. Smith B: The ultimate in financial analysis. *DVM Manage* 17(8):3-4, 1986.
7. 15 USCS 1692.
8. California Civil Code § 1788.2(f) (c).
9. General Business § 600.
10. California Civil Code § 1788.12 (b) (c).
11. *Black's Law Dictionary*, ed 5. St. Paul, MN, West Publishing Co, 1979, pp 115, 612.
12. 15 USCA § 1673(a), § 1674.
13. Epstein: *Debtor—Creditor Law in a Nutshell*, ed 3. St Paul, MN, West Publishing Co, 1985 pp51, 61-62.

CHAPTER 14

Medical Records: Content, Requirements, and Legal Implications

The business, medical, and legal aspects of veterinary practice require the creation of complete patient medical records in order to serve the needs of patients, owners, and attending veterinarians. At veterinary schools and at veterinary practices with residency programs, special measures must be taken so that those records provide detailed data for the clinical research of students, residents, and faculty.

Records range from overly brief in private practices to detailed journals at the university teaching hospitals. Medical records at veterinary colleges may contain from 10 to 15 different forms and are often 25 to 100 pages in length for one case. The massive bulk of these records can hinder rather than raise the quality of care. Practitioners, on the other hand, often become obsessed with brevity. Both lengthiness and brevity of medical records can pose serious problems in conveying competence to the client, practicing quality veterinary medicine, and developing a legal defense.

This chapter focuses on the legal requirements for medical records. It also presents examples of brief record forms; however, other references also should be reviewed for discussions of the business and diagnostic aspects of record keeping.[1, 2]

Types of Records

Medical and Business Documents

Although the patient's medical history and treatment chart are usually the primary components of a medical record, a host of other data also are important. The following veterinary medical and business documents are considered medical records:

- client registration forms
- appointment books

Well of course you can find Pookie's record! We were here just yesterday.

- client consent forms
- radiographs
- estimate sheets
- financial records
- anesthesia records
- telephone consultations
- controlled drug logs
- surgery logs
- radiology logs
- laboratory logs
- patient discharge records
- routine hospital handouts
- electrocardiograms and electromyograms
- electroencephalograms and electroretinograms
- radiographs and CT scans
- patient history and treatment records
- master and minor problem lists
- consultation reports from other veterinarians
- laboratory reports, including:
  1. clinical pathology reports (blood chemistry, hematology, and urinalysis reports);

  2. clinical immunology reports (antibody titers and radioimmunoassay test results);

  3. microbiology reports (bacterial, viral, and fungal cultures and sensitivities); and

  4. cytology, pathology, radiology, and necropsy reports.

Additional records and reports of medical significance may exist. Any document that is relevant to the care, discussion, and outcome of a case may be of importance and could be subpoenaed for presentation as evidence in a trial.

Source versus Problem-Oriented Records

There are three types of medical records: (1) the conventional and source-oriented record, (2) the problem-oriented record, and (3) combinations of these two.

The conventional, source-oriented medical record consists of data entered on the record from various sources in chronological order for each office visit or period of hospitalization.

According to the American Animal Hospital Association's (AAHA's) *Medical Records Manual*, the record should include entries on up to 36 different items.[2] The major elements of this type of record in the proper order include:

1. owner information
2. animal identification
3. vaccination history
4. chief complaint
5. history (Hx)
6. physical exam (PE)
7. diagnosis (Dx) or tentative diagnoses (TDx)
8. chronological order of medical and surgical events
9. prognosis (Px)
10. treatment (Rx)
11. various reports (e.g., laboratory, radiography, cardiology, etc.)
12. financial records

The trend in veterinary medicine has been away from source-oriented records and toward the use of problem-oriented veterinary medical records (POVMR), or combinations of these two techniques. The POVMR system is kept in chronological order according to each medical problem that has been identified. This system links all information to specific medical problems. The ideal POVMR system has four sections:

1. the defined data base comprised of the chief complaint, patient profile, history, physical examination, and laboratory and radiology reports;
2. the problem list with its three sections, the major problem list, a minor problem list, and a medication table;
3. the plans section written with discussion of further diagnostic procedures, therapy, and client education; and
4. a progress note section written in the "SOAP" format. This divides the written material into four different areas; S is for the subjective information including presenting complaint and history; O is for objective and obser-

vational information derived from the physical examination and various laboratory reports; A is the assessment of the data including a provisional diagnosis and results of consultations; and P stands for plans being made or suggested for further diagnostic studies, the differential rule outs, and for treatment or surgery.[2]

The structured nature of POVMR makes data and information easier for veterinarians to find, provides better organization for making a diagnosis, and permits a rapid evaluation of the status of a medical problem at any time. The use of this system, however, requires considerably more effort, and it will probably never gain wide acceptance in its pure form with veterinarians outside the university environment. Record-keeping systems that employ some of its concepts but adhere to the conventional formats will be the most common types used in practice.

Anyone who tries to decipher medical records from various sources is likely to encounter a variety of abbreviations. Similarly, veterinarians are always searching for abbreviated ways of recording data. The in-depth medical abbreviation list found in Appendix M can help in deciphering and writing medical records.

Recording Information in the Record

It is not generally agreed what information must be recorded in patient medical records. Regulations adopted by some state boards of examiners help determine the standard, and additional information may be gleaned from the manual *Standards for AAHA Hospitals*.[3] Although the standards associated with membership in this association are for those practices that aspire to be a step above the average, the standards are a well-conceived representation of what is expected of most small animal practices.

The History

The process of establishing a diagnosis centers on the owner's primary complaint and the initial entry made by the receptionist. Clients often describe their pet's problem to more than one person before meeting with the veterinarian and, therefore, they expect practitioners to have some idea of the nature of the difficulty before any evaluation is initiated. The primary complaint should be briefly recorded by the receptionist after the date entered on the patient's chart.

An organized history should be extracted from the owner and recorded before any effort is expended examining the animal. A few minutes of intense questioning and discussion shows owners that the veterinarian cares about and respects their assessment of the animal's problem. This also gives the animal time to become accustomed to the doctor's presence and to relax. Most exam room biting or scratching injuries occur when an entry is hurried and an examination is begun before animals become accustomed to the veterinarian's voice, odor, and demeanor.

A good way for practitioners to assure that an accurate history is being recorded is to orally relate the facts to the client as they are being entered in the record so that the client hears precisely what is being recorded. Clients produce a more accurate history when they know their account is being written in the animal's medical record. Veterinarians remember facts with greater accuracy if all entries are made while the client is still available to produce the information.

significant or not. Likewise, if a practitioner can recognize, for example, that a cat has lost 3 lb since the previous year, which amounts to almost 30% of its weight, a recommendation to run diagnostic tests will seem more reasonable than if no distinct cause for concern can be cited.

The notation of normal physical findings is often as important as recording abnormalities. Even when maladies are obvious, they should be recorded in detail. Practitioners cannot remember everything, and even if they have superb recollection, very few judges or juries will believe them without corroborative evidence. Documented changes in the appearance of visible lesions via written notes or photographs are valuable, especially with dermatological problems. Recommendations for diagnostic procedures and notations designating which laboratory or pathology service blood or tissue samples were sent to also are useful. Entries such as "Complete panel to A&B Lab" or "Biopsy to Dr. C" help other veterinarians or staff members track down results not found in the medical record.

Descriptions of visible or palpable masses, lymph nodes, or body organs, including dimensions in centimeters and specific anatomical locations, should be recorded. Documented changes in the character of such items can help veterinarians convince owners to proceed with surgery or a more complete work-up at the time the change is discovered rather than the next time the animal is seen. Such notations are also invaluable in the development of a good legal defense, if one is ever needed.

The Examination

The patient's temperature, weight and, if possible, heart rate should be noted in some consistent location on the chart. It is frequently important to be able to refer to these figures over several visits to note and comprehend changes in a patient's condition. Unless body temperature is recorded nearly every time a patient is seen, it will be hard to determine whether a one-time temperature of 103° F is

The Diagnosis

After the examination portion of the record has been completed, a diagnosis or tentative diagnoses should be entered. Owners who consult veterinarians expect a diagnosis, pet health insurance companies require one and base their coverage of fees on it, and state boards of examiners that require medical records stipulate that some form of diagnosis should appear. Practices that use master problem lists establish a chronological list of conditions that may or may not contain a diagnosis associated with each one. Nevertheless, a master problem record usually is an adequate substitute for a specific diagnosis associated with each examination.

Treatment

The next important entry concerns the choice of treatment. If an anesthetic is administered, the type and dosage of preanesthetic and anesthetic drugs should be recorded. If surgery is performed, a description of the procedure and type of suture materials or orthopedic hardware should be noted, as well as whether or not subcutaneous or intramuscular sutures were placed. These notations can help determine if a subsequent swelling might be attributed to a suture reaction instead of an infection.

Of critical importance is information about medications administered. The standard of care is for practitioners to record injectable drug doses in cubic centimeters or milliliters. To prevent confusion, however, it is advisable for these amounts to be recorded in milligrams or units instead, unless the injectable drug used comes in only one concentration. It is also good practice to record how and where the drug was administered, for example, SQ, IM, right rear, IV, left cephalic, left jugular. These entries are invaluable, for example, if it becomes necessary to convince a client or the court that it was not an injection that caused a problem to an animal in a certain body location.

When oral medications have been given or dispensed, the medical record should indicate the name of the drug, the number of tablets or capsules, the unit size, and the dosage instructions. It is imperative that the veterinarian be able to tell owners how many pills were dispensed should a child or pet get into the container.

Some veterinary clinics use daily treatment logs. In such cases treatments for hospitalized patients are entered only on the daily log and not on the individual patient chart. This type of

record keeping necessitates searching in two locations whenever pertinent medical information is needed. Because of this, it is advisable to keep all information together in one location within the patient's chart. Although additional space is required within the chart, important information for billing and medical purposes also can be retrieved much more easily.

Special instructions to owners should be placed at the bottom of the written entries before an animal is released. Notes like "Owner to remove bandage in two days," or "recheck in one week" should stand out for easy reference. Staff members who release patients should enter their initials next to these entries so that it can be determined what was said to an owner and by whom.

Other Important Entries

A huge array of information can and should be included in the patient record. In private practice, though, time is often of the essence, and brevity is essential. In addition to the routine history and treatment information discussed previously, the following list of important items should be included in the record if possible:

- Requests and demands from owners that differ from the recommendations of the veterinarian.

- Client refusals of specific recommendations by the veterinarian for higher-quality care. Simple notes like "rec'd x-rays, owner declined" may be invaluable at a later date.

- Recommendations regarding referrals of patients to specialists for consultations or additional medical care.

- All telephone consultations with the owner, consultations with colleagues from within the same practice or outside of it, and consultations with any specialists. If an employee, rather than the doctor, talks to the owner, but the doctor makes the entry in the record, the note should read "telephone consult—Dr.

W.—DNT" plus the information discussed. The "DNT" simply means Dr. W. did not talk with the owner. Notations made by employees should contain their initials along with the entry.

- Discussions with owners concerning notification of laboratory results. Simple notes saying "O.N. lab results" (owner notified of lab results) allow the attending veterinarian and all the other staff people to easily determine what an owner has been told.

Omissions from the Medical Record

Care must be exercised in the wording and substance of all medical record entries, because at the time the entry is made there is no way of knowing who may read it later on. The following items do not belong in the medical record:

- any derogatory statements about a client, a patient, or another veterinarian
- any negative comments about an owner's personality, credit rating, or apparent chemical addictions
- comments about inferior equipment, personnel, or surgical instruments that led to an inadequate resolution of the case

It is understandable that important notations about a client's financial status or state of mind might be essential to the business. When information like this is needed, it is best to indicate it in the form of codes or abbreviations unique to the practice so that errant photocopying and distribution of a patient record to some other party cannot result in any legal action.

Alterations in the Record

As mentioned previously, the recording of medical information chronologically and in a timely manner is critical to the credibility of the record. No matter how careful one is,

however, errant or incorrect entries will be made. Usually any effort to alter the content or chronology will raise suspicions. Lines, pages, or paragraphs from the animal's chart should never be deleted or rendered illegible. When corrections must be made, they should be made overtly, not covertly. The best procedure is to draw one or two lines through the material to be eliminated and add the correct information in the margin, somewhere later in the chart, or on an addendum.

New entries or alterations should be dated, initialed or signed by the writer and should include proper explanations for the changes. Text that is blacked out automatically raises skepticism and makes it look like something is being hidden.

Explaining an overt amendment to the medical record under the stress of cross-examination is very difficult under any circumstances. Disclosure of covertly amended records under cross-examination, however, can devastate the veterinarian's credibility and significantly affect the verdict.[4] Furthermore, tampering with medical records is unprofessional conduct, and proof thereof can result in actions by the state board of examiners.

Medical Record Requirements

Some of the legal reasons why practitioners should maintain complete medical records are as follows:

- Some states have specific laws and regulations that require maintenance of medical records.
- Medical records are essential for the defense of civil or criminal suits for malpractice, negligence, incompetence, fraud, deception, unprofessional conduct, or cruelty to animals filed by animal owners, state boards of examiners, or district attorneys.

- Medical records are indispensable to the defense of grievances filed by clients with veterinary association ethics or peer review committees.

- Records are necessary for the documentation of income and sales taxes.

- Medical records are required to show compliance with controlled drug laws.

- They are a component of the evidence needed to show that a veterinarian-client-patient relationship exists.

- The equine mortality insurance industry and the growing pet health insurance industry require medical records to determine the extent of coverage under insurance policies.[5]

- At least one professional association—AAHA—requires that medical records meet certain standards in order for a hospital to be accredited by the association.

- Medical records can help verify that an enforceable contract was present for the care of a patient and collection of a fee.

Statutory Requirements

Medical records are specifically required by law in some states. California veterinarians performing any acts requiring a veterinary license on any animals in their custody or in the custody of their hospitals must prepare written records concerning the animals.[6] The phrase "in their custody" has been interpreted to mean under the veterinarian's care and thus pertains to animals seen on ambulatory calls as well as patients examined and treated in hospitals. According to the California Board of Examiners, large animal and poultry practitioners must have medical records for each client's flock or herd but not necessarily for each individual animal.

In Virginia, veterinarians are required to keep a written daily record of all the animals they treat.[7] The Virginia State Board has interpreted the word *treat* to include every

patient the veterinarian sees, whether or not any treatment was rendered. There is an exception for "economic animals," wherein records may be maintained on a per-client basis. Regardless of state statutes or regulations, practicing veterinary medicine without medical records or with inadequate record keeping procedures is considered to be unprofessional conduct or negligence. It could be determined that inadequate records constitute a violation of a state practice act.

Under California law, each patient's medical record must include (1) the name, address, and telephone number of the owner; (2) the name and identity of the animal; (3) the age, sex, and breed of the animal; (4) the beginning and ending dates of custody; (5) a short history of the animal's condition at the beginning of custody; (6) medications and treatments given or dispensed including amounts and frequencies of administration; and (7) an indication of the progress and disposition of the case.[8] Veterinarians also must maintain surgery logs, although the regulations do not state what facts must be on the log. California's regulations stipulate that medical records be retained a minimum of three years after the last visit.

In 1987, Massachusetts adopted a lengthy list of requirements for veterinary medical record keeping including such things as the chief complaint of each visit, results of examinations, and the type and dosage of anesthesia used.

Many of the California regulations were adopted in the late 1970s. Those codes and the ones in Virginia are among the most explicit regarding the necessity for medical records. Nevertheless, committees of the California Veterinary Medical Association have been extremely active in 1986 and 1987 revising many of the previous regulations in that state. Although the exact language of the regulations will not be finalized until after public hearings are held in the summer of 1988, the proposals for these regulations are well conceived (see Appendix C).

California's new standards also propose the first specific medical record keeping requirements for food animal veterinary practitioners. Although this document is only a proposal, its passage is advocated by the California Veterinary Medical Association, and it will be subjected to considerable scrutiny during the public hearing process. Practitioners who maintain their medical records in a manner that would meet the requirements proposed by the California Veterinary Medical Association probably will withstand legal challenges in other states as well.

The regulatory requirements for maintaining veterinary medical records vary significantly from one state to another. Each state's board of examiners in veterinary medicine should be contacted before a record system is established in order to assure that the system will meet the minimum requirements of that state.

In regard to owner access to medical records, some state practice acts require veterinarians to provide a summary of an animal's medical record to the owner within a reasonable time after it has been requested.[9] This requirement applies to medical records for all forms of veterinary medicine; i.e., food-producing, companion, and exotic animal practices.

Medical Records in a Legal Defense

One of the most important reasons for complete medical records is their importance in defending against a lawsuit or complaint filed with a state board of veterinary examiners, a veterinary association ethics committee, or a peer review committee.

Medical records prepared in a systematic fashion can be summoned to aid in one's legal defense at any time. Poorly prepared medical records may make the defense of a case difficult or impossible. Attorneys working for professional liability insurance companies often must recommend that cases be settled out of court rather than defended, primarily because of the inadequacy of the medical record. There is an old and often-quoted saying: "One line of faded blue ink is worth one thousand memories."[10] This statement is especially apt in a profession where patients cannot talk.

In most cases, the medical record is of primary importance to a practitioner's defense of a lawsuit. In other cases, it may be of grave importance to a legal action brought by a client against a third party. For example, when an animal inflicts an injury on a client's pet, it is not uncommon for the client to try to recover the costs for veterinary services. This can involve a small claims court action against the owner of the offending animal as well as a claim against the party's homeowner or renter's insurance company.

When such a claim is filed, the medical record is critical to ascertaining the cause and extent of an injury and the reasons for the veterinary fees incurred. In anticipation of receiving reimbursement, the client may request and authorize veterinary services, and veterinarians may extend credit for those services until reimbursement is made. If adequate documentation in medical records is lacking, clients may be unable to recoup their costs for veterinary care from the liable party, leaving the veterinarian unpaid and partially at fault.

Trials are exercises in truth and proof. The truth may be that the quality of medical treatment provided met the standard of care for the profession. Without written corroborative proof, though, a veterinarian's recollection of a case can be seriously impugned during examination on the witness stand. In addition, the judge or jury might assume that the failure to maintain adequate medical records reflects a lack of competence and a failure to attend to other details of proper medical care.

Basic Rules of Evidence

There are some general rules of evidence that explain further why the medical record is important. Trials often occur long after the event, and a risk of this time lapse is the witness's loss of memory. Therefore, rules of evidence permit the introduction of writings that help refresh a witness's memory, as long as those writings are relevant and authenticated.[11]

Medical records are used in a trial to show what was or was not done for an animal. Court rules of evidence require that the best evidence be presented whenever possible. Generally, the best evidence is direct evidence, i.e., the information provided by persons who witnessed with their senses what actually occurred. Examples include testimony by a veterinarian who examined and admitted a patient to the hospital, an animal health technician who helped treat the case, a kennel person who discovered the patient dead in its cage, or a pathologist who performed a necropsy on the animal.

Another type of evidence is hearsay. This is evidence based on what someone else said about a fact instead of what a witness actually observed. Ordinarily, hearsay evidence is not admissible in a trial. The courts have made a large list of exceptions to this rule, though, and will allow certain types of hearsay evidence to be admitted. One type of hearsay that is allowed consists of entries on business records. In order for the medical or business record to be admissible, the following criteria must be established:[12]

- The document must have been made at or near the time of the event.

- The writing must have been derived from information given by a person with knowledge of what occurred.

- It must be a record that is kept in the course of a regularly conducted business activity as shown by the testimony of a qualified witness.

Under the business records exception to the hearsay rule, the plaintiff in a malpractice case can introduce a relevant medical record to show what a veterinarian did or failed to do. This can occur whether or not the veterinarian testifies at the trial and even if the practitioner did not want such evidence introduced. This exception is very important, because properly documented and authenticated hearsay evidence plays a key role in determining the outcome of many cases.

Computer-Generated Medical and Business Records

Two types of records are generally kept in veterinary practices: business records (financial information) and medical records (patient information). Many computer systems today can accommodate both; however, most automated practices use computers primarily for accounting, marketing (mailing and reminder lists), inventory, and limited medical data storage.

No specific legal cases have yet dealt with the validity of computerized medical records as evidence. At least one state has elected to handle this issue in a statutory manner, rather than on a case-by-case basis. Section 1500 of the California Evidence Code says, "Except as otherwise provided by statute, no evidence other than the original of a writing is admissible to prove the content of the writing." This statute, known as *The Best Evidence Rule*, is standard in most, if not all, states. As computer technology has gained wider acceptance, especially for storing data, a change was needed in this rule. Therefore, in 1983, California passed another statute that provides the following:

> Notwithstanding the provisions of Section 1500, a printed representation of computer information... which is being used by or stored on a computer... shall be admissible to prove the existence and content of the computer information or computer program.

> Computer recorded information...or copies of computer recorded information or computer programs shall not be rendered inadmissible by the best evidence rule. Printed representations of computer information...will be presumed to be accurate representations of the computer information...that they purport to represent.[13]

The statute goes on to say that if a party to a judicial proceeding introduces evidence that the computer information is inaccurate or unreliable, the party who initially introduced such evidence will have the burden of proving that the printed information is the best available evidence of the existence and content of the computer information that it purports to represent.

The existence of similar statutory law must be researched on a state-by-state basis before it can be relied upon elsewhere. Nevertheless, the rule is reasonable and should go a long way toward reassuring practice owners that computer-generated business and medical records will be admissible in a court of law.

Although no appellate court cases discussing computerized medical records have been discovered to date, many courts have reviewed the admissibility of computerized general business records. Consequently, the court's views of business record admissibility will be used as an example by which the computerized veterinary medical record might also be evaluated.

The Three-Prong Test

In order to evaluate the authenticity and credibility of computer-generated information in a standard manner, many state courts have adopted the "three-prong test."[14] This test considers the following criteria: (1) whether testimony is given by an individual with reasonable knowledge of the computer system to satisfy the court that the information is trustworthy,[15] (2) whether the entries were made in the regular course of business at or near the time of the event recorded, and (3) whether the computer is recognized as standard equipment in the business environment.

Admissibility According to the Courts

A 1981 study of 117 cases involving the admission of computerized business records as evidence demonstrates the overall favorable opinion held by the legal system.[16] Most cases utilized the testimony of lay witnesses rather than that of a computer professional to intro-

duce data into evidence. The study also noted that computer-stored data appear to be treated like other business records.

Out of the 117 cases studied, there were only 16 objections (14%) to the admissibility of the electronic record, and of these, only 4 objections were sustained. In addition, it was found that objections to computer-stored data are "more likely to be offhand, pro forma, or a result of 'the heat of the battle'," indicating a lack of premeditated objection to the computerized record.[16]

Admissibility According to Others

According to the editor of the monthly newsletter *Legal Aspects of Medical Practice*, the issue of computerized medical records has been presented in trials involving medical malpractice cases. The editor's discussions with attorneys who have tried these cases established that the records have been admitted in court provided that a proper foundation has been laid. However, no cases are reported in that journal, and the editor knew of no appellate decisions.[17]

An article in the *Legal Aspects of Medical Practice* journal on the issue of medical records indicates that in some cases state statutory requirements could be an impediment. According to one source, "Most statutes mandate that the patient records must be written or typed and must be signed by the physician."[18] Although this may be the case with medical records for humans, requirements for signed handwritten records are not the rule in veterinary medicine. That article went on to say:

> An attorney must be extremely assiduous in laying a foundation for the introduction of these records. ... The entire record computerization process must be explained lucidly to the court and opposing party for the records to be introduced. However, if an attorney is diligent in laying a thorough foundation, there should be no problem in having computerized medical records accepted into evidence at trial.[18]

From this information, it appears that the groundwork already laid for the admissibility of business records has set a satisfactory precedent for the admission of computerized medical records. All that is needed are appellate court cases or state statutes upholding that contention.

Computer Record Reliability

One of the criteria of the three-prong test is that testimony as to the trustworthiness or reliability of the information presented in evidence is required. Computerized record reliability is based primarily on evidence that the computer-stored data are resistant to alteration.

The level of security of the electronic medical record is often compared with that of its traditional written counterpart. One of the major criticisms of computers is the alleged ease with which data can be altered. The written documentation found in most practices, though, is not entirely safe from alteration or complete replacement either.

Although some people have doubts about computerized record reliability, the potential to expand electronic security is great, whereas the handwritten record has little chance of becoming a more trustworthy form of documentation. Given a choice of data storage media, there is every reason to seek the most efficient and secure record keeping system available. This is an important point to keep in mind whether or not an individual is concerned with the legal implications of computerized medical records.

The Strengths and Weaknesses of Current Security Techniques

Although computers potentially can produce credible business and medical records, most software systems presently on the market provide limited security. Practitioners should be aware of some of the specific weaknesses inherent in this new technology: They include the following problems: (1) data entry errors, (2) electrical failures which erase or alter data, (3) errors caused by computer software or hardware systems, (4) intentional and unintentional errors and alterations produced by employees, (5) an ease of data alteration in some software systems that damages the credibility of the records, and (6) the fact that experienced operators and programmers can bypass security measures in order to enter and modify the program of even the most sophisticated software.[19]

The three methods that follow are some of the more common security features of veterinary-related software.

Unalterable Medical Records

Many methods have been designed to discourage accidental or purposeful alteration and protect the integrity of electronic information. The most stringent method is to block all personnel from editing data that have been entered and thus create an unalterable medical record. A major difficulty with this system is that data entry errors cannot be corrected. To overcome this problem, most systems allow alterations for a finite period of time, determined by the user, until the invoice is posted. The most frequent time period is 24 hours or until the end of the business day. At least one manufacturer provides for copies of the posted medical record to be sent to the client, thus ensuring the existence of an unaltered copy.

Passwords

Passwords are a very common form of low-level security. Their usage varies greatly, according to the number of security levels offered and the features protected. While passwords are definitely a step in attaining security, they do not afford sufficient protection alone. The best employment of passwords is in the prevention of accidental data alteration or destruction by innocent personnel who find themselves in an unfamiliar section of the program.

Passwords have at least two serious shortcomings. They can be discovered relatively easily by motivated individuals, and they do not protect data from those with the greatest desire to alter records, namely the administrative staff and the veterinarians themselves.

Audit Trails

The specific mechanisms for establishing an audit trail vary, but the general concept for all of them is the same. Each time a piece of information has been changed while working within the software, it is permanently identified as having been altered. Most systems have an option that will list all of the manipulated information. Some software packages even keep track of the individual making the alterations by recording the currently active password. A record of changes is stored in code along with the other data and is contained on the original data disk as well as on the backup copies.

With well-conceived audit trails, the only way to remove all evidence of alteration is complete erasure of the data-storage device, resulting in loss of all information stored on the computer. Although extremely difficult, it is conceivable that an experienced computer programmer could locate the incriminating information and alter it without the data being marked or eliminate that specific section from the system's memory. While this is a concern for large institutions, it is not of significant importance to the average veterinary practice and is unlikely to create legal difficulties.

The Future of Computer-Generated Medical Records

While computer security will never be ideal, there is no question that it has the potential to be more reliable than the traditional written medical record. The key to realistic computer security is to anticipate potential personnel and machine problems and safeguard against them. Equipment and software from proven manufacturers who offer complete support is mandatory. The next step is to guard against both accidental and intentional errors.[20] This can be accomplished through various means, including limiting access to trusted personnel, usage of passwords, cross-checking for error detection, and backing up data frequently.

The computer is currently a valuable adjunct to keeping medical records. Its legal acceptance seems to be a foregone conclusion as long as moderate security measures are taken.

Insurance Requirements

Mortality Insurance for Horses

The success and acceptance of mortality insurance in the horse industry create a significant need for quality medical records. As values for horses have risen and medical and surgical technologies have advanced, insurance carriers have become increasingly reluctant to pay claims on insured horses unless there is no chance that the sick or injured animal can recover. Because of this, proper documentation of diagnoses, treatments, failures of treatment, and excessive patient suffering may be required to ensure that an insurance company will pay benefits when an insured patient must be euthanatized.

When insured horses are seriously ill or injured and euthanasia is being considered, the insurance policy usually dictates that no death benefit will be paid unless the company has authorized euthanasia before it was performed. This poses an unusual consent situation wherein the insurance company's approval or denial of euthanasia may be more critical than the owner's.

In many cases, agents for the insurance companies will authorize euthanasia based on the attending veterinarian's description of the horse's condition. Other times, agents will provide an open-ended authorization for a veterinarian to euthanatize a horse if it continues to deteriorate during a time period when an insurance company agent is unavailable. Occasionally, the insurance company will send its own adjustor and veterinary representative out to examine the horse and review the medical care and condition of the animal before a decision is made. Therefore, for security reasons, whenever telephone authorizations for euthanasia are provided by owners or insurance agents, notations should be written on the patient's chart along with the authorizing person's name and phone number, the date, and the time of the conversation.

An added caution regarding euthanasia or necropsies on insured horses involves animal identification. If possible, veterinarians should retain a color photograph and a detailed description of the horse, and perhaps even preserve the tatooed lip in formalin.

Whenever a medical case involves the economic interests of the insurance industry, considerable care must be exercised to create a complete medical record. A failure to accomplish this can result in a refusal by the insurance company to pay benefits. This action, in turn, could precipitate suits by horse owners for financial damages related directly to improper and substandard medical record keeping, separate from any claims for the negligent practice of veterinary medicine.

A recent turn of events, coinciding with the equine mortality insurance industry's reluctance to pay claims on expensive insured horses, has been their willingness to bring suits against the veterinarians who provided medical care for horses that died or were euthanatized. In these cases veterinarians and their insurance companies become third-party participants in suits brought by horse owners against the equine mortality insurance company. The contention of the equine mortality companies is that, "But for the negligence of the attending veterinarian, they would not have been placed in a position where their insured horse would have died." Consequently, they seek reimbursement for their expenses to pay for the dead horse by referring the liability back to veterinarians and their professional liability insurance carriers. The medical record is crucial to the outcome of these cases.

Pet Health Insurance

The availability of pet health insurance is also growing, and it too enhances the importance of complete medical records. Although currently only a relatively low percentage of pets are insured, medical records have a major impact on individual cases.

Pet health insurance carriers frequently seek medical records to determine whether an insurance claim should be paid. Sometimes they only need to check that the condition for which the claim was filed originated after the insurance policy became effective. Other

times, the company needs to verify a diagnosis or substantiate the extent of injuries suffered by the insured patient in order to justify payment of the amount for which the claim was submitted.

In some respects, insurance company analysis of medical records is a form of peer review. Inadequate records can result in the insurance company's withholding payment for medical services rendered. This could induce a client to bring legal action for the amount of the claim that was denied due to incompetent record keeping or file a complaint with the state's insurance commissioner.

In addition, unsubstantiated claims, submitting claims on preexisting conditions, and padding of fees could provoke legal actions at the state court level by the insurance company for insurance fraud. The company or client could concurrently file a complaint with the appropriate state board of examiners against the licensed veterinarian for fraud, deception, or unprofessional conduct in the practice of veterinary medicine. In any of these situations, the quality of the medical record would be crucial to the outcome of the allegations or complaints.

Professional Association Requirements

An additional reason to maintain good medical records is that certain professional associations require them. Hospital accreditation by the AAHA requires that a practice's medical records meet certain criteria. The AAHA recognizes that medical records are an important tool in the practice of quality veterinary medicine, and it has compiled the 75-page *Medical Records Manual*, which includes sample record forms, log books, client education materials, and other information.[21]

AAHA's *Standards for AAHA Hospitals* state that (1) medical records must be available for examination by AAHA field representatives, (2) there must be evidence on the medical record that the diagnosis was made based on the information given by the client in the history, a careful physical examination, and a scientific interpretation of the findings, and (3) sufficient data must be recorded to justify the treatment of the patient and the results.

Contractual Requirements

Good medical records help establish that an enforceable agreement exists between the veterinarian rendering services and the animal owner who agrees to pay for such care. The following elements must be present for a contract to be valid: (1) an offer, (2) an acceptance, (3) a meeting of the minds as to the terms of the agreement, (4) an intent to make a contract, and (5) the exchange of an item called "consideration"—usually in the form of money.

Although most contracts for veterinary care are oral, these agreements are enforceable provided the necessary five elements are present. Whenever possible, agreements with new clients should be initiated with the client's completion of a written document. This gives the veterinarian considerably more clout if any disagreement arises regarding authorization for medical services. As shown in Figure 14.2, an initial consent form also can be used to notify clients in writing what action will be taken with animals abandoned at the practice.

Although it is common policy in veterinary emergency clinics to initiate each client visit with a signed written document, this is seldom done for routine daytime visits to small animal practices or by large animal practitioners. Requiring signed consents at every visit can raise feelings of distrust and is usually unnecessary.

A written agreement is advisable whenever major surgical or medical procedures are scheduled. New agreements for veterinary care also should be signed whenever a change of practice ownership or key veterinarians takes place. Emergency clinics should require signed agreements for each visit, because most people at these facilities are not regular clients and will not be part of an ongoing veterinarian-client-patient relationship.

Contractual Language and Consent

There are a variety of ways to establish a contractual relationship between clients and veterinarians. Some hospitals use client registration forms without any contract or consent language in them (Figure 14.1). Other forms combine client and patient information with contract and consent language (Figure 14.2).

Practitioners who want some type of contract language other than that in Figure 14.2 can use a simple statement on their client registration form as follows:

I hereby authorize the_____
_____ Veterinary   Hospital
and its designated associates or assistants
to treat, anesthetize, prescribe medication
for, or perform specified   diagnostic tests
or surgery upon my animal named
_____ . I agree to pay for services
rendered at the time my animal is discharged from the hospital or when service
is otherwise terminated.

Owner's or agent's signature

Date

For those who prefer more explicit wording, all or portions of the following can be used:

I, the undersigned owner or authorized
agent of the animal named_____
_____ , hereby   authorize
_____ Veterinary Hospital,
Dr. _____, and his/her assistants, to administer such treatments and to perform
such procedures as are considered therapeutically and/or diagnostically necessary for the care of my animal, including
the administration of anesthesia. In the
event that emergency treatment is required and I cannot be reached, I authorize
Dr._____ and assistants to perform such
medical and surgical treatment as is necessary to preserve the life of the patient until
I can be contacted for further authorization. I understand that no guarantee of

---

Jacket _____

Quest. No. _____

Meow Gram _____

Vacc. Reminder _____

Client Tally _____

CLIENT REGISTRATION FORM

Clients visiting our hospital for the first time are most welcome. Please complete this form as fully as possible. Please PRINT.

Date: _____

Name: _____ Spouse/Co-owner: _____

Address: _____

City: _____ State: _____ Zip: _____ Phone: _____

In case of emergency, do you have an alternate phone? _____

Is there someone we may thank for recommending our hospital to you? _____

Employer and address (If unemployed, give spouse's employment): _____

_____ Phone: _____

Name of Bank: _____ Branch: _____

All payments must be made at the time the services are performed. Please circle the payment method you find most convenient.

Cash   Check   Visa   Mastercard   American Express

We will gladly prepare a written estimate if you desire. Please ask the receptionist or doctor for your written estimate.

BIRD REGISTRATION AND MEDICAL HISTORY FORM

Bird's name: _____ Species: _____ Age: _____

Length of time owned: _____ Sex: _____ Bird's diet: _____

Vitamins? _____ Any recent changes in environment? _____

Is your pet allergic to any drugs or foods: _____ Name them: _____

Any previous history of illness? _____ Describe: _____

Reason for this visit: _____

If your pet is ill, please check changes seen at home:

Appetite:	_____ Urination changed	_____ Limping	_____ Fainting	_____ Bleeding
_____ normal	_____ Listless	_____ Crouched with	_____ Growths	_____ Swelling
_____ abnormal	_____ Weight loss	fluffed feathers	Eyes:	where _____
Bowel Movement:	_____ Shaking/	_____ Sneezing	_____ discharge	_____ Discharge
_____ diarrhea	Shivering	_____ Vomiting	_____ puffy	where _____
_____ straining	_____ Scratching	_____ Coughing	_____ closed	_____ Laceration
				where _____

Other: _____

How long have these problems been apparent? _____ days _____ weeks _____ months

I am the legal owner or representative of the legal owner of the animal being presented for treatment, and I am over the age of 18 years.

Signature _____

Figure 14.1   A client registration form that makes no referral to contracts, agreements, or authorization. (Courtesy of North Rockville Veterinary Hospital, Inc., Rockville, Maryland)

OWNER AND PATIENT REGISTRATION FORM

Name _____   Home phone _____
        Last   First   Middle

Address _____
            Street   City   Zip Code

Occupation _____   Work phone _____

Employer _____
            Name   Street   City   Zip Code

Spouse or co-owner's name _____
                            Last   First   Middle

Spouse or co-owner's occupation _____   Work phone _____

Spouse's employer _____
                    Name   Street   City   Zip Code

Referred by _____
                    (name of person, yellow pages, sign, etc.)

Pet No. 1		Pet No. 2	
Pet's name	Birth date	Pet's name	Birth date
Species Cat Bird Other Dog Reptile		Species Cat Bird Other Dog Reptile	
Breed	Sex	Breed	Sex
Color	Neutered?	Color	Neutered?
Date last vaccination		Date last vaccination	
Last Rabies vaccination		Last Rabies vaccination	
Allergies?		Allergies?	
List any long-term medical problems		List any long-term medical problems	
List any medications used routinely		List any medications used routinely	

I hereby authorize _____ Veterinary Hospital to examine, prescribe for, treat, or perform surgery upon the above-described pet(s). I also consent to the administration of such anesthetics as are necessary. Furthermore, I agree to pay fees for services rendered at the time the pet is discharged from the clinic or when service is otherwise terminated. _____ Veterinary Hospital is authorized to humanely dispose of said animal(s) unless I, the owner, or an authorized agent of mine, calls for and pays all accrued charges on the animal(s) within ____ days after written or oral notification that the animal is ready to be released from the hospital. I further understand that veterinary service is provided during night time hours as necessary in the judgement of the veterinarian in charge. Continuous presence of qualified personnel may not be provided at all times.

Please circle your preferred method of payment: **Cash   Check   Visa   Master Card   Veterinary Pet Insurance**

Signature of owner or responsible agent _____   Date _____

Figure 14.2 A client registration form that includes a client consent and authorization agreement. (Courtesy of Four Corners Veterinary Hospital, Concord, California)

successful treatment is made. I accept financial responsibility for the treatment of the above-named patient and understand that payment in full is due upon release of this animal from the hospital or when service is otherwise terminated. I certify that I have read and fully understand this authorization for medical and/or surgical treatment, the reason why such medical and/or surgical treatment is considered necessary, as well as its advantages and possible complications, if any. I hereby release Dr. _____ and assistants from any and all claims, except claims for negligence, arising out of or connected with the performance of his/her treatment.

_____
Owner or Agent's Signature

_____
Date

Another paragraph that can be included as part of the initial agreement is:

I realize that in many cases it is impossible to determine in advance the extent of medical or surgical treatment required for an animal. In such cases staff from the _____ Veterinary Hospital will attempt to estimate the cost of treatment, but it is understood that the actual cost may exceed or be lower than this estimate, depending upon the extent of treatment required.

Disclaiming all liability in some consent forms is seen by some people as inflammatory and should not be done. Because it is nearly impossible to disclaim liability for negligence, and most courts will never uphold statements in which the animal owner assumes all risks, wording to that effect is undesirable. It may, in fact, alienate some clients and make them distrustful rather than serve any valid legal purpose. The question practitioners should ask regarding their consent form is, "If I were a client at this practice, would I object to signing this?"

Consents for Euthanasia

Written Consents

Obtaining a client's consent is important prior to many different procedures. The most crucial time, though, is before euthanasia. There is no legal requirement for owners to sign an authorization for this life-ending act, but there are several legal and business reasons why the formality should be performed routinely.

1. A signed document helps verify that the individual who has signed it is in fact the owner or an agent of the owner of the animal.

2. Because of public health concerns about rabies exposure, it is important to ascertain whether or not any person or animal has been bitten by an animal that is about to be euthanatized. In some cases public health authorities quarantine the biting animal for several days prior to euthanasia. Other times, the practice must hold the animal's body or head until public health authorities can be contacted for a decision regarding the course of action. Identification of a potentially rabid animal after it has been euthanatized and the body has been disposed of can necessitate numerous people's undergoing rabies prophylaxis treatments. This can lead to considerable liability for veterinarians who failed to recognize their public health responsibility regarding this communicable disease.

3. Collecting fees that are still owed becomes a more difficult task once the animal is dead. Thus, asking owners to sign an authorization for euthanasia also provides an opportunity to request payment of charges or at least to make arrangements for remuneration.

4. Requiring that owners formally sign euthanasia forms helps ensure that their decision to euthanatize the animal is firm. It also averts a situation wherein clients argue that they thought putting

their animal to sleep meant giving an anesthetic. This can be an important consideration with clients who are senile, mentally ill, inebriated, affected by drugs, or have language barrier difficulties.

Some practices rubber stamp the patient's record to maximize efficiency and minimize additional forms. A stamp can read as follows:

I certify that I am the owner or authorized agent for the owner of the animal described above and that, to the best of my knowledge, this animal has not bitten any person or animal within the past 10 days. I hereby authorize Dr._____to euthanatize _____.

   Name of Patient

_____
Signature

_____
Date

There are also more formal euthanasia release forms. Figure 14.3 is an example of one used at a veterinary school. This form separates the bite incidents statement from the rest of the document and requires a separate signature. This additional measure is probably more important in larger institutions where less personal client-hospital relationships require that more formality be exercised with consent forms.

To deal with situations wherein a known bite incident has occurred, the statement found in Figure 14.4 can be placed unobtrusively on the back of the record form. This format provides a broad consent for necropsy and histopathology as directed by public health authorities. It also requires information needed by public health authorities to identify animals and people exposed to rabies.

Telephone Consents

When it is impossible for an owner to come to the practice to sign a euthanasia release, it is best to have a veterinarian use one telephone and a hospital employee listen on an extension telephone, identify his or her presence, and witness the owner's verbal authorization for euthanasia. The date, time, name of the authorizing party, and name of the witness are recorded on the patient's chart. Although this is not as good as a signed consent, it is superior to no written documentation at all.

Abandoned Animal and Nonpayment Agreements

Client registration contracts also can establish hospital policies on animals abandoned at the facility and nonpayment of fees. Some of the options regarding abandoned animals and liens are governed by state statutes (see Chapter 4).

Whether or not statutes exist, the client registration form should address the issue of abandoned animals. States without abandoned animal statutes will probably uphold any contractual agreement that is reasonable and that provides for notice to the owner. The following is one format:

In the event my animal is abandoned at _____ Veterinary Hospital, I hereby authorize Dr. _____ or the staff to humanely dispose of such pet if it has not been picked up within seven calendar days after notice by registered or certified mail has been sent to me at the address the hospital shows as my last current address.

An alternative to notice by registered mail is to state that notice may be simply written or oral. The following is an example of that approach as it pertains to abandonment or a failure to pay for all veterinary care.

_____ Veterinary Hospital is authorized to humanely dispose of the animal described above unless I, the owner or an authorized agent of mine, calls for the animal and pays all accrued charges within seven days after written or oral notification has been made to me that the animal is ready to be released from the hospital.

_____ **Veterinary Hospital**   **EUTHANASIA RECORD**

Date _____ Case No. _____

Owner's Name _____

Address _____

City, State _____ Phone _____

Description of Animal _____ Breed _____ Sex _____

Color and/or Markings _____ Patient's Name _____ Age _____

    I, the undersigned, hereby certify that I am the owner or authorized agent for the owner of the animal described above. I understand that by signing this agreement I authorize the _____ Veterinary Hospital and its agents or representatives to humanely euthanize this patient. I agree to release this hospital and its agents or representatives from any and all liability associated with the performance of this service.

Signature _____ Date _____

Address (if different from above) _____

Witness _____ Date _____

I certify that, to the best of my knowledge, this patient has not bitten any person or animal in the past 10 days.

Signature _____ Date _____

(If patient has been involved in a bite incident see reverse side of form)

Figure 14.3 This formal euthanasia release form would most commonly be used by a veterinary school, where client-hospital relationships are less personal. (Courtesy of the University of Pennsylvania)

I, the undersigned, hereby certify that my animal, named _____ , has bitten the following people or animals

Name of person bitten or owner of animal bitten   Name of animal bitten

_____   _____

_____   _____

_____   _____

_____   _____

_____   _____

To the best of my knowledge, the bite(s) occurred on _____
                                                       (date)

at the following address (es) _____

I hereby agree that the _____ Veterinary Hospital and its agents or representatives may contact appropriate Public Health Authorities regarding this bite incident(s) and undertake procedures for the diagnosis of rabies as deemed necessary by hospital personnel or Public Health Authorities.

Owner's Signature_____   Date _____

Figure 14.4 A section to be included on euthanasia forms for use in cases of a known bite incident.

(Hospital retains Original — Copy to Owner-Agent)

FEE ESTIMATE FOR VETERINARY SERVICES TO BE RENDERED BY _____
                                                                      Name of Hospital

To: _____
                             Patient's name

Breed _____ Sex _____ Age _____ Color _____   Owner/Authorized agent _____

Address _____   Phone _____   _____
                                                    (Home)   (Business)

Office visit	$ _____	Surgery:	
Examination	$ _____	Description _____	$ _____
Vaccinations	$ _____ Type: _____	Description _____	$ _____
	$ _____ Type: _____	Hospitalization & treatment	
Radiology	$ _____	Daily professional care _____	$ _____
Laboratory/Diagnostic service		Fluid Therapy _____	$ _____
	$ _____ Description _____	Injections _____	$ _____
	$ _____ Description _____	Medication used _____	$ _____
Other	$ _____ Description _____	Sedation and/or Anesthesia _____	$ _____

                                                        Total estimated fees . . . . $ _____

Some surgical and medical problems require more than a physical examination (blood tests, urine analysis, radiographs, etc.) before a total expense can be approximated by the doctor. The initial tests, care and treatment that have been recommended for the first 24 to 48 hours will be approximately $ _____ . If additional testing, care and treatment are needed, these will be discussed with you, based on information gained earlier. The first 24 to 48 hours are generally the most expensive proportionately to time, because the information needed for diagnosis, prognosis and treatment is gathered at that time. It is understood that these are estimated fees. If the animal's condition dictates, an effort will be made to contact you before additional treatment is rendered. Thank you for your understanding and cooperation.

_____   _____
Admitting veterinarian   Date

Figure 14.5 A duplicate-copy estimate sheet, wherein both the client and veterinarian retain a copy. This ia a more formal approach to fee estimation. (Courtesy of the Southern California Medical Association)

Serious problems of proof arise, though, if this is the only form of notification used, so registered mail is recommended.

Some states, like California, have abandoned animal acts that prohibit veterinarians, dog kennels, groomers, etc. from disposing of abandoned animals for 14 days after they were due to be picked up and for an additional 10 days during which a new owner must be sought.[22] Because this places a heavy burden on businesses holding abandoned animals, numerous California veterinarians have attempted to alter the terms of the statute by contract (Figure 14.2). When a state statute specifically provides for the disposition of an abandoned animal, there is some question as to whether a signed contractual release in a client registration form can alter a right granted to the animal owner by law.

Estimate Sheets— The Roots of a Contract

Discussions between client and doctor usually establish the terms of the agreement since most contracts for treatment are oral. Even though the client may have signed a contract or consent form, the terms of the agreement may be too vague to make it enforceable unless an estimate sheet is used.

The biggest concern with oral discussions and agreements is the difficulty of proving the contents of the conversation. Thus, written estimates take on considerable importance. The routine use of written estimates reduces client misunderstandings and complaints.

Estimates should be prepared whether or not clients request them so that the terms of the agreement are determined and understood by both parties. In the process, veterinarians are forced to develop an organized, cost-effective approach to solving the case, and clients can be urged to discuss any budgetary limitations they have. The list of procedures to be performed and medications to be dispensed becomes the basis for the agreement to render care. The fact that this information is contained in a written document provides legal and business proof of what transpired.

Duplicate-copy estimate sheets like the one

designed by the Southern California Veterinary Medical Association (Figure 14.5) or single-copy formats (Figure 14.6) can be used. Some owners want a copy to take with them, and some veterinarians feel better if they get an owner's signature on the estimate. Usually, though, owners simply want an idea of the projected costs without undue formality. In such cases, single-copy estimates left in the medical record usually suffice.

A sign or placard in the examination room similar to the one below invites discussion and can often encourage clients to request an estimate.

> Please Feel Free
> to Discuss Fees Before
> Services are Rendered
> We Accept
> VISA, Mastercard, Checks, Cash,
> and Pet Insurance

Since absolute estimates are unrealistic, broad ranges of fees for services like surgery or x-rays should be given to allow for difficulties encountered and amount of time required. When unexpected events require that the estimate be exceeded, authorization should be obtained by phone from the owner. The necessity for this action can be reduced by using broad ranges of fees or by including a statement in the estimate form that says owners will be notified only if the estimate will be exceeded by 10%.

If owners cannot be reached for additional fee authorization, practitioners should either not pursue the more expensive care or proceed only after efforts to reach the owner have been documented on the patient's medical record. Phone numbers called and time of day should be written on the record whenever attempts to contact owners were unsuccessful. The only exception to this is in a true emergency wherein there is legal justification for exceeding the estimate and collecting for extra services rendered without the owner's approval. The material on the "Law of Unjust Enrichment" or "Quasi-Contract" covered in Chapter 8 should be reviewed for additional information.

ESTIMATE & ITEMIZED DAILY HOSPITAL CHART

Patient _____   Owner _____

Date Service Performed

Service						Total
1. Prof'l Service / O.C.						
Initial Exam						
In-Hospital Exam						
Recheck Exams						
Tech. Ass't. Fee						
Consultations						
2. Immunizations						
3. Lab/Blood Panel						
Heartworm Test						
Culture & Sensitivity						
Cytology						
Fecal						
Pathology						
Skin Scrapings						
Urinalysis						
4. Radiology						
5. Anesthetic/Sed						
6. Surgery						
7. Operating Room						
8. Dentistry/Hygiene						
Extractions						
9. Medical Services						
Injections						
Pharmacy						
Fluids						
Casting & Bandages						
Ear Flush						
Intensive Care						
E K G						
Enemas						
I V Catheter						
Other						
10. Hospitalization						
11. Special Diets						

Total $ _____

Figure 14.6   A single-copy estimate sheet, meant to be left with the medical record until after the services have been completed.

Tax and Documentary Purposes

It is the taxpayer's responsibility to show that the information provided to a federal, state, or local taxing agency is correct. The medical record is one of the keys to providing accurate information, because it is the source from which all documented financial transactions originate.

Assuming federal income tax returns have been filed and there has been no fraud, information regarding income (including the medical record and expenses) must be retained for three years after taxes have been filed.[23] If a charge of fraud is made by the Internal Revenue Service, there is no time limit for retention of business and medical records. Although it varies from state to state, investigations and assessments of state income taxes can go back for a period of three to four years.

Sales tax information in jurisdictions that tax veterinary services or products also is derived in part from the medical record. Thus, it is equally important to retain these records for several years in case of audits by state or local governments.

Informed Consent Requirements

The issue of whether a client's *informed consent* was obtained before rendering veterinary services arises repeatedly under the law of negligence and malpractice. Traditionally, courts have applied either negligence or legal concepts of tortious battery to cases where physicians perform surgery without informed consent. Liability for battery originated with the common law concept of unlawful bodily contact. Liability for negligence can be imposed as a remedy for the physician's breach of duty to inform patients of material risks inherent in prescribed medications and surgery.[24]

In the human medical field the legal requirements under the negligence theory impose two duties on doctors: (1) a duty to disclose information about what will transpire

in terms that the patient can understand and (2) a duty to obtain the patient's consent for the contemplated procedures before they are rendered.[25]

The invasion of a person's body (who is often anesthetized) without that person's full understanding of what will transpire can be considered an assault or battery on the person. In veterinary medicine, animals do not have a right to be free from assault or battery unless the injurious action is classified as cruelty to animals. Thus, the law of informed consent in veterinary medicine has more overtones of contract law or the law of negligence than it does of tortious battery. It is in this context that veterinary consent forms should be approached. Clients who lack adequate information about risks and benefits from various medical therapies, diagnostic procedures, or surgical treatments are unable to contract for those services. Furthermore, veterinarians who fail to provide adequate information to their clients can be held to have been negligent.

Although there is no guarantee that a court will uphold a particular consent form, there is no justification for not using them. If consent forms are too broadly written, giving the veterinarian unlimited authority to perform treatment, they can be worthless. If they are too exculpatory, holding the practitioner harmless as a result of any claim arising out of the treatment, the court may hold that the consent is unenforceable.[25]

Sometimes all-inclusive consent forms like those previously discussed are satisfactory. When more specificity is desired, for example, regarding the administration of different types of drugs, sample consent forms like those found in Chapter 9 can be employed. However, consent forms also are valuable when anesthetics will be administered or surgery performed.

Many veterinarians defend their failure to obtain informed consent for surgery or anesthesia by claiming that full disclosure would so alarm clients that they might decide against a procedure that is essential for the patient's well-being. The courts have not viewed this as an adequate defense. In a study conducted by the medical profession, most patients not only have a right to know but want to understand

PRESURGERY INFORMATION

It is important to understand the steps that will be taken to protect your pet and to assure the best possible results. Please read this information sheet carefully.

Patient _____ Date of Surgery _____ Time of Surgery _____

——————— How to Prepare for Surgery ———————

Please follow these instructions:

1. No food or water after _____ the day before.
2. Drop off the animal at _____ on the day of surgery.
3. Inform us of all medications given during the previous 24 hours.

——————— Vaccination Status ———————

☐Current

until_____

☐We have no record of vaccination. Bring proof.

——————— What Will Happen in the Hospital? ———————

1. *Presurgical Examination*—Whenever an animal undergoes anesthesia and surgery, some risk is involved. The amount of risk depends on many factors, including age, general physical condition, and the condition of the heart and other organs. It has been found that risks can be greatly reduced if certain bodily functions are evaluated before giving an animal an anesthetic. In some instances, the presurgical exam may cause the operation to be delayed or even canceled.

2. *Preparation and Sterilization*—Skin around the surgical site is clipped and scrubbed thoroughly with an antiseptic. Drapes and instruments are sterilized. The surgeon and assistants scrub with antiseptic soap and wear gloves, caps, gowns and masks during surgery.

3. *Monitoring*—Heart and respiratory functions are monitored during the operation.

——————— What Will Happen After Surgery? ———————

1. *Postsurgical Care*—If your pet is hospitalized, it will be seen by the doctor during rounds each day. In addition, it will be attended by staff personnel, under the doctor's direction and will be examined by the doctor prior to discharge.

2. *Discharge Instructions*—Routine discharges are made by trained staff members. If you feel you must talk with the doctor personally, please make arrangements in advance.

Figure 14.7   A presurgery information and consent form. (Courtesy of Perry Pet Hospital, Duncannon, Pennsylvania)

the possible complications of a procedure regardless of how they may feel. Since risk disclosure is more likely to be traumatic for humans undergoing medical care than for animal owners whose animals are being cared for, this defense seems even less plausible for veterinarians.[22]

Sample Surgery or Anesthesia Consent Forms

An ideal alternative to a formally signed consent agreement is shown in Figure 14.7. If this presurgery information form is handed to clients prior to surgery or anesthesia on their animals, it can eliminate the necessity for in-depth discussions of anesthetic risks with every owner whose animal is about to be anesthetized. It includes information regarding the preparation of patients for surgery, presurgical and surgical procedures, and medical risks. Consistent use of a client handout such as this documents that clients have had access to the information contained therein.

When anesthetic risks for a particular patient are greater than average, the doctor can refer to the form and provide additional emphasis without frightening the client. At that time recommendations for presurgical blood panels, radiographs, EKGs, etc. can be made. For practices that routinely require preanesthetic blood work on all patients, the following can be printed as a section of the presurgery form in Figure 14.7:

If your pet is scheduled for anesthesia or surgery, you can feel fortunate that advances in anesthesia and surgery have made routine procedures relatively safe, with a low rate of complications. Occasional problems can occur due to preexisting conditions not evident during routine examination. To avoid these problems, we recommend that your pet be screened prior to surgery by means of the following laboratory tests: (1) white blood cell count, (2) packed cell volume, (3) kidney function test (BUN), (4) clotting time, (5) other tests as stated

---

These tests will be performed and you will be billed for them or they may be waived as indicated below:

I do not want the tests performed prior to anesthesia and surgery on my pet.

_____

Signature

_____

Date

Please perform these tests as recommended.

_____

Signature

_____

Date

For practices that prefer not to take this type of approach on all cases but that would like to use it for specific high-risk patients, the above waiver can be printed on the back of a second set of forms identical to those in Figure 14.7 or established as a separate form. In this way, the waiver is used only in applicable cases and does not appear on forms for routine cases where it would only induce unnecessary questions and concern.

When anesthetic and surgical risks are minimal, the Figure 14.7 form is enough, and no additional risk discussion by the doctor is necessary. This handout is ideal when surgery is being scheduled for the future. The same form also can be used, though, for patients scheduled for surgery immediately after an examination. When this occurs, the veterinarian checks off the blanks discussing food, water, medications given, and vaccination status as these questions are asked and then hands the form to clients for them to take with them. In this manner, clients can be invited to read the remaining information and ask questions they might have about hospital care before they leave the facility.

A postsurgery instruction form is shown in Figure 14.8. This form also provides specific written instructions for owners to review at home when they cannot remember what they were told at the hospital. Practices that regularly use forms such as these are unlikely to experience problems with informed consent for surgical or anesthetic procedures.

POSTSURGERY HOME CARE

Patient _____

Release date _____   Next appointment _____

To help continue your pet's recovery at home, it is important that you follow these instructions. If you have any questions, please call us.

1. Food and Water

- Allow nothing by mouth during the first _____ hours after the patient returns home.
- Water in small amounts may be given after _____ hours.
- Food, also in small amounts, may be given after _____ hours.
- Be careful—excessive water or food will cause vomiting.
- Resume normal water in _____ days and normal diet in _____ days.

2. Exercise

- Restrict all activity for _____ days.
- Mild exercise on a leash is permissible, but do not allow unrestrained running or jumping.

3. Incision

- Check the incision at least twice a day. As long as the incision remains closed, clean, and free of discharge, it is progressing normally.
- Try to prevent the patient from licking or scratching the surgical area.

4. Weakness

- Expect your pet to be weak for a period lasting up to 24 hours. This is an aftereffect of the anesthetic.

5. Problems to watch for

Call us if you detect any of the following:
- No appetite
- Repeated vomiting
- Persistent bleeding
- Chewing and loss of sutures
- Excessive swelling or discharge

6. Special Instructions:

_____
_____
_____
_____
_____

Figure 14.8   A postsurgery instruction and consent form. (Courtesy of Perry Pet Hospital, Duncannon, Pennsylvania)

Owner Consent Form

Veterinary Hospital University of Pennsylvania
Investigative Clinical Therapy

I, the undersigned, hereby certify that I am the owner (or duly authorized agent for the owner) of the _____ year old dog, cat, bird (circle one) named _____. I further understand that I have been asked to participate in a VHUP investigative clinical therapy study to determine the safety and effectiveness of a new modality of treatment. The study my animal is participating in involves (1) drug therapy _____, (2) surgery _____, (3) radiation therapy _____, and/or (4) other forms of therapy as listed _____
_____(circle appropriate types of treatment and place initials in spaces).

I agree to carry out the instructions given to me and to return for examinations as requested by the attending veterinarian. Before giving my consent by signing this form, I acknowledge that I have been informed of the costs, purpose and nature of this study and the most commonly experienced known adverse effects that might result from this course of treatment. Among those, the most serious adverse effects include _____
_____.

I understand that this therapy is experimental in nature and that no guarantees of its effectiveness can be made at this time. However, I acknowledge that the potential benefit from this treatment is important enough to my pet that I am willing to assume all the financial and treatment obligations involved, including potential increased costs related to adverse effects.

I understand that any time I have questions about the procedure to which I am consenting, I am welcome to ask the clinician involved. With a thorough understanding of the information described above, I voluntarily consent to have my animal participate in this study.

_____   _____
Owner or agent's signature   Date

_____   _____
Witness   Date

Form Control No._____

Figure 14.9   An investigative clinical therapy consent form.

Veterinary Hospital University of Pennsylvania

Consent for Surgical Repair
of Inherited Defect(s)

I, _____, hereby certify that I am the owner
(or duly authorized agent of the owner) of an animal named
_____, a _____ year old
_____ (dog, cat, etc.). I understand that
_____(name) has been diagnosed as
affected with _____,
a condition known or believed to be hereditary in nature.

   I hereby consent to the surgical repair of this condition
understanding, and having been advised, that the repair of this
heritable defect is intended solely for medical health reasons and
not to conceal the presence of a defect.

   I have been advised, and understand, that the presence of this
heritable defect makes it inadvisable to breed this animal, and
that surgical repair of the defect does not alter this situation.

   I understand and agree that the repair of this heritable defect
is being performed on the condition that _____(animal's
name) will not subsequently be entered or exhibited in any breed
shows.

_____   _____
Owner or agent's signature   Date

_____   _____
Witness   Date

Figure 14.10   Consent form for surgical repair of inherited defect(s).

Sample Clinical Investigative Study Consent Forms

Occasionally private practitioners will engage in clinical investigative studies on behalf of pharmaceutical or biological companies or in conjunction with a veterinary school. Clinicians at universities, on the other hand, often engage in new investigative studies. In either case, the procedures performed or treatments rendered are generally experimental in nature and, thus, not within the standard of care for veterinary practices. When this situation arises, the use of a consent form like that in Figure 14.9 is indicated.

Consents for Repair of Inherited Defects

Veterinarians are occasionally placed in an awkward ethical position when they recommend or clients request surgery that would intentionally or inadvertently conceal an animal's inherited defect. This ethical concern stems from the "Genetics Defects" section of the AVMA *Principles of Veterinary Medical Ethics*. It says

> Performance of surgical procedures in all species for the purpose of concealing genetic defects in animals to be shown, raced, bred, or sold as breeding animals is unethical. However, should the health or welfare of the individual patient require correction of such genetic defects, it is recommended that the patient be rendered incapable of reproduction.

Practitioners often fear that if they insist upon the animals being neutered, their clients will seek another veterinarian who will agree to perform the procedure without demanding that the animal be neutered. This outcome would result in lost income or the greater impact of the loss of a client. Veterinarians also fear that unless they have some type of written documentation, their clients can selectively "not remember" any prior discussion of this subject. They also fear that if their recommendation is an oral one the client can easily elect "not to remember" any such discussion.

Conversely, veterinarians feel that if they agree to perform the surgical repair they may be promoting or perpetuating serious medical problems for that animal's progeny as well as for the breed. In most cases their concern would be alleviated if they could be assured by the client that the animal would not be bred, shown, or raced.

It is an extremely difficult prerequisite to demand of clients that they have their animals neutered or agree never to race, breed, or show them before inherited defects are surgically corrected. The consent in Figure 14.10 has been drafted to capture the philosophy underlying this ethical principle without categorically requiring clients to neuter their animals.

Ownership, Possession, and Access to the Medical Record

Medical records are the physical property of the hospital or the proprietor of the practice that prepares them.[26] Records may be held against the demands of outsiders until proper legal process is completed. When a court has ordered that a medical record be provided to legal counsel for an opponent, a copy—not the original—should be provided unless the court demands the original. If an original is required, a copy is retained for the veterinarian's records. The medical record is such an important legal document that practitioners must always preserve a copy of a patient's entire file.

Some states require that the owner be provided with a summary of a record within a reasonable time or within 30 days after it has been requested.[27-29] It is usually best for the veterinarian to be open with clients and allow them to view certain portions of the medical record. In most states clients do not have a right to the record itself or a copy thereof without a court order. In New York, however, failing to make copies of medical records prepared and paid for by a patient or client available upon request is considered to be unprofessional conduct and a violation of state law.[30]

If legal action is likely, the decision to withhold a copy of the record until a court order is received should be made in consultation with an agent from the veterinarian's professional liability carrier or with legal counsel. When patient records are of high quality and the medical care delivered is clearly within the standard of care, a decision to provide the client with a copy of the record may discourage legal action.

Copies of or information from veterinary records may be provided without the owner's consent to governmental agencies or other people who have a legitimate interest in their contents. Examples include public health authorities who have a legitimate interest in the health of the client's animals, animals belonging to others, or for human health reasons, such as with positive tuberculosis or brucellosis test results. The standard test is whether or not the party has a "legitimate interest" and "needs to know."[31]

The hospital director or practice proprietor decides whether information contained in a medical record or the record itself should be released. Consent from the veterinarian who attended the case is not needed if that person is an employed veterinarian, because any right of nondisclosure belongs to the owner of the patient or the owner of the practice. Once a record has been completed and properly filed in the hospital, that record becomes the property of the practice owner.

Confidentiality of Medical Records

It is the duty of the veterinary proprietor or medical records librarian to maintain the confidentiality of the medical record. In the university setting this becomes a monumental task because many cases are referred to the school for in-depth care and involve numerous veterinary personnel.

Serious problems with breaches of confidentiality occur less frequently in veterinary medicine and usually with less potential monetary damage than they do in human medicine. In the human health care field, courts frequently have upheld the right of a patient to recover damages from a physician for unauthorized disclosure of

information. One of the legal theories applied is that such disclosure constitutes an objectionable invasion of the patient's privacy. Recoveries also have been granted on the grounds that disclosure by the physician constitutes a breach of the legally recognized confidential or privileged relationship between the patient and physician.[32] To understand their rationale, a discussion of the legal *privilege* for professionals is necessary.

Many courts in the criminal justice system recognize a legal privilege to withhold certain types of information from discovery by the court. This exclusion of evidence involves incriminating statements occurring in the course of a relationship between particular professional people and their clients or patients. Examples include the physician-patient, attorney-client, and pastor-parishioner relationships. No privilege to withhold incriminating information exists in veterinary medicine. In the few jurisdictions where communications between patients and physicians are not considered to be privileged, the courts have refused to recognize any liability for disclosure of confidential information.[32]

In veterinary medicine, a suit for invasion of privacy with subsequent personal injury damages is less likely to occur than a suit based upon the interference in the financial relationship between a client and another party. Examinations and veterinary care for patients with hereditary defects, for expensive animals being offered for sale, and for valuable breeding stock pose the biggest risks for serious damages.

Other veterinarians, including those providing for subsequent health needs for a patient, do not have a right to receive a copy of a patient's record unless the owner requests that it be provided. (See Chapter 15 for discussion of this problem relative to prepurchase examinations.) Disclosures of ordinary facts not related to professional veterinary services, however, can be made without authorization from an owner. Such things as patient age, name, breed, species, sex, and probably vaccination history and medications dispensed can be released without the owner's authorization. Disclosures of more detailed information like a patient's history, examination findings, diagnosis, and full course of therapy should be withheld until the owner's consent to provide information has been received.

To maintain the confidentiality of medical records, hospital directors and medical record administrators must establish a specific procedure for the release of information and adhere to it. The following information printed on a postcard can simplify and document an owner's authorization to release information from an animal's medical record.

Request for release of
medical records

To: veterinarian's name_____
address_____
city, state, zip_____

I hereby request that a copy
of the medical records of my
animal(s) named _____
_____ be released to
veterinarian's name_____
address_____
city, state, zip_____

Owner's signature

_____

Date

_____

Veterinarian's approval

_____

Date

When well-established clients are moving and have not yet determined who their next veterinarian will be, it is common practice to provide them with a copy of their animal(s) record. If for any reason this makes a practitioner uncomfortable, .the use of a postcard consent is a practical alternative.

Although most veterinary practices routinely provide copies of patient records at no cost to owners, there is no legal reason why a fee for this service cannot be charged. Clients must be informed beforehand of the practice's policy, and veterinarians should recognize that many clients will object to this policy. An acceptable procedure in some hospitals is to provide copies of records that are less than

three to five pages in length at no charge but to assess a fee for those that are longer.

Retention of Medical Records

The aspect of record retention is one of the areas pertaining to medical record keeping that all state boards of veterinary examiners should address. Unless a state board regulation exists, veterinarians will always be in jeopardy of discarding records too soon or retaining them longer than they need to. If there is no specific state board policy, practitioners cannot know whether the rules covering physicians will be applied to them or whether some unknown common law precedent in the jurisdiction will apply.

California and Virginia require that records be retained three years from the last patient visit or discharge of the patient from the hospital.[6,33] Massachusetts has proposed that the medical record be retained for four years after the last "encounter" with the patient.[29] Theoretically, this would mean four years from the last telephone call pertaining to the care of the patient unless encounter is interpreted to include an examination. New Jersey requires that records be retained for five years from the date of the patient's last visit unless the patient is deceased, in which case the time period is three years from the last date of entry.[28] When a veterinary board has not published any direction on this subject, the safest tack would be to retain patient records for at least three years after the last visit.

Questions may arise regarding records remaining after a veterinarian dies, retires, or simply closes the practice. Since there is a paucity of precedent in veterinary medicine regarding this issue, the policy applied to human medicine must be examined. In general, record retention by physicians is required for longer time periods (10 years is common) than for animals, because life expectancies for people are so much longer. According to one author, "the judicial qualities of the physician-patient relationship require retention of medical records that may be of value to patients and that are not transferred to a new physician."[34] Therefore, it would appear that any medical records remaining at the time of a veterinarian's death or retirement must be retained the same length of time as would otherwise be required in the jurisdiction for veterinary medical records. If the records are sold or given to another practice, that practice will have a legal duty to fulfill the required time period before destroying the records.

Ownership of Radiographs, Electrocardiograms, and Laboratory Reports

Most of the following discussion deals with policies for handling radiographs, because these records pose some unique problems regarding duplication. However, other portions of the patient record can be equally important to a case. Most states have established that, along with radiographs, all electrocardiograms, electroencephalograms, and other laboratory test results belong to the medical practice that made them.[35]

In 1935, the Michigan Supreme Court held that radiographs are the property of the physician or hospital that produced them regardless of how the cost is charged to the patient.[36] The Michigan case involved a human patient, but the reasons given by that court for its decision are also applicable to radiographs of animals. Four reasons for the ruling were given:

- Radiographs are part of the history of the case, like notes made by the physician, and therefore are a part of the medical file of the patient.

- They represent a professional service involving a skill and judgment, like anything else the physician does.

- Radiographs have extraordinary and irreplaceable value to the physician.

- They are meaningless to most lay persons and are useful only when associated with other factors in the case and when expertly interpreted.[31]

This precedent leaves no doubt that radiographs are the property of the medical facility that produced them, and this fact has been reiterated in some state board regulations.[6] Because radiographs are an irreplaceable part of the medical record, they should not be released from the practice except under certain circumstances and then only by following a specific protocol.

Radiograph Transfers

Clients usually request the release of radiographs for one of two reasons: (1) they are dissatisfied and are seeking second opinions from other veterinarians, and (2) they are being referred to another veterinarian for consultation or for further care. The procedures in releasing radiographs depend greatly upon the reason the client wants them.

If the client is involved in a friendly referral wherein there is little or no question of negligence, it is satisfactory to release the radiographs to the client. This should never be done, though, without obtaining a signed statement in the medical record as follows:

I hereby accept custody of _____ (the number of films) x-ray films of my pet named_____, taken by _____ Veterinary Hospital, for transport to

Dr. _____

at_____ (name of facility) for the purpose of consultation and/or additional veterinary care.

_____

Owner or agent's signature

_____

Date

This statement can be written longhand on the patient's chart or placed on a separate form. Although it is probably safer from a legal viewpoint to send the films through the mail, this may be unsatisfactory because of the imminent need for a consultation. The use of a signed statement that makes the owner the responsible agent is an acceptable alternative.

A different approach should be taken if a dissatisfied owner requests the radiographs or if there is a potential for a claim of malpractice.

In such a situation the referring practice should require the following:

- a statement signed by the owner authorizing and requesting the release of the radiographs
- a documented oral or written request from the veterinarian who will be receiving the radiographs noted in the patient record
- that an employee deliver the radiographs personally to the practice that has requested them or send them by registered or certified mail with a return receipt requested

Radiograph Identification

At least two states have either proposed or current regulations directing that all exposed radiographic films contain some form of permanent identification legibly exposed in the film emulsion. The specific requirements include (1) the hospital or clinic name and/or the veterinarian's name, (2) client identification, (3) patient identification, (4) date the radiograph was taken, and (5) left and right imprints.[37] Even if other states do not have specific regulations regarding identity of the radiograph, a failure to do so generally would be considered to be below the standard of care for veterinary medicine. This is because the authenticity of a radiograph is lost without some form of permanent identification on the developed film. This does not prevent films with phony identification from being created by practices trying to cover up an omission. However, that situation can be dealt with by reviewing the practice's radiology logbook.

Radiology Logbooks

At least one state board of examiners requires veterinarians to maintain radiology logbooks as part of a practice's medical records.[38] In addition, the AAHA recommends their use in order for a hospital to be accredited.[3] This is (1) because it constitutes good medical practice, (2) because the exposure settings must be recorded each time a film is taken so that they may be duplicated when follow-up films are taken, and (3) because the presence of a logbook is invaluable corroborative evidence when attempts are made to prove that radiographs were taken as indicated on the patient record.

If radiographs are sequentially numbered, the radiology logbook provides a running tally of all patients that were radiographed. Any time a patient's number is out of order or absent from the sequential logbook, the authenticity of that radiograph is diminished. This is true even if the film emulsion contained proper information about the patient in question.

The best way to authenticate a radiograph with a high degree of accuracy is to compare the information on the film with the data in the logbook and on the medical record. If the film information looks accurate but the logbook seems too perfect or has two animals with identically numbered radiographs, the credibility of the film(s) is impaired. If the film information looks correct and the logbook appears accurate, but the bone structure of the patient does not match that of the patient described on the medical record, the radiograph is suspect. Right and left markers

RADIOLOGY										
Date	Owner & Patient	Age	Sex	Breed	X-ray No	CM	KV	MA	SEC	View Taken & Diagnosis

Figure 14.11   A complete format for a radiology log book.

on the film are also critical in order to properly identify the patient and the location of the animal's lesion.

An example of a complete format for a radiology logbook can be found in Figure 14.11.

Radiograph Retention

Since radiographs are part of the medical record, the same retention time applicable to medical records should apply to them. That time period varies from three to five years after the patient was last seen at the veterinary facility. If a state has no specified time period for retention of veterinary medical records, a court could apply the same time period required for the retention of radiographs or medical records by physicians.

Theft of Mailing Lists and Computer-Generated Records

The availability of photocopy machines and application of computer technology to veterinary medical record keeping have heightened opportunities for thefts of important and valuable information. Probably the most vulnerable and valuable record is a veterinary practice's manually created or computer-generated client mailing list. Theft of a hard copy (paper) print-out or a floppy disk containing the list can occur with considerable ease. Theft of other computer information or computer software, and alterations or destruction of the practice's financial data base, i.e., accounts receivable, or other business or medical data are additional concerns. The theft or unauthorized use of a manually created mailing list by a competing veterinarian could produce a significant loss for most practices. An act of this type could be prosecuted under criminal statutes, civil law (for compensation), and possibly as an administrative action by a state board of examiners.

In recent years numerous states have passed specific statutes dealing with computer access problems. In California, for example, any person who intentionally and without authorization accesses any computer system or data, with knowledge that the access was not authorized, is guilty of a public offense.[39] If the unauthorized access does not result in any injury or damage, conviction of the infraction is punishable by a fine not exceeding $250. For a second infraction or where injury or damages occur, the fine may not exceed $5000 or imprisonment in the county jail not exceeding one year, or both.[39] New Jersey has statutes similar to those in California providing for prosecution of individuals who have knowingly and without authorization altered, damaged, taken, or destroyed any data from a computer system.[40]

Although laws in other states have not been cited, concerned practitioners can look in the index of any state's statutory code under the heading "Computers" to locate the state statutes pertaining to the theft, alteration, or destruction of computer software, hardware, or data. Conviction of a crime of this nature by a veterinarian would most certainly be considered unprofessional conduct. Under the typical state veterinary practice act, proof that unprofessional conduct has occurred is grounds for veterinary license revocation, suspension, fines, or admonishment.

Lost Medical Records

An interesting case involving lost medical records occurred in the human health care industry in 1974.[41] During discovery, the physician defendant was unable to produce the original clinical records concerning his treatment of the plaintiff. He claimed that the original records were recopied in a more legible form when he was informed that the plaintiff was seeing another physician so that the other doctor would have readable medical records available. The original records could not be located, and the defendant assumed that they had been thrown away.

On appeal, the court held that the fact that the defendant was unable to produce his original clinical records concerning his treatment of the plaintiff *after* he had been charged with malpractice created the inference of consciousness of guilt on his part. Even though he admitted partial liability and attempted to use that admission to counter arguments regarding the missing records at trial, the court held that that was not good enough. Instead, the court held that his partial admission did not neutralize the effect of spoilation (altering or destroying medical records) and that a party's suppression of evidence by spoilation can be used to create an inference against him as an indication of his consciousness that his case is a weak or unfounded one.

This case is a good example of spoilation not only hindering the defense of a case involving malpractice but also indirectly supporting a plaintiff's cause of action and likelihood for a recovery.[42] Although it may appear preferable to have no patient record rather than a mediocre one, legal cases repeatedly show that this is untrue.

Improving the Routine Medical Record

Many different techniques can be used to improve the efficiency, usefulness, credibility, and accuracy of medical records.

Timeliness

One of the exceptions to the hearsay rule permits authenticated business records to be admitted as evidence. Two of the criteria for admission are that the record be made at or near the time of the event and in the regular course of business. This reflects the fact that the longer it is before pertinent information is recorded, the less accurate the information is likely to be. Therefore, entries should be made as near as possible to the time the information was discovered or treatment rendered.

When nonveterinary staff members render treatments to patients, they too should record each treatment performed on the medical record. One method for handling this is for the doctor to write down various treatments and times and for staff people to check them off as they are performed. It is helpful with large staffs for assistants who administered medications or treatments to place their initials after the entries.

For maximal credibility, notations on the record should appear chronologically. When information must be entered by technicians or other doctors before the attending veterinarians have made all their notations, enough empty lines should be left so that additional comments and material can be entered later. It is best to leave excess room when additional entries must be made rather than to skimp. Insufficient space requires that added information be entered out of sequence. This makes the record more difficult to read and impairs the credibility of the medical record and the medical care provided.

Gaps left in the record should alert those people responsible for filing the record that information is lacking. Establishing a hospital policy that patient records with gaps be returned to the attending doctor helps prevent these records from being filed in an incomplete state.

Dealing with Incomplete Records

The best technique to prevent incomplete records from being filed is to tag those that need additional information. A small 2-in. by 3-in. hard paper marker printed with **"Doctor Needs to Write Up This Record"** is clipped to the record. Whenever an attending veterinarian or a staff person plans to complete a record later or notices that it is incomplete, one of these tags is used. Placing the tags at strategic locations throughout the hospital helps doctors and staff people prevent records from being filed until the additional data have been entered. This system allows partially completed records to be used by other staff people without the concern that the records will be filed before they are completed.

Differentiating Staff Entries on the Record

Medical records should always be in ink. If records are typed, the practitioner's initials or signature should appear at the end of the entry. The ease with which pencil records can be changed reduces their credibility and admissibility in court.

A problem in multiperson practices is the difficulty in identifying which doctor wrote what in the patient's record. A simple solution is to have each doctor use different-colored ink. If the photocopy equipment used by the practice is carefully set, often four to five different-colored inks can be used, and legible copies will be produced. Red, green, blue, brown, and black seem to photocopy well on quality machines. One of the positive effects of this system is that it tells practitioners quickly when and by whom the patient was seen. This impresses clients and makes the entire staff look efficient.

Flow Sheet
Laboratory Forms

Practitioners should be searching constantly for the simplest and most efficient way to compile medical records. Now that diagnostic laboratory work is so commonplace, a means must be devised to provide easy access to all of that information. A multiple-entry laboratory form such as the one in Figure 14.12 provides a running tally of CBC, blood chemistry, and urinalysis results on one sheet of paper. The sequence for recording values should mimic that of the external laboratory used most often. Because there are spaces for seven different samples and places for many different tests, six to 15 extra sheets of paper can be eliminated from the medical record before a second page is needed.

There are three basic problems with this arrangement: (1) if different laboratories are used with different reporting sequences and numbering systems, practices will have difficulty transferring data; (2) once several year's worth of lab data are recorded on a specific flow sheet set up to match that of the laboratory, it is difficult to change labs and switch all the old records to a new format; and (3) it takes time to transcribe information received from the laboratory onto this type of form.

In addition to minimizing bulky patient charts, there are some other pluses: (1) it is much easier to develop a chronology for a patient, (2) it is easier to compare specific blood values, (3) upward or downward trends in individual items are more apparent, and (4) anyone picking up the record can instantly find all of the laboratory history without having to piece it together from individual entries on the medical history.

Hospital Census List

A daily release list like the one shown in Figure 14.13 is a simple way to provide the front desk with basic information about hospitalized patients and thereby save unnecessary phone calls. These forms should be printed on tear-off pads. For maximum benefit, they are filled out each morning and updated each afternoon. For larger institutions with a higher in-patient census, the form shown in Figure 14.14 may be more practicable. Notes placed in the status or comments columns directing when patients are ready to be released assist the receptionist in creating an orderly release schedule.

This is also a perfect location to place notes about personal phone calls expected at the practice that day. This can prevent many missed telephone calls while allowing the receptionist to give knowledgeable status reports with minimal time and effort. Because all this information is readily available to the receptionist, the practice appears and is well organized.

The Use of Photographs

A great practice builder and technique for improving medical records is to have a high-quality Polaroid camera at the practice. Just as "one line of faded blue ink is worth a thousand memories," "a photograph is worth a thousand words." When photos of alopectic patients and various skin or oral lesions are taken, clients are impressed by the thoroughness of the examination. When clients ask why the picture is being taken, they can be informed that it enhances the attending veterinarian's recollection and allows other members of the hospital staff to evaluate the

Clinical Pathology Flow Sheet

Owner   Animal   Species   Sex   Age

Clinical history and comment

	HEMATOLOGY		"AVIAN NORMALS"	CANINE REFERENCE RANGE	FELINE REFERENCE RANGE						
1	WBC	X10³	3-10	6.0-17	5.5-195	1	1	1	1	1	1
2	RBC	X10⁶		5.5-8.5	5.0-10.0	2	2	2	2	2	2
3	HGB	gm%		12-18	8-15	3	3	3	3	3	3
4	HCT	%	40-55	37-55	24-45	4	4	4	4	4	4
5	MCV	U³		60-77	39-55	5	5	5	5	5	5
6	MCH	uug		19.5-24.5	12.5-17.5	6	6	6	6	6	6
7	MCHC	%		32-36	32-36	7	7	7	7	7	7
8	Reticulocyte	%		0.5-1.5	0 – 1 +	8	8	8	8	8	8
9	NRBC/100 WBC			0	0	9	9	9	9	9	9
10	Neutrophil Seq	%	30-75	60-77	35-75	10	10	10	10	10	10
11	Neutrophil Band	%	< 2	0-3	0-3	11	11	11	11	11	11
12	Lymphocyte	%	25-70	12-30	20-55	12	12	12	12	12	12
13	Monocyte	%	0-4	3-10	1-4	13	13	13	13	13	13
14	Eosinophil	%	0-2	2-10	2-12	14	14	14	14	14	14
15	Basophil		0-5	Rare	Rare	15	15	15	15	15	15
16	Metamyeiocytes			0	0	16	16	16	16	16	16
17	Myelocytes			0	0	17	17	17	17	17	17
18	Promyeiocytes			0	0	18	18	18	18	18	18
19	Blast cells			0	0	19	19	19	19	19	19
20	Platelets	x10³		200-500	300-700	20	20	20	20	20	20
21	Platelets Est.	☐ Increased	☐ Decreased	☐ Adequate		21	21	21	21	21	21
22	Polychromasia	1+	2+	3+	4+	22	22	22	22	22	22
23	Anisocytosis	′1+	2+	3+	4+	23	23	23	23	23	23
24	Polkilocytosis	1+	2+	3+	4+	24	24	24	24	24	24
25	Leptocytes	1+	2+	3+	4+	25	25	25	25	25	25
26	Howell Jolly Bodies	1+	2+	3+	4+	26	26	26	26	26	26
27	Heinz Bodies	1+	2+	3+	4+	27	27	27	27	27	27
28	Other					28	28	28	28	28	28
29	FIA	☐ Positive		☐ Negative		29	29	29	29	29	29
30	Microfilaria	☐ Positive Appears to be_____		☐ Negative		30	30	30	30	30	30
31	FeLV-Ag	☐ Positive Titer_____		☐ Negative		31	31	31	31	31	31
32	FIP	☐ Positive Titer_____		☐ Negative		32	32	32	32	32	32
33	Parvovirus-HA	☐ Positive Titer_____		☐ Negative		33	33	33	33	33	33
34	Parvovirus-HI	☐ Titer_____				34	34	34	34	34	34
35	Brucella	☐ Positive Titer_____		☐ Negative		35	35	35	35	35	35
36	Sed Rate	MM		/Min.		36	36	36	36	36	36
37	Coombs	☐ Weak 1+ 2+ 3+ 4+		☐ Negative		37	37	37	37	37	37
38	ANA	☐ Positive Titer_____		☐ Negative		38	38	38	38	38	38
39	LE Prep	☐ Positive		☐ Negative		39	39	39	39	39	39
40	PTT					40	40	40	40	40	40
41	PT					41	41	41	41	41	41
42	Fibrinogen					42	42	42	42	42	42
43	FDP					43	43	43	43	43	43

Figure 14.12 A multiple-entry laboratory form such as this provides easy access to all laboratory information.

Clinical Pathology Flow Sheet

Owner   Animal   Species   Sex   Age

Clinical history and comment

CHEMISTRY		"AVIAN NORMALS"	CANINE REFERENCE RANGE	FELINE REFERENCE RANGE						
1 Alk. Phosphatase	IU/L		10-150	10-80	1	1	1	1	1	1
2 SGPT (Alt)	IU/L		5-60	5-60	2	2	2	2	2	2
3 SGOT (Alt)	IU/L	120-130	5-25	5-25	3	3	3	3	3	3
4 CPK	IU/L		10-60	10-60	4	4	4	4	4	4
5 LDH	IU/L	100-420	50-305	80-305	5	5	5	5	5	5
6 Amylase	IU/L		200-1900	200-700	6	6	6	6	6	6
7 Lipase	IU/L		15-150	5-95	7	7	7	7	7	7
8 Albumin	gm%		2.3-3.4	2.1-3.3	8	8	8	8	8	8
9 Protein total	gm%	2.25-5.5	5.4-7.8	5.4-7.8	9	9	9	9	9	9
10 Globulin	gm%		3.1-4.2	3.3-4.5	10	10	10	10	10	10
11 Bilirubin, Total	mg%		0.1-0.6	0.1-0.4	11	11	11	11	11	11
12 Bilirubin, Direct	mg%		0.1-0.1	0.1-0.1	12	12	12	12	12	12
13 Bun	mg%		10-25	20-30	13	13	13	13	13	13
14 Creatinine	mg%	0-0.7	0.8-1.8	0.8-1.8	14	14	14	14	14	14
15 Uric Acid	mg%	2.0-10.0	0.0-2.0	0.0-1.0	15	15	15	15	15	15
16 Cholesterol	mg%		150-300	95-130	16	16	16	16	16	16
17 Glucose	mg%	200-300	60-115	70-150	17	17	17	17	17	17
18 Calcium	mg%	9.0-12.0	8.4-11.2	7.5-10.2	18	18	18	18	18	18
19 Phosphorous	mg%		2.5-6.0	4.0-7.0	19	19	19	19	19	19
20 Potassium	mEq/L	2.5-4.7	4.0-5.6	4.0-4.5	20	20	20	20	20	20
21 Sodium	mEq/L	135-150	141-156	147-156	21	21	21	21	21	21
22 T-4	ug/dl		1.0-3.6	1.1-3.9	22	22	22	22	22	22
23 T-3	ng/dl		75-150	27-95	23	23	23	23	23	23
24 Cortisol	ug/dl		1-6		24	24	24	24	24	24
25 BSP			Less than 5%		25	25	25	25	25	25
26 Other					26	26	26	26	26	26

URINALYSIS

1 Date:					
2 Method:					
3 Volume:					
4 Color:					
5 Clarity:					
6 Specific Gravity: 1.0					
7 pH:					
8 Protein:					
9 Glucose:					
10 Ketones:					
11 Bilirubin:					
12 Blood:					
13 WBC/HBF:					
14 RBC/HBF:					
15 Bacteria/HPF:					
16 Epl. Cell/LPF:					
17 Mucous/LPF:					
18 Casts/LPF:					
19 Crystals:					
20 Others:					

patients' improvement. These photos must be properly labeled with the correct date, location on the animal, and client and patient information in order to be admissible as evidence.

Photographs are required whenever practitioners suspect that they are seeing a case involving alleged cruelty to animals. Before and after photos or videotapes of these cases comprise some of the best evidence available for use in court.

Incidental Notations

Notations about clients and their interests can be valuable information in the medical record. Interest in the client as well as concern about the patient is demonstrated if such things are remembered.

Many practices find it useful to record a number or letter at the top of the medical record indicating something about the clients' responsiveness to the needs of their animals. For example, a "1" may indicate a client who is extremely cooperative and will agree to all recommended procedures without question. A "2" can mean a client who prefers an estimate before authorizing any significant care but who will usually accept the doctor's recommendations. A "3" can indicate a cautious client who needs to be convinced that each expenditure for care is essential and who may not be as likely to follow through with recommendations. Lastly, a "4" may connote a client who has defaulted on payments in the past or who is notoriously irresponsible regarding follow-up care.

Many owners who peruse the medical record while waiting for the doctor will be offended by literal descriptions on the chart of themselves or their animals. This is good justification for the use of code systems like the one just described. Also, reminding staff people about idiosyncrasies of the animals are much better if done in code. A "C," or "CAUTION" can indicate a fractious animal. Notations about the client must always be in code, for example, "OTL" can mean that this client is "out to lunch," and it is not worth spending much time on explanations.

Notations about the special status of certain clients can also be helpful in avoiding embarrassing situations. Statements like "personal friend of Dr. A" or "neighbor of Dr. B" will allow for immediate recognition of these people by staff who are unaware of this hierarchy of clients.

Arm Twisters and Bail Outs

Sometimes young veterinarians who have not yet mastered sales techniques or who lack experience can be placed in difficult situations by strong-willed clients. In these cases a statement such as the following can be of immense value on the medical record. In fact, the mere request that owners sign this subtle "arm twister" often convinces them to allow the practitioner to proceed with the recommended course of treatment.

I understand that the surgery/medical care for the above-named patient _____ will, upon my request, be performed in a manner other than that recommended by Dr. _____.
Since this is at my request, I hereby accept all risks of complications resulting from this unorthodox or unrecommended procedure.

_____
Signature

_____
Date

In other situations, when it appears that attempts to provide additional medical care will only create greater stresses for the staff, it is often best to simply "bail out." Legally, however, doctors cannot leave patients in a precarious medical state. In such a situation the following statement placed on the medical record could either convince an owner to cooperate or seek care elsewhere.

Daily Release List

Owner	Patient	Problem	Status	Med?	Releasor

Figure 14.13 A hospital daily release list.

Daily Hospital Census Report

Services: _____   Date: _____

Time Report Compiled: _____   Clinicians: _____

Owner's Name	Patient's Name	Breed	Sex	Food Eaten %	Tentative Diagnosis	Attending Clinician	Comments: Patient Attitude (alert, depressed, active - etc.) Patient Status (stable, improved, temp. ↑ or ↓ Vomiting, diarrhea, urination, etc.)	Owner Needs Call Back

Figure 14.14 An alternative daily release form for larger institutions.

I, the owner of the following animal(s) _____ hereby request that _____ Veterinary Hospital provide no further medical care for my animal(s). I acknowledge that further veterinary medical care is/may be essential to my animal's well-being, and will seek such care on my own. I understand that Dr. _____ will provide a summary of my animal's medical record to the veterinarian of my choice within a reasonable time period after I request that the medical records be transferred. I hereby agree not to hold Dr. _____ liable

for any medical complications occurring as a result of my decision to seek veterinary attention for my animal(s) elsewhere.

_____
Signature

_____
Date

Veterinarians have no legal duty to see every client and patient that requests their care. When they or their staff dislike some clients (or patients) and find that they are impossible to work with, it is best to terminate the relationship. The stress created is not worth the income derived.

References

1. Wilson JF: *Business Guide for Veterinary Practice*. Princeton, NJ, Solvay Veterinary, Inc, pp 76-97, 1983.
2. *Medical Records Manual*. Denver, American Animal Hospital Assoc, pp 2.0-2.01, 2.2.00, 1978.
3. *Standards for AAHA Hospitals*. Denver, American Animal Hospital Assoc, 1983, § 1.00-1.07.
4. Jevicky JE: Medical records addenda. *Legal Aspects Med Pract* 14(4):6, 1987.
5. One company, Veterinary Pet Insurance, 400 N Tustin Ave, Suite 375, Santa Ana, CA 92705-9940 has already processed over 100,000 claims and paid out in excess of $2 million for medical care.
6. California Administrative Code, Title 16, Chap 20, 2031.
7. Virginia Board of Veterinary Medicine Regulations § 4.2 (4).
8. California Business and Professions Code, Chap 11, 4855.
9. California Administrative Code, Title 16, Chap 20, 2031.
10. Pritchard WR: Legal aspects of the veterinary medical record. *JAVMA* 172(2):176-180, 1978.
11. California Evidence Code § 711.
12. Federal Rules of Evidence § 803(6).
13. California Code of Evidence § 1500.5.
14. Medina AM: The admissibility of computer records as evidence. *Wash State Bar News* 39:14-19, 1978.
15. 222 So. 2d. 393 (Miss.) (1969).
16. Bronstein DA, Engelberg D: A preliminary assessment of the reception of computer evidence: Report of the computer evidence survey project. *Jurimetrics J* 29:329-332, 1981.
17. Hirsch H: Personal communication, Pharmaceutical Communications, Inc, Long Island City, NY, 1987.
18. Berenato MA: Keeping your patient's medical records. *Legal Aspects Med Pract* 12(3):7, 1984.
19. *Office Information Systems Security User Manual*. Wang Laboratories, Inc, 1982.
20. Reichenbach T: Data security: Keeping high-tech crime out of your practice. *Mod Vet Pract* (Oct/Nov):840-841, 1986.
21. *Medical Records Manual*. Denver, American Animal Hospital Association, 1978.

22. California Civil Code § 1834.5.

23. Internal Revenue Code 6401.

24. Rumore JJ, Al-Bagdadi FK: The doctrine of informed consent and its applicability to the field of veterinary medicine. *JAVMA* 181(5):450, 1982.

25. Hannah HW: Informed consent and consent forms. *JAVMA* 182(7):850, 1982.

26. Pritchard WR: Legal aspects of the veterinary medical record. *JAVMA* 172(2):178, 1978.

27. California Business and Professions Code § 4855.

28. New Jersey Administrative Code § 13:44-2.12.

29. 256 Code of Massachusetts Regulations § 5.01(3).

30. New York Education Law § 6506, Chapter 1, Board of Regents, Part 27.1(7).

31. Rumore JJ, Al-Bagdadi FK, Titkemeyer C: Medical records and the law. *JAVMA* 178(3):203, 1981.

32. Sh! Patient privacy and confidentiality in a lawsuit. *Legal Aspects Med Pract* 13(2):7, 1985.

33. California Administrative Code, Title 16, § 2031 (b)(2).

34. Lydon DR: Physician's advocate. *Legal Aspects Med Pract* 14(10):7, 1986.

35. Regan LJ: *Doctor and Patient Law*, ed 3. St Louis, The CV Mosby Co, 1956, p 530.

36. *McGarry v JA Mercier Co*, 262 NW 296, Michigan Supreme Court (1935).

37. Virginia Board of Veterinary Medicine Regulations § 4.2 (5). See also California Proposed Minimum Standards of Practice § 2030 IV.(C) found in Appendix B, this text.

38. Marasco JV: Medical records keeping: Part II. *Calif Board Exam Vet Med Newslet* (Fall): 4, 1983.

39. California Penal Code § 502.5 (d), (f).

40. New Jersey Code of Criminal Justice § 2C:20-30.

41. *Thor v Boska*, 113 Cal Rptr 296 (1974).

42. Shemonsky NK: The impact of "lost" medical records. *Legal Aspects Med Pract* 14(9):6, 1986.

CHAPTER 15

Legal Principles Associated with Prepurchase Examinations

Prepurchase examinations, unfortunately, mark the beginning of many ethical, moral, and legal problems.[1] This chapter focuses on the equine prepurchase examination because it is the one most commonly performed. The same principles and pitfalls, however, apply to prepurchase physical examinations of other species such as racing greyhounds and field trial and sled dogs, as well as to breeding soundness examinations of cattle, swine, horses, and dogs. Many references that detail the standard of care for breeding soundness examinations of cattle are available.[2–8]

The problems associated with prepurchase examinations are far more complex than those inherent in routine veterinary practice, because prepurchase examinations deal with immense variations in the value of those animals, predictions about future health and function of patients, and numerous people and personalities. Many of the difficulties that occur in veterinarians' relationships with buyers, sellers, and agents of these parties are discussed herein.

Terminology

Equine practitioners have been called upon for many years to render opinions about the basic soundness of horses to be sold; these traditionally were called *soundness examinations*. Considerable disagreement arose, however, because of the connotation of the word *sound*. Opinions on whether a horse was sound for use as a cutting horse, a pleasure horse, a broodmare, or as a show or racehorse were disputable. To some people, sound means fit for the intended use, while to others it means free from any evidence of lameness. These variations in understanding have created considerable and often difficult problems for equine practitioners performing this service.

Because of the inherent inadequacy of the term *soundness examination*, some practitioners now use the term *purchase examination* or *prepurchase examination* as the title for this service. It is also called *physical examination* by some since that is truly what is being performed. This choice coincides with the terminology used in the world of professional sports in which

359

pretrade physical examinations for athletes are standard operating procedure. All of these terms have fewer connotations than "soundness," apply better to all species of animals, and can include examinations for factors other than soundness to work or perform athletically. It is anticipated that these titles will continue to be adopted throughout the industry.

Liability Concerns

Increasing Liability Risks

The price of many breeding and show animals has risen recently to that of a car or a home. Concurrently, buyers have become more selective about the health, temperament, identification, and/or athletic abilities of the animals they purchase. Since there are ever-increasing numbers of people but only a finite number of animals achieving the status of champion, best of show, or Derby winner, this trend toward higher prices will continue.

As the price for an exceptional animal climbs, so does the buyer's tendency to sue. In addition, often times sellers try to force a purchase once a horse passes its examination, while buyers tend to hedge, saying that their purchase is entirely dependent upon the veterinarian's findings at the time of the exam. This places a heavy burden on veterinarians who serve as medical evaluators and leaves them increasingly vulnerable to liability suits. If a veterinarian performs a prepurchase examination in a negligent manner, and the buyer suffers financial loss by relying on that exam, the veterinarian can be liable for damages.

The Issue of Confidentiality

There are numerous pitfalls in performing prepurchase examinations on horses. An awkward situation can occur, for example, when a buyer asks an equine practitioner to perform a prepurchase examination on an animal owned by one of the practitioner's regular clients.

In order to understand some of the issues associated with breaches of confidentiality, it helps to review legal doctrines in other areas of the law. In the criminal justice system, there are legal privileges to withhold certain types of information from the court. One can exclude, for example, incriminating statements made in the course of a relationship between professional people and their clients or patients. Such relationships include the physician-patient, attorney-client, and pastor-parishioner relationships. With regard to civil suits, legally enforceable confidential relationships exist, but there is no absolute privilege to withhold incriminating or confidential information from the court.

In veterinary medicine there is no privilege to withhold information in either civil or criminal cases. The legal system does recognize, however, confidential relationships between veterinarians and clients.[9] Practitioners who breach the integrity of this relationship can be liable for damages.[10]

When prior care has been rendered to a seller's horse, the veterinarian may have considerable knowledge about the medical history of the horse being examined. The confidential relationship with the seller, however, precludes the veterinarian from providing pertinent information to an inquiring buyer.

One question that arises, then, is what information about prior medical care rendered to a horse being examined during a prepurchase exam can be divulged to prospective buyers without breaching a veterinarian's confidentiality with the seller? And conversely, how much information can be legally withheld from a buyer without breaching one's agreement with that party to perform a quality prepurchase exam? In many cases, these questions remain unasked or unanswered because the parties are uncomfortable with the subject and would rather avoid it. The issues and answers surrounding the confidentiality of medical records are not clear cut. They are influenced by ethical and legal factors, which are addressed herein.

Conflicts of Interest

A complication of the confidentiality issue occurs when the relationship between a veterinarian and a seller is likely to be harmed by a finding that the horse is unsuitable. This can damage present and future seller-veterinarian relationships. If this is a possibility, veterinarians should decline as examiners because of the conflict of interest. Forgoing the fee is better than risking one's reputation and credibility.

A related problem involves the question as to which party veterinarians can represent when performing a prepurchase examination. According to the *AVMA Principles of Veterinary Medical Ethics*:

> When employed by the buyer to inspect an animal for soundness, it is unethical to accept a fee from the seller. The acceptance of such a fee is *prima facia* evidence of fraud. On the other hand, it is deemed unethical to criticize unfairly an animal about to be sold. The veterinarian's duty in this connection is to be a just and honest referee.[11]

Clearly, if practitioners abide by the code of ethics, they should be involved only in performing prepurchase examinations for buyers.

Occasionally, the seller will disagree with the findings of the veterinarian who performed the prepurchase examination. If this occurs, the veterinarian or the seller can recommend that a second opinion be sought. Second opinions, however, pose problems for sellers, because not many buyers are anxious to pay for a second examination when their veterinarian found the animal unsuitable on the first exam. Because of this,

To tell or not to tell, that is the question.

recommendations for second opinions usually are received more favorably by buyers if veterinarians rather than sellers make them.

Another difficult problem to be dealt with is that horses that fail a prepurchase examination may become unsellable. Word travels rapidly within the small community of the horse world, so practitioners must be as fair as possible when performing prepurchase examinations.

Areas of Legal Concern

Three basic areas of legal concern exist with regard to prepurchase exams:

1. the buyer's involvement in the process,
2. the examination itself, and
3. the seller's position in the relationship.

The Buyer's Involvement in the Prepurchase Exam

Attendees at the Examination

The presence or absence of buyers and sellers at the time of the examination is an issue of concern. If possible, sellers or their agents should be present during the entire course of the examination. If no one representing the seller is in attendance and a lameness or other defect is discovered, sellers are apt to blame the attending veterinarian for causing an injury and thwarting the sale. Buyers or someone representing their interests also should be present during the examination so that they can ask questions and see first hand exactly what transpired.

If either party is absent during the examination and the practitioner discusses the findings with each party individually, any disparities in what the parties are told will be magnified by disparities in what they remember. The veterinarian is caught in the middle and easily can become the scapegoat for a reluctant buyer. Because of this, practitioners should create accurate medical records, provide good written summaries of their findings, and maintain well-documented telephone consultation notes.

On the other hand, when the buyer and seller are both present during the examination, different problems occur. For example, every time the buyer or veterinarian wants a more in-depth evaluation of some aspect of the horse's condition, the seller might interject commentary that defends the horse. These comments can intimidate the buyer, upset the veterinarian, or limit the additional evaluation.

Some practitioners overcome these potential obstacles by having buyers at the scene for the majority of the examination and requesting that the sellers join them for a summary near the end. This allows the veterinarian and buyer to work in private for the primary examination but still gives the seller the opportunity to answer questions and listen to the veterinarian's conclusions in the buyer's presence. It does not, however, provide for the seller's observation of the entire examination. This is an important legal consideration in that the veterinarian can more easily be blamed for injuring the patient during the exam if the seller is not present. A better solution is to have both parties present but have them separated by enough distance so that conversations with each can be held privately.

A frequent problem with prepurchase examinations is that the buyer lives a great distance from the horse being sold and cannot be in attendance. It is best in such cases to have buyers employ or appoint an agent to represent them at the exam. If this is impossible, a conference telephone call to discuss the findings can be helpful. By doing this or by sending a written report, both parties hear the same discussion or see the same written summary, and communication gaps are minimized.

The Horse's Intended Use

A problem that can stem from the buyer's absence at the examination is a failure on the part of the veterinarian to ascertain how that party intends to use the horse. It is essential for an equine practitioner to know the intended use of an animal in order to determine its suitability. A notation of the intended use should be made on the examination record. An oral discussion and recollection by the three separate parties is totally inadequate, especially if any legal question arises. Figure 15.1 is an example of a buyer's statement and prepurchase examination agreement form, which includes the intended use of the horse as one of the first entries.

Identifying the Horse

Since similarities in markings and coloring are common among horses, another concern is proper identification. Unless the patient is tattooed, it is advisable to include a photo of the horse on the prepurchase examination form. In the absence of a photograph, a thorough description of the animal is critical. Opportunities for substitution of horses following examinations are greatly reduced if animals are properly identified and information is recorded on the buyer's consent form or the medical record.

Disclosing the Value of the Horse

Opinions regarding whether practitioners who perform prepurchase exams should know the horse's sale price differ greatly among veterinarians. Most practitioners say that they would rather not know the value, because they feel the quality of the examination should not vary according to the sales price. Others say that they would like some oral information on the price, because they are likely to recommend more extensive screening tests on expensive horses. The vast majority feel that the asking price should not be written anywhere on the medical record where future buyers might possibly gain access to the information.

A parallel issue concerns whether the fee for a prepurchase exam should vary depending upon the value of the horse. Most practitioners charge a set fee for the basic physical examination, but the total fee depends on whether the buyer demands more sophisticated diagnostic tests. It seems reasonable, though, that the fee could vary based partially upon the sale price simply because the liability risk for the examination of a $500,000 horse is considerably higher than it is for a $5,000 animal.

Evaluating Behavior and/or Reproductive Capabilities

Behavior evaluations can and often should be of concern to the buyer. A good pre-

purchase exam form should routinely state the buyer's desires regarding temperament, performance, and reproductive capability along with information on what kind of stabling is expected. If temperament and train-ability are critical issues to the buyer, veterinarians should recommend that buyers seek opinions from competent trainers. In addition, a horse's willingness and ability to get in and out of a horse trailer can be an important concern to some buyers and may need to be evaluated by a trainer.

Practitioners who do not feel confident evaluating reproductive soundness or temperament should indicate that their examination will not cover those areas. An example of such a disclaimer is found in Figure 15.2. Referrals to qualified colleagues are appropriate in these cases and should be noted in the examination record.

The Buyer's Consent

It is difficult to formulate an ideal buyer's consent form that accomplishes every goal. Practitioners feel differently about the amount of time and effort that should be spent on this aspect of the prepurchase exam. In some cases, little or no information is available regarding the desires, needs, and expectations of the buyer. When this occurs, practitioners are well advised not to perform the examination. If no other veterinarian is available to fulfill the buyer's request, however, and the practitioner agrees to do it, considerable attempts should be made to determine what the buyer wants. Although some form of written documentation is important in all cases, written annotations regarding the buyer's knowledge of the horse and intended use take on added importance when the buyer is a stranger.

The value of the horse in question also has an impact upon the examination process, with examinations of high-priced animals generally requiring better documentation than examinations of lower-priced ones (even though the exams are much the same). The use of buyer's consent forms, like those shown in Figures 15.1 and 15.2, provides a

Buyer's Statement and Prepurchase Examination Form

Prospective buyer's name _____ Phone _____

Address _____

Seller's name & address _____ Phone _____

Intended use of the horse _____

Identification of the animal (attach photograph or make drawings of both side views and head)

1. Name _____

2. Age _____

3. Sex _____

4. Color _____

5. Markings _____

    _____

6. Gelded _____

7. Age when gelded _____

8. Tatoo number _____

Proposed principal rider: Name _____ Relationship to buyer _____

Age _____ Height _____ Weight _____ Ability _____

How long has the buyer known the horse? _____

Which of the intended uses have been attempted? _____

Of what importance are the following (use 0-10 rating system):

  Blemishes _____

  Performance _____

  Temperament _____

  Reproduction _____

What type of stable care is anticipated for this horse? _____

_____

I, the undersigned, hereby request that Dr. _____ perform a prepurchase examination on the above-named horse. Estimated fees for the various examination procedures are listed on the next page.

Figure 15.1   A buyer's statement and prepurchase examination agreement form.

A. Required Portion of Examination   **Fee**

    1. Thorough physical examination of those organs routinely available for examination   _____

    2. Other procedures   _____   _____

                                       _____   _____

                                       _____   _____

B. Optional Diagnostic Procedure	Estimated Fee Ranges	Comments		Estimated Fee Ranges	Comments
1. Breeding Exam			**3. Laryngoscopic Exam**	_____	_____
a. Mares: uterine culture	_____	_____	**4. Blood Tests**	_____	_____
uterine biopsy	_____	_____	a. CBC	_____	_____
b. Stallions: semen analysis	_____	_____	b. Blood chemistries	_____	_____
semen culture	_____	_____	c. Coggin's test	_____	_____
			d. Other	_____	_____
2. Radiological Exam					
a. Feet: left front	_____	_____	**5. Fecal Analysis**	_____	_____
right front	_____	_____	**6. Urinalysis**	_____	_____
left rear	_____	_____	**7. Blood or**		
right rear	_____	_____	**Urine Drug Tests**	_____	_____
b. Carpus left	_____	_____	**8. EKG**	_____	_____
right	_____	_____	**9. Other**	_____	_____
c. Hock left	_____	_____			
right	_____	_____			
d. Other areas, e.g., chest	_____	_____			

The above procedures, their advisability, and their cost have been explained adequately to me by Dr.
and I have requested those procedures that I wish to have performed.   _____

_____   _____
Signature of prospective buyer or agent   Date

VETERINARIAN'S FINDINGS

Abnormal or Undesirable Finding   Potential Impact on Intended Use

1.   1.

2.   2.

3.   3.

4.   4.

5.   5.

6.   6.

_____   _____
Veterinarian's signature   Date

Buyer's Statement and
Prepurchase Examination Agreement Form
(Buyer's Section)

A. Proposed buyer's name _____ Phone _____

   Address _____

   Seller's name _____ Intended use of horse _____

   How long has the buyer known the horse? _____

   Which of the intended uses have been attempted? _____

B. Horse's name _____ Age _____ Sex _____

   Color _____ Markings _____

C. Special exams/tests requested (Fee): Initial those desired

     1. Radiology (x-rays) _____

       Front feet (_____) _____ Hocks (_____) _____ Other (_____) _____

     2. Endoscopy (scoping of upper airways) (_____) _____

     3. Blood tests: CBC (_____) _____ Chemistry screen (_____) _____

       Coggin's test (_____) _____

     4. Blood/urine drug tests (_____) _____

     5. Fecal (_____) _____

     6. Urinalysis (_____) _____ (Buyer/attendant to provide sample)

     7. Other (_____) _____

I, the undersigned, hereby request that Dr. _____ perform a prepurchase exam

on _____ . The seller/person responsible for this horse's care

has stated to me, the buyer, that this horse has/has not received any medication within 14 days.

If the horse has received medication within the past 14 days, when and what was administered? _____

_____

This page must be completed and signed, in duplicate, before the doctor will complete Part 2.

_____	_____
Buyer's signature (or buyer's agent)	Date

Page 1 of 2

Figure 15.2   An alternate buyer statement and prepurchase examination agreement form.

Buyer's Statement and
Prepurchase Examination Agreement Form
(Doctor's Section)

Buyer's name ——————————————————— Horse's name ————————————————

Seller's name ——

Listing of abnormal or undesirable findings and blemishes:

——
——
——
——
——
——
——
——
——
——
——
——

Results of special exams/tests:

——
——
——
——
——
——
——
——

This prepurchase examination is an observation only of the external organs capable of examination by this doctor. It is a listing of the results of the examination and not a guarantee of the horse's future usefulness. This doctor does not perform breeding soundness exams and makes no statement about this horse's breeding abilities.

———————————————————————————— ——————————————————
Veterinarian's signature   Date

place to document important information that should reduce significantly the liability associated with equine prepurchase examinations and generate more complete examinations in the process.

Reviewing the Components of the Exam

The last and, perhaps, most important concern to the practitioner is the buyer's understanding of all the components of a quality prepurchase examination. The psychology of explaining a thorough prepurchase exam is different than that associated with routine examinations. Animals under discussion in prepurchase exams are usually healthy, whereas most of the animals seen by veterinarians in normal practice are not. Owners expect numerous diagnostic tests to determine why their animal is sick; buyers do not expect to be offered the gamut of tests to prove that the horse for sale is well.

Because of these factors, many buyers have an errant idea of what constitutes a prepurchase examination. They often expect that their veterinarian can make an accurate assessment of the horse's condition based entirely on a physical examination, without the additional information provided by other diagnostic tests. In this respect they are frequently undereducated. The use of a written fee schedule that separates the cost for the physical examination from the optional diagnostic tests helps practitioners inform clients about all the services offered.

Recommendations for the performance of various diagnostic tests can differ depending upon the value and intended use of the horse, the wishes of the buyer, the animal's previous medical history, and the experience of the attending veterinarian. However, only when the buyer is aware of all the options (preferably in writing) can veterinarians be assured that their clients will not claim later on that they failed to tell them about the availability of the less common tests. The forms in Figures 15.1 and 15.2 can be used to educate buyers as to exactly how involved prepurchase examinations can be. Ranges of

fees within each category should be used to show that significant variations will occur depending upon how many radiographs are needed or which blood or urine tests are performed.

The Examination

The Veterinarian's Findings

Tradition has pushed veterinarians to conclude prepurchase examination forms with opinions as to whether the horse is sound or unsound, suitable or unsuitable, or satisfactory or unsatisfactory. Providing buyers with a declaration that a horse is sound has always placed equine practitioners in a vulnerable position because they cannot completely comprehend each buyer's expectations and needs. Consequently, it makes a great deal more sense to conclude an examination in a different manner.

According to a chairman of the American Association of Equine Practitioners Purchase Examination Committee, the trend is that "the veterinarian is no longer looked on as an advisor to buying or selling, but rather as a medical evaluator of an animal for an intended purpose."[12] If this tack is taken, practitioners can list the abnormal or undesirable findings and provide buyers with a brief assessment of the potential impact each of these might have on the performance of the horse in question (see Figures 15.1 and 15.2).

The need for information on the potential impact of medical findings varies considerably depending upon the purchaser's knowledge of and experience with horses and should be taken into consideration. The ultimate decision whether or not to buy the horse has always been and should continue to be the buyer's, with the veterinarian's role simply to provide the medical information. Upon completion of the examination, buyers will always want a pass-fail grade or a recommendation whether or not to buy. Instead of giving such an answer under the buyer's pressure, it is better to compare the exam process with a dressage event where the horse's performance is given a numerical grade based upon a perfect score of 10. If this is done, the veterinarian's grade for a horse can be questioned just like that of any other judge, but practitioners will avoid making overly definitive recommendations about the purchase.

Laws Regarding Medical Records

The requirements for medical records for prepurchase examinations vary from state to state and veterinarian to veterinarian. In California and many other states, state board regulations require that licensed veterinarians prepare written records in conjunction with examinations of animals in their custody.[13] Board policy has been that any animal examined by a licensed veterinarian at the request of the owner or agent is "in the custody of the veterinarian." Thus, a medical record reflecting the examination and treatment must be created and maintained.

Other states also require the creation of medical records when animals are examined.[14] Even if such medical records are not required, though, they should be produced routinely for prepurchase examinations to enhance client relations, provide for a better exam, help clients better understand the fees charged, improve the professional image of the veterinarian, and provide for a legal defense if needed.

The Physical Examination

Unlike routine calls to diagnose and treat illnesses, with prepurchase examinations there is minimal opportunity to perform follow-up examinations. As such, the practitioner has virtually no chance to extract any additional medical history, alter the diagnosis, or monitor the client's satisfaction or the patient's response to the course of therapy. Buyers usually want a complete report immediately upon completion of the examination. Because of these factors, documentation of how an examination was performed and

exactly what was found for each component of the examination is essential.

Evidence that an organ or extremity was examined and found to be normal is as important as a finding that it was abnormal. Notes about the use of diagnostic tools like hoof testers, pen lights, otoscopes, and endoscopes should be recorded. Since vision is a major concern with many performance horses, thorough ophthalmic examinations should be conducted on these animals and notations made regarding ophthalmic instruments used and whether or not the eyes were dilated during the ophthalmic exam.

The scope of a physical examination and the interpretation of the findings vary based upon differences among veterinarians. Practitioners who do prepurchase examinations should review some of the material that has been published to ensure that they are performing thorough examinations.[15,16]

The Examination Form

An in-depth examination form helps ensure a systematic exam and aids practitioners in remembering all the details of their findings (Figure 15.3). It also provides for excellent documentation and can serve as a checklist for use in completing a thorough examination. Normal findings can be noted with a simple "N." Abnormal findings are listed and discussed on the proper line or in an expanded section entitled *footnotes*.

When abbreviations are used to simplify the note-taking process, and someone assists in taking notes at the doctor's direction, a minimal amount of time can be spent completing a comprehensive written record. Ideally, this examination form serves as a practitioner's reference for the production of a written report to the buyer and seller.

The Seller's Involvement

Veterinarians performing prepurchase examinations work under contractual agreements with prospective buyers just as a house inspector works by agreement with a

Prepurchase Examination Form

Date _____

Buyer's name _____ Buyer's phone no. _____
Seller's name _____ Seller's phone no. _____
Address _____
Species _____ Breed _____ Age _____ Color _____
Sex: M ____ F ____ SF ____ CM ____ Name _____ Referred by _____

1. Vaccination status (dates of most recent vaccines)
   Encephalitis _____ Tetanus toxoid _____ Influenza _____ Rhinopneumonitis _____ Rabies _____ Other _____
2. Medical history _____
   _____
   _____

3. Examination in stall
   A. Temperature _____ B. Pulse _____ C. Respiration _____
   D. Vices observed _____
   E. Standing leg lameness _____
4. Examination out of stall
   A. Shivering _____
   B. Stringhalt _____
   C. Other lameness _____
5. Visual physical examination
   A. Head
      1) Facial bones, sinuses _____
      2) Nasal cavity _____
      3) Eyes
         a. Cornea _____ c. Naso-lacrimal duct _____
         b. Retina _____ d. Vision _____
      4) Ears _____
      5) Poll _____
      6) Teeth
         a. Estimated age _____ d. Dental irregularities _____
         b. Parvinathism _____ e. Points _____
         c. Alveolar periostisis _____
   B. Neck
      1) Salivary glands _____
      2) Mandibular lymph nodes _____
      3) Larynx _____
      4) Pharynx _____
      5) Thyroid _____
      6) Jugular veins _____
      7) Muscle hypertrophy or atrophy _____
      8) Old wounds _____
   C. Forelimb
      1) Confirmation _____
      2) Scars _____
      3) Muscle hypertrophy or atrophy _____
      4) Withers _____
      5) Joints & bones _____ Tendon sheaths _____ Tendons _____ Ligaments _____
         a. Shoulder _____ f. Fetlock _____
         b. Elbow _____ g. Pastern _____
         c. Carpus _____ h. Coffin _____
         d. Splint bones _____ i. Navicular _____
         e. Sesamoids _____
      6) Hoof
         a. Contraction _____ d. Thrush _____
         b. Cracks _____ e. Laminitis _____
         c. Corns _____ f. Other _____
      7) Old wounds _____

Figure 15.3   A prepurchase examination medical record form.

D. Hindlimb
   1) Confirmation _____
   2) Scars _____
   3) Muscle hypertrophy or atrophy _____
   4) Pelvis _____
      a. Tuber coxae _____
      b. Tuber sacralae _____
   5) Joints & bones _____ Tendon sheaths _____ Tendons _____ Ligaments _____
      a. Hip _____
      b. Stifle _____
      c. Hock _____
      d. Splint bones _____
      e. Sesamoids _____
      f. Fetlock _____
      g. Pastern _____
      h. Coffin _____
      i. Navicular _____
   6) Hoof
      a. Contraction _____
      b. Cracks _____
      c. Corns _____
      d. Thrush _____
      e. Laminitis _____
      f. Other _____
   7) Old wounds _____
E. Trunk
   1) Vertebrae & ribs _____
   2) Muscles _____
   3) Abdomen _____
   4) Old wounds _____
F. Skin & genitalia
   1) Current or previous lesions _____
   2) Testicles _____
   3) Mammary glands _____
   4) External Genitalia _____
G. Rectal examination
   1) Pelvic fractures _____
   2) Hernia _____
   3) Aorta _____
   4) Iliacs _____
   5) Anterior mesenteric _____
   6) Uterus/ovaries _____
   7) Kidney _____
   8) Bladder _____
   9) Other _____
H. Lameness examination
   1) Walk   LF _____ LH _____ RF _____ RH _____
   2) Trot   LF _____ LH _____ RF _____ RH _____
I. Heart & lungs
   1) Before exercise _____
   2) After exercise _____
J. Observation back in stall
K. Suggested laboratory examinations
   ____ Blood analysis _____
   ____ Urine analysis _____
   ____ Radiographs _____
   ____ Other _____

6. Footnotes

prospective home buyer. The accuracy of the veterinarian's report can be affected significantly by information provided by the seller. Therefore, it is helpful to obtain as much pertinent information as possible from the seller.

Disclosures by Sellers

Historically, the sale of goods has been based upon the principle that buyers had to take what they got, good or bad. This attitude has changed dramatically in the past 20 years because of numerous consumer-oriented alterations in contract law and the adoption of the Uniform Commercial Code by 49 states (see Chapter 8). Legislative and judicial pressures broadening the requirements for disclosures associated with the sale of goods, securities, and real estate have placed buyers (consumers) on more equal footing with sellers. The trend has extended to other areas of the law as well, including the sales of livestock[17] and implied warranties of merchantability associated with the sales of all goods.[18]

A key question arises as to how much disclosure veterinarians should expect or demand from sellers or their agents with regard to prepurchase examinations involving the sales of horses and other livestock. Historically, disclosure requirements have been minimal.

The issue of disclosure becomes extremely important regarding the administration of drugs to horses within 5 to 10 days prior to the exam. The failure to disclose the use of a drug that could mask symptoms of lameness on the day of the examination predisposes a veterinarian to liability for an incompetent or negligent exam. In addition, the seller's failure to disclose the proper age of the patient, previous lamenesses requiring treatment, known vices, prior injuries, or proper vaccination histories can also affect the accuracy of and professional liability for prepurchase examinations.

A formal, written seller's consent and disclosure statement (Figure 15.4) is a new concept and may be met with resistance from people in the horse business. Its use, however, will maximize client communications and minimize practitioners' vulnerability to legal actions for negligence in performing prepurchase examinations.

An alternative method for gathering information is used routinely by some experienced practitioners. This procedure involves asking the seller a series of eight questions in the presence of both the buyer and the seller or their respective agents. This occurs just prior to the examination, and answers are recorded on a medical record form, just as is done with routine physical examinations. The following questions are posed.

1. What is the current use of this horse and at what level of competition has it been performing?
2. Has this animal had any surgery?
3. Has the horse had any medical problems?
4. Have there been any lameness problems?
5. Has the horse been on medication within the past few days or today?
6. Does he or she need medication in order to compete?
7. Does this animal have any vices?
8. Are there any objectionable characteristics of which we should be aware?

Veterinarians who elect not to use a written disclosure form are encouraged to ask these questions in a formal history-taking session before the physical examination begins. When practitioners are skeptical about answers provided by the sellers or their agents, they should ask them to initial the answers to the questions as they were recorded.

Drug-Use Disclosure

As technology in drug testing continues to advance and prices for horses escalate, the entire area of drug detection should be considered more carefully.

Blood versus Urine Testing

It must be decided whether to recommend testing of the urine, blood, or both. Each test type has advantages and disadvantages. Urine testing outranks blood as a source because urine is available in relatively large volumes, tends to contain higher levels of parent drugs, and has greater concentrations of drug metabolites. Collecting urine samples, however, can be slow and difficult. Depending upon the state of hydration and frequency of urination, samples may not correspond with contemporaneous blood samples.

Blood samples, on the other hand, are relatively easy to collect. Once drug concentrations are quantified, experts can usually estimate the pharmacological effect of the drug on the patient. The principal problems with blood are the small sample volumes and the difficulty in accurately measuring low levels of drugs and drug metabolites. Consequently, both blood and urine testing may be needed in order to accurately assess the presence of a drug at the time of the prepurchase examination.

Choices must be made about which types of drugs to include in the testing. The most common drugs used to mask defects of wind, limb, or temperament in horses being offered for sale include the phenylbutazone-like drugs, corticosteroids, local anesthetics, and tranquilizers.[20] Phenylbutazone's widespread availability makes it the most commonly used drug to mask a horse's soreness before a prepurchase examination or sale. Levels of this drug are detectable in blood samples for about 48 hours after a clinically effective dose is administered.[20] There are always uncertainties regarding interpretations of laboratory results, and therefore consultations with experts are sometimes necessary to accurately evaluate drug levels and determine their medical significance.[21]

The Issue of Disclosure

Veterinarians should always be concerned about performing exams on horses that have been treated recently with drugs. It is advisable to obtain information on the medication status for the 5 to 10 days prior to the examination date because of liability risks and concerns about accurate prepurchase examinations. When it is disclosed that drugs have been administered recently, the veterinarian can decide whether the prepurchase exam should be completed on the date requested or postponed.

One method used to help assure a drug-free examination is to have the seller or an agent of the seller certify that no drugs have been used (Figure 15.4). An alternative is to have buyers certify that sellers have stated that no medications were administered within the past 5 to 10 days (Figure 15.2). Asking this question of sellers and having them sign the statements may produce more honest answers. However, having a buyer sign (as in the Figure 15.2 form) rather than the seller (Figure 15.4) alleviates the veterinarian of responsibility and may be a more palatable way to approach this problem within the equine industry. Perhaps the best method, though, is to ask questions about medications as described previously, i.e., during the history-taking session in front of the buyer and seller, writing the answers in the medical record.

Previous Medical Records

Legal precedent rules that the medical record is the property of the veterinarian who created it.[9] As previously mentioned, some state practice acts and regulations say that veterinarians must keep written daily records of all animals receiving veterinary services, and provide a summary of that record to the owner of animals receiving veterinary services when requested.[13, 14]

The legal principles regarding ownership and access to information in routine medical records (as opposed to prepurchase examination records) pose a serious question. If the veterinarian owns the record, and the owner (seller) has the right to a summary of that record, does the buyer acquire a right to that summary or copies of the entire medical record once the sale is completed? In other

Seller's Statement and
Consent to a Prepurchase Examination

Owner's name _____ Phone _____

Address _____

Co-owner's name _____ Phone _____
(if applicable)

Address _____

Agent's name _____ Phone _____
(if applicable)

Identification of the animal (attach photograph or make drawings of both side views and head):

1. Name _____

2. Age _____

3. Sex _____

4. Color _____

5. Markings _____
   _____

6. Gelded _____

7. Age when gelded _____

8. Tattoo no. _____

How long have you been acquainted with the horse? _____

Do you have knowledge of any lameness or disease process affecting this
horse's performance in the past year? If so, explain _____
_____
_____
_____
_____

Medical treatments rendered within the past year _____
_____
_____
_____
_____

Figure 15.4 Seller's statement and consent to a prepurchase examination.

Vices _____

Disabilities _____

Idiosyncracies _____

Knowledge of prospective buyer's intended use of the animal _____

I hereby certify that the above statements are, to the best of my knowledge, true and complete responses to items asked. I further certify that I am the owner, or duly authorized agent for the owner, of the above-described animal. I hereby grant my consent to the examination of the above-named horse by Dr. _____ for the purposes of determining the status of _____'s health prior to sale.
                    (horse's name)

Additional Information

I certify that, to the best of my knowledge, the above-named horse has not been treated with any oral, intravenous, subcutaneous or intramuscular drugs within 10 days of the time of the prepurchase examination except for the following drugs or worming compounds: _____

_____

I hereby authorize/do not authorize the release of information on this horse's previous medical records from _____
               (name of veterinarian)

to _____
     (name of veterinarian performing examination)

_____   _____
Signature of Seller or Agent for Seller   Date

_____   _____
Signature of Co-owner (if applicable)   Date

words, is access to the record tied to the person who paid for its creation or to the animal itself and the current owner of that animal?

Although good arguments can be made for ownership by either party, it is most practical that access to the medical records go with ownership of the horse, and that the records not be controlled by a previous owner. A good comparison can be made with professional sports, wherein the medical record is confidential information between an athlete and the doctor who provided medical care and not the property of the sports franchise that held the playing rights to a player and paid for the medical care. After all, the medical records will be important to the future well-being of the professional athlete or the animal no matter who the owner is.

When buyers who have arranged for prepurchase examinations, or veterinarians who are performing these examinations request that copies or summaries of medical records be forwarded to them before the exam is completed, it is wise for sellers to consent to such requests. In cases in which they have failed to comply and the buyer (as the new owner) obtains a summary showing serious prior medical problems, grounds may exist for an action to void the contract of sale based upon nondisclosure of pertinent information.

When sellers contact their regular veterinarians requesting that prior medical records be provided for an upcoming prepurchase examination, copies of the records should be sent only to the veterinarian performing the prepurchase examination. Unless a contract indicates otherwise, prospective buyers have no legal right to the medical record and should not receive copies without specific legal authorization by the seller.

The Prepurchase Examination Record

Two questions arise concerning the medical record of the prepurchase examination. First, when the buyer contracts for a prepurchase examination and the veterinarian produces a medical record thereof, does the owner (seller) have a right to a copy or summary? Under the previously quoted California law,[13] the answer appears to be affirmative, even though the seller was not the client who paid for the exam. Since the seller is the owner, this seems a just result and would probably hold true in other jurisdictions as well. The seller usually will have heard an oral report on the results of the prepurchase examination anyway.

The second question on this issue revolves around how veterinarians should store medical records of prepurchase exams. If the horse has a prior medical record at the practice, should the prepurchase record be attached to the rest of the horse's record or stored separately under the buyer's name?

In many cases, this is not a serious problem because the horse has no prior record, and the results of the exam are routinely filed under the buyer's name. If the results of a prepurchase exam are detrimental to the seller, though, and the record of the exam is stored in the animal's file under the seller's name, serious problems can occur. For example, if a seller requests that his or her veterinarian provide a copy of the horse's prior medical record to another veterinarian performing a subsequent prepurchase examination, and the prior prepurchase examination medical record is included therein, the new veterinarian, and thus the new buyer, receive information they had no right to obtain.

Legal theory indicates that only the prospective buyer who paid for the exam has authority to release that information. Since this information can be detrimental to sellers, who did not pay for the prepurchase examinations and who never requested or authorized the placement of that information in their horse records, veterinarians might find themselves vulnerable to a lawsuit for interference with prospective contractual relations. The fact that there was no intent to interfere with the contractual relations of the seller would tend to minimize the potential for legal recourse.[10]

To resolve this problem, a separate medical record file on the horse under the prospective buyer's name should be created. Once this is done, a reference is placed in the horse's regular medical record indicating that a prepurchase examination occurred and that the information thereon can be found under the buyer's name. When done this way, veterinarians avoid the risk of sending confidential information and perhaps even some radiographs that could adversely affect sellers.

Summary

With litigation involving equine practices increasing and the potential for liability dramatically rising as the value of quality horses escalates, veterinarians must be cautious. Better prepurchase examinations and medical records may cost more money to complete, but as long as the risks of liability continue to increase, improved examinations and more complete records are the best defense against client complaints or litigation. Veterinarians must perceive the full impact of the examination on the success or failure of the sale of a horse and handle that responsibility with maximal professional and legal competence.

References

1. Dinsmore J: Personal communication, AVMA Professional Liability Trust, Schaumburg, IL, 1987.
2. Nichols MT: Field application of a bull breeding soundness examination. *Iowa State Univ Vet* 49(1):48-54, l987.
3. Morrow DA: Examination of the reproductive tract of the cow and heifer. *Current Therapy in Theriogenology 2.* Philadelphia, WB Saunders Co, 1986, pp 95-100.
4. Larson LL: Examination of the reproductive system of the bull, in Morrow DA: *Current Therapy in Theriogenology 2.* Philadelphia, WB Saunders Co, 1986, pp 101-116.
5. Ott RS: Breeding soundness examination of bulls, in Morrow DA: *Current Therapy in Theriogenology 2.* Philadelphia, WB Saunders Co, 1986, pp 125-130.
6. Manual for breeding soundness examination of bulls. *J Soc Theriogenol* XII(Feb):1-65, 1983.
7. Wenkoff MS: *The Valuation of Bulls for Breeding Soundness.* Ottawa, Ontario, Canadian Veterinary Medical Assoc, 1987.
8. Bowen J, Brooke D, Forfa R: Reproduction: Evaluating the stallion. *Equine Data* 8(12):185, 1987.
9. Pritchard WR: Legal aspects of the veterinary medical record. *JAVMA* 172(2):176-180, 1978.
10. Hunter HO: *Modern Law of Contracts, Breaches and Remedies.* New York, Warren, Gorham and Lamont, l986, § 44.01, p 415. A relatively new tort (civil wrong) known as business interference, or interferences with prospective contractual relations occurs when someone who does not have any privilege induces or otherwise purposely causes another person not to enter into, or continue, a business relationship with a third party. This topic is discussed in more detail in Chapter 8 on contract law.
11. *AVMA Principles of Veterinary Medical Ethics.* Schaumburg, IL, American Veterinary Medical Assoc, 1987, p 3 (see Appendix D).
12. DeAngelis V: Purchase examinations benefit or burden? *Equus* (Sept):22, 1985.
13. California Business and Professions Code § 4855 and Title 16, Professional and Vocational Regulations § 2031.
14. Virginia Board of Veterinary Medicine Regulation § 4.2 (4).
15. Panel report. Purchase exams in horses. *Mod Vet Pract* 65(1):66-68, 1984.
16. Anderson GF, Landsheft B: Purchase examinations for performance horses. *Mod Vet Pract* 65(9):692-695, 1984.
17. Hannah HW: Is caveat emptor still alive? *JAVMA* 158(7):1268, 1971.
18. Hannah HW: Legal brief. Veterinarians, animal sales, and the Uniform Commercial Code. *JAVMA* 178(1):18, 1981.
19. Blake JW, Tobin T: Testing for drugs in horses. *J Equine Vet Sci* 6(2):93-97, 1986.
20. Tobin T: Prepurchase testing for drugs in horses: A review. *J Equine Vet Sci* 6(1):35-36, 1986.
21. Tobin T: Uncertainty in the "detection times" for drugs in horses. *J Equine Vet Sci* 6(3):124-128, 1986.

CHAPTER 16

Wildlife Law

Jo Anne L. Garbe, D.V.M., J.D.
United States Fish and Wildlife Service
Department of Interior

The Laws, Treaties, and Authorities Governing Wildlife

The impact of wildlife on the general population worldwide has changed dramatically over the last 200 years, and the conceptual basis for wildlife regulation has evolved significantly, as well. In the days when people were more dependent upon the land, wildlife was viewed as an integral part of existence, and the individual's right to hunt and fish on owned or unowned land was recognized despite the law of trespass which traditionally would have forbidden such activity.[1]

There was almost no wildlife legislation in the United States prior to 1900. Until the end of the 19th century, wildlife served as an essential food source and an important component of commercial trade. The intent of the legislation enacted during this period was to maintain the continued existence of beneficial wildlife for consumption or trade, manage game species, and eliminate harmful or pest species.

Individual states elected to regulate the taking and disposal of wildlife. Wildlife was viewed as property of the citizens of the state, to do with as they saw fit. Regulation, then, allowed wildlife to be taken either for consumption or to protect livestock.

The federal government first became involved in wildlife regulation in 1900 with the enactment of the Lacey Act. This early attempt at federal regulation focused on supporting state fish and game laws that were geared toward limiting or prohibiting the killing or taking of indigenous wildlife. As the federal domain grew with the establishment of national parks and wildlife refuges, issues such as states' rights arose. These issues were finally resolved by the courts, which ruled that the federal government had ultimate jurisdiction over the regulation of wildlife in the United States. Currently, the federal government and the states cooperate in wildlife management.

It was not until the late 1960s that the federal government considered legislation that dealt comprehensively with conservation of wildlife. In fact, the terms *conservation* and *environment* have recent origins dating from the mid 1960s, the heyday of the environmental movement. Viewing wildlife from the perspective of its inherent value is also a relatively new concept. It came to fruition when Congress passed the Marine Mammal Protection Act in 1972 and the Endangered Species Act in 1973.

International Law

Until fairly recently, the international community did not act cohesively with regard to wildlife issues. Decisions about wildlife management were left to the negotiation of individual countries. This approach led to a multitude of documents including over 70 international wildlife treaties and agreements to which the United States is a party.

Typically, these agreements involved two or three countries that found it in their best interest to regulate some shared aspect of wildlife management. Often subsequent treaties, drafted by different parties, would use the concepts and terminology of previous treaties as their basis.

International Agreements

Protection of Migratory Birds

The first international agreement to which the United States was a party was the Convention for the Protection of Migratory Birds, drafted by the United States and Great Britain (acting on behalf of Canada) in 1916.[2] The provisions of the treaty included establishment of three groups of migratory birds: migratory game birds, migratory insectivorous birds, and nongame migratory birds. The treaty designated a closed hunting season year round for the latter two groups. For migratory game birds, the treaty provided an open hunting season to extend three and

one-half months per year. Although the treaty made no reference to habitat protection, it did prohibit the taking of nests and eggs except for scientific purposes. Since this treaty was written during a period when wildlife was thought of only in terms of commercial value, it authorized issuance of permits to kill any migratory bird if it became *injurious* to agricultural or other community interests.

Three subsequent treaties regarding migratory birds have been signed by the United States, based on the 1916 migratory bird treaty, each with slightly different provisions. These treaties were ratified as follows: Mexico (1936),[3] Japan (1972),[4] and the Soviet Union (1976).[5] All three treaties allow take for scientific and educational purposes (*take* in this context means removal from the wild). The agreement with Mexico provides for take by private game farms, while those with Japan and the Soviet Union focus on maintaining habitat sufficient to ensure the survival of the species. These three treaties clearly reflect an evolving environmental orientation. Whereas the 1936 treaty focuses on limiting hunting seasons, the 1976 treaty takes the environmentalist position that habitat must be protected, particularly to prevent disturbance of nesting sites.

Marine Mammal Protection

The international community has been the moving force behind marine mammal protection. This aspect of wildlife management has been the focus of both individually drafted treaties and a global treaty. As early as 1911, international concern regarding the excessive harvest of fur seals fostered the ratification of the Treaty for Preservation and Protection of Fur Seals signed by the United States, the United Kingdom, Japan, and Russia.[6] This international legislation focused on preserving adequate stocks of fur seals so that harvest could continue, albeit at a lower level. In 1957, this treaty was superseded by the Interim Convention on the Conservation of North Pacific Fur Seals.[7] This interim agreement has been renewed continuously since its enactment and has not been significantly affected by passage of the Marine Mammal Protection Act, discussed subsequently in this text.

Whale Protection

The first comprehensive move in the international community to deal seriously with the whaling issue was made with the ratification of the International Convention for the Regulation of Whaling in 1946.[8] This treaty established the International Whaling Commission (IWC), composed of delegates from each signatory country. The commission has a dual function: (1) to conserve species of whales and (2) to coordinate the development of the whaling industry.

The IWC decides on a schedule consisting of when and if whaling will be allowed to take place, the species and size of whales that may be taken, methods of capture, and the catch limit. Three-fourths concurrence of the commission is needed to amend an approved schedule. Any IWC member may register an objection to the schedule within 90 days of the amendment adoption. The objecting member, then, is not subject to the schedule's provisions. Allowing any member to exclude itself from these provisions is considered by many to be a major weakness of this legislation.

For many years the IWC's inactivity allowed it to serve as an "overseer of the successive depletion of individual whale stocks."[9] In the early 1970s the international environmental community became outraged at the tremendous depletion of whale stocks. Pressures brought by political and ecological interests have now forced the IWC to become more responsive.

The United States has been able to influence IWC policy through passage of statutory levers such as the Marine Mammal Protection Act (MMPA) and various amendments to existing legislation.[10] The MMPA directs the federal government to seek amendments to international treaties so that they are consistent with the conservation aims of the act. Consequently, the United States delegation to the IWC has the author-

ity to work ardently for the conservation of marine mammals.

Additionally, the Pelly Amendment to the Fisherman's Protective Act of 1967 provides the president of the United States some discretionary options.[11] The most important of these allows the exercise of economic sanctions prohibiting the importation of fisheries products from countries continuing to act in a manner inconsistent with the conservation goals of the United States.

Another avenue of redress involves invocation of the Packwood Amendment. This law mandates a penalty against violators of the whaling convention of a 50% reduction in the allocation of fish that the violating country is entitled to take under the Fishery Conservation and Management Act.[12]

In 1979, the IWC designated the Indian Ocean as a whale sanctuary, prohibiting commercial whaling in that region. In 1982, the IWC voted 25 to 7 to halt all commercial whaling by 1986. Four nations, including Japan and the Soviet Union, filed objections. To date, the United States has not determined whether or not to impose sanctions on these four nations.

The United States has long pursued a complete ban on commercial whaling. However, it has fought to protect the right of its native people to take whales in a traditional manner, and actually has persuaded the IWC to allow limited aboriginal harvesting.

Other International Agreements

There have been numerous international treaties regarding commercial fisheries management. In fact, this area comprises the majority of wildlife treaties. Generally, the emphasis in these international agreements is on producing a sustainable yield population as opposed to considering that fish have any inherent value or addressing issues of habitat protection.

A number of other significant international treaties dealing with the ocean environment and conservation of the resources of Antarctica have been passed. Although a detailed analysis is beyond the scope of this text, readers are encouraged to refer to the list of treaties contained in Appendix H.

International Regulation of Trade

The international community regulates trade of endangered and threatened wildlife through the Convention on the International Trade in Endangered Species of Wild Fauna and Flora (CITES), which was enacted in 1973.[13] To date, 95 countries have acceded to this international convention.

The intent of CITES is to conserve endangered species of wild fauna and flora by limiting international trade and transportation of such species. All affected animals and plants that appear in the international market are afforded some type of protection. If, however, a species is either endangered or threatened but does not enter into trade, it is not included within the scope of this international legislation.

The treaty provides that member countries (*parties*) meet every two years to evaluate the effectiveness of CITES implementation, to exchange scientific and administrative information, and to decide how best to achieve the future goals of the treaty internationally.

The method of determining which species should receive protection and the extent of that protection continues to be of concern to the parties to CITES. At the time the treaty was enacted, three appendices were developed that defined various levels of vulnerability to extinction and the consequent restriction on trade in the particular species listed. To implement CITES, the parties created a system of permits to regulate movement of affected animals across national boundaries. Depending on the level of species endangerment, permits must be issued for import, export, or both.

Species Threatened with Extinction

Appendix I of CITES provides the most stringent restrictions on trade and, thus, the greatest protection for a listed species. Species included in Appendix I are recognized as threatened with extinction due to excessive exploitation by trade. The CITES treaty states that species on this list may not be traded primarily for commercial purposes. Limited trade does occur, however, between zoos and educational facilities. To trade an animal listed in this appendix, both an export permit from the country of origin and an import permit from the importing country are required. Examples of listed species are gorillas; most whales, tigers, leopards, and Asian elephants; all rhinoceros species; sea turtles; ostrich; bald eagles, and scarlet macaws.

Species Not Threatened with Immediate Extinction

Appendix II of CITES lists species that may not be immediately threatened with extinction but that will become so if trade is not controlled. Included are many species similar in appearance to those in Appendix I. Although not endangered themselves, these species are difficult to differentiate from endangered animals.

Appendix II species may be traded for commercial purposes, but only if it is determined that such trade is not detrimental to the survival of the species. Trade in Appendix II species requires only an export permit from the country of origin. Examples of listed species are all parrots except budgerigars, cockatiels, rose-ringed parakeets, and those parrots listed on Appendix I; golden eagles; African elephants; grizzly and polar bears; alligators; iguanas; boa constrictors; pythons; monitor lizards; gopher tortoises; and birdwing butterflies.

Additional Trade Restrictions

CITES' Appendix III contains species nominated by an individual party that regulates the species within its borders and needs the cooperation of other parties to control trade in the listed species. The nomination is unilateral and, thus, does not require consensus by the other parties to CITES. Trade requires an export permit from the nominating party or a certificate from the country of origin stating that the animal did not originate in the country that proposed the listing. Examples of listed species are walrus (Canada), water buffalo (Nepal), the great white egret, and the hippopotamus (Ghana).

At the biennial conference, species are either listed or removed from Appendices I and II by a vote supported by two-thirds of the parties. Changes to Appendix III require action by the nominating party for that species.

CITES Exemptions

Although trade in species listed on the three appendices is limited, the parties to CITES agreed that various exemptions to this trade barrier should be recognized for specific activities. This includes trade in live or dead specimens that fall within the following categories: (1) specimens that were acquired prior to either their listing on an appendix or the time that the exporting government became a party to CITES; (2) specimens that were part of someone's personal or household effects; (3) specimens that were bred in captivity; or (4) trade that involved a noncommercial loan or exchange between scientific or educational institutions.[14]

Additionally, each party to CITES has an opportunity to make a *reservation* regarding the listing of any species. This means that the party so reserving is treated as a nonparty to CITES as far as trade in that species is concerned; however, nonparties must provide *comparable documentation* when trading in listed species.[15] As an example, when Japan became a party to CITES, it made several reservations concerning species such as the crocodile that were already listed in a CITES Appendix. The other parties to CITES, then, treated Japan as a nonparty with regard to trade in those reserved species. Although CITES requires Japan to document the origins of the species traded, it does not mandate that Japan adhere to the restrictions

normally provided for the protection of the listed species for which Japan made a reservation. A party's ability to make a reservation does not end once the party has become a member of CITES. Any party can make a reservation within 90 days of the announcement of a species listing. The United States has not made any reservations on CITES-listed species.

CITES National Authority

Notably absent from the CITES treaty is mention of either an international enforcement organization or the structure to develop such an agency. CITES does, however, provide that each party authorize a management and a scientific authority. The party's management authority develops national policy implementing CITES and issues trade permits. The scientific authority assesses the potential impact of trade on the listed species and recommends whether or not the management authority should issue a permit.

In the United States both of these agencies are within the Department of the Interior, Fish and Wildlife Service. The Office of Management Authority (formerly the Federal Wildlife Permit Office) functions as the management authority for CITES. The Office of the Scientific Authority functions as its name implies. A detailed description of the permitting process can be found later in this chapter in the section headed "The Permit Process Pertaining to Wildlife."

An additional task created by the treaty provides that a party's scientific authority monitor the export of species listed in CITES Appendix II and make recommendations to the management authority to limit the issuance of export permits when the number of individuals of a species falls below a certain level. Individual parties may act in whatever manner necessary to protect indigenous wildlife (wildlife that is native to the exporting country). As a way of counteracting depletion of such species, whether or not they are listed in an appendix, many parties have instituted export bans on species recognized as being traded too heavily.

Impact on World Wildlife

The impact of CITES on the status of wildlife worldwide is not entirely clear. The treaty limits its application to international trade—domestic trade is beyond its scope. Furthermore, domestic activity that affects species populations only indirectly such as habitat destruction, pesticide application, and exotic species introduction, is not regulated by this treaty.[16] The CITES treaty, however, has focused world attention on the plight of endangered wildlife and has furthered the use of trade restrictions to conserve natural resources.

Federal Legislation and Regulation

The Lacey Act of 1900[17]

The Lacey Act was the first federal legislation concerning wildlife passed by Congress. It has been amended several times, most significantly in 1981. Initially, the Lacey Act served a dual purpose. First, it provided federal support for enforcement of state game laws and, second, it promoted agriculture and horticulture by prohibiting the importation of *injurious* wildlife. Further, it authorized the Department of Agriculture to adopt all measures necessary for the preservation of game and other wild birds.

In 1949, Congress amended the Lacey Act to prohibit the importation of animals under inhumane or unhealthful conditions. Responsibility for promulgating regulations pertaining to that provision was delegated to the United States secretary of the treasury. The regulatory process was never initiated by the secretary, though, so in 1981, Congress again amended the Lacey Act, this time shifting responsibility for developing rules regarding humane transport to the United States secretary of the interior. After a six-year delay, these regulations were published on November 10, 1987.

The 1981 amendments changed the scope of the Lacey Act dramatically. It is currently a violation of federal law to import or export animals taken, possessed, transported, or sold in violation of the laws of any state, Indian tribe, foreign country, or international treaty. Additionally, protection has been extended to cover plants and captive-bred animals, as well as those caught in the wild. This legislation, then, provides the cornerstone of the federal program to conserve wildlife through regulation of trade.

The Endangered Species Act

The Endangered Species Act (ESA) of 1973 was the first comprehensive federal legislation to deal with wildlife conservation.[18] This act authorized the federal government to develop a list of species threatened with worldwide extinction and to prohibit import of those species into the United States except for certain purposes such as education, zoological display, scientific investigation, and captive propagation. The United States government was further directed by this act to encourage foreign countries to ensure the survival of their own wildlife and to provide technical assistance to countries developing conservation programs.

The scope of the ESA far exceeds that of previous legislation because it emphasizes the need to acquire and preserve the habitat of endangered and threatened species. It also authorizes the protection of endangered populations of existing healthy species. This means that if an animal population within a certain geographic area is in danger of extinction, even though the species as a whole is stable, that particular population can be protected. Because of these provisions, the spectrum of protection is much broader than any prior legislation. The ESA also requires all federal agencies to act to conserve endangered and threatened species of wildlife. Further, the ESA expands the definition of affected species to include any member of the animal or plant kingdom.

The ESA is the implementing legislation for CITES in the United States. The purposes of the two documents differ somewhat, though.[19] While CITES attempts to conserve wildlife through regulation of international trade, the ESA approaches wildlife conservation on basic scientific grounds. Under the ESA, species are evaluated as to their conservation status based solely on scientific parameters and whether they are considered endangered or threatened. Human activity with regard to these species is limited whether or not these animals enter into trade. As an example, the Morro Bay kangaroo rat, indigenous to California, is protected under the ESA due to its vanishing numbers and habitat; however, it is not protected under CITES since it does not enter into commercial trade.

Endangered and Threatened Species Lists

The ESA's protection program has two species lists—one for endangered and one for threatened species—and a list of areas designated as habitats critical to the survival of the affected species. The major drawback of this law is that it protects only habitats on federally owned land or where activity requires federal approval.[20]

The ESA defines *endangered* as "any species which is in danger of extinction throughout all or a significant portion of its range"[21] and *threatened* as "any species which is likely to become an endangered species within the foreseeable future throughout all or a significant portion of its range."[22]

Protection varies depending upon the list on which the species (or population) is placed. Further, it is possible under this regulatory scheme to have varying levels of protection for the same species depending on its geographic location. This is the situation with the bald eagle, which is considered threatened in five states (Washington, Oregon, Minnesota, Wisconsin, and Michigan) and endangered in the remainder of the United States. In practical terms, the United States Fish and Wildlife Service has decided, as a matter of national policy, to treat endangered and threatened species in the same manner from a regulatory standpoint unless a special rule has been established with

regard to the species in question. This is the case with the grizzly bear. Although it is only listed on the threatened species list, taking grizzly bears from the wild within the United States is prohibited except under certain circumstances and in particular regions of the country.[23]

The ESA also provides that a nonaffected species may be listed in either category due to its similarity of appearance to a threatened or endangered species. This is especially important when dealing with refined products of species that are often indistinguishable to the lay individual. A case in point is the American alligator, which is no longer considered endangered within the southern United States. It is often difficult to differentiate products made from the skins of this species from products of other endangered crocodilian species. The American alligator continues to be listed so that protection remains adequate for its endangered and threatened counterparts.

The procedures developed for listing a species as endangered or threatened are complex and involve consultation with affected foreign and state governments and open hearings if requested. Listing authority rests with the secretary of the interior acting through the United States Fish and Wildlife Service for most species and with the secretary of commerce through the National Marine Fisheries Service (NMFS) for specifically designated animals such as some species of marine mammals. Listing can be initiated by either secretary or by interested private parties. Once a decision has been made to list a species, a proposal to that effect must be published in the *Federal Register* and local newspapers with an ensuing period open to receive public comments. Final listing must take place within one year following the proposal and, thereafter, *critical habitat* must be designated within a year of listing if unknown at the time of listing.

Listing can occur under emergency circumstances, but such listings automatically terminate in 240 days unless action has been taken to list the species in the normal manner during the intervening period.

Examples of species on the endangered list are bactrian camel, Columbian white-tailed deer, red kangaroo, spider monkey, and gray wolf. Examples of species on the threatened list are American alligator, gopher tortoise, brown or grizzly bear, and southern sea otter.

Exceptions to the Provisions of the ESA

Originally, the ESA designated four exceptions to its prohibitions: (1) if the specimens were possessed for noncommercial purposes at the time that the ESA was passed; (2) in cases of economic hardship; (3) for certain Alaskan residents that relied on the taking of species for survival; and (4) for scientific and/or propagation purposes. The progeny of any of the above exempted animals continue to be protected under the provisions of the ESA.

Subsequent amendments to the ESA provided several additional exemption categories. Scrimshaw is exempt if it is sold by a person who owned the item at the time of enactment. Raptors (except the bald eagle) are exempt if legally held in captivity on the date of the 1978 amendments and banded under the terms of a valid Migratory Bird Treaty Act (MBTA) permit. The exemption extends to their progeny also. People acting in self-defense with regard to listed species are exempt from ESA coverage, although civil penalties still may be imposed.

In 1982, Congress recognized three more exemptions. The first, involving *experimental* populations of endangered species, provides that, in order to encourage local cooperation in conservation efforts, introduced populations are to be treated less stringently than under ordinary circumstances. This is the situation with the Delmarva Peninsula fox squirrel, which is listed as endangered in most of its range. The remainder of its range encompasses the area of introduction of a *nonessential experimental* population. Due to the determination that this population is nonessential, it is considered threatened rather than endangered.

A further exemption involves *incidental take*, meaning take in the course of some other legitimate activity such as commercial fishing. This type of take can be a permitted activity, but the permit applicant must submit a conservation plan providing information about reduction of incidental take prior to permit issuance.

The final exemption involves incidental take by federal agencies pursuant to § 7 of the ESA. Detailed analysis of this section, which deals with federal agency responsibility, is beyond the scope of this text. For further analysis of the workings and impact of this section, see the accompanying references.[24]

Prohibitions Under the ESA

A particularly important aspect of the ESA is its articulation of prohibitions. Most significantly, no person may take an endangered or threatened species. *Take* under the ESA means to harass, harm, pursue, hunt, shoot, wound, kill, trap, capture, collect, or attempt to engage in any such conduct whether intentional or unintentional.[25] Inclusion of the term *harass* is important because it has been determined that recreational activity can be construed as harassment. Prohibition is extended to include activities such as import and export, sale, interstate shipment involved with a commercial activity, and possession when taken in violation of the ESA. Further, the ESA prohibits trade in contravention of CITES and possession of CITES-listed species traded unlawfully, and it requires that importers and exporters of wildlife be licensed.

The International Component of the ESA

The ESA directs the executive branch to implement CITES and the Convention on Nature Protection and Wildlife Preservation in the Western Hemisphere. The federal government is instructed to encourage the development of endangered species programs in foreign countries and to provide financial and personnel assistance to those countries.

It also authorizes law-enforcement investigations and research abroad. Further, Section 7, which prohibits federal agencies from contributing to the demise of species domestically, applies to agency activity in foreign countries as well.[24]

The ESA authorizes the government to use an embargo to halt the import of products from countries whose nationals are in violation of CITES. Significantly, this authorization includes taking as well as trade, so that the implications for use of an embargo are much broader than if just applicable to traded species.[26]

The Marine Mammal Protection Act[27]

In 1972, Congress recognized that many species of marine mammals were on the brink of extinction, and it passed the MMPA. This federal legislation declared that species and populations of marine mammals should not be permitted to diminish to the point where they ceased to be a significant functioning element in the marine ecosystem. "In particular, efforts should be made to protect the rookeries, mating grounds, and areas of similar significance for each species of marine mammal from the adverse effect of [hu]man's actions."[28] Further, "negotiations should be undertaken immediately to encourage the development of international arrangements for research on, and conservation of, all marine mammals."[28]

The MMPA preempts any state control over marine mammal resources; however, it provides a mechanism for states to resume responsibility for managing such species, with federal financial aid, if states develop a conservation plan consistent with federal goals.

As mentioned above, the MMPA authorizes the federal government to begin a coordinated program for the conservation of marine mammals. A fundamental feature of this program is a moratorium on the take of any marine mammal under the jurisdiction of or imported into the United States. Under the terms of the MMPA, *take* means "to

harass, hunt, capture, or kill."[29] Significantly, this broad definition includes unintentional take such as that involved in recreational activity, in addition to that which is traditionally considered take for intentional purposes.

Exceptions Under the MMPA

Although the MMPA provides for a moratorium on the take of marine mammals, there are exceptions. Take by native peoples in Arctic regions for subsistence or for creating and selling authentic handicrafts is provided for in this act.

Additionally, permits can be issued for the taking and importation of marine mammals for scientific research and public display. Before such permits are issued, though, the Marine Mammal Commission must determine that the species involved is not depleted within the marine environment.

In general, as with the ESA, the MMPA deals with marine mammals on the basis of population concerns rather than solely along species lines. A population is considered depleted if it falls below the optimal sustainable population (defined as the number of animals that will result in the maximum productivity of the population)[29] or is listed on either the endangered or threatened lists of the ESA. If the population is considered depleted, animals may be taken only for scientific purposes and under humane circumstances. It is in this regard that a veterinarian is most likely to become involved, for example, in consulting on the capture and transport of such animals.

The MMPA provides for waiver of the moratorium in the event that the affected species or population falls within the optimal sustainable population and that harvesting the stock will not put the species below that level.

Incidental take related either to commercial fishing or pursuant to international treaty obligations or to other federally approved activities is permitted but is strictly controlled. This is because fishing techniques used by the tuna industry have caused a lasting impact on porpoise populations. The incidental take occurring in the tuna fishing industry was so significant in the early 1970s that maximum quotas were established to limit porpoise loss. These quotas have decreased in subsequent years, but incidental take still accounts for the death of approximately 20,000 porpoises per year.

Because of this problem, federal regulations provide for observers to be present on about one-third of the tuna fishing vessels. It is interesting to note that the reported number of porpoise killed on observer ships is significantly lower than on ships without observers. Also, incidental take may be on the rise since reports indicate that more porpoise were killed in 1982 than in 1976. The incidental take in other commercial fisheries operations is considered negligible and thus is regulated by guidelines rather than regulations. Other incidental take, such as that which occurs with recreation or development of natural resources, is to be regulated through the development of specific regulations regarding the particular activity.

International Aspects of the MMPA

A major thrust of the MMPA is to maintain the marine habitat. As such, the MMPA directs the secretaries of commerce and the interior to act through the secretary of state to negotiate new international agreements in three specified areas: (1) general marine mammal protection; (2) fisheries operations that unduly harm marine mammals; and (3) protection of specific ocean areas important for marine mammal survival. Although the federal government is mandated by the MMPA to pursue these efforts, very little has happened since its passage.

Other Federal Wildlife Legislation

Other pieces of federal legislation affecting wildlife have been passed. Congress approaches it either directly, designating a particular species of concern, or indirectly, through regulation of commerce. Interestingly, all federal statutes that restrict the taking of wildlife also restrict commerce in the

protected species. A brief synopsis of federal statutes that fall within this category follows.[30]

The Bald Eagle Protection Act[31]

In 1940, Congress enacted the Bald Eagle Protection Act (BEPA) to prevent the extinction of this species from the United States. The BEPA made it illegal to take or possess a bald eagle, a part of a bald eagle, or a nest. An exception was provided for take and possession by scientific organizations and for the protection of wildlife and agricultural interests.

The BEPA has been amended substantially twice. In the 1962 revision, protection was extended to golden eagles because of the difficulty in distinguishing immature eagles of the two species from one another. Also, take and possession were permitted for religious purposes by Indians. Finally, the secretary of the interior was given authority to take golden eagles if the governor of any state requested such action to protect agricultural interests, such as flocks or herds of domesticated animals, within his/her state.

The second revision, passed in 1972, extended the definition of *take* to include poisoning of bald eagles and increased the penalties for take. A new provision was included which allowed for an individual's grazing rights on federally owned lands to be suspended upon conviction of a violation under the BEPA. Additionally, payment of a bounty to any person providing information that resulted in a conviction under the provisions of the BEPA was authorized. Finally, these amendments provided that golden eagles could be taken for falconry purposes.

In 1978, Congress further exempted from protection the taking of golden eagle nests if they interfered with resource development. Although this exemption was primarily aimed at the coal mining industry, the language of the amendment did not limit application specifically to coal field situations.

The BEPA has not been especially effective. Even though it was enacted in 1940 and has been amended twice, it became necessary to place the bald eagle on the endangered species list and the golden eagle on the threatened list.

The Wild Free-Roaming Horses and Burros Act[32]

Another piece of legislation that approaches conservation on a species basis is the Wild Free-Roaming Horses and Burros Act. This 1971 act attempts to protect a symbol of the old west by prohibiting the shooting or poisoning of wild horses and burros.

Penalties Under Federal Wildlife Law

All the federal wildlife laws outlined above provide some form of penalty for violators of a provision. The penalties range from fines of $5000 to $20,000 per violation and prison terms of six months to one year. Forfeitures of wildlife seized and equipment used to perpetrate the offense also are authorized. Certain laws, such as the MMPA, authorize the restriction of importation of products from countries not adhering to the conservation principles of the United States. The spectrum of penalties overall is quite broad.

The Permit Process Pertaining to Wildlife

The Departments of Interior, Commerce, Agriculture, and Health and Human Services regulate activities concerning wildlife. One of their principal functions is to issue permits or licenses to conduct activity that is normally prohibited. The permit process is complex, and the volume of materials pertaining to it can be overwhelming. Therefore, only those areas of wildlife law directly applicable to veterinarians in private practice will be discussed herein. Additional information and answers to specific questions can be obtained from the agencies cited in the references.

Permit Procedures Under the Department of Interior Authority

Primary responsibility for administering wildlife legislation rests with the Department of the Interior. Its agency, the United States Fish and Wildlife Service (Service), has promulgated regulations concerning the permitting process under the following federal laws or international treaties: the ESA, the MMPA, the BEPA, the Lacey Act, and CITES.

The Permit Application Process Under the Jurisdiction of the United States Fish and Wildlife Service[33]

Applicants for permits to possess protected wildlife or conduct otherwise prohibited activity must submit a completed federal fish and wildlife license/permit application, Form 3-200 (Figure 16.1). Migratory bird banding permit applications are handled differently, however, and are submitted on other forms. The offices that process the different permit applications are as follows:

- Office of Management Authority
    Feather quota
    Injurious wildlife permits
    Endangered and threatened species permits
    Marine mammal permits
    CITES permits and certificates
    Captive-bred wildlife registrations
- Bird Banding Laboratory
    Migratory bird banding permit
- Special agent-in-charge
    Exception to the designated port
    Import/export license
    Migratory bird permit (other than bird banding)
    Bald or golden eagle permits

SEND TO:
Director, U.S. Fish & Wildlife Service
Office of Management Authority
P.O. Box 27329, Central Station
Washington, D.C. 20038-7329
Call 202/343-4955 for help or information

OMB NO. 42-R1670

DEPARTMENT OF THE INTERIOR
U.S. FISH AND WILDLIFE SERVICE

FEDERAL FISH AND WILDLIFE
LICENSE/PERMIT APPLICATION

1. APPLICATION FOR *(Indicate only one)*

☐ IMPORT OR EXPORT LICENSE   [XX] PERMIT

2. BRIEF DESCRIPTION OF ACTIVITY FOR WHICH REQUESTED LICENSE OR PERMIT IS NEEDED.

Re-export of African elephant ivory

Single Shipment

APPLICANT. *(Name, complete address and phone number of individual, business, agency, or institution for which permit is requested)*

4. IF "APPLICANT" IS AN INDIVIDUAL, COMPLETE THE FOLLOWING:

☐ MR. ☐ MRS. ☐ MISS ☐ MS. | HEIGHT | WEIGHT

DATE OF BIRTH | COLOR HAIR | COLOR EYES

PHONE NUMBER WHERE EMPLOYED | SOCIAL SECURITY NUMBER

OCCUPATION

ANY BUSINESS, AGENCY, OR INSTITUTIONAL AFFILIATION HAVING TO DO WITH THE WILDLIFE TO BE COVERED BY THIS LICENSE/PERMIT

5. IF "APPLICANT" IS A BUSINESS, CORPORATION, PUBLIC AGENCY, OR INSTITUTION, COMPLETE THE FOLLOWING:

EXPLAIN TYPE OR KIND OF BUSINESS, AGENCY, OR INSTITUTION

NAME, TITLE, AND PHONE NUMBER OF PRESIDENT, PRINCIPAL OFFICER, DIRECTOR, ETC.

IF "APPLICANT" IS A CORPORATION, INDICATE STATE IN WHICH INCORPORATED

6. LOCATION WHERE PROPOSED ACTIVITY IS TO BE CONDUCTED

7. DO YOU HOLD ANY CURRENTLY VALID FEDERAL FISH AND WILDLIFE LICENSE OR PERMIT? ☐ YES ☐ NO
(If yes, list license or permit numbers)

8. IF REQUIRED BY ANY STATE OR FOREIGN GOVERNMENT, DO YOU HAVE THEIR APPROVAL TO CONDUCT THE ACTIVITY YOU PROPOSE? ☐ YES ☐ NO
(If yes, list jurisdictions and type of documents)

9. CHECK OR MONEY ORDER *(if applicable)* PAYABLE TO THE U.S. FISH AND WILDLIFE SERVICE ENCLOSED IN AMOUNT OF
$ 25.00 (U.S.currency)

10. DESIRED EFFECTIVE DATE

11. DURATION NEEDED

12. ATTACHMENTS. THE SPECIFIC INFORMATION REQUIRED FOR THE TYPE OF LICENSE/PERMIT REQUESTED (See 50 CFR 13.12(b)) MUST BE ATTACHED. IT CONSTITUTES AN INTEGRAL PART OF THIS APPLICATION. LIST SECTIONS OF 50 CFR UNDER WHICH ATTACHMENTS ARE PROVIDED.

See Reverse

CERTIFICATION

I HEREBY CERTIFY THAT I HAVE READ AND AM FAMILIAR WITH THE REGULATIONS CONTAINED IN TITLE 50, PART 13, OF THE CODE OF FEDERAL REGULATIONS AND THE OTHER APPLICABLE PARTS IN SUBCHAPTER B OF CHAPTER I OF TITLE 50, AND I FURTHER CERTIFY THAT THE INFORMATION SUBMITTED IN THIS APPLICATION FOR A LICENSE/PERMIT IS COMPLETE AND ACCURATE TO THE BEST OF MY KNOWLEDGE AND BELIEF. I UNDERSTAND THAT ANY FALSE STATEMENT HEREIN MAY SUBJECT ME TO THE CRIMINAL PENALTIES OF 18 U.S.C. 1001.

SIGNATURE *(In ink)* ★ | DATE

3-200
(6/74) *Applicant listed in 3 above or principal officer listed in 5 above must sign.

Figure 16.1 A federal fish and wildlife licence/permit application (Form 3-200).

When submitting permit applications for activities processed by a special agent-in-charge, it must be mailed to the agent for the district in which the applicant resides.[34] Appendix J lists the addresses of offices involved in the permitting process.

The Service requires certain information from applicants to help it make appropriate decisions regarding permit issuance. Baseline information includes (1) the professional background of the applicant, (2) the type of animal for which the permit is requested, (3) the number of animals involved in the activity, and (4) the type of facilities and intended disposition of the animal if the permit is granted. Additional information may be requested depending upon the type of permit needed.

Applications for endangered species and marine mammal permits should be submitted at least 75 days prior to the permit's effective date. All other permits require a minimum of 30 days to process.

The fee for processing and issuing a permit is $25 unless the activity is governed by one of the following nonstandard fees:[35]

- import/export license—$250 and inspection fees
- marine mammal—$100
- migratory bird—none
- bald or golden eagles—none

These fees may be waived in the case of public institutions and are waived when any governmental agency is sponsoring the activity.

General Permit Issuance[36]

The director of the Service is authorized to issue a permit unless one of the following circumstances is present: (1) the applicant has been assessed a civil penalty or convicted of a criminal act related to the permitted activity that shows a lack of responsibility; (2) the applicant has not disclosed necessary data or has provided false information; (3) the applicant has failed to justify adequately the need for a permit; (4) the activity potentially threatens wildlife with harm; or (5) the direc-

tor determines that the applicant is unqualified.

Permits can be renewed or amended by contacting the office that granted the permit and asking for instructions. The Service has the authority to recall or modify any permits it issues. Applicants or those with permits who are dissatisfied with the outcome of the application results may file appeals.[37]

Accurate records of transactions involving permitted animals must be kept for a minimum of five years from the date the permit was issued.[38] Any agent of the Service can inspect the premises listed in the permit at any reasonable time and is authorized to inspect the physical facilities as well as any records or books.[39] Lastly, the Service can exact penalties for any violations of the regulatory provisions. However, the Service must give notice of impending actions unless the public health is at risk.[40]

Importation, Exportation, and Transportation of Wildlife[41]

The regulations implementing wildlife legislation devote considerable attention to the transportation of imported or exported wildlife. These provisions are in addition to other regulations that deal with international trade in wildlife.[42]

The first provision states that import and export of wildlife must take place through a *designated port of entry*. The nine United States designated ports are as follows:[43]

- Los Angeles, California
- San Francisco, California
- Miami, Florida
- Honolulu, Hawaii
- New Orleans, Louisiana
- New York, New York
- Chicago, Illinois
- Seattle, Washington
- Dallas/Fort Worth, Texas

Animals that are being shipped through the United States but that are not ultimately destined for a point within the country are exempted from the requirement to use a designated port.[44] If a permit is not required under provisions elsewhere in the regulations and the wildlife originates in the United States, Mexico, or Canada, it can be imported or exported at a number of different border ports in addition to those designated ports. This provision, however, pertains only to wildlife taken lawfully in these countries that do not require permits for transport.[45]

Personally owned pet birds may be imported through ports designated by the Department of Agriculture including New York; Miami; Hidalgo, Texas; Los Angeles; San Francisco; and Honolulu.[46] Marine mammals taken lawfully in accordance with regulations implementing the MMPA may be imported through any port. [47]

The director of the Service can issue permits exempting individuals from the designated port requirement if the purpose of the wildlife import or export is of a scientific nature.[48] The application procedures for issuance of such permits are the same as for the general permits described previously.[49]

Inspection of Wildlife[50]

All wildlife imported into the United Sates must be cleared by an agent of the Service prior to being admitted by customs officials. Agents will deny the wildlife's entry into the United States if the required documentation is not in order or if the wildlife specimens are different from those that are described in the documentation.

There are three exceptions to this rule. Unless required under the ESA, clearance of the following is not required: (1) shellfish and fish products intended for consumption, (2) lawfully taken marine mammals, and (3) certain antique wildlife items (worked ivory and taxidermy specimens).[51]

At the time of clearance, importers must file a completed Form 3-177, *Declaration for Importation or Exportation of Fish or Wildlife*. No form need be filed for (1) shellfish or fish products, (2) fish taken recreationally from Canada or Mexico, (3) game mammals or birds from Canada or Mexico if the appropriate customs forms have been filed, and (4)

wildlife products that are not intended for sale or those that are part of personal or household effects.

Exporters of wildlife also must complete Form 3-177 and file it with the Service before the wildlife leaves the country. Shellfish and fish products, wildlife not intended for sale and valued at less than $250, and personal items of baggage are again exempted from the requirements of this provision.

Humane Transport Regulations for the Importation of Wildlife[52]

On November 10, 1987, the Service adopted regulations dealing with the transport of mammals and birds into the United States in a humane manner that is conducive to their safety and well-being. These regulations establish general conditions under which birds and mammals are to be transported.

The regulations require the establishment of suitable holding facilities to be provided by carriers at points of departure (exporting country), arrival (the United States), and at any stopover points in between. Environmental parameters are to be monitored and maintained within certain levels both in transporting vehicles and in holding facilities. The regulations also require that a veterinarian certify that, prior to initiating the journey, the specimen appears to be healthy and able to withstand the rigors of transport.

Further details regarding transport requirements can be obtained by reviewing the regulations or contacting the Office of Management Authority (Appendix J).

The Permit Process Under the Endangered Species Act[53]

The following activities are prohibited under the ESA without a permit: (1) import or export (including shipment through the United States to another country); (2) transport, sale, or receipt of lawfully taken wildlife in interstate or foreign commerce in the course of conducting a commercial activity; (3) take; (4) possession, transport, receipt, or sale of unlawfully taken endangered or threatened wildlife; or (5) violation of any federal regulation regarding a listed species.[54] The intent of these prohibitions is to prevent listed species from entering commercial trade. Activity with unlawfully obtained species is prohibited under any circumstances.

Permits are issued for these prohibited activities when dealing with endangered species in order to allow scientific research, to enhance the propagation or survival of the species, or for incidental take. Individuals who wish to conduct a prohibited activity other than research or propagation may apply for a permit within one year after a species has been listed as endangered. A permit may be granted if a claim of undue economic hardship can be substantiated as a result of the species having been listed.[55] Applicants must show, however, that they entered into a commercial contract regarding the particular species before they received any indication that it would be placed on the endangered species list.

The normal course of applications made for ESA permits is as follows:

- submit completed forms
- 30-day public comment period
- decision regarding permit issuance
- appeal procedure

To obtain an ESA permit, a completed Form 3-200 (Figure 16.1) is submitted to the Service. Information concerning the applicant's expertise in working with the particular species is required, as well as a description of the physical facilities and the use for which the permit is being sought.[56]

Commercial activity involving lawfully obtained endangered or threatened wildlife occurring entirely within one state is not prohibited by the ESA. Advertisements that have interstate circulation must say that a federal permit is required for purchase of the specimen, however.

No permits are issued for the maintenance of endangered or threatened wildlife as pets. Additionally, if the animal covered by the permit escapes into the wild, it must be reported immediately to the Service.[57]

The Captive-Bred Wildlife Permit Process

Special procedures accommodate individuals wishing to conduct activity with endangered animals bred and raised in captivity. The Code of Federal Regulations defines *captive-bred wildlife* as any living, exotic (nonnative) specimen listed under the ESA that was conceived and born in captivity within the United States.[58] Indigenous (native) captive bred wildlife do not fall within the scope of this exemption.

Various kinds of activities are authorized under this provision, including conduct in the course of a commercial enterprise.[59] In order for the activity to be approved, however, applicants must show that it will enhance the propagation or survival of the species.[60]

To transact business involving captive-bred wildlife, both buyer and seller must be registered with the Service and, thus, each must possess a captive bred wildlife permit number.[61] Registration under this procedure authorizes activity involving taxonomically classified families of wildlife rather than individual species, somewhat like a multiple-animal permit. Applicants must submit a completed Form 3-200 (Figure 16.1) to the Service describing both the physical facilities that will be available and the applicant's wildlife propagation expertise. Registrants also must maintain complete records regarding activities conducted with the captive bred wildlife and submit copies of these records to the Service annually. Since both buyer and seller must be registered, both must submit annual reports.

Individuals claiming a captive bred wildlife exemption must supply appropriate documentation and comply with state laws as well. Since native species are not covered by this exemption, individuals who possess these animals must obtain permits for each transaction involving interstate or foreign commerce and import or export of native endangered species.

Currently, the Service is reevaluating its approach to the regulation of captive-bred exotic wildlife, and it is anticipated that significant practical changes will be made in the near future.

Special Rules Regarding Threatened Species

The Service policy is to treat threatened species in the same manner as their endangered counterparts[62]; however, a number of threatened species come under what is termed *special rules*. This means that either limited commercial activity is allowed with these species or that there are fewer restrictions pertaining to their use than to threatened species that are fully protected.

These special rules frequently are modified either by changing the species to which the rule applies or by altering the conditions under which the special rule can be invoked. Changes are based primarily on new scientific data which induce a reevaluation of the status of the species in question. For special rules pertaining to grizzly bears, nonhuman primates, American alligators, and fish, as examples, see regulations in reference.[63]

Other Permits

Permits for prohibited activity affecting threatened species are issued only under the following circumstances: for scientific research, enhancement of propagation or survival of the species, zoological exhibition, educational purposes, special purposes consistent with the ESA, and economic hardship.[64]

The ESA allows a species to be designated threatened due to its similarity of appearance to another species already classified as endangered or threatened. Except for two additional requirements, the permit application process that deals with these species is the same as for species listed as endangered or threatened. First, the wildlife must be marked in accordance with directions on the permit and, second, a copy of the permit must be available during any permit-authorized activity.[65]

The Service is authorized by the ESA to reintroduce into the wild endangered or threatened species that may be extinct from their historic range. These reintroductions are classified as experimental populations. In processing permit requests, the Service treats these populations as threatened species. Presently, there are three species so classified: the Delmarva Peninsula fox-squirrel, the Colorado squawfish, and the woundfish.[66]

Scientific Research and the ESA

In most cases, if scientific research involves the use of endangered or threatened species, an ESA take permit must be obtained from the Service. The reason for this is that use of these animals in research has been construed to be harassment, which is an integral part of the definition of take. The issuance of such a permit is research specific, that is, the permit is issued only for the particular experiment the investigator wishes to conduct.

There are several exceptions to this policy. If the investigator can fulfill the requirements of any of the exemptions or if the species is one about which a special rule has been adopted, a permit under the ESA may not be needed. A permit is required, however, whether or not the specimen is captive bred. Further information can be obtained from the appropriate authorities listed in Appendix J.

The Permit Process Used by the National Marine Fisheries Service[67]

The National Marine Fisheries Service (NMFS) shares responsibility with the United States Fish and Wildlife Service in issuing permits for particular species under the ESA. The permitting process is somewhat different than that used by the Fish and Wildlife Service. Refer to the section entitled "Permit Procedures Under Department of Commerce Authority" for further information.

The Permit Process Under the Migratory Bird Treaty Act[68]

The Migratory Bird Treaty Act (MBTA) protects over 800 avian species. In accordance with this act, it is unlawful for individuals to take, possess, buy, transport, or sell listed species without a permit.[69] The United States Fish and Wildlife Service issues permits for marking and banding listed birds, scientific collection, taxidermy, predator control, waterfowl sale and disposal, falconry, and special purposes.[70] Import and export are allowed if the individual is working under an existing MBTA permit or if the specimen is possessed by a scientific or educational institution, museum, or zoo. No permit is required for import or export if the migratory bird is lawfully possessed.[71] These regulations, with the exception of the banding and marking provisions, do not apply to bald or golden eagles, as they are covered elsewhere.[72] As with other legislation, exemptions are provided.

Banding or Marking Permits[74]

A permit must be obtained in order to capture any migratory bird for marking or banding. In addition to the general permit requirements, applicants must provide information relevant to the purpose of the activity, the number and type of birds to be used, and the states involved. Service-issued bands must be used and applied in a fashion consistent with the *North American Bird Banding Manual*. Accurate records must be maintained. Permits are usually issued for a two-year period.

Waterfowl Sale and Disposal Permits[75]

A permit is required before an individual may sell, trade, donate, or dispose of any captive-reared, properly marked waterfowl or eggs, excluding mallard ducks. Permit applications are sent to the special agent-in-charge for the district in which the activity is to take place (Appendix J). Applicants must agree not to take any birds from the wild, to properly mark all birds, and to submit annual reports. Form 3-186 must be filed with the Service, the carrier, and the buyer whenever transactions with one of the permitted birds take place. These permits usually are issued for two years.

Special Purposes Permit[76]

This category allows Service personnel the discretion of granting a permit for any activity that can be justified due to its benefit to the species or the public. When activities do not fall within a usual category of permitted activity, applicants should contact the special agent-in-charge for the appropriate district to determine if a permit can be granted under the authority of this provision.

Falconry Permits[77]

A permit is required to take, possess, or transport raptors for falconry purposes. The issuance of a permit is contingent upon the existence of a federal/state agreement allowing such activity. All but 10 states have federally recognized programs regulating falconry. Individuals residing in states with such programs must submit permit applications to state offices administering these programs. If an application is approved, a joint federal-state permit will be issued. In nonparticipating states, applicants must submit separate applications to the appropriate special agent-in-charge, including documentation that they also have applied for a state permit.

The conditions of the federal permit focus on the trading aspects of falconry activity. If no money is involved, permit holders may transfer raptors to other permit holders within the same state without notifying the Service. Gratuitous transfers also may occur interstate provided that the appropriate state authorities are notified. Interstate or international commercial transactions involving captive-bred raptors can take place when the recipients are authorized to take possession of the raptor. Annual reports are required of permit holders, and permits are valid for 18 months.

The federal government regulates the standards for falconry activity.[78] There are three classes of falconer, designating varying degrees of skill in conducting the activity. Falconers are required to comply with state regulations pertaining to this activity and in some cases will find state regulations to be more restrictive than their federal counterparts.

Raptor Propagation Permits[79]

Individuals who wish to take, possess, transport, or sell raptors, eggs, or semen for propagation must obtain a federal permit. Species that are under the jurisdiction of the ESA may not be taken unless an ESA permit also has been issued. Applications are submitted to the special agent-in-charge. Conditions of the permit include the submission of an annual report of breeding activity and a prohibition on trading raptors until they are banded and at least two weeks of age. Trading of raptors, eggs, or semen obtained from the wild is prohibited.

The Service requires that it be notified when the permit holder's raptors have laid their first eggs. Any offspring must be banded using bands issued by the Service. Permit holders can hybridize these raptors only if the offspring are imprinted on humans or sterilized, eliminating any possibility that these hybridized specimens will be added to the wild gene pool.

When a permitted raptor dies, the Service is to be notified immediately and the body destroyed unless the permit holder requests otherwise. Raptors may not be released into the wild without authorization by the director of the Service. Tenure of the raptor propagation permit is five years.

The Permit Process Under the Bald Eagle Protection Act[80]

The Bald Eagle Protection Act (BEPA) prohibits the take, possession, or transportation of bald or golden eagles, nests, or eggs without a permit.[81] Conduct involving the purchase, sale, barter, import, or export of these species is prohibited, and no permits are issued authorizing such activity.[82] Permits are available for scientific or display purposes, Indian religious purposes, and predation control.[83]

Completed applications for permitted activities should be sent to the special agent-in-charge in the region in which the activity is to occur. Information beyond that required by the general permit conditions of the regulations is necessary to obtain permits for scientific or display purposes. A detailed explanation of the purpose of the take, the species involved, and the names of the parties participating must be provided. There also are certain reporting requirements, including a description of the activities conducted during the permit period. This report is to be filed within 30 days of permit expiration.[84]

Falconry Permits Under the BEPA[85]

After evaluating a completed application, the Service may issue permits to possess and transport golden eagles for falconry purposes. Applications are submitted to the special agent-in-charge and must include a copy of the applicant's masters class permit,[86] a description of the applicant's experience in handling large raptors, two letters of recommendation from individuals recognized for their expertise in working with eagles, a description of the applicant's housing facilities, and several additional items.[87] Permit conditions include prohibitions on breeding these eagles, requirements for banding specimens, prohibitions on any type of transaction with the permitted specimens without the written permission of the Service, and notification of the special agent-in-charge upon the death of any of the specimens. Permit holders also must abide by any state laws that are more restrictive than the federal regulations. A golden eagle falconry permit is valid as long as the person holds a master's permit or until revoked.

Golden eagles may be trapped for falconry purposes if permission has been granted by the state animal damage control unit authorizing and overseeing the activity.[87] Nests may be taken, but only under strict control and for purposes of resource development or recovery operations.[88]

The Permit Process Under CITES[89]

The constraints of the CITÈS apply only to situations involving international movement of wildlife. It is unlawful under CITES for any individual to import, export, or reexport any animal or plant listed in a CITES appendix unless a permit has been issued or an exemption invoked. It also is unlawful to possess any animal that has been transported contrary to the provisions of CITES.[90]

Regulations require that proper CITES documentation accompany any import, export, or reexport of listed specimens. Export permits are always required; import permits are required only for CITES Appendix I species or Appendix II species that are introduced from the sea.

CITES Permits and Certificates[91]

A uniform permit is used by all parties to CITES. The documents accompanying the shipment must be original and filled out entirely. There must be a valid signature and seal from the appropriate management authority, and the document must be current. Sample permits are provided in Figures 16.2 and 16.3.

If a specimen listed on a CITES appendix also is covered by the ESA or the MMPA, only one application for a permit need be submitted to the Office of Management Authority.[91] A joint permit then will be issued by this office.

Information to be provided in a CITES permit application includes (1) a description of the wildlife involved and whether or not it comes from the wild; (2) the type of shipping container to be used; (3) how the importer will provide for the needs of the specimen; and (4) the purpose of the activity. Permits or certificates must be presented to a Service agent at designated ports either at the time of import or prior to the time of export or reexport. Permits are issued for periods not to exceed six months. Three CITES appendices regulate trade in the CITES-listed species.

CITES Appendix I Permits[92]

Listing in Appendix I indicates endangerment, and thus the most stringent restrictions apply. Any activity with an Appendix I species requires that both an export permit from the country of origin and an import permit from the country of destination be issued. Import permits must be obtained first since issuance of the export permit is contingent upon already having obtained an import permit.

Individuals applying for an Appendix I permit must provide their credentials, an explanation of the purpose of the activity, an indication of the mortality experienced by the applicant in caring for similar species over the past two years, and the steps taken to avoid future mortality.

The Office of Management Authority must determine the following to issue an export permit for Appendix I species originating in the United States:

- that the specimen has been taken lawfully;
- that the risks of injury, damage to health, or cruel treatment will be minimized in transportation;
- that an import permit has been issued by the country importing the specimen; and
- that the Office of the Scientific Authority has determined that export will not be detrimental to the survival of the species.[93]

To issue an import permit for Appendix I species, the Office of Management Authority must determine that the specimen will not be used for primarily commercial purposes. Additionally, the Office of the Scientific Authority must determine that the applicant is able to care for the animal(s) and that the purposes for import will not be detrimental to the species survival.[94]

CITES Appendix II Permits

Appendix II restrictions are somewhat less stringent than those of Appendix I in that only one permit is required. For imports into the United States, the importer must obtain either an export (or reexport) permit or a certificate of exemption from the country of origin. For all listed specimens exported from the United States, a federal CITES export permit or reexport certificate must be obtained. An exception to the one permit requirement occurs in the case of specimens taken from the sea where both import and export permits are required.[92]

Activities allowed under a permit for an Appendix II species are broad. Almost

FORM 3-201A (12/82)

CONVENTION ON INTERNATIONAL TRADE IN ENDANGERED SPECIES OF WILD FAUNA AND FLORA

☑ IMPORT PERMIT
☐ EXPORT PERMIT
☐ RE-EXPORT CERTIFICATE
☐ OTHER CERTIFICATES (See block 9)

Page ___ 1 ___ of ___ 1 ___

1. Original Permit/Certificate No.
US 723100

2. Valid until
2/28/89

3. Permittee (name and address, country)

Mary Doe
RT. 1, BOX 11
RED BLUFF   CA 96080
U.S.A.

4. Consignee/Consignor (name and address, country)
XXXX
AVICENTRA PVBA
11 GOUDBLOEMLOAN
SCHILDE   2230
BELGIUM

5. Special conditions

-MUST COMPLY WITH ATTACHED GENERAL PERMIT CONDITIONS.
-U.S. ENDANGERED SPECIES (50 CFR 17.22): FOR PROPAGATION.
-ALL SPECIMENS MUST BE PHYSICALLY INSPECTED BY A FISH & WILDLIFE SERVICE INSPECTOR & THIS DOCUMENT STAMPED BY SAME.

6. U.S. Management Authority

FEDERAL WILDLIFE PERMIT OFFICE
U.S. FISH AND WILDLIFE SERVICE
DEPARTMENT OF THE INTERIOR
WASHINGTON, D.C. 20240
UNITED STATES OF AMERICA

2/29/88
Issuing Date

US 9131680

AUTHORITY   Endangered Spe

7/8. Common Name and Scientific Name (genus and species) of Animal or Plant	9. Description of part or derivative. Including identifying marks or numbers (age/sex if live)	10. Appendix No. and source (W, C, A or O)	11. Quantity, number of specimens, and/or net weight (kg. or lbs.)
A. COMMON NAME **GOLDEN CONURE** SCIENTIFIC NAME **ARATINGA GUAROUBA**	0.0.10; LIVE; ALL BIRDS CAPTIVE-BORN AT AVICENTRA ALL CLOSE-RINGED; RING NOS. MUST BE IDENTIFIED ON BELGIUM EXPORT PERMIT.	10. 1 C 12. Country of origin* BELGIUM Country of origin permit/certificate no.	11. 10
B. COMMON NAME ___ SCIENTIFIC NAME		10. 12. Country of origin* Country of origin permit/certificate no.	11.
C. COMMON NAME ___ SCIENTIFIC NAME		10. 12. Country of origin* Country of origin permit/certificate no.	11.
D. COMMON NAME ___ SCIENTIFIC NAME		10. 12. Country of origin* Country of origin permit/certificate no.	11.

* Country in which the specimens were taken from the wild, bred in captivity or artificially propagated.

13. Export/Re-export Endorsement:

The official who inspects shipment upon exportation/re-exportation must enter the actual quantities of specimens being exported/re-exported in this block.

14. Bill of Lading/Air Way-Bill Number

Port of Exportation/Re-exportation

15. This document valid only with inspecting official's ORIGINAL stamp, signature and date in this block.

See block 7	Quantity
A	
B	
C	
D	

Total No. of Shipping Containers

Figure 16.2   A CITES import permit.

FORM 3-201A (12/82)

CONVENTION ON INTERNATIONAL TRADE IN ENDANGERED SPECIES OF WILD FAUNA AND FLORA

☐ IMPORT PERMIT
☑ EXPORT PERMIT
☐ RE EXPORT CERTIFICATE
☐ OTHER CERTIFICATES (See block 9)

Page __1__ of __1__

1. Original Permit/Certificate No.
US 725493

2. Valid until
8/31/88

3. Permittee (name and address, country)

John Doe
111 JUANITA DR. N.E.
KIRKLAND   WA   98034
U.S.A.

4. Consignee/Consignor (name and address, country)

John Doe
C/O AMERICAN CONSULATE GENERAL
CALCUTTA, DEPT. OF STATE
WASHINGTON, D.C.   20520
U.S.A.

5. Special conditions

-MUST COMPLY WITH ATTACHED GENERAL PERMIT CONDITIONS.
-PERSONAL PET ACCOMPANYING PERMITTEE TO CALCUTTA, INDIA, IN HOUSEHOLD MOVE.

6. U.S. Management Authority

FEDERAL WILDLIFE PERMIT OFFICE
U.S. FISH AND WILDLIFE SERVICE
DEPARTMENT OF THE INTERIOR
WASHINGTON, D.C. 20240
UNITED STATES OF AMERICA

2/25/88
Issuing Date

US 9131650

AUTHORITY: Endangered ... seq.)

7/8. Common Name and Scientific Name (genus and species) of Animal or Plant	9. Description of part or derivative. Including identifying marks or numbers (age/sex if live)	10. Appendix No. and source (W, C, A or O)	11. Quantity, number of specimens, and/or net weight (kg. or lbs.)
A. COMMON NAME **YELLOW-CROWNED AMAZON** SCIENTIFIC NAME **AMAZONA OCHROCEPHALA**	**0.0.1; LIVE; BORN IN MARCH 1987; CLOSED LEG BAND #84 87 DGB. - SEE BLOCK 5 -**	10. **2** C	11. **1** 12. Country of origin* **U.S.A.** Country of origin permit/certificate no. **US NO. 725493**
B. COMMON NAME SCIENTIFIC NAME		10. 12. Country of origin* Country of origin permit/certificate no.	11.
C. COMMON NAME SCIENTIFIC NAME		10. 12. Country of origin* Country of origin permit/certificate no.	11.
D. COMMON NAME SCIENTIFIC NAME		10. 12. Country of origin* Country of origin permit/certificate no.	11.

* Country in which the specimens were taken from the wild, bred in captivity or artificially propagated.

13. Export/Re-export Endorsement:

The official who inspects shipment upon exportation/re-exportation must enter the actual quantities of specimens being exported/re-exported in this block.

See block 7	Quantity
A	
B	
C	

14. Bill of Lading/Air Way-Bill Number

Port of Exportation/Re-exportation

Total No. of Shipping Containers

15. This document valid only with inspecting official's ORIGINAL stamp, signature and date in this block.

Figure 16.3   A CITES export permit.

anything is permitted unless it is determined to be detrimental to the survival of the species.

The federal government has developed a number of different programs dealing with the export of Appendix II species that are indigenous to the United States. The species involved are the American alligator, bobcat, lynx, river otter, Alaskan gray wolf, and the Alaskan brown or grizzly bear. Essentially, these programs offer ways of allowing state regulation of and commercial trade in these species.[95]

CITES Appendix III Permits

A valid export permit or certificate of origin must be issued from the listing country to import an Appendix III species into the United States. Alternatively, a reexport certificate may be issued prior to transport from the country of reexport.[92]

Permit Exemptions[96]

Certain activities are exempted from the prohibitions associated with CITES, and in these cases a certificate of exemption is required instead of a permit. This certificate must be displayed at the port of entry or exit but is not collected by Service personnel.

Two activities are of particular interest. First, CITES has defined *captive-bred wildlife* to include only offspring of parents that were maintained in a captive environment during conception. This means that eggs taken from the wild and hatched in captivity do not fall within the definition of captive-bred wildlife. Further, "... specimens of animal species in Appendix I bred in captivity for commercial purposes shall be treated as if they were in Appendix II...."[97] Individuals wishing to use this exemption.must obtain a CITES certificate of exemption for captive-bred wildlife from the specimen's country of origin.

Second, no CITES permit is needed for specimens being transshipped through the United States to another destination if the shipment remains in the custody of the United States Customs authority while passing through the country. In other words, if the specimen is in the United States as a stopover to accommodate travel arrangements, no special documentation is required to proceed to a destination in another country. This exemption does not apply, however, to such shipment of species that are on an ESA or MMPA list in addition to a CITES list. Transshipment of these animals is allowed only after a proper permit has been issued.

Permit Procedures Under the Department of Commerce Authority

The Commerce Department implements wildlife legislation that impacts marine species. The department acts in that capacity through its agency the National Marine Fisheries Service (NMFS), which promulgates and administers regulations affecting such species. As part of this responsibility, the NMFS issues permits for marine species over which it has jurisdiction including cetaceans, pinnipeds (except walrus), and sea turtles, as well as commercial fisheries. The Fish and Wildlife Service has jurisdiction over marine species that spend part of their lives on land, such as the polar bear and sea otter. Interestingly, in the case of the sea turtle, NMFS has jurisdiction while the turtle is in the water, and the Service has jurisdiction when the animal is on land. The NMFS permitting regulations pertain to the implementation of the MMPA, the ESA, and the Fur Seal Act.

The Permit Process Under the National Marine Fisheries Service

The MMPA prohibits the taking, transport, purchase, or sale of marine mammals; the importation of such species into the United States; or the possession of unlawfully taken marine mammals.[98]

Permits may be issued for marine mammal take and importation for purposes of scientific research, public display, or incidental take in commercial fishing.[99] It continues to be unlawful to take marine mammals in an inhumane fashion; from depleted populations; or if they are pregnant, nursing, or younger than eight months of age. Application procedures are the same as for granting a general permit; however, additional information is required of the applicant. Of critical significance is the requirement that a written certification be made by a veterinarian experienced with marine mammals that the transport proposal is in order and that it is realistic in terms of expected outcome. The shipper must state whether or not a veterinarian will accompany the animal specimen. The veterinarian also must certify that the applicant will be able to provide for the needs of the specimen once it reaches its destination. Applications are submitted to the director of NMFS (Appendix J), and permit processing requires a minimum of 45 days.

The Service and the NMFS issue permits for take from the wild, but maintenance in captivity of these animals comes under the jurisdiction of the Department of Agriculture's Animal and Plant Health Inspection Service (APHIS). Failure to comply with the Department of Agriculture's regulations is cause for revocation of a permit issued either by the Service or the NMFS.

Procedures Under the Department of Agriculture Authority That Affect Wildlife

The United States Department of Agriculture is congressionally mandated to safeguard the well-being of animals within the United States. The scope of this authority extends from the protection of agricultural interests to the provision of standards for the care and treatment of laboratory animals. Through its agency APHIS, the department has developed regulations regarding the quarantine of recently imported animals; the interstate movement of animals; and the humane care and treatment provided animals in the hands of researchers, dealers, handlers, and exhibitors.

Wildlife Aspects of the Animal Welfare Act Regulations[100]

The Animal Welfare Act authorizes APHIS to draft, adopt, and administer regulations.[101] The purpose of this law is to insure the humane treatment of animals used in research, for public display, and as pets. Its application is limited to warm-blooded animals. The regulations authorized by this legislation specifically exclude birds, rats, mice, and livestock from coverage. The Animal Welfare Act regulations affect wildlife species to the extent that they fall within three categories: they must be warm-blooded, used in research or display, and involved in interstate commerce.

Under the Animal Welfare Act, APHIS has the authority to adopt regulations regarding animal care standards and to license or register animal dealers, operators of animal auctions, research facilities, carriers, intermediate handlers, and exhibitors.

Licensing Under the Animal Welfare Act Regulations[102]

An individual who wishes to operate as a dealer, exhibitor, or operator of an animal auction (where dogs and cats are sold) must obtain a license from APHIS (Appendix J).

A *dealer* is anyone who, for commercial purposes, delivers or sells animals for use in research, exhibition, or as pets. Retail pet stores are not included unless they sell animals to research facilities, exhibitors, or other dealers. Further, persons who do not sell wild animals, dogs, or cats but who sell other types of animals and do not gross more than $500 per year from such activity are not dealers either.

An *exhibitor* is defined by APHIS as a zoo, carnival, circus, or animal act. It does not include retail pet stores, rodeos, cat and dog shows, or county fairs.

The licensure procedure requires that the applicant comply with all the standards developed by APHIS for the humane care and treatment of the animal for which the license is being acquired. This means that the applicant must allow APHIS personnel to inspect the facility in which the licensed activity is to take place. Once the inspection and processing have been completed, a license can be issued. Thereafter, an annual report must be submitted as long as an individual is licensed. Applications for licensure can be obtained by writing to the federal veterinarian-in-charge for the state in which the operation will take place. The fee is based on the type of activity conducted by the licensee.[103]

Registration Under the Animal Welfare Act Regulations[104]

Any research facility, carrier, intermediate handler, or exhibitor that is not required to be licensed must register with APHIS and should obtain a registration form from the area veterinarian-in-charge. Research facilities that are registered under this provision must submit annual reports to APHIS. A detailed accounting of the number of animals used for both painful and nonpainful experimentation is to be included in this report as well as a certification by the staff veterinarian that pain-relieving medications were utilized where appropriate.

Maintenance of Records and Requirements for Health Certificates[105]

Dealers, operators of auction sales, and exhibitors are required to maintain records of all transactions involving animals other than dogs and cats.[106] Two forms, available from APHIS and entitled *VS Form 18-19* (*Record of Animals on Hand*) and *VS Form 18-20* (*Record of Acquisition, Disposition, or Transport of Animals*), must accompany any transaction or transport of an animal. Copies of such documentation must be provided to the purchaser and retained by the operator.[107] Records are to be maintained for a minimum of one year.

A health certificate including identification of the animal signed by a licensed veterinarian within 10 days of anticipated transport must accompany any nonhuman primate being moved from one location to another. Forms are available from APHIS.[108]

Inspection, Confiscation, and Destruction of Animals

APHIS officials are authorized to inspect records and physical facilities of all licensees and registrants at reasonable times.[109] Inspection can be for the purpose of finding missing animals or to establish compliance with federal standards for the humane care and treatment of the animals involved. If APHIS personnel find animals that are suffering, they may take whatever action is necessary to alleviate the situation.

Standards for the Humane Care, Handling, Treatment, and Transport of Animals[110]

The Department of Agriculture has promulgated regulations that provide for the humane care, handling, treatment, and transport of many types of animals. The wildlife species included in the provisions are guinea pigs, hamsters, rabbits, nonhuman primates, and marine mammals. Additionally, there is one section that specifically addresses the requirements of warm-blooded animals other than those listed here. The salient feature of these standards is the provision for adequate veterinary care.

All sections pertaining to wildlife species allow carriers who are unable to meet the temperature requirements of the transport regulations to accept animals for transport that have been acclimated to a lower temperature for a minimum of 10 days. Certification by a USDA-accredited veterinarian must accompany animals being transported in such a manner.

The sections pertaining to the maintenance of marine mammals in captivity are detailed and contain items such as standards for pool dimensions. These regulations also provide that newly acquired marine mammals be isolated from resident populations until it is clear that the new animals have no infectious diseases. Variances can be issued.

Marine mammals that die in captivity must be necropsied, and facilities must maintain a copy of the necropsy report for three years after the animal's death.[111]

Department of Agriculture Regulations on Importation of Wildlife[112]

The Department of Agriculture's mission is to protect the interests of animals within the United States. More specifically, it regulates as much as possible the exposure of animals to foreign disease organisms. Its primary interest is in monitoring the nation's livestock industry. As a secondary objective, however, the department is concerned with the well-being of animals in laboratory situations. Only to the extent that wildlife either impacts these interests or is directly involved in some aspect of this mission is activity with wildlife regulated by the department. Finally, it is not the function of this agency to protect the interests of wildlife at the expense of domestic populations of animals.

The Department of Agriculture, through APHIS, controls the importation of all species of animals into the United States. Those provisions pertaining to wildlife follow.

Import Permits Required by APHIS[113]

APHIS requires that import permits be acquired from the Veterinary Services office of APHIS prior to the importation of animals into the United States. This requirement also covers semen and animal test specimens.

Import permits can be denied based upon inadequate information provided by applicants or the existence of diseases contagious to livestock in the country of origin or en route to the United States.

Permits issued by this agency are sent to the importer, who then forwards the original and a copy to the shipper in the country of origin. Thereafter, the original permit must accompany the shipment to the point of import in the United States.

Wild ruminants and wild swine imported from countries having rinderpest or foot and mouth disease must enter the United States only through the port of New York and be quarantined there. Permits to import these animals are issued only if the animals are destined for exhibition in an approved zoo. APHIS has procedures for approval of zoological facilities consisting of on-site inspections and evaluations. It is further required that a veterinarian be available for consultation, treatment, and postmortem evaluation when necessary. The veterinarian must report any evidence of contagious disease among the zoo population to the appropriate state or federal livestock officials. APHIS also requires a quarantine period of 60 days under the supervision of a veterinarian in the country of origin prior to shipment of animals to the United States. The shipment must be direct, and the animals may not be unloaded at any point other than at entry in New York. No other ruminants or swine may be on board the transporting vehicle. Upon arrival in New York, animals are quarantined for 30 days and are then shipped to the zoo that has been issued the permit and retained by that facility. Prior approval by Veterinary Services is necessary to move any animals from the authorized zoo.[113]

Health Certification Required for Importation of Wildlife[114]

A health certificate signed by a veterinarian employed by the country of origin must accompany the shipment of all wild ruminants and wild swine into the United States. This certificate must specify that the area from which these animals were obtained was free of a number of contagious diseases for a period of 60 days prior to the date of shipment.[115]

Provisions also exist for health certification of imported pet, commercial, research, and zoo birds. Certificates must indicate that the birds have been personally inspected by the government veterinarian and that they are free of Newcastle's disease, psittacosis, and any other disease contagious to poultry, and that the birds originate from areas free of these contagious diseases. To qualify, areas must have been free of disease for a minimum of 90 days preceding export. It also must be clear that the birds have not been vaccinated with Newcastle's disease vaccine and that they were placed in new containers at the time of shipment.[114]

Animals being transshipped through the United States to some other destination are not bound by these requirements. An import permit from APHIS' Veterinary Services, however, must be obtained for this type of shipment. If any stopover will occur in the United States, the carrier must be able to prove to APHIS that the animals will be confined in such a way that the spread of disease is impossible.[116]

Department of Agriculture Ports of Entry for the Importation of Animals

The Department of Agriculture has designated the ports of Los Angeles, California; Miami, Florida; Honolulu, Hawaii; and Newburgh, New York for the importation of animals other than nondomestic birds into the United States. The department has also designated various ports for entry along the border between the United States and Canada and between the United States and Mexico.[117]

Department of Agriculture ports of entry for the importation of birds vary depending upon the purpose for the importation.[118]

All animals that come under the jurisdiction of the Department of Agriculture are subject to inspection at the port of entry into the United States.[119]

Regulations Regarding the Importation of Birds

Importation of birds into the United States is prohibited except under certain circumstances.[120] Pet birds may be imported from Canada if, upon inspection at the port, the birds are found to be free of disease and the

owner documents that they have not been exposed to other birds and have been in the owner's possession for the last 90 days.[121]

Pet birds that originate in this country and have been abroad for less than 60 days may reenter the United States using the same health certificate issued prior to leaving the country. This health certificate must clearly indicate the band or tattoo number of the individual pet. If the period out of the country exceeds 60 days, the owners must furnish the inspector with a notarized document indicating that the pet bird has not been in contact with any other birds. Additionally, the owner must agree (using VS Form 17-8) to quarantine the pet bird for 30 days following import and to report any sign of disease occurring within that period.[121]

If a pet bird is entering the United States for the first time, it must be accompanied by a health certificate issued by a veterinary officer employed by the country of export. This certificate must indicate that the veterinarian examined the pet bird and found it to be healthy and free of any communicable diseases and that export is legal under the laws of the country of export. Further, the pet bird must be quarantined at a facility operated by the United States Department of Agriculture—for a minimum of 30 days.

It is suggested that the importer make a formal reservation for space with the quarantine facility prior to the actual import. If no space is available at the time of arrival, the animal without a reservation will be refused entry into the United States.[121] Clearance through this quarantine procedure requires that the port veterinarian issue an agricultural release for entry through United States Customs. The owner of the bird is responsible for all costs incurred during the quarantine process. Importation of zoo or performing birds also requires compliance with these regulations.

Import from Canada[122]

Animals originating in the United States, traveling to Canada, and returning to this country may enter the United States without a Canadian health certificate if they have the original United States export health certification. Certificates must be signed by the Canadian veterinarian who inspected the animal at the time of entry into Canada.

Exhibition animals traveling within Canada will be allowed reentry into the United States without Canadian health certification if the travel occurs within 90 days of departure from the United States and if they are traveling under valid United States health certification. These animals still must be inspected by a federal veterinary inspector at the time of reentry into the United States.

Miscellaneous Import Regulations Under the Authority of the Department of Agriculture

Other interesting Department of Agriculture regulations dealing with importation of animals into the United States include provisions governing the import of eggs from foreign countries to avoid spread of Newcastle's disease[123] and the importation of animal embryos.[124] Imported embryos must comply with regulations similar to those affecting live animal import. Embryos must be accompanied by a health certificate issued by the exporting country and a permit allowing such import issued by APHIS.

Wildlife Aspects of Quarantine Regulations

The goal of quarantine regulation is to protect domestic livestock and poultry within the United States from the transmission of infectious diseases. Thus, wildlife species are included in these quarantine regulations only insofar as their health affects or has the potential to affect livestock interests.

Animals recognized as having any of a number of different communicable diseases generally are prohibited from being transported interstate.[125] Movement of these animals is allowed, but only under strict control.

Wild ruminants and swine are quarantined for a minimum of 15 days after arrival in the United States. Birds imported for research, commercial, or zoological purposes or as pets (exclusive of those from Canada or those reentering the United States) must be quarantined at an approved facility for a minimum of 30 days after entry. The purpose of the quarantine is to prevent the introduction of exotic Newcastle's disease into the poultry population of the United States.

Within 72 hours of arrival at the quarantine facility, all psittacines must be individually identified by use of leg bands supplied by the Department of Agriculture. Also, they must be placed on prophylactic tetracycline for the period of quarantine.[126] Veterinary Services personnel may order any tests they feel necessary to effectively evaluate the health of the quarantined birds. An extensive record-keeping system is required, and all records must be maintained for one year following the animal's release from quarantine.

Animals that die during this process must be held for necropsy and evaluation. If Newcastle's disease is discovered during the quarantine period, all birds within that shipment are either destroyed or refused entry into the United States. Importers may elect to reexport the birds to any country that will accept the shipment.

Exotic Newcastle's Disease Regulations That Affect Wildlife[127]

APHIS has determined that since all species of birds are susceptible to Newcastle's disease, regulations that apply to poultry are also to be applied to nonpoultry species.[128] If an outbreak of Newcastle's disease occurs in a facility, a quarantine order is issued. All birds in that facility are destroyed, and all equipment is either disinfected or destroyed if disinfection is not possible. Repopulation can take place only when the federal veterinarian-in-charge or an appropriate state official has found the facility to be disease free. When endangered species are involved, APHIS must contact the Department of the Interior prior to initiating any action.[129]

Interstate transport of birds originating from a quarantine area is prohibited except when the bird or birds (not to exceed two) are privately owned. In that case, the owner must submit a notarized document to a federal official stating that the bird has been in the owner's possession for a minimum of 90 days and has not been exposed to other birds or to Newcastle's disease. The owner also must quarantine the bird for 30 days upon arrival at the destination and allow federal inspection until the bird has been cleared through the quarantine process.[130] Finally, provision is made for the disinfection of vehicles used in the transport of birds affected with this disease.[131]

Permit Procedures Under the Department of Health and Human Services Authority

The Department of Health and Human Services regulates certain aspects of wildlife importation. This department focuses primarily on the public health aspects of the activity. The department acts through its agency, the Public Health Service, whose job it is to protect the public health.

Activity Under the Public Health Service Act[132]

The United States surgeon general, the administrator of the Public Health Service, is authorized by the Public Health Service Act to promulgate regulations to prevent the introduction, transmission, or spread of communicable diseases from foreign countries. The regulations articulate concerns regarding the effect of diseases transmitted by recently imported animals, as well as those transmitted by humans.[133] Wildlife regulation under this act occurs only to the extent that the public health of the nation is involved. Of particular interest is the importation of nonhuman primates, turtles, and psittacine birds.[134] Enforcement rests with the Centers for Disease Control in Atlanta.

Importation of Turtles Under the Public Health Service Act[135]

Generally, the importation of viable turtle eggs or turtles with a carapace length of less than 4 inches is prohibited.[136] The reason for this restriction is to prevent human exposure to *Salmonella* and *Arizona* infections.

Permits are required for importation of these animals and are issued for scientific, educational, or exhibition purposes. Permit applicants must be able to demonstrate that they have taken precautions to reduce the opportunity for human exposure to *Salmonella* and *Arizona* organisms.

No permit is needed in the following circumstances: (1) marine turtle importation, (2) shipments that are not for commercial purposes and that contain less than seven specimens or eggs, and (3) turtles whose shell length is greater than 4 inches.

Importers also are required to comply with any other federal laws regulating the importation of these species. Requests for a permit should be submitted to the Centers for Disease Control.

Importation and Transport of Psittacines Under the Public Health Service Act[137]

The importation of psittacines as pets is limited to two specimens per person per year under the authority of the Public Health Service Act.

The interstate transport of psittacine birds is regulated by the Food and Drug Administration, an agency within the Department of Health and Human Services. According to the regulations, any transport of these birds shall be accompanied by a permit issued by the health department in the state of destination if such permit is required by state law. The criteria for issuance are at the discretion of the individual state involved.

The regulations also provide that the surgeon general can declare an area infected with psittacosis and thus restrict movement of psittacine birds into and out of such an area if there is cause for concern about spread of disease to humans. Transport can be allowed at the discretion of the surgeon general for medical research and if accompanied by a permit.

Federal Regulation of Other Wildlife Activities

Wildlife Rehabilitation Facilities

Facilities that provide care and attempt to rehabilitate wildlife for eventual release to the wild or to zoos are regulated by the federal government and by states, counties, and/or municipalities.

Since many of the animals that are being rehabilitated come under the jurisdiction of federal law, a federal permit for such rehabilitation is frequently required. For example, the MBTA requires that persons *in possession* of animals falling within the purview of the act obtain a permit. Thus, a permit is required for simple *possession* of a migratory bird, regardless of the type of activity to be performed with the specimen. Other federal laws do not prohibit possession per se but do prohibit unlawful possession. Possession permits can be obtained from the special agent-in-charge of the region in which the rehabilitation is to occur (see Appendix J for address).

Activities involving rehabilitation of eagles come under the purview of the BEPA. Again, the special agent-in-charge for the region in which the activity is to take place should be contacted. If an animal to be rehabilitated is either endangered or threatened, its possession should be reported to the federal wildlife law enforcement officials of that region.

Ideally, permits should be obtained prior to possession of any protected species. Because of the need for emergency care, however, veterinarians may encounter situations for which they could not have anticipated the need for a permit. If this occurs, they should contact the appropriate special agent when they come into possession of such animals so that they do not violate federal law.

Local regulation of wildlife rehabilitation varies significantly. The reader is advised to contact authorities such as the state fish and game department within the area in which the rehabilitation is to occur to discover what regulations pertain to conducting this activity. Appendix K provides a list of all state wildlife conservation agencies.

Pet Stores

Pet stores are regulated primarily on a state or local level. If, however, these stores sell wild mammals, the United States Department of Agriculture considers that they have become *animal dealers*. In such cases, the pet store operator is required to be federally licensed and is subject to the provisions described for animal dealers. Pet stores that only exhibit such animals and do not remove them from the premises are not required to be licensed by the Department of Agriculture.

Persons involved with pet store operation are advised to contact local authorities such as health departments or licensing agencies to determine the extent to which their activity is being regulated locally, as well.

Wildlife Auctions

The Department of Agriculture currently has jurisdiction over the regulation of activities conducted at animal auctions. This regulatory authority extends only to auctions where dogs and cats are sold (exclusive of domestic livestock sales, where disease prevention is an issue). Unless these auctions include domestic small animal sales or the operators are licensed concurrently as animal dealers, this type of activity involving wildlife is not regulated on a federal level. Local officials should be contacted to determine the breadth of local regulation in this area.

State Regulation of Wildlife

State governments are structured much like the federal government. For example, every state has a department that deals with issues of natural resource management, analogous to the Department of the Interior. In some states this agency is called the *Department of Fish and Game*; in others, *the Department of Natural Resources*.

The breadth of activity in each state varies considerably, but all states regulate activity involving wildlife to some degree. Regulation may consist of monitoring hunting activity, protecting agricultural interests, or implementing both state and federal wildlife conservation programs.

Federal law requires that states develop and enforce their wildlife conservation laws in a manner consistent with the federal mandate. States may employ wildlife conservation practices, however, that are more restrictive than those of the federal government.

Implementation of federal law often involves state cooperation. In many cases, federal wildlife conservation programs provide funding to help states implement federal legislation. Further information regarding federally funded state conservation programs can be obtained by contacting the appropriate state conservation agency (see Appendix K).

The approach to wildlife conservation and the legal basis for implementation vary greatly from state to state. Most states employ some type of protection for indigenous wildlife; however, the volume and type of indigenous species differ among states.

Additionally, there is concern about the degree to which nonindigenous wildlife might become pests if established as wild populations within a state. To illustrate, several southern states are concerned that certain species of parrots might be introduced, become established as wild populations, and cause harm to the public. Problems with these species are of less concern to states like Montana, however, where the climate is unsuitable for the establishment of such a population.

The degree to which a state depends economically on agriculture also determines the focus of wildlife regulation. In California, where agriculture is a primary industry and the geography and climate would support feral populations of crop-destructive ferrets, personal ownership of pet ferrets is prohibited.

New York Regulation of Wild Bird Importation

New York's recent legislation to control the importation of wild birds is a good example of how one state has attempted to promote wildlife conservation. In 1985, New York's legislature passed a bill to prohibit the sale of all wild-caught birds within the state.[138] The prohibition on sale included all birds not domestically bred.[138] Additionally, coverage was extended to all imported birds, not only those endangered or threatened species that were protected under federal law.

The purpose of the New York law is to decrease the demand for wild-caught birds.[139] Importers can continue to import wild birds into New York; however, they may not sell these imported birds within the state.[140] Individuals can continue to import exotic birds as private pets. Exceptions exist for scientific, zoological, educational, and governmental purposes.[141]

This law has two major components: (1) For the first time, it regulates aviculturists within the state by requiring that they be licensed[142] and (2) it provides that all captive birds held within the state must be identified by the use of leg bands.[143] Species of birds that are primarily captive bred (such as cockatiels and budgerigars) are exempt from such identification and registration.[141] A list of exempt species is available from New York's Department of Environmental Conservation.

Recognizing the potential impact of this law, the state legislature attempted to accommodate all interests. It created a two-year transition period to allow pet stores adequate time to liquidate supplies of wild-caught birds. Additionally, breeders may continue to import wild-caught breeding stock until 1991 to encourage a greater gene pool.[144]

This law has endured considerable criticism focused primarily on allegations that its implementation would produce increased incidence of smuggling. Despite such criticism, however, the banding requirements do allow for positive identification of captive-bred or exempt species of birds. No other method exists at this time to distinguish these captive-bred birds from those caught in the wild and smuggled into New York. Thus, the law is based on sound principles. Many other states have attempted to pass similar legislation based on the New York law; it seems that this is the current trend in the future of state wildlife conservation and regulation.

Other Areas of Concern to Wildlife Veterinarians

Extra-Label Use of Pharmaceutical Products with Wildlife

Veterinarians who treat wildlife with pharmaceutical or biological products that have not been specifically approved for use in wild animals often express concern about the legality of their actions. For example, what are the consequences of vaccinating nondomestic animals with vaccines intended for use in dogs or cats or treating pet ferrets, raccoons, or raptors with drugs approved only for use in food animals.

Chapters 9 and 10 discuss the extra-label use of drugs and biologicals pertaining to domestic animals. However, legal precedents or regulations dealing with the use of drugs, biologicals, and pesticides for wildlife are virtually nonexistent. One must presume, therefore, that veterinarians will be held to standards similar to those applied in the treatment of domestic animals. In other words, veterinarians will be held to the professionally accepted standard of care for practitioners providing similar care to non-domestic animals.

A court will likely use literature references such as Fowler's *Zoo and Wild Animal Medicine*[145] or *Veterinary Clinics of North America* as well as opinions from members of professional associations like the American Association of Zoo Veterinarians to establish the appropriate standard of care. For example, a veterinarian who uses a product that is considered by the zoo community to be inappropriate might be found liable for malpractice. Practitioners who treat wildlife, therefore, are advised to learn the commonly accepted practices within the field of wildlife medicine before engaging in extensive medical care.

Another interesting issue arises when veterinarians who treat wildlife use food animal drugs with established withdrawal periods. Theoretically, if veterinarians use these products to treat fish, game birds, deer, or other game animals and these animals are released into the wild before the drug withholding period has lapsed, they could be held liable for injuries suffered by humans who eat the meat containing these drug residues. Although federal law does not specifically address this issue, federal agencies generally do not consider wild game animals to be food animals. Nevertheless, the Food and Drug Administration has recommended that veterinarians delay the release of these animals into the wild until after the withdrawal period has been completed.

Liability of Wildlife Veterinarians

Zoo veterinarians may find themselves in unique circumstances in terms of personal liability regarding the animals they treat. Zoo animals usually are owned by zoological societies, and veterinarians may contract with these entities to provide their veterinary care or they may serve in the capacity of employees. If a rare or endangered species animal dies while under a practitioner's care, the potential for liability can be considerable. In most respects this is no different than situations wherein practitioners work for equine breeding farms, specific dairies, or even for clients who own their animals.

Veterinarians who are working under full- or part-time employment contracts should ensure that the issue of professional liability insurance is clearly addressed by their employment contract. Those who become independent contractors providing veterinary care for these wildlife-management centers or zoos should notify their insurance carriers of such professional activity to ascertain that they have adequate insurance coverage.

A somewhat more complicated liability question arises when the animal is not owned by the zoological society but is on loan from another zoo. Veterinarians in this situation should ensure that the zoo managers have dealt with these veterinary care and liability issues in their loan agreements. Otherwise, negligent veterinary care might provoke personal liability.

Veterinarians who are employed full-time by a zoo or governmental agency and who provide veterinary care for animals belonging to someone other than their employers should purchase their own professional liability coverage separate from anything provided by their employers.

References

1. Favre DS: Wildlife rights: The ever-widening circle. *Environ Law* 9:241, 1979.
2. Convention for the Protection of Migratory Birds, Aug 16, 1916, United States-United Kingdom (on behalf of Canada), 39 Stat 1702, TIAS No 628.
3. Convention for the Protection of Migratory Birds and Game Mammals, Feb 7, 1936, United States-Mexico, 50 Stat 1311, TIAS No 913.
4. Convention for the Protection of Migratory Birds and Birds in Danger of Extinction, and their Environment, March 4, 1972, United States-Japan, 25 UST 3329, TIAS No 7990.
5. Convention Concerning the Conservation of Migratory Birds and their Environment, Nov 19, 1976, United States-Union of Soviet Socialist Republics, 29 UST 4647, TIAS No 9073.
6. Treaty for the Preservation and Protection of Fur Seals, July 7, 1911, 37 Stat 1542, TIAS No 564.
7. Interim Convention on Conservation of North Pacific Fur Seals, Feb 9, 1957, 8 UST 2283, TIAS No 3948, 314 UNTS 105.
8. International Convention for the Regulation of Whaling, Dec 2, 1946, 62 Stat 1716, TIAS 1849.
9. Bean MJ: *The Evolution of National Wildlife Law*. New York, Praeger Scientific, 1983, note 42, p 264.
10. The Marine Mammal Protection Act of 1972, 16 USC § 1361-1407 (1976 and Supp V 1981).
11. Fisherman's Protective Act of 1967, 22 USC § 1978 (Supp V 1981).
12. Fishery Conservation and Management Act, 16 USC § 1821(e)(2) (Supp V 1981).
13. The Convention on the International Trade in Endangered Species of Wild Fauna and Flora (CITES), March 3, 1973, 27 UST 1087, TIAS No 8249.
14. CITES, article VII.
15. For further information on what constitutes "comparable documentation," see CITES, article X.
16. Comment, The convention on international trade in endangered species: No carrot, but where's the stick? *Environ Law R* 17:10, 222, 1987.
17. Lacey Act of 1900 CH553, 31 Stat 187, 16 USC § 701, 3371-78, 18 USC § 42 (1976 and Supp V 1981).

18.   The Endangered Species Act of 1973, 16 USC § 1531-43 (1976 and Supp V 1981).

19.   ESA § 2(b): "The purposes of this chapter are to provide a means whereby the ecosystems upon which endangered and threatened species depend may be conserved..." CITES preamble: "International cooperation is essential for the protection of certain species of wild fauna and flora against over-exploitation through inter national trade.

20.   Favre p 271 (supra note 1).

21.   16 USC § 1532(6) (Supp V 1981).

22.   16 USC § 1532(20) (Supp V 1981).

23.   50 CFR § 17.40(b) (1986).

24.   Bean MJ: *The Evolution of National Wildlife Law.* New York, Praeger Scientific, pp 355-373, 1983.

25.   16 USC § 1532(19) (Supp V 1981).

26.   See the Pelly Amendment to the Fisherman's Protective Act of 1967, 22 USC § 1978 (Supp 1981).

27.   The Marine Mammal Protection Act of 1972, 16 USC § 1361-1407 (1976 and Supp V 1981).

28.   16 USC § 1361(2),(4).

29.   16 USC § 1362(13),(8).

30.   Examples of other federal legislation which has impacted wildlife law even though such was not its primary purpose are the Tariff Acts of 1930 and 1962 which prohibit the importation of wildlife if the exporting country restricts the take, possession, or killing of such wildlife. See Appendix I for citation to further federal legislation in this regard.

31.   The Bald Eagle Protection Act of 1940, 16 USC § 668-668(d) (1976 and Supp V 1981).

32.   The Wild Free-Roaming Horses and Burros Act, 16 USC § 1331-1340 (1976 and Supp V 1971).

33.   50 CFR § 13 (1986).

34.   50 CFR § 13.11(b)(2) (1986).

35.   50 CFR § 13.11(d)(4) (1986).

36.   50 CFR § 13.21(b) (1986).

37.   See 50 CFR § 13.32 for details of the appeals procedure.

38.   50 CFR § 13.46 (1986).

39.   50 CFR § 13.47 (1986).

40.   See CFR § 13.51 (1986) for a description of the penalties.

41.   50 CFR § 14 (1986).

42.   These "other" regulations include those implementing CITES domestically; see 50 CFR § 23 (1986).

43.   50 CFR § 14.11, 14.12 (1986); transporting marine mammals under the jurisdiction of the NMFS requires shipment though designated ports including all but Dallas/Ft. Worth; 50 CFR § 216.40 (1986).

44.   50 CFR § 14.14(b) (1986).

45.   50 CFR § 14.16 (1986).

46.   50 CFR § 14.17 (1986), 9 CFR § 92.3(f) (1987).

47.   50 CFR § 14.18 (1986).

48.   50 CFR § 14.31 (1986).

49.   See 50 CFR § 14.32 and 14.33 (1986) for other exceptions.

50.   50 CFR § 14.51 (1986).

51.   50 CFR § 14.55 (1986).

52.   50 CFR § 14(j) (1988).

53.   50 CFR § 17 (1986).

54.   50 CFR § 17.21 (1986).

55.   50 CFR § 17.23 (1986).

56.   See 50 CFR § 17.22 (1986) for additional information about permit requirements.

57.   50 CFR § 17.22(a)(3) (1986).

58.   Application of this provision is extended to threatened species also. 44 FR 54006 (1979).

59.   Under this rule, persons are authorized to "take, import/export, deliver, receive, carry, transport or ship in interstate or foreign commerce in the course of a commercial activity, or sell or offer for sale in interstate or foreign commerce..." 44 FR 54006 (1979).

60.   This can include exhibition for public education also. 50 CFR § 17.21(g) (1986).

61. If one of the participants is not registered, the transaction is regulated through the normal permitting process.
62. 50 CFR § 17.31 (1986).
63. 50 CFR § 17.40(b)(c), 1744 (1986); 52 FR 21059 (1987).
64. 50 CFR § 17.32 (1986).
65. 50 CFR § 17.50 (1986).
66. Specifics regarding regulation of these species can be found at 50 CFR § 17.84 (1986).
67. 50 CFR § 220 (1986).
68. 50 CFR § 13, 21 (1986).
69. 50 CFR § 21.11 (1986).
70. 50 CFR § 21.23, 21.24 (1986).
71. 50 CFR § 21.2(d) (1986); however, if the bird is a species listed on a CITES appendix, an import or export permit is required. Refer to the CITES permit section in the text for further information.
72. 50 CFR § 21.2(b) (1986).
73. See 50 CFR § 21.13, 21.14 (1986) for details.
74. 50 CFR § 21.22 (1986).
75. 50 CFR § 21.25 (1986).
76. 50 CFR § 21.27 (1986).
77. 50 CFR § 21.28 (1986).
78. 50 CFR § 21.29 (1986).
79. 50 CFR § 21.30 (1986).
80. 50 CFR § 22 (1986).
81. 50 CFR § 22.11 (1986).
82. 50 CFR § 22.12 (1986).
83. See 50 CFR § 22.22 (1986) for details pertaining to Indian religious and predation control permits.
84. 50 CFR § 22.21 (1986).
85. 50 CFR § 22.24 (1986).
86. Issued by the Service, 50 CFR § 21.28 (1986).
87. 50 CFR § 22.24(a),(f) (1986).
88. 50 CFR § 22.25 (1986).
89. 50 CFR § 23 (1986).
90. 50 CFR § 23.11 (1986).
91. 50 CFR § 23.15, 23.15(a) (1986).
92. 50 CFR § 23.12 (1986).
93. CITES, Article III, § 2 (1976).
94. CITES, Article III, § 13 (1976).
95. 50 CFR § 23.52-23.56 (1986).
96. 50 CFR § 23.13 (1986).
97. CITES Resolution, Conf 2.12, Costa Rica, 1979.
98. 50 CFR § 18.11, 18.12, 18.13 (1986).
99. 50 CFR § 18.31, 216.24 (1986).
100. 9 CFR § 1 (1987).
101. The Laboratory Animal Welfare Act of 1966, 7 USC § 2131-2155 (1976).
102. 9 CFR § 2 (1987).
103. See 9 CFR § 2.6 (1987) for the fee schedule.
104. 9 CFR § 2.25 (1987).
105. 9 CFR § 2.79 (1987).
106. 9 CFR § 2.75(b) (1987).
107. 9 CFR § 2.77 (1987).
108. *USDA Individual Health Certificate and Identification Form* (VS Form 18-1) and *USDA Multianimal Health Certificate and Identification Form* (VS Form 18-2).
109. 9 CFR § 2.126 (1987).

110. 9 CFR § 3 (1987).
111. 9 CFR § 3.110 (1987).
112. 9 CFR § 92 (1987).
113. 9 CFR § 92.4, 92.4(c) (1987).
114. 9 CFR § 92.5, 92.5(c) (1987).
115. Foot and mouth disease, rinderpest, contagious pleuropneumonia, and surra are listed in the provision.
116. 9 CFR § 92.2(d) (1987).
117. 9 CFR § 92.3(a) (1987).
118. 9 CFR § 92.3, 92.3(f), 92.8(b) (1987).
119. 9 CFR § 92.8 (1987).
120. 9 CFR § 92.2(b) (1987).
121. 9 CFR § 92.2(c)(1), 92.2(c)(2), 92.2(c)(3) (1987).
122. 9 CFR § 92.25 (1987).
123. 9 CFR § 94.6 (1987).
124. 9 CFR § 98 (1987).
125. 9 CFR § 71.3(a) (1987).
126. As a point of information, it is clear that treatment with tetracycline for the 30-day quarantine period only is insufficient to clear a bird of psittacosis.
127. 9 CFR § 82 (1987).
128. 9 CFR § 82.2 (1987).
129. 9 CFR § 82.3 (1987).
130. 9 CFR § 82.4 (1987).
131. 9 CFR § 82.5 (1987).
132. The Public Health Service Act, 42 USCA 201 (1982).
133. 42 CFR § 71 (1986).
134. See 42 CFR 71.53(1986) for information regarding nonhuman primates.
135. 42 CFR § 71.52 (1986).
136. The Food and Drug Administration (also a part of the Department of Health and Human Services) has authority in this area also and has promulgated regulations that provide for the destruction of turtles found to be in the possession of persons in violation of the regulations and an appeals procedure. See 21-CFR § 1240.62 (1987) for further explanation.
137. 21 CFR § 1240.65 (1987).
138. 6 NYCRR § 174.1(h), 174.1(f) (1985).
139. Memorandum by Governor Cuomo, Aug 13, 1984.
140. 6 NYCRR § 174.2 (1985).
141. 6 NYCRR § 174.3, 174.3(a) (1985).
142. 6 NYCRR § 174.4, 174.8 (1985).
143. 6 NYCRR § 174.9 (1985). Closed bands to be applied in the first two weeks of life for use in birds bred outside the state and butt-end bands (open) to be issued, with identifying numbers by New York State, to licensed breeders located within the state.
144. 6 NYCRR § 174.4(a) (1985).
145. Fowler ME: *Zoo and Wild Animal Medicine*, ed 2.

Table of Contents:
Appendices

Appendix A	Compilation of Laws Relating to the Practice of Veterinary Medicine	414
Appendix B	Model Veterinary Practice Act	438
Appendix C	Proposed Minimum Standards of Practice	447
Appendix D	Principles of Veterinary Medical Ethics	456
Appendix E	National Drug Withdrawal Guide	467
Appendix F	The Commonwealth of Massachusetts Code of Professional Conduct	469
Appendix G	Revised Contra Costa County, CA, Animal Control Ordinance	472
Appendix H	International Treaties	487
Appendix I	Federal Legislation	488
Appendix J	Addresses of Federal Agencies or Offices Issuing Wildlife Permits	489
Appendix K	Offices Involved with State Regulation of Wildlife	491
Appendix L	DEA Divisional Domestic Field Offices	495
Appendix M	Medical Abbreviations	499
Appendix N	AVMA Guidelines for Supervising Use and Distribution of Veterinary Prescription Drugs	507

Compilation of Laws Relating to the Practice of Veterinary Medicine

Excerpts from Business and Professions Code

CHAPTER 11. VETERINARY MEDICINE

Article 1. Administration

4800. Board and Appointment of Members
4801. Qualification of Members
4802. Tenure of Members; Vacancies
4803. Removal of Members
4804. Officers of Board; Bonds
4805. Oaths Perjury
4806. Compensation of Members and Secretary
4807. Quorum
4808. Rules and Regulations; Meetings; Licensing Powers
4809. Record of Meetings; Registration of Licensed Applicants; Registration
4809.5. Inspection of Premises
4809.6. Enforcement of Cleanliness; State Pre-emption
4809.7. Establishment of Regular Inspection Program

Article 2. Practice Provisions

4825. Practice Without License
4826. Practice Defined
4826.1. Emergency Treatment; Immunity
4827. Practice Exemptions
4828. 12 Month Licensing Exemption
4829. Duration of License
4830. Licensing Exemption
4830.5. Report of Dog Injured or Killed in Staged Animal Fight; Civil Liability
4831. Violations; Misdemeanors; Penalty

Article 2.5. Animal Health Technicians

4832. Animal Health Technician Examining Committee; Creation; Membership
4833. Powers of Committee
4834. Removal of Committee Members From Office
4835. Per Diem and Expenses
4836. Regulations and Authority
4836.5. Unauthorized Practices
4837. Revocation and Suspension of Registration; Grounds
4838. Continuing Education; Rules and Regulations
4839. Animal Health Technician Defined
4840. Authorized Acts for Animal Health Technicians and Unregistered Assistants
4840.7. Operation of Radiographic Equipment
4840.9. Qualified Members of Technicians and Unregistered Assistants
4841. Certification of Registration Required
4841.5. Eligibility for Examination
4842. Disqualification of Applicants
4842.1. Issuance of Registration
4842.2. Revenues; Reports; Deposits
4842.5. Fees
4843. Approval of Schools Offering Training
4843.2. Duration of Certificates
4843.5. Renewal of Expired Certificates
4844. Renewal of Certification; Certificates Expired Five Years or More

Article 3.   Issuance of Licenses

4846.   Application for Licenses; Diploma
4846.1.   Graduates of Unrecognized Veterinary Colleges; Determination of Qualification; Rules and Regulations
4846.2.   Graduates of Unrecognized Veterinary Colleges; Deficiencies in Qualification; Remedial Requirements
4847.   Numbering and Disposition of Applications
4848.   Examination; Waiver
4849.   Time and Scope of Examination
4850.   Display of License
4852.   Notification of Board Upon Change of Place of Practice
4853.   Premises; Registration; Certification; Form; Definition; Application; Name of Licensing Manager
4853.5.   Administrative Adjudication of Failure to Keep Premises and Equipment Clean; Penalties
4853.6.   Withhold; Suspension or Revocation of Registration; Grounds
4854.   Premises and Equipment to be Kept Clean and Sanitary and in Conformance with Minimum Standards
4855.   Record of Animals Receiving Veterinary Services

Article 3.5.   Diversion Evaluation Committees

4860.   Legislative Intent
4861.   Authorization of Committees; Composition; Qualification and Appointments
4862.   Per Diem and Expenses
4863.   Quorum
4864.   Chairperson; Vice-Chairperson
4865.   Administration of Article
4866.   Criteria for Inclusion of Persons in Program and Examiners
4867.   Program Information Supplied to Applicants
4868.   Duties of Committees
4869.   Closed Sessions of Committees
4870.   Agreements of Participants to Cooperate With Treatment Program
4871.   Records; Distruction and Confidentiality
4872.   Defamation Actions
4873.   Program Registration Fees

Article 4.   Revocation and Suspension

4875.   Powers; Fines; Causes; Proceedings; Conduct
4875.2.   Citation and Fine Authority
4876.   Probation of Licensee; Grounds
4881.   Entry on Register; Records as Evidence
4883.   Grounds
4885.   "Conviction" Defined; Time of Action by Board
4886.   Reinstatement; Terms and Conditions
4887.   Petitioning for Reinstatement; Procedures

Article 5.   Revenue

4900.   Expiration of Licenses; Renewal of Unexpired License; Application; Fees
4901.   Renewal of Expired Licenses; Application; Fee; Effective Date of Renewal
4901.1.   Expiration of Suspended License; Renewal
4901.2.   Expiration of Revoked License; Renewal; Reinstatement
4902.   Failure to Renew License Within Five Years; Issuance of New License; Conditions
4903.   Disposition of Fines and Forfeiture
4904.   Report and Disposition of Fees and Receipts
4905.   Schedule of Fees

Article 6.   Veterinary Corporations

4910.   Definition
4911.   Corporation Name
4912.   Officer
4913.   Income
4914.   Unprofessional Conduct
4915.   Unprofessional Conduct—Moscone-Knox Professional Conduct Act
4916.   Formulation of Rules and Regulations
4917.   Premise Incorporation

Article 1.   Administration

4800.   Board and Appointment of Members

There is in the Department of Consumer Affairs a Board of Examiners in Veterinary Medicine in which the administration of this chapter is vested. The board consists of six members, two of whom shall be public members.

4801.   Qualification of Members

Each member, except the public members, shall be a graduate of some veterinary college authorized by law to confer degrees, a bonafide resident of this state for a period of at least five years immediately preceding his appointment and shall have been actually engaged in the practice of his profession in this state during this period. The public members shall have been residents of this state for a period of at least five years last past before their appointment and shall not be licentiates of the board or of any other board under this division or of any board referred to in Sections 1000 and 3600. At no time shall there be two members on the board from the same congressional district.

No person shall serve as a member of the board for more than two consecutive terms.

4802.   Tenure of Members; Vacancies

The members of the board shall hold office for a term of four years. Each member shall serve until the appointment and qualification of his successor or until one year shall have elapsed since the expiration of the term for which he was appointed, whichever first occurs. A member may be reappointed subject to the limitation contained in Section 4801.

Vacancies occurring shall be filled by appointment for the unexpired term, within 90 days after they occur.

The Governor shall appoint four members qualified as provided in Section 4801. The Senate Rules Committee and the Speaker of the Assembly shall each appoint a public member, and their initial appointment shall be made to fill, respectively, the first and second public member vacancies which occur on or after January 1, 1983.

4803.   Removal of Members

The Governor may, in his judgment, remove any member of the board for neglect of duty or other sufficient cause, after due notice and hearing.

4804. Officers of Board; Bonds

The board shall elect a president, vice president, and such other officers as shall be necessary, from its membership. The board may require any or all officers of the board to give a bond to the State of California in such form and penalty as it deems proper. The Attorney General shall act as counsel for the board and the members thereof in their official or individual capacity for any act done under the color of official right,

4805. Oaths Perjury

The secretary of the board may administer oaths or affirmations upon such matters as pertain to the business of the board. Any person wilfully making any false oath or affirmation is guilty of perjury.

4806. Compensation of Members and Secretary

Each member of the board shall receive a per diem and expenses as provided in Section 103. The secretary of the Board of Examiners in Veterinary Medicine shall receive expenses.

The secretary shall not receive a salary for acting in such capacity.

4807. Quorum

Four members of the board constitute a quorum for transaction of business at any meeting of the board.

4808. Rules and Regulations; Meetings; Licensing Powers

The board may in accordance with the provisions of the Administrative Procedure Act, adopt, amend, or repeal such rules and regulations as are reasonably necessary to carry into effect the provisions of this chapter. The board may hold such meetings as are necessary for the transaction of business. It shall issue all licenses to practice veterinary medicine in this State.

4809. Record of Meetings; Registration of Licensed Applicants; Registration

The board shall keep an official record of its meetings, and it shall also keep an official register of all applicants for licenses.

The register shall be prima facie evidence of all matters contained therein.

4809.4. Repealed; Statutes 1979, Ch. 522.

4809.5. Inspection of Premises

The Board may at any time inspect the premises in which veterinary medicine, veterinary dentistry, or veterinary surgery is being practiced.

4809.6. Enforcement of Cleanliness; State Pre-emption

The enforcement of Sections 4809.5 and 4854 of this chapter is a function exclusively reserved to the Board of Examiners in Veterinary Medicine and the state has preempted and occupied this field of enforcing the cleanliness and sanitary requirements of this chapter.

4809.7. Establishment of Regular Inspection Progam

The board shall establish a regular inspection program which will provide for random, unannounced inspections.

4810. Repealed; Stats. 1978, Ch. 1161.

Article 2.   Practice Provisions

4825. Practice Without License

It is unlawful for any person to practice veterinary medicine or any branch thereof in this State unless at the time of so doing, such person holds a valid, unexpired, and unrevoked license as provided in this chapter.

4826. *Practice Defined*

Any person practices veterinary medicine, surgery, and dentistry, and the various branches thereof, when he does any one of the following:

(a) Represents himself as engaged in the practice of veterinary medicine, veterinary surgery, or veterinary dentistry in any of its branches.

(b) Diagnoses or prescribes a drug, medicine, appliance or application or treatment of whatever nature for the prevention, cure or relief of a wound, fracture, or bodily injury or disease of animals.

(c) Administers a drug, medicine, appliance or application or treatment of whatever nature for the prevention, cure or relief of a wound, fracture, or bodily injury or disease of animals, except where such drug, medicine, appliance or application or treatment is administered by an animal health technician or an unregistered assistant at the direction of and under the direct supervision of a licensed veterinarian subject to the provisions of Article 2.5 (commencing with Section 4832) of this chapter. However, no person, other than a licensed veterinarian, may induce anesthesia unless authorized by regulation of the board.

(d) Performs a surgical or dental operation upon an animal.

(e) Performs any manual procedure for the diagnosis of pregnancy, sterility, or infertility upon livestock.

(f) Uses any words, letters or titles in such connection or under such circumstances as to induce the belief that the person using them is engaged in the practice of veterinary medicine, veterinary surgery or veterinary dentistry. Such use shall be prima facie evidence of the intention to represent himself as engaged in the practice of veterinary medicine, veterinary surgery or veterinary dentistry.

4826.1. *Emergency Treatement; Immunity*

A veterinarian who on his own initiative, at the request of an owner, or at the request of someone other than the owner, renders emergency treatment to a sick or injured animal at the scene of an accident shall not be liable in damages to the owner of such animal in the absence of gross negligence.

4827. *Practice Exemptions*

Nothing in this chapter prohibits any person from:

(a) Practicing veterinary medicine upon his own animals.

(b) Being assisted in such practice by his employees when employed in the conduct of such person's business.

(c) Being assisted in such practice by some other person gratuitously.

(d) The lay testing of poultry by the whole blood agglutination test.

(e) Making any determination as to the status of pregnancy, sterility, or infertility upon livestock at the time an animal is being inseminated, providing no direct charge is made for such determination.

(f) Administering sodium pentobarbitol for euthanasia of sick, injured, homeless, or unwanted domestic pets or animals, without the presence of a veterinarian when such person is an employee of a public pound or humane society and has received proper training in the administration of sodium pentobarbitol for such purposes.

4828. *12 Month Licensing Exemption*

All veterinarians actually engaged and employed as such by the state, or a county, city, corporation, firm or individual are practicing veterinary medicine and shall secure a state license issued by the State Board of Veterinary Examiners; provided, however, that veterinarians employed by the California Department of Food and Agriculture as fulltime veterinary meat inspectors shall not be required to have a license so long as they do not practice any other branch of veterinary medicine. Notwithstanding the provisions of this section, a veterinarian employed to perform official veterinary services for the state, a county, city and county, or city, shall not be required to secure the state license herein required until 12 months after having entered the employment of such governmental agencies.

4829.   Duration of License

Any license granted to any person to practice veterinary medicine, or any branch thereof, in this State issued under any preceding act relating to veterinary medicine whall remain in force until the renewal fee becomes due and thereafter so long as the holder complies with the provisions of this chapter relating to the renewal of the license and not otherwise. Notwithstanding the payment of this fee his license at any time may be suspended or revoked as provided in Article 4 of this chapter.

4829.5.   Repealed; Statutes 1980; Ch. 471.

4830.   Licensing Exemption

This chapter does not apply to:

(a) Veterinary surgeons while serving in any armed branch of the military service of the United States or the United States Department of Agriculture while actually engaged and employed in their official capacity.

(b) Regularly licensed veterinarians in actual consultation from other states.

(c) Regularly licensed veterinarians actually called from other states to attend cases in this State, but who do not open an office or appoint a place to do business within this State.

(d) Veterinarians employed by the University of California while engaged in the performance of duties in connection with the College of Agriculture, the Agricultural Experiment Station, the School of Veterinary Medicine, or the agricultural extension work of the university.

(e) Students in the School of Veterinary Medicine of the University of California who participate in diagnosis and treatment as part of their educational experience, including those in off-campus educational programs under the direct supervision of a licensed veterinarian appointed by the University of California, Davis.

4830.5.   Report of Dog Injured or Killed in Staged Animal Fight; Civil Liability

Whenever any licensee under this chapter has reasonable cause to believe that a dog has been injured or killed through participation in a staged animal fight, as prescribed in Section 597b of the Penal Code, it shall be the duty of such licensee to promptly report the same to the appropriate law enforcement authorities of the county, city, or city and county in which the same occurred.

No licensee shall incur any civil liability as a result of making any report pursuant to this section.

4831.   Violations; Misdemeanors; Penalty

Any person, who violates or aids or abets in violating any of the provisions of this chapter, is guilty of a misdemeanor and upon conviction thereof shall be punished by a fine of not less than five hundred dollars ($500), nor more than two thousand dollars ($2,000), or by imprisonment in the county jail for not less than thirty days nor more than one year, or by both such fine and imprisonment.

Article 2.5.   Animal Health Technicians

4832.   Animal Health Technician Examining Committee; Creation; Membership

(a) There is hereby created within the jurisdiction of the board, an Animal Health Technician Examining Committee, hereinafter referred to as the examining committee.

(b) The examining committee shall consist of eight members. The examining committee shall consist of three veterinarians licensed to practice veterinary medicine in the State of California, one of whom shall be involved in educating animal health technicians, two public members and three members who shall be registered as animal health technicians in the State of California, who shall serve at the pleasure of the appointing power. Appointments may be made from lists, if any, submitted by appropriate professional associations and societies.

The Governor shall appoint the six licensed and registered members qualified as provided in this subdivision. The Senate Rules Committee and the Speaker of the Assembly shall each appoint a public member, and their initial appointment shall be made to fill, respectively, the first and second public member vacancies which occur on or after January 1, 1983.

The Governor shall appoint the additional animal health technician member, provided for by the statute enacted during the 1984 portion of the 1984–85 Regular Session upon the expiration of the term of the public member appointed by the Governor.

(c) All members of the examining committee shall be citizens of the United States and residents of the State of California. All doctors of veterinary medicine who are appointed members of the examining committee, shall have been licensed to practice veterinary medicine, at least five years preceding their appointments.

(d) The members of the examining committee shall serve for a term of four years, except that the original examining committee appointments may be staggered to achieve rotational terms. No person may serve as a member of the committee for more than two consecutive terms.

(e) The first animal health technician appointed to the committee shall upon appointment become a registered animal health technician, provided such person meets the eligibility requirements to take the written and practical examination as established in Section 4841.5.

4833. Powers of Committee

(a) The examining committee shall assist the board in the examination of applicants for animal health technician registration. Such examination shall be held at least once a year at the times and places designated by the board.

(b) As directed by the board, the examining committee may investigate and evaluate each applicant applying for registration as an animal health technician and may recommend to the board for final determination the admission of the applicant to the examination and eligibility for registration.

(c) The examining committee shall make recommendations to the board regarding the establishment and operation of the continuing education requirements authorized by Section 4838 of this article.

(d) The Examining Committee shall assist the board in the inspection and approval of all schools or institutions offering a curriculum for training animal health technicians.

4834. Removal of Committee Members From Office

The board has the power to remove from office at any time any member of the examining committee for continued neglect of any duty required by this article, for incompetency, or for unprofessional conduct.

4835. Per Diem and Expenses

Each member of the examining committee shall receive a per diem and expenses, as provided in Section 103.

4836. Regulations and Authority

(a) The board shall adopt regulations establishing animal health care tasks and an appropriate degree of supervision required for those tasks which may be performed only by a registered animal health technician or a licensed veterinarian.

(b) The board also may adopt regulations establishing animal health care tasks which may be performed by an unregistered assistant as well as by a registered animal health technician or a licensed veterinarian. The board shall establish an appropriate degree of supervision by a registered animal health technician or a licensed veterinarian over an unregistered assistant for any tasks established under this subdivision and the degree of supervision for any of those tasks shall be higher than, or equal to, the degree of supervision required when a registered animal health technician performs the task.

Such regulations required by this section shall take effect at such time as the board determines that a sufficient number of animal health technicians have been registered pursuant to this article to insure that no decrease occurs in the level of animal health care services provided in this state, but in any event no later than January 1, 1983.

4836.5.   Unauthorized Practices

The board shall take action pursuant to Article 4 (commencing with Section 4875) of this chapter against any veterinarian licensed or authorized to practice in this state who permits any registered animal health technician or unregistered assistant to perform any animal health care services other than those allowed by this article.

4837.   Revocation and Suspension of Registration; Grounds

The board may revoke or suspend the registration of an animal health technician in this state after notice and hearing for any cause provided in this article. The proceedings under this article shall be conducted in accordance with the provisions for administrative adjudication in Chapter 5 (commencing with Section 11500) of Part 1 of Division 3 of Title 2 of the Government Code, and the board shall have all the powers granted therein. The board may revoke or suspend a certificate of registration for any of the following reasons:

(a) The employment of fraud, misrepresentation or deception in obtaining a registration.

(b) Conviction of a crime substantially related to the qualifications, functions and duties of an animal health technician in which case the record of such conviction will be conclusive evidence.

(c) Chronic inebriety or habitual use of drugs.

(d) For having professional connection with or lending one's name to any illegal practitioner of veterinary medicine and the various branches thereof.

(e) Violating or attempts to violate, directly or indirectly, or assisting in or abetting the violation of, or conspiring to violate, any provision of this chapter, or of the regulations adopted under this chapter.

4838.   Continuing Education; Rules and Regulations

Effective with the 1976 renewal period, if the board determines that the public health and safety would be served by requiring all registrants under the provisions of this article to continue their education after receiving such registration, it may require, as a condition of renewal, that they submit assurances satisfactory to the board that they will, during the succeeding renewal period, inform themselves of the developments in the field of animal health technology since the issuance of their certificate of registration by pursuing one or more courses of study satisfactory to the board or by other means deemed equivalent by the board.

The board shall adopt regulations providing for the suspension of registration at the end of each annual renewal period until compliance with the assurances provided for in this section is accomplished.

4839.   Animal Health Technician Defined

For purposes of this article, an animal health technician means a person who has met the requirements of Section 4841.5, has passed the written and practical examination, and is registered by the Board of Examiners in Veterinary Medicine.

4840.   Authorized Acts for Animal Health Technicians and Unregistered Assistants

Animal health technicians and unregistered assistants are approved to perform those animal health care services prescribed by law under the supervision of a veterinarian licensed or authorized to practice in this state.

Animal health technicians may perform animal health care services on those animals impounded by a state, county, city, or city and county agency pursuant to the direct order, written order or telephonic order of a veterinarian licensed or authorized to practice in this state.

4840.2. Prohibited Acts for Animal Health Technicians and Unregistered Assistants

Animal health technicians and unregistered assistants shall not perform the following health care services:
(a) Surgery
(b) Diagnosis and prognosis of animal diseases.
(c) Prescribing of drugs, medicine and appliances.

4840.5. Emergency Powers

Under conditions of an emergency, a registered animal health technician may render such lifesaving and treatment as may be prescribed under rules and regulations adopted by the board pursuant to Section 4836. Such emergency aid and treatment if rendered to an animal patient not in the presence of a licensed veterinarian must only be continued under the direction of a licensed veterinarian. "Emergency" for the purpose of this section, means that the animal has been paced in a life-threatening condition where immediate treatment is necessary to sustain life.

4840.6. Liability for Damages; Emergency Services

Any animal health technician registered in this state who in good faith renders emergency animal health care at the scene of the emergency, or his employing veterinarian or agency authorized under Section 4840.9, shall not be liable for any civil damages as the result of acts or omissions by such animal health technician rendering the emergency care. This section shall not grant immunity from civil damages when the animal health technician is grossly negligent.

4840.7. Operation of Radiographic Equipment

(a) An animal health technician who has been examined by the board in the area of radiation safty and techniques may operate radiographic equipment under indirect supervision of a licensed veterinarian.

(b) An unregistered assistant may operate radiographic equipment under the direct supervision of an animal health technician or a licensed veterinarian.

4840.9. Qualified Members of Technicians and Unregistered Assistants

Registered animal health technicians and unregistered assistants may be employed by any veterinarian licensed or authorized to practice in this state or by any governmental agency which employs veterinarians. However, the employer must be fully aware of the provisions of this article as stated by regulations adopted by the board pursuant to Section 4836.

4841. Certification of Registration Required

Any person performing any of the tasks designated by the board pursuant to Section 4836 and any person representing himself as an animal health technician in this State, shall hold a valid unexpired certificate of registration as provided in this article.

4841.5. Eligibility for Examination

To be eligible to take the written and practical examination for registration as an animal health technician, the applicant shall:
(a) Be at least 18 years of age.
(b) Furnish satisfactory evidence of graduation from a two-year curriculum in animal health technology, or the equivalent thereof as determined by the board, in a college or other institution approved by the board, except that in lieu of such graduation, a person who files his application within four years of the effective date of this section, may furnish satisfactory evidence that within the seven-year period

between January 1, 1972, and January 1, 1979, he has received three years of equivalent practical experience under a licensed veterinarian who will attest by affidavit that such person has had such training.

4842.   Disqualification of Applicants

The board may deny an application to take a written and practical examination for registration as an animal health technician if the applicant has one any of the following:

(a) Committed any act which would grounds for the suspension or revocation of registration under this chapter.

(b) While unregistered, committed or aided and abetted the commission of, any act for which a certificate of registration is required by this chapter.

(c) Knowingly made any false statement in the application.

(d) Been convicted of a crime substantially related to the qualifications, functions and duties of an animal health technician.

(d) Committed any act which resulted in a revocation by another state of his license, registration, or other procedure by virtue of which one is licensed or allowed to practice animal health technology in that state.

4842.1.   Issuance of Registration

The board shall issue a certificate of registration to each applicant who passes the examination. The form of the certificate shall be determined by the board.

4842.2.   Revenues; Report; Deposits

The board shall certify to the State Controller at the beginning of each month for the month preceding, the amount and source of all revenue received by it pursuant to this chapter, and shall pay the entire amount thereof to the State Treasurer for deposit in the Animal Health Technician Examining Committee Fund, which fund is hereby created and is continuously appropriated to carry out the purposes of this chapter.

4842.5.   Fees

The amount of fees prescribed by this article is that fixed by the following schedule:

(a) The fee for filing an application for examination shall be set by the board at not more than fifty dollars ($50).

(b) The fee for registration shall be set by the board at not more than forty dollars ($40).

(c) The renewal fee shall be set by the board at not more than fifty dollars ($50).

(d) The delinquency fee shall be ten dollars ($10).

(e) Any charge made for duplication or other services shall be set at the cost of rendering such services.

(f) The fee for filing an application for approval of a school pursuant to Section 4843 shall be set by the board at an amount not to exceed the cost of the approval process.

4843.   Approval of Schools Offering Training

The Board of Examiners in Veterinary Medicine shall approve all schools or institutions offering a curriculum for training animal health technicians. Application forms for schools requesting approval shall be furnished by the board. Approval by the board shall be for a two-year period. Reapplication for approval by the board shall be made at the end of the expiration date. The board shall report to the Legislature on January 1, 1977, the schools or institutions which have applied for approval and those which have been approved.

4843.2.   Duration of Certificates

Certificates under this article shall expire at midnight on February 1 of each year, if not renewed.

4843.5. Renewal of Expired Certificates

Except as otherwise provided in this article, an expired certificate of registration may be renewed at any time within five years after its expiration on filing of application for renewal on a form prescribed by the board, and payment of the renewal fee in effect on the last regular renewal date. If the certificate of registration is renewed more than 30 days after its expiration, the registrant, as a condition precedent to renewal, shall also pay the delinquency fee prescribed by this article. Renewal under this section shall be effective on the date on which the application is filed, on the date the renewal fee is paid, or on the date on which the delinquency fee, if any, is paid, whichever occurs last.

4844. Renewal of Certification; Certificates Expired Five Years or More

A person who fails to renew his certificate of registration within five years after its expiration may not renew it, and it shall not be restored, reissued, or reinstated thereafter, but such person may apply for and obtain a new certificate of registration if:

(a) He is not subject to denial of registration under Section 480.

(b) No fact, circumstance, or condition exists which, if the certificate of registration were issued, would justify its revocation or suspension.

(c) He takes and passes the examination, if any, which would be required of him if he were then applying for a certificate of registration for the first time, or otherwise establishes to the satisfaction of the board that, with due regard for the public interest, he is qualified to be a registered animal health technician.

(d) He pays all of the fees that would be required of him if he were applying for the certificate of registration for the first time.

The board may, by regulation, provide for the waiver or refund of all or any part of the examination fee in those cases in which a certificate of registration is issued without an examination pursuant to the provisions of this section.

Article 3. Issuance of Licenses

4846. Application for Licenses; Diploma

Applications for a license shall be upon a form furnished by the board and in addition, shall be accompanied by a diploma from a veterinary college recognized by the board.

4846.1. Graduates of Unrecognized Veterinary Colleges; Determination of Qualification; Rules and Regulations

If the veterinary college from which an applicant is graduated is not recognized by the board, the board shall have the authority to determine the qualifications of such graduates and to review the quality of the educational experience attained by them in an unrecognized veterinary college. The board shall have the authority to adopt rules and regulations to implement this provision.

4846.2. Graduates of Unrecognized Veterinary Colleges; Deficiencies in Qualification; Remedial Requirements

If the board finds in evaluating the graduate described in Section 4846.1 that such applicant is deficient in qualification or in the quality of his educational experience the board may require such applicant to fulfill such other remedial or other requirements as the board, by regulation, may prescribe.

4847. Numbering and Disposition of Applications

The board shall number consecutively all applications received, note upon each the disposition made of it, and preserve the same for reference.

4848. Examination; Waiver

(a) The board shall by means of examination, ascertain the professional qualifications of all applicants for licenses to practice veterinary medicine in this state and shall issue a license to every person which it finds to be qualified.

The examination shall consist of a written examination and a practical examination which may be given at the same time or at different times as determined by the board. The written examination may be waived by the board in any case in which it determines that the applicant has taken an examination for license in another state substantially equivalent in scope and subject matter to the written examination last given in California before such determination is made, and has achieved a score on the out-of-state examination at least equal to the score required to pass such California written examination. Nothing in this chapter shall preclude the board from permitting a person who has completed a portion of his educational program, as determined by the board, in a veterinary college, recognized by the board under Section 4846, to take the examination or any part thereof prior to satisfying the requirements for application for a license established by Section 4846.

(b) No license shall be issued to anyone who has not demonstrated his competency by examination.

(c) The board may waive the examination requirements of subdivision (a), and issue a license to an applicant to practice veterinary medicine, surgery and dentistry, provided such applicant meets the following requirements and would not be declined issuance of a license by any other provision of this code:

(1) The applicant is licensed in one or more other states in which the board has determined that he has taken licensing examinations consisting of a written and a practical examination each equivalent in scope and subject matter to the written and practical examinations last given in California, and he has achieved a score on each of the out-of-state exainations at least equal to the score required to pass such California examination.

(2) The applicant has been lawfully and continuously engaged in the practice of veterinary medicine, surgery and dentistry for four years or more in one or more states immediately preceding filing his application for licensure in this state.

(3) The applicant has graduated from a veterinary college recognized by the board under Section 4846.

(4) The board determines that no disciplinary action has been taken against the applicant by any public agency concerned with the practice of veterinary medicine and that the applicant has not been the subject of adverse judgments resulting from the practice of veterinary medicine which the board determines constitutes evidence of a pattern of incompetence or negligence.

(5) The applicant passes a practicing veterinarian examination administered by a committee authorized by the board. It shall be oral or practical or clinical in nature and full consideration shall be given to the duration and character of the applicant's practice.

4849.   *Time and Scope of Examination*

The complete examination shall be given at least once each year. It shall include all such subjects as are ordinarily included in the curricula of veterinary colleges in good standing and may include such other subjects as the board may by rule authorize and direct.

4850.   *Display of License*

Every person holding a license under the provisions of this chapter shall conspicuously display it in his principal place of business.

4852.   *Notification of Board Upon Change of Place of Practice*

Every person holding a license issued under the provisions of this chapter who changes his place of practice shall notify the board of his new address within 30 days after moving to such address. The board shall not renew the license of any person who fails to comply with the provision of this section unless such person pays the penalty fee prescribed in Section 4905. An applicant for the renewal of a license shall specify in his application whether he has changed the address of his place of practice and the board may accept such statement as evidence of such fact.

4853. *Premises; Registration; Certification; Form; Definition; Application; Name of Licensing Manager*

All premises where veterinary medicine, veterinary dentistry, or veterinary surgery is being practiced shall be registered with the board. The certificate of registration shall be on a form prescribed in accordance with Section 164.

"Premises" for the purpose of this chapter shall include a building, kennel, mobile unit, or vehicle. Mobile units and vehicles shall be exempted from independent registration with the board when they are operated from a building or facility which is the licensee manager's principal place of business and the building is registered with the board, and such registration identifies and declares the use of such a mobile unit or vehicle.

Every application for registration of veterinary premises shall set forth in the application the name of the responsible licensee manager who is to act for and on behalf of the licensed premises. Substitution of the responsible licensee manager may be accomplished by application to the board providing the person substituted qualifies by presenting satisfactory evidence that he possesses a valid, unexpired, and unrevoked license as provided by this chapter and that such license is not currently under suspension, and providing further that no circumvention of the law is contemplated by such substitution.

4853.5. *Administrative and Adjudication of Failure to Keep Premises and Equipment Clean; Penalties*

When it has been adjudicated in an administrative hearing that the licensee manager has failed to keep the premises and all equipment therein in a clean and sanitary condition as provided for in subdivision (h) of Section 4883, or is in violation of any of the provisions of Section 4854, the board may withhold, suspend or revoke the registration of veterinary premises, or assess a fine of not less than fifty dollars ($50) nor more than five hundred dollars ($500) per day until such violation has been rectified, or both such suspension and fine. The total amount of any fine assessed pursuant to this section shall not exceed five thousand dollars ($5,000).

4853.6. *Withhold; Suspension or Revocation of Registration; Grounds*

The board shall withhold, suspend or revoke registration of veterinary premises:

(a) When the licensee manager set forth in the application in accordance with Section 4853 ceases to become responsible for management of the registered premises and no substitution of the responsible licensee manager has been made by application as provided for in Section 4853.

(b) When the licensee manager has, under proceedings conducted in accordance with Chapter 5 (commencing with Section 11500) of Part 1 of Division 3 of Title 2 of the Government Code, the license to practice veterinary medicine, surgery, and dentistry revoked or suspended.

4854. *Premises and Equipment to be Kept Clean and Sanitary and in Conformance with Minimum Standards*

All premises where veterinary medicine, veterinary dentistry, or veterinary surgery is being practiced, and all instruments, apparatus and apparel used in connection with those practices, shall be kept clean and sanitary at all times, and shall conform to those minimum standards established by the board.

4855. *Record of Animals Receiving Veterinary Services*

A veterinarian subject to the provisions of this chapter shall, as required by regulation of the board, keep a written record of all animals receiving veterinary services, and provide a summary of that record to the owner of animals receiving veterinary services, when requested. The minimum amount of information which shall be included in written records and summaries shall be established by the board. The minimum duration of time for which a licensed premise shall retain the written record or a complete copy of the written record shall be determined by the board.

Article 3.5.   Diversion Evaluation Committees

4860. Legislative Intent

It is the intent of the Legislature that the Board of Examiners in Veterinary Medicine seek ways and means to identify and rehabilitate veterinarians and animal health technicians with impairment due to abuse of dangerous drugs or alcohol, affecting competency so that veterinarians and animal health technicians so afflicted may be treated and returned to the practice of veterinary medicine in a manner which will not endanger the public health and safety.

4861. Authorization of Committees; Composition; Qualification and Appointments

One or more diversion evaluation committees is hereby authorized to be established by the board. Each diversion evaluation committee shall be composed of five persons appointed by the board.

Each diversion evaluation committee shall have the following composition:

(a) Three veterinarians licensed under this chapter. The board in making its appointments shall give consideration to recommendations of veterinary associations and local veterinary societies and shall consider, among others, where appropriate, the appointment of veterinarians who have recovered from impairment or who have knowledge and expertise in the management of impairment.

(b) Two public members.

Each person appointed to a diversion evaluation committee shall have experience or knowledge in the evaluation or management of persons who are impaired due to alcohol or drug abuse.

It shall require the majority vote of the board to appoint a person to a diversion evaluation committee. Each appointment shall be at the pleasure of the board for a term not to exceed four years. In its discretion the board may stagger the terms of the initial members appointed.

The board may appoint a program director and other personnel as necessary to carry out provisions of this article.

4862. Per Diem and Expenses

Each member of a diversion evaluation committee shall receive per diem and expenses as provided in Section 103.

4863. Quorum

Three members of a diversion evaluation committee shall constitute a quorum for the transaction of business at any meeting. Any action requires the majority vote of the diversion evaluation committee.

4864. Chairperson; Vice-Chairperson

Each diversion evaluation committee shall elect from its membership a chairperson and a vice chairperson.

4865. Administration of Article

The board shall administer the provisions of this article.

4866. Criteria for Inclusion of Persons in Program and Examiners

(a) The board shall establish criteria for the acceptance, denial, or termination of veterinarians and animal health technicians in a diversion program. Only those veterinarians and animal health technicians who have voluntarily requested diversion treatment and supervision by a diversion evaluation committee shall participate in a program.

(b) The board shall establish criteria for the selection of administrative physicians who shall examine veterinarians and animal health technicians requesting diversion under a program. Any reports made under this article by the administrative physician shall constitute an exception to Sections 994 and 995 of the Evidence Code.

(c) The diversion program may accept no more than 100 participants who are licensees of the board.

(d) The board shall evaluate the effectiveness and necessity of the diversion program and report its findings to the Senate Committee on Business and Professions and the Assembly Committee on Agriculture on or before March 1, 1989.

4867. Program Information Supplied to Applicants

The diversion evaluation committee shall inform each veterinarian and animal health technician who requests participation in a program of the procedures followed in the program, of the rights and responsibilities of the veterinarian and animal health technician in the program, and of the possible results of noncompliance with the program.

4868. Duties of Committees

Each diversion evaluation committee shall have the following duties and responsibilities:

(a) To evaluate those veterinarians and animal health technicians who request participation in the program according to the guidelines prescribed by the board and to consider the recommendation of the administrative physician on the admission of the veterinarian or animal health technician to the diversion program.

(b) To review and designate those treatment facilities to which veterinarians and animal health technicians in a diversion program may be referred.

(c) To receive and review information concerning veterinarians and animal health technicians participating in the program.

(d) To call meetings as necessary to consider the requests of veterinarians and animal health technicians to participate in a diversion program, and to consider reports regarding veterinarians and animal health technicians participating in a program from an administrative physician, or from others.

(e) To consider in the case of each veterinarian and animal health technician participating in a program whether he or she may with safety continue or resume the practice of veterinary medicine or the assisting in the practice of veterinary medicine.

(f) To set forth in writing for each veterinarian and animal health technician participating in a program a treatment program established for each such veterinarian and animal health technician with the requirements for supervision and surveillance.

(g) To hold a general meeting at least twice year, which shall be open and public, to evaluate the program's progress, to review data as required in reports to the board, to prepare reports to be submitted to the board, and to suggest proposals for changes in the diversion program.

4869. Closed Sessions of Committees

Notwithstanding the provisions of Chapter 1 (commencing with Section 11120) of Part 1 of Division 2 of Title 2 of the Government Code, relating to public meetings, a diversion evaluation committee may convene in closed session to consider reports pertaining to any veterinarian or animal health technician requesting or participating in a diversion program. A diversion evaluation committee shall only convene in closed session to the extent that it is necessary to protect the privacy of such a veterinarian or animal health technician.

4870. Agreements of Participants to Cooperate With Treatment Program

Each veterinarian and animal health technician who requests participation in a diversion program shall agree to cooperate with the treatment program designed by a diversion evaluation committee. Any failure to comply with the provisions of a treatment program may result in termination of the veterinarian's or animal health technician's participation in a program.

4871. Records; Destruction and Confidentiality

(a) After a diversion evaluation committee in its discretion has determined that a veterinarian or animal health technician has been rehabilitated and the diversion program is completed, the diversion evaluation committee shall purge and destroy all records pertaining to the veterinarian's or animal health technician's participation in a diversion program.

(b) All board and diversion evaluation committee records and records of proceedings pertaining to the treatment of a veterinarian or animal health technician in a program shall be kept confidential and are not subject to discovery or subpoena.

4872. Defamation Actions

The board shall provide for the representation of any persons making reports to a diversion evaluation committee or the board under this article in any action for defamation.

4873. Program Registration Fees

The board shall charge each veterinarian and animal health technician who is expected to participate in the diversion program a diversion program registration fee. The diversion program registration fee shall be set by the board in an amount not to exceed sixteen hundred dollars ($1600). In the event that the diversion program registration fee exceeds two hundred dollars ($200), the Board may provide for quarterly payments.

Article 4.   Revocation and Suspension

4875. Powers; Fines; Causes; Proceedings; Conduct

The board may revoke or suspend for a certain time the license of any person to practice veterinary medicine or any branch thereof in this state after notice and hearing for any of the causes provided in this article. In addition to its authority to suspend or revoke a license, the board shall have the authority to assess a fine not in excess of five thousand dollars ($5,000) against a licensee for any of the causes specified in Section 4883. Such fine may be assessed in lieu of or in addition to a suspension or revocation. The proceedings under this article shall be conducted in accordance with Chapter 5 of Part 1 of Division 3 of Title 2 of the Government Code, and the board shall have all the powers granted therein. Notwithstanding the provisions of Section 4903, all fines collected pursuant to this section shall be deposited to the credit of the Board of Examiners in the Veterinary Medicine Contingent Fund.

4875.2. Citation and Fine Authority

If, upon completion of an investigation, the executive officer has probable cause to believe that a veterinarian or an unlicensed person acting as a veterinarian has violated provisions of this chapter, he or she may issue a citation to the veterinarian or unlicensed person, as provided in this section. Each citation shall be in writing and shall describe with particularity the nature of the violation, including a reference to the provision of this chapter alleged to have been violated. In addition, each citation may contain an order of abatement fixing a reasonable time for abatement of the violation, and may contain an assessment of a civil penalty. The citation shall be served upon the veterinarian or unlicensed individual personally or by any type of mailing requiring a return receipt. Before any citation may be issued, the executive officer shall submit the alleged violation for review and investigation to at least one designee of the board who is a veterinarian licensed in or employed by the state. The review shall include attempts to contact the veterinarian or unlicensed person to discuss and resolve the alleged violation. Upon conclusion of the board designee's review, the designee shall prepare a finding of fact and a recommendation. If the board designee concludes that probable cause exists that the veterinarian or unlicensed person has violated any provisions of this chapter, a civil citation shall be issued to the veterinarian or unlicensed person.

4875.4.

(a) The board shall, in the manner prescribed in Section 4808, adopt regulations covering the assessment of civil penalties under this article which give due consideration to the appropriateness of the penalty with respect to the following factors:

(1) The gravity of the violation.

(2) The good faith of the person being charged.

(3) The history of previous violations.

(b) In no event shall the civil penalty for each citation issued be assessed in an amount greater than two thousand dollars ($2,000).

4875.6.

(a) If a veterinarian or an unlicensed person desires to administratively contest a civil citation or the proposed assessment of a civil penalty therefor, he or she shall, within 10 business days after service of the citation, notify the executive officer in writing of his or her request for an informal conference with the executive officer or his or her designee. The executive officer or his or her designee shall hold, within 60 days from the receipt of the request, an informal conference. At the conclusion of the informal conference, the executive officer may affirm, modify, or dismiss the citation or proposed assessment of a civil penalty, and he or she shall state with particularity in writing his or her reasons for the action, and shall immediately transmit a copy thereof to the board, the veterinarian or unlicensed person, and the person who submitted the verified complaint. If the veterinarian or unlicensed person desires to administratively contest a decision made after the informal conference, he or she shall inform the executive officer in writing within five business days after he or she receives the decision resulting from the informal conference.

If the veterinarian or unlicensed person fails to notify the executive officer in writing that he or she intends to contest the citation or the proposed assessment of a civil penalty therefor or the decision made after an informal conference within the time specified in this subdivision, the citation or the proposed assessment of a civil penalty or the decision made after an informal conference shall be deemed a final order of the board and shall not be subject to further administrative review.

(b) If an alleged violation is resolved by payment of the assessed civil penalty, or by an agreement to comply with the order of abatement, at or prior to the informal conference, the civil citation and any records relating thereto shall be confidential and shall not be subject to public disclosure.

(c) A veterinarian or an unlicensed person may, in lieu of contesting a citation pursuant to this section, transmit to the board the amount assessed in the citation as a civil penalty, within 10 business days after service of the citation. An unlicensed person may notify the board that he or she wishes to proceed directly to a judicial hearing which may be brought by the board under subdivision (e), without engaging in an informal conference or administrative hearing.

(d) If a veterinarian or an unlicensed person has notified the executive officer in a timely manner that he or she intends to contest the decision made after the informal conference, the executive officer shall arrange a hearing to be held in accordance with Section 11512 of the Government Code, except that the hearing shall be held before the board and an administrative law judge. After the hearing, the board and administrative law judge shall issue a decision, based on findings of fact, affirming, modifying, or vacating the citation, or directing other appropriate relief which shall include, but need not be limited to, a notice that the failure of a veterinarian or unlicensed person to comply with any provision of the board's decision constitutes grounds for suspension, or denial of licensure, or both. The proceedings under this section shall be conducted in accordance with Chapter 5 (commencing with Section 11500) of Part 1 of Division 3 of Title 2 of the Government Code, and the board shall have all the powers granted therein.

(e) After the exhaustion of the review procedures provided for in this section, the board may bring an action in the appropriate court in the county in which the offense occurred to recover the civil penalty and obtain an order compelling the cited person to comply with the order of abatement. In that action, the complaint shall include a certified copy of the final order of the board, together with the factual findings and recommendation of the board's designee. The findings of the board's designee shall be prima facie evidence of the facts stated therein, and in the absence of contrary evidence may serve as the basis for the issuance of the judgment and order.

(f) Any civil penalties received under this chapter shall be deposited in the Board of Examiners in Veterinary Medicine Contingent Fund.

4876. Probation of Licensee; Grounds

In addition to its authority to suspend or revoke a license, or assess a fine of a person licensed under this chapter, the board shall have the authority to place a licensee on probation. The authority of the board to discipline by placing the licensee on probation shall include, but is not limited to, the following:

(a) Requiring the licensee to complete a course of study or service, or both, as prescribed by the board, and to demonstrate renewed competence to the satisfaction of the board.

(b) Requiring the licensee to submit to a complete diagnostic examination by one or more physicians appointed by the board. If the board requires a licensee to submit to such an examination, the board shall receive and consider any other report of a complete diagnostic examination given by one or more physicians of the licensee's choice.

(c) Restricting or limiting the extent, scope, or type of practice of the licensee.

4881. Entry on Register; Record as Evidence

The secretary in all cases of suspension, revocation or restriction of licenses or assessment of fines shall enter on the register the fact of suspension, revocation, as the case may be. The record of such suspension, revocation or restriction or fine so made by the county clerks shall be prima facie evidence of the fact thereof, and of the regularity of all the proceedings of the board in the matter of the suspension or revocation or restriction or fine.

4883. Grounds

The board may deny, revoke, or suspend a license or assess a fine as provided in Section 4875 for any of the following:

(a) Conviction of a crime substantially related to the qualifications, functions, or duties of veterinary medicine, surgery, or dentistry, in which case the record of such conviction shall be conclusive evidence.

(b) For having professional connection with or lending one's name to any illegal practitioner of veterinary medicine and the various branches thereof.

(c) Violation or attempting to violate, directly or indirectly, any of the provisions of this chapter.

(d) Fraud or dishonesty in applying, treating or reporting on tuberculin or other biological tests.

(e) Employment of anyone but a veterinarian licensed in the State of California to demonstrate the use of biologics in the treatment of animals.

(f) False or misleading advertising having for its purpose or intent deception or fraud.

(g) Unprofessional conduct, which includes, but is not limited to, the following:

(1) Conviction of a charge of violating any federal statutes or rules or any statute or rule of this state, regulating narcotics, dangerous drugs or controlled substances, and the record of the conviction is conclusive evidence. A plea or verdict of guilty or a conviction following a plea of nolo contendere is deemed to be a conviction within the meaning of this section. The board may order the license suspended or revoked, or assess a fine, or decline to issue a license, when the time for appeal has elapsed, or the judgment of conviction has been affirmed on appeal or when an order granting probation is made suspending the imposition of sentence, irrespective of a subsequent order under the provisions of Section 1203.4 of the Penal Code allowing such person to withdraw his plea of guilty and

to enter a plea of not guilty, or setting aside the verdict of guilty, or dismissing the accusation, information or indictment.

(2) The use of or prescribing for or administering to himself or herself, any of the controlled substances specified in Schedule I of Section 11054, or Schedule II of Section 11055, or any narcotic drug specified in Schedule III of Section 11056, of the Health and Safety Code; or the use of any of the dangerous drugs specified in Section 4211 of this code, or of alcoholic beverages to the extent, or in such a manner as to be dangerous or injurious to a person licensed under this chapter, or to any other person or to the public, or to the extent that such use impairs the ability of such person so licensed to conduct with safety the practice authorized by the license; or the conviction of more than one misdemeanor or any felony involving the use, consumption or self-administration of any of the substances referred to in this section or any combination thereof and the record of the conviction is conclusive evidence; a plea or verdict of guilty or a conviction following a plea of nolo contendere is deemed to be a conviction within the meaning of this section; the board may order the license suspended or revoked or assess a fine, or may decline to issue a license, when the time for appeal has elapsed or the judgment of conviction has been affirmed on appeal or when an order granting probation is made suspending imposition of sentence, irrespective of a subsequent order under the provisions of Section 1203.4 of the Penal Code allowing such person to withdraw his or her plea of guilty and to enter a plea of not guilty, or setting aside the verdict of guilty, or dismissing the accusation, information or indictment.

(3) A violation of any federal statute, or rule or regulation or any of the statutes or rules or regulations of this state regarding narcotics, dangerous drugs, or controlled substances.

(h) Failure to keep one's premises and all equipment therein in a clean and sanitary condition.

(i) Fraud, deception, negligence, or incompetence in the practice of veterinary medicine.

(j) Aiding or abetting in any acts which are in violation of any of the provisions of this chapter.

(k) The employment of fraud, misrepresentation, or deception in obtaining such license.

(*l*) The revocation by a sister state or territory of a license or certificate by virtue of which one is licensed to practice veterinary medicine in that state or territory.

(m) Conviction on a charge of cruelty to animals.

(n) Disciplinary action taken by any public agency for any act substantially related to the practice of veterinary medicine.

4885.   "Conviction" Defined; Time of Action by Board

A plea or verdict of guilty or a conviction following a plea of nolo contendere made to a charge of a felony or of any offense related to the practice of veterinary medicine is deemed to be a conviction within the meaning of this article. The board may order the license suspended or revoked, or assess a fine as provided in Section 4883, or may decline to issue a license, when the time for appeal has elapsed, or the judgment of conviction has been affirmed on appeal or when an order granting probation is made suspending the imposition of sentence, irrespective of a subsequent order under the provisions of Section 1203.4 of the Penal Code allowing such person to withdraw his plea of guilty and to enter a plea of not guilty, or setting aside the verdict of guilty, or dismissing the accusation, information or indictment.

4886.   Reinstatement; Terms and Conditions

In reinstating a license which has been revoked or suspended under Section 4883, the board may impose terms and conditions to be followed by the licensee after the certificate has been reinstated. The authority of the board to impose terms and conditions includes, but is not limited, to the following:

(a) Requiring the licensee to obtain additional professional training and to pass an examination upon completion of the training.

(b) Requiring the licensee to pass an oral, written, practical or clinical examination, or any combination thereof to determine his or her present fitness to engage in the practice of veterinary medicine.

(c) Requiring the licensee to submit to a complete diagnostic examination by one or more physicians appointed by the board. If the board requires the licensee to submit to such an examination, the board shall receive and consider any other report of a complete diagnostic examination given by one or more physicians of the licensee's choice.

(d) Restricting or limiting the extent, scope, or type of practice of the licensee.

4887.   *Petitioning for Reinstatement; Procedures*

A person whose license has been revoked or who has been placed on probation may petition the board for reinstatement or modification or penalty including modification or termination of probation after a period of not less than one year has elapsed from the effective date of the decision ordering such disciplinary action. The petition shall state such facts as may be required by the board.

The petition shall be accompanied by at least two verified recommendations from veterinarians licensed by the board who have personal knowledge of the activities of the petitioner since the disciplinary penalty was imposed. The petition shall be heard by the board. The board may consider all activities of the petitioner since the disciplinary action was taken, the offense for which the petitioner was disciplined, the petitioner's activities since the certificate was in good standing, and the petitioner's rehabilitation efforts, general reputation for truth, and professional ability. The hearing may be continued from time to time as the board finds necessary.

The board reinstating the license or modifying a penalty may impose such terms and conditions as it determines necessary. To reinstate a revoked certificate or to otherwise reduce a penalty or modify probation shall require a vote of four of the members of the board.

The petition shall be considered while the petitioner is under sentence for any criminal offense, including any period during which the petitioner is on court-imposed probation or parole. The board may deny without a hearing or argument any petition filed pursuant to this section within a period of two years from the effective date of the prior decision following a hearing under this section.

Article 5.   Revenue

4900.   *Expiration of Licenses; Renewal of Unexpired License; Application; Fees*

(a) All veterinary licenses and animal health technician certificates shall expire at 12 midnight of the last day of the birth month of the licensee or certificate holder during the second year of a two-year term if not renewed.

(b) The board shall establish by regulation procedures for the administration of a birth date renewal program, including, but not limited to, the establishment of a system of staggered license and certificate expiration dates and a pro rata formula for the payment of renewal fees by veterinarians and animal health technicians affected by the implementation of the program.

(c) To renew an unexpired license or certificate, the licensee or certificate holder shall, on or before the date of expiration of the license or certificate, apply for renewal on a form provided by the board, accompanied by the prescribed renewal fee.

(d) Removal under this section shall be effective on the date on which the application is filed, on the date on which the renewal fee is paid, or on the date on which the delinquency fee, if any, is paid, whichever occurs last. If so renewed, the license or certificate shall continue in effect through the expiration date provided in this section which next occurs after the effective date of the renewal, when it shall expire, if it is not again renewed.

4901. Renewal of Expired License; Application; Fee; Effective Date of Renewal

Except as otherwise provided in this chapter, an expired license may be renewed at any time within five years after its expiration on filing of application for renewal on a form prescribed by the board, and payment of the renewal fee in effect on the last regular renewal date. If the license is renewed more than 30 days after its expiration, the licensee, as a condition precedent to renewal, shall also pay the delinquency fee prescribed by this chapter. Renewal under this section shall be effective on the date on which the application is filed, on the date on which the renewal fee is paid, or on the date on which the delinquency fee, if any, is paid, whichever last occurs. If so renewed, the license shall continue in effect through the expiration date provided in Section 4900 which next occurs after the effective date of the renewal, when it shall expire if it is not again renewed.

4901.1. Expired License

A license which is suspended is subject to expiration, and shall be renewed as provided in this chapter, but such renewal does not entitle the licensee, while the license remains suspended and until it is reinstated, to engage in the licensed activity, or in any other activity in violation of the order or judgment by which it was suspended.

4901.2. Reinstatement Fee of a Revoked License

A revoked license is subject to expiration as provided in this article, but it may not be renewed. If it is reinstated after its expiration, the licensee, as a condition precedent to reinstatement, shall pay a reinstatement fee in an amount equal to the renewal fee in effect on the last regular renewal date before the date on which it is reinstated plus the delinquency fee, if any, accrued at the time of its revocation.

4902. Failure to Renew License Within Five Years; Issuance of New License; Conditions

A person who fails to renew his license within five years after its expiration may not renew it, and it shall not be restored, reissued, or reinstated thereafter, but such person may apply for and obtain a new license if:

(a) He is not subject to denial of licensure under Section 480.

(b) He takes and passes the examination, if any, which would be required of him if he were then applying for a license for the first time, or otherwise establishes to the satisfaction of the board that, with due regard for the public interest, he is qualified to practice veterinary medicine, and

(c) He pays all of the fees that would be required of him if he were then applying for the license for the first time.

The board may, by regulation, provide for the waiver or refund of all or any part of the examination fee in those cases in which a license is issued without an examination pursuant to the provisions of this section.

4903. Disposition of Fines and Foreiture

Of all fines or forfeitures of bail in any case wherein any person is charged with a violation of any of the provisions of this act, fifty percent shall be paid upon collection by the proper officer of the court to the State Treasurer, to be deposited to the credit of the Board of Examiners in the Veterinary Medicine Contingent Fund. The other fifty percent shall be paid as provided by law, for the payment of fines or forfeitures of bail in misdemeanor cases.

4904. Report and Disposition of Fees and Receipts

All fees collected on behalf of the board and all receipts of every kind and nature shall be reported each month for the month preceding to the State Controller and at the same time the entire amount shall be paid into the State Treasury and shall be credited to the Board of Veterinary Examiners Contingent Fund. This contingent fund shall be for the use of the Board of Veterinary Examiners and out of it and not otherwise shall be paid all expenses of the board.

4905.   Schedule of Fees

The following fees shall be collected by the board and the same shall be credited to the Board of Examiners in Veterinary Medicine Contingent Fund:

(a) The fee for filing an application for examination shall be fixed by the board in such amount as it determines is reasonably necessary to provide sufficient funds to carry out the purpose of this chapter, but not to exceed one hundred eighty dollars ($180) for the practical examination, and at not more than one hundred eighty dollars ($180) for the written examination.

(b) The initial license fee is in an amount equal to the renewal fee in effect on the last regular renewal date before the date on which the license is issued, except that, if the license is issued less than one year before the date on which it will expire, then the fee is an amount equal to 50 percent of the renewal fee in effect on the last regular renewal date before the date on which the license is issued. The board may, by appropriate regulation, provide for the waiver or refund of the initial license fee where the license is issued less than 45 days before the date on which it will expire.

(c) The renewal fee shall be fixed by the board for each biennial renewal period in such amount as it determines is reasonably necessary to provide sufficient funds to carry out the purpose of this chapter, but not to exceed one hundred fifty dollars ($150).

(d) The delinquency fee shall not exceed twenty-five dollars ($25).

(e) The fee for issuance of a duplicate license is ten dollars ($10).

(f) The board may make a charge for records, transcripts, and other official documents pertaining to the affairs of the board.

(g) The fee for failure to report a change in the place of practice is fifteen dollars ($15).

(h) The initial and annual renewal fees for registration of veterinary premises shall be set by the board in an amount not to exceed fifty dollars ($50) annually.

Article 6.   Veterinary Corporations

4910.   Veterinary Corporations

A veterinary corporation is a corporation which is authorized to render professional services, as defined in Section 13401 of the Corporations Code, so long as that corporation and its shareholders, officers, directors, and employees rendering professional services who are licensed veterinarians are in compliance with the Moscone-Knox Professional Corporation Act (Part 4 (commencing with Section 13400) of Division 3 of Title 1 of the Corporations Code), this article, and all other statutes and regulations pertaining to the corporation and the conduct of its affairs. With respect to a veterinary corporation, the governmental agency referred to in the Moscone-Knox Professional Corporation Act (Part 4 (commencing with Section 13400) of Division 3 of Title 1 of the Corporations Code) is the Board of Examiners in Veterinary Medicine.

4911.   Corporation Name

Notwithstanding any other provision of law, the name of a veterinary corporation and any name or names under which it renders professional services shall include the words "veterinary corporation" or wording or abbreviations denoting corporate existence.

4912.   Officer

Except as provided in Section 13403 of the Corporations Code, each director, shareholder, and officer of a veterinary corporation shall be a licensed person as defined in Section 13401 of the Corporations Code.

4913.   Income

The income of a veterinary corporation attributable to professional services rendered while a shareholder is a disqualified person (as defined in Section 13401 of the Corporations Code) shall not in any manner accrue to the benefit of that shareholder or his or her shares in the veterinary corporation.

4914.   Unprofessional Conduct

A veterinary corporation shall not do or fail to do any act the doing of which or the failure to do which would constitute unprofessional conduct under any statute, rule, or regulation now or hereafter in effect. In the conduct of its practice, it shall observe and be bound by such statutes, rules and regulations to the same extent as a person holding a license under Section 4848.

4915.   Unprofessional Conduct—Moscone-Knox Professional Conduct Act

It shall constitute unprofessional conduct and a violation of this chapter, punishable as specified in Section 4831, for any person licensed under this chapter to violate, attempt to violate, directly or indirectly, or assist in or abet the violation of, or conspire to violate, the Moscone-Knox Professional Corporation Act (Part 4 (commencing with Section 13400), of Division 3 of Title 1 of the Corporations Code), this article, or any regulation adopted pursuant to those provisions.

4916.   Formulation of Rules and Regulations

The board may formulate and enforce rules and regulations to carry out the purposes and the objectives of this article, including rules and regulations requiring (1) that the articles of incorporation or bylaws of a veterinary corporation shall include a provision whereby the capital stock of the corporation owned by a disqualified person (as defined in Section 13401 of the Corporations Code), or a deceased person, shall be sold to the corporation or to the remaining shareholders of the corporation within such time as such rules and regulations may provide, and (2) that a veterinary corporation shall provide adequate security by insurance or otherwise for claims against it by its patients arising out of the rendering of professional services.

4917.   Premise Incorporation

Nothing in this article requires an applicant for or a holder of a certificate of registration of veterinary premises described in Section 4853 to be a veterinary corporation.

Model Veterinary Practice Act

Preamble

This statute is enacted as an exercise of the police powers of the state to promote the public health, safety, and welfare by safeguarding the people of this state against incompetent, dishonest or unprincipled practitioners of veterinary medicine. It is hereby declared that the right to practice veterinary medicine is a privilege conferred by legislative grant to persons possessed of the personal and professional qualifications specified in this act.

Section 1—Title

This act shall be known as the (name of state) Veterinary Practice Act. Except where otherwise indicated by context, in this act the present tense includes the past and future tenses and the future tense includes the present, each gender includes the other two genders; and the singular includes the plural, and the plural the singular.

Section 2—Definitions

When used in this act these words and phrases shall be defined as follows:

1. "Accredited or approved college of veterinary medicine" means any veterinary college or division of a university or college that offers the degree of Doctor of Veterinary Medicine or its equivalent and that conforms to the standards required for accreditation or approval by the American Veterinary Medical Association.

2. "Animal" means any animal other than man and includes fowl, birds, fish, and reptiles, wild or domestic, living or dead.

3. "Board" means the State Board of Veterinary Medicine.

438

4. "ECFVG certificate" means a certificate issued by the American Veterinary Medical Association Educational Commission for Foreign Veterinary Graduates, indicating that the holder has demonstrated knowledge and skill equivalent to that possessed by a graduate of an accredited or approved college of veterinary medicine.

5. "Licensed veterinarian" means a person who is validly and currently licensed to practice veterinary medicine in this state.

6. "Person" means any individual, firm, partnership, association, joint venture, cooperative, corporation, or any other group or combination acting in concert; and whether or not acting as a principal, trustee, fiduciary, receiver, or as any other kind of legal or personal representative, or as the successor in interest, assignee, agent, factor, servant, employee, director, officer, or any other representative of such person.

7. "Practice of veterinary medicine" means:

    a. to diagnose, treat, correct, change, relieve, or prevent animal disease, deformity , defect, injury, or other physical or mental conditions; including the prescription or administration of any drug, medicine, biologic, apparatus, application, anesthetic, or other therapeutic or diagnostic substance or technique, and the use of any manual or mechanical procedure for artificial insemination, for testing for pregnancy, or for correcting sterility or infertility, or to render advice or recommendation with regard to any of the above.

    b. to represent, directly or indirectly, publicly or privately, an ability and willingness to do an act described in subsection (a).

    c. to use any title, words, abbreviation, or letters in a manner or under circumstances which induce the belief that the person using them is qualified to do any act described in subsection (a).

    d. to apply principles or environmental sanitation, food inspection, environmental pollution control, animal nutrition, zoonotic disease control, and disaster medicine in the promotion and protection of public health.

8. "Veterinarian" means a person who has received a professional degree from a college of veterinary medicine.

9. "Veterinarian-client-patient relationship" means that:

    a. the veterinarian has assumed the responsibility for making medical judgments regarding the health of the animal(s) and the need for medical treatment, and the client (owner or other caretaker) has agreed to follow the instruction of the veterinarian.

    b. there is sufficient knowledge of the animal(s) by the veterinarian to initiate at least a general or preliminary diagnosis of the medical condition of the animal(s). This means that the veterinarian has recently seen and is personally acquainted with the keeping and care of the animal(s) by virtue of an examination of the animal(s), and/or by medically appropriate and timely visits to the premises where the animal(s) is(are) kept.

    c. the practicing veterinarian is readily available for follow-up in case of adverse reactions or failure of the regimen of therapy.

10. "Veterinary medicine" includes veterinary surgery, obstetrics, dentistry, and all other branches or specialties of veterinary medicine.

Section 3—License Requirement and Exceptions

No person may practice veterinary medicine in the state who is not a licensed veterinarian or the holder of a valid temporary permit issued by the board. This act shall not be construed to prohibit:

1. An employee of the federal, state, or local government performing his official duties.
2. A person who is a regular student in an accredited or approved college of veterinary medicine performing duties or actions assigned by his instructors, or working under the direct supervision of a licensed veterinarian during a school vacation period.
3. A person advising with respect to or performing acts which the board by rule has prescribed as accepted livestock management practices.
4. A veterinarian regularly licensed in another state consulting with a licensed veterinarian in this state.
5. Any merchant or manufacturer selling at his regular place of business medicines, feed, appliances, or other products used in the prevention or treatment of animal diseases.
6. The owner of an animal and the owner's full-time regular employee caring for and treating the animal belonging to such owner, except where the ownership of the animal was transferred for purposes of circumventing this act.
7. A member of the faculty of an accredited college of veterinary medicine performing his regular functions or a person lecturing or giving instructions or demonstrations at an accredited college of veterinary medicine or in connection with a continuing education course or seminar.
8. Any person selling or applying any pesticide, insecticide, or herbicide.
9. Any person engaging in bona fide scientific research which reasonably requires experimentation involving animals.
10. Any person approved by the Board performing artificial insemination.
11. Any person otherwise appropriately licensed or approved by the state performing the functions described in Section 2(7)(d) of this Act.
12. Any employee of a licensed veterinarian performing duties other than diagnosis, prescription, or surgery under the direction and supervision of such veterinarian who shall be responsible for his or her performance.
13. A graduate of a foreign college of veterinary medicine who is in the process of obtaining an ECFVG certificate performing duties or actions under the direction or supervision of a licensed veterinarian.

Section 4—Board of Veterinary Medicine

1. A board of veterinary medicine shall be appointed by the governor, which shall consist of five members each appointed for a term of five years or until his successor is appointed, except that the terms of the first appointees may be for shorter periods to permit a staggering of terms whereby one term expires each year. Members of the veterinary board appointed under the chapter which this act replaces may continue as members of the Board until the expiration of the term for which they were appointed. Whenever the occasion arises for an appointment under this section, the state veterinary medical association may nominate three or more qualified persons and forward the nomination to the governor at least 30 days before the date set for the appointment. The governor may appoint one of the persons so nominated. Vacancies due to death, resignation, or removal shall be filled for the remainder of the unexpired term in the same manner as regular appointments. No person shall serve two consecutive five-year terms, but a person appointed for a term of less than five years may succeed himself.

    A person shall be qualified to serve as a member of the Board if he is a graduate of an accredited or approved college of veterinary medicine and holds an ECFVG certificate, is a resident of this state, and has been licensed to practice veterinary medicine in this state for the five years preceding the time of his appointment. No person may serve on the Board who is, or was during the two years preceding his appointment, a member of the faculty, trustees, or advisory board of a veterinary school.

Each member of the Board shall be paid $___ for each day or substantial portion thereof he is engaged in the work of the Board, in addition to such reimbursement for travel and other expenses as is normally allowed to state employees.

Any member of the Board may be removed by the governor after a hearing by the Board determines cause for removal.

2. The Board shall meet at least once each year at the time and place fixed by rule of the Board. Other necessary meetings may be called by the president of the Board by giving notice as may be required by the rule. Except as may otherwise be provided, a majority of the Board constitutes a quorum. Meetings shall be open and public except that the Board may meet in closed session to prepare, approve, administer, or grade examinations, or to deliberate the qualification of an applicant for license or the disposition of a proceeding to discipline a licensed veterinarian.

3. At its annual meeting, the Board shall organize by electing a president, a secretary-treasurer, and such other officers as may be prescribed by rule. Officers of the Board serve for terms of 1 year and until a successor is elected, without limitation on the number of terms an officer may serve. The president shall serve as chairman of Board meetings.

The duties of the secretary-treasurer shall include carrying on the correspondence of the Board, keeping permanent accounts and records of all receipts and disbursements by the Board and all Board proceedings, including the disposition of all applicants for licenses, and keeping a register of all persons currently licensed by the Board. All Board records shall be open to public inspection during regular office hours. The secretary-treasurer shall give a surety bond to the Board in such sum as the Board may require by rule, the cost of such bond to be paid by the Board.

At the end of each fiscal year, the president and secretary-treasurer shall submit to the governor a report on the transactions of the Board, including an account of monies received and disbursed.

4. All revenues received by the Board shall be accepted by the secretary-treasurer and deposited by him with the treasurer of the state to be credited to an account to be known as the Board of Veterinary Medicine Fund. All expenses of the Board shall be paid from the fund by voucher signed by secretary-treasurer of the Board, and no part of the state's general fund shall be expended for this purpose. This fund shall be a continuing account and shall not be subject to revision to the state's general fund, except to the extent that the balance in the fund at the close of any fiscal year exceeds the Board's current budget by 200%, in which case the excess shall be transferred to and becomes a part of the state's general fund.

5. The Board shall have the power to:

a. Examine and determine the qualifications and fitness of applicants for a license to practice veterinary medicine in the state.

b. Issue, renew, deny, suspend, or revoke licenses and temporary permits to practice veterinary medicine in the state or otherwise discipline licensed veterinarians consistent with the provisions of the act and the rules and regulations adopted thereunder.

c. Regulate artificial insemination by establishing standards of practice and issue permits to persons found qualified by the Board.

d. Establish and publish annually a schedule of fees for licensing and registration of veterinarians. The fee schedule shall be based on the Board's anticipated financial requirements for the year.

e. Conduct investigations for the purpose of discovering violations of this act or grounds for disciplining licensed veterinarians.

f. Hold hearings on all matters properly brought before the Board and in connection thereto to administer oaths, receive evidence, make the necessary determinations, and enter orders consistent with the findings. The Board may require by subpoena the attendance and testimony of witnesses and the production of papers, records, or other documentary evidence and commission depositions. The Board may designate one or more of its members to serve as its hearing officer.

g. Employ full- or part-time personnel—professional, clerical, or special—necessary to effectuate the provision of this act and purchase or rent necessary office space, equipment, and supplies.

h. Appoint from its own membership one or more members to act as representatives of the board at any meeting within or without the state where such representation is deemed desirable.

i. Bring proceedings in the courts for the enforcement of this act or any regulations made pursuant thereto.

j. Adopt, amend, or repeal all rules necessary for its government and all regulations necessary to carry into effect the provision of this act, including the establishment and publication of standards of professional conduct for the practice of veterinary medicine.

The powers enumerated above are granted for the purpose of enabling the Board to effectively supervise the practice of veterinary medicine and are to be construed liberally to accomplish this objective.

Section 5—Status of Persons Previously Licensed

Any person holding a valid license to practice veterinary medicine in this state on the date this act becomes effective shall be recognized as a licensed veterinarian and shall be entitled to retain this status so long as he complies with the provisions of this act, including annual renewal of the license.

Section 6—Application for License: Qualifications

Any person desiring a license to practice veterinary medicine in this state shall make written application to the Board. The application shall show that the applicant is a graduate of an accredited or approved college of veterinary medicine or the holder of an ECFVG certificate. The application shall also show that the applicant is 21 years of age or more, and a person of good moral character and such other information and proof as the Board may require by rule. The application shall be accompanied by a fee of the amount established and published by the Board.

If the Board determines that the applicant possesses the proper qualifications, it shall admit the applicant to the next examination, or if the applicant is eligible for license without examination under Section 8, the Board may forthwith grant him a license. If an applicant is found not qualified to take the examination or for a license without examination, the secretary-treasurer of the Board shall immediately notify the applicant in writing of such finding and the grounds therefor. An applicant found unqualified may require a hearing on the question of his qualification under the procedure set forth in Section 13. Any applicant who is found not qualified shall be allowed the return of his application fee.

Section 7—Examinations

The Board shall hold at least one examination during each year and may hold such additional examinations as are necessary. The secretary-treasurer shall give public notice of the time and place for each examination at least 120 days in advance of the date set for the examination. A person desiring to take an examination shall make application at least 60 days before the date of the examination.

The preparation, administration, and grading of examinations shall be governed by rules prescribed by the Board. Examinations shall be designed to test the examinee's knowledge of and proficiency in the subjects and techniques commonly taught in veterinary schools. To pass the examination, the examinee must demonstrate scientific and practical knowledge sufficient to prove himself a competent person to practice veterinary medicine in the judgment of the Board. All examinees shall be tested by written examination, supplemented by such oral interviews and practical demonstrations as the Board may deem necessary. The Board may adopt and use the examination prepared by the National Board of Veterinary Examiners.

After each examination, the secretary-treasurer shall notify each examinee of the result of his examination, and the Board shall issue licenses to the persons successfully completing the examination. The secretary-treasurer shall record the new licenses and issue a certificate of registration to the new licensees. Any person failing an examination shall be admitted to any subsequent examination on payment of the application fee.

Section 8—License Without Examination

The Board may issue a license without a written examination to a qualified applicant who furnished satisfactory proof that he is a graduate of an accredited or approved college of veterinary medicine or holds an ECFVG certificate and who:

1. Has for five years just prior to filing his application been a practicing veterinarian licensed in a state, territory, or district of the United States having license requirements, at the time the applicant was first licensed, which were substantially equivalent to the requirements of this act or

2. Has within the three years just prior to filing his application successfully completed the examination provided by the National Board of Veterinary Medical Examiners.

At its discretion, the Board may orally or practically examine any person qualifying for licensing under this section.

Section 9—Temporary Permit

The Board may issue without examination a temporary permit to practice veterinary medicine in this state:

1. To a qualified applicant for license pending examination, provided that such temporary permit shall expire the day after the notice of results of the first examination given after the permit is issued. No temporary permit may be issued to an applicant who has previously failed the examination in this state or in any other state territory, district of the United States, or a foreign country.

2. To a nonresident veterinarian validly licensed in another state, territory, or district of the United States or a foreign country who pays the fee established and published by the Board provided that such temporary permit shall be issued for a period of no more than 60 days and that no more than one permit shall be issued to a person during each calendar year.

A temporary permit may be summarily revoked by majority vote of the Board without a hearing.

Section 10—License Renewal

All licenses shall expire annually on December 31 of each year but may be renewed by registration with the Board and payment of the registration renewal fee established and published by the Board. On December 1 of each year, the secretary-treasurer shall mail a notice to each licensed veterinarian that his license will expire on December 31 and provide him with a form for reregistration. The secretary-treasurer shall issue a new certificate of registration to all persons registering under this act.

Any person who shall practice veterinary medicine after the expiration of his license and willfully or by neglect fail to renew such license shall be practicing in violation of this act. Any person may renew an expired license within five years of the date of its expiration by making written application for renewal and paying the current renewal fee plus all delinquent renewal fees. After five years have elapsed since the date of the expiration, a license may not be renewed, but the holder must make application for a new license and take the license examination.

The Board may waive the payment of the registration renewal fee of a licensed veterinarian during the period when he is on active duty with any branch of the armed services of the United States, not to exceed three years or the duration of a national emergency.

Section 11—Discipline of Licensees

Upon written complaint sworn to by any person, the Board may, after a fair hearing and by a concurrence of four members, revoke or suspend for a certain time the license of, or otherwise discipline, any licensed veterinarian for any of the following reasons:

1. The employment of fraud, misrepresentation, or deception in obtaining a license.
2. An adjudication of insanity.
3. Chronic inebriety or habitual use of drugs.
4. The use of advertising or solicitation which is false, misleading, or is otherwise deemed unprofessional under regulations adopted by the Board.
5. Conviction or cash compromise of a felony or other public offense involving moral turpitude.
6. Incompetence, gross negligence, or other malpractice in the practice of veterinary medicine.
7. Having professional association with or employing any person practicing veterinary medicine unlawfully.
8. Fraud or dishonesty in the application or reporting of any test for disease in animals.
9. Failure to keep veterinary premises and equipment in a clean and sanitary condition.
10. Failure to report, as required by law, or making false report of, any contagious or infectious disease.
11. Dishonesty or gross negligence in the inspection of foodstuffs or the issuance of health or inspection certificates.
12. Cruelty to animals.
13. Revocation of a license to practice veterinary medicine by another state, territory, or district of the United States on grounds other than nonpayment of registration fee.
14. Unprofessional conduct as defined in regulations adopted by the Board.

15. The use, prescription, or sale of any veterinary prescription drug, or the prescription of an extra-label use of any over-the-counter drug in the absence of a valid veterinarian-client-patient relationship.

Section 12—Hearing Procedure

A hearing shall be held no sooner than 20 days after written notice to a licensed veterinarian of a complaint against him under Section 11 or, in the case of a person whose application for license is denied, no sooner than ten days after receipt by the Board of a written request for a hearing. Notice of the time and place of the hearing, along with a copy of the complaint filed, shall be served on a licensee in the same manner required for original service of process in a civil suit.

The applicant or licensee shall have the right to be heard in person and by counsel, the right to have subpoenaed the attendance of witnesses in his behalf, and the right to cross-examine witnesses appearing against him. Strict rules of evidence shall not apply. The Board shall provide a stenographer to take down the testimony and shall preserve a full record of the proceeding. A transcript of the record may be purchased by any person interested in such hearing on payment to the Board of the cost of preparing such transcript.

The Board shall notify the applicant or licensee of its decision in writing ten days after the conclusion of the hearing. The secretary-treasurer in all cases of suspension or revocation shall enter the fact on the register. Any person whose license is suspended or revoked shall be deemed an unlicensed person for purposes of this act.

The fees and expenses allowed witnesses and officers shall be paid by the Board and shall be the same as prescribed by law in civil cases in the courts of this state.

Section 13—Appeal

Any party aggrieved by a decision of the Board may appeal the matter to a court of general jurisdiction within 90 days after receipt of notice of the Board's final determination. Appeals shall be taken by filing the action with the court and serving upon the secretary-treasurer of the Board written notice of the appeal stating the grounds thereof. The court shall review the decision of the Board as it would the decision of an inferior court. The decision of the reviewing court shall be final and no further appeal shall be taken.

Section 14—Reinstatement

Any person whose license is suspended or revoked may, at the discretion of the Board, be relicensed or reinstated at any time, without an examination, by majority vote of the Board on written application made to the Board showing cause justifying relicensing or reinstatement.

Section 15—Enforcement

1. Any person who shall practice veterinary medicine without a currently valid license or temporary permit shall be guilty of a misdemeanor and upon conviction shall be fined not less than $50 nor more than $500, or imprisoned for no more than 90 days, or both fined and imprisoned; provided that each act of such unlawful practice shall constitute a distinct and separate offense.

2. No person who shall practice veterinary medicine without a currently valid license or temporary permit may receive any compensation for services so rendered.

3. The Board or any citizen of this state may bring an action to enjoin any person from practicing veterinary medicine without a currently valid license or temporary permit. If the court finds that the person is violating, or is threatening to violate, this act it shall enter an injunction restraining him from such unlawful acts.

4. The successful maintenance of an action based on any one of the remedies set forth in this section shall in no way prejudice the prosecution of an action based on any other of the remedies.

Section 16—Severability

If any part of this act is held invalid by a court of competent jurisdiction, all valid parts that are severable from the invalid part remain in effect.

Section 17—Repeal

(Repealers)

Section 18—Effective Date

This act shall become effective on —1st, 19—. This act does not affect rights and duties that matured, penalties that were incurred, and proceedings that were begun before its effective date.

Proposed Minimum Standards of Practice

Proposed Minimum Standards of Practice:

CVMA Seeks Your Input

The current minimum standards of practice for the veterinary profession in California were adopted almost a decade ago. At the request of the Board of Examiners, CVMA accepted the challenge to propose minimum standards that would provide guidelines from the time of their adoption to the advent of the 21st century. An Ad Hoc Committee on Small Animal Medicine Standards of Practice was appointed almost two years ago, and CVMA's Agricultural Interrelations Committee formed a Food Animal Standards of Practice Subcommittee shortly thereafter.

The CVMA Board of Governors and House of Delegates reviewed drafts of the proposed standards in March, and agreed that they should be published in this issue of the *CV* prior to our making a formal submission to the Board of Examiners. Any recommendations made by CVMA will have to undergo a lengthy public hearing and/or legislative process. The CVMA Equine Committee's recommendations will be printed in a future issue.

We ask that you review the following drafts of proposed minimum standards of practice.

Should you have comments or questions concerning CVMA's proposals, please submit them in writing to the CVMA office, and/or contact one of the committee members listed at the end of the standards of practice.

Note: The current minimum standards of practice are included in this draft. Sections added to the draft by the committee are italicized; sections deleted from the present standards are struck through.

Article 4. Practice

2030. Minimum Standards

I. *The delivery of veterinary care shall be provided in a competent and humane manner. All aspects of veterinary medicine shall be performed in a manner compatible with current veterinary medical practice.*

II. *For a veterinarian/client/patient relationship to exist, and for a veterinarian to exercise properly the rights granted by the veterinary license, the following must be present:*
   (A) *A minimal physical examination of an animal shall be performed, which shall employ the veterinarian's senses of vision, touch, hearing and smell. Any physical deficiency of senses will not prevent the veterinarian's ability to practice. A superficial or minimal physical examination shall be defined as an examination that does not utilize diagnostic tools other than the veterinarian's senses of perception and clinical judgment. When a group of animals of one species is under a single ownership, it may be considered as a single entity. A veterinarian/client/patient relationship will be considered to have been established for the whole group if a representative number of animals have been examined.*

   (B) *A diagnostic assessment and treatment plan, to include recommendations and medications, will be discussed with the client and shall be entered into the patient's medical record.*
   (C) *Followup recommendations shall be discussed with the client.*

III. *All premises where veterinary medicine and its various branches are being practiced shall conform to the following minimum standards:*
   (A) *Premises.* All premises where veterinary medicine, ~~veterinary dentistry or veterinary surgery~~ *and its various branches* ~~is~~ *are* being practiced, and all instruments, ~~apparatus,~~ *equipment* and apparel used in connection with those practices, shall be kept clean and sanitary at all times. ~~and shall conform to the following minimum standards.~~ *A veterinary facility where animals are housed shall contain the following:*

   ~~(a) Indoor lighting for halls, wards, reception areas, examining and surgical rooms shall be adequate for their intended purpose. All surgical rooms shall be provided with emergency lighting.~~

   ~~(b) A veterinary facility where animals are housed shall contain the following:~~

   (1) A reception room and office, or a combination of the two.
   (2) An examination room separate from other areas of the facility and of sufficient size to accommodate the doctor, assistant, patient and client.
   (3) A surgery room separate and distinct from all other rooms. A single purpose room for surgery only ~~will be~~ *is* required for those premises for which a premises permit application is received by the Board for new construction. ~~only after January 1, 1981.~~
   (4) Housing. In those veterinary hospitals where animals are retained for treatment or hospitalization, the following shall be provided:
   ~~(A)~~ *(a)* Separate compartments, one for each animal, maintained in a *comfortable and* sanitary manner. ~~so as to assure comfort.~~
   ~~(B)~~ *(b)* ~~Facilities allowing~~ *A means* for the effective separation of contagious and noncontagious cases.
   ~~(C)~~ *(c) Exercise runs which provide and allow effective separation of animals and their waste products.* ~~Where animals are kept in clinics for 24 hours or more,~~ *Provisions for walking the animals meets this requirement. The exercise areas are to be* ~~cleaned daily,~~ *kept clean and sanitary.*
   ~~(c) If there are to be no personnel on the premises any time an animal is left at the veterinary facility, it is required that prior written notice of this fact be given to the animal's owner.~~
   ~~(d) Practice Management~~

(d) Indoor lighting for halls, wards, reception areas, examining and surgical rooms shall be adequate for their intended purpose, and in compliance with local building codes. All surgical rooms shall be provided with effective emergency lighting.

(e) Fire precautions shall meet the requirements of local and state fire prevention codes. A fire-and-smoke alarm system should be utilized to protect living beings.

~~(1)~~ *(f)* Veterinary facilities shall maintain a sanitary environment to avoid sources and transmission of infection. This is to include the proper routine disposal of waste materials and proper sterilization or sanitation of all equipment used in diagnosis or treatment.

~~(2) Fire precautions shall meet the requirements of local and state fire prevention codes.~~

~~(3)~~ *(g)* The temperature and ventilation of the facility shall be maintained so as to assure the comfort of all patients.

(5) A library of current veterinary journals and textbooks shall be available on the premises for ready reference.

(6) If there are to be no personnel on the premises during any time an animal is left at the veterinary facility, it is required that prior notice of this fact be given to the animal's owner.

IV. Radiological Services

~~(4)~~ *(A)* ~~The~~ Full service veterinary ~~facility~~ practices must have the capacity to render adequate diagnostic radiological services, either in the hospital or through other commercial facilities. Radiological procedures shall be in accordance with State Public Health standards.

(B) A radiograph is the property of the veterinarian or the veterinary facility which originally ordered it to be prepared, and it shall be released within 10 working days upon the request of another veterinarian who has the authorization of the owner of the animal to which it pertains. Such radiograph shall be returned to the originating veterinarian within 10 working days of receipt of a written request. Radiographs originating at an emergency hospital shall become the property of the next attending veterinary facility upon receipt. Documented proof of transfers of radiographs shall be verifiable.

(C) Radiographs should be stored and maintained for a minimum of three years. All exposed radiographic films shall have a permanent identification legibly exposed in the film emulsion, which will include the following: the hospital or clinic name and/or the veterinarian's name, client identification, patient identification, and the date the radiograph was taken.

~~(5) Laboratory and pharmaceutical facilities must be available either in the hospital or through commercial facilities.~~

V. Laboratory Services

(A) Clinical pathology and histopathology diagnostic laboratory services must be available within the veterinary facility or through outside services.

(B) Laboratory data is the property of the veterinarian or the veterinary facility which originally ordered it to be prepared, and a copy shall be released within 10 working days upon the request of another veterinarian who has the authorization of the owner of the animal to which it pertains.

VI. Pharmacological Services

(A) No legend drug or biologic shall be prescribed, dispensed or administered without the establishment of a veterinarian/client/patient relationship.

(B) The veterinarian in charge is responsible for assuring that any legend drugs and biologicals prescribed for use in the veterinary hospital are properly administered, for maintaining accurate records to include strength, dosage and quantity of all medications used or prescribed, and for instructions to clients on the administration of drugs when the veterinarian will not be providing direct supervision.

(C) (1) All drugs and biologicals shall be maintained, administered, dispensed and prescribed in compliance with state and federal laws.

(2) All repackaged legend drugs dispensed for companion animals shall be in approved safety closure containers, except that this provision shall not apply to drugs dispensed to any person who requests that the medication not be placed in such containers, or in such cases in which the medication is of such form or size that it cannot be dispensed reasonably in such containers.

(3) All drugs dispensed shall be labeled with the:
(a) Name, address and telephone number of the facility
(b) Client's name
(c) Patient's name
(d) Date dispensed
(e) Directions for use
(f) Name, strength (if more than dosage form exists), and quantity of drug, and the expiration date when available
(g) Name of prescribing veterinarian

(D) Records shall be maintained of all medications prescribed and dispensed for any animal in that animal's individual file. Such pharmacy records may be transferred, in whole or in part, from one veterinarian to another, in writing or by telephone, at the request of the client/owner, when necessary to continue treatment or disease prevention medication started by the original attending veterinarian.

VII. Vaccinations

(A) A vaccination is the administration of a vaccine to an animal in an attempt to prevent disease.

(B) A veterinarian/client/patient relationship must exist prior to administration of a vaccine in order to ensure that the patient is medically fit to receive it.

(C) A plan for initial vaccination and subsequent revaccinations shall be formulated, be communicated to the client, and become a part of the medical record of that animal.

(D) No vaccine shall be administered unless provision has been made for treatment of vaccination-related emergencies. If such treatment is not to be provided on site, clients will be advised where emergency service is provided. (Please refer to Section XII, Emergency Service.)

VIII. Euthanasia

Euthanasia shall be performed in a competent and humane manner.

IX.   *Disposal of Dead Animals*

~~(6)~~ Sanitary methods for the disposal of deceased animals shall be provided and maintained. ~~Where~~ *When* the owner of a dèceased animal has not given the veterinarian authorization to dispose of his or her animal, the veterinarian shall be required to ~~maintain~~ *retain* the carcass in a freezer for a maximum of fourteen days~~.~~*, or a lesser time if authorization for disposal is obtained from the owner or his agent.*

X.   *Anesthesia Services* (Please note: The committee added this language to this section of the Practice Act. Refer to Section 2032, located on page 17 of the Act, to find the current requirements for anesthesia.)

(A) General anesthesia is a condition caused by the administration of a drug or combination of drugs sufficient to produce a state of unconsciousness or dissociation and blocked response to a given pain or alarming stimulus. Appropriate and humane methods of anesthesia, analgesia and sedation shall be utilized to minimize pain and distress during surgical procedures.

(B) Anesthesia Guidelines

A veterinarian shall comply with the following standards when administering a general anesthetic:

(1) Every animal shall be given a physical examination within twelve (12) hours prior to the administration of an anesthetic. Reference Section II (A).

(2) The animal under general anesthesia shall be under continuous observation until at least the swallowing reflex has returned.

(C) (1) Anesthetic equipment in accordance with the level of surgery performed will be available at all times. The minimum amount of support equipment required for the delivery of assisted ventilation will be: (a) resuscitation bags of appropriate volumes, and (b) an assortment of endotracheal tubes with cuffs in working condition.

(2) Oxygen equipment will be available at all times.

(3) Some method of respiratory monitoring is mandatory, such as observing chest movements, watching the rebreathing bag, or use of a respirometer. Some method of cardiac monitoring is recommended, and may include use of a stethoscope or electrocardiographic monitor.

(D) No patient shall be released from veterinary supervision to the owner/client until it is ambulatory unless it is not ambulatory for reasons unrelated to anesthesia. This shall not preclude direct transfer of an animal under anesthesia to a suitable emergency facility for referred observation.

(E) Effective means shall be provided for exhausting waste gases from hospital areas in which inhalation anesthesia is used. Such means shall comply with existing federal, state and local regulations and may include use of filtration canisters, gravitational and/or negative-suction venting.

(F) Anesthetic equipment will be maintained in proper working condition.

XI.   *Surgical Services*

(A) Sterile surgery shall be defined as procedures in which aseptic technique is practiced in patient preparation, instrumentation and surgical attire.

(B) Surgery Room

(1) A room shall be reserved for aseptic surgery and used for no other purpose. [Refer to Section III (A) (3).] Storage in the surgery room will be limited to items and equipment normally related to surgery and surgical procedures.

(2) Nothing in this section shall preclude performance of emergency aseptic surgical procedures in another room when the room designated for such purpose is already occupied.

(3) The surgery room will be well-lighted, will have proper illumination for reviewing radiographs and will be provided with effective emergency lighting. [Refer to Section III (A) (4) (d).]

(4) The surgery room will be clean, orderly and properly maintained. [Refer to III (A) (4) (f).]

(5) The floors, table tops, and counter tops of the surgery room will be of a material suitable for regular disinfection and cleaning, and will be cleaned and disinfected regularly.

(C) Instruments and Equipment

(1) Instruments and equipment will be: (1) adequate for the type of surgical service provided, and (2) sterilized by a method acceptable for the type of surgery for which they will be used. [Refer to Section XI (D).]

(2) In any sterile procedure, a separate sterile pack will be used for each animal.

(D) Sterilization

(1) Aseptic surgery requires sterilization of all appropriate equipment. An acceptable method of sterilization sufficient to kill spores must be used on all instruments, packs and equipment intended for use in aseptic surgical procedures.

(2) External use of tape-type indicators on surgical/gown packs and the use of "steam clock" type indicators deep in surgical packs shall be required to monitor sterilization efficacy. The date that the items were sterilized must be indicated.

(E) Attire for Surgical Service

(1) The following attire and techniques shall be required for sterile surgery:

(a) Prior to disinfection of the surgeon's hands via scrubbing, an appropriate sanitary cap and sanitary mask must be put on to sufficiently cover the surgeon's head hair and mouth, nose and any facial hair, respectively. Clean clothing and footwear are required.

(b) After disinfection of the surgeon's hands, a gas or steam/pressure sterilized surgical gown with long sleeves and gas or steam/pressure sterilized gloves must be worn.

(c) Ancillary personnel in the surgery room shall wear clean clothing and footwear. Sanitary cap and mask shall be required of personnel in the immediate proximity of the sterile field.

(2) When performing clean surgery, the surgeon(s) and ancillary personnel shall wear clean clothing and footwear.

~~(e) Practice Techniques~~

(1) Equipment Requirements:
~~Sterilizing of all appropriate equipment is required.~~
~~(A) (1) Surgical packs include drapes, gloves, sponges and proper instrumentation.~~
~~(B) In any surgical procedures, including invading the body cavity, a separate sterile surgical pack will be used for each animal.~~
~~(C) A library of current journals and textbooks shall be available on the premises for ready reference.~~
~~(D) Anesthetic equipment in accordance with the level of surgery performed will be available at all times.~~
~~(E) Oxygen equipment will be available at all times.~~
~~(F) Surgeons and assistants shall wear clean attire and sterile gloves for any clean and sterile procedures.~~
~~(G) Surgical packs shall be properly prepared for sterilization by heat or gas (sufficient to kill spores) for each sterile surgical procedure.~~
~~(H) In any sterile procedures, including invading the body cavity, a separate sterile surgical pack will be used for each animal.~~

XII. ~~(f)~~ Emergency Service
(A) (1) Emergency service is the delivery of veterinary care during the hours when the majority of regional, daytime veterinary practices have no regularly scheduled office hours (are closed).
(2) Such emergency service is provided by veterinary facilities known as emergency veterinary clinics or hospitals.
(3) ~~(1)~~ Emergency service *or referral* shall be provided at all times. This requirement does not mean that ~~a hospital~~ *an emergency facility* must be open to the public at all times but that the provisions of professional services must be accomplished by appropriate means including the assignment of staff and cooperation between hospitals and the after-hours emergency ~~hospital~~ *facility* serving the area. In remote areas with only one veterinarian in the area, the hospital phone shall be answered at all times so that inquirers can be told when the veterinarian is available.
(4) The minimum staffing requirements for an emergency facility shall include a licensed veterinarian on the premises at all times during the posted hours of operation.
(B) Advertisements (Ed. Note: This section replaces Section 2030.5, Emergency Hospital Advertisements, which appears on page 11 of *CV*.)
(1) *Any veterinary practice that represents itself as an emergency veterinary facility shall be required to conform to the standards of care required of emergency facilities.*
(2) *Advertisements for emergency facilities shall clearly state:*
(a) A licensed veterinarian is on the premises during the posted emergency hours.
(b) The hours of the facility will provide emergency service.
(c) The address and telephone number of the facility.

(3) The phrase "veterinarian on call" shall mean that a veterinarian is not present at the facility but is able to respond within a reasonable time to requests for emergency veterinary services, and has been designated to so respond by a daytime veterinary facility after regular office hours. Such a facility's services are not to be considered or advertised as an emergency clinic or hospital.
(C) Medical Records
(1) When continuing care of the patient is required following emergency clinic service, the pet owner shall be provided with a legible copy of the medical record to be transferred to the next attending veterinarian. The minimum information included in the medical record shall consist of the following:
(a) Physical examination findings.
(b) Dosages and time of administration of medications.
(c) Copies of diagnostic data or procedures.
(d) All radiographs, for which the facility shall obtain a signed release when transferred.
(e) Surgical summary.
(f) Tentative diagnosis and prognosis.
(g) Followup instructions.
(D) Equipment
(1) All emergency facilities shall have the equipment necessary to perform standard emergency medical procedures.
(E) Specialized Services
(1) The emergency facility must have the capacity to render timely and adequate diagnostic radiologic services on premises.
(2) The emergency facility must have the capacity to render timely and adequate laboratory services.
(3) The emergency facility must have the ability to provide diagnostic cardiac monitoring.

XIII. ~~(g)~~ Mobile ~~Clinics~~ *Veterinary Practice*
(A) Mobile veterinary practice is that form of clinical veterinary practice that may be transported or moved from one location to another for delivery of service. Mobile veterinary practice may be general service, limited service, and/or outcall service.
(1) General mobile veterinary practice may be defined as providing a wide range of medical or surgical services in a movable trailer or mobile home type of vehicle modified to function as a veterinary practice facility.
(2) Limited service mobile veterinary practice may be defined as the public or private delivery of preventive health care, such as mass or group vaccinations, and is represented as limited to such practice.
(a) Public immunization clinics are practices for public health protection, operated by local veterinary associations, and performed on a volunteer basis at the request of local health departments or animal licensing agencies. (Reference Section 1920 of the Health and Safety Code.)
(b) Private limited service mobile veterinary practices are practices restricted to the deliv-

ery of animal health protection through vaccination and/or minor diagnostic testing.

(3) An outcall service is an ambulatory extension of a general service veterinary practice.

(a) It is located within the same region as the related general service practice, but is physically removed from the practice premises. It provides vaccinations, physical examinations, minimal treatments, and minimal diagnostic screenings.

(b) All house call veterinary practices that are not extensions of a fixed veterinary facility must have an affiliation with a general service facility in the same region.

(B) General Requirements

(1) Premise license requirements as defined by the BEVM (Reference Section 4853 of the Practice Act) shall apply to general service mobile practices and private limited service mobile practices. Outcall practices (or services) shall operate under the premise permit of the parent hospital or clinic. Public health immunization clinics shall be exempt from premise permit requirements.

(2) In all types of mobile veterinary practice, minimum standards of practice must be adhered to and a veterinarian/client/patient relationship must exist.

~~"Mobile Clinic" means a trailer and/or a mobile home established to function as a hospital and which is required by Section 4853 of the code to be registered with the board. A mobile clinic does not include ambulatory clinics. Mobile clinics shall have:~~
~~(1) hot and cold water,~~
~~(2) a 110 volt power source for diagnostic equipment,~~
~~(3) a collection tank for disposal of waste material,~~
~~(4) adequate lighting,~~
~~(5) table tops and counter tops, such as formica or stainless steel, which can be cleaned and disinfected,~~
~~(6) floor coverings which can be cleaned and disinfected,~~
~~(7) adequate heating, cooling, and ventilation,~~
~~(8) instruments which meet the requirements of subsection (e) (1) (A), and (B),~~
~~(9) separate compartments when it is necessary to transport or hold animals. Mobile clinics shall also comply with the other provisions of this section when applicable to the mobile clinic type of practice.~~
~~(h) The standards and requirements of this section shall not apply to equine or food animal veterinary medical practices.~~

XIV. Advertising

(1) Advertising is the use of any form of communication designed to inform the general public about the availability, nature, or prices of products or services, or to attract clients.

(B) A veterinarian may not initiate or knowingly participate in any form of advertising or solicitation that contains a false, deceptive or misleading statement or claim.

(C) Additional requirements for advertising for emergency facilities are included in Section XII (B).

(D) Refer to Section 651 of the Business and Professions Code for further regulations regarding advertising.

XV. Continuing Education

All licensed veterinarians are obliged to remain current in their knowledge of the science and art of veterinary medicine.

XVI. Specialist Practitioners

(A) Limited licenses shall not be issued.

(B) A specialist may represent himself as such only if he is a bonafide board-certified specialist. Claims for specialization shall be restricted to those disciplines for which there is a specialty board approved by the American Veterinary Medical Association (AVMA). A veterinarian may not use the term specialist for an area of practice for which there is no AVMA recognized certification. A diplomate of the American Board of Veterinary Practitioners can claim only a specialty for the class of animals in which he specializes, not for medical specialties unless he is board-certified in those medical specialties.

(C) The term "specialty" or "specialists" is not permitted to be used in the name of a veterinary hospital unless all veterinary staff are Board certified specialists.

XVII. Consultant Practitioners

(A) Consultant veterinary services may not be provided to more than one privately held, animal-owning client or agent unless the practitioner acting as the consultant possesses a valid California veterinary license.

(B) Consulting veterinarians in laboratory animal medicine who are full time employees of a single owner of privately held animals must pass the examination for licensure in the state of California within one year of beginning such employment. Diplomates of the American College of Laboratory Animal Medicine employed in California by a single owner of privately held animals on the date of enactment of this subsection shall be exempt from the licensing requirements of Section XVII (B).

~~2030.5. Emergency Hospital Advertisements.~~
~~A veterinarian who advertises a veterinary emergency hospital or clinic shall include in all such emergency hospital or clinic advertisements the hours during which such emergency services are provided and the availability of the veterinarian who is to provide the emergency service.~~
~~The availability of the veterinarian who is to provide emergency service shall be specified as either "veterinarian on premises" or "veterinarian on call".~~
~~The phrase "veterinarian on premises" shall mean that there is a veterinarian actually present at the hospital who is prepared to render emergency veterinary services.~~
~~The phrase "veterinarian on call" shall mean that a veterinarian is not present at the hospital, but is able to respond within a reasonable time to requests for emergency veterinary services and has~~

been designated to so respond.

2031. Recordkeeping.

(A) (a) Every veterinarian *involved in a veterinarian/client/patient relationship and* performing any act requiring a license pursuant to the provisions of Chapter 11, Division 2, of the code, upon any animal or group of animals in his *or her* custody or in the custody of an animal hospital, shall prepare a *legible*, written, *individual (or group) animal and client* record concerning the animal or animals which shall contain the ~~following information, requirements listed below.~~ *requirements listed below.* ~~in legible form, if available:~~ *The medical record will provide documentation that an adequate physical examination was performed.*

(1) Name, address and phone number of animal's owner *or agent.*

(2) Name and identity of the animal~~.~~*., including age, sex, breed, weight, and color.*

(3) ~~Age, sex and breed of the animal.~~ *The medical record shall contain:*

(a) A history or pertinent information as it pertains to the animal's medical status.

(b) Notation of the physical exam and when instrumentation is performed resulting in absolute data (i.e., temperature, pulse rate, respiration rate, laboratory data, etc.), that data shall be noted in the record.

(c) Treatment and/or an intended treatment plan including medications, their amount and frequency of use. Records for surgical procedures shall be kept in the medical record or in the surgical log and shall include the type of sedative/anesthetic agents used, the procedure and the name of the surgeon.

(d) A diagnosis or tentative diagnosis will be placed in the record. A prognosis will be placed in the record when pertinent.

(e) Progress notes and disposition of the case will be entered into the record.

~~(4)~~ *(f)* Dates (beginning and ending) of custody of the animal.

(4) In the case of vaccination clinics, a certificate including the information required by subsections (1) and (2) may serve as the medical record.

(5) ~~A short history of the animal's condition as it pertains to the animal's medical status.~~

(6) ~~Diagnosis or condition at the beginning of custody of animal.~~

(7) ~~Medication and treatment, including amount and frequency.~~

(8) ~~Progress and disposition of the case.~~

(9) ~~Surgery log.~~

(B) (b) Record *and Radiograph* Storage.

(1) ~~Records~~ *All records and radiographs* shall be maintained for a minimum of three years after the last visit. *Copies or a summary of records will be made available within ten working days upon the client's request. Transfers of radiographs will be verifiable. Reference IV (B).*

(2) *Radiographs.* ~~A radiograph is the property of the veterinarian who originally ordered it to be prepared, and it shall be released upon the written request of another veterinarian who has the authorization of the owner of the animal to whom it pertains and such radiograph shall be returned to the veterinarian who originally ordered it to be prepared within a reasonable time.~~ *Reference Section IV (B).*

(3) *Laboratory Data. Reference Section V (B).*

2032. ~~Anesthesia.~~

(a) ~~General anesthesia is a condition caused by the administration of a drug or combination of drugs sufficient to produce a state of unconsciousness or dissociation and blocked response to a given pain or alarming stimulus.~~

(b) ~~Anesthesia Guidelines.~~

~~A veterinarian shall comply with the following standards when administering general anesthesia:~~

(1) ~~Within twelve (12) hours of surgery, every animal shall be given a preanesthetic examination.~~

(2) ~~The animal under general anesthesia shall be under continuous observation until at least the swallowing reflex has returned.~~

(3) ~~Appropriate and humane methods shall be utilized to minimize pain and stress during surgical procedures (such as anesthesia).~~

Proposed Minimum Standards of Practice for Food Animal Veterinary Practitioners

I.	*The delivery of veterinary care shall be provided in a competent and humane manner according to standards commonly accepted by the veterinary profession.*

II.	*For a veterinarian/client/patient relationship to exist, and for a veterinarian to exercise properly the rights granted by the veterinary license, the following must be present:*

A.	*An examination of the animal, herd or flock is conducted or, under certain circumstances, such as with large herds or flocks, adequate prior familiarity on the part of the veterinarian with the client and the operation to enable proper evaluation of reported signs.*

B.	*A diagnosis which must be entered by the veterinarian into his permanent records. The method of arriving at a diagnosis is to be consistent with that considered "normal" or "accepted" for a given practice type or field. Because methods of practice vary among species, and what is considered to be proper practice in one type may not be proper practice in another type, grievances will be brought before a review committee of the practitioner's peers to determine if good veterinary medicine has been practiced in a particular case.*

C.	*A treatment plan, to include all recommendations and medications, is provided. The veterinarian in charge is responsible for maintaining accurate records to include strength, dosage and quantity of all medications prescribed, for proper instructions to clients on the administration of drugs when the veterinarian will not be providing direct supervision, and for informing clients of potential drug residues and probable withdrawal times, when applicable.*

D.	*The practicing veterinarian is responsible for followup in the case of adverse reactions or failure of the regimen of therapy.*

III. For a veterinarian to exercise properly the rights granted by the veterinary license, the food animal practitioner may provide the following services:

A. *Non-diagnostic professional services.*

B. *Diagnostic services. Such situations may involve an individual animal or group of animals. In such cases, the veterinarian should:*

   1. *Identify the problem or problems and assess their magnitude.*

   2. *Gather data as needed:*

     a. *History.*

     b. *Observations.*

     c. *Physical examination may be used to contribute meaningful information to the data base in order to evaluate a problem presented. The practitioner may use his visual, tactile, auditory and/or olfactory senses to evaluate abnormal functions of organ systems.*

     d. *Laboratory tests and other diagnostic aids.*

   3. *Develop an approach or plan.*

     a. *Diagnostic plan.*

     b. *Resolution (i.e., treatment, management, animal husbandry practices, appropriate client education, etc.)*

   4. *Provide services for followup reassessment, if needed.*

IV. Recordkeeping

A. *Records of veterinary services shall be maintained for a minimum of three years. The records shall be the property of the practice contacted by the client for such services. They must be filed in such a manner that they are readily retrievable. Records jointly compiled by the client and the veterinarian may be used to record data and approaches taken (e.g., individual cow records accrued during routine sterility programs). The records are the property of the client, if he maintains them, and the veterinarian is not responsible for them.*

When diagnostic veterinary services are performed, it is the practitioner's responsibility to identify the animals in whatever manner is practical, i.e., description of group, string or lot numbers, individual numbers, etc. The problem(s), data, approaches, and any resulting followups shall be recorded.

B. *When the practitioner takes possession of an animal at the veterinary clinic for the purpose of treatment, an individual record shall be kept for that animal. That record will include the following:*

   1. *Description of the problem(s).*

   2. *History, observations, information derived from the physical examination, laboratory findings and other diagnostic data, if any.*

   3. *Approach:*

     a. *Diagnosis.*

     b. *Resolution or attempted resolution of the problem(s).*

   4. *Description of the daily care and condition of the animal including any change in approach.*

   5. *Instructions to the owner.*

V. Pharmaceutical Services

A. *No legend drug shall be prescribed or dispensed without the establishment of a veterinarian/client/patient relationship.*

B. *The veterinarian is responsible for issuing instructions to clients on the administration of drugs and for maintaining accurate records to include strength, dosage and quantity of all medications prescribed.*

C. *Food animal veterinarians shall be required to utilize a drug authorization form when prescribing and dispensing pharmaceuticals that require authorization by a licensed veterinarian. There will be three copies of the drug authorization form, one copy for the veterinarian, one for the client and one for the pharmaceutical distributor. The drug authorization form shall include the following information:*

   1. *Name and address of client.*

   2. *Species of animal.*

   3. *Date issued.*

   4. *Name of drug, strength, size, quantity and expiration date.*

   5. *Signature of owner or agent.*

   6. *Instructions for use.*

   7. *Cautionary statements and suggested withdrawal time if there is extra-label use.*

   8. *Name, address and telephone number of prescribing veterinarian.*

   9. *Expiration date of drug authorization form, which should clearly state, "Void after 90 days."*

   10. *The number of repeat refills permissible.*

   11. *That a veterinarian/client/patient relationship exists.*

D. *All repackaged drugs dispensed shall be labeled with:*

   1. *Name, address and telephone number of the facility.*

   2. *Client's name.*

   3. *Patient's name or species of animal(s).*

   4. *Date dispensed.*

   5. *Directions for use.*

   6. *Name, strength (if more than one dosage form exists) and quantity of drug, and the expiration date when available.*

   7. *Name of prescribing veterinarian.*

   8. *Cautionary statements.*

   9. *Withdrawal time.*

VI. Premises

A. *Veterinary premises where food animal medicine is practiced should be required to have a reception room and office or a combination of the two. The premises should include the following:*

   1. *Facilities for cleaning and sterilizing instruments and equipment.*

   2. *Telephone and/or answering service.*

   3. *Recordkeeping system.*

   4. *Facilities for proper storage of pharmaceuticals and biologicals.*

   5. *When the food animal practitioner maintains his own hospitalization facilities, indoor holding facilities must have adequate*

temperature, ventilation and space to maintain the comfort and well-being of the animals housed.

6. If there are to be no personnel on premises during any time an animal is left at the veterinary facility, it is required that notice of this fact be given to the animal's owner.

7. A library of current journals or textbooks shall be available for ready reference.

8. Laboratory services must be available.

VII.   *Ambulatory Units*

A. Ambulatory units as utilized by food animal practitioners shall be maintained in a clean and sanitary fashion. The vehicle shall contain those items of equipment that are necessary for the veterinarian to perform physical examinations, surgical procedures and medical treatments consistent with the standards of the profession and the type of veterinary services being rendered. Standard items equipping the

unit should include but not be limited to the following:

1. If sterile surgery is to be performed, sterile surgical instruments, suturing materials, syringes and needles should be carried.

2. Protective clothing, rubber boots and a means to clean and sanitize them between each visit to each premises.

3. Current and properly stored pharmaceuticals and biologicals.

4. A means of cold sterilization.

5. OB sleeves for rectal palpation which shall be cleaned and sanitized between each premises. If disposable sleeves are used, a new sleeve shall be used at each premises.

6. Antiseptic intravenous equipm. nt shall be used for each intravenous injection.

7. When working with known infectious disease within a herd, precautions shall be used to prevent transmission of infectious agents.

Ad Hoc Committee on Small Animal Standards of Practice:
Richard Le Vine, DVM, Chairman (209) 523-3245
Ben Alegado, DVM, Board Liaison (818) 288-0600
John Andersen, DVM (415) 837-7246
Hermann Bonasch, DVM (415) 278-8440
James Burns, DVM (916) 343-1234
Charles Edgerly, DVM (209) 638-2373
Alonzo Edmiston, DVM (619) 475-9770
Robert Garcia, DVM (209) 951-8911
Harold Kopit, DVM (714) 828-5891
Roger Kuhn, DVM (415) 921-0410
Michael Murray, DVM (408) 373-5620

John Switzer, DVM (707) 938-8198
Kelly Akol, 1986 UCD Student Representative (213) 372-8881
Cassie Jones, 1987 UCD Student Representative (916) 756-2989

Agricultural Interrelations Committee
Standards of Practice Subcommittee:
Wilbur Delph, DVM, Chairman (209) 931-4117
Robert Bushnell, DVM (916) 752-0853
J. Kendall Harding, DVM (209) 383-4722
Edward Kearley, DVM, MS (209) 634-1980
Hugh Kieley, DVM (209) 869-3693
Jack Morse, DVM (209) 634-5801

California Veterinarian July/August 1987

Principles of Veterinary Medical Ethics

Of The American Veterinary Medical Association (AVMA)

*(**Bold print states the Principles,** standard print explains or clarifies the Principle to which it applies)*

I. *Introduction*

A. Veterinarians are members of a scholarly profession who have earned academic degrees from comprehensive universities or similar educational institutions. Veterinarians practice the profession of veterinary medicine in a variety of situations and circumstances.

B. Exemplary professional conduct upholds the dignity of the veterinary profession. All veterinarians are expected to adhere to a progressive code of ethical conduct known as the Principles of Veterinary Medical Ethics (the Principles). The basis of the Principles is the Golden Rule. Veterinarians should accept this rule as a guide to their general conduct, and abide by the Principles. They should conduct their professional and personal affairs in an ethical manner. Professional veterinary associations should adopt the Principles or a similar code as a guide for their activities.

C. Professional organizations should establish ethics, grievance, or peer review committees to address ethical issues. Local and state veterinary associations should also include discussions of ethical issues in their continuing education programs.

1. Complaints about behavior that may violate the Principles should be addressed in an appropriate and timely manner. Such questions should be considered initially by ethics, grievance, or peer review committees of local or state veterinary associations and, if necessary, state veterinary medical boards. Members of local and state committees are familiar with local customs and circumstances, and those committees are in the best position to confer with all parties involved.

2. All veterinarians in local or state associations and jurisdictions have a responsibility to regulate and guide the professional conduct of their members.

3. Colleges of veterinary medicine should stress the teaching of ethical and value issues as part of the professional veterinary curriculum for all veterinary students.

4. The National Board Examination Committee is encouraged to prepare and include questions regarding professional ethics in the National Board Examination.

D. The AVMA Judicial Council is charged to interpret the AVMA Constitution and Bylaws, the Principles of Veterinary Medical Ethics, and other rules of the Association. The Judicial Council should review the Principles periodically to insure that they remain complete and up to date.

II. *Professional Behavior*

A. Veterinarians should first consider the needs of the patient: to relieve disease, suffering, or disability while minimizing pain or fear.

B. Veterinarians should obey all laws of the jurisdictions in which they reside and practice veterinary medicine. Veterinarians should be honest and fair in their relations with others, and they should not engage in fraud, misrepresentation, or deceit.

1. Veterinarians should report illegal practices and activities to the proper authorities.

2. The AVMA Judicial Council may choose to report alleged infractions by nonmembers of the AVMA to the appropriate agencies.

3. Veterinarians should use only the title of the professional degree that was awarded by the school of veterinary medicine where the degree was earned. All veterinarians may use the courtesy titles *Doctor* or *Veterinarian.* Veterinarians who were awarded a degree other than DVM or VMD should refer to the *AVMA Directory* for information on the appropriate titles and degrees.

C. **It is unethical for veterinarians to identify themselves as members of an AVMA recognized specialty organization if such certification has not been awarded.**

D. **It is unethical to place professional knowledge, credentials, or services at the disposal of any nonprofessional organization, group, or individual to promote or lend credibility to the illegal practice of veterinary medicine.**

E. **Veterinarians may choose whom they will serve. Once they have started patient care, veterinarians must not neglect their patients, and they must continue to provide professional services until they are relieved of their professional responsibilities.**

F. **In emergencies, veterinarians have an ethical responsibility to provide essential services for animals when it is necessary to save life or relieve suffering. Such emergency care may be limited to euthanasia to relieve suffering, or when the client rejects euthanasia, to stabilize the patient sufficiently to enable transportation to another veterinary hospital for definitive care.**

1. When veterinarians cannot be available to provide services, they should arrange with their colleagues to assure that emergency services are available, consistent with the needs of the locality.

2. Veterinarians who are not qualified to manage and treat certain emergencies should arrange to refer their clients to other veterinarians who can provide the appropriate emergency services.

G. **Regardless of practice ownership, the interests of the patient, client, and public require that all decisions that affect diagnosis, care, and treatment of patients are made by veterinarians.**

H. **Veterinarians should strive to enhance their image with respect to their colleagues, clients, other health professionals, and the general public**. Veterinarians should be honest, fair, courteous, considerate, and compassionate. Veterinarians should present a professional appearance and follow acceptable professional procedures using current professional and scientific knowledge.

I. Veterinarians should not slander, or injure the professional standing or reputation of other veterinarians in a false or misleading manner.

J. Veterinarians should strive to improve their veterinary knowledge and skills, and they are encouraged to collaborate with other professionals in the quest for knowledge and professional development.

K. **The responsibilities of the veterinary profession extend beyond individual patients and clients to society in general.** Veterinarians are encouraged to make their knowledge available to their communities and to provide their services for activities that protect public health.

L. **Veterinarians and their associates should protect the personal privacy of patients and clients.** Veterinarians should not reveal confidences unless required to by law or unless it becomes necessary to protect the health and welfare of other individuals or animals.

M. **Veterinarians who are impaired by alcohol or other substances should seek assistance from qualified organizations or individuals.** Colleagues of impaired veterinarians should encourage those individuals to seek assistance and to overcome their disabilities.

III. *The Veterinarian-Client-Patient Relationship*

A. **The veterinarian-client-patient relationship (VCPR) is the basis for interaction among veterinarians, their clients, and their patients.** A VCPR exists when all of the following conditions have been met:

1. The veterinarian has assumed responsibility for making clinical judgements regarding the health of the animal(s) and the need for medical treatment, and the client has agreed to follow the veterinarian's instructions.

2. The veterinarian has sufficient knowledge of the animal(s) to initiate at least a general or preliminary diagnosis of the medical condition of the animal(s). This means that the veterinarian has recently seen and is personally acquainted with the keeping and care of the animal(s) by virtue of an examination of the animal(s), or by medically appropriate and timely visits to the premises where the animal(s) are kept.

3. The veterinarian is readily available, or has arranged for emergency coverage, for follow-up evaluation in the event of adverse reactions or the failure of the treatment regimen.

B. When a VCPR exists, veterinarians must maintain medical records (See section VII).

C. Dispensing or prescribing a prescription product requires a VCPR

1. Veterinarians should honor a client's request for a prescription in lieu of dispensing.

2. Without a valid VCPR, veterinarians' merchandising or use of veterinary prescription drugs or their extra-label use of any pharmaceutical is unethical and is illegal under federal law.

D. Veterinarians may terminate a VCPR under certain conditions, and they have an ethical obligation to use courtesy and tact in doing so.

1. If there is no ongoing medical condition, veterinarians may terminate a VCPR by notifying the client that they no longer wish to serve that patient and client.

2. If there is an ongoing medical or surgical condition, the patient should be referred to another veterinarian for diagnosis, care, and treatment. The former attending veterinarian should continue to provide care, as needed, during the transition.

E. Clients may terminate the VCPR at any time.

IV. *Attending, Consulting and Referring*

A. An *attending veterinarian* is a veterinarian (or a group of veterinarians) who assumes responsibility for primary care of a patient. A VCPR is established.

1. Attending veterinarians are entitled to charge a fee for their professional services.

2. When appropriate, attending veterinarians are encouraged to seek assistance in the form of consultations and referrals. A decision to consult or refer is made jointly by the attending veterinarian and the client.

3. When a consultation occurs, the attending veterinarian continues to be primarily responsible for the case.

B. A *consulting veterinarian* is a veterinarian (or group of veterinarians) who agrees to advise an attending veterinarian on the care and management of a case. The VCPR remains the responsibility of the attending veterinarian.

1. Consulting veterinarians may or may not charge fees for service.

2. Consulting veterinarians should communicate their findings and opinions directly to the attending veterinarians.

3. Consulting veterinarians should revisit the patients or communicate with the clients in collaboration with the attending veterinarians.

4. Consultations usually involve the exchange of information or interpretation of test results. However, it may be appropriate or necessary for consultants to examine patients. When advanced or invasive techniques are required to gather information or substantiate diagnoses, attending veterinarians may refer the patients. A new VCPR is established with the veterinarian to whom a case is referred.

C. **The *referral veterinarian or receiving veterinarian* is a veterinarian (or group of veterinarians) who agrees to provide requested veterinary services. A new VCPR is established. The referring and referral veterinarians must communicate.**

1. Attending veterinarians should honor clients' requests for referral.

2. Referral veterinarians may choose to accept or decline clients and patients from attending veterinarians.

3. Patients are usually referred because of specific medical problems or services. Referral veterinarians should provide services or treatments relative to the referred conditions, and they should communicate with the referring veterinarians and clients if other services or treatments are required.

D. **When a client seeks professional services or opinions from a different veterinarian without a referral, a new VCPR is established with the new attending veterinarian. When contacted, the veterinarian who was formerly involved in the diagnosis, care, and treatment of the patient should communicate with the new attending veterinarian as if the patient and client had been referred.**

1. With the client's consent, the new attending veterinarian should contact the former veterinarian to learn the original diagnosis, care, and treatment and clarify any issues before proceeding with a new treatment plan.

2. If there is evidence that the actions of the former attending veterinarian have clearly and significantly endangered the health or safety of the patient, the new attending veterinarian has a responsibility to report the matter to the appropriate authorities of the local and state association or professional regulatory agency.

V. Influences on Judgement

A. **The choice of treatments or animal care should not be influenced by consider-ations other than the needs of the patient, the welfare of the client, and the safety of the public.**

B. **Veterinarians should not allow their medical judgement to be influenced by agreements by which they stand to profit through referring clients to other providers of services or products.**

C. **The medical judgements of veterinarians should not be influenced by con-tracts or agreements made by their associations or societies.**

VI. Therapies

A. **Attending veterinarians are responsible for choosing the treatment regimens for their patients.** It is the attending veterinarian's responsibility to inform the client of the expected results and costs, and the related risks of each treatment regimen.

B. **It is unethical for veterinarians to prescribe or dispense prescription products in the absence of a VCPR.**

C. **It is unethical for veterinarians to promote, sell, prescribe, dispense, or use secret remedies or any other product for which they do not know the ingredi-ent formula.**

D. **It is unethical for veterinarians to use or permit the use of their names, signa-tures, or professional status in connection with the resale of ethical products in a manner which violates those directions or conditions specified by the manufacturer to ensure the safe and efficacious use of the product.**

VII. Medical Records

A. **Veterinary medical records are an integral part of veterinary care.** The records must comply with the standards established by state and federal law.

B. **Medical Records are the property of the practice and the practice owner.** The original records must be retained by the practice for the period required by stat-ute.

C. **Ethically, the information within veterinary medical records is considered privileged and confidential. It must not be released except by court order or consent of the owner of the patient.**

D. Veterinarians are obligated to provide copies or summaries of medical records when requested by the client. Veterinarians should secure a written release to document that request.

E. Without the express permission of the practice owner, it is unethical for a veterinarian to remove, copy, or use the medical records or any part of any record.

VIII. *Fees and Remuneration*

A. Veterinarians are entitled to charge fees for their professional services.

B. In connection with consultations or referrals, it is unethical for veterinarians to enter into financial arrangements, such as fee splitting, which involve payment of a portion of a fee to a recommending veterinarian who has not rendered the professional services for which the fee was paid by the client.

C. Regardless of the fees that are charged or received, the quality of service must be maintained at the usual professional standard.

D. It is unethical for a group or association of veterinarians to take any action which coerces, pressures, or achieves agreement among veterinarians to conform to a fee schedule or fixed fees.

X. *Advertising*

A. Without written permission from the AVMA Executive Board, no member or employee of the American Veterinary Medical Association (AVMA) shall use the AVMA name or logo in connection with the promotion or advertising of any commercial product or service.

B. Advertising by veterinarians is ethical when there are no false, deceptive, or misleading statements or claims. A false, deceptive, or misleading statement or claim is one which communicates false information or is intended, through a material omission, to leave a false impression.

C. Testimonials or endorsements are advertising, and they should comply with the guidelines for advertising. In addition, testimonials and endorsements of professional products or services by veterinarians are considered unethical unless they comply with the following:

1. The endorser must be a bonafide user of the product or service.

2. There must be adequate substantiation that the results obtained by the endorser are representative of what veterinarians may expect in actual conditions of use.

3. Any financial, business, or other relationship between the endorser and the seller of a product or service must be fully disclosed.

4. When reprints of scientific articles are used with advertising, the reprints must remain unchanged, and be presented in their entirety.

D. **The principles that apply to advertising, testimonials, and endorsements also apply to veterinarians' communications with their clients.**

E. **Veterinarians may permit the use of their names by commercial enterprises (e.g. pet shops, kennels, farms, feedlots) so that the enterprises can advertise 'under veterinary supervision', only if they provide such supervision.**

X. Euthanasia

Humane euthanasia of animals is an ethical veterinary procedure.

I. Glossary

1. PHARMACEUTICAL PRODUCTS

Several of the following terms are used to describe veterinary pharmaceutical products. Some have legal status, others do not. Although not all of the terms are used in the Principles, we have listed them here for clarification of meaning and to avoid confusion.

A. *Ethical Product*: A product for which the manufacturer has voluntarily limited the sale to veterinarians as a marketing decision. Such products are often given a different product name and are packaged differently than products that are sold directly to consumers. "Ethical products" are sold only to veterinarians as a condition of sale that is specified in a sales agreement or on the product label.

B. *Legend Drug*: A synonymous term for a veterinary prescription drug. The name refers to the statement (legend) that is required on the label (see *veterinary prescription drug* below).

C. *Over the Counter (OTC) Drug*: Any drug that can be labeled with adequate direction to enable it to be used safely and properly by a consumer who is not a medical professional.

D. *Prescription Drug:* A drug that cannot be labeled with adequate direction to enable its safe and proper use by non-professionals.

E. *Veterinary Prescription Drug*: A drug that is restricted by federal law to use by or on the order of a licensed veterinarian, according to section 503(f) of the federal Food, Drug, and Cosmetic Act. The law requires that such drugs be labeled with the statement: " Caution, federal law restricts this drug to use by or on the order of a licensed veterinarian."

2. DISPENSING, PRESCRIBING, MARKETING AND MERCHANDISING

A. *Dispensing* is the direct distribution of products by veterinarians to clients for use on their animals.

B. *Prescribing* is the transmitting of an order authorizing a licensed pharmacist or equivalent to prepare and dispense specified pharmaceuticals to be used in or on animals in the dosage and in the manner directed by a veterinarian.

C. *Marketing* is promoting and encouraging animal owners to improve animal health and welfare by using veterinary care, services, and products.

D. *Merchandising* is the buying and selling of products or services.

3. ADVERTISING AND TESTIMONIALS

A. *Advertising* is defined as communication that is designed to inform the public about the availability, nature, or price of products or services or to influence clients to use certain products or services.

B. *Testimonials* or endorsements are statements that are intended to influence attitudes regarding the purchase or use of products or services.

4. FEE SPLITTING

The dividing of a professional fee for veterinary services with the recommending veterinarian (See Section VIII B).

07/99

National Drug Withdrawal Guide

BEEF CATTLE DRUG LIST

INJECTABLE USE

Active Ingredients	Withdrawal DAYS
Dihydrostreptomycin	30
Erythromycin	14
Ivermectin	35
Levamisole phosphate	7
Oxytetracycline	15-22[1]
Procaine penicillin G	5-30[1]
Procaine penicillin G and dihydrostreptomycin sulfate	30
Sulfamethoxine	5
Sulfamethazine	10
Tylosin	21

ORAL USE

Amprolium	1
Chlortetracycline hydrochloride	2-3[3]
Chlortetracycline sulfamethazine	7
Haloxon	7
Levamisole	2
Melengestrol acetate	2
Morantel Tartrate	14
Neomycin	30
Oxytetracycline	5
Ronnel	10
Sulfabromomethazine	10
Sulfadimethoxine	7-12[1]
Sulfamethazine	10
Sulfaquinoxaline	10
Tetracycline hydrochloride	5
Thiabendazole	3

TOPICAL USE

Active Ingredients	Withdrawal DAYS
Famphur	35
Fenthion	35-45[4]
N-(mercaptomethyl) phthalimide S-(o. o-dimethyl phosphorodithioate)	21

IMPLANT USE

Estradiol benzoate and testosterone propionate	60
Progesterone and estradiol benzoate	60
Zeranol	65

BEEF CALF DRUG LIST

INJECTABLE USE

Sodium sulfachlorpyridazine	5
Sulfadimethoxine	7

ORAL USE

Chlorhexidine dihydrochloride and dihydrostreptomycin sulfate	3
Chlortetracycline hydrochloride	1
Chlortetracycline bisulfate	3
Dihydrostreptomycin	30
Streptomycin	30
Sulfachlorpyridazine	7
Sulfamethazine, streptomycin phthalylsulfathiazole, and kaolin	10
Tetracycline hydrochloride	12

DAIRY CATTLE DRUG LIST

DRUG	TRADE NAME	PRESLAUGHTER WITHDRAWAL (DAYS)	MILK DISCARD (HRS)
INTRAMAMMARY APPLICATION (NONLACTATING)			
Benzathine cephapirin		42	
Benzathine cloxacillin		3-30	
Dihydrostreptomycin sulfate (plus Procaine penicillin G)		60	
NOVOBIOCIN		30	
INTRAMAMMARY APPLICATION (LACTATING)			
Novobiocin		15	72
Potassium hetacillin		10	72
*Procaine Penicillin G		4	60
*Sodium Cephapirin		4	98
*Sodium Cloxacillin		10	48
INTRAMAMMARY APPLICATION (LACTATING AND NONLACTATING)			
Erythromycin			36
Furaltadone			96
Oxytetracycline		4	96
Procaine Penicillin G		14	72
INJECTABLE APPLICATION (NONLACTATING)			
Amoxicillin		25	
Dihydrostreptomycin		30	
Oxytetracycline		19-28	
Procaine Penicillin G (plus Benzathine Penicillin G)		30	
Sulfamethazine		10	
Tylosin		21	
INJECTABLE APPLICATION (LACTATING AND NONLACTATING)			
Ampicillin Trihydrate		6-9	48
Dihydrostreptomycin sulfate		30	48
Erythromycin		14	72
Eurosemide		2	48
Hydrochlorothiazide			72
Ivermectin (Not for use Ivomec in dairy cattle of breeding age)		35	
Levamisole		7	
Procaine Penicillin G		4-10	72
Pen-Strept		30	72
Sodium Selenite (plus vitamin E)		30	
Sodium Sulfachlorpyridazine		5	
Sulfadimethoxine		5	60

ORAL APPLICATION (NONLACTATING)

Chlortetracycline	1-4
Oxytetracycline	7
Sulfachloropyridazine	7
Sulfadimethoxine	7-12
Sulfamethazine	10-28
Sulfaquinoxalene (water)	10
Sulfathiazole plus Sulfamethazine	10

ORAL APPLICATION (LACTATING AND NONLACTATING)

Amoxicillin	20	
Ampicillin	15	
Amprolium	1	
Chlortetracycline	1-3	
Chlorothiazide		72
Crufomate	7	
Fenbendazole	8	
Furosemide	2	48
Haloxon	7	
Levamisole	2	
Neomycin Sulfate	30	
Oxytetracycline	5	60
Ronnel	10	240
Sodium Sulfachlorpyridazine	7	
Streptomycin Sulfate (water)	2	
Tetracycline Hydrochloride	5-14	
Thiabendazole	3	96
Trichlormethiazide Naquasone Bolus (plus Dexamethasone) (bolus)		72

MISCELLANEOUS (LACTATING AND NONLACTATING)

Nitrofurazone	3

MISCELLANEOUS (NONLACTATING)

Fenthion	35-80
Famphur (plus xylene)	35

*Be sure to check label - some of these drugs are not for use in dairy cattle of breeding age

DAIRY CALF DRUG LIST

DAIRY CALF DRUGS (INJECTABLE USE)

Active Ingredients	Withdrawal DAYS
Dihydrostreptomycin sulfate	30
Erythromycin	14
Levamisole	7
Oxytetracycline	15-22
Procaine penicillin G	5
Procaine penicillin G and dihydrostreptomycin sulfate	30
Sodium sulfachlorpyridazine	5
Sulfamethazine	10
Sulfadimethoxine	7
Tylosin	0

DAIRY CALF DRUGS (ORAL USE)

Amprolium	1
Chlortetracycline hydrochloride	1
Chlortetracycline bisulfate (water)	3
Chlortetracycline and neomycin	1
Haloxon	7
Levamisole hydrochloride	2
Streptomycin	30
Sulfabromomethazine	10
Sulfachlorpyridazine	7
Sulfadimethoxine	7
Sulfamethazine	10
Sulfamethazine, streptomycin phthalylsulfathiazole, and kaolin	10
Tetracycline hydrochloride (water)	5

SWINE DRUG LIST

INJECTABLE USE

Active Ingredients	Withdrawal DAYS
Ampicillin	15
Dihydrostreptomycin	30
Erythromycin	7
Gentamycin	40
Ivermectin	18
Lincomycin	2
Oxytetracycline	18-28
Procaine penicillin G	6-7
Sodium selenite	14
Sulfamethazine	10
Sulfapyridine	10
Tylosin	14

ORAL USE

Ampicillin	1
Apramycin	28
Arsanilic Acid	5
Carbadox	70
Chlortetracycline	1-5
Chlortetracycline and Sulfamethazine	15
Furazolidone	5
Gentamycin	3-14
Hygromycin B	15
Levamisole	3-11
Lincomycin	6
Neomycin	20
Nitrofurazone	5
Oxytetracycline	5
Pyrantel tartrate	1
Roxarsone	5
Sodium Arsanilate	5
Spectinomycin	10
Sulfachloropyradazine	4
Sulfamethazine	10-15
Sulfamethazine and chlortetracycline and Penicillin G	15
Sulfaquinoxaline	10
Sulfathiazole, Chlortetracycline, and Procaine Penicillin G	7
Tetracycline	4
Thiabendazole	30
Tiamulin	3
Tylosin	2
Tylosin and Hygromycin B	15
Tylosin and Sulfamethazine	15

FOOT-NOTES
1 Withdrawal times vary with different commercial brand names. Consult labels for specific times.
2 Withdrawal times vary with different dosage forms. Consult label for specific times.
3 Withdrawal times vary with dosages
4 Withdrawal is longer when animals are retreated
5 Withdrawal for both slaughtering and freshening

  This table is intended only as a guideline and is subject to change. Always refer to label instructions on the product you are using. Be sure to read the label carefully and follow the instructions. If you have any questions on the proper use of any drug, consult your veterinarian

Courtesy of Nebraska Veterinary Medical Association

The Commonwealth of Massachusetts

7.01: *Code of Professional Conduct*

1. A veterinarian shall bill accurately and truthfully for services rendered.

2. A veterinarian shall not overutilize his/her practice. Overutilization of practice is practice excessive in quality or amount to the needs of the patient. Overutilization may be determined from such sources as the patient's history, subjective symptoms, objective findings and reasonable clinical judgment as well as other relevant information.

3. A veterinarian shall promptly notify the Board of any disciplinary action taken against him/her, and/or the voluntary surrender of his/her license to practice veterinary medicine in another jurisdiction.

4. A veterinarian's practice shall conform to the currently accepted standards in the profession of veterinary medicine.

5. A veterinarian shall not engage in any fraud, deceit, or misrepresentation in the procurement of a license to practice veterinary medicine.

6. A veterinarian shall not practice veterinary medicine as to endanger the health and welfare of his/her patients or the public. A veterinarian shall not practice veterinary medicine if his/her ability to practice with reasonable skill and safety is adversely affected by reason of illness, excessive use of alcohol, drugs, narcotics, chemicals, or any other substance or as a result of any mental or physical disability.

7. A veterinarian shall not engage in fraud, deceit, or misrepresentation in the practice of veterinary medicine.

8. A veterinarian shall at all times conduct professional activities in conformity with federal, state and municipal laws, ordinances and/or regulations and with the Regulations of the Board.

9. A veterinarian shall cooperate with any request by the Board to appear before the Board and/or provide information to the Board.

10. A veterinarian shall comply with any restrictions on his/her practice of veterinary medicine imposed by the Board with the licensee's consent or after notice and hearing.

11. A veterinarian shall at all times maintain his/her service premises and all equipment thereon in a clean and sanitary condition. A veterinarian shall maintain clean and sanitary attire.

12. A veterinarian shall notify the Board of the suspension, revocation, or voluntary surrender of his/her federal Drug Enforcement Administration DEA, registration, and his/her state controlled substances license.

13. A veterinarian shall not represent conflicting interests except by the express consent of all the parties after full disclosure of all the facts. A conflict of interest shall include, but not be limited to, accepting a fee from a buyer to inspect an animal for soundness and accepting a fee from the seller. Acceptance of a fee from both the buyer and the seller is prima facie evidence of a conflict of interest.

14. A veterinarian shall not dispense or prescribe controlled substances except in the course of his/her professional practice and when a bona fide veterinarian/client/patient relationship has been established.

15. A veterinarian shall maintain a confidential relationship with his/her clients, except as otherwise provided by law or required by considerations related to public health and/or animal health.

16. A veterinarian shall not issue a certificate of health unless he/she shall have personal knowledge by means of actual examination and appropriate testing of the animal that the animal meets the requirements for the issuance of such a certificate.

17. A veterinarian shall not in any way aid or abet the unlawful practice of veterinary medicine.

18. A veterinarian shall not engage in verbal abuse or harassment of a client, nor shall a veterinarian physically threaten or assault a client or an employee.

19. A veterinarian shall not physically abuse or engage in unnecessary rough handling of an animal under his/her care.

20. A veterinarian shall not delegate to an assistant who is not licensed as a veterinarian any aspect of the practice of veterinary medicine as defined in M.G.L.C. 112, s. 58, without direct supervision by the veterinarian himself/herself.

21. A veterinarian shall not refuse treatment of an animal on the basis of the owner's race, color, sex, religion, national origin, or handicap.

22. A veterinarian shall not refuse to provide treatment to an animal unless such refusal is based on reasons such as the inadequacy of the facilities then available or the unavailability of all-night veterinary medical care for the animal. Where treatment is refused for such reasons, a veterinarian shall provide advice for or arrange an alternative source of veterinary medical care. [Ed. note: The application of this section as it is presently worded means veterinarians are required to render emergency care regardless of the owner's ability to pay.]

23. A veterinarian shall not refuse to return an animal to its owner on the grounds that the owner has failed to fully pay for veterinary medical services rendered, as distinguished from boarding services rendered pursuant to M.G.L.C. 255, c. 24.

24. A veterinarian shall not neglect an animal under his/her care.

25. A veterinarian shall not permit a veterinary technician or other assistant to evaluate the medical condition of a patient by telephone or otherwise without the veterinarian being on the office premises.

26. A veterinarian shall, where possible, preserve the body of any patient which dies while in the veterinarian's care while its owner is away, except as otherwise provided by law.

27. A veterinarian shall obtain the consent of the owner before disposing of any patient which dies while in the veterinarian's care, provided such consent is given within a reasonable time.

28. A veterinarian shall obtain the consent of the patient's owner before administering general anesthesia and/or performing any surgical procedure.

29. A veterinarian shall have the right to refuse to admit as an in-patient to his/her hospital or clinic an animal that is not currently vaccinated.

30. A veterinarian shall have the right to establish his/her own policy regarding the hours, emergency coverage, and other similar provisions for the operation of his/her facility, provided that this information is posted at the facility and may be obtained over the telephone.

31. A veterinarian shall have the right to refuse to render veterinary medical services for any owner who uses physical or verbal abuse towards the veterinarian or towards any employee of the veterinarian.

32. A veterinarian shall ascertain, before hiring, whether a potential veterinarian employee has a valid, current Massachusetts license to practice veterinary medicine.

33. A veterinarian shall be responsible for ascertaining whether the license to practice veterinary medicine of any veterinarian employee is current.

34. A veterinarian shall obtain the consent of a patient's owner before transporting a patient to another facility for veterinary medical care or any other reason, unless circumstances qualifying as an emergency do not permit obtaining such consent.

35. A veterinarian shall not engage in any other conduct which reflects unfavorably on the profession of veterinary medicine.

APPENDIX G

Revised Contra Costa County, CA Animal Control Ordinance

Chapter 416-2 Definitions.

§ 416-2.002 Generally.

As used in Division 416, the following terms have the meanings set forth in this chapter, unless the context clearly requires otherwise.

§ 416-2.004 Animal Services Director.

"Animal Services Director" means the head of the Animal Services Department and his or her designated subordinates.

§ 416-2.010 Owner.

"Owner" includes the legal owner, equitable owner, and any person, association, partnership, or corporation harboring or having custody or control of an animal.

§ 416-2.012 License Tag.

"License tag" means a numbered tag, stamped with the name of the county, and issued by the licensing authority for the purpose of identifying the owner and the dog or cat described in the license application and worn by that dog or cat.

§ 416-2.014 Veterinarian.

"Veterinarian" means a person authorized to practice veterinary medicine in California.

§ 416-2.016 Wild or Exotic Animal.

"Wild animal" or "exotic animal" means any of the following:

1. Any animal described in California Fish and Game Code Sections 2116 and 2118.
2. Any animal described in any addition to Fish and Game Code Section 2118 by regulation of the Fish and Game Commission as provided in Section 2118(j).
3. Class Aves: (birds)

a. Order Falconiformes (including, but not limited to hawks, eagles, and vultures).

b. Subdivision Ratitae (including, but not limited to ostriches, rheas, cassowaries, and emus).

4. Class Reptilia: (snakes, lizards, turtles, alligators)

a. Order Ophidia (including, but not limited to racers, boas, water snakes, and pythons) over six feet long.

b. Order Loricata (including, but not limited to alligators, caymans, and crocodiles) over 12 inches long.

5. Any class, order, family, genera, or species of wild animals which may be designated by the Animal Services Director as a menace to public peace, health or safety, or to native wildlife or agricultural interests, by a written designation filed with the Clerk of the Board of Supervisors.

6. Any non-domestic species when kept, maintained or harbored in such numbers or in such a manner as to create or constitute a nuisance or, in any event, a likelihood of danger to such animals, other animals, the environment or the persons or property of human beings.

7. Any species of animal which is venomous to human beings, whether by bite, sting, touch or otherwise, except honey-producing bees.

Chapter 416-4 General Provisions.

Article 416-4.2 Control.

§ 416-4.202 Animal Services Director.

a. The County's animal control activities are functions of the Animal Services Department under the Animal Services Director. The Animal Services Director shall supervise, control and report concerning such activities as provided in this Ordinance Code and in Chapters 1 and 2 of Division 2 of the Food and Agricultural Code (Sections 2001 ff); and he or she is the appointing authority for the other positions in the department.

b. The Animal Services Director is authorized to adopt regulations to interpret and carry out the provisions of Division 416 or this code.

c. The Animal Services Director may adopt regulations exempting:

1. handicapped people and animals being raised, trained or used to aid handicapped people,

2. police dogs on duty,

3. persons participating in animal rescue programs, from specific requirements of Division 416 of this code.

§ 416-4.204 Officers' Status, Weapons, and Arrests.

The Animal Services Director and the subordinate animal control officers, when acting in the course and scope of their employment, are as a class designated as entitled to carry weapons within the meaning of Penal Code Section 12031, and as public officers for the purposes of enforcing all laws on animal control, and they are authorized to arrest persons for violation of these laws pursuant to Section 14-2.203.

Article 416-4.4 Restraint.

§ 416-4.402 Animals at Large.

a. No person owning, possessing, harboring, or controlling any animal shall allow such animal to be at large.

  b. As used in this section, "at large" means an animal which either:

    1. In the case of dogs, is not under effective restraint by a leash; or

    2. In the case of animals other than dogs or cats, is not in the immediate presence and under the effective control of such person; or

    3. Is tethered or leashed on any street, or other public place, not set aside for such tethering or leashing for a period of longer than fifteen minutes, or in such a way as to block a public walkway or thoroughfare; or

    4. Is pastured, tethered, tied, or otherwise present on private property or in any public building without the consent of the owner or occupant; or

    5. Is in any place or position with the capacity to injure persons or property; or

    6. Fights, bites, or causes harm to any other animal or person unless such animal or person has entered the private property owned by, or in the possession of the person owning or controlling the offending animal without permission when such property is properly fenced and posted as to the presence of the offending animal; or

    7. Is not on the private property owned by, or in the possession of, the person owning or controlling the animal and is not wearing a required license tag; or

    8. Is left at any place without provision for its care. Provided, nevertheless, that a dog is not required to be under restraint by a leash when the dog has not strayed from and is upon private property owned by, or in the possession of, the person owning or controlling the dog.

  c. **Exemptions.** A working dog, performing acts such as herding under the control and supervision of an owner/handler shall not be considered at large while performing his duties. A hunting, obedience, tracking or show dog shall not be considered at large while performing in the above capacities. Dogs being exercised under the control of their owners in public areas designated for animal exercise shall not be considered at large.

  d. **Females in Heat.** In the case of female dogs or cats in heat and for the purposes of Food and Agricultural Code Section 30954, "at large" means outside a house, vehicle, or other secure enclosure adequate to prevent unplanned male access.

  e. **Animals in Vehicles.**

    1. A dog or any other animal in or upon a vehicle is deemed to be upon the property of the operator of such vehicle. No dog or any other animal shall be transported on any public thoroughfare in any vehicle unless such dog or animal is totally enclosed within such vehicle, within a secured container carried upon such vehicle, or securely cross-tethered to such vehicle in such a way as to prevent a falling out of or off such vehicle, and to prevent injury to the animal.

    2. No dog or any other animal shall be left completely enclosed in a parked vehicle without adequate ventilation, or in such a way as to subject the animal to temperatures sufficiently above ambient to affect the animal's health and welfare.

§ 416-4.404 Abandonment.
No owner of an animal shall abandon it.

Article 416-4.6 Enforcement.

§ 416-4.604 Penalties.
Notwithstanding Section 14-8.004, and pursuant to Food and Agricultural Code § 31401, violations of Division 416 of this code, excepting Chapter 416-10 and Article 416-12.2, are punishable by a fine of not more than fifty dollars for the first offense, and not more than one hundred dollars for the second or subsequent offense.

Chapter 416-6 Individual Licenses.

Article 416-6.0 Licenses.

§ 416-6.002 Dog and Cat Licenses.

a. Every person owning, possessing, harboring, or having custody of any dog over four months old shall annually obtain a license and pay a license fee.

b. Every such person shall obtain a license within thirty days after a dog reaches the age of four months.

c. Every such person shall obtain a license within thirty days after acquiring a dog over four months old.

d. An added late fee shall be charged for late licensing.

e. Any person may voluntarily license any domestic cat subject to proper application and payment of the required license fee.

f. Any person who transfers any licensed dog or cat to another person and any person who acquires a licensed dog or cat must give written notice of the name and address of the person to whom possession is transferred and of the person acquiring such animal, and the license tag number, to the Animal Services Department within thirty days.

g. No person shall own, possess, harbor, or keep any dog over four months old without a license for which all fees have been paid; but this does not apply during the thirty-day grace period under subsections (b) and (c) of this section.

§ 416-6.004 Exemptions.

a. **Non-residents.** The provisions of this article shall not apply to dogs or cats whose owners are non-residents temporarily within the county for thirty days or less, nor to dogs or cats brought into the county to participate in any dog or cat show or field trial.

b. **Handicapped.** Dogs being raised, trained and used to aid handicapped persons shall be licensed without fee.

c. **Government.** Dogs owned or used by the county, municipal corporations, or other public agencies shall be licensed without fee.

d. **Senior Citizens.** One dog kept in a household where the owner of the dog is over the age of sixty-five shall be licensed without fee.

§ 416-6.006 Tags.

The licensing authority shall issue dog or cat license tags, stamped or imprinted with the name County of Contra Costa and an identification number.

§ 416-6.008 Applications.

a. Application for dog or cat licenses shall be made in writing to the licensing agency on forms approved by the licensing agency. They shall include for each animal the name and address of owner; age, sex, color, breed, and description of the animal; and a current rabies certificate issued by an authorized veterinarian. In addition, the applicant shall certify to receipt of a copy of Article 416-4.4 of this ordinance.

b. Tag Numbers. The licensing authority shall enter on the application the number of the license tag issued. All applications shall be kept on file in an office of the licensing authority, open to public inspection during the term of the licenses applied for.

§ 416-6.016 Prohibition.

No person may use any license for any animal other than the animal for which it was issued. Article 416-6.2 Multiple Pet Licenses.

§ 416-6.200 License Required.

a. No more than three dogs and no more than five cats over six months of age may be kept, harbored, possessed or maintained for more than thirty days in a single dwelling or business unit without a multiple pet license in an area zoned for uses other than agriculture.

b. No more than twenty dogs and no more than twenty cats over six months of age, and no dogs or cats for commercial purposes may be kept, harbored, possessed or maintained in any single dwelling or business unit without a kennel license. Commercial purposes shall include but not be limited to boarding, training, or wholesaling of animals but shall not be construed to mean the sale of individual animals to private owners.

§ 416-6.202 Applications.

a. Application for a multiple pet license shall include an application fee and shall be made in writing to the Animal Services Director, who shall issue the license when the application is approved.

b. Application for a kennel license shall include an application fee and shall be made in writing to the Director of Planning, who shall issue the license jointly with the Animal Services Director if the application is approved.

c. The Director of Planning and the Animal Services Director may jointly or severally promulgate regulations governing the application for, and issuance of, kennel licenses.

d. Applications for multiple pet licenses or kennel licenses shall show that the following conditions have been met:

   1. facilities exist at the location to adequately secure, feed, house and maintain the animals;

   2. possession and maintenance of the animals at the location has not resulted in and is not likely to result in the animals being subjected to neglect, suffering, cruelty or abuse;

   3. neither the applicant, the owner, nor the possessor of the animals has had a county license revoked or been convicted for a violation of this ordinance or any law regulating animals within one year;

   4. all dogs maintained under a multiple pet license shall be confined on the premises and shall be enclosed in a secure shelter during the hours of darkness except when they are shown, exercised, tried, worked, hunted, or trained under the owner's control. The required showing may be made by declaration under penalty of perjury.

e. Each application for a multiple pet license or kennel license must list every dog to be included. An updated list shall be submitted to the Animal Services Director upon application for a renewal of a multiple pet license. Each application must also include a current rabies immunization certificate issued by an authorized veterinarian for every dog listed.

§ 416-6.204 License Approval.

a. At the receipt of a complete application for a multiple pet license, the Animal Services Director may investigate the application including investigation of the premises at which the animals will be kept prior to the approval of the application.

b. In the case of kennels, after receipt of a complete application the Animal Services Director or the Director of Planning may investigate the application including the premises on which the kennel will be operating, and shall ascertain that the kennel is authorized by a land use permit prior to approval of the application.

c. The Animal Services Director or the Director of Planning may require such information pertinent to the keeping of the animals from an applicant as they deem necessary with respect to their action on a multiple pet or kennel license application or renewal application.

d. The Animal Services Director or the Director of Planning may impose conditions on the approval or renewal of any multiple pet or kennel license. Such conditions must be in writing and must serve to effectuate the intent of this ordinance, the well-being of the animals, or the public health, welfare, convenience or necessity.

e. Prior to the denial of any multiple pet license or renewal thereof, or any approval to which conditions are attached, the Animal Services Director shall notify the applicant in writing of the intended action. Any conditions to be attached to an approval or renewal shall be specified in the notice. The applicant, in writing, may request a hearing before the Animal Services Director within five days after receipt of such notice if he/she wishes to contest a decision of denial or approval with conditions. If the applicant requests a hearing, the Animal Service Director shall give the applicant no less than five days notice, in writing, of the time and place of such hearing, by mail. After hearing, the Animal Services Director shall determine whether the license should be issued, issued subject to conditions, or denied.

f. A multiple pet license shall be renewed without review upon the filing of a complete application and payment of the necessary fees unless renewal has been protested or the Animal Services Department has received or lodged two or more complaints concerning the licensed location within the last year.

§ 416-6.206 Periods.
Multiple pet licenses and kennel licenses shall be valid for such periods not less than one year, and the license fees shall become due and payable at such times, as shall be determined by resolution of the Board of Supervisors.

§ 416-6.203 Fees.
Multiple pet license fees, kennel license fees, application fees, and late license fees shall be established by resolution of the Board of Supervisors. Separate fee schedules may be established for dog enthusiasts or cat fanciers.

§ 416-6.210 Exemptions.
Multiple pet license fees and kennel license fees shall not be charged to veterinary hospital, except when such hospitals offer boarding or breeding services separately from veterinary medical services.

§ 416-6.212 Late Fees.
Late fees shall be payable upon failure to obtain a multiple pet license or a kennel license within sixty days of keeping, harboring, possessing or maintaining animals in excess of those specified herein, or upon failure to pay a renewal license fee within sixty days after it is due and payable.

§ 416-6.214 Dog Tags.
Any dog for which a license is required and which is covered under a multiple pet or kennel

license, which is removed for more than one day from the licensed premises shall wear its current, valid license tag unless performing in the capacity of hunting, working, obedience, tracking or showing.

§ 416-6.216 Breeding Limitation.

a. No person, except as provided below, shall allow the parturition and rearing of more than one litter of dogs and one litter of cats in any one calendar year.

b. Persons holding multiple pet or kennel licenses may allow the parturition and rearing of no more than one litter per bitch registered by a nationally-recognized dog registering body and one litter per queen registered by a nationally-recognized cat registering body, in any one calendar year.

§ 416-6.218 Existing Licensees.

Persons holding Dog Fancier Licenses or Commercial Kennel Licenses on the effective date of Ordinance 80-97 are entitled to a multiple pet license, and persons holding a Commercial Kennel License on the effective date of Ordinance 80-97 are entitled to a kennel license, without prior approval, upon filing complete application documents and tendering the required fees.

Article 416-6.4 License Revocation.

§ 416-6.400 License Revocation.

a. A license may be revoked by the Animal Services Director on one or more of the following grounds:

1. falsification of facts in the license application;

2. violation of any provisions of this ordinance or any California State law, statute rule, order or regulation governing the activity for which the license was issued;

3. conviction of cruelty to animals in this or any other state;

4. failure to meet and maintain the conditions of the license;

5. inhumane and/or cruel treatment of animals;

6. violations of health and sanitation codes.

b. Prior to revocation of a license, the Animal Services Director shall hold a public hearing to determine whether the grounds described in § 416-6.400 (a) exist.

c. At least ten days prior to hearing, the Animal Services Director shall mail or otherwise deliver to the possessor of the animals a notice containing a statement of the charges supporting license revocation and/or impoundment and notice of the time and place of hearing before the Animal Services Director as to the truth of the charges.

d. If the Animal Services Director determines, after hearing, that charges supporting such action are true, he/she may revoke the license and may impound any animals covered under such license.

e. On revocation of license, if the cause is not inhumane treatment of animals or violation of health and sanitation codes, the owner of the license so revoked shall have a sixty day grace period prior to the effective date of revocation to attempt to find new adoptive owners for the animals involved.

f. If a license has been denied or revoked for cause, the Animal Services Director shall not accept a new application by the same person less than twelve months after such denial or revocation unless the applicant affirmatively shows, and has verified by the Animal Services Director, that the grounds upon which the first license or application was denied or revoked no longer exist.

g. On revocation of license, no part of the license fee shall be refunded.

h. Evidence must be relevant, non-cumulative, and of such nature as responsible persons are accustomed to rely on in the conduct of serious affairs. Written statements by a county officer or employee, an officer or employee of the State of California, or an officer or employee of any law enforcement or fire protection agency acting in the course and scope of their official duties or employment, written records of the animal services department, and statements under penalty of perjury may be accepted as evidence that the fact(s) or condition(s) expressed therein do or do not exist.

§ 416-6.402 Inspection.
For the sole purposes of determining inhumane treatment of animals and/or violations of state and local health and sanitation laws, the Animal Services Director, upon reasonable notice and having in his/her possession a search warrant, shall be permitted to inspect all animals, and the premises so specified in said search warrant at which any such animal(s) are kept, harbored, possessed or maintained.

Chapter 416-8 Impoundment.

§ 416-8.002 Impoundment Required.
a. All dogs found at large in violation of the provisions of Division 14 of the Agricultural Code, or any provisions of Division 416 of this Ordinance Code, shall be taken up and impounded, and are subject to destruction by humane injection.

b. All animals, including dogs and cats, that are abandoned, found at large, taken into custody by the Animal Services Director, or otherwise found to be in violation of Division 416 of the Ordinance Code, shall be taken up and impounded, and are subject to destruction by humane injection.

c. Any person taking up and/or holding a stray animal the owner of which is unknown or cannot be immediately contacted, shall notify the Animal Services Department within twenty-four hours and, upon request, shall immediately surrender it for impounding. Any person participating in a rescue program authorized for such purposes by the Animal Services Director is exempt from the surrender requirement.

§ 416-8.004 Exceptions.
The Animal Services Director shall not impound any animal (including fowl) not otherwise in violation of Division 416, staked or tied for grazing on private property or any fowl at large on private property except on the complaint of the owner or occupant or the property, or of any other property if he claims injury.

§ 416-8.006 Holding Period, Notice.
a. Except for rabies control purposes, impounded animals shall be kept at a facility of or authorized by the Animal Services Department for seventy-two hours, except:
   1. stray dogs or cats with valid licenses shall be held 10 days after written notice is mailed or otherwise given to the owner, if the owner is identified; and
   2. Stray bovine animals, horses, mules or burros shall be held for five days and, if unclaimed after that period, shall be disposed of in such manner as the Board of Supervisors shall specify by resolution.

b. If the owner of an impounded animal, other than a dog or cat with a valid license, is identified, the Animal Services Department shall notify the owner by telephone or mail within two days after such identification and hold the animal for at least five working days after notice is mailed or otherwise given.

c. The Animal Services Director may dispose of animals unclaimed after expiration of the holding period by humanely destroying them by injection or by placing the animal in an adoptive home. No live animal shall be released for teaching or experimental purposes.

§ 416-8.008 Summary Destruction.

The Animal Services Director may, without waiting for the holding periods to elapse, cause any impounded animal to be destroyed when such an animal is severely injured, or infected with a dangerous or communicable disease, and only after reasonable efforts under the circumstances have been made to apprise the owner of such animal, if such owner can be reasonably identified, of the condition of the animal.

§ 416-8.010 Owner Claims.

a. The owner of any impounded animal is liable for all accrued impoundment fees. The owner of any impounded animal may claim it from the Animal Services Department before its destruction, sale, or other disposition, after obtaining all required licenses and permits and paying all accrued impoundment fees.

b. If the owner claims that an animal was unlawfully impounded, the owner may request a hearing which shall be provided by the Animal Services Director within three working days of such request. The Animal Services Director shall hear the evidence and argument of the owner and make such further investigation as is deemed appropriate. The animal shall be released to the owner without payment of fees or penalties, except applicable license or permit fees, if the Animal Services Director concludes there is reasonable doubt as to the lawfulness of the impoundment. No fees shall be charged on account of continued impoundment after a hearing has been requested.

§ 416-8.014 Abandonment.

The refusal or failure of the owner of any animal to apply for all required licenses or permits, and to pay all applicable license, permit, and impoundment fees, within ten days after notice of impoundment is mailed to such owner's last known address or otherwise given to such owner constitutes abandonment and relinquishment of the owner's rights to the county.

§ 416-8.016 Adoption.

a. Animals subject to disposition by the county may be sold if the Animal Services Director finds that the sale of any such animal is not contrary to law, to policy of the department, or to the public interest. Dogs or cats may not be sold for purposes other than keeping as pets, and may not be sold without first having been licensed, neutered or spayed, and vaccinated against rabies, or a fee therefore having been deposited.

b. Fees for the purchase of animals from the Animal Services Department shall be established by resolution of the Board of Supervisors.

Chapter 416-10 Rabies Control.

§ 416-10.006 Suspected Rabies.

a. **Knowledge and Report.** If the owner and/or keeper of any animal observes or learns (from any source whatsoever) that the animal shows symptoms of rabies, that person shall immediately confine the animal in a veterinary hospital, an Animal Services Department facility, or other adequate facility; including the owner's premises if approved by the Animal Services Director; notify the Animal Services Director, and make the animal available to the Animal Services Director for examination and/or confinement.

b. **Examination.** The Animal Services Director shall cause the animal to be examined by a veterinarian.

c. **Confinement.** If the Animal Services Director, on the advice of a veterinarian, deems it advisable for the protection of the public health, he/she shall have the animal confined in a veterinary hospital, an Animal Services Department facility, or other adequate facility, and shall keep the health officer advised of the animal's condition.

d. **Release.** No person shall release any animal so confined until release is authorized by the Animal Services Director.

e. **Charge.** The animal's owner shall be charged for all costs incurred or fees applicable with respect to examination or confinement of the animal.

§ 416-10.008 Bites.

a. **Knowledge and Report.** If the owner and/or keeper of any animal knows or learns from any source whatsoever that the animal has bitten any person, any other animal, or has been bitten by another animal having rabies or reasonably suspected of having rabies, such owner or keeper shall immediately confine the animal in a veterinary hospital, an Animal Services Department facility or other adequate facility, notify the Animal Services Director, and shall make the animal available to the Animal Services Director for examination and/or confinement. The victim of such biting shall report the incident to the Animal Services Director where the owner or keeper of the animal is unknown, or where the owner or keeper is unable or refuses to make the required report.

b. **Examination.** The Animal Services Director may cause the animal to be examined by a veterinarian.

c. **Confinement.** The Animal Services Director shall confine or have the animal confined in a veterinary hospital, an Animal Services Department facility, or other adequate facility for the period prescribed by state law, and shall keep the health officer advised of the animal's condition.

d. **Release.** No person shall release any animal so confined until release is authorized by the Animal Services Director.

e. **Charges.** The animal's owner shall be charged for all costs incurred or fees applicable with respect to examination or confinement of the animal.

§ 416-10.010 Rabies Reports.

a. Rabies is declared to be a reportable disease. Every veterinarian practicing in this county and every person providing professional medical treatment for animal bite by an animal of a species subject to rabies shall immediately notify the health department whenever rabies is suspected.

b. Every veterinarian practicing in this county shall provide the Animal Services Director with a copy of every rabies immunization certificate which he/she issues.

Chapter 416-11 Wild or Exotic Animals.

§ 416-11.002 Registration Required.

All persons owning, maintaining, or possessing any wild or exotic animal must register such animal with the Animal Services Director.

§ 416-11.004 Registration Form.

All persons registering wild or exotic animals with the Animal Services Director shall submit the following information on a form provided by the Animal Services Department:

1. The true name and address of the owner or possessor of such animals, and the names and addresses of two persons who may be contacted in case of emergency.

2. The number and true scientific name(s) of the type(s) of wild or exotic animal(s) for which registration is requested.
3. The address or place where the animal(s) will be located.
4. The purpose for which the animal(s) will be possessed.
5. If the animal(s) are described in Fish and Game Code § 2118, a copy of a current, valid permit from the State of California for possession of such animal(s).
6. Any other information as the Animal Services Director may require.
7. There shall be no fee for registration of wild or exotic animals.

§ 416-11.006 Impoundment.

Any wild or exotic animal in this county which is at large, or for which the Animal Services Director does not have a current registration, is subject to impoundment under the provisions of Chapter 416-8, at the discretion of the Animal Services Director, or to summary destruction if the Animal Services Director concludes that the animal poses a threat to public health and safety and cannot be immediately and safely impounded.

Chapter 416-12 Miscellaneous.

Article 416-12.0 Disposal.

§ 416-12.002 By Owner.

Any person possessing a dead animal or fowl shall dispose of it in a safe and sanitary manner. Upon receipt of information that the body of any animal or fowl has not been properly disposed of in accordance with this section, the Animal Services Director shall dispose of the body.

§ 416-12.004 Requested Disposal.

On request by any person, the Animal Services Director may remove and dispose of any small animal such as dog, cat, fowl or rabbit lawfully in the possession of the person.

§ 416-12.006 Fees.

Animal disposal services by the Animal Services Director shall be subject to such fees as shall be established by resolution of the Board of Supervisors.

Article 416-12.2 Nuisances.

§ 416-12.202 Animal Noise.

a. No person shall own, possess, harbor, control, or keep on any premises any dog, fowl, or other animal, that barks, bays, cries, howls, or makes any other noise so continuously or incessantly as to unreasonably disturb the peace or quiet of any two persons living in different households within three hundred feet of the location of the disturbance.
b. Any person who shall keep or permit to remain on any premises any animal as defined in part (a) above is guilty of a violation of this ordinance, provided that during the time that the animal is making such a noise, no person or other animal is trespassing or threatening to trespass or no person is teasing or provoking the animal. This section shall not be construed to prohibit the keeping of any watchdog, provided that the keeper thereof takes immediate steps to quiet such dog whenever it barks, and provided that such keeper never leaves such dog unattended on the premises in a place where its barking, if prolonged or repeated an undue number of times, disturbs the peace or quiet of any two persons living in different households within three hundred feet of the location of the disturbance.

§ 416-12.204 Animal Wastes.

Any person having the ownership, custody, or control of any animal which defecates on public walks, in public recreation areas, in public buildings, or without the owner's consent on private property shall immediately remove the excrement from any such place to a site not prohibited by law. This restriction shall not apply in areas identified as horse trails or areas specifically set aside for exercise of animals.

Article 416-12.4 Dangerous Animals.

§ 416-12.402 Dangerous Animals.

Any animal, except a dog assisting a peace officer engaged in law enforcement duties, which demonstrates any of the following behavior, is rebuttably presumed dangerous:

a. An attack which requires a defensive action by any person to prevent bodily injury and/ or property damage in a place where such person is conducting himself peacefully and lawfully.

b. An attack on another animal or livestock which occurs off the property of the owner of the attacking animal.

c. An attack that results in an injury to a person in a place where such person is conducting himself peacefully and lawfully.

d. Any behavior that constitutes a physical threat of bodily harm to a person in a place where such person is conducting himself peacefully and lawfully.

For the purposes of this section, a person is peaceably and lawfully upon the private property of an owner or possessor of the animal when he is on such property in the performance of any duty imposed upon him by the laws of this state or any city or county, or by the laws or postal regulations of the United States, or when he is on such property upon invitation, express or implied.

§ 416-12.404 Finding of Danger.

After notice and hearing upon charges following the procedure expressed in §416-6.400, the Animal Services Director may declare that an animal is dangerous and thereafter such animal is a dangerous animal.

§ 416-12.406 Dangerous Animal Permit Required.

No person shall own, maintain, or possess any dangerous animal without having obtained a permit from the Animal Services Director, including payment of any and all fees required, and compliance with all conditions of such permit, within thirty days after a declaration that the animal is dangerous.

§ 416-12.408 Dangerous Animal Permit Application.

An application for a dangerous animal permit shall include:

a. The true name and address of the applicant and of the owner or possessor of the animal, and the names and addresses of two persons who may be contacted in the case of emergency;

b. An accurate description of the dangerous animal for which the permit is requested;

c. The address or place where the animal will be located;

d. The purpose for which the animal will be possessed or kept;

e. Such other information as the Animal Services Director may require; and

f. An application fee for each animal.

§ 416-12.410 Investigation.

a. At the receipt of a complete permit application, the Animal Services Director may investigate the application and may grant a county permit if in his/her discretion, he/she finds the following conditions satisfied:

1. Facilities exist at the location to adequately secure, feed, house and maintain the animal;

2. Possession and maintenance of the animal at the location is not likely to endanger the peace, quiet, health, safety or comfort of persons in the vicinity of the location;

3. Possession and maintenance of the animal at the location is not likely to be detrimental to agriculture, native wildlife, or the public peace, health or safety in the county;

4. Possession and maintenance of the animal at the location has not resulted in, and is not likely to result in, the animal being subjected to neglect, suffering, cruelty, or abuse;

5. Neither the applicant, owner, nor the possessor of the animal has had a County Dangerous Animal Permit or any other license required under this ordinance revoked, or been convicted of a violation of this ordinance or any law regulating animals within three years;

6. Possession of the animal at the location specified will not violate any law, ordinance, or regulation.

b. Persons residing in the vicinity of the location shall be notified of the application and be given an opportunity for comment.

§ 416-12.412 Dangerous Animal Permit.

A county dangerous animal permit shall be issued to the possessor of the animal and shall be valid for not more than one calendar year but may be renewed for subsequent years upon the filing of a renewal application conforming to the requirements of § 416-12.400 not later than December 31 of each year, and meeting all the requirements of this chapter as upon the issuance of the original permit. No person holding a dangerous animal has any right to a renewal of that permit. Failure to file application for renewal by February 1 shall result in a delinquent fee for each animal. County permits shall include the name and address of the applicant, the owner and possessor of the animal, the number and accurate description of the animal(s), and the address or place where the animal will be located.

§ 416-12.414 Permit Conditions.

All county dangerous animal permits are subject to compliance with all relevant state laws and ordinances and are subject to the following conditions:

a. The permit is non-transferable;

b. The animal may not be possessed or maintained at any location other than that expressed on the permit;

c. The animal must be securely maintained;

d. The animal may not be permitted to be loose, or to create any detriment or danger to the peace, health, or safety of the people in the vicinity of the location, nor to agriculture, native wildlife, or public peace, health, or safety in the county;

e. The animal may not be subject to neglect, suffering, cruelty, or abuse;

f. The location where the animal is possessed or maintained is kept clean and sanitary; and the animal is provided with proper and adequate food, water, ventilation, shelter, and care at all times;

g. The Animal Services Director shall be allowed at any reasonable time to inspect the animal and place where the animal is located;

h. Payment of a permit fee if imposed by resolution of the board of supervisors.

§ 416-12.417 Unpermitted Dangerous Animals.

In the event that within ten (10) days after mailing notice that an animal is declared to be a dangerous animal an application for a dangerous animal permit is not received, and (10) days after mailing notice that a dangerous animal permit has been denied or revoked, the Animal Services Director may dispose of any dangerous animal by humanely destroying it by injection.

§ 416-12.420 Dangerous Animal at Large.

Any dangerous animal found at large shall be destroyed, impounded, or impounded subject to destruction at the discretion of the Animal Services Director.

Article 416-12.8 Sales or Gifts of Animals.

§ 416-12.604 Public Display Prohibited.

No person under the age of eighteen shall place any dog, cat, puppy or kitten on display for the purpose of sale, offer for sale, barter or give away upon any street, sidewalk, parking lot, shopping center walkway or other public place, and no transfer of any such animal shall be made to any person under the age of eighteen.

§ 416-12.804 Sale of Dogs or Cats.

a. The seller of a dog or cat shall provide to the buyer at the time of sale a signed statement attesting to the seller's knowledge of the animal's health. Such statement shall also include the animal's immunization history and the record of any known disease, sickness or internal parasites that the animal is afflicted with at the time of transfer of ownership, including treatment and medication.

b. Any person purchasing a dog or cat from a person or an establishment required to be licensed or registered pursuant to Chapter 416-6 of this code may within five days of such purchase cause such animal to be examined by a veterinarian licensed by the State of California. If such examination reveals clinical signs of contagious or infectious disease or serious congenital defects not otherwise disclosed to the purchaser as required by this article, the purchaser may, within one business day of the examination, return such animal to the seller. When returned, such animal must be accompanied with a certificate signed by the examining veterinarian stating examination findings. Upon return of such animal for the reasons stated in this section, the seller shall reimburse the purchaser for the cost of the animal. If the seller refuses to reimburse the purchaser for the cost of the animal upon the purchaser's offer to return it, the purchaser may file a civil complaint.

Ordinance No. 80-98

§ 82-4.220 Kennel.

a. "Kennel means any lot, building, structure, enclosure, or premises where one or more dogs or cats are kept or maintained for commercial purposes, excluding places where veterinarians board animals for medical care only; or where over twenty dogs or over twenty cats over the age of six months are owned or kept;

b. Whenever "commercial dog kennel" is used in Title 8 of this Ordinance Code, it refers to "kennel" as defined herein.

§ 82-20.002 Kennels.

a. A kennel may be allowed after the issuance of a land use permit in any of the following districts:

Light Agricultural District (A-1), General

Agricultural District (A-2), Heavy

Agricultural District (A-3), Retail

Agricultural District (A-4)

Business District (R-B), General

Commercial District (C)

Light Industrial District (L-1), and the

Heavy Industrial District (H-1).

b. All animals maintained in kennels shall be confined on the premises or trained or exercised or bred under the owner's control and shall be enclosed in a secure shelter during the hours of darkness, except when they are shown, tried, worked, or hunting under the owner's control.

International Treaties

Agreement on the Conservation of Polar Bears, Nov. 15, 1973, TIAS No. 8409.

Antarctic Treaty, Dec. 1, 1959, 12 UST 794, TIAS No. 4780.

Convention Concerning the Conservation of Migratory Birds and Their Environment, Nov. 19, 1976, United States-USSR, 29 UST 4647, TIAS No. 9073.

Convention for Conservation of Antarctic Seals, June 1, 1972, 29 UST 441, TIAS No. 826.

Convention for the Protection of Migratory Birds and Birds in Danger of Extinction, and Their Environment, March 4, 1972, United States-Japan, 25 UST 3329, TIAS No. 7990.

Convention for the Protection of Migratory Birds and Game Mammals, Feb. 7, 1936, United States-Mexico, 50 Stat. 1311, TS No. 913.

Convention for the Protection of Migratory Birds, Aug. 16, 1916, United States-United Kingdom (on behalf of Canada), 39 Stat. 1702, TIAS No. 628.

Convention for the Regulation of Whaling, Sept. 24, 1931, 49 Stat. 3079, TIAS No. 880.

Convention on Conservation of Antarctic Marine Living Resources, in Senate document "Executive X," 96th Cong., 2d Sess. (1980).

Convention on the International Trade in Endangered Species of Wild Fauna and Flora (CITES), Mar. 3, 1973, 27 UST 1087, TIAS No. 8249.

Convention on Nature Protection and Wildlife Preservation in the Western Hemisphere, Oct. 12, 1940, 56 Stat. 1354, TIAS No. 981, UNTS No. 193.

Interim Convention of Conservation of North Pacific Fur Seals, Feb. 9, 1957, 8 UST 2283, TIAS No. 3948, 314 UNTS 105.

International Convention for the Regulation of Whaling, Dec. 2, 1946, 62 Stat. 1716, TIAS 1849.

Treaty for the Preservation and Protection of Fur Seals, July 7,

Federal Legislation

Animal Welfare Act, 7 USC § 2131-2155 (1976).

Bald Eagle Protection Act of 1940, 16 USC § 668-668(d) (1976 and Supp. V 1981).

Endangered Species Act of 1973, 16 USC § 1531-1543 (1976 and Supp. V 1981); The Endangered Species Act Amendments of 1982, 96 Stat. 1411.

Endangered Species Conservation Act of 1969, Pub. L. No. 91-135, 83 Stat. 275 (repealed 1973).

Federal Aid in Wildlife Restoration Act, 16 USC § 669-669(i) (1976 and Supp. V 1981).

Fish and Wildlife Conservation Act of 1980, 16 USC § 2901-2911 (Supp. V 1981).

Fish and Wildlife Coordination Act, 16 USC § 661-667(e) (1976).

Fishermen's Protective Act of 1967, 22 USC § 1978 (Supp. V 1981).

Fishery Conservation and Management Act of 1976, 16 USC § 1801-1882 (1976 and Supp. V 1981).

Fur Seal Act, 16 USC § 1151-1187 (1976).

Lacey Act of 1900, Ch 553, 31 Stat. 187, 16 USC § 701, 3371-3378, 18 USC § 42 (1976 and Supp. V 1981).

Marine Mammal Protection Act of 1972, 16 USC § 1361-1407 (1976 and Supp. V 1981).

Marine Protection Research and Sanctuaries Act, 33 USC § 1401-1444 and 16 USC § 1431-1434 (1976 and Supp. V 1981).

Migratory Bird Conservation Act, 16 USC § 715-715(d), 715(e), 715(f))715(k), 715(n)/715(r) (1976).

National Environmental Policy Act of 1969, 42 USC § 4321-4361 (1976).

Public Health Service Act, 42 USC § 264 (1976).

Tariff Act of 1930, 19 USC § 1527 (1976).

Tariff Act of 1962, 19 USC § 1202 (1976).

Whaling Convention Act of 1949, 16 USC § 916-916(1) (1976).

Wild Free-Roaming Horses and Burros Act of 1971, 16 USC § 1331-1340 (1976 and Supp. V 1971).

Addresses of Federal Agencies or Offices Issuing Wildlife Permits

Bird Banding Laboratory
Office of Migratory Bird Management
U.S. Fish and Wildlife Service
Laurel, MD 20810

Office of Management Authority
U.S. Fish and Wildlife Service
P.O. Box 27329, Central Station
Washington, DC 20038-7329

Office of Protected Species and Habitat
    Conservation
National Marine Fisheries Service
U.S. Dept. of Commerce
Washington, DC 20235

Assistant Administrator for Fisheries
Attn: Marine Mammals and Endangered
    Species Division
National Marine Fisheries Service
U.S. Dept. of Commerce
Washington, DC 20235

National Marine Mammal Laboratory
National Marine Fisheries Service
7600 Sand Point Way, NE
Seattle, WA 98115

The Department of Agriculture
Animal Care Staff
APHIS, USDA
765 Federal Building
Hyattsville, MD 20782

Import-Export Operations Staff
Veterinary Services
APHIS, USDA
Federal Building
6505 Belcrest Rd.
Hyattsville, MD 20782

Chief Bacterial Zoonoses Branch
Bacterial Diseases Division
Bureau of Epidemiology
Centers for Disease Control
Atlanta, GA 30333

Center for Prevention Services
Division of Quarantine
Attn: Director
Centers for Disease Control
Atlanta, GA 30333

Director, Centers for Disease Control
Public Health Service
Dept. of Health and Human Services
Atlanta, GA 30333

Special Agent-In-Charge

Region 1
California, Nevada, Oregon, Hawaii, Idaho, Washington
847 NE 19th Ave.
Suite 225
Portland, OR 97232
(503) 231-6125

Region 2
Arizona, New Mexico, Oklahoma, Texas
P.O. Box 329
Albuquerque, NM 87103
(505) 767-2091

Region 3
Illinois, Indiana, Iowa, Michigan, Minnesota, Missouri, Ohio, Wisconsin
P.O. Box 45
Twin Cities, MN 55111
(612) 725-3530

Region 4
Alabama, Arkansas, Florida, Georgia, Kentucky, Louisiana, Mississippi, North Carolina, Puerto Rico, South Carolina, Tennessee
P.O. Box 4839
Atlanta, GA 30302
(404) 331-3555

Region 5
Connecticut, District of Columbia, Delaware, Maine, Maryland, Massachusetts, New Hampshire, New Jersey, New York, Pennsylvania, Rhode Island, Vermont, Virginia, West Virginia
P.O. Box 129 New Town Branch
Boston, MA 02258
(617) 965-2298

Region 6
Colorado, Kansas, Montana, Nebraska, North Dakota, South Dakota, Utah, Wyoming
P.O. Box 25486
Denver Federal Center
Denver, CO 80225
(303) 236-7540

Region 7
Alaska
P.O. Box 4-2597
Anchorage, AK 99509
(907) 786-3311

Offices Involved with State Regulation of Wildlife

List of State Conservation Agencies

Director
Division of Game and Fish
Department of Conservation & Natural
    Resources
64 N. Union Street
Montgomery, AL 36130
(205) 832-6300

Commissioner
Department of Fish & Game
P.O. 3-2000
Juneau, AK 99802
(907) 465-4190 (Mammals/Birds)

Director
Game & Fish Department
Nongame Branch
2222 West Greenway Road
Phoenix, AZ 85023
(602) 942-3000 (ext. 245)

Director
Department of Fish & Game
#2 Natural Resources Drive
Little Rock, AR 72205
(501) 223-6300

Director
Department of Fish & Game
1416 Ninth Street
Sacramento, CA 95814
(916) 445-3531

Director
Division of Wildlife
6060 Broadway
Denver, CO 80216
(303) 825-1192

Deputy Commissioner
Department of Environmental Protection
Preservation & Conservation Division
State Office Building
165 Capitol Building
Hartford, CT 06106
(203) 566-4522

Director
Division of Fish and Wildlife
Richardson and Robbins Building
P.O. Box 1401
Dover, DE 19903
(302) 736-5295

Director
Game & Fresh Water Fish Commission
620 South Meridian
Tallahassee, FL 32301
(904) 488-1960

Director
Department of Natural Resources
Game & Fish Division
270 Washington Street, S.W.
Atlanta, GA 30334
(404) 656-3523

Director
Division of Fish and Game
Department of Land & Natural Resources
1151 Punchbowl Street
Honolulu, HI 96813
(808) 548-4002 (Fish & Aquatic Mammals)
(808) 548-2861 (Birds/Terrestrial Wildlife)

Director
Fish and Game Department
600 South Walnut Street
P.O. Box 25
Boise, ID 83707
(208) 334-2920

Director
Department of Conservation
524 South Second Street
Springfield, IL 62706
(217) 782-6302

Director
Division of Fish & Wildlife
Department of Natural Resources
607 State Office Building
Indianapolis, IN 46204
(317) 232-4080

Director
State Conservation Commission
Wallace State Office Building
300 Fourth Street
Des Moines, IA 50319-0034
(515) 281-5145

Director
Fish & Game Commission
R.R. 2, Box 54A
Pratt, KS 67124
(316) 672-5911

Commission
Department of Fish & Wildlife Resources
Capitol Plaza Tower
Frankfort, KY 40601
(502) 564-3400

Director
Department of Wildlife & Fisheries
Ecological Studies Section
P.O. Box 15570
Baton Rouge, LA 70895
(504) 342-9274

Commissioner
Dept. of Inland Fisheries and Wildlife
284 State Street
Augusta, ME 04333
(207) 289-2766

Director
Department of Natural Resources
Maryland Forest, Park & Wildlife
Tawes State Office Building
Annapolis, MD 21401
(301) 269-3776

Natural Heritage and Endangered
    Species Program
Division of Fisheries & Wildlife
100 Cambridge Street
Boston, MA 02202
(617) 727-3151

Director
Department of Natural Resources
Wildlife Division, Permit Specialist
Box 30028
Lansing, MI 48909
(517) 373-1263

Commission
Department of Natural Resources
Box 20, 500 Lafayette Road
St. Paul, MN 55146
(612) 296-0598

Director of Wildlife Conservation
Game & Fish Commission
Southport Mall, P.O. Box 451
Jackson, MS 39205
(601) 961-5311

Director
Department of Conservation
P.O. Box 180
Jefferson City, MO 65102
(314) 751-4115

Director
Fish and Game Department
1420 East Sixth
Helena, MT 59601
(406) 444-2452

Director
Game & Parks Commission
2200 N. 33rd St.
P.O. Box 30370
Lincoln, NB 68503
(402) 464-0641

Director
Department of Wildlife
Box 10678
Reno, NV 89520
(702) 789-0500

Director
Fish and Game Department
34 Bridge Street
Concord, NH 03301
(603) 271-3421

Director
Division of Fish, Game, and Wildlife
CN 400
Trenton, NJ 08625
(609) 292-9400

Director
Department of Game & Fish
Villagra Building
Santa Fe, NM 87503
(505) 827-7899

Director
Division of Fish & Wildlife
Dept. of Environmental Conservation
50 Wolf Road
Albany, NY 12233
(518) 457-3400

Executive Director
Wildlife Resources Commission
Archdale Building
512 N. Salisbury Street
Raleigh, NC 27611
(919) 733-3391

Commissioner
Game and Fish Department
2121 Lovett Avenue
Bismarck, ND 58505
(701) 224-2180

Director
Department of Natural Resources
Fountain Square D-3
Columbus, Ohio 43224
(614) 265-6877

Director
Department of Wildlife Conservation
1801 N. Lincoln
P.O. Box 53465
Oklahoma City, OK 73152
(405) 521-3851

Director
Fish & Wildlife Department
P.O. Box 59
Portland, OR 97207
(503) 229-5551

Executive Director
Fish Commission
P.O. Box 1673
Harrisburg, PA 17105
(717) 657-4515

Chief
Division of Fish and Wildlife
Government Center
Wakefield, RI 02879
(401) 789-3094

Executive Director
Wildlife and Marine Resources
Bldg. D, Dutch Plaza
P.O. Box 167
Columbia, SC 29202
(803) 758-0015

Secretary
Department of Game, Fish & Parks
Sigurd Anderson Building
Pierre, SD 57501
(605) 773-3387

Chief of Law Enforcement
Wildlife Resources Agency
Ellington Agricultural Center
P.O. Box 40747
Nashville, TN 37204
(615) 360-0581

Executive Director
Parks & Wildlife Department
4200 Smith School Road
Austin, TX 78744
(512) 389-4864

Director
Division of Wildlife Resources
Department of Natural Resources
1596 West North Temple
Salt Lake City, UT 84116
(801) 533-9333

Commissioner
Fish and Game Department
State Office Building
Montpelier, VT 05602
(802) 828-3371

Executive Director
Commission of Game & Inland Fisheries
4010 W. Broad Street
P.O. Box 11104
Richmond, VA 23230
(804) 257-1000

Director
Department of Game
600 North Capitol Way
Olympia, WA 98504
(206) 753-5728

Director
Department of Natural Resources
1800 Washington Street, East
Charleston, WV 25305
(304) 348-2754

Secretary
Department of Natural Resources
Box 7921
Madison, WI 53707
(608) 226-2621

Director
Game & Fish Division
Cheyenne, WY 82002
(307) 777-7632

Chief
Aquatic & Wildlife Resources
Agana, Guam 96910
011-671-734-3941

Secretary
Department of Natural Resources
P.O. Box 5887
San Juan, PR 00906
(809) 722-1429

Governor of American Samoa
Pago Pago, Tutuila
American Samoa 96799

Commissioner
Department of Conservation and
    Cultural Affairs
P.O. Box 4340
Charlotte Amalie
St. Thomas, VI 00801

For a copy of "State Lists of Endangered and Threatened Species of Reptiles and Amphibians and Laws and Regulations Covering Collecting of Reptiles and Amphibians in Each State," contact:

William B. Allen, Jr.
Supervisor of Reptiles and Amphibians
The Pittsburgh Zoo
Pittsburgh, PA 15206

DEA Divisional Domestic Field Offices

Location	Jurisdiction
Atlanta Division Richard B. Russell, FB 75 Spring St., S.W., Rm. 740 Atlanta, Georgia 30303 (404) 221-4401	Georgia North Carolina South Carolina
Boston Division G-64 JFK Federal Building Boston, Massachusetts 02203 (617) 223-4730	Maine Massachusetts New Hampshire Rhode Island Vermont
Chicago Division 219 South Dearborn Street Suite 500 Dirksen Federal Building Chicago, Illinois 60604 (312) 353-7889	Minnesota North Dakota Northern Illinois Wisconsin
Cleveland Resident Office 601 Rockwell Room 300 Cleveland, Ohio 44114 (216) 522-3705	Kentucky Ohio

Dallas Division
1880 Regal Row
Dallas, Texas 75235
(214) 767-7250

Oklahoma
Northern Texas

Denver Division
U.S. Custom House
Room 316
P.O. Box 1860
Denver, Colorado 80201
(303) 844-3951

Colorado
New Mexico
Utah
Wyoming

Detroit Division
231 W. Lafayette
Room 357
Detroit, Michigan 48226
(313) 226-7290

Michigan

Hartford Resident Office
450 Main Street
Room 628-E
Hartford, Connecticut 06103
(203) 244-3230

Connecticut

Houston Division
333 W. Loop North
Suite 300
Houston, Texas 77027
(713) 229-2950

Southern Texas

Indianapolis Resident Office
575 N. Pennsylvania
Room 290
Indianapolis, Indiana 46204
(317) 269-7977

Indiana

Kansas City Resident Office
812 N. Seventh Street
Room 206
Kansas City, Kansas 64106
(913) 236-3974

Kansas
Nebraska
South Dakota
Western Missouri

Los Angeles Division
350 South Figueroa Street
Suite 800
Los Angeles, California 90071
(213) 688-4016

Hawaii
Southern California
Southern Nevada

Miami Division
8400 N.W. 53rd Street
Miami, Florida 33166
(305) 591-4980

Florida

Nashville Resident Office Estes Kefauver Building, A929 F.B.-USCH 801 Broadway Nashville, Tennessee 37203 (615) 251-5988	Tennessee
New Orleans Division 1661 Canal Street Suite 2200 New Orleans, Louisiana 70112 (504) 589-2171	Alabama Arkansas Louisiana Mississippi
Newark Division Federal Office Building 970 Broad Street Newark, New Jersey 07101 (201) 645-5940	New Jersey
New York Division 555 W. 57th Street New York, New York 10019 (212) 399-5018	New York
Philadelphia Division William J. Green Federal Building 600 Arch Street Room 10224 Philadelphia, Pennsylvania 19106 (215) 597-9540	Delaware Eastern Pennsylvania
Phoenix Division 1 North First Street Suite 201 Phoenix, Arizona 85004 (602) 261-4866	Arizona
Pittsburgh Resident Office 2306 Federal Building 1000 Liberty Avenue Pittsburgh, Pennsylvania 15222 (412) 644-3390	Western Pennsylvania
San Francisco Division 450 Golden Gate Avenue Room 12215 San Francisco, California 94102 (415) 556-3325	Northern California Northern Nevada

San Juan District Office   Puerto Rico
Housing Investment Building
Suite 514
416 Ponce de Leon Avenue
Hato Rey, Puerto Rico 00918
(809) 754-6450

Seattle Division   Alaska
220 W. Mercer   Idaho
Suite 301   Montana
Seattle, Washington 98119   Oregon
(206) 442-5990   Washington

St. Louis Division   Eastern Missouri
Chromalloy Plaza, Suite 200   Iowa
120 South Central Avenue   Southern Illinois
St. Louis, Missouri 63105
(314) 425-3264

Washington Division   District of Columbia
400 Sixth Street, S.W.   Maryland
Washington, D.C. 20024   Virginia
(202) 724-7834   West Virginia

Medical Abbreviations

I. PHARMACEUTICAL TERMS

A. Prescription Writing & Medical Records

od, sid	once daily
bid	twice daily
tid	thrice daily
qid	four times daily
h	hour
qh, oh	every hour
q 2 hr	every 2 hours
q 6 hr	every 6 hours
q.d.	every day
q.o.d.	every other day
I.V.	intravenous
I.M.	intramuscular
I.P.	intraperitoneal
I.C.	intracardial
S.C., S.Q.	subcutaneous
per os	peroral, by mouth, orally
O., os	orally, per os
per r	per rectum, rectally
p.r.n.	as needed, repeat as needed
q.s.	quantity sufficient, as needed
q.n.s.	quantity not sufficient
n.r.	do not repeat, non-renewable
s.o.s.	if necessary
ac	before meals
pc	after meals
$\bar{a}$	before
$\bar{p}$	after
$\bar{c}$	with
$\bar{s}$	without
$\bar{o}$	no, none
$\overline{ss}$	half
$\overline{aa}$	of each
No., #	number
amt	amount
vol.	volume
sol.	solution
tab., tabs	tablet, tablets
caps	capsules
ung.	ointment
Tr, Ti.	tincture
gtt.	drop
cc	cubic centimeter
ml	milliliter
tsp	teaspoon
tbsp	tablespoon
ʒ	dram
℥	ounce
lb, #	pound
O.	pint
qt.	quart
C.	gallon

Rx	take thou of
eq. pts.	equal parts
Sig.	directions, instructions
ad. lib.	freely, as wanted

B. Physical Terms, Weights, Measures

C	Centigrade
F.	Fahrenheit
gtt.	drop
cc	cubic centimeter
ʒ	dram
℥	ounce
m	minim
tsp	teaspoon
tbsp	tablespoon
O.	pint
qt.	quart
C.	gallon
%	percent
lb.,#	pound
mol wt	molecular weight
ppm	parts per million
rpm	revolutions per minute
w/w	weight in weight
w/v	weight by volume
min.	minutes
sec.	seconds
liq.	liquid
ht	height
wt	weight

C. Metric Weights and Measures

km	kilometer
m	meter
cm	centimeter
mm	millimeter
mu	millimicron
u	micron (1/1000 mm)
ml	milliliter
L	liter
ma	milliampere
mgq	microvolt
kg	kilogram
gm, Gm	gram
mg	milligram
mcg	microgram
mg %	milligrams percent
mol	molar, molecular
mol wt	molecular weight
kv	kilovolt
kw	kilowatt

D. **Minerals, Elements, Compounds**

1. **Essential & Trace Minerals**

Ca	Calcium
P	Phosphorus
Fe	Iron
Na	Sodium
K	Potassium
Mg	Magnesium
Mn	Manganese
S	Sulfur
Co	Cobalt
Cu	Copper
Zn	Zinc
Cr	Chromium
Se	Selenium
Mo	Molybdenum

2. **Other Minerals & Heavy Metals**

Ag	Silver
Al	Aluminum
As	Arsenic
Au	Gold
Ba	Barium
Bi	Bismuth
Hg	Mercury
Li	Lithium
Ni	Nickel
Pb	Lead
Pt	Platinum
Ra	Radium
Si	Silicon
Sn	Tin
Sr	Strontium
Ta	Tantalum
Th	Thorium
Ti	Titanium
Tl	Thallium
U	Uranium
V	Vanadium
W	Tungsten
Zr	Zirconium

3. **Essential Elements**

N	Nitrogen
O_2	Oxygen
H	Hydrogen
Br	Bromine
Cl	Chlorine
F	Fluorine
I	Iodine
HOH	Water
CO_2	Carbon Dioxide
C	Carbon

4. **Other important Natural Elements & Compounds**

HOH, H_2O	Water
H_2O_2	Hydrogen Peroxide
N_2O	Nitrous Oxide
$C\tilde{O}_2$	Carbon Dioxide
CO	Carbon Monoxide
SO_2	Sulfur Dioxide
Oz	Ozone
ETOH	Alcohol
He	Helium
NaCl	Sodium Chloride
KI	Potassium Iodide
$CuSo_4$	Copper Sulfate

E. **Vitamins**

A	Vit. A. Palmitate	
B_1	thiamine hydrochloride	
$B_2(G)$		riboflavin
$B_3 B_4 B_5$		(Not named)
B_6		pyridoxine hydrochloride
B_{12}		cyanocobalamin
C		ascorbic acid
D		irradiated ergosterol
D_2		calciferol
D_3		dehydrocholesterol
E		d-alpha tocopherol
K		menadione
LTF		lipotrophic factor
CH		choline
Bio.		biotin
FA		folic acid
In.		inositol
NA		niacin (niacinamide)
PPF		pellagra preventing factor
Pan.		pantothenic acid
PABA		para-aminobenzoic acid

F. **Antibiotics**

Amp.	Ampicillin
CHPC	Chloramphenicol
Eryth.	Erythromycin
Kan.	Kanamycin
Lin.	Lincomycin
Neo.	Neomycin
Pen.	Penicillin
Strep.	Streptomycin
Pen/Strep	Penicillin & Streptomycin
TC	Tetracycline

G. **Other Drugs & Medicines**

AA	amino acids
ACTH	adrenocorticotropic hormone
AT	atropine
BaCl	barium chloride
CGG	canine gamma globulin
CaGlu	calcium gluconate
CGH	chorionic gonadotrophic hormone

CS	corticosteroid
DES	diethylstilbesterol
Dex	dextrose
D/S	dextrose & saline
DMSO	dimethysulfoxide
DNA	desoxyribonucleic acid
EDTA	ethylenediamne triacetate
ETOH	alcohol, ethanol
FA	folic acid
FSH	follicle stimulating hormone
G	glucose
LH	leuteinizing hormone
LTF	lipotrophic factor
PI	proinsulin, protamine insulin
Pro	protein
PSS	physiological saline sol.
PZI	protamine zinc insulin
RaCo	radioactive cobalt
RaI	radioactive iodine
RNA	ribonucleic acid
TAT	tetanus antitoxin
TT	tetanus toxoid
TSH	thyroid stimulating hormone

H. Poisons

ANTU	alphanaphthylthiourea
As	arsenic
Cl	chlorine
CO	carbon monoxide
$CuSo_4$	copper sulfate
ClHC	chlorinated hydrocarbons (DDT, Chlordane, BHC, Dieldrin etc.)
F	fluorine
Hg	mercury
I	iodine
K	potassium
KI	potassium iodide
LSD	d-lysergic acid diethylamide
NaCl	salt, sodium chloride
NO_2	nitrites
NO_3	nitrates
2-4-d	one of group of nitrate p.
O.P., Org. P	Organic Phosphate poisons (parathion, TEPP, Co-ral, etc.)
P	phosphorus
Pb	lead
Ra	radium
S	sulfur
SO_2	sulfur dioxide
Se	selenium
Stry.	strychnine
Tl	thallium
Thi.	thiabendazole
1080	sodium fluoracetate

| War. | warfarin |
| r,X-Ray | roentgen |

II. MEDICAL–CLINICAL TERMINOLOGY

A-1 General Terms

AT	additional terms
B&A	bright and alert
cath.	catheterize, catheter
chg	charge
CM	complications
DOA	dead on arrival
deh	dehydrated, dehydration
DC	discontinue
DX	diagnosis, diagnostic
E & D	Euthanasia and Disposal
ET	etiology
emac.	emaciated
FD_{50}	median fatal dose
Fl. Th.	fluid therapy
FUO	fever of undetermined origin
Fx	fracture
GIU	Gastrointestinal upset
Gyn	gynecological
HBC	hit by car
HBS	harsh bronchial sounds
H/O	history of
hosp.	hospital, hospitalize
hyd.	hydrated
IC	intensive care
Inj.	injection
Lab.	laboratory, lab. data
(L)	left
LD_{50}	Median lethal dose
(LR)	left to right
LR	left rear
lg	large
med.	medium
Med.	medicine, medication
MLD	minimum lethal dose
neg	negative
No., #	number
NSF	no significant findings
NR	not remarkable
NPO	nothing per os
N&V	nausea and vomiting
OB	obstetrics
obj.	object, objective
$\bar{o}$	no, none
OR	operating room
palp.	palpate, palpated
path.	pathology, pathological

P	pulse
p	after
prog.	prognosis, progress
pos.	positive, position
P.D.Q.	pretty darned quick
Pd,pd	paid
pt	patient
per os	by mouth
PE	physical examination
PO, post op	postoperative
PRT	Pulse – Resp – Temp
preop	preoperative
prof.	professional
per r	per rectum, rectally
R	Respiration
(R)	Right
(RL)	right to left
R/O	rule out
RR	right rear
Rx	therapeutic, med. given or dispensed
SG	signs, physical signs
sm.	small
SP, S.prep.	surgical prep.
S&W	soap and water
stat.	immediately
S/P	status post
superf.	superficial
T	Temperature
"TLC"	tender loving care
thru, via	through, by way of
V & D	Vomiting and diarrhea
Xr, X-ray	X-ray, radiograph

A-2 Other Symbols

@	at rate of
&	and
/	per
/or	and or
#	number
♂	male
♀	female
↑	increased
>	greater than normal / increase
<	less than normal / decreased
⇒	shows, implies
↓	decreased
Rx	dispensed, dispense, medicine given
Dx	diagnosis, diagnostic of
Fx	fracture
X	multiplied by
H/O	history of
N/C, No. Chg	no charge
R/O	rule out

$\overline{o}$	none
p	after
qd	every day
S/P	status postoperative
(R)	right
(L)	left
U/A	urine analysis
F/A	fecal analysis

B. Anatomical Terms

abd.	abdominal
ant.	anterior
A&P	anterior and posterior
caud.	caudal
ceph.	cephalic
cerv.	cervical
CNS	central nervous system
conj.	conjunctiva
CV	cardiovascular
CVS	cardiovascular system
dist.	distal
dor.	dorsal
ENT	ears, nose and throat
EENT	eyes, ears, nose and throat
GB	gall bladder
GI	gastrointestinal
GU	genitourinary
H/L	heart/lungs
IVD	intervertebral disc
int.	intestines
LN	lymph node
med.	medial
MM	mucous membrane
ophth.	ophthalmic
PA	pulmonary artery
prox.	proximal
PS	pulmonary system
post.	posterior
RES	reticuloendothelial system
thor.	thoracic
vent.	ventral
RFL	right forelimb
LFL	left forelimb
RRL	right rear limb
LRL	left rear limb
C_1 to C_7	cervical vertebrae
T_1 to T_{13}	thoracic vertebrae
L_1 to L_7	lumbar vertebrae
Cr_1 to Cr_{11}	cranial nerves

C. Physiological Terms

AN	anemic
app	appetite
BM	bowel movement
BMR	basal metabolic rate

BP	blood pressure	
CR	conditioned reflex	
CVP	central venous pressure	
Emac.	emaciated	
GW	generalized weakness	
HR	heart rate	
N&V	nausea and vomiting	
PR	pulse rate	
PTD	permanent total disability	
RR	respiratory rate	
SOB	shortness of breath	
T	body temperature	
TPR	temperature, pulse, respiration	
U	urine, urinations	
VS	vital signs	

D. Neurological Terms

ANS	autonomic nervous system
CDE	canine distemper encephalitis
Enc.	encephalitis
CNS	central nervous system
CR	conditioned reflex
CN	cranial nerves
IVD	intervertebral disc
IVDS	intervertebral disc syndrome
LMN	lower motor neuron
PNS	peripheral nerves
SNS	sympathetic nervous system
UMN	upper motor neuron
VS	vasomotor

E. Surgical Terms

AR	artificial respiration
BWR	bite wound repair
cast.	castration
cath.	catheter, catheterize
Cor. S.	corrective surgery
CS,C-Sect.	Cesarean section
Dr.	drain, drainage
Dr. T.	drain tube
neut.	neuter, neutered
OHE	ovariohysterectomy, spay
mast.	mastectomy
Orth. S.	orthopedic surgery
OR	operating room
pat.lux.	patellar luxation
PO, post op	postoperative
PPB	positive pressure breathing
Preop	preoperative
PU	perineal urethrostomy
RACL	ruptured anterior cruciate ligament
SR	surgical repair
tons.	tonsillectomy
EA, Exc. arth.	excision arthroplasty

F. Dental Terms

al. peri.	alveolar periostitis
cal.	calculus
cav.	cavitron
D. pro.	dental prophylaxis
ext.	extractions
Inc.	incisor teeth
Mol.	molar teeth
Perio D.	periodontal disease
Pre M.	premolar teeth
R.C.	root canal
tar.	tartar
USProf.	ultra sound prophylaxis

G. Cardiovascular Terms

A-Fib	atrial fibrillation
BP	blood pressure
BV	blood volume
CHF	congestive heart failure
CI	cardiac insufficiency
CV	cardiovascular
CVP	central venous pressure
ECG	electrocardiogram
RHF	right heart failure
HOCM	hypertrophic obstructive cardiomyopathy
HR	heart rate
HWD	heart worm disease
LHF	left heart failure
MI	mitral insufficiency
PAP	pulmonary artery pressure
PAT	paroxysmal auricular tachycardia
PRAA	persistent right aortic arch
PDA	patent ductus arteriosus
PS	pulmonic stenosis
TI	tricuspid insufficiency
VHD	valvular heart disease
VR	venous return
VSD	ventral septal defect
V-tach.	ventricular tachycardia
VW	vessel wall

H. Urogenital Terms

ARF	acute renal failure
cast.	castration,castrated
CGN	chronic glomerular nephritis
CIN	chronic interstitial nephritis
CRF	chronic renal failure
cyst.	cystitis
GU	genitourinary
met.	metritis
neph.	nephritis

OHE	ovariohysterectomy
prost.	prostate, prostatitis
PU	perineal urethrostomy
pyom.	pyometritis, pyometra
RC	retention catheter
UTI	urinary tract infection
UO	urethral obstruction
vag.	vaginitis

I. **Orthopedic Terms**

CJ, carp.j.	carpal joint
CFJ	coxofemoral joint
EA	excision arthroplasty
fem.	femur
F	fracture
HD	hip dysplasia
CHD	canine hip dysplasia
HOD	hypertrophic osteodystrophy
HPO	hypertrophic pulmonary osteoarthropathy
hum.	humerus
IVD	intervertebral disc
N-UFx	nonunion fracture
pat.	patella
pat. J.	patellar joint
pel.	pelvis
PP	plaster of paris, cast, splint
OCD	osteochondritis dissecans
rad.	radius
R/U	radius/ulna
ROM	range of motion
sh. j.	shoulder joint
tib.	tibia
T/F	tibia/fibula
UAP	ununited anconeal process
ul.	ulna
RFL	right forelimb
LFL	left forelimb
RRL	right rear limb
LRL	left rear limb

J. **Ophthalmic Terms**

AC	acute conjunctivitis
CC	chronic conjunctivitis
conj.	conjunctivitis
DR	detached retina
ERG	electroretinogram
glau.	glaucoma
KCS	keratoconjunctivitis sicca
Ker.	keratitis
O.D.	right eye
O.O.	ophthalmic ointment
O.S.	left eye
O.U.	both eyes

K. **Animal Species Abbreviations**

Amp.	amphibian
Av.	avian
Bov.	bovine
Can.	canine
Cap.	caprine
Eq.	equine
Fel.	feline
Mar.	marsupial
Ov.	ovine
Prim.	primate
Rep.	reptile
Rac.	raccoon
Rod.	rodent

III. **PATHOLOGICAL AND RELATED TERMS**

A. **Disease Terms**

AGN	acute glomerular nephritis
AIHA	autoimmune hemolytic anemia
an.	anemia
ARD	acute respiratory disease
ARF	acute renal failure
arth.	arthritis
CA	cancer
CD	canine distemper
CDE	canine distemper encephalitis
CGN	chronic glomerulonephritis
CH	canine hepatitis
CHD	coronary heart disease, canine hip dysplasia
CHF	congestive heart failure
CND	central nervous disorder
CIN	chronic interstitial nephritis
cocci.	coccidioidomycosis (valley fever)
conj.	conjunctivitis
CRD	chronic respiratory disease
CRF	chronic renal failure
CUC	chronic ulcerative colitis
CVD	cardiovascular disease
DM	diabetes mellitus
emac.	emaciated
FB	foreign body
FD	feline distemper
FP	feline panleukopenia
FPL	feline pneumonitis
FVR	feline viral rhinotracheitis
GE	gastroenteritis
GI	gastrointestinal
GYN	gynecology
HGE	hemorrhagic gastroenteritis
histo.	histoplasmosis
HWD	heart worm disease

ICH	infectious canine hepatitis	EKG, ECG	electrocardiogram
IFP	infectious feline peritonitis	EEG	electroencephalogram
IVD	intervertebral disc disease	FA	fecal analysis
ker.	keratitis	FC	fecal culture
KCS	keratoconjunctivitis sicca	FF	fecal flotation
lepto.	leptospirosis	Glu.	glucose
LSA	lymphosarcoma	Hgb, Hb	hemoglobin
mast.	mastitis; mass cell tumor	HC,HTC	hematocrit
MEI	middle ear infection	IVP	intravenous pyelogram
MLV	modified live virus	LFT	liver function test
MI	myocardial infarction	lab.	laboratory
met.	metritis	neg.	negative
PE	pulmonary embolism	O&P	ova & parasites
PPLO	pleuropneumonia-like organism	PB-Fe	protein-bound iron
pyo.	pyogenic	PB-I	protein-bound iodine
pyom.	pyometra	PCV	packed cell volume
OM	osteomalacia	pH	hydrogen ion concentration
osteo.	osteoarthritis	PL	phospholipid
spond.	spondylitis, spondylosis	PMN	polymorphonuclear leucocytes
T.B.	tuberculosis	prot.	protein
tet.	tetanus	PT	prothrombin time
ton.	tonsillitis	pos.	positive
toxo.	toxoplasmosis	r	roentgen
URI	upper respiratory infection	P.E.	physical examination
U/O	urethral obstruction	RBC	red blood cell count
UTI	urinary tract infection	SC	skin scraping
VD	venereal disease	spec.	specimen
VG	venereal granuloma	SD	standard deviation
VHD	valvular heart disease	SMA12	12 blood chemistries
vag.	vaginitis	SR, sed.rate	sedimentation rate
		SGOT	serum glutamic oxaloacetic transaminase
		SGPT	serum glutamic pyruvic transaminase

B. **Vaccinations and Immunizations**

CD	canine distemper vaccine	SHBD	serum hydroxybutyric acid dehydrogenase
CGG	canine gamma globulin (antiserum)	sp.gr.	specific gravity
CH	canine hepatitis vaccine	TL	total lipids
DHL	canine distemper-hepatitis-	TP	total protein
	leptospirosis vaccine	tr.	trace
DHL-T	canine distemper-hepatitis-leptospirosis-	UA	urine analysis
	tracheobronchitis vaccine	UB	urobilinogen
FD	feline distemper vaccine	UC	urine culture
FP	feline pneumonitis vaccine	UGI	upper gastrointestinal series
FVR	feline viral rhinotracheitis vaccine	UU	urine urobilinogen
Lepto	leptospirosis vaccine	WBC	white blood cell count
M-V, M-D	measles vaccine, measles-distemper vaccine	WNL	within normal limits
RV	rabies vaccine	X-ray	radiograph

C. **Laboratory Terms and Tests**

Alka-Tase	alkaline phosphatase
bili.	bilirubin
BUN	blood urea nitrogen
CBC	complete blood count
CSF	cerebrospinal fluid
CVP	central venous pressure
Diff.	differential leucocyte count
C & S	culture and sensitivity

AVMA Guidelines for Supervising Use and Distribution of Veterinary Prescription Drugs

In an effort to assist practicing veterinarians who supervise the use and distribution of veterinary prescription drugs and over-the-counter drugs that, for clinical effectiveness, must be used in an extra-label manner, the Council on Biologic and Therapeutic Agents has developed the following guidelines. The guidelines were approved by the 1988 House of Delegates and are being published in a pull-out section that may be retained by the practitioner for easy reference.

The guidelines were designed to heighten the practitioner's level of awareness on the subject and to promote appropriate animal drug use by practi-tioners as well as animal owners. The Council emphasizes that the guidelines must not be interpreted as hard and fast rules. Each practitioner must exercise sound clinical judgment as well as common sense when making decisions regarding the use of therapeutic agents, regardless of whether the drugs in question actually are being used or dispensed by the practitioner, or whether they are dispensed on the order of the veterinarian and used by the animal owner or his agent.

The Council acknowledges the extensive efforts of Dr. Jack Morse, Turlock, California, who as a member of the Council, was a principal author of these guidelines.

Fred W. Scott, Chairman
Council on Biologic and
Therapeutic Agents

INTRODUCTION

Society is pressing for changes in the way animal drugs are distributed and used, because consumers are concerned that meat, milk, and eggs may contain harmful drug residues. Although food animal products of US origin are among the most wholesome and safe in the world, the perception of hazardous residues still exists in the minds of consumers because contaminants are occasionally detected.

Unless the livestock industry, the pharmaceutical industry, drug distributors, and the veterinary profession work together to eliminate harmful residues, the possibility exists that, eventually, few drugs will be available for use in food animals. Despite health management techniques and disease prevention programs, there will always be a need for therapeutic drugs. Failure to act could result in further erosion of public confidence in the wholesomeness of food animal products.

The veterinary profession should take the leadership in assuring a supply of meat, milk, and eggs that is free of harmful residues. Veterinarians can assume this responsibility if their proper role in supervising use and distribution of drugs used in food animals is recognized and supported by regulatory agencies, livestock owners, and pharmaceutical distributors. The veterinary profession must adhere to high ethical and scientific standards to merit this support.

Nonprofessional Staff

The guidelines for supervising veterinary prescription drugs dispensed by veterinarians in private practice are designed to decrease the possibility of inadvertent inappropriate dispensing by clinic staff, and to aid the staff in carrying out the veterinarian's instructions. Methods should be devised to assure that employees comply with instructions in the veterinarian's absence. Staff members authorized to dispense drugs should be properly trained.

Because of potential confusion, veterinary prescription drugs labeled "Caution: Federal law restricts the drug to use by or on the order of a licensed veterinarian" should be segregated and identified with an easily noticed mark or sticker.

Client Relationships

Parts of these guidelines relate to the relationship between the veterinarian and the client and the client's employees. Of necessity, this relationship requires honesty, openness, and a commitment to a common cause.

Owner treatment records decrease the possibility of violative residues, and comply with the FDA guide for preserving the identity of food animals treated with drugs used in an extra-label manner.

Drug storage recommendations are made to protect children and unauthorized persons from access to potentially dangerous drugs.

The additional set of instructions for veterinary prescription drug use will provide the client with another source of reference on proper drug usage. Labels on containers may become dirty and blurred through repeated use. Suggested ways to accommodate these additional instructions are clear plastic covers for instruction inserts that can be posted in the drug room area, loose-leaf notebooks for instructions, and computer printouts or farm or ranch visit reports posted under plastic.

Veterinary Prescription Drugs

By FDA's definition, veterinary prescription drugs are those drugs restricted by federal law to use by or on the order of a licensed veterinarian. Any other drugs used in animals in a manner not in accordance with their labeling (extra-label uses) should be subjected to the same supervisory precautions that apply to veterinary prescription drugs. In this document, when the term "veterinary prescription drug" is used, the precautions noted apply to all drugs used for extra-label purposes as well as those defined by FDA to be veterinary prescription drugs.

There are vast differences among types of practices, species of animals treated, and production-management circumstances. These guidelines provide a basis for responsible professional decisions. Each veterinarian must use clinical judgment, current medical information, good sense, and high ethical standards when applying them to practice situations.

Veterinarians should be responsible for supervising use of veterinary prescription drugs that are dispensed or administered in the course of private practice, delivered to a client by drug distributors upon the veterinarian's order, or obtained from a pharmacist on the prescription of a veterinarian. For clarity, these guidelines are restated for each of the above situations.

GUIDELINES

Veterinary Prescription Drugs Dispensed or Used by Veterinarians in Private Practice

Veterinary prescription drugs should be dispensed only by or on the order of a licensed veterinarian in the presence of a valid veterinarian-client-patient relationship (VCPR).

Nonprofessional staff may dispense veterinary prescription drugs only after receiving specific instructions from a veterinarian.

Records should be maintained to show the prescription drugs that may be supplied to clients with whom a valid VCPR exists. Such records should indicate the veterinarian(s) who has the animals under his or her care. The dispensing of veterinary prescription drugs should be based on records and medical histories of animals seen or treated. The record of drugs that may be dispensed should not be changed without signed authorization of the responsible veterinarian, who should update each record no less often than on a quarterly basis. The drugs dispensed should be invoiced with the name and address of the client to provide records for follow-up evaluation, if needed.

Training for all staff should be regular and effective to assure that veterinary prescription drugs are dispensed only on the order of a veterinarian, and only when a valid VCPR exists.

Drugs labeled with the FDA precaution "for use by or on the order of a licensed veterinarian" should be stored separately from other drugs on the practice premises. These drugs should be clearly distinguishable and separated from over-the-counter drugs. They should not be openly displayed or be accessible to the public.

Proper labeling should accompany all veterinary prescription drugs dispensed.

Quantities dispensed should be no greater than needed for treatment of the animal, herd, or flock.

Clients should be advised that veterinary prescription drugs should be securely stored, with access limited to key personnel. Each client should be advised to keep a complete record of all animals treated, including identification of animal(s), drug(s) used, routes of administration, amounts used, duration of treatment, and final disposition of the animal(s), ie, date sold, returned to herd, or died. This could be in the form of a simple table or chart issued by the veterinarian.

Instructions for the use of each veterinary prescription drug dispensed should be written by the veterinarian, when applicable. These instructions should be kept in the client's drug storage area. Ideally, these instructions, the drug storage area, and the drugs themselves should be examined at least quarterly with the client, to assure cleanliness, orderliness, purity, and nonexpired dating.

Records should be kept for at least two years when veterinary prescription drugs are dispensed or used in practice.

Veterinary Prescription Drugs Delivered to Clients by Drug Distributors on the Order of a Veterinarian

Orders issued by licensed veterinarians authorizing drug distributors to deliver veterinary prescription drugs to a specific client should be based on a valid VCPR and should contain the following information:

- The veterinarian's name, address, telephone number, and license number (not DEA number)
- Name and address of client
- Species
- Name and quantity of drug(s) to be delivered
- Directions for use
- Cautionary statements including, if applicable, expiration date and withdrawal time
- Date of issue
- Number of refills
- Veterinarian's signature

Drug orders must be initiated by the veterinarian, based on dialogue with the client or his agent. Requests coming directly from drug distributors are not within the bounds of a valid VCPR.

Telephone orders require prompt completion and processing of the drug order form.

When a drug order is issued, the quantity should be limited to an appropriate usage period.

Clients should be instructed that veterinary prescription drugs should be securely stored, with access limited to key personnel. Each client should be advised to keep a complete record of all animals treated, which would include identification of animal(s), drug(s) used, route of administration, amounts used, duration of treatment, and final disposition of the animal(s), ie, date sold, returned to herd, or died.

Additional instructions for use of each veterinary prescription drug should be written by the veterinarian. These instructions should be kept in the client's drug storage area. Ideally, these instructions, the drug storage area, and the drugs themselves should be examined at least quarterly with the client, to assure cleanliness, orderliness, purity, and nonexpired dating.

Veterinarians should keep records of prescription drug orders for at least two years.

Veterinary Prescription Drugs Obtained from a Pharmacist on the Order of a Veterinarian

Prescriptions/orders issued by licensed veterinarians authorizing pharmacists to dispense veterinary prescription drugs to a specific client should be based on a valid VCPR and should contain the following information:

- The veterinarian's name, address, telephone number, and license number (not DEA number)
- Name and address of client
- Species
- Name and quantity of drug(s)
- Directions for use
- Cautionary statements including, if applicable, expiration date and withdrawal time
- Date of issue
- Number of refills
- Signature of issuer (prescriber)

The prescription/order must be initiated by the veterinarian from dialogue with the client or his agent. Requests coming directly from the pharmacist are not within the bounds of a valid VCPR.

Telephone orders require prescription/order forms identical to written orders, with identical processing.

Quantities prescribed/ordered should be limited to an appropriate usage period.

Clients should be instructed that veterinary prescription drugs dispensed by the pharmacist should be stored securely, preferably under lock, with access limited to key personnel. Each client should be advised to keep a complete record of all animals treated, which would include identification of animal(s), drug(s) used, routes of administra-

tion, amounts used, duration of treatment, and final disposition of the animal(s), ie, date sold, returned to herd, or died.

Instructions for use of each veterinary prescription drug dispensed by the pharmacist should be written by the veterinarian, when applicable. These instructions should be kept in the client's drug storage area. Ideally, these instructions, the drug storage area, and the drugs themselves should be examined at least quarterly with the client, to assure cleanliness, orderliness, purity, and nonexpired dating.

Records of prescriptions/orders should be kept for at least two years.

DEFINITIONS AND BACKGROUND

Veterinary Prescription Drugs

According to FDA, drugs that, because of toxicity or other potential for harmful effect, or because of the method of use, cannot be approved for animal use except under the supervision of a veterinarian are classified as veterinary prescription drugs. The agency requires that such drugs be labeled with the statement "Caution: Federal law restricts this drug to use by or on the order of a licensed veterinarian." Phrases such as "For Veterinary Use Only," and "Sold to Veterinarians Only" do not refer to the drug's prescription status. For purposes of these guidelines, when any other drugs are used for extra-label purposes, they should be afforded the same precautions that apply to the FDA definition of a veterinary prescription drug.

Extra-Label Use of Drugs

Extra-label use means the administration or application of a drug in a manner that is not in accordance with the drug's labeling. Extra-label use of drugs in treating food-producing animals may be considered only in special circumstances. For such usage, the FDA specifies that the following criteria must be met:

- A careful clinical diagnosis is made by an attending veterinarian within the context of a valid VCPR
- A determination is made that there is no marketed drug specifically labeled to treat the condition diagnosed, or that

treatment at the dosage recommended by the labeling has been found clinically ineffective

- Procedures are instituted to assure that identity of the treated animals is carefully maintained
- A significantly extended time period is assigned for drug withdrawal prior to marketing meat, milk, or eggs; steps are taken to assure that the assigned time frames are met; and no harmful residues occur

Certain drugs (chloramphenicol, diethylstilbestrol, and dimetridazole) may not be used in treating food-producing animals even under the cited criteria.

Veterinarian-Client-Patient Relationship

The VCPR exists when all of the following conditions have been met:

- The veterinarian has assumed the responsibility for making clinical judgments regarding the health of the animal(s) and the need for medical treatment, and the client has agreed to follow the veterinarian's instructions.
- The veterinarian has sufficient knowledge of the animal(s) to initiate at least a general or preliminary diagnosis of the medical condition of the animal(s). This means that the veterinarian has recently seen and is personally acquainted with the keeping and care of the animal(s) by virtue of an examination of the animal(s) or by medically appropriate and timely visits to the premises where the animal(s) are kept.
- The veterinarian is readily available for follow-up evaluation in the event of adverse reactions or failure of the treatment regimen.

This definition of the VCPR is of necessity broad in scope. Its general terms are intended to apply to many types of practices covering several species of animals.

Concept of a Veterinary Practice

Veterinary prescription drugs are to be used, ordered, dispensed, or prescribed by the licensed veterinarian within the course of professional practice. This means the veterinarian is licensed or otherwise properly authorized under state law to practice veterinary medicine in the state, and that a valid VCPR exists. Veterinarians who are employees of drug manufacturers or distributors, or veterinarians who operate drug distributorships cannot legally sell veterinary prescription drugs or issue prescriptions or orders for such drugs outside the scope of a professional veterinary practice.

Dispensing Labels

All veterinary prescription drugs should be properly labeled when dispensed. The label should ordinarily contain information that would appear on a veterinarian's prescription/order to a pharmacist or drug distributor (*see* page 6).

As long as the drug is properly identified, the above information may be supplied separately in writing in lieu of the dispensing label.

Veterinary Drug Orders

Orders authorizing pharmacists to dispense veterinary prescription drugs are called "prescriptions." There is no standard form for the "prescription," but information the prescription should include is specified in each state's pharmacy regulations and rules. Some states have reserved the term "prescription" as an order only a pharmacist may process. Additionally, some states have decreed that instructions to a person other than a pharmacist to dispense a veterinary prescription drug be called a "drug order."

These guidelines enumerate the information the prescription or drug order should include, based on the usual requirements of boards of pharmacy, and should be adequate for trained pharmacists. This information may not be adequate for nonprofessionals. For example, Idaho has special requirements for dispensers who are not pharmacists or veterinarians.

For any state without stringent qualifications for the nonprofessional processor of the veterinarian's order, a detailed order would be indicated. The veterinarian would retain the third copy, and the drug distributor the original, while the second copy would accompany the drugs delivered to the client.

The drug order should be designed to provide the following information:

Name and address of the client and evidence that the client understands and will follow directions given.

Name and address of the drug distributor, including evidence of the distributor's commitment that only those drugs listed at the strength and quantity noted on the order will be provided, that drugs will not be delivered after expiration of the order date, and that the drug order will be processed exactly as written by the veterinarian and no substitutions of a different brand or product will be made without consulting the issuing veterinarian.

Name and address of the issuing veterinarian, including his or her signature or other evidence that a valid VCPR exists with the client to whom the drugs are to be delivered, that written instructions on the use of the drugs have been provided to the client, and that the order may or may not be refilled and, if so, the number of refills.

The name of the drug(s) to be delivered, including the strength, unit size, and quantity. This should be a list of only those drugs to be delivered.

Written instructions on the use and withdrawal times of the drugs listed.

The date of issue and a statement that the order is void in 90 days.

Index

AAHA, *see* American Animal Hospital Association (AAHA)

Abandoned animals, 86–89
  defined, 86–87
  fees and, 88–89
  human officers and, 89
  liability and, 135
  lien laws and, 91
  medical records requirements, 333, 336
  statutory language problems, 88
  stray animals contrasted, 87–88
  veterinary hospitals/kennels, 87

Abortion, 39

Abuse of animals, *see* Cruelty to animals

Abuse of process (countersuits), 163

Acceptance:
  contracts, 193
  implied versus express contracts, 193–194
  Uniform Commercial Code, 194

Accident scenes, 97–98

Accounts receivable, 296

aging accounts, 302–303
  see also Credit management and debt collection

Action in reliance (consideration), 196–197

Addison's disease, 138

Adulterated drugs, 218

Adversary system, 11–12

Adverse drug reactions:
  consent considerations, 243–248
  drug regulation and, 235–236, 237

Advertising, 27, 185–188

Agister's laws, 90

Alcohol abuse, *see* Substance abuse

Ambiguity, 30

American Animal Hospital Association (AAHA):
  medical records, 318, 328–329
  radiology logbooks, 348
  standards of care, 141

American Arbitration Association, 23

American Association of State Veterinary Boards, 53, 55, 60, 65

American Association of Zoo Veterinarians, 408
American College of Veterinary Ophthalmologists, 177–178
American Heart Association, 63
American Horse Show Association, 248, 250
American Law Institute, 191
American National Red Cross, 63
American Veterinary Medical Association (AVMA):
   advertising, 186
   antitrust, 177
   bulk drugs, 224
   code of ethics of, 3, 27, 31, 124, 125
   domestic/wild animal classification, 73
   drug labeling, 233
   drug use, 220
   examinations, 61
   inherited defects repair, 344
   licensing, 59–60, 62
   ownership regulations, 65
   peer review, 125, 126, 127
   prepurchase examinations, 361
   specialists, 139
   standards of care, 57–58, 141
   substance abuse, 65, 282
   veterinarian-client-patient relationship, 227
   veterinary practice acts, 53
American Veterinary Medical Association Professional Liability Insurance Trust (AVMAPLIT), 131–132, 143, 232
Amputation, 36
Anesthetics:
   consent, 243, 340
   ethics, 35–36
   state board requirements, 58
Animal abuse, *see* Cruelty to animals
Animal and Plant Health Inspection Service (USDA, APHIS), 216, 400–404
   import/export, 402
   quarantine regulations, 404
Animal bites:
   liability for, 80–81

reporting requirements, 81–82
Animal confinement laws, 76–79
Animal control officers, *see* Humane officers and societies
Animal control ordinances, 85, 472–486
Animal cruelty laws, *see* Cruelty to animals
Animal custody, *see* Custody
Animal ethics, *see* Ethics
Animal fights, *see* Staged animal fights
Animal health technician (AHT):
   controlled substances, 266–267
   defined, 55, 415
   good samaritan acts, 62–63
   tasks of, 55–56
   veterinary practice acts, 51
Animal licensing requirements, 79
Animal noise, 83–84
Animal regulation departments, 97
Animal restraint, *see* Restraint
Animal rights, *see* Ownership rights; Property
Animal rights movement:
   ethics and morality, 2, 26, 35–36
   law and, 72
   veterinary profession and, 36
Animals, 72–110
   bailments, 105–107
   definitions and categories, 72–75
   domestic/wild classification of, 73–74
   emergency care/euthanasia, 107–109
   ownership limitations, 76–94
   property laws (unique), 75–76
   rights, 94–105. *See also* Ownership rights
Animal shelters, 267–268
Animal waste laws, 84–85
Animal Welfare Act, 47
   licensing regulations, 400–401
   registration regulations, 401
   wildlife permits, 400
Antibiotics, 226
Antitrust, 175–185
   covenants not to compete, 207, 209–213
   Federal Trade Commission Act, 184–185

Goldfarb v. *Virginia Bar* case, 176
    liability insurance and, 184
    licensing and, 52
    prior to 1975, 175–176
    Sherman Antitrust Act, 176–184
APHIS, *see* Animal and Plant Health
    Inspection Service (USDA, APHIS)
Appeals, 20
Appellate jurisdiction, 8–9
Appellate procedures, 21
Arbitration, 23
Aristotle, 24–25
Arrest warrant, 17
Assault and battery, 164–166
    defenses for, 165–166
    defined, 164–165
    informed consent, 338
Assumption of risk, 158–159
Atomic research, 26–27
Attachment, 313
Attorneys, 12–15
    equality in adversariness/
        competence, 12
    expert witnesses and, 287
    fees of, 14–15
    jury selection, 19
    selection of, 12–13
    specialty practice, 13
Auctions (wildlife), 406
Audit trails, 327
Auto industry, 239
AVMA, *see* American Veterinary
    Medical Association (AVMA)

Bailments:
    described, 105–107
    liability insurance coverage, 161–162
Bald Eagle Protection Act:
    described, 387–388
    permit process under, 395
Banding/marking (migratory birds), 394
Barratry, 164
Bates and O'Steen v. *State Bar of Arizona*,
    186–187
Beef Quality Assurance Program, 227
Billing fees, 299–300
Billing system, 299–302. *See also* Credit

    management and debt collection
Biologicals, 254–258
    defined, 255
    extra-label use of, 257
    packaging/labeling requirements, 256
    product efficacy concerns, 256–257
    rabies vaccine administration, 258
    testing procedures, 255
    testing products, 255–256
    veterinarian-client-patient
    relationship, 257
    Virus-Serum-Toxin Act of 1913,
        254–255
    see also Controlled substances; Drug
    categories; Drug use; Pesticides
Birds:
    importation regulations, 403
    state regulation, 407–408
    U.S. Department of Health and
    Human Services, 405–406
Bites, *see* Animal bites
Blood testing, 373
Board certification, 139
Brand name drugs, 225
Breaches of contract:
    covenants not to compete, 210
    remedies for, 200–203
Bullfighting, 64
Burden of proof, 19
Business records; *see* Documentation;
    Medical records; Record keeping

Cadavers, 98–102, 103
Canada, 403–404
Canine Eye Registration Foundation,
    177–179
Captive-bred wildlife permits, 392–393
Cardozo, Benjamin N., 236
Case headings, 9–10, 11
Case law, 1–2
CCT (examination), 60–61
Census list (hospital), 351, 355
Chafee, John H., 226
Charge (judge's to jury), 20
Chemotherapeutic drugs, 244–245,
    247–248, 249
Child abuse, 33

Chlamydia vaccine, 257
Chloramphenicol, 222
Citation (law), 9–10, 11
Citations (penalties), 68–70
CITES, *see* Convention on the
    International Trade in Endangered
    Species of Wild Fauna and Flora
    (CITES)
Civil actions and laws:
    burden of proof in, 19
    contract law versus tort law, 5–6
    course of events in, 15–17
    criminal law compared, 5
    jury selection, 19
    nolo contendere plea, 19
    settlement conferences, 18
    see also Criminal actions and law; Law
Civil rights, 39
Clayton Act, 183–184, 185
Cleary v. *American Airlines*, 170
Clients:
    ethics, 33, 34
    medical records and, 354
    see also Veterinarian-client-patient
        relationship
    see also Complaints (client); Dispute
        resolution
Closing statements (trials), 20
Cock fighting, 64
Codes of ethics, 3, 27, 31, 469–471. *See
    also* American Veterinary Medical
    Association, code of ethics of
Codes of professional conduct, 68,
    469–471
Codification systems, 9–10, 11
Colleagues:
    communications with, 123
    complaints, 120–123
    ethics, 33, 34
    medical records, 321
Collection, 332. *See also* Credit manage-
    ment
Collection agencies, 307–308
Combinations (antitrust), 180
Commissions, 136–138
Common law:

acceptance, 193
contracts, 190, 191
evidence, 285
liens, 89–90
offers, 191–193
standard form contracts, 195
Uniform Commercial Code
    contrasted, 194
unwritten law, 7
see also English common law; Law
Communication:
    colleagues, 123
    debt collection, 304–306
    drug use, 243
    product liability, 240, 241
Comparative negligence standard, 158
Compassion, 119–120
Compensatory damages:
    breaches of contract, 201
    described, 146
    see also Damages
Competency, 51, 52
Competition:
    covenants not to compete, 205–207,
        209–213
    unfair methods of, 184–185
    see also Antitrust
Complaining party, 15–16
Complaint (legal):
    civil actions, 16
    criminal actions, 17
Complaints (client), 111–123
    aggravating factors in, 120–123
    communication breakdowns, 111–117
    compassion, 119–120
    fees, 114–117
    quality/quantity of care, 117–118
    referrals, 118–119
    see also Dispute resolution
Comprehensive Drug Abuse Prevention
    and Control Act, 262–263
Comprehensive general liability policies,
    161
Computer:
    billing statements, 299
    controlled substances record keeping,
        277

security, 326
theft of records, 349
Confidentiality:
cruelty reporting requirements and, 64
ethics, 32–33
medical records, 345–346
peer review committees, 127
prepurchase examinations, 360–361
Confinement laws, 76–79
Confiscation, 401
Conflict of interest, 361
Consent:
cadaver disposal, 99–100, 103
contracts and, 90
medical records requirements, 329–333
necropsies, 100–102
prepurchase examination, 374–375
veterinary practice act violations, 67
Consequential damages, 147–148
Consideration (contracts), 195–197
Conspiracies, 180
Constitution (U.S.), *see* United States Constitution
Consultations, 320–321. *See also* Referrals
Consumer law and movement, 175
advertising, 185
contracts, 191
food chain drugs, 226
Consumer Products Safety Commission, 233
Continuing education:
drug use, 233
nonstandard treatment, 242–243
standards of care, 138
see also Veterinary education
Contracts and contract law, 190–214
acceptance in implied versus expressed contracts, 193–194
acceptance under common law, 193
antitrust, 180
breaches of contract, 200–203
capacity to contract, 197–199
consent forms and, 90

consideration, 195–197
covenants not to compete, 205–207, 209–213
credit management, 295–296
defined, 190–191
ethics, 35
intent, 194–195
medical records requirements, 329–337
meeting of the minds, 194
negligence/malpractice, 133
offer/acceptance under Uniform Commercial Code, 194
offer under common law, 191–193
parol (oral) evidence, 200
personal service contracts, 204–205, 206–207, 208, 209
quasi contracts (unjust enrichment), 203–204
remedies in equity, 7
standard form (contracts of adhesion), 195
Statute of Frauds, 199–200
termination of, 135
tort law compared, 5–6
Contracts of adhesion, 195
Contributory negligence:
defense of, 157–158
product liability defense, 241–242
Controlled substances, 262–283
classification of, 263–264
federal regulation of, 262–263
importance of regulation of, 262
inventory of, 277
ordering of, 269–273
record keeping, 273–277
registration requirements, 278–282
security requirements, 264–269
state governments, 263
substance abusing veterinarians, 282
see also Biologicals; Drug categories; Drug use; Pesticides
Controlled Substances Act, 216, 263
Convention for the Protection of Migratory Birds, 379
Convention on the International Trade

in Endangered Species of Wild Fauna
and Flora (CITES), 381–383
Endangered Species Act and, 383–384,
385
permit process under, 395–399
Counsel, *see* Attorneys
Counterclaims:
civil actions, 16
enforcement procedures, 21
small claims court, 311
Countersuits, 162–164
abuse of process, 163
barratry/defamation/emotional/
distress/invasion of privacy/prima
facie tort, 164
debt collection, 295
malicious prosecution, 162–163
negligence (plaintiff's lawyer), 163
Courts:
dispute resolution, 129–130
tort law, 6
see also Law; Judicial system
Covenants not to compete, 205–207, 209–
213
Crawford, Lester, 230
Credit management and debt collection,
294–315
aging accounts, 302–303
billing system, 299–302
client debt management, 296–299
collection agencies, 307–308
contracts, 295–296
debt avoidance techniques, 294–295
fair debt collection statutes, 304–307
in-house collection techniques, 303–
304
small claims court, 308–314
Criminal actions and laws:
assault and battery, 165
burden of proof in, 19
civil law compared, 5
course of events in, 17–18
jury selection, 19
plea bargaining, 18–19
see also Law(s)
Criminal Fines Act of 1984, 231

Cruelty to animals, 91–94
analysis of laws, 92
documentation needs, 94
ethics and, 32–34, 43–44, 45
ground rules, 93–94
humane officer and, 93
reporting requirements, 63–64, 94
samples of laws, 92
staged animal fights, 64
veterinarian involvement in, 92–93
Custody:
bailment liability insurance, 161–162
fees (unpaid), 89–91

Damages:
breaches of contract, 200–201
compensatory damages, 146
consequential damages, 147–148
general damages, 149–150
libel and slander, 168
lost use/income/profits, 148–149
nominal damages, 146
pets/heirlooms comparisons, 151–152
punitive damages, 152–154
special damages, 146–147
unique property theory of, 147
see also Fines; Penalties
Dangerous dogs, 82–83
Debt avoidance techniques, 294–295. *See
also* Credit management and debt
collection
Debt collection, *see* Credit management
and debt collection; Small claims court
Decision making, *see* Ethical decision
making; Ethics
Declawing, 34
Defamation, 164
Defamatory statement, 167
Demurrer, 17
Deposition, 18
Devocalizations, 34
Diagnosis, 319–320
Dialogue, 37–38. *See also*
Communication
Diethylstilbestrol, 221–222
Dimetridazole, 222

Dinsmore, Jack, 232
Diphrenorphine, 278, 282
Directed verdicts, 20
Director's liability insurance, 161
Direct supervision, 56
Disciplinary action, 67–68. *See also* Fines;
  Penalties
Disclosure, 143, 144
Discovery phase:
  civil actions, 16
  legal actions, 18
  pretrial motions, 18
Discretion, *see* Judicial discretion
Discrimination, 29–30
Disposal, *see* Euthanasia and disposal
Dispute resolution, 123–130
  courts of law, 129–130
  ethics committees, 124–125
  peer review committees, 125–127
  personal contact, 123–124
  state boards of examiners review,
    127–129
  see also Complaints (client)
Dockings, 34
Doctrine of proximate cause, 133
Doctrine of unconscionability, 195
Documentation:
  adverse drug reactions, 235–236, 237
  expert witnesses, 288
  medical records, 338
  see also Medical records; Record
    keeping
Dogfighting, 64
Dogs:
  livestock attacks by, 104–105
  vicious, 82–83
Domestic animals, 73–74
Drug abuse, *see* Substance abuse
Drug categories, 218–225
  adulterated drugs, 218
  extra-label drug use, 220–221
  generic versus brand name drugs, 225
  minor use drugs, 225
  misbranded drugs, 218–219
  over-the-counter drugs, 219
  prescription (legend) drugs, 219–220

prohibited in livestock, 221–223
unapproved drugs, 223–225
unrelated drugs, 218
see also Biologicals; Controlled
  substances; Drug use; Pesticides
Drug suppliers/distributors, 231–232
Drug use, 215–253
  adverse drug reactions, 235–236
  consent issues in, 243–248
  drug categories, 218–225
  Federal Drug and Cosmetic Act,
    216–218
  Food and Drug Administration
    changes, 225–229
  Food and Drug Administration
    investigations/penalties, 229–231
  horses (show and racehorses), 248,
    250–251
  labeling and packaging, 233–235
  management issues, 231–233
  nonstandard treatment rights,
    242–243
  pharmaceutical terms used in,
    499–506
  prepurchase examination, 370–373
  product liability, 236, 238–242
  regulatory system for, 215–216
  wildlife law, 408
  withdrawal guide, 467–468
  see also Biologicals; Controlled
    substances; Drug categories;
    Pesticides
Duty:
  emergency care, 134–135
  negligence, 134
  referrals, 154–156

Ear cropping, 27, 28
Education, *see* Veterinary education
Egotistical veterinarians, 122–123
Electrocardiography:
  liability, 138–139
  medical records ownership, 347–349
Emergency care:
  duty to provide, 134–135
  ethics and, 3–4

good samaritan acts, 62–63
legal requirements, 107–109
negligence, 155
strays, 96–97
Emergency clinics, 120–121
Emotional distress (countersuits), 164
Employees:
   compassion and, 119–120
   contracts, 196–197, 204–205
   controlled substances, 266–267
   covenants not to compete, 205–207,
     209–213
   debt collection, 303
   drug product liability, 240–241
   ethics, 4
   medical records identification, 350–
     351
   sample contracts, 206–207, 208, 209
   wrongful discharge, 170–172
   zoos, 408–409
Endangered species:
   international protection, 381–383
   permits, 390
Endangered Species Act (U.S.), 383–386
   international component of, 385–386
   permit process under, 391–392
Enforceability, 2–3
Enforcement:
   animal licensing requirements, 79
   described, 21
   veterinary practice acts, 66–70
   see also Fines; Penalties
English common law, 1
   adversary system, 12
   assault and battery, 164–165
   remedies in equity, 7
   see also Common law; Law
Epistemic values, 25. *See also* Ethics
Equality, 41
Equality in adversariness/competence,
   12
Equine electrocardiography, 139. *See also*
   Electrocardiography
Equity, 7
Estimates:
   credit management, 296

fees, 113–116
medical records requirements, 336–
   337
Ethical decision making:
   morally relevant differences and, 29–
     30
   rational approach to, 29
Ethics, 24–49
   adjudication, 42–45
   advertising, 185–188
   animals and, 45–48
   codes of ethics, 3. *See also* American
     Veterinary Medical Association
     (AVMA), code of ethics of
   colleague neglect, 123
   enforceability and, 2–3
   inherited defects repair, 344
   law and, 2–5, 35
   moral principles and, 38–41
   moral value judgments and, 25–26
   neglect of, 26–28
   overview of, 24–25
   principles recommended, 456–466
   rationality and, 28–31
   resolution of conflicts, 36–38
   theory and, 41–42
   valuational assumptions in, 25
   veterinary medicine and, 31–36
Ethics committees, 124–125
Etorphine hydrochloride, 278, 282
Euthansia and disposal:
   abandoned animals, 87–88
   ethics, 4, 27, 28, 35, 36
   legal requirements, 107–109
   medical records requirements, 332–
     333, 334, 335
   moral value judgements, 26
   ownership rights, 102
   U.S. Department of Agriculture, 401
   wills and trusts, 96
Evidence:
   expert witnesses, 285–287
   medical records, 323–324
   trial procedures, 20
Examination (medical records), 319
Examinations (state boards), 60–61

Exemplary damages, *see* Damages; Punitive damages
Exotic animals, 278, 282
Expert witnesses, 284–293
  appearance, 291
  attributes of, 292–293
  cadaver disposal, 99
  definitions, 284
  documentation for, 288
  duty of, 284–285
  evidence and, 285–287
  modesty and, 288
  opinion/hypothetical questions, 291–292
  payment for, 289
  preparation for, 287–288
  qualification as, 289–290
  questioning process, 290–291
  stance and, 288
  standards of care, 57, 137, 141
  types of, 285
Export, *see* Import/export
Express contracts, 193–194
Extinction, *see* Endangered species
Extra-label drug use:
  biologicals, 257
  described, 220–221
  drug residues in food, 232
  nonstandard treatments, 242–243
  pesticides, 260
  prohibition in livestock, 222
  unapproved drugs contrasted, 223
  wildlife, 408
  see also Labeling

Falconry, 395
Falconry permits, 394
False imprisonment, 166
Family, 2
Favre, D. S., 75, 136, 148
Federal courts:
  judicial system, 8, 10
  jury selection, 19
  U.S. Attorney, 17
Federal law and government:
  biologicals regulation, 254–258

CITES and, 382
controlled substance regulation, 262–263
drug regulation agencies, 215–216
household pet regulations, 74–75
veterinary practice acts, 51
wildlife, 378–379, 488
wildlife permits, 388, 489–490
see also entries under United States
Federal Insecticide, Fungicide and Rodenticide Act, 216, 258–260
Federal Trade Commission, 184–185
  licensing reciprocity, 62
  veterinary practice acts, 52
Fees:
  abandoned animals, 87, 88–89
  attorneys, 184
  complaints, 114–117
  consequential damages, 147–148
  credit management, 296–299
  estimates, 336–337
  expert witnesses, 289
  liens for, 89–91
  medical records requirements, 332
  stray animal emergency care, 97
  third-party payers and, 78–79
  veterinary ethics, 27
  wildlife permits, 390
  see also Credit management and debt collection
Felony:
  assault and battery, 165
  criminal actions, 17
Fighting, *see* Staged animal fights
Fines:
  abandoned animals, 86–87
  drug violations, 231
  penalties, 68–70
  veterinary practice act violations, 67
  wildlife law, 388
  see also Damages; Penalties
Fisheries, 380–381
Fisherman's Protective Act, 380
Fleas, 260
Flow sheet laboratory forms, 351, 352
Food animals, *see* Livestock

Food chain, 226
Food, Drug and Cosmetic Act, 215, 216–218
  inspections, 229
  penalties, 231
Food Security Act of 1985, 255
Foreign veterinary graduates, 59–60
Foreseeability, 239
Forms, *see* Medical records; Record keeping
Fowler, M. E., 408
Fur seals, 379–380

Garnishment, 21, 313–314
General damages, 149–150
Generic drugs:
  brand name drugs versus, 225
  unapproved drugs, 223–224
Genetics, *see* Inherited defects
Gentamicin, 219
Gloyd, Joe, 223, 233
Goldfarb v. *Virginia Bar*, 52, 175, 176, 180, 181, 182, 185, 209
Good samaritan laws:
  described, 62–63
  emergency care liability, 135
  strays, 96
Grand jury, 17, 18
Grievances, *see* Dispute resolution
Guest, Gerald, 223
Guilt, *see* Personal guilt

Hannah, H. W., 157, 230, 239
Health certification:
  import/export, 402–403
  U.S. Department of Agriculture, 401
Health insurance (pets), 328
Hearsay evidence, 286
Heirloom/pet comparison, 151–152
Henningsen v. *Bloomfield Motors, Inc.*, 195
Herron, T. J., 22
History (medical), 319. *See also* Medical records
Hit-and-run accidents, 97–98
Honesty, 4–5. *See also* Truth
Horse:
  drug use with, 248, 250–251

identification of, 362–363
medical records requirements, 327–328
prepurchase examinations, 359
restraint, 142, 143
see also Prepurchase examination
Hospital census list, 351, 355. *See also* Veterinary premises
Housing and Urban Development Department, *see* U.S. Department of Housing and Urban Development
Humane officers and societies:
  abandonment and, 89
  animal cruelty laws and, 93
  strays, 97
Human subjects, 32

Impartial tribunal, 11
Implied contracts:
  acceptance in, 193–194
  credit management, 295
Implied warranties, 236, 238
Import/export:
  biologicals, 255
  CITES, 395–399
  controlled substances, 263
  U.S. Department of Agriculture, 402–404
  wildlife permits, 390–391
Inconsistency, 30
Independent contractors, 267
Indictment, 17, 18
Indirect supervision, 56
Individual, 41–42
Informed consent:
  defined, 143
  drug use, 243–248
  medical records requirements, 338–344
  standards of care, 143–145
  tests for, 143–144
  veterinarians and, 144–145
  see also Consent
Inherited defects, 343, 344
Injunction, 7
Injury, 168
Insecticides, 218. *See also* Pesticides

Inspections:
  state boards, 57
  U.S. Department of Agriculture, 401
  U.S. Food and Drug Administration,
    229–230
Instructions, *see* Jury instructions
Insurance:
  consequential damages, 148
  medical records requirements,
    327–328
  payment for services by, 78–79
  pet health insurance, 328
  standards of care, 139
  see also Liability insurance
Intent, 194–195
Interest charges, 299–302
Interim Convention on the Conservation
  of North Pacific Fur Seals, 379–380
International animal rights movement,
  see Animal rights movement
International law and regulation:
  Endangered Species Act (U.S.),
    385–386
  Marine Mammal Protection Act
  (U.S.), 387
  treaties listed, 487
  wildlife, 381–383
  see also Convention on the
    International Trade in Endangered
    Species of Wild Fauna and Flora
  (CITES)
International Whaling Commission, 380
Interrogatories, 18
Interstate commerce:
  antitrust, 181
  biologicals, 255
  covenants not to compete, 209–210
  drug regulation, 217, 218–219
Intoxication, 199. *See also* Substance
  abuse
Intrastate commerce, 255
Invasion of privacy, 164
Inventory, 277

Judges:
  appellate courts, 21
  jury trials, 20

Judicial collection, 313–314
Judicial discretion, 1
Judicial system, 7–9
  courts of appellate jurisdiction, 8–9
  courts of original jurisdiction, 8
Jurisdiction:
  courts of appellate jurisdiction, 8–9
  courts of original jurisdiction, 8
  state boards of examiner, 66
  variations in, 2
Jury instructions, 20
Jury selection, 19
Jury system, 11

Kant, Immanuel, 41, 42
Karpinski v. *Ingrasci*, 210
Katz, Jay, 32
Kennels, 87. *See also* Veterinary premises

Labeling:
  biologicals, 256
  drug product liability, 241
  drug use, 233–235
  pesticides, 259, 260
  prescription drugs, 219–220
  unapproved/bulk drugs, 224
  see also Extra-label drug use
Laboratory reports:
  flow sheets, 351, 352
  medical records, 321, 347–349
Lacey Act, 378, 383
Law, 1–23
  adversary system and, 11–12
  alternative settlement methods, 21–22
  animal cruelty laws, 91–94. *See also*
    Cruelty to animals
  animals, 72–110. *See also* Animals
  attorneys, 12–15
  classification of, 5–7
  codification/citation/library system
    in, 9–10, 11
  course of events (civil action), 15–17
  course of events (criminal action),
    17–18
  course of events (end stages), 20–21
  course of events (mid stages), 18–19
  debt collection statutes, 304–307

defined, 2
enforceability of, 2–3
enforcement procedures, 21
equity compared, 7
ethics/morality and, 2–5, 35, 39
ignorance of, 50–51
judicial system and, 7–9
medical records requirements, 322–324
negligence/malpractice, 132–133
origins of, 1–2
prepurchase examination records, 369
standards of care, 141–142
trial, 19–20
unapproved drugs, 223
see also Veterinary practice acts
Lawsuits:
computer-generated records, 324–326
medical records in, 323–324
see also Liability; Malpractice;
Negligence
Lawyers, *see* Attorneys
Legal detriment, *see* Consideration
Legend drugs, *see* Prescription drugs
Legislatures, 6
Levine v. *Knowles,* 153
Liability, 131–174
abandoned animals, 86
animal bites, 80–81
animal confinement laws, 76–79
assault and battery, 164–166
countersuits, 162–164
drug distributor products, 231–232
drug residues in food, 232
false imprisonment, 166
good samaritan acts, 62–63
libel and slander, 166–170
livestock ownership, 104–105
magnitude of problem, 131–132
medical records requirements, 332
necropsies, 100
negligence/malpractice and, 132–160.
see also Malpractice; Negligence
nonstandard treatment rights,
242–243
over-the-counter drugs versus

prescription drugs, 232
peer review committees, 127
pesticides, 260
prepurchase examinations, 360–361
product liability, 236, 238–242
standard of care, 135–145
wildlife law, 408–409
wrongful discharge, 170–172
see also Malpractice; Negligence
Liability insurance:
antitrust and, 184
civil actions, 15–16
confinement laws, 78
dangerous dogs, 82
types of, 160–162
see also Insurance
Libel and slander, 166–170
defenses in, 169–170
definitions, 166–167
elements in, 167–168
Library systems, 9–10
Licenses and licensing:
Animal Welfare Act Regulations,
400–401
protectionist nature of, 52
reciprocity of, 61–62
revocation of, 67
state boards and, 50–51, 58–60
substance abuse and, 65–66
suspension of, 262
veterinary practice acts and, 51
veterinary premises, 64
Licensing requirement (of animals), 79
Liens:
abandoned animal statutes, 91
enforcement procedures, 21
fees, 89–91
Limitations on numbers of animals,
85–86
Liquidated damages, 201
Livestock:
bailments, 105–107
biologicals, 256, 257
custody/liens, 90–91
damages, 146–147
drug prohibitions, 221–223

drug regulation, 226
drug residues in, 232
drugs for, 220
feed chain drugs, 226–227
nonstandard treatments, 242
ownership rights, 102, 104–105
state boards, 57–58
Loring M., 75, 136, 148
Lost use/income/profits (damages), 148–149

Mailing list theft, 349
Malicious prosecution, 162–163
Malpractice:
    countersuits, 162–164
    disciplinary actions, 68
    duty, 134
    ethics, 4–5, 35, 38
    informed consent forms, 338–344
    medical records in defense, 323–324
    nonstandard treatment rights, 242–243
    omission/commissions, 137–138
    peer review committees, 127
    referrals, 140–141
    standards of care, 57, 136
    statutes of limitation, 7, 159–160
    see also Liability; Negligence
Marine Mammal Protection Act, 380, 386–387, 399
Marine mammals:
    import/export permits, 391
    international protection, 379–380
    National Marine Fisheries Service, 399–400
    permits, 390
Mediation, 22–23
Medical records, 316–359
    computer-generated, 324–327
    confidentiality, 345–346
    contractual requirements, 329–337
    corrections to, 321
    discovery phase, 18
    dispute resolution, 123–124
    evidence, 286
    improvements in, 350–356

information included in, 318–321
informed consent requirements, 327–328
legal defense requirements, 323–324
loss of, 349–350
omissions from, 321
ownership/possession/access, 344–345
prepurchase examination, 369, 370–371, 373, 376–377
professional association requirements, 328–329
radiographs/electrocardiograms/ laboratory reports, 347–349
requirements for, 321–322
retention of, 346
state board requirements, 58
statutory requirements for, 322–323
tax/documentary purposes, 338
thefts, 349
types of, 316–318
see also Documentation; Record keeping
Meeting of the minds (contracts), 194
Mental disability, 198–199
Migratory bird banding permits, 388
Migratory bird protection, 379
Migratory Bird Treaty Act, 385, 393–395
Milk quality control programs, 57–58
Minor use drugs, 225
Misbranded drugs, 218–219
Misdemeanor, 17
Mitigation of damages, 202–203
Model State Poison Prevention Packaging Act, 235
Model Veterinary Practice Act, 53
Morality, 2–5
Moral principles, 38–41
Moral value judgments, 25–26
Motions, *see* Preliminary motions

Nader, Ralph, 175
National Association of State Racing Commission, 250–251
National Marine Fisheries Service, 384, 393, 399–400

NBE (examination), 60
Necropsy:
    cadaver disposal, 98, 99
    consent for, 100–102
Negligence:
    countersuit for plaintiff's attorney's
        negligence, 163
    damages, 145–154
    defined, 132–133
    duty in, 134
    emergency care duty, 134–135
    essential proofs required, 133–134
    informed consent, 338–344
    law of, 132–133
    legal defenses in, 157–160
    nonstandard treatment rights,
        242–243
    proximate causation, 145
    referral duty, 154–156
    res ipsa loquitur, 156–157
    tort law, 6
    see also Liability; Malpractice
Negotiated settlements, 21–22
Neighbors, 83–84
New animal drug approval:
    generic versus brand name drugs, 225
    minor use drugs, 225
    process of, 217–218
    unapproved/bulk drugs, 224
Newcastle's disease, 404–405
New York State, 407–408
Noise, *see* Animal noise
Nolo contendere, 19
Nominal damages:
    breaches of contract, 201
    described, 146
Nuclear research, 26–27
Nuisance:
    animal noise, 83–84
    animal waste, 84–85
    limitations on numbers of animals,
        85–86

Oath, *see* Veterinarian's oath
Offer (contracts), 191–193, 194
Officer's liability insurance, 161

Omissions, 136–138
Ongoing care, 135
Opening statements, 19–20
Opinion, 28–29
Oral contracts, 295–296
Original jurisdiction, 8
Over-the-counter drugs, 219, 232
Ownership rights, 94–105
    abandoned animals, 87
    accident stop requirements, 97–98
    cadavers, 98–102, 103
    destruction of animals, 102
    livestock, 102, 104–105
    medical records, 344–345, 347–349
    overview of, 94–95
    rights and duties of, 73–74
    stray animals, 96–97
    veterinary practice acts, 64–65
    wills and trusts, 95–96
    see also Property

Packaging:
    biologicals, 256
    drug use, 233–235
    see also Labeling
Packwood Amendment, 380
Pain, 31–32, 35–36
Pain and suffering damages, 149–151
Parol (oral) evidence, 200
Passwords (computer), 326
Payment, 3–4. *See also* Credit
    management and debt collection; Fees
Peer review committees, 125–127
Peers, *see* Colleagues
Pelly Amendment (Fisherman's
    Protective Act), 380
Penalties, 67–70
    abandoned animals, 89
    antitrust, 183–184
    citations, 68–70
    disciplinary action, 67–68
    drug violations, 231, 262
    licensed veterinarians, 67
    unprofessional conduct, 68
    usury, 302
    wildlife law, 388

see also Damages; Fines

Penicillin, 219

Permits, *see* Wildlife permits

Per se rule, 182

Personal guilt, 2, 5

Personality (veterinarian's), 122–123

Personal service contracts, 204–205, 206–207, 208, 209

Pesticides, 258–260
active versus inert ingredients, 259
concerns about, 258–259
Federal Insecticide, Fungicide, and Rodenticide Act (FIFRA), 258
labels and labeling, 259, 260
liability, 260
misbranding, 259
state laws, 260

Pet:
classification as, 74–75
drug use and, 227
heirloom comparison (damages), 151–152

Pet health insurance, 328

Pet stores, 406

Pharmaceuticals, *see* Biologicals; Controlled substances; Drug categories; Drug use; Pesticides

Philosophy, 24–25, 41–42

Photographs, 351, 354

Physical examination, 369. *See also* Prepurchase examination

Pit bulls, 82–83

Plea bargaining, 18–19

Pleadings, 16

Poisonings, 233

Poison Prevention Packaging Act, 234–235

Political climate, 226–227

Ports of entry, 403. *See also* Import/ export

Power of attorney, 272–273

Preemptory strike, 19

Preexisting duty rule, 196

Preliminary hearing, 17–18

Preliminary motion, 16–17

Premises, *see* Veterinary premises

Prepurchase examination, 359–378
buyer's involvement in, 362–368
examination process in, 368–369
legal concerns in, 361
liability concerns in, 360–361
seller's involvement in, 369, 372–377
terminology in, 359–360

Prescription drugs:
described, 219
hospital policies regarding sales of, 232–233
over-the-counter drugs distinguished from, 219, 232
see also Biologicals; Controlled substances; Drug categories; Drug use

Pretrial motions, 18

Prima facie tort, 164

Privity theory, 236

Probable cause, 17, 18

Probation, 67

Problem-oriented records, 317–318

Procedural law, 6–7, 18

Product liability, 236, 238–242

Product recall, 239–240

Professional associations, 328–329

Professional liability, *see* Liability; Malpractice; Negligence

Promissory estoppel, 196–197, 203

Property:
animals, 75–76
assault and battery defense, 165–166
cadavers, 98
ethics, 35, 44
legal classification, 74
medical records, 344–345, 347–349
possession/liens, 90–91
see also Ownership rights

Prosser, W. L., 157

Proximate causation, 145

Psittacosis, 405–406

Psychotherapy, 74

Psychotropic drugs:
consent, 243–244
written consent form for, 247
see also Controlled substances; Drug

categories; Drug use
Publication, 167–168
Public health:
    cadavers, 98
    rabies, 79–80
    U.S. Department of Health and
    Human Services requirements, 405–406
Public Health Service Act, 405
Public officials and figures, 169–170
Pugh v. *See's Candies*, 170
Punitive damages, 152–154. *See also*
    Damages
Purchase examination, *see* Prepurchase
    examination

Quality/quantity of care:
    complaints, 117–118
    peer reporting, 123
    see also Standards of care
Quarantine regulations, 404–405
Quasi contract law, 203–204

Rabies:
    liability, 138
    vaccination administration, 258
    vaccination requirements, 79–80
Racehorses:
    drug use, 248, 250–251
    see also Horse
Radiographs, 347–349
Raptor propagation permits, 395
Rationality, 28–31, 46–47
Reasonable man theory, 136
Reasonableness rule, 182
Recall, *see* Product recall
Record keeping:
    adverse drug reactions, 235–236, 237
    animal cruelty, 94
    computer-generated records, 324–327
    confinement laws, 77
    controlled substances, 273–277
    prepurchase agreements, 364–367
    tax purposes, 338
    U.S. Department of Agriculture, 401
    wildlife permits, 390
    see also Documentation; Medical

records
Referrals:
    complaints, 118–119
    criticism, 123
    duty to refer, 154–156
    medical records and, 320
    standards of care, 140–141
    see also Specialization
Rehabilitation facilities (wildlife), 406
Religion, 2, 41, 46
Remand of case, 21
Remedies at law, 7
Remedies in equity, 7
Removal for cause, 19
Reporting requirements:
    adverse drug reactions, 236, 237
    animal bites, 81–82
    animal cruelty, 94
    staged animal fights, 64
    veterinary practice acts, 63–64
Res ipsa loquitur, 156–157
Restitution, 202
Restraint (of animals), 142–143
Restraint of trade, 181
Rhulen Insurance Agency of New York,
    139
Rickards v. *CERF*, 178
Rule of reason, 182

Salmonella infection, 226
Science, 26–27, 28
Scienter doctrine, 80–81
Seals, 379–380
Search warrants, 230–231
Security:
    computer-generated records, 326
    controlled substances, 278–282
Self-defense, 165
Senility, 198
Service of process, 16, 310–311
Settlement conferences, 18
Sherman Antitrust Act, 176, 176–184
    covenants not to compete, 207,
    209–212
    see also Antitrust
Show horses, 248, 250–251

Side effects, 243
Similar locality rule, 136
Slander, *see* Libel and slander
Slavery, 75
Small claims court, 308–314
  answers to actions, 311
  considerations in, 309–310
  counterclaims, 311
  debt collection, 294
  decision and appeals, 313
  drawbacks to, 308–309
  filing of claims, 310
  judicial collection devices, 313–314
  preparation for trial, 311–312
  service of process, 310–311
  testimony, 312
  types of complaints, 308
  venue, 311
  see also Credit management and debt
    collection
Socialization, 38–39
Society:
  abandoned animals, 86
  animal laws, 72
  ethics, 34, 36, 44
  moral principles, 41
Society for the Welfare of Animals, Inc. v.
  Walwrath, 187
Socrates, 30
Soundness examination, *see* Prepurchase
  examination
Source-oriented records, 317–318
Special damages, 146–147
Specialization:
  complaints, 121
  duty to refer, 154–156
  ethics, 37
  lawyers, 13
  reciprocity of licensing and, 62
  standards of care, 139–140
  see also Referrals
Specific performance:
  breaches of contract, 201–202
  contract law, 7
Staff members, *see* Employees
Staged animal fights, 64

Standard form contracts, 195
Standards of care, 135–145
  animal restraint, 142–143
  changes in, 138–139
  continuing education, 138
  informed consent and, 143–145
  malpractice law and, 136
  minimum proposed standards,
    447–455
  negligence law and, 135–136
  omission and commissions, 136–138
  referrals, 140–141
  similar locality rule, 136
  specialists, 139–140
  state boards, 57–58
  statutory, 141–142
  see also Veterinary practice laws
Stare decisis, 2
State bar associations, 14
State boards:
  appointments to, 51
  described, 50–51
  dispute resolution, 127–129
  examinations given by, 60–61
  powers of, 56–61
  see also Veterinary practice acts
State courts, 8, 9, 19
State law and governments:
  computer-generated records, 324–325
  controlled substances, 263, 277
  covenants not to compete, 212–213
  drug labeling requirements, 233–234
  drug regulation by, 216
  examples of, 415–437
  fair debt collection statutes, 304–307
  horse drugging, 250
  medical records, 322–323, 344
  pesticides, 260
  prepurchase examination records, 369
  rabies vaccines, 258
  veterinary practice acts, 51–52
  wildlife regulation, 407–408, 491–494
  see also Federal law and government;
  Law; Veterinary practice acts
State veterinary associations:
  abandoned animals, 87

codes of ethics, 3
Statute of Frauds, 199–200
Statute of limitations:
    antitrust, 184
    negligence defense, 159–160
    procedural law, 6–7
Stay of execution, 20
Stray animals:
    abandoned animals contrasted, 87–88
    emergency care, 96–97
    see also Abandoned animals
Strict liability, 238–239
Subpoenas, 17, 18
Substance abuse:
    controlled substances, 262
    vetirinarians, 282
    veterinary practice acts, 65–66
    see also Controlled substances
Substantive law, 6–7
Summons:
    civil actions, 15, 16, 17
    criminal actions, 17

Tail dockings, 34
Tamemy v. *Atlantic Richfield*, 170
Taxes, 338
Technology:
    antitrust, 175
    standards of care, 138–139
Telephone consent, 333
Testimony:
    small claims court, 312
    see also Expert witnesses
Tests and testing, 137
Tetracycline, 219
Third-party payers, *see* Insurance;
    Liability insurance
Threatened species, 393. *See also*
    Endangered species
Three-prong test (medical records),
    325–326
Timeliness:
    abandoned animals, 88
    medical records, 350
Tort law and actions:
    contract law compared, 5–6
    emergency care, 4

liability, 131, 132
    strict liability, 238–239
    substantive law, 6
    wrongful discharge, 170
Trade (international), 381–383
Transportation:
    U.S. Department of Agriculture,
    401–402
    wildlife permits, 391
Treatment, 320
Trials, 19–20
Trusts, 95–96
Truth:
    computer-generated records, 325–326
    ethics, 34–35, 42–43
    expert witnesses, 286
    libel and slander defense, 169
    moral principles, 40

Unapproved drugs:
    described, 223–225
    drug residue in food, 232
    nonstandard treatments, 242–243
    see also Drug categories; Drug use
Uniform Commercial Code:
    contracts, 191
    implied warranties, 236
    offer and acceptance under, 194
    prepurchase examination, 372
    standard form contracts, 195
    Statute of Frauds, 199
Unique property theory, 147
United States Attorney, 17
United States Constitution:
    jury system, 11
    libel and slander law, 166–167
United States Department of
    Agriculture:
    Animal and Plant Health Inspection
    Service of, 400–404
    auctions, 406
    biologicals, 254–258
    described, 215–216
    food chain drugs, 227
    import/export, 402–404
    pet stores, 406

wildlife permits, 400–405
United States Department of Commerce, 399–400
United States Department of Health and Human Services, 405–406
United States Department of Housing and Urban Development, 74–75
United States Department of Justice, 177, 184
United States Department of the Interior, 388–399
United States Drug Enforcement Agency, 216, 263 *ff*, 495–498
United States Environmental Protection Agency, 218
  described, 216
  pesticides, 258–260
United States Federal Trade Commission, 177, 179
United States Fish and Wildlife Service, 384
United States Food and Drug Administration, 216–218
  adverse drug reactions, 235–236
  approval applications, 217–218
  changing efforts of, 225–229
  controlled substances, 282
  described, 215
  interstate commerce, 217
  investigations and penalties of, 229–231
  nonstandard treatments, 242
  priorities of, 229
  product recalls, 239–240
United States Supreme Court:
  advertising, 185–187
  antitrust, 175, 176, 178
  licensing, 52
  veterinary ethics, 27
United States v. *Article of Device...Therametic*, 230
Unjust enrichment law, 203–204
Unprofessional conduct, 68
Unresolvable issue, 11
Unwritten law, 7
Urine test, 373

Usury, 301–302
Utilitarianism, 41, 42

Vaccines, *see* Biologicals
Valuational assumptions, 25. *See also* Ethics
Veracity, *see* Truth
Verdicts, 20
Veterinarian-client-patient relationship:
  AVMA's definition of, 227
  California law and, 228
  controlled substances and, 282
  drug use and, 227
  see also Clients
Veterinarian's oath, 36
Veterinary associations, 37–38
Veterinary drugs, *see* Drug categories; Drug use
Veterinary education:
  communications, 112
  complaints, 121–122
  continuing education, 138, 233, 242–243
  cruelty reporting requirements, 64
  ethics, 26, 28, 30–31, 37
  licensing and, 59–60
  morality and, 2
Veterinary ethics, *see* Ethics
Veterinary hospitals, *see* Veterinary premises
Veterinary practice acts, 50–71, 416–438
  animal health technician definition, 55–56, 416
  cruelty reporting requirements, 63–64
  definitions in, 52
  direct supervision term, 56
  examples of, 415–437
  exemption/exclusions, 53–55
  good samaritan acts, 62–63
  indirect supervision, 56
  licensing of premises, 64
  licensing reciprocity, 61–62
  model act, 438–446
  ownership regulations, 64–65
  penalties for violations of, 66–70
  practice of veterinary medicine

definition, 52–53
purpose of, 51–52
staged animal fights, 64
state boards, 50–51, 56–61
substance abuse, 65–66
see also State boards; State law and
governments
Veterinary premises:
abandonment at, 87
census list, 351, 355
inspections, 57
licensing requirements, 64
U.S. FDA investigations, 230–231
zoning laws, 85–86
Veterinary technician, *see* Animal health
technician
Vicious dogs, 82–83
Virginia Board of Pharmacy v. *Virginia
Consumer Council*, 185
Virus-Serum-Toxin Act of 1913, 216,
254–255
Voir dire, 19

Warranties, 236, 238
Waste laws, 84–85
Waterfowl sale and disposal permits,
394
Weiss, Ted, 226
Whale protection, 380
Wild Free-Roaming Horses and Burros
Act, 388
Wildlife law, 378–412
auctions, 406
controlled substances, 278, 282
drug use (extra-label), 408
federal regulation, 383–388
international agreements on, 379–381
international law, 379, 493
international regulation of trade,
381–383
legal classification, 73–74
liability, 408–409
overview of, 378–379
penalties for violation of, 388
permit process pertaining to, 388–406

See also Wildlife permits
pet stores, 406
rehabilitation facilities, 406
state regulations, 407–408, 491–494
Wildlife permits, 388–406
Bald Eagle Protection Act, 395
captive-bred permit process, 392–393
CITES and, 395–399
Endangered Species Act, 391–392
federal agencies listed, 489–490
general issuance, 390
import/export/transport, 390–391
inspection for import/export, 391
Migratory Bird Treaty Act, 393–395
National Marine Fisheries Service,
393, 399–400
quarantine regulations, 404–405
threatened species, 393
U.S. Department of Agriculture,
400–405
U.S. Department of Commerce,
399–400
U.S. Department of Health and
Human Services, 405–406
U.S. Department of the Interior,
388–399
waterfowl sale/disposal, 394
see also Wildlife law
Wills, 95–96
Witnesses:
discovery phase, 18
evidence and, 20
see also Expert witnesses
Women:
exclusion of, 26
licensing procedures, 62
Written contracts, 296
Written law, 7
Wrongful discharge, 170–172

Zoning laws, 85–86
Zoos:
controlled substances, 278, 282
extra-label drug use, 408
liability, 408–409